Children
The Early Years

Dr. Celia A. Decker
Professor of Family and Consumer Sciences, retired
Northwestern State University of Louisiana
Natchitoches, Louisiana

Publisher
The Goodheart-Willcox Company, Inc.
Tinley Park, Illinois

Library of Congress Catalog Card Number 2002021474

International Standard Book Number 1-56637-945-8

5 6 7 8 9 10 – 04 – 08 07 06 05

Library of Congress Cataloging-in-Publication Data

Decker, Celia Anita.
    Children: the early years / Celia A. Decker.
        p. cm.
    Includes index.
    ISBN 1-56637-945-8
      1. Child development. 2. Child psychology. I. Title.

HQ767.9.D43 2004
305.231—dc21   2002021474

Introduction

Children: The Early Years will help you understand how to work with and care for children as they grow. It explains how children develop physically, intellectually, socially, and emotionally. *Children: The Early Years* will also help you apply what you have learned to meet children's needs in the best possible ways.

Children are different from adults. You need to know how children grow and develop in order to work with them effectively. This text begins by explaining the study of children. It helps you understand why studying child development is important—whether you become a parent, work in a child-related field, or just spend time with children. The text also discusses the choices and preparation involved in becoming a parent.

This text takes you from the prenatal stage through the child's school-age stage of development. The text presents the facts and theories about the child's development. Many examples are provided to help you apply this information when working with children of all ages.

Children: The Early Years helps you explore how family situations affect children. It explores the special needs and concerns of children with special needs. You will also learn about ways to care for children, including play activities, ways to keep children healthy and safe, group programs, and child-related careers.

About the Author

After a 38-year career in education, Celia A. Decker retired as a professor in the Department of Family and Consumer Sciences at Northwestern State University of Louisiana. She taught courses in early childhood education, child development, and family relations. Dr. Decker was coordinator of graduate studies in early childhood education. Before her position at Northwestern State University, she taught college courses at East Texas State University (now Texas A&M at Commerce) and at the University of Arkansas at Fayetteville. Dr. Decker also taught public school kindergarten in Kansas City, Kansas.

In addition to writing this text, she and her husband, Dr. John R. Decker, wrote *Planning and Administering Early Childhood Programs*. Dr. Decker has also published numerous chapters in books and articles. She presents papers at national and state annual meetings of professional associations, such as the National Association for the Education of Young Children, Southern Early Childhood Association, Association for Childhood Education International, National Association of Early Childhood Teacher Educators, and the Society for Research in Child Development. She does extensive consultant work for Head Start, Even Start, and local school systems.

During her years of teaching, Dr. Decker was named to *Who's Who in Child Development Professionals, Who's Who in Personalities of the South, Who's Who in American Women,* and the *World's Who's Who in Education.* In 1994, she was selected as the Outstanding Professor at Northwestern State University.

Contents in Brief

Table of Contents

Part 3   Infants 202

Part 1
Children in Today's World

In the past, people thought training in child development was unnecessary. They thought all the knowledge and skills that adults need for child-related careers—including parenting—come naturally. Many felt just being raised in a family teaches adults all they need to know about children and child care skills.

Today, experts know that understanding children requires careful study. Changes that are taking place in society and in families require people to know more about child development than what they observed in their own families.

In **chapter 1**, you will learn many reasons for studying children. You will also study the basic concepts of a child's growth and development. Finally, you will learn more about children through observation. By studying **chapter 2**, you will learn about the family's role in a child's development. You will read about the many family types in which children live, the family life cycle, and parenting styles. **Chapter 3** will introduce you to the roles of parents and the questions adults should consider before they have children.

Sasha and Benji are brother and sister, but they are very different. Four-year-old Sasha has black hair, dark skin, and deep brown eyes. She is quiet, talking as little as possible. At the child care center, Sasha prefers to play alone in quiet activities, such as dolls or puzzles. She also watches the other children rather than joining in their play. Two-year-old Benji has brown hair, fair skin, and light brown eyes. He prefers playing with tractors, trucks, and blocks with the other children. Benji is talkative and thinks playing alone is boring.

Chapter 1
Learning
About
Children

After studying this chapter, you will be able to

- list reasons for learning about children.
- define the term *child development*.
- describe the individual life cycle.
- describe three factors that promote growth and development.
- explain how brain development occurs.
- identify differences in the rate of growth and development.
- explain and give examples of some major principles and theories of growth and development.
- develop observation skills.

would use a cardboard box for a house, a race car, or a submarine? If you have spent any time with children, you know they can be lovable and challenging.

How will studying children help you? Whether you are interested in caring for children or being a parent someday, learning about children will help you better understand them as well as yourself. As you learn, you will see that children go through many stages of growth and development. This book emphasizes the early years because these years are important in shaping children's lives.

Studying children will also help you learn positive ways to care for them. People like to think they live in a **child-centered society**—a society that sees children as important and works for their good. However, some children also experience a great deal of harm through abuse and neglect. Children need safe environments. They need homes, schools, and other places where they can develop to their full potential, 1-1. All children should have the chance to grow in an environment that will promote their health and well-being. By studying children, you will learn how to provide these safe places.

Child development is one of the most fascinating subjects you can study. Children are constantly changing and discovering. They are also curious and creative. Who else

child-centered society. A society that sees children as important and works for their good.

1-1 Activities that are fun and challenging encourage intellectual and social development.
© John Shaw

Why Study Children?

Knowing how to meet children's needs is not easy. Before studying how adults can help children develop and learn, you must understand why you should study children.

To Understand Yourself

Studying how children grow and develop can help you grow, too. It can help you appreciate all that goes into taking a first step or saying a first word. When you help a child overcome a fear or learn a skill, you feel good. Adults often enjoy just being with children, 1-2. Their awe of beauty, their frankness, and their world of magic please adults.

1-2 Just being around children is a happy experience for many adults.
© John Shaw

Children can share gifts that, sadly, adults often outgrow. Many times, adults are not fully aware that who they are today is a result of the children they once were. As you study children, you can gain insight into your own growth, development, and personal priorities. You can also understand how your personal priorities affect your feelings about, and reactions to, children. This knowledge can help you serve children in better ways.

To Be a Responsible Parent

By studying children, parents know their children's needs at each stage of development. They also know the best ways to respond to those needs. Parenting is a mind-boggling task! How much adults know about children, however, can determine the kind of parents they become. Studying children also helps parents have realistic expectations about their parenting abilities. Parents must be responsible for meeting all their children's needs, which include the following:

❖ **physical needs.** Children need the right diet to nourish their growing, active bodies. They need well-fitting clothes that also promote self-esteem. They need shelter and physical protection, 1-3. Children also need proper health and medical care. Parents must provide for these needs.

❖ **intellectual needs.** Parents need to provide good experiences for their children. Experiences can help

1-3 Infants and young children have many safety needs.
Fisher-Price

children learn and develop skills they need to survive. Parents must also meet children's creative needs.

❖ **social needs.** Learning to form relationships is a key social need. All children need to form strong relationships with their parents. These relationships can help children feel secure and teach them how to respond and relate to other people. Children also need a sense of belonging. To build this sense, parents must socialize their

socialize. To train a child to live as a part of a group, such as the family, culture, or society.

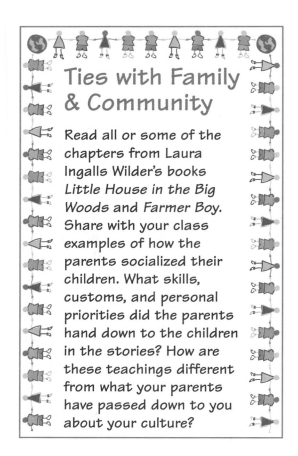

Ties with Family & Community

Read all or some of the chapters from Laura Ingalls Wilder's books *Little House in the Big Woods* and *Farmer Boy*. Share with your class examples of how the parents socialized their children. What skills, customs, and personal priorities did the parents hand down to the children in the stories? How are these teachings different from what your parents have passed down to you about your culture?

1-4 Learning family rituals and celebrations is part of a child's culture.
© John Shaw

children, or train them to live as part of the group. Parents must teach children about their **culture**, or way of life within the group. Each culture may have its own language, beliefs, attitudes, personal priorities, rituals, and skills, 1-4. Parents help children learn what the culture expects of its members. (You will learn more about the role of culture in families by reading chapter 2.)

❖ **trust needs.** Children need to feel they can cope with demands of family, friends, and society. Being able to trust their parents helps children gain confidence. Trust begins early in life when parents meet their needs. It continues to grow when parents allow them the freedom to develop.

❖ **love/guidance needs.** Children need love and support from their parents. In loving children, parents must listen to their children, set limits, and share their reasons for limits, 1-5. As a part of guidance, parents help their children develop character. **Character** is an inward force that guides a person's conduct. It helps people make choices that meet acceptable

1-5 Setting limits is part of loving and disciplining children.
© John Shaw

standards of right and wrong. Through love and guidance, parents help their children grow into self-directed adults.

To Protect Children's Rights

Children are easily hurt because they are physically weaker than adults and cannot reason as adults do. Society must protect them. By learning about children, lawmakers can pass laws that will keep children safe.

The Convention on the Rights of the Child (United Nations International Children's Education Fund) wrote 54 articles that set out the rights of every child in the world. These rights can be given under 11 major categories. The following categories explain children's rights to:

* **an identity** (government should protect children's names, family ties, and nationalities)
* **a family** (children should be able to live with their parents unless this is not in the children's best interest; parents have the responsibility for raising children with government support)
* **express themselves and have access to information** (children have the right to: express their views; have freedom of thought, conscience, and religion; and obtain information)
* **a safe and healthy life** (children have the right to life; the government should do all it can to make sure children survive and develop; children should have access to medical services and a decent standard of living)
* **special protection in times of war** (children who are refugees are entitled to special protection; children who are under 15 should not take part in armed conflict)
* **an education** (primary education should be free and required of all children; secondary education should be accessible to all children)

culture. The way of life within a group that includes language, beliefs, attitudes, values, rituals, and skills.

character. An inward force that guides a person's conduct.

❖ **special care for the disabled** (children with disabilities have the right to special care, education, and training)

❖ **protection from discrimination** (all rights apply to all children; children have the right to practice their own cultures, religions, and languages)

❖ **protection from abuse** (children shall be protected against abuse and neglect; government shall be involved with laws and programs concerned with abuse)

❖ **protection from harmful work** (children have the right to rest, leisure, play, and participation in cultural and artistic activities; children have the right to be protected from having to participate in work that threatens their health, education, and development)

❖ **special treatment if arrested** (children are entitled to assistance and treatment that respects their rights)

In the United States, parents have the rights of guardianship and determine their children's upbringing. For example, they control the children's level of financial support. They also control religious and moral teachings, as well as education and health care choices. The state can come between a parent and child only if the court feels the child needs more protection. For example, the state may require foster care.

Each state can make laws and policies to protect children. For example, laws have been passed regarding school attendance, child labor, and illegal drug sales to help protect children and society.

State laws protect children from the results of their own lack of judgment. For example, young children are not responsible legally for their contracts. They are also treated differently in court than adults. The state can also make laws to develop child welfare services. For instance, a state office checks on the quality of child care programs.

Children have gained rights, too. Examples are the rights of due process and fair treatment in schools and juvenile courts. In some states, children may receive medical help without parental consent.

Laws can be enacted on the local level, too. An example is a curfew law. In addition, local citizen groups often become advocates of children's rights. These groups attempt to get needed laws passed and notify the appropriate persons when it seems a child's rights have been violated.

To Work with Children

Adults with child-related careers should study children. (See chapter 25 to read about these careers.) Most careers focus on only one area of children's needs. A school cook is concerned with children's nutritional needs, while a teacher may focus more on intellectual needs. However, the child is a whole person. Anyone in a child-related field should know about all aspects of children's growth and development, 1-6. Learning more about children allows people in child-related careers to serve them better.

1-6 Classroom teachers are mainly prepared to meet children's mental needs. They must also be aware of children's other needs and learn how these affect mental growth.
© John Shaw

What Is Child Development?

Development is the gradual process through which babies become adults. The process has many stages, such as infancy, childhood, adolescence, and adulthood, 1-7. Development begins at conception and continues until death.

For many years, scientists and researchers have been studying children. The goal of these professionals was to learn more about how children grow and develop. Their research has made them experts in the field of child

1-7 Between infancy and adulthood, children go through many stages of development.

development. **Child development** is the scientific study of children from conception to adolescence.

Child development focuses on changes that occur in children over time. This includes how children's bodies change and how children think and learn. Child development also

 development. The gradual process of growth through many stages, such as infancy, children, adolescence, and adulthood.

child development. The scientific study of children from conception to adolescence.

focuses on how children feel about themselves and interact with others.

By doing research, experts in medicine, education, family and consumer sciences, and sociology help gather knowledge about children. People then use these facts to learn about children. Child development is not just for experts, though. Anyone who is around children can use this knowledge. Child development teaches people how to care for children.

Individual Life Cycle

The **individual life cycle** is a description of the stages of change people experience throughout life. To help them study development over time, experts divide life into age-related stages. These stages were chosen based on changes in growth and behavior that occur as a result of age. The exact ages for a specific person may vary, but average ages are given. These provide a basic idea of when stages may begin and end. Because this book is about child development, only the first six stages (those that involve children) are described here. The life cycle also includes stages for teens and adults.

❖ The *prenatal stage* begins at conception and ends about nine months later at birth. The rate of growth at this stage is the fastest it will be in life. In this stage, a child grows from a single cell to a complete organism.

❖ The *neonatal stage* extends from birth through the second week. During this period, the baby physically adapts to life outside of the mother's body.

❖ The *infancy stage* begins at two weeks and continues through the first birthday (12 months). The infant develops the foundation for motor, thinking, language, and social skills.

❖ The *toddler stage* begins at 12 months and ends at 36 months (the child's third birthday). In the toddler stage, the child makes great strides in motor, thinking, and language skills and begins to test his or her dependence on adults.

❖ The *preschool stage* begins at three years and ends at the sixth birthday. During this stage, the child becomes more self-sufficient, spends many hours in play exploring the physical and social world, and develops a rather stable self-concept.

❖ The *school-age stage,* or middle childhood, begins at 6 years and ends at 12 years. This stage corresponds to the typical ages of children in the elementary school years. Achievement is the central goal of these years. School-age children master the basics of reading, writing, and arithmetic. They are exposed to many other school learnings, too. In school, children interact with peers more and learn by group instruction. This makes it important for them to learn self-control.

Factors That Influence Growth and Development

Why is each child different? Two main factors influence growth and development. First, each child has unique, inborn traits. Secondly, a child's surroundings also play a large role. The way these two factors combine also makes children different from one another.

Heredity and environment influence growth and development. **Heredity** includes all the traits that are passed to a child from blood relatives. **Environment** includes all the conditions and situations that affect a child. Experts have done many studies to help them understand how these two factors affect children's growth and development. They have learned much, but unanswered questions remain.

Heredity

You have many traits in common with all the other members of your family. These traits were passed to you in complex ways through your parents' genes at the moment of conception. **Genes** are sections of the DNA molecule found in a person's cells that determine the individual traits each person will have. Genes carry the inborn instructions that have helped to make you who you are.

Genetics is the study of the factors involved in the passing of traits from one generation of living beings to the

next. In short, genetics is the study of heredity. *Geneticists* (biologists who study heredity) have made many strides in learning which traits are passed from parents to child. They have found that almost every physical, mental, and social-emotional trait is affected by genes. Thus, genes influence your growth and development in many ways. The following points are known about heredity:

❖ The genes' instructions are life-long. They carry the same message throughout life. For instance, the genes for eye color remain the same for life.

❖ Genes affect some parts of growth and development more than others. For instance, genes determine body features like blood type, facial structure, and color of hair, eyes, and skin, 1-8. Other

individual life cycle. A description of the stages of change people experience throughout life.

heredity. The sum of all the traits that are passed to a child from blood relatives.

environment. The sum of all the conditions and situations that affect a child's growth and development.

genes. Sections of the DNA molecule found in a person's cells that determine the individual traits the person will have.

genetics. The study of the factors involved in the passing of traits from one generation of living beings to the next.

1-8 Brothers and sisters may look alike in many ways because they both inherit genes from their parents.

traits, such as mental ability and social-emotional traits, are affected by both genes and the environment.

❖ Some genes determine whether a person will have a trait. For example, a person either is or is not an albino. (An *albino* is a person with white skin, almost white hair, and pink eyes.) This is determined by genes.

❖ Other genes affect the range of a trait. Traits like height (very short to very tall) and athletic ability (almost no ability to greatness) come from these genes. These genes determine a trait's potential. (*Potential* is the greatest amount or level possible.) Whether a person will show or use that trait to its potential depends on the person's life. For instance, a good diet will help a child reach his or her height potential. The child cannot grow beyond this potential, however. On the other hand, children with poor nutrition may not achieve their full potential.

Environment

The environment affects growth and development, too. Physical conditions, such as food and rest, are part of the environment. These conditions shape the experiences children have, 1-9. A child's environment also includes relationships with others, as well as everything children hear or see. All these factors affect the way a child grows and develops.

Factors in the environment can affect physical traits. For example, studies show that babies' brains develop at a slower rate if no one holds or talks to them. When children receive attention and many chances to learn, their brains develop to their full potential, 1-10.

Intellectual and social-emotional traits are also affected by factors in the environment. For instance, a child whose family members show affection openly may be more likely to show affection,

1-9 Children learn through firsthand experiences.
© John Shaw

1-10 An environment with appropriate play materials encourages much concentration and learning during play.
Lakeshore Learning Materials, Carson, Calif.

too. A child whose family members show little affection might be less comfortable hugging or kissing others.

Heredity and Environment Combined

For years, people argued about which affected growth and development more—heredity or environment. Now, experts agree they work together.

Genes control how quickly a baby's muscles and bones grow (heredity). A proper diet is needed for the baby to grow (environment). However, a better diet does not make bones and muscles bigger than heredity allows (heredity and environment).

Going one step further, parents can exercise their baby's muscles to help strengthen them (environment). Nevertheless, the baby cannot walk until muscles and bones are ready (heredity). When the baby's body is ready, parents can help the baby walk as soon as possible through exercise and encouragement (heredity and environment).

This interaction can also be observed in the developing brain. Genes and environment work together to shape a child's brain. The effects of each are unique.

Brain Development

The command center of the body—the brain—has always fascinated scientists. People who study and work with children have also been curious about how the brain grows and changes in childhood. Until recently, the brain was mostly a mystery. However, in recent years, scientists have learned much more about brain development. Much of this knowledge has come from the use of high technology and advances in biochemistry. An abundance of brain research is now in progress. Although many questions have been answered, many more remain for scientists to unravel.

Basic Wiring Occurs

The brain is responsible for controlling most body functions. These include operation of the body systems, movements, thinking, memory, and feelings. Brain cells called **neurons** control these tasks. The neurons do their work by sending and receiving electrical impulses throughout the brain. These impulses are like messages that tell body parts or systems what to do.

Electrical impulses can be passed within a single brain cell or between two brain cells. Special chemicals send both types of impulses (within one cell or between two cells). When a message must travel between cells, however, it needs a pathway along which to travel. For this "talk" between neurons, the brain builds a web of fibers to serve as links between cells. Think of these fibers as microscopic cables that carry brain signals. This network of fibers is called the brain's **wiring**.

Each neuron can develop two types of cables, 1-11. Longer, heavier cables called **axons** send signals. Each cell can have only one axon. This axon transmits all the signals from this neuron to other neurons. Short, bushy cables called **dendrites** receive signals. One cell can have as many as 15,000 dendrites. The axon from one neuron does not touch the dendrite of another. Instead, there is a tiny gap called **synapse** between them. As the signal leaves the axon, it jumps the synapse to travel to the dendrite. The brain's complex wiring allows one axon to send signals to many dendrites at the same time.

Heredity and Environment Interact

Scientists now know that heredity and environment work together to develop the brain. Heredity affects how many neurons a baby will have

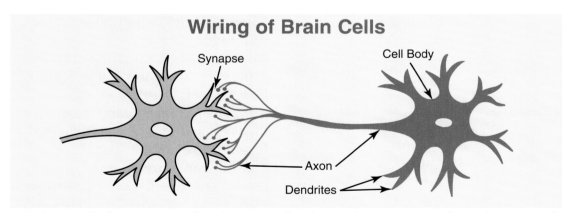

Wiring of Brain Cells

Synapse

Cell Body

Axon

Dendrites

1-11 Brain cells "communicate" with one another by sending messages from the axons of one neuron across the synapse to the dendrites of another.

throughout life. All these neurons will be present at birth. In addition, half of a person's 80,000 genes are involved in brain growth and development. These genes cause cells to divide and grow. They are also responsible for basic wiring between the axons and dendrites before birth. When the baby is born, he or she will have about 50 trillion synapses in the brain. These synapses are the ones the baby must have to survive outside the mother's body.

Unlike a computer that is built and then turned on, the brain starts working even before it is finished. The basics are present at birth, but the baby's brain continues to grow after birth, 1-12. When stimulated, the axon sends electrical impulses to the dendrites of other cells. These messages help the brain form more synapses (connections) between the neurons. Repeating a positive experience causes the impulses to be sent again, which strengthens the connection.

The brain can use a stronger connection more easily than a weak one. Over time, the brain continues to strengthen used pathways, but begins to weed out the unused ones. This process is called **pruning**. Healthy pruning allows the remaining connections to become strong. This increases the speed and efficiency for often-used brain signals. Too much pruning

1-12 At birth, babies come with only the basic wiring needed to survive—much brain development still lies ahead.

neurons. Brain cells that send and receive electrical impulses amongst each other that direct the various tasks of the brain.

wiring. Network of fibers that carry brain signals between neurons.

axons. Long, thick cables that transmit all the signals from a neuron to other neurons.

dendrites. Short, bushy cables that allow each neuron to receive signals sent by other neurons.

synapse. A tiny gap between a dendrite of one neuron and the axon of another across which electrical impulses can be transmitted.

pruning. The process of weeding out underused or weak connections between neurons.

means the person will not be able to develop certain needed skills and abilities. Pruning begins in the very first years of a child's life and is almost completed by age 10 years.

In this system of wiring, the environment is crucial. Rich sensory experiences create new dendrites, which builds new networks for learning. Examples of rich experiences are getting a hug, hearing music, learning a skill, and exploring a toy. In the first year of life, the number of synapses increases to more than 1,000 trillion. This allows for the rapid rate of learning among babies and young children, 1-13.

1-13 Until recently, few people understood that holding and talking to babies and young children stimulates their brain development.

Rich sensory experiences strengthen and refine the brain's wiring. A lack of stimulation can prevent some connections from forming and cause others to be pruned away. In fact, early experiences have such a dramatic effect on brain wiring they can increase or decrease the final number of synapses by as much as 25 percent. The effects this has on future learning potential are lifelong.

Windows of Opportunity

Timing is an important concept when it comes to brain development. The entire brain is not wired at one time. Genes control the general order and timetable in which regions of the brain develop. Each region has a specific function, such as processing a person's movement, language, memory, emotions, or sensory experiences. By observing children's skills, experts have learned which parts of the brain are being wired at various ages.

For best results, parents and people who work with children should offer specific types of stimulation at certain times. These times are called windows of opportunity. A **window of opportunity** is a prime period in a child's life for developing a particular skill. In this window, the child reaches a peak capacity to learn this skill if given the opportunity. At this time, a certain type of stimulation is more critical than others.

Each area has its own window of opportunity. Some windows are large, which means the favorable time for learning this skill is several years.

Language development is a good example. Some windows are small, which means the most favorable time for learning is less than a year. For instance, wiring for vision is completed in a few months. Once the window of opportunity has passed, it is more difficult (sometimes impossible) for the brain to develop this skill or acquire this learning.

Often, the windows of opportunity for various tasks overlap. This means more than one learning can happen at the same time. For instance, the window for learning to respond to stress lasts from birth to a little more than three years. The window for basic motor skills opens and closes at about the same times. This means a child will likely be learning both skills at the same time if given the opportunity.

Why is this information useful? Knowing when the windows of opportunity for various skills occur helps parents and teachers offer the right kinds of experiences for a child at the best possible times. They will know which skills they should encourage most and which will likely come at a later time. This can help children's brains reach their full potential.

Brain Plasticity

When working with children, it's also good to know that a child's brain has the ability to change or adapt to the environment. This ability to be shaped and reshaped is called plasticity (technically *brain plasiticity).*

Plasticity can have both positive and negative effects on brain development. This depends largely on the environment. In a favorable environment, the brain receives a great deal of stimulation. This stimulation comes from the child's experiences and surroundings. Stimulation causes the brain to send signals that strengthen the wiring for these types of activities.

The following are basic suggestions for offering a positive environment for young children:

❖ The best experiences are interaction with loving adults engaged in daily tasks and family-type activities. (Even child care programs for children under three years of age should have a home-like atmosphere.) Babies and very young children need not be taught in a formal way. These children learn by playing, especially with caring adults.

❖ Children need choices in what and how to learn. For example, adults should never insist that a baby or toddler play with a certain toy or listen to a certain story.

❖ Children need time to practice and master skills. Repetition of

window of opportunity. A prime period in a child's life for developing a particular skill if given the chance to do so.

plasticity. The ability of the brain to be shaped and reshaped, which is greatest early in life.

experiences develops the brain. Even with a small quantity of playthings, children can learn and develop.

Because of plasticity, brain development can be easily injured by abuse, neglect, and other negative experiences. Stress has a harmful effect on brain function. When a person fears or senses a threat, the body prepares for "fight or flight." The resulting chemical change in the brain has been described as an acid bath washing over the wiring. This acid prunes away the synapses needed for caring for and understanding others. Furthermore, because stress signals occur in the brain cortex (the part of the brain in which we do most of our thinking), a child cannot learn well while distressed. If stress is constant, these unused connections will also be pruned.

Plasticity lessens with age. Even the brain of a three-year-old is far less changeable than it was at birth. Ten-year-olds have very little plasticity, and adults have even less. This short period of brain plasticity tells us the following:

❖ The infant and toddler years are times of great brain activity and learning.

❖ Children who have developmental delays, live in unsafe environments, or lack stimulating experiences need early professional help to overcome these obstacles.

❖ A good early environment provides the best foundation for all areas of

development. It also promotes *resilience* (the ability to recover from or adjust easily to change).

Cutting-edge science on brain development confirms what many parents and caregivers have known for years, 1-14. The earliest years are the most important for all areas of growth and development (physical, intellectual, and social-emotional). Prenatal care, loving relations between young children and adults, and quality experiences play a lasting role in brain development. Learning about brain development can help adults shape children's potential in positive ways.

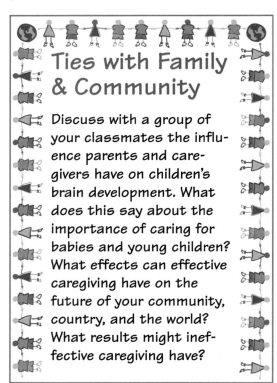

Ties with Family & Community

Discuss with a group of your classmates the influence parents and caregivers have on children's brain development. What does this say about the importance of caring for babies and young children? What effects can effective caregiving have on the future of your community, country, and the world? What results might ineffective caregiving have?

1-14 Parents can offer play experiences, such as blockbuilding, at the appropriate times to help their children master these skills.

Differences in the Rate of Growth and Development

All people change with time. They grow and develop certain skills and behaviors in expected sequences called *stages*. As you just read, many factors influence growth and development. These factors make each person develop at a unique rate.

Some people enter a stage earlier and some later than the typical age.

Developmental acceleration is when a child performs like an older child. For example, a 30-month-old child who speaks in long, complex sentences is developmentally accelerated in language. On the other hand, **developmental delay** is when a child performs like a younger child. For example, a three-year-old who speaks in two-word sentences may have a developmental delay in language. With support and encouragement, children with delays usually catch up with other children over time.

People do not advance in all areas of development at the same rate. For example, a child may develop at a fast rate in motor skills and a slower rate in language usage. A child may be developmentally accelerated or delayed in one or more areas. It's even possible for a child to be delayed in one area and accelerated in another. Some children have a favorable heredity and environment. These children may be developmentally accelerated in most areas. Sometimes unfavorable conditions can delay most areas of development. For example, a child born too early may be developmentally delayed in most areas.

developmental acceleration. When a child performs like an older child.

developmental delay. When a child performs like a younger child.

Principles of Growth and Development

Each person is unique, yet people are more alike than different. Experts study these likenesses to find patterns in the way people generally grow and develop. These patterns, or **principles of growth and development**, do not fit every person exactly. However, they are true enough to be used as a guide when learning about children. The following sections describe key principles of growth and development.

Growth and Development Are Constant

Many aspects of a person's growth and development are unchanging. This is called *constancy*. What a child is today is a good hint—but not proof—of what he or she will be tomorrow. For example, tall two-year-olds tend to be tall adults. Children who are good students in elementary school are likely to be good students in high school. Happy, secure children tend to be cheerful, confident adults.

Why is this so? There are two reasons for constancy in growth and development. First, traits controlled by heredity do not change. Second, people often live in the same environment for years. For major changes to take place in growth and development, major changes must take place in the environment.

Growth and Development Are Gradual and Continuous

Growth and development are gradual and continuous because changes that take place happen in little, unbroken steps. A child does not grow or develop overnight. Consider a baby taking his or her first steps on a certain date. Each day before walking, the baby grew, the body matured, and the baby practiced motor skills, such as crawling and pulling to a stand. All these small changes led to the baby's first steps, 1-15.

In a positive way, the principle also suggests development does not reverse overnight. A few mistakes or stresses usually do not cause severe problems. As an example, a one-day junk food binge does not seriously harm a healthy person.

The principle also suggests that if people do not develop when they are supposed to, they may be able to do so later in life. For instance, if children are not taught to read at age six, they can learn a few years later, although it may be more difficult. Making up these learnings may require professional help. In a few cases, once an opportunity has passed, it might never be possible to gain this development.

This principle can also work to a person's disadvantage. It suggests that poor growth and development are not easily reversed. For example, consider a child with poor health due to a lifelong poor diet. It may take many months or years of eating a carefully planned diet to restore the child's health. In

A   **B**

C   **D**   **E**

1-15 Children must practice many motor skills before they take their first steps. Before walking, children pull themselves mainly by their arms (A), creep on all fours (B), pull themselves onto their feet (C), stand without support (D), and try standing on one foot (E).
Photographs courtesy of Carter's; Photography by Bruce Plotkin

some cases, the body may never be able to overcome these obstacles.

Growth and Development Happen in Sequenced Steps

In order for growth and development to be continuous, change must build on what children have already learned. For instance, writing comes from making random marks. The steps

principles of growth and development. Statements of the general patterns in which growth and development take place in people.

in growth and development follow each other in a set order called **sequenced steps**. Think about the changes that happen in children in ranked stages—one stage always occurs before the next.

A **teachable moment** is a time when a person can learn a new task. It occurs when the body is physically ready (during the brain's windows of opportunity), when caregivers encourage and support the child, and when the child feels a strong desire to learn. If a child has not reached the teachable moment, he or she will feel stressed when trying to master a task or skill. Waiting too long after the teachable moment occurs may cause problems, too. For example, a child who was ready to ride a bicycle but did not have the chance to learn may have trouble learning the skill as an adult.

Growth and Development Happen at Different Rates

Growth and development happen at different rates throughout life. Experts know when fast and slow periods of growth and development occur. Height and weight increases are fast in infancy, for example. The increases are moderate in preschool, slow in elementary school, and fast again in junior and senior high school.

Rates of growth and development also vary from one child to another. Some children develop quickly and others slowly. Although the sequence of growth and development is similar for all children, the rates of change differ.

Why do these rates differ? Children grow and develop at different rates because of heredity, environment, and motivation.

Heredity determines different growth rates. For example, girl's bones and organs are more mature than boy's at all ages because of heredity.

Children need a good environment to grow at the best rate. If the environment is lacking, *lags* or delays in growth and development occur. Does this mean trying to speed up development is good? No—an adult's attempts to hurry growth and development may cause a child harmful stress.

Motivation, which is a child's desire to achieve, also makes growth and development rates vary. Some children are eager to achieve and others are more poorly motivated.

Growth and Development Have Interrelated Parts

In this book, the physical, mental, and social-emotional aspects of growth and development are often discussed in separate sections or chapters. This is so you can better understand each aspect. In reality, however, all aspects interact in complex ways. For instance, as children's bodies grow and mature, their motor skills improve. Increased motor skills, in turn, can improve children's social skills, 1-16. As social skills improve, children talk to more people and learn about new ideas. This helps their mental skills. As mental skills improve, children can play in more complex sports, which helps their motor skills.

1-16 Having the needed motor skills to catch crawfish (crayfish) can lead to a fun time with a friend.
Louisiana Department of Wildlife and Fisheries

People who work with children must understand how areas of growth and development affect each other. For instance, a teacher's job is to improve children's intellectual growth. However, how teachers treat children also affects their social-emotional growth. Understanding these interrelationships improves the way people work with children.

Theories of Growth and Development

Many researchers have studied children. Some of the more famous were Erik Erikson and Jean Piaget. Their theories about child development are described in later chapters of this text. Researchers Robert J. Havighurst and Abraham Maslow also studied children. Their research led them to form the following theories about growth and development.

Havighurst's Theory of Developmental Tasks

Each child masters skills and activities that fit his or her level of growth and development. In all cultures, children are expected to learn

Ties with Family & Community

Interview a person who is over 60 years of age. If possible, ask him or her for permission to record the interview on audio- or videotape. Share with the person what you have learned about developmental tasks. Ask the person to describe developmental tasks he or she mastered that people seldom master today. Examples might include chores, hobbies, games, and job duties of the past. Share your findings or your recorded interview with the class.

sequenced steps. Steps in growth and development that follow one another in a set order.

teachable moment. A time when a person can learn a new task because the body is physically ready, caregivers encourage and support, and the child feels a strong desire to learn.

skills like crawling, self-feeding, and dressing at a time that is right for them. These are called **developmental tasks**, or tasks that should be mastered at a certain stage in life.

Havighurst, a well-known educator and behavioral scientist, believed achieving developmental tasks leads to happiness and success with later tasks, 1-17. Failure to achieve tasks leads to unhappiness and problems with later tasks.

Havighurst identified the developmental tasks of children as coming from the following three sources:

❖ physical growth. A baby comes into the world as a helpless being. As its body matures, the child is able to learn many new skills, such as walking and reading.

❖ social pressures. Through rewards and penalties, society pressures the child to master the tasks seen as important. Developmental tasks

differ from culture to culture, because each group may value different skills. For instance, playing to win has no value to Hopi Indian children. However, most other American children feel winning is important. Tasks differ from region to region, too. Over time, tasks also change to reflect changes in society.

❖ inner pressures. The actual push to achieve comes from within children. In the end, it is the child who is responsible for mastering each task. Children work harder to learn tasks they like, 1-18.

Maslow's Theory of Human Needs

Maslow, a noted psychologist, believed that development is a result of meeting personal needs. His theory states all people work to fulfill basic needs and higher-level needs.

Basic needs are both physiological (related to the body) and psychological (related to feelings). Maslow divides basic needs into four categories. One category includes all physiological needs. The other three categories are the psychological needs of safety; belonging and love; and esteem.

In addition to basic needs, Maslow also created a category for higher-level needs, which he called *self-actualization needs*, 1-19. These are the needs to grow and feel fulfilled as a person. They include the drive to pursue talents and hobbies, gain skills, and learn more about the world.

1-17 Mastering school tasks is important for success in later life.
Courtesy of the Perfection Learning Corporation

Developmental Tasks

Area: **Motor Task**
Task for middle chilhood: **Learning physical skills needed for common games**
Example of task: **Learning skills needed to play ball.**

Source: Physical growth
Child needs bone and muscle growth; eyes and hands must work smoothly together

Source: Social pressures
Other children reward skillful players (praise or accept them as friends) and punish failures (tease or reject them as friends). Parents and coaches may also expect children to master the skills.

Source: Inner pressures
Child desires to be admired by other children, parents, and coaches.

Source: Must see new possibilities for behavior
Child sees older children playing ball.

Source: Must form new concept of self
Child thinks, "I can be a player."

Source: Must cope with conflicting demands
Child thinks, "I can get hit with a ball or be teased for striking out. But if I do not play, the other kids will make fun of me and my parents and coaches will not consider me grown-up."

Source: Wants to achieve the next step in development enough to work for it
Child now spends hours in practice.

1-18 Children master developmental tasks when their bodies are ready, when others place pressure on them, and when they want to learn a new skill.

Education meets self-actualization needs. Complete self-actualization is a lifelong process. Many people never attain complete self-actualization.

Maslow ranked these basic and higher-level needs in an order he called the *hierarchy of human needs*. This means lower-level needs (basic needs) must be somewhat fulfilled before higher-level needs can be pursued.

All adults who study about and care for children need to understand this hierarchy of human needs.

Maslow's work implies the further up the hierarchy a person can go, the more growth and fulfillment he or she will seek. Maslow sees humans as driven by the need to become more fulfilled.

Adults need to learn and practice ways to help children meet their needs.

developmental tasks. Skills that should be mastered at a certain stage in life.

Maslow's Needs

Basic Needs

physiological needs
food, water, air, shelter, clothing

safety needs
avoidance of illness, danger, and disruption; security

belonging and love needs
affiliation (belonging to groups such as family), acceptance, and love

esteem needs
mastery, adequacy, achievement, competence, and recognition

Higher-Level Needs

aesthetic needs, cognitive needs, and self-actualization needs
knowledge and appreciation of beauty, goodness, freedom, and a realistic view and acceptance of self and others

1-19 Maslow sees two kinds of needs in all humans—basic needs and higher-level needs.

The first step is to help children meet basic needs. For instance, adults can offer children nutritious foods. Once basic needs are met, adults can help children meet higher-level needs. For example, well-fed children can turn their attention from eating to psychological needs. These might include building relationships with friends. Higher-level skills help children reach their full potential as adults, which is called self-actualization.

Observing Children

Observation is the oldest, most common, and best way to learn about human behavior, including the behavior of children. One reason observation is so commonly used is because humans enter the world with their own observation equipment— their senses. As you watch and listen to children, you can learn about their behavior. By watching carefully, you can respond quickly if dangers arise.

When you observe adults who work with children, you can learn to imitate their successful behaviors. This can help you interact with children in a more positive way. Because many skills are learned through imitation, this type of observation is important.

Because the senses are the main tools used, you might think observation skills come naturally. To some extent, they do. You see and hear what goes on around you every day. Interpreting what you see and hear in a way you can use takes training, however. For this reason, many observation skills must be learned. These skills come with knowledge and practice. Pretend you are looking at an X ray with your doctor. Where you might see only shadows and lines, your doctor sees a bone fracture. Why would your doctor see more? With his or her experience, your doctor can see meaning in these images you may not notice.

If you have ever cared for or worked with children, you might have already begun to use observation. For instance, you would react instantly when you see a child in danger. Observation may have also helped you learn skills through imitation. If you observed a teacher sitting on the floor working with children, you might later try this, too.

You will learn more about children when you use your mind to "see" more. Observing children will help you understand what you read in this book and what you hear about children. At the same time, what you learn from your reading will help you see more when you observe, too, 1-20.

Why Observe Children?

How do researchers know so much about children? They have been observing and writing about children for many years. As you observe, you will behave like a researcher, too.

Usually, a researcher has a question and then observes children to learn the answer. What you observe will

1-20 Each time this student observes and takes notes, she learns to see more.
© John Shaw

depend on the purpose of your observation. Because this book looks at the sequence of children's growth and development, you will consider these principles when you observe. Your teacher will assign you a task from the book. As you observe, you will look for answers to each task.

What Do Researchers Want to Know?

Sometimes researchers, while observing, think of another idea to study. You, too, will notice behaviors that were not part of your assigned work. You will want to ask questions about what you see. This is how researchers learn.

Other times, researchers want to know more about a behavior and decide to observe further. For example, you may hear three-year-olds reciting numbers from 1 to 10. Does this mean they can count objects to 10, also? To find out, you may need to observe behavior more closely.

Researchers may also look for causes that affect behavior, such as factors that cause a child to feel secure. You may also try to understand the behaviors of children or note why a certain game worked well with children.

Observing children can also help you better interact with the children in your care. You can learn this by observing how others work with children and how the children react to them.

Ways to Observe

There are many ways to observe children. The best way is to observe children directly. However, many observations are done indirectly.

Direct Observations

A **direct observation** means watching children in their natural environments. These environments include home, play groups, child care programs, schools, and public places, such as shopping centers, parks, and restaurants, 1-21. Most direct observations occur in places such as these.

Researchers often set up special laboratory settings where they can study what they do not often see in the natural environment. They may need to observe, for example, how a baby reacts when the mother leaves the room and a stranger enters. Researchers also use laboratory observations to speed up the observation process. Suppose researchers want to observe a child's balancing skills. If

they go to a park with a balance beam, they may wait hours before they can observe enough children to form a sample for their study. In a laboratory, however, children would arrive at the setting, walk the beam, and leave. Researchers also use laboratory settings when special equipment is needed.

Observations set in laboratories cannot answer all questions. For instance, it would be hard for researchers to know if children really like playing on a balance beam. Although some information in this book comes from research done in the laboratory setting, you will not start by observing in this way. You will begin observing in the natural setting, as all researchers do.

Indirect Observations

Although direct observation is the main way to learn about children, researchers also use other observation methods to study them. Sometimes they want to see something in more detail or check direct observations. One important method is **indirect observation**. This may include asking questions of

1-21 Researchers carefully observe and record many aspects of children's development.
© John Shaw

direct observation. Watching children in their natural environments.

indirect observation. Observation done by methods other than watching children, including asking other people questions about the children and observing the products children make.

parents, teachers, or children. Indirect observation also includes observing products children make, such as artwork or the stories children dictate or write. This method helps you gather information you could not obtain directly from observing the child.

You can learn a lot from children's work. You can learn even more when you observe children making these products. For example, it is easy to look at a drawing and notice a child has colored outside the lines. How can you tell if this is due to lack of motor control, a damaged crayon, or a rushed coloring job? Only direct observation will tell you.

Guidelines for Observing

Anyone observing children should follow certain guidelines, 1-22. These guidelines are important for several reasons. First, they protect the rights of the subject and the observer. They also list proper behaviors you should follow when visiting a child care center. Finally, these guidelines will help you make meaningful and accurate observations.

Guidelines for Observations

Guidelines	Details About Guidelines
Know your objectives.	Objectives tell us ❖ what age children to observe ❖ what type of activity to observe ❖ where to observe (in some cases) ❖ how much time to spend observing ❖ what type of records to keep
Obtain permission to observe.	In public places (a park or shopping center), you may observe children without permission. Parents or other adults are more cooperative, however, when they know what you are doing. Explain that you will keep children's names or other information confidential. To observe in private places (homes or child care programs), you will need prior approval from your teacher and permission from the adult at the home or program. Observe only on dates and times approved by your teacher. If observing in a home, call the day before to be sure the time is still convenient for the parent.
Know what to do at the site.	Remember, you are an invited guest. ❖ Always introduce yourself and state your purpose. ❖ Try not to distract children or adults from their activities. Move quietly, and do not talk unless you are working with children. ❖ Thank the parent or teacher when leaving. (continued)

1-22 Care must be taken when doing observations.

Guidelines for Observations (Continued)

Guidelines	Details About Guidelines
Know what to do at the site. (continued)	Sites also have different procedures. At some sites, you observe in an observation room looking through a one-way mirror. At other sites, you may help with the children. In still other sites, you sit away from the children. Find out in advance what you will be expected to do.
Be sure observations do not distract children from regular activities.	❖ Get acquainted with the children and setting before observing. ❖ Unless asked to help, do not get any closer to the children than necessary. (When making language observations, however, you must be close.) ❖ Do not smile at children or wear jewelry or clothing that will distract them. If children come to you, answer them briefly but encourage them to return to their activities. ❖ Avoid talking directly to children, including giving hints about how to do an activity. ❖ Your objectives should never interfere with the program objectives.
Observe carefully and objectively.	Observations require intense mental activity. You want to watch closely so you can remember the situation vividly. Many situations can affect objectivity, such as distractions, fatigue, or discomfort. Biases also affect objectivity. For these reasons, observers should not study their own children or children of close friends or relatives.
Record accurately.	Avoid the following three errors when recording information: ❖ Leaving out information that may help you understand the situation. ❖ Recording behaviors that did not occur. This happens when the observer does not pay close attention or relies on memory to complete notes. Sometimes biases cause the observer to use inaccurate words. Avoid using too many adjectives in your descriptions. ❖ Having notes out of sequence. Control this by writing the time in your notes every three to five minutes.
Protect the rights of all observed.	People have privacy rights observers must protect in the following ways: ❖ Never discuss a child in front of that child or an adult except the child's teacher. ❖ Use no name or the child's first name only during class discussions. (Researchers often use letters or numbers to identify children.) ❖ Respect parents' rights to refuse your request to observe. ❖ Keep information confidential. Take notes discreetly so others cannot read them as you write. File notes in a secure place when you are not using them. ❖ Destroy notes carefully when they are no longer useful. This applies to handwritten, typed, or word-processed notes and notes on disks. (If notes placed in the trash are easy to read, they are not destroyed.)

Summing It Up

The scientific study of children is called child development. Children's growth and development depends on three factors—heredity, environment, and the combination of heredity and environment. Most children follow similar patterns called principles of growth and development.

Brain development research helps people better understand how to help children learn. To help a child's brain wire itself to perform at its inherited potential, adults can offer a positive environment and rich sensory experiences.

Researchers have formed a number of theories about how children grow and develop. Havighurst and Maslow are two researchers with such theories.

Observing children is the best way to learn about their behavior. Child observations are done to answer questions, get new ideas, and look for causes that affect behavior.

Learning about children will help you understand the basic concepts of a child's growth and development.
© John Shaw

Reviewing Key Concepts

Write your answers on a separate sheet of paper.

1. True or false. Only people who will be parents someday need to know how to care for and guide children.
2. List four reasons that people study children.
3. Define the term *child development*.
4. List the six stages of the individual life cycle that include children.
5. What are the three factors that promote growth and development?
6. True or false. Genes affect the physical, mental, and social aspects of development to the same degree.
7. The environment _____(does, does not) greatly affect growth and development.
8. True or false. Brain development is a good example of how heredity and environment interact to affect development.
9. Explain the difference between developmental acceleration and developmental delay.
10. Describe one principle of growth and development and provide an example.
11. Which of the following statements is most true about child growth and development?
    A. Most children grow and develop at about the same rate of change and in the same ordered steps. The order of the steps and the rate of change in growth and development are about the same for most children.
    B. Most children grow and develop at about the same rate of change. The rate of change in growth and development is about the same for most children.
    C. The steps in which most children grow and develop occur in about the same order. The order of the steps in growth and development is about the same for most children.
12. Match each source of mastering developmental tasks with the correct example.
    _____ physical growth
    _____ social pressures
    _____ inner pressures
    A. The child's teacher says learning math skills is important.
    B. The child's brain cells develop.
    C. The child reads about space industry careers and thinks that such a career would be fun.
13. Explain Maslow's hierarchy of human needs.
14. List five guidelines for observing children.

Using Your Knowledge

1. **Social Studies.** Make a display called "Children in Our Society." In the display, use newspaper clippings, magazine articles, and

other information on children and products for children.

2. **Technology.** Use the Internet to research child labor laws. Share with your class how the needs of children led to these laws.

3. **Science/Art.** Research the anatomy of the brain and design a poster illustrating the various parts. You could also choose to research more about brain development and design a poster showing how stimulation changes the wiring of the brain.

4. **Language Arts.** Read about the life of a famous person in any career. Write a paper giving examples of constancy in the person's growth and development. How did this constancy lead to fame in his or her career?

Making Observations

1. List examples of culture you have observed being handed down from one generation to another. Examples of culture include language, attitudes, beliefs, rituals, and skills.

2. Observe a person working with children in a child-related career such as a child care teacher or child care provider. What characteristics does this person exhibit when working with children?

3. Observe a group of people. List characteristics you see that are due to heredity and characteristics you see that are due to environment. Compare your lists with a classmate and discuss.

4. Observe infants or toddlers and note examples you see that illustrate the principles of development.

Thinking Further

1. With a group of classmates, list some ways society is child-centered and some ways society is adult-centered. Discuss your lists. Can a society resolve these opposing interests? How can a new family find a balance for a happier family life?

2. If you were asked to recruit other students in your school to take a child development course, what would you say or do to convince them child development is a worthwhile subject? Be specific and explain the reason behind your idea(s).

3. Havighurst said one source for developmental tasks comes from social pressures. Given the situations in society today, what developmental tasks do you predict will be important for future children? Why?

4. With a small group, discuss how areas of development are interrelated. Each group should trace the effects of a different problem, such as poor nutrition or lack of affection, on all areas of development.

Chapter 2
Families Today

Latrice, age five, and Sheri, age three, attend a child care center while their mother works as a nurse. Since their parents' divorce two years ago, the girls have spent two weekends each month with their father. Recently, their father remarried a woman who has two children. Latrice and Sheri are having problems adjusting to these new family members. They show signs of stress before and after weekend visits with their father.

After studying this chapter, you will be able to

- describe changes affecting families today.
- explain the role of families in today's society.
- list the main advantages and disadvantages of living in different types of families.
- explain changes that take place during the family life cycle.
- describe the major roles of parents.
- define three parenting styles.
- list characteristics of healthy families.
- describe ways that culture influences the family.

The family is the oldest known social group. Why did it come into being? Experts do not know exactly. Most believe people began living in families for children's well-being. Throughout history, families have held different ideas about children's needs. These ideas have changed the roles of parents and family structures. However, families continue to be the basic unit of society.

Changes Affecting Families Today

Changes in society have caused major changes in the family. Before the Industrial Revolution, most families lived on farms. Farm families met most of their own needs. They were producers who built their own homes, made their own clothing, and grew their own food. These families consisted of the *immediate family* (parents and their children) as well as grandparents and other family members. These families often lived in nearby houses or shared the same house.

During the Industrial Revolution, many families moved off the farms and into the cities to work in factories, leaving relatives and friends behind. In the cities, families began to depend on others outside the family to produce most of the needed goods and services. City families became consumers. Earning an income, rather than making things, was most important.

Away from other relatives, people began to turn to their immediate family members for companionship and emotional support. The immediate family became more important for love and security. When these needs were not met within the family, divorce rates increased.

Today, the following changes affect families:

❖ Age at first marriage has increased. The median age at first marriage is now 25.1 years for women and 26.8 years for men. Although about 95 percent of people will marry during life, postponing marriage is common. Almost one-third of men and one-fourth of women have not married by 30 to 34 years of age.

❖ Birthrates declined for most of the 1990s, but slight increases are now being seen. (About 14.6 babies are born per 1000 people. The highest birthrate increase occurred in women ages 30 to 34 years. Teens were the only group to have a decrease in birthrate.)

❖ Family size has remained small. (Only 6 percent of all Americans with children have four or more children. More than half of adults prefer fewer than three children, while 38 percent say three children is ideal.)

❖ More women are working for economic reasons and personal fulfillment. (Over 60 percent of women with children under the age of six are employed and are earning incomes closer to equaling those of men.)

❖ The rate of marital separation and divorce rate is still high, but it is starting to level after a 30-year increase. (About 13 percent of women and 10 percent of men are currently separated or divorced. In any given year, separation/divorce affects about 1 in 60 children.)

❖ The rate of single-parent families is increasing. This is due to the high rate of divorce and separation, as well as the increased rate of people raising children outside of marriage. (About 43 percent of women and 34 percent of men who head single-parent families have never been married. In any given year, one-fourth of all children live in a single-parent family. About half of all children will live in a single-parent family at some point in their childhood.)

❖ The number of **multicultural families** (families with members from two or more cultural groups) is increasing. This trend is due to increases in interracial marriages and adoptions in which children and adoptive parents are from different cultures.

❖ Poverty continues to be a major concern for families. (Of today's children, about 1 in 5 was born poor; 1 in 6 is now poor; and 1 in 15 lives at less than half the poverty level.)

Changes in Family Roles

The roles of family members have changed through the years. Until the 1700s, parents were the only ones to meet children's physical needs for food, clothing, shelter, and safety. When children reached age four to seven years, they were expected to work long days in factories or on farms. Children were considered an asset to the family, for they helped the family earn money.

As adults learned more about children's needs, parent-child roles changed. Today, adults still must meet children's physical needs. However, they also see childhood as a special time in each person's life. A child's "job" is to learn about the world. Families serve as a support system from whom children can learn and be as free from stress as possible. Most people believe children's needs are best met first in a loving family and later by other social groups.

Family Types

In the United States, children are members of many types of families. The family type describes which people live in the household and how these people are related. Families can be two-parent, single-parent, or extended families. These families include children, their parent or parents, and (in extended families) other relatives.

Children usually enter families through birth and live in these families throughout childhood. Some children have families who formed differently, however. These types of families include stepfamilies, families with adoptive children, and foster families. In these cases, children can have more than one type of family. The following sections describe each family type and its effect on children.

2-1 This young boy lives with his biological parents in a two-parent family.

Two-Parent Families

A father, a mother, and their biological child or children who live together form a **two-parent family**. This type of family exists in most societies, 2-1. In two-parent families, children often leave home when they

multicultural families. Families with members from two or more cultural groups.

two-parent family. Family consisting of a father, a mother, and their biological child or children who live together.

become adults. When these children marry, they begin their own families separate from their parents.

When you think of the "typical family," what type of family comes to mind? Many think of the two-parent type, with a working father and a mother who cares for children at home. Is this type of family really typical in the United States? No—actually, only a small number of American families have two parents. Even fewer of those families have mothers who stay home with children.

Compared to other family types, two-parent families can have some disadvantages. In this tight family unit, relatives and others don't live in the home. Children in a two-parent family may be exposed less often to various kinds of people, including the elderly. This also means the children may lose out on the skills these other people can teach them. Finally, the family may live too far from relatives to rely on them for support in times of stress. This family type can also be a drawback for children if the parents do not get along. Children may be exposed to stress in the parents' relationship. This is especially true if the relationship is abusive.

On the other hand, two-parent families have advantages. Both the adults and the children may have their needs met more easily because family members can share responsibilities. Children may be apt to learn more flexible home and child care roles in the two-parent family. Adults often share these tasks, and children who see role sharing may be better prepared for the future than those who do not. Children also have the chance to see how spouses should relate to each other.

Single-Parent Families

Single-parent families are headed by one adult. These families form when a parent dies, parents divorce or separate, or a single parent adopts children. A single parent may also head the family if parents have children outside of marriage or a parent deserts the family.

The number of single parents in America is growing. The greatest increase is among parents who have never been married. The high rate of marital separation and divorce is also a factor. Women head most single-parent families. However, a growing number of single fathers are gaining custody and raising their children, 2-2.

Raising children alone is hard. Single parents face the responsibility of providing care, supervision, and guidance for their children alone. Both parents still have a legal responsibility to provide financial support for the children, but often one provides the bulk of the support. Single parents often lack support and feel overwhelmed by all they must do. How well they handle their parenting roles depends on their family situation. For instance, a sudden change from having two parents to having only one can bring a difficult adjustment for the remaining parent and the children.

2-2 More single men are opting to raise their children.
© Nancy P. Alexander

Being a single parent is not easy, but it can be very rewarding. Children in well-adjusted single-parent homes are more stable than children in unhappy two-parent homes. The relationship between the children and their parent is often very strong. In addition, recent studies show that children of single parents may show independence at an earlier age than those in other family types. In these studies, children with one parent performed some self-care tasks, such as using the toilet, earlier than children living with two parents.

Living with a single parent does not always mean the other parent cannot take an active role in the children's lives. In fact, children are often happier when both parents are involved. When possible, parents should work together to raise the children even if they do not live in the same house. Some co-parents go to court to seek **joint custody.** This is the shared legal right to provide care and make decisions about their children's lives. Joint custody is becoming more common.

If only one parent participates in the child's life, he or she should be sure to find other sources of support and help. Families and friends can serve as role models for the children. These loved ones can offer help and love to the parent and the children. Often, social service agencies offer emotional, practical, and financial help, too.

Extended Families

In an **extended family**, more than two generations of a family live together. In the past, the extended family was most often an older couple

single-parent families. Families headed by one adult.

joint custody. The shared legal right of parents who are not married to provide care and make decisions about their children's lives.

extended family. Family in which several generations live together.

2-3 Many of today's extended families include parents, children, and one or more grandparents.

with their children, in-laws, and grandchildren. Today, many other family groups may form an extended family, 2-3.

Sometimes the extended family lives in one home. Each family unit may have some space to call its own. The extended family might cook and eat together and share some common space in the home. Extended family members may live together if they run a family business. In these families, members often share housework and child care. Each member does a certain task, and members may not change roles often. For instance, the same person may cook each day.

Extended families are very common in many countries around the world. In the United States, these families are generally less common than they once were. For the most part, fewer family businesses and less economic need for large families caused the decline. In some cultures and regions of the country, however, this family type is still quite common.

Sometimes an extended family forms temporarily. For example, young adults may move back home while trying to establish their careers. A divorced family member may need a temporary residence while trying to save money. Aging family members may need short-term care.

Extended families do experience certain problems more often than members of other kinds of families. Sometimes children and even adults find they must deal with too many people. Also, decisions are often made for the good of the entire family rather than the needs of each person.

These families also have many advantages. Children learn to interact with people of all ages because young and old members are in daily contact. This helps family members know and respect each other. Extended families are good at handing down family beliefs and *family history* (stories of a family's past), 2-4. Because there are so many members, extended families can perform more duties than small family groups. For example, some members can care for the children of working parents. When stressful events, such as death, happen in extended families, many people are there to help children and adults.

Stepfamilies

Stepfamilies are formed when a single parent marries another person. In many cases, two single parents marry each other. Families in which the children of both spouses will live with the couple are sometimes called *blended families*.

The stepfamily is a fairly common family form. As more single parents marry or remarry, it grows even more common. In fact, many of today's children have two stepfamilies—that

2-4 Grandfathers often take pride in handing down family history and sharing their talents with their grandchildren.
© John Shaw

of the father and his new wife and that of the mother and her new husband. Often children live with only one of these stepfamilies. Other

stepfamilies. Families formed when a single parent marries another person.

times, children live with each step-family part of the year. Each situation is unique.

When a stepfamily forms, it can be a big adjustment for everyone. Family members find themselves in instant relationships—stepparents must relate with stepchildren and stepchildren must relate with each other. The parents must also adjust to their new roles of husband and wife. Children usually maintain relationships with the family of their other parent, too. All this adds up to many changes for everyone, especially the children.

Children may have problems adjusting to a new family. Many children are asked to adjust to two sets of rules. This can be a major problem for school-age children, who are weighing family and peer priorities in search of self-identity. Dealing with two families may further confuse their self-identity.

One study reported that, although they do face problems, almost two-thirds of stepfamilies have good relationships. In this study, both mothers and children tended to rate stepfathers as good parents—just as good as biological fathers. It can take special effort, however, to help the family adjust smoothly.

Families with Adopted Children

Adoption occurs when a child of one pair of parents legally becomes the child of another parent or parents. Adoption legally ends the rights and responsibilities between a child and the birthparents (biological parents). The adoptive parents are then granted these rights. Adoption gives the child a new family.

People want to adopt for a number of reasons. Among them are the following:

❖ The couple cannot give birth or can give birth only with great difficulty.
❖ The couple may want to add to their current family.
❖ The couple know a child who needs a home.
❖ A single person wants to be a parent and provide a home for children.

Fewer birthparents plan adoptions now than in the past. This means fewer babies are available to be adopted. Many of the children available for adoption are older, have special needs, are born outside the U.S., or living in foster families and group homes.

Adoption Agencies and Independent Adoptions

Most parents who have adopted children have spent much effort finding them. There are two ways to adopt children legally—through an adoption agency and through an independent source.

An **adoption agency** is an agency licensed by the state to handle adoptions. It is either state funded (such as the agency that also handles foster care) or private (managed by a church or organization). The agency works out the details between the birthparents and adoptive parents. Final legal aspects of the adoption are handled in state courts.

In an **independent adoption**, a person, such as a lawyer or physician, works out the details between the birthparents and adoptive parents. In some independent adoptions, fewer details must be worked out. Such cases include adoption of relatives or stepchildren. All independent adoptions are handled in state courts and thus follow state laws. Foreign adoptions can be either agency or independent adoptions. You can use Figure 2-5 to help you compare the pros and cons of each type of adoption.

Adoption Options and Rights

The laws of each state govern adoption options and rights. In all states, when people pay money that exceeds medical and legal costs to an agency, independent source, or birthparents, they are "buying" a child. This is called an **illegal market adoption**.

In an adoption, birthparents sign forms to release the baby from the hospital for adoption purposes. They also sign papers consenting to the adoption. Then the matter must be presented in court and a judge must declare the adoption final. Each state sets laws about what papers must be signed and what waiting periods may occur between various steps of the process. When the adoption is complete, the child's original birth certificate will be placed under court

seal. A new one will be issued listing the adoptive parents as the child's parents.

Both agency and independent adoptions may be either closed or open adoptions. Birthparents and adoptive parents can choose the type they prefer. The two options differ in how much information is exchanged and how much contact occurs between the birthparents and the adoptive family.

In a **closed adoption**, the identity of the birthparents and adopting family are not revealed to each other. The two sides do not meet or contact each other. The adoption agency, attorney, or

adoption. The process by which a child of one pair of parents legally becomes the child of other parents (or parent).

adoption agency. A state-funded or private agency licensed by the state to handle adoptions.

independent adoption. An adoption in which a person, such as a lawyer or physician, works out the details between the birthparents and adoptive parents.

illegal market adoption. An adoption in which adoptive parents pay money to an agency, independent source, or birthparents other than medical and legal costs that are approved by state law.

closed adoption. An adoption in which the identity of the birthparents and adopting family are not revealed to each other.

Types of Adoption

Type	Pros	Cons
Agency	❖ Agency handles the legal aspects to meet the needs of all involved. ❖ Children are closely matched with adoptive families to ensure good placement. Emphasis is on meeting the child's needs. ❖ Birthparents can request certain types of adoptive families. (They can choose or meet adoptive parents in an open adoption.) ❖ Adoptive parent can choose a child of a certain gender, age, and family background. ❖ Information is exchanged between birthparents and the adoptive family (nonidentifying information only in a closed adoption). ❖ Social workers counsel both sets of parents. ❖ Adoptive families are supervised from the time children are placed until the adoption is final. ❖ Cost may be lower for the adoptive parents. Agency may charge based on parents' ability to pay.	❖ Agency sets criteria for adoptive parents. Many suitable homes may be turned down in favor of "more qualified" homes. People who are newly married, remarried, single, or older may have a harder time using an agency. ❖ Income, religious, and housing guidelines may also exclude some people wanting to adopt. ❖ The study of people wanting to adopt is extremely detailed and goes into all aspects of personal and married life. ❖ Fewer babies are available for adoption. Also, available children may not be of the same culture as the adoptive parents. ❖ When fewer children are available for adoption, long waiting periods are common. ❖ People wanting to adopt may wait a long time before a good match with a child is found.
Independent	❖ There are no stated qualifications for adoptive parents. Thus, many people who might not be chosen to adopt through agency (people who are newly married, remarried, single, or older) can become adoptive parents. ❖ If they wish, birthparents can arrange for someone they already know as adoptive parents. ❖ It may be easier to adopt a baby or to adopt a child of the same culture as the adoptive parents.	❖ Less emphasis may be placed on the child's welfare. ❖ Adoptive parents are screened less thoroughly. Placement occurs before a study is done, so child may be in an unsuitable home. ❖ Adoptive parents may receive less information about child's background and health history. ❖ Adoptive parents need to hire lawyers to help them with legal details. ❖ May be less privacy for both sets of parents than in an agency adoption. ❖ Counseling is not provided as part of the adoption. ❖ Cost may be higher than with an agency. (Some adoptive parents enter illegal market adoptions without knowing it.)

2-5 Adoptive parents should consider the advantages and disadvantages of each type of adoption before choosing one.

doctor works out the details of the adoption. Addresses, names, and other identifying facts are kept private.

Other information can be exchanged through the agency or person handling the adoption. The adoptive family and child have a right to know the medical history and social backgrounds of the birthparents. The birthparents have a right to know about the type of family in which the child will be placed. Sometimes birthparents write a letter for the child to read when he or she is old enough to understand it. (This letter would be signed with a nonidentifying signature, such as *Your Birthmom*.)

In closed adoptions, state laws govern what identifying information can be made available and to whom it can be given. Sometimes even an adult who was adopted as a child cannot obtain information about his or her birthparents.

Fewer closed adoptions occur today. These are being replaced by **open adoption**, a type of adoption that involves some degree of communication between the birthparents and adoptive family. The *openness* of the adoption refers to how much information is exchanged and how much contact occurs. In an open adoption, the birthparents might choose and meet the adoptive parents. They could also choose the adoptive parents from resumes and/or photographs.

In the last 20 years, open adoptions have grown more common. The birthparents feel they have more choice in the decision. Adopting families will not think of the adoption process as something secret and will also have the information and support to best parent their children. Children benefit from knowing their adoptions were loving decisions that involved open communication between both sets of parents. In open adoptions, all adoption records are usually accessible to adopted children when they become adults.

Adoption rights protect those involved in adoption. In most states, the birthfather has legal rights. State laws may permit him to deny *paternity* (fathering of a child), give all rights to the birthmother, or give permission along with the birthmother for the child to be adopted. In some states, if the father cannot be found, steps can be taken to end his rights to make decisions about the child.

Adoption Issues

Children who are adopted generally have stable, happy home lives. This is because their adopted families wanted them very much, 2-6. Some problems can exist, however. In most cases, adoptive parents don't have the nine months of pregnancy to make the transition to parenthood. Instead,

open adoption. An adoption that involves some degree of communication between birthparent(s) and adoptive family.

2-6 Adoption is often a happy situation for both adoptive parents and children.
© John Shaw

they take on their new roles very quickly. Persons wanting to adopt may be on a waiting list for many years. Then one day the adoption agency may call and announce a child will be ready for them the next day!

Other problems may arise related to the adopted child's birthparents, especially if the adoption is closed. Birthparents may want to see the child. There is a chance they may want to become part of the child's life. Adoptive parents may not agree this is best for the child. Children who are adopted often ask questions about the adoption. They may want to know about or meet their birthparents. Older children who have lived with their birthparents and are then adopted by a new family need time to adjust. These children may

miss their birthparents or want to be with them again. Adoptive parents may need to seek counseling to help them guide the children and offer them the support needed to make the adjustment.

Adoptive parents should answer their children's questions about adoption in direct and honest ways. Adopted children should be told from the beginning they are adopted. Their adoptions should not be kept secret. This would cause more turmoil for the child when he or she found out the truth.

It can take time for each member to adjust to living in an adoptive family. Soon, however, this family will likely adapt. Most adoptive parents create a loving family life that helps adopted children overcome any stress they may feel.

Foster Families

Some children live at least part of their lives in **foster families**. These are families in which adults provide temporary homes for children who cannot live with their birthparents. Foster parents assume the parenting responsibilities for the children in their care. They fill these roles until the children are reunited with their birthparents or placed in adoptive homes.

Children often enter foster families because of problems in their birthfamilies. These problems often include abuse, neglect, and substance abuse by the birthparents or other family members. In these cases, the courts intervene to protect the children. The court places the children in a foster family and provides counseling, treatment, and other help for the birthparents. The goal is to reunite children with their birthparents if possible. However, the birthparents must be able to provide a safe, secure home for their children. In serious or prolonged cases, the court may sever the rights of the birthparents. The children are then placed in a foster family until they can be adopted and given a permanent home. Sometimes children can be adopted by their foster parents.

A foster family may have one or two parents. It may include other biological, adoptive, or foster children. A foster child may be placed with brothers and sisters or apart from them, depending on the situation. Foster families can offer a stable, secure home for children. Joining a foster family is a big adjustment, however. In many cases, foster children need counseling for the problems they faced in their birthfamilies. They may also miss their birthparents and other family members. To ease separation stress, contact or visitation is sometimes granted. Other children may grieve if they know they will never return to live with their birthparents. Each situation is unique. Foster parents need to be flexible, supportive, and understanding of the children in their care.

In recent years, three main changes in the foster care system have greatly helped foster children. The following paragraphs describe each of these changes.

First, foster families get more support in the task of raising children. Better screening and training for foster parenting is now more common. Caseworkers are making more frequent visits to foster families to check on the welfare of the children. Therapists counsel for the foster family as a whole and each member separately.

Second, the courts have recognized that all children need permanent homes. In the past, birthparents were given many years to work out their problems. Their children spent this year waiting for a permanent home life, which some of them never received. Foster children were also moved from foster home to foster home due to a large number or less-than-ideal placements. Moving foster children was also meant to prevent too strong of attachments between foster parents and foster children. Such actions were not in the best interest of the children. Today, birthparents must become fit parents more quickly or sign papers allowing their children to be adopted. Foster children who are not reunited with their birthparents are placed for adoption sooner than in the past—many as babies or very young children. Now foster parents

foster families. Families in which adults provide temporary homes for children who cannot live with their birthparents.

who care for a given child may even be eligible to adopt the child.

Third, states are recognizing foster children may need help and support even after they reach 18 years of age. In most states, foster family care stops when the child reaches this age. At this age, young adults may not have completed high school. Even fewer are enrolled in further education or have careers. Today, some provisions are being made to further help young adults from foster families. Programs are available to help these young adults find housing, learn work skills, and gain life-management skills. These programs can help foster children become independent and live on their own. Having this help can make the transition from foster care to adulthood easier for them.

The Family Life Cycle

Families change through the years, just as individuals do. Most families change in similar stages that are called the **family life cycle**. The family life cycle can be divided into six stages, 2-7.

In the *beginning stage*, the couple is a family of two. During this time, they get to know each other better. They also decide whether they want to become parents and how soon, if ever, they will parent. (Families without children will stay in this stage until they reach the mid-years stage.)

For families who will have children, the next stage is the *childbearing*

stage. In this stage, the family grows as parents give birth to one or more children. Parents learn their roles in caring for and guiding children through their earliest years. As parents enter later stages, their roles will continue to change.

The *parenting stage* begins when the family is complete. Parents focus on guiding and nurturing their children. They are preparing their children to become productive members of society. During these years, parents also realize other people will be teaching and guiding their children. Children begin to learn more from teachers and peers. Parents need to stay involved with their children's growth.

Children's adolescent years can be confusing for both parents and children. Adolescents are striving to become more independent. They are not always ready to handle as much responsibility as they want to, however. Adolescents may want more privacy, but they still need to know they can talk to their parents. At this stage, parents need to begin treating their children as adults. They also need to know when to provide guidance and help.

The *launching stage* brings new feelings for parents. During this stage,

family life cycle. A series of six stages through which many families go over the years.

The Family Life Cycle

Beginning stage

A couple marries and gets to know each other. This stage lasts until a child is born.

Launching stage

The couple's children begin leaving home to live on their own. This stage ends when all children have left home.

Childbearing stage

The couple starts having children. This stage lasts until the birth of the last child.

Mid-years stage

The couple focuses on their marriage, planning for their future, and becoming grandparents. This stage last until the couple retires.

Parenting stage

The couple focuses on guiding their children through the school-age and teen years. This stage lasts until children start to leave home.

Aging stage

The couple retires and adjusts to this change in lifestyle. This stage lasts throughout life.

2-7 Families with children pass through the six stages of the family life cycle.

children start to leave home to make their own lives. As each child leaves home, parents may feel lonelier. They may also feel their children no longer need them. In this stage, parents must acknowledge their children are adults. Now their relationships may be more equal. Parents may continue to be an important part of their children's lives.

In the *mid-years stage*, parents may find more time for themselves than they did when their children lived at home. They may devote more time to new interests or hobbies. Keeping in touch with their children is still important. They may be involved with their grandchildren. The couple also begins to focus on its retirement.

The final stage of the family life cycle is the *aging stage*. This stage lasts from retirement to death of both partners. In this stage, the couple may pursue new hobbies and spend time with family and friends. They may have health problems that cause them to need help from their children. The couple may face different challenges and have new concerns. During this stage, all family members may need to make many adjustments.

A new challenge for families occurs when grown children return home after the launching stage. Economic troubles, divorce, or other situations may cause them to move back home again. Parents may have to learn new ways to relate to these children. They may have adjusted to their children becoming adults. Now, however, they may not know how to treat them as adults when they all live in the same home. Likewise, adult children may not know what parents expect of them. Family members need to communicate openly to make sure family members continue to get along.

Roles of Parents

Parents are responsible for the well-being of their children. In American society, parents' roles mainly involve socialization, nuturance, guidance, and discipline. Children must be socialized into their culture by their parents and other members of their family. Children thrive in a nurturing environment and need guidance and discipline to learn right from wrong.

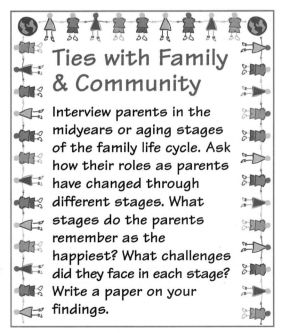

Ties with Family & Community

Interview parents in the midyears or aging stages of the family life cycle. Ask how their roles as parents have changed through different stages. What stages do the parents remember as the happiest? What challenges did they face in each stage? Write a paper on your findings.

Socialization

As you learned in chapter 1, socialization is the training children receive to help them learn to live in a group. Each group or culture has its own rules and ways of doing things. Children are not born knowing what their parents' cultural group or society expects of its members. All this must be learned, 2-8. These learnings occur early in life, with the foundation being laid by as early as five years of age. In these early years, children interact mostly with their parents. For this reason, parents are the people most responsible for socializing children.

Socialization is complex and requires the passing down of many personal priorities that work toward the same end, 2-9. Socialization is a major role of parents, for it allows children to fit into their culture. As you read the next sections, keep in mind the way parents nurture, guide, and discipline their children is part of the socialization process.

Nurturance

Nurturance, in a narrow sense, includes the physical aspects of child care, such as feeding, dressing, and bathing children. In a broader sense, nurturance also includes meeting emotional and social needs, such as helping children feel secure and loved. Studies in child development show that physical care, love, and

Aspects of a Person's Culture

History, folklore, heroes

Language (written, verbal, slang, body language, and gestures)

Humor

Names (surname and given name)

Holiday celebrations, traditions, and rituals

Methods of greeting (such as eye contact, handshakes, hugs, kisses, and bowing)

Preferences about personal space and touching

Foods, eating methods, eating manners

Dress and body decorations

Home furnishings and decorations

Arts and crafts

2-8 Culture touches many aspects of a person's life. What others can you list?

concern are important for children's healthy growth. Both mothers and fathers play an important role in nurturing their children.

Guidance and Discipline

Child guidance and discipline are important responsibilities of parenthood. Parents guide their children in

 nurturance. Providing all aspects of care for a child, which includes meeting physical, emotional, and social needs.

Examples of Cultural Priorities

Family and family roles:
- ❖ Does the family include immediate family only, immediate and extended family, or family and other friends and loved ones?
- ❖ How important is the family compared to nonfamily persons?
- ❖ How important are elders, the husband-wife bond, and children?
- ❖ Do family members live in the same house?
- ❖ Who makes decisions?

Parenting methods:
- ❖ Are adults in the family child-centered or adult-centered?
- ❖ Who cares for young children, and how is this care given?
- ❖ By what age is the child viewed as an adult?

Health practices:
- ❖ Is care given for prevention and/or disease/injury?
- ❖ Are natural approaches (herbs, etc.) or high technology treatments given?

Moral learnings:
- ❖ What is good character?
- ❖ Which actions are considered misbehavior?
- ❖ When children misbehave, how is it handled?

Achievement:
- ❖ What aspects of achievement are most important?
- ❖ Is ability or effort seen as more important?

Attitudes:
- ❖ independence vs. dependence
- ❖ child-centered vs. family-centered
- ❖ regard for things vs. regard for people
- ❖ direct and assertive interaction style vs. less open and passive interaction style
- ❖ change is positive vs. hold to tradition
- ❖ aggressive vs. submissive
- ❖ work to "get ahead" vs. work for present needs
- ❖ saving for future vs. sharing wealth
- ❖ self-support vs. depends on others for support
- ❖ individual identity vs. group identity
- ❖ time orientation vs. flexible use of time

2-9 Priorities may differ greatly from one culture to the next.

their daily interactions with them. **Guidance** includes the words and actions parents use to influence their child's behavior. For example, when parents face frustrations but react calmly, they guide their children to do the same. By showing children they are not upset when they don't get their way, parents are modeling good behavior. Guiding children in a positive way is an important parental role, 2-10.

Discipline is part of guidance. **Discipline** is the use of methods and techniques to teach children self-control. Through discipline, children learn to act in ways that society finds acceptable.

The goal of guidance and discipline is to teach children behaviors that will help them guide themselves. Guidance and discipline teach children to think and act in safe and acceptable

2-10 Teaching children to make their homework a priority is only one guidance task of parents.

ways. There are various ways to help children learn this, and some are more effective than others.

Types of Discipline

Most parents would like to find the perfect method for handling their children's unpleasant or disruptive behaviors. Although there is no perfect method for use with every child, some forms of discipline are

better than others. These methods teach children self-control. This is important because parents will not always be able to guide children, especially as they become older. Studies have found that parents and other adults use three types of discipline—power assertion, love withdrawal, and induction.

Power Assertion

Power assertion occurs when parents use or threaten to use some form of physical punishment. The main problem with physical punishment is that it can hurt or harm children. Certainly, many people can name children who were occasionally spanked and are now healthy, happy adults. Some adults even claim spankings were good for them. If this is true, why are most parenting experts against power-assertive techniques?

There are several reasons that power-assertive techniques are not healthy forms of discipline. First, power assertion works because the child fears the adult. As the child

guidance. The words and actions parents use to influence their children's behavior.

discipline. The use of methods and techniques to help teach children self-control.

power assertion. A discipline technique in which parents use or threaten to use some form of physical punishment.

grows physically, however, fear lessens and the technique no longer works. Even for young children, fear is based on being caught and punished. Many power-assertive adults will threaten, "Don't let me catch you doing that again!" Thus, the child weighs the chances of being caught and the likely punishment. The child is not being guided by what is right or wrong.

Another reason power-assertion techniques are poor is because, to children, being physically punished for an act of aggression such as hitting another child seems like a double standard. The child may think, "You are hitting me; why can't I hit others?"

In addition, power-assertive techniques are often used when parents are angry. If parents are prone to losing their tempers, their intended light physical punishment could become abusive when done in anger.

Finally, all discipline techniques are imitated or modeled by children. Children disciplined through power assertiveness are more apt to use these methods in their own relationships. If they see their parents lose control, children may become violent during the teen years or abusive to their own spouses or children as adults.

Love Withdrawal

In a discipline technique called love withdrawal, parents threaten children or suggest some form of parent/child separation. An extreme example is parents telling children they do not want or love them. Some parents even tell their children they are going to give them away. Milder forms of love withdrawal include ignoring the child or giving the child the "silent treatment." Experts consider love withdrawal to be emotional abuse. Even in its milder forms, the technique creates stress and prevents the expression of feelings.

Induction

The third technique, induction, happens when parents discipline by reasoning and explaining. Adults, as older and wiser people, explain why children should or should not use certain behaviors. Children disciplined by this technique tend to show better self-control, display more concern for others, and take responsibility for their own failures.

By using the induction method, parents can use several discipline techniques. The technique used will vary for each age group, 2-11. These techniques are described in more detail in later chapters on meeting children's needs.

Parenting Styles

Most parents want to raise their children to become responsible, well-mannered adults. They realize guidance and discipline are important. New parents need to give some thought to the style they will use to guide and discipline their children. Parenting styles can be grouped into

Examples of Specific Discipline Techniques

0 – 3 months
None. Parents try to sooth babies with routines.

3 – 6 months
None. Parents try to interact with babies as much as possible.

6 – 12 months
None. Parents still try to interact with babies and make their houses childproof.

12 – 18 months
Parents provide a secure base for normal exploration and childproof their houses and yards. They can also direct their babies away from undesired behavior and dangerous situations.

18 – 36 months
Parents should remove children from dangerous situations. They should say no and give one- or two-word explanation, such as "Hot!" or "Hurt baby." Parents should also keep their houses childproof.

3 – 4 years
Parents should explain why children cannot do or continue to do something. After the first offense, take or send children to a quiet place where they are alone but not afraid. Children should remain alone for three or four minutes.

4 years – school age
Parents should use the induction method. Adjust reasons to the child's age. Some good techniques include the following:
- ❖ Listen to the child's story.
- ❖ Acknowledge the child's feelings with statements like "I know you feel angry."
- ❖ Express your feelings about the consequences and your expectations with statements like, "I was furious you left your wagon outside in the rain. The wagon goes in the garage each day."
- ❖ Avoid attacking a child's character. For example, do not call the child stupid.
- ❖ Allow the child to make amends.
- ❖ Give the child a choice of meeting a standard or losing a privilege. For example, "If you cannot rinse your dish, I cannot let you eat a snack."

Parents may need to send some children to a quiet, safe place for about one minute per age, when misbehavior occurs.

2-11 At every age, parents should discipline their children with love and understanding.

three main categories: authoritarian, permissive, and democratic.

Authoritarian

Some parents use an **authoritarian** parenting style, in which the main objective is to make children completely obedient. These parents think obedience is the most important behavior their children should learn. They expect

love withdrawal. Discipline techniques in which parents threaten children with being unloved or suggest some form of parent/child separation.

induction. A technique in which parents discipline by reasoning and explaining.

authoritarian. Parenting style in which the main objective is to make children completely obedient.

children to respect their authority with little or no explanation as to why children should obey. Such parents are likely to use physical punishment when children do not behave. They seldom reward good behavior.

Authoritarian parenting may teach children to obey their parents. However, these children may not understand why they should act as their parents wish. They may not be able to develop self-control. They may also fear their parents and even rebel against them when they become older. Authoritarian parenting does not have good outcomes for the child. As a result, most parenting experts do not recommend this style of parenting.

Permissive

Permissive parents give children almost no guidelines or rules. They feel children should make their own decisions about right and wrong. They may think setting limits for their children will make the children feel unhappy or unloved. The truth is, without guidelines, these children may feel lost. They may have trouble getting along with others later in life because they have never needed to follow rules. Permissive parenting can also give children the impression parents do not care enough to guide and teach them. Parenting experts do not recommend this style of parenting.

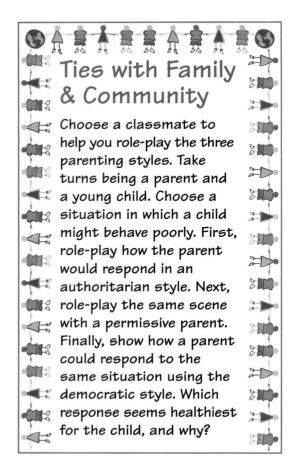

Ties with Family & Community

Choose a classmate to help you role-play the three parenting styles. Take turns being a parent and a young child. Choose a situation in which a child might behave poorly. First, role-play how the parent would respond in an authoritarian style. Next, role-play the same scene with a permissive parent. Finally, show how a parent could respond to the same situation using the democratic style. Which response seems healthiest for the child, and why?

Democratic

Most parents find a compromise between these two styles of parenting. They use a **democratic** style, in which parents set some rules but allow children some freedom. When these parents set rules, they explain to children why the rules are needed. Children may even be allowed to help set some rules and decide some punishments. These children learn self-discipline in a positive, encouraging setting. Parenting experts endorse a democratic parenting style as healthiest for children and families.

Characteristics of Healthy Families

Families may be healthy or unhealthy. What determines a family's health? In the past, it was measured mainly by durability (family staying together for many years). Often, durability can be a sign of a family's health. Sometimes, however, families may stay together even though members may seem to be family in name only.

There is no magic recipe to create a healthy family. Families can be very different and yet strong. Some characteristics are often seen in healthy families. The most common is that spouses enter marriage with shared personal priorities. They use these priorities to decide on goals throughout their marriage and guide them in parenting their children.

Closely tied to shared priorities is the belief that family members are individuals. Strong families accept that even people who share many priorities will be somewhat different. They also realize life itself can change the family's goals. Healthy families are willing to adjust as needed.

Healthy families seem to share a mutual commitment to family life. In these families, parents want their own relationship to succeed, 2-12. They want to be successful parents. Part of

2-12 In healthy families, parents take time to work on their marriage and keep it strong. This helps them be successful parents and role models for their children.

the commitment involves growth—becoming more loving, caring, and understanding. These members also want to do many things as a family unit.

In healthy families, members want to help each other rather than being self-centered. Members share responsibilities. Although each family may divide

permissive. Parenting style in which parents give children almost no guidelines or rules.

democratic. Parenting style in which parents set some rules but allow children some freedom.

tasks differently, healthy families seem to happily follow their own choices about duties. Each member can depend on the others to keep promises, fulfill commitments, and be honest.

Healthy families communicate. They are polite and consider each other's feelings. They talk about their feelings and problems. Healthy families use problem-solving skills to work on problems rather than trying to change others. Above all, the members support each other's efforts and show appreciation for each other.

Cultural Influences on Families

Families are alike in many ways, but they may differ in the cultural groups to which they belong. Culture, a way of life for a certain group of people, greatly affects a family's life. Because not every family belongs to the same culture, the effects of culture differ widely from one family to the next.

People of many cultural groups live in the United States. Families who once came from many parts of the world call this country home. The U.S. is an example of a nation with great **cultural diversity**, which means it has more than one culture represented among its people.

Families often identify their culture in terms of their origin or ancestors. Some people refer to their *region of origin*. An example is saying a person has a Native American, European, or African heritage. Other people refer to

culture by the *specific country* from which their ancestors came. These people might say they are Mexican rather than Latino or Chinese rather than Asian. Still other groups refer to the *language* they speak, such as Spanish-speaking or German-speaking peoples.

All families are affected by each culture to which they belong. The influence might be subtle or more profound, depending on how involved the family is in the culture. The degree of involvement can vary widely, even among members of the same culture.

Culture affects the beliefs and customs families have. Each culture's practices support its particular beliefs and customs. For example, families in some cultures view academic learnings as the top priority for children, whereas other cultures emphasize play as well as academic skills. Because they have such different views, these two families will differ in their parenting practices, modeling, praise, and criticism regarding the role of education.

Parents model, reward, and praise what their culture values. They criticize and correct that which doesn't fit with their cultural beliefs. In this socialization process, children learn most of their culture's values at home. These concepts are also taught indirectly by living within the culture.

cultural diversity. Having more than one culture represented.

Some cultural concepts, such as history and heroes, are taught more directly. The reasons behind traditions of the culture are also often taught to children from an early age. Older family members may help impart values to children through storytelling and answering children's questions about the culture or its practices.

Cultures differ in the way they view the concept of family. In some cultures, *family* includes only the immediate family. In others, this term has a broader meaning that includes extended family members, close family friends, and neighbors.

The importance of the family also varies from culture to culture, 2-13. In

Cultures See Families Differently

Group-Oriented Culture	Individually-Oriented Culture
Family includes kin and perhaps others.	Family includes parents and their children.
Family members live in same house or near each other.	Family members may live far from kin.
Status in the family (and possibly in the group) is achieved by age and/or gender.	Status is determined by achievement.
Elders make decisions based on the welfare of the whole family (collective responsibility).	The individual considers his or her own welfare when making decisions for himself or herself (individual responsibility).
Members take pride in their family name, family history, and family honor.	Members take pride in their own talents, achievements, and status.
Conform to those in authority.	Challenge or question those in authority.
Cooperate in all tasks.	Competitive.
Family harmony is emphasized.	Individual pursuit of happiness is emphasized.
Early dependence on group is encouraged. Group members help each other, even at their own expense.	Early independence encouraged. Each person is expected to help himself or herself with little assistance from family.
Parent-child bond stressed. Children are seen as extensions of parents (children bring honor to and help family throughout life).	Husband-wife bond stressed. Children are individuals who as adults take care of themselves.
Parents ask, "What can we do to help each other?"	Parents ask, "What can I do to help you?"
Expression of emotion is more indirect (emotionally controlled; modest; formal toward elders to show respect).	Expression of emotion is more direct (emotionally expressive; more "I-centered;" informal).

2-13 Group-oriented cultures see families differently from cultures that are individual-oriented. These two sets of beliefs affect family life in different ways.

cultures with a group orientation, family is most important. As the name suggests, cultures with an individual orientation focus on each person as an individual more than on the family as a group.

Goals for achievement vary from culture to culture. Some cultures stress academic achievement as a way to honor the family and achieve economic success that will help the entire family. Other cultures stress achievement in social interactions. In these cultures, showing dignity and respect in inter-actions with others brings honor to the individual or family.

Language can vary from one culture to the next, too. Families generally use their culture's native language and teach this language to their children. Using the language of their people can bring a sense of unity and belonging. Families may use language as a way to foster this involvement in the culture.

Speaking different languages is not the only way communication differs across cultures. The role of language can differ, too. For instance, some cultures teach children to talk often, be open and direct, and be informal. These children might address people by their first names without asking and soon after meeting, use slang, and talk to strangers. Other cultures value silence; that is, talking only when necessary. These cultures teach children to notice other body language clues (such as "reading the eyes") to help

them understand without being told. These cultures prefer formal word choice and the use of courtesy titles when addressing elders or strangers. In these cultures, children are taught to address elders in a way that shows respect.

The use and meaning of body language can vary from group to group. This explains the well-known saying: *Not all people smile in the same language.* In some cultures, smiling expresses friendliness, pleasure, or understanding of humor. In other cultures, a smile is used to acknowledge a fault. Some cultures might use smiling to mask emotion (hurt or disagreement) or avoid conflict. In other cultures, people smile in response to a compliment if they feel verbal response would show a lack of modesty.

The family also teaches children how to respond to people of other cultures. Families who value diversity point out the benefit of learning from people who are not like themselves. These families teach children to appreciate people of all cultures. They believe each group is different from, but equal to, other groups. Other families do not value diversity. They believe their group is better than others and that people of different groups should not interact with one another. Whatever their viewpoints, parents should be aware they are passing these views to their children.

Multicultural Families

As the United States increases in cultural diversity, the number of multicultural families continues to grow. In these families, more than one culture is represented. This happens when people of different cultures marry or when single people of different cultures have children together. Children and their adoptive or foster parents might also come from different cultures.

Multicultural families are like other families in many ways. They have many of the same joys and problems as other families. In some ways, however, these families are unique. The diversity within their families can bring added joy as well as added challenges.

Everyone in a multicultural family needs to learn about the cultures of its members. Parents need to understand the roles and expectations of each of these cultures. This takes some time and effort, but it can help the family avoid misunderstandings and conflicts.

In some multicultural families, parents do not know enough about the culture into which they are marrying or from which adopted or foster children are coming. Problems in these families may occur because of the following:

❖ communication differences between cultures
❖ differing cultural expectations, roles, beliefs, and priorities
❖ differing traditions, rituals, and holidays
❖ differing views regarding family life
❖ expressions of bias or exclusion from others, especially family members

Most children raised in multicultural homes are happy and are high achievers in school. They grow up to respect diversity and have a strong sense of self. The strongest multicultural families seem to have much in common, 2-14.

These parents often explain to their children that people who express

What Makes Multicultural Families Strong?

Studies have shown the strongest multicultural families often have the following in characteristics:

❖ parents have strong cultural identities and feel good about their multicultural family
❖ the family talks about cultural issues in the home
❖ parents and children develop creative ways to solve problems that show equal respect for both cultures
❖ the family surrounds itself with supportive family and friends
❖ parents work with child care staff and teachers on behalf of their children
❖ the family celebrates all cultures
❖ parents tolerate no biased remarks within their circle of family, friends, and peers

2-14 Having or lacking these characteristics may influence the strength of multicultural families.

bias toward them may not know any better. The unkind words and actions of biased people may come from not knowing others who are different from them. Parents in strong multicultural families discourage their chil-dren from fighting in response to bias. They make it clear it is not right to hurt people who are different or assume all people in a group behave the same way.

Summing It Up

The family is the basic unit of society. Many changes affect families today. One major difference from years past is the variety in family types that occurs. Family types include two-parent, single-parent, stepfamilies, extended families, families with adopted children, and foster families. Each family type has unique problems and strengths.

Many changes occur during the six stages of the family life cycle. From the beginning stage through the childbearing, parenting, launching, mid-years, and aging stages, the family grows and develops.

Parents have many responsibilities with respect to their children. They have parental roles to fulfill. The main roles are socialization, nurturance, and guidance and discipline.

Several factors contribute to the health of a family. These include shared priorities, a mutual commitment to family life, shared responsibilities, and good communication.

Culture greatly influences how each family lives its life. Because the United States has such cultural diversity, the effects of culture vary widely from one family to the next. Multicultural families are also becoming more common. These families may have more challenges, but they can be as happy and healthy as other families.

If they are taught to appreciate cultural diversity, children make friends easily with people of all cultures.

Reviewing Key Concepts

Write your answers on a separate sheet of paper.

1. Describe two changes affecting families today.
2. For each statement below, write the letter of the family type it best describes.
   A. extended families
   B. families with adopted children
   C. foster families
   D. single-parent families
   E. stepfamilies
   F. two-parent families
   _____ Child care responsibilities are shared by both spouses.
   _____ Many family members are there to help during stressful times.
   _____ Children have many family members in the home who can teach and care for them.
   _____ Children may want to learn about or meet their birthparents when they become teens or adults.
   _____ Children see only one parent as a role model.
   _____ Children often have to adjust to new family relationships and rules quickly.
   _____ Adults provide temporary homes and serve as parents until the child can be placed in a permanent home.
3. Match each step of the family life cycle to the description it best fits.
   A. beginning stage
   B. childbearing stage
   C. parenting stage
   D. launching stage
   E. mid-years stage
   F. aging stage
   _____ Parents focus on guiding and teaching the children.
   _____ Spouses adjust to marriage and get to know each other better.
   _____ Spouses may feel lonely as teen or adult children begin leaving home.
   _____ Spouses focus on planning for their retirement and enjoying their relationship.
   _____ Adult children may have to provide care for parents as they near the end of life.
   _____ Spouses become parents and complete their families by having children.
4. Being responsible for their children's welfare involves the parental roles of _____, _____, and _____ and _____.
5. Describe three types of discipline and their effects on children.
6. The _____ parenting style allows children to have some freedom but sets rules for their well-being.
7. The _____ parenting style allows children to do as they please without interference.
8. The _____ parenting style pushes children to be obedient to their parents above all else.
9. List three factors that contribute to the health of a family.
10. What is cultural diversity?
11. List five characteristics of successful multicultural families.

Using Your Knowledge

1. **Language Arts.** Write a fiction story entitled, "The Joys and Trials of Living in a _____ Family Type." Base the story on your own family type or describe what you think it would be like to live in a family type different from your own.
2. **Role-Play.** In small groups, play the roles of family members in various stages of the family life cycle. Emphasize the changes that take place in each stage.
3. **Library Skills.** Ask an elementary school librarian for children's books about divorce and/or stepfamilies. Give the bibliographical information, the age for which the book was written, and a few statements about the main ideas the book conveys.
4. **Technology.** Use the Internet to research disciplining of children. Use the computer to compose a short paper on your findings.
5. **Art.** Design a poster illustrating one aspect of your cultural heritage or celebrating cultural diversity. Display your poster in your classroom or other approved area of your school.

Making Observations

1. Observe how couples with young children share their responsibilities. What techniques do they use to help them meet their obligations?
2. Observe families in an informal setting, such as a shopping mall or park. Do parents seem comfortable in their parenting roles? What behaviors help form your opinion?
3. If possible, observe a family of a culture different from your own. What similarities do you notice between this family and your own? What differences seem to exist?

Thinking Further

1. What are some of the advantages and disadvantages of joint custody over sole custody for parents? for children?
2. What are some possible benefits and problems of open adoption for each of the following: birthparents, adoptive family, adopted child? Whose benefit do you think should take priority, and why?
3. Many adults know reasoning rather than power assertion is a better form of discipline, yet many adults still use threats to discipline children. Why do adults use threats? Can threats be justified? Why or why not?
4. Discuss with a small group what makes a family healthy or strong. Compile a checklist someone could use to "test the health" of his or her family. Have the teacher photocopy each group's list. Compare other lists to that of your group and discuss.
5. In what ways do you think your cultural background will influence the way you parent or care for children? How can children benefit from these influences?

Bettina and Boris have been married for four months. They live in a one-bedroom apartment near the clinic where Bettina works as a medical receptionist. Boris is working as a car sales associate in the same city. Bettina wants to have a baby and she wants to begin planning for one. Boris is not sure if he will ever want to be a father. He feels their friends with children have too many problems. Bettina and Boris argue frequently about these issues.

After studying this chapter, you will be able to

- explain why parenting is more difficult than other jobs.
- analyze some of the motivations for and against parenthood.
- identify factors to consider before becoming a parent.
- describe effects of family planning.
- explain physical and psychological problems of infertility.
- describe fertility methods.

Chapter 3
Preparing for Parenting

Define...

indirect costs
foregone income
maternity leave
paternity leave
Family and Medical Leave Act
family planning
birth control methods
infertile
sterile
fertility counseling
assisted reproductive
    technologies (ART)
artificial insemination
in vitro fertilization (IVF)
gamete intrafallopian transfer
    (GIFT)
surrogate mother

Parenting is a rewarding and difficult task. Many people invest more money, time, and emotions in their children than they do in any investment in their life. Most parents hope their children will inherit all their strengths and avoid their weaknesses. They also hope their children will have opportunities they did not have.

Before having a child, a couple must seriously consider all aspects of parenting. This chapter discusses some of the important decisions people must make to prepare for parenting.

Why Is It Hard to Be a Good Parent?

Parenting skills are not automatic—a person does not just become a good parent. Just because a person is biologically able to reproduce does not mean he or she will be a good parent. If a person has long, agile fingers, does that mean he or she can automatically play the piano well?

Becoming a good parent is harder than becoming a good pianist for a few reasons. First, parenting involves relationships with people. In a good

Ties with Family & Community

Interview several couples who have young children. Ask each couple about how they learned the skills they would need for parenting before they had children. What skills did they have to learn after having children? Ask them to share some funny stories about trying to care for their children. Take notes about these stories or record them on audio- or videotape. Share your findings with the class.

relationship, each person wants what is best for the other. They support each other. Sometimes, because of people's individual differences, this is hard. In addition, the parent-child relationship is difficult because it is more one-sided than other relationships. For many years, parents are the "givers" and children are the "takers," 3-1.

Parenting also is hard because training to become a parent is not nearly as clear as training for most jobs. Parents probably have studied and trained more for their careers than for their roles as parents. Their job skills may be better than their child care skills, for which they have had little or no training.

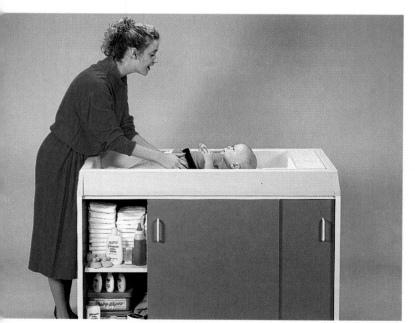

3-1 Children require much care in their first years. They are not able to give much in return.
Lakeshore Learning Materials, Carson, Calif.

Another reason parenting is difficult is that, years ago, children could see their parents handling younger brothers and sisters. They even may have helped care for them. Families are becoming smaller these days, however, and many children do not have this chance. Also, most young parents of the past turned to relatives for parenting help. However, in the United States today, there are fewer extended families. Today young parents often live many miles away from their relatives.

Being a good parent is hard but it is also most parents' greatest wish. Because of this desire, couples are becoming better informed about parenting skills and child development. A parent can best measure success if his or her adult children can say, "If I could have chosen my parent, I would have chosen you."

Learning Parenting Skills

Many couples feel they need help learning how to become good parents. They want to find the following resources to help them learn about child care and development:
- ❖ professionals and/or successful parents to give advice
- ❖ literature (books, journals, magazines) that is accurate, practical, and available
- ❖ child care and parenting classes (Community colleges and local American Red Cross chapters may offer such classes.)

❖ families with infants and young children (Spending time with children by babysitting and volunteering in schools and churches can help you understand what it is like to care for children, 3-2.)

New parents should also realize there is not one right way to parent. Although some methods may be more respected than others, many factors influence parenting. The culture in which a child is raised affects how parents raise children. The personalities of parents and children also affect parenting. The ways couples have seen their parents or friends care for children influences how they care for their own. All these factors are important to think about when learning child care skills.

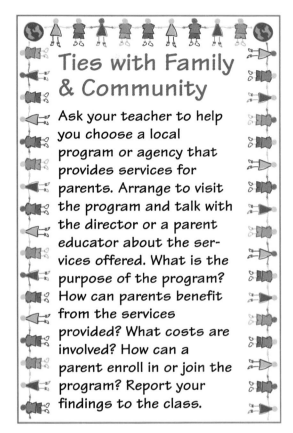

Ties with Family & Community

Ask your teacher to help you choose a local program or agency that provides services for parents. Arrange to visit the program and talk with the director or a parent educator about the services offered. What is the purpose of the program? How can parents benefit from the services provided? What costs are involved? How can a parent enroll in or join the program? Report your findings to the class.

3-2 A couple can learn about children by babysitting the children of friends.
© John Shaw

Deciding About Parenthood

Deciding whether to have children is a personal choice. For the sake of the couple and the future child, the husband and wife should agree on the decision. Couples should discuss their feelings about parenthood before they marry.

The decision to parent is unlike many life decisions in two ways. First, the decision to parent is a permanent choice. Once a child is born, he or she is part of the parent's life forever. A person can choose to change careers, for example, but having a child is different. Once a person is a parent, he or she will always be a parent.

Second, a decision not to parent is not permanent. People must make many life choices within a limited amount of time. For example, if a person wants a career in ballet, he or she must begin studying as a youngster and continue for many years. Couples have a longer period of time to decide whether to become parents. Young couples have 15 or more safe childbearing years. The option of adopting a child may increase this time by a few years. Thus, some couples may want to be parents, but may choose to wait until a better time. Other couples may not be sure about parenthood and wait to decide. Even couples who decide they never want children can change their minds later.

Couples have different motivations for and against parenthood. Some of these are described in this chapter. In the end, each couple must make the choice by respecting their feelings and needs.

Reasons for Choosing Parenthood

Couples have various reasons for choosing parenthood. Although they may not always be able to explain why, they see children as part of their life. The following are reasons couples give for wanting to become parents. Some are better reasons than others.

"We want to share our love with a child."

This is perhaps the most important reason for wanting a child. A couple's desire to share their love and time with a child is the best reason for parenthood, 3-3. Parents should want a child with no strings attached. If parents hope a child will fulfill other needs or goals, the parent-child relationship may not be healthy.

"Wouldn't it be nice to have a cute, little baby?"

When some couples see others with babies, they think it would be nice to have a cute, little baby, too. It's good for couples to think positively about babies. The problem is, babies aren't always cute. All babies are sick, fussy, and cranky at times. In addition, children do not stay babies long.

3-3 Parenting involves sharing knowledge and love with a child.

"Our parents want grandchildren."

Some couples want to fulfill their parents' wishes to be grandparents. It is fine for the parents of each spouse to want a grandchild. Grandparents can give a child much love. It is more important, however, for parents to want and love a child.

"Our older child needs a brother or sister."

When a couple wants a playmate for an older child, the parents are fulfilling someone else's needs, not their own. This reason is similar to having a baby because parents want grandchildren. Although a child might enjoy a brother or sister, there are other ways to meet an only child's needs for playmates.

"A child can make us proud."

Some couples see children as sources of pride. They want children to carry on the family name and customs, inherit the family business or money, or achieve certain goals. It is good for parents to be proud of their children and want them to achieve. They must be careful, however, not to let their hopes stifle their children's goals. Parenthood is not a good choice if a child is wanted only to boost the parents' ego or meet their unfulfilled goals.

Parent-child relationships suffer when children cannot meet their parents' goals. Not meeting parents' goals can make children feel inadequate. The relationship also suffers when children meet the parents' goals, but feel they can't be themselves. This often leads children to resent their parents.

"Others will see me as a stable, reliable person."

A few couples see having children as giving them the image of stable community members and reliable employees. Fortunately, such ideas are beginning to break down. People are judged more today on their own merits and not on family status. Parents should not want children simply to help them create an image or fulfill their goals.

"A child will comfort us in our old age."

Sometimes couples think of children as sources of help in their old age. It is natural for people to think about being helpless or lonely when they grow old. However, an aging parent cannot count on a child's help. In fact, parents may outlive their children.

"A child will make us love each other."

Some couples hope that having a child will save a failing marriage. Children may enrich family life for stable couples. Unstable couples may find that having children makes their problems worse. Studies show couples with children often argue about parenting practices—especially discipline. Children also add a financial burden. Usually, these problems add to the instability of marriages. Couples who stay together "because of the children" may always be unhappy.

Sadly, their children often feel responsible for the problems at home.

Reasons for Not Choosing Parenthood

Some couples decide to postpone parenthood. Three to five percent of all couples plan to be childless permanently. These couples feel parenthood does not suit them—at least at the present time. Even couples who want children should think about how children will change their lives.

"We're not ready for a child."

When couples say they're not ready for children, they usually mean they need to mature. They may want to pursue their interests before caring for a child. They may feel they need more time as a couple for their marriage to mature. They may need more time for education or job maturity. Some jobs take many years of education or training. Many people want to spend time establishing themselves in a career before becoming parents.

"A baby costs a lot."

Babies do cost a lot. At one time, a large family was an economic asset because children helped with the work. Today, children cannot contribute a great deal, if anything, to family income. (Later in this chapter, you will look more closely at the cost of having a child.)

"A child will tie us down."

With children comes endless responsibility. Unlike many other responsibilities, child care tasks cannot be put off until later. Children cannot be ignored while on vacation. Even with the best babysitters in charge, parents cannot completely forget their roles. They are always called if children are hurt, ill, or need help. However, the couple can arrange to have personal time with a little planning.

"A child will interfere with our careers."

Both children and careers require time and attention. When tending to both their career and children, parents face two common problems. First, it is hard for parents to have enough time and energy for both parenting and succeeding at work, 3-4. Second, it is difficult to find good child care services.

Some careers make parenting easier than others. For example, school

3-4 One of the challenges of parenting is having enough time and energy to devote to both parenthood and career.
© John Shaw

teachers have hours and vacation times similar to those of their older children. Other careers make parenting more difficult. For example, they may require parents to work long hours, night shifts, or at irregular times. Other examples include jobs that make parents feel stressed, demand parents to travel, or ask families to move often. Jobs that require families to live in areas that are unsafe or don't have schools are also hard for parents. Couples who combine these types of jobs with parenting must plan carefully.

"Our child could be sick or disabled."

There is no guarantee a child will be in perfect health when he or she is born. Babies can be disabled or become seriously ill or injured. Good medical care before and after birth reduces—but does not eliminate— these risks. Disabled, ill, or injured children have special needs beyond those of other children. However, most parents feel that raising disabled children is highly rewarding.

"Our marriage could fail, and I don't want to be a single parent."

Couples whose marriages are unstable may feel this way. Couples with marital problems may want to solve them before having children. Being a single parent is hard. Single parents may lack money, help with household and child care tasks, and the support of a spouse. Without these resources, the single parent can't always take part in adult activities, which can lead to feelings of isolation. However, many single parents can solve such problems.

Factors to Consider

Parenthood happens quickly. When a child is born or placed (during adoption), the mother and father instantly become parents. Few, if any, other jobs give a beginner such responsibility. No wonder some people refer to their first child as an "experimental child." To prepare for parenthood, couples need to know how children will change their lives.

How Children Affect Relationships

People who think about having children must look at their lives. They should look at the strengths and weaknesses of their present relationships. Couples should remember that, for children's healthy growth, their strengths should balance each other. In addition, the couple should think about other changes parenthood will bring.

Children and the Couple

Couples should begin looking at their relationships by asking questions about their feelings for others. These kinds of questions relate directly to parenting. For starters, couples might ask themselves the following:

❖ Are we loving and sensitive to others' needs?
❖ Are we careful not to judge people and their ideas?

* Can we recognize and respect others' rights?
* Are we self-disciplined?
* Do we relate well to others?
* Are we flexible enough to accept changes?
* Are we brave about challenges?
* Can we be honest about our feelings for others?

After answering these questions, couples should think about how their relationship with their partner would change if they were parents, 3-5. The following questions may help:

* Do we have the time and energy to give to children?
* Do we want to share much of our time together with children?
* Are we doing in our daily lives what we want our children to do? (Children model parents' behavior.)

3-5 When couples have happy, sharing relationships and want children, their children have the best chance for growth and development.

Couples can't set up a "formula" for successful parenting. They must realize children bring extra work to a marriage. Children usually do not strengthen a weak marriage. However, if a couple can answer most of these questions positively, their relationship may be strong enough for parenthood.

Children and Relatives and Friends

Couples must also look at their present relationships with relatives and friends. Good relationships with others are positive for the couple and their possible children. Couples might want to ask themselves the following questions about their relationships with others:

* Do our relatives and friends share our basic priorities?
* Can we ignore small differences in beliefs?
* Can we ask for advice and also use our own judgment?
* Can we tell others about our needs and accept the help they offer?
* Can we recognize others' needs and offer our help?
* Can we avoid abusing others' generosity, including time and money?
* Can we share fun times with others?

If couples can answer most of these questions positively, having a child should not cause problems in relationships outside the family. When couples enjoy their relationships with others before parenthood, these relationships can often be enriched by including children, 3-6.

Couples must also think about how their relationships with others can affect their children. There are at least three advantages to children's relationships with others. First, relatives and friends provide children with their first link to the outside world. Second, grandparents and older relatives can teach children about the past. Third, when many relatives and friends care for children, they feel more rooted to their family. Because each relative and friend is unique, children learn to understand that people are different. They also learn to accept people's unique traits.

This interaction will help children get along well with others as they grow.

Sharing Responsibilities

Couples should examine how they feel about home care responsibilities. Some couples practice more traditional roles. For example, the husband brings home the paycheck and the wife cares for the home and children.

Today, many wives work outside the home. In these families, husbands often help with home and child care tasks more than they would in traditional roles, 3-7. Many men enjoy taking on some of these tasks. In many families, however, wives still do far more in the home, even if both spouses

3-6 Strong relationships with other adults can provide support for a couple when they decide to have children.
© John Shaw

3-7 Dividing tasks saves time and allows a parent to spend time alone with children.

work outside the home. In a few families, the wife works outside the home and the husband cares for the home and children. In this way, husbands and wives switch traditional roles.

Couples must consider how they feel about the way they share tasks. They need to ask themselves the following questions:

❖ Are we happy with the way we share responsibilities?
❖ Do we appreciate each other's help?
❖ Do we feel equally important in efforts to reach our goals?

Next, the couple must consider how children will affect how they share responsibilities. They should ask themselves the following questions:

❖ If we become parents, will there be major changes in the way we share responsibilities?
❖ Can we agree on how to divide home and child care tasks?
❖ If one of us works outside the home and the other cares for children, will we feel we are contributing to our goals equally? How will the full-time employee develop a close relationship with the children? How will the full-time homemaker meet personal needs for adult time and interaction?

Couples who want to share responsibilities should answer these questions. How they choose to divide tasks can depend on each person's needs. If couples plan carefully and try all ideas, they can divide tasks so both partners are happy.

Managing Finances

Couples must realize children cost a lot. The first year is expensive, and expenses grow as the child grows. The first baby is often the most expensive, 3-8. Later children may use some of the firstborn's items. However, each extra child increases the costs. A second child usually doubles costs. Couples should think about finances before becoming parents. They should ask themselves the following questions:

❖ How do we earn and spend our money now?
❖ Are we happy with our budget?

3-8 Even with baby shower gifts from family and friends, parents-to-be must make many purchases as they prepare for their first baby.
© John Shaw

- ❖ Do we have regular savings we could use to meet child-related expenses? If not, can we adjust our budget to meet such expenses?
- ❖ Can we expect more income or lower expenses during the next few years to help offset child-related costs?
- ❖ What type of savings goals do we need for a child?
- ❖ What is an estimate of child-related expenses for the first and next several years?

In addition, spouses should consider the indirect costs of having a child.

Indirect costs are resources parents use to meet child-related costs that could have been used to meet other goals. They are not actual expenses.

Indirect costs vary from couple to couple. For one couple, an indirect cost of having children might be giving up time to pursue a hobby because this time must be spent interacting with their child. For another couple, one spouse might change work hours to take a shift opposite the other spouse. This would allow the couple to avoid child care costs, but it would have an indirect cost. The spouse with the job change might give up certain job tasks that can only be done in the previous shift. Giving up this task might have an effect on career goals.

If one parent stays home to raise the child, there will be the indirect cost of **foregone income**. This is the potential income lost by not being in the workforce. Foregone income is greater for the parent who could earn the higher salary.

Another indirect cost is the impact that time out of the labor force will

indirect costs. Resources used to meet child-related costs that could have been used to meet other goals.

foregone income. Potential income given up by a parent who leaves the workforce and stays home to raise a child.

have on career opportunities. A worker who is out of the workforce for several years may miss promotions and may even need to be retrained before working again. The cost of time out of the workforce is the most difficult indirect cost to calculate.

Couples must think about many factors when they estimate the direct and indirect costs of parenting. Each family is different, and these differences show in the way families spend their money.

Carefully planning financial resources is important for everyone, 3-9. In some ways, financial planning becomes more important when couples begin to think about children.

This is because children rely on their parents for financial support for many years. Parents are also models of either good or poor consumers for their children.

Managing Careers

Couples must decide whether they will both work or whether one will care for children at home. Some fathers do choose to stay home while mothers work, but this is far less common than the reverse situation. Usually mothers decide whether to stay home with children or to work outside the home, 3-10.

Today, because most women work, child care decisions are extremely important. Parents must decide who will care for the baby, as well as how much time they will take from work

3-9 Parents must carefully budget their income to meet the high costs of having a baby.
© John Shaw

3-10 Working parents often have dual pleasures and dual responsibilities.
© John Shaw

when the baby is born. (You will learn about child care options in later chapters of this text.)

Maternity and Paternity Leave

The time mothers take off work for the birth or adoption of a child is called maternity leave. Women generally take time off work after giving birth or adoption. Some women take time off just before the birth, as well, although this is less common than in the past. Today, many pregnant women can stay on the job until just before their babies are born.

The length of maternity leave varies from company to company. Six weeks is often the minimum length offered. Maternity may be paid, partially paid, or unpaid. Some companies grant benefits and a percentage of salary during maternity leave. Others grant a longer unpaid leave. Some companies allow several months or a year off. Most working mothers return within three months of the birth or adoption, although many would prefer more time off. They may decide not to take more leave for financial or career reasons.

Maternity leave allows the new mother time to regain her strength and get to know her newborn. It takes time to recover from pregnancy, labor, and delivery. Life with a newborn is usually hectic and exhausting for the first few weeks. The mother needs time to rest and adjust to her new role. This time also helps her to bond with the baby.

Some employers grant paternity leave to fathers. Paternity leave is time off (usually unpaid) for a set period after a child's birth or adoption. At the end of paternity leave, the company must offer the father a job and salary comparable to the one he left. A few companies pay for this leave.

Paternity leave is growing more common. This time helps the new father care for his recovering wife and child. It allows him to share in this special time and bond with his child.

Men sometimes face some problems in taking paternity leave. One is the economic hardship caused if the leave is unpaid. Some men say their companies might not give them salary raises and promotions if they choose to take leave. These problems may change as more men take paternity leave.

A law called the Family and Medical Leave Act protects the rights of many women and men to take unpaid maternity or paternity leave.

maternity leave. Time a woman takes off from work for the birth or adoption of a child.

paternity leave. Time a man takes off from work (usually without pay) for a set period after a child's birth or adoption.

Family and Medical Leave Act. Law that protects the rights of the workers of large companies to take up to 12 weeks of unpaid leave per year for various family-related reasons.

This law applies to U.S. companies with more than 50 employees. It grants these workers a total of 12 weeks unpaid leave per year to provide care for family members in certain situations. One of these situations is the birth or adoption of a child, 3-11. During this leave, the employee's job must be held or an equal job must be available when the worker returns.

A second federal law also applies to maternity leave. This law states employers are required to treat leave for childbirth and recovery as a medical disability. If employers have provisions for people with other medical disabilities, they must apply these same rules to a woman on maternity leave. This law may require partial pay during the maternity leave.

Before children are born or adopted, it's good for parents to review their employers' leave policies. Understanding these polices will help them calculate forgone income costs of various lengths of leave. When they know these costs, a couple can plan its budget accordingly and decide what leave each partner wants to take.

Problems with Family and Work

Working parents often encounter problems as they care for their families and strive to do well at their jobs. These roles can be tough to balance. Dual-career couples will need to answer the following questions:

❖ Can we find good child care during working hours?
❖ Can we balance job demands and children's needs? For example, will we be able to give complete or only partial attention to our children after work?
❖ Can we work out mutual responsibilities for child and home care tasks?
❖ Can we make enough time for ourselves as individuals and as a couple free of other concerns?
❖ Can we be organized? Can we be flexible and meet changes in our schedules? What will we do to meet the needs of a sick child? What will we do when job demands are heavy for a short time?

3-11 Maternity and paternity leaves allow parents the time they need to adjust to having a new baby.
Jacob Cullen Darlinger

❖ If we are uncomfortable with our answers to any of these questions, what other options do we have?

Parents may worry about how their children will be affected when they work outside the home. Studies show that, when children had good care, being separated from parents during work hours did not harm them. However, the mother's attitude about work seemed to be most important. The happiest children came from homes where the mother wanted to work and did or wanted to stay home and could. If seems if the mother is happy about her situation, children benefit from her attitude. Children may suffer if their mother's is unhappy about her situation.

Family Planning

After considering all these factors, many couples practice family planning. **Family planning** happens when a couple decides how many children they want and when to have them. It is easier to plan a family now than in the past, because many options are available for controlling conception. Couples can use these **birth control methods** to help them delay having children until they decide to conceive.

To learn about the birth control options available, couples should consult their doctor. The doctor can explain each method in terms of the following:

❖ how the method works to prevents pregnancy (For example, does the method block sperm's travel or provide hormones that prevent ovulation?)

❖ how successful the method is at preventing pregnancy when used properly

❖ directions for using the method

❖ the method's possible side effects and risks

❖ effects, if any, the method has on future fertility

❖ the method's cost

Before advising a particular option, however, the doctor will review the couple's health history and give them a complete checkup. The couple should think about which method they prefer. This will depend on their religious beliefs and their likes and dislikes of certain methods.

Family planning is a couple's personal choice. There are some points couples should keep in mind as they plan families. First, to protect the health of mother and child, doctors advise a year or more between pregnancies. After several pregnancies, mothers may need even more time. A woman should consult a doctor about her health before becoming pregnant.

family planning. Decisions couples make about the desired number and spacing of future children.

birth control methods. Methods couples use to prevent conception.

In addition, there is often less jealousy between children when they are born about three years apart. This is because older children can help with the new baby and still feel needed. Also, some research shows this spacing may allow each child to develop better. It gives parents time to work with each child alone before they must divide their attention.

Not all couples feel they can handle another child right away. These feelings depend on their finances, emotional and physical energy, career, age, and lifestyle. Couples should not feel guilty if they want only one child. They should realize an only child will not necessarily be spoiled or lonely. The best reason for having another child is wanting to share their love and time with this child, too.

Infertility and Sterility

About 80 to 85 percent of all couples who try to conceive will do so within a year. Couples who do not conceive within a year are known as infertile. About half of these infertile couples will later conceive. Most will need medical assistance, but some will conceive on their own. The remaining couples will not successfully conceive, for one or both partners are sterile. This means the couple will be permanently unable to conceive or the wife is unable to carry their fully biological child.

People often think that women account for almost all fertility problems. However, a fair number of cases involve fertility problems in the male. In some cases, both partners are infertile. These couples have much lower chances to conceive than couples with only one infertile partner. In at least 10 percent of infertility cases, no cause can be determined.

Reproductive diseases and problems with the reproductive organs are the main causes of infertility and sterility, 3-12. Being exposed to drugs, chemicals, and radiation can hamper fertility. The same is true of sexually transmitted diseases, smoking, and being overweight. Excessive exercise, being underweight, and aging can also lead to fertility problems.

Major Causes of Infertility and Sterility

Women	Men
lack of ovulation	low sperm count
hormone deficiencies	hormone deficiencies
irregular ovulation	inability of sperm to move
damage to reproductive organs	damage to reproductive organs

3-12 Infertility can have many causes, some of which are unknown.

Overcoming Infertility

Infertile couples who want to pursue having biological children can seek fertility counseling. **Fertility counseling** consists of determining the reasons for the fertility problems and exploring treatment options. First, both partners are given several tests. These might reveal the fertility problem involves the woman, the man, or both partners.

If a problem is found, the doctor may suggest steps to restore fertility, 3-13. Hormones or drugs might be given to stimulate ovulation or balance hormone levels. Surgery might be able to repair problems with the reproductive organs.

If these treatments do not work, couples can look into other options. They might consider adopting a child or being foster parents. Other couples try what are called **assisted reproductive technologies (ART)**. These are methods to help infertile couples conceive. Three of the most common ART procedures are the following:

❖ **Artificial insemination** occurs when the sperm is introduced into the vagina or uterus by a medical procedure rather than by sexual relations.

❖ **In vitro fertilization (IVF)** occurs when some of the mother's eggs are surgically removed and fertilized with sperm in a laboratory dish. After a few days, the fertilized egg is implanted into the mother's uterus. Babies conceived by this method were once referred to as test-tube babies.

❖ **Gamete intrafallopian transfer (GIFT)** occurs when a mixture of sperm and eggs is placed in the woman's fallopian tubes, where fertilization can occur. Because more than one egg is present, conception is more likely, but a multiple pregnancy can occur, too.

infertile. Unable to conceive after a year of trying.

sterile. The condition of being permanently unable to conceive or carry fully biological children.

fertility counseling. Medical evaluation that seeks to determine the reasons for fertility problems and explore available treatment options.

assisted reproductive technologies (ART). Methods infertile couples can use to help them conceive.

artificial insemination. ART procedure that involves introducing sperm into the vagina or uterus by a medical procedure rather than by sexual relations.

in vitro fertilization (IVF). ART procedure occurs when some of the mother's eggs are surgically removed, fertilized with sperm in a laboratory dish, and then implanted in the mother's uterus.

gamete intrafallopian transfer (GIFT). ART procedure in which a mixture of sperm and eggs is placed in the woman's fallopian tubes, where fertilization can occur.

Fertility Methods

Method	Used to...	Problems
Artificial insemination	Provide increased number of sperm for conception in biological mother Impregnate surrogate mother	Slight risk of infection If sperm is not husband's, moral issues and legal issues (legitimacy and biological father's rights)
Hormone therapy (fertility drugs)	Stimulate ovaries to function properly	Multiple pregnancies Possible increased risk for female cancers
Microsurgery	Attempt to open the fallopian tubes	Risks of surgery, such as anesthetic and infection risks
In vitro fertilization (IVF)	Allow a woman with permanently blocked fallopian tubes to have her eggs surgically removed and fertilized with her husband's sperm in a laboratory dish. After a few days, the fertilized eggs are implanted in the mother's uterus. Impregnate surrogate mother	Risks of surgery Multiple births Moral and legal issues
Gamete Intrafallopian Transfer (GIFT)	Increased chances of conception if men have a low sperm count or women have problems ovulating. (A mixture of sperm and several eggs are surgically placed in the fallopian tubes.)	Risks of surgery Multiple births
Surrogate mother	Replace the infertile couple's role in bearing a child. (Surrogate mother (a) may bear a child who is the infertile couple's biological child conceived by in vitro fertilization, (b) may bear a child with her egg and the husband's sperm (of the infertile couple) that were introduced to the surrogate mother through artificial insemination, or (c) may bear a child not biologically related to the infertile couple by using her own eggs and donor sperm introduced through artificial insemination.	Moral issues Legal issues

3-13 Infertile couples now have many options for having children.

In some cases, problems exist with the sperm, eggs, or both sperm and eggs of the couple. For example, one or both partners may be sterile. When these problems exist, couples may opt to use an ART with the germ cells (sperm, eggs, or sperm and eggs) that were donated by other people. These donor cells would be used to attempt conception.

If the wife cannot carry a baby, the couple might consider using a **surrogate mother**. This is a woman who bears (sometimes both conceives and bears) a child for a couple. The surrogate would carry the baby in her uterus, give birth to the baby, and sign her parenting rights over to the couple. She could conceive using an ART with the wife's eggs (or donate her own eggs if the wife's eggs cannot be used).

There are many drawbacks to ART. Even with advances in fertility treatments, over half of all ART attempts do not succeed. Older couples have the least chance of conceiving, because fertility, especially for the woman, declines with age. Fertility problems are emotionally painful for couples. They may feel very disappointed if they use ART and it is not successful. Couples may also feel their privacy is violated during fertility testing and treatment. Some couples begin to lose hope about their life plans. The partner with the fertility problem may feel damaged, defective, or guilty.

Another drawback to ART is the cost. These methods are very expensive—each try costs thousands of dollars. Couples may need to try the procedure more than once for it to succeed. They may have to travel some distance to major hospitals for fertility treatments. Even still, there is no guarantee the couple will ever conceive. Couples may lessen the costs of ART by seeking treatment through research or teaching hospitals.

ART also raises some ethical and legal issues. When donor cells are used, the donor of the egg or sperm is the biological parent of the child born to the couple. Problems can result if the donor wants parenting rights or changes his or her mind. Other problems can occur if the couple decides, for whatever reason, they don't want the baby. These complex issues can lead to legal battles. Couples may want to seek legal advice before agreeing to use donor cells in an ART procedure.

Likewise, the use of a surrogate raises moral and legal issues. First is the moral issue of whether someone other than the couple wanting to parent should be involved in the pregnancy. Legal issues are raised concerning any fee and what happens

surrogate mother. A woman who bears (sometimes both conceives and bears) a child for a couple.

if the oral or written agreement is broken. These questions include the following:

❖ Who pays if the surrogate mother's and/or the newborn's medical fees are much higher than the contract fee?

❖ What happens if the surrogate decides she wants to keep the baby who may be her child biologically?

❖ What happens if the couple decides they do not want this child because they have conceived in the meantime or the child has a disability?

Because of these drawbacks, many couples choose not to pursue their options regarding ART. Others try but find they cannot restore their fertility. Both types of couples may face or experience a crisis as they adjust to this reality. For some people who deeply desire children, there may be a lasting sense of being unfulfilled. Counseling may help them resolve these feelings. Many other couples become fulfilled parents through adoption or foster parenthood. Some childless couples find fulfillment in other endeavors involving families and children.

Summing It Up

Parenting is more difficult than other tasks because it involves relationships. Parents usually are not trained to be parents. Most jobs require training, but parenting, one of the most important jobs of all, is often undertaken without preparation. With fewer extended families today and more mobility, having supportive relationships is more difficult.

Those considering parenting need to find out what resources are available to them. They should learn as much about children as possible. These resources include professionals, successful parents, books, magazines, or child care classes. Spending time with other infants and children also will increase a couple's knowledge of children. The way the couple was raised will also affect their parenting roles.

Couples have different reasons for wanting or not wanting children. There are a number of factors couples must think about when deciding on a family. They must consider how having a baby will change their relationships with each other, relatives, and friends. Couples should also think about how children will affect their shared responsibilities at home. In addition, they should also understand how children will affect their finances and career.

Many couples today practice family planning. The use of birth control methods can make family planning more successful. A couple should consult their doctor when selecting a method.

Some couples who plan for children find they are infertile or sterile. These problems have many causes, some of which are unknown. In some cases, infertile couples choose to pursue an ART method, such as artificial insemination, IVF, or GIFT, to help them conceive. Some consider becoming parents of adopted or foster children or seek other ways to include time with children in their lives.

Reviewing Key Concepts

Write your answers on a separate sheet of paper.

1. True or false. For most couples, parenting is a natural, automatic response that immediately follows a baby's birth or adoption.
2. List three poor reasons people give for wanting to become parents.
3. Which is the best reason for wanting to have a baby?
   A. Our parents want to be grandparents.
   B. Babies are so cute.
   C. We need a child to carry on the family business.
   D. We want to share our life and love with a child.
   E. A child will give us a reason to love each other again.
4. What are the most common problems of meeting both career and parenthood demands?
5. Define foregone income.
6. Why might a woman consider taking maternity leave after the birth of a child?
7. What is the Family and Medical Leave Act?
8. How does family planning affect children?
9. True or false. Infertility is a problem that affects only women.
10. Explain how infertility might affect a couple.
11. Describe two ways an infertile couple might be able to become parents.

Using Your Knowledge

1. **Technology.** Use a computer to compose a short paper giving your views on the kinds of maturity couples should have before becoming parents.
2. **Art.** Construct a poster or collage showing different parenting responsibilities.
3. **Technology/Library Skills.** Collect some books, magazines, and pamphlets about child care. Use the computer to create a bibliography that includes the title of the publication, name and address of publisher, topics covered, age of children discussed, and other important information.
4. **Mathematics.** Child care is an indirect cost of parenting when both parents work. Ask a local child care provider what rate is charged to provide child care for one infant full-time (all day, five days a week). Use this weekly rate to calculate the cost of child care during the first year of life (from age six weeks until the first birthday).
5. **Science.** Working with a small group, research one of the ART methods that can help infertile couples conceive. Prepare a group report on your chosen method.

Making Observations

1. In an informal setting, observe parents who are having a difficult time with a child. What parenting skills might they need to help them with their children? For example, do they need to know more about appropriate developmental tasks for the child's age, discipline methods, or how to childproof their home?
2. Observe examples of literature and professional services for parents in your local school and community.
3. Observe how dual-career families share responsibilities for home and child care.
4. Observe how an employer in your community helps parents meet their family and work obligations. For example, does the employer offer maternity leave, paternity leave, child care programs, job sharing, and/or flexible work schedules?

Thinking Further

1. If a married couple chooses not to have children or wants to wait several years before having a child, what can they say to their parents who want grandchildren? Why do older people often want grandchildren? Besides having grandchildren, what are some ways older people can fulfill their need to be with young children?
2. What are some specific ways a dual-career couple can equally share home care tasks? What could be done to make the sharing of home tasks fair if the demands of one person's job involve travel, very long work hours in comparison to the partner's work hours, being on-call, or bringing work home?
3. Why might companies choose to offer paternity leave to their employees? Why might companies choose not to offer paternity leave to their employees?
4. Suppose you and your future spouse could not conceive. Do you think you would consider using an ART or surrogate mother to help you become parents? Explain.

Part 2
Prenatal Development and the Newborn

Pregnancy is a special time for a couple. The feelings of parents-to-be range from great excitement to anxiety. However, when both spouses want children, they adjust to parenthood rather easily.

The prenatal period, which lasts about 280 days, is the shortest stage in the life span. This formative stage also is the most critical time for a child's development. For this reason, proper prenatal care is crucial for all mothers-to-be.

Childbirth ends the prenatal period and begins the baby's life as a separate person. Through labor and delivery, the mother's body works to bring the baby into the world. At the end of this process, parents can finally meet their precious newborn.

In the first two weeks following birth, the baby is called a neonate. During this time, the neonate adjusts to life outside the mother's body. Parents adjust during this time, too, by adapting to the first challenges and demands of parenthood.

In **chapters 4** and **5**, you will learn about pregnancy, prenatal care, and childbirth. **Chapter 6** will introduce you to the new baby.

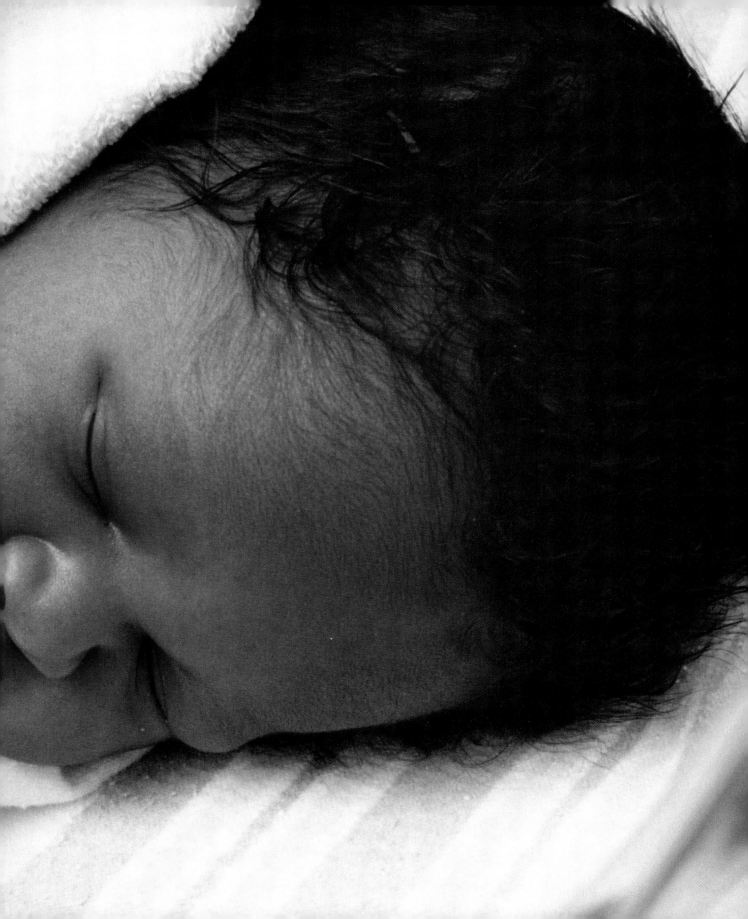

Chapter 4
Pregnancy

Julio and Carla have identical two-year-old twins named Raquel and Rosita. They look just alike and like the same things! In fact, Julio and Carla worried at first about how to tell them apart. Luckily, Julio noticed a difference right away. Rosita has a small birthmark on her right leg, and Raquel has a similar one on her left leg. In the last year, the twins have become easier to tell apart. Quiet Rosita is easygoing, while energetic Raquel gets upset easily. Julio and Carla wonder how the twins will change in the coming years.

After studying this chapter, you will be able to
- describe what happens during conception.
- explain how genetic factors affect prenatal development.
- describe how a person inherits traits through genes.
- list the three different types of multiple pregnancies.
- describe the three main stages of prenatal development.

the baby grows and develops at a fast rate. Before the baby actually is born, however, many complex changes must take place.

Many factors influence these changes. One factor is a baby's genes. Genes determine much about a person's looks, personality, and physical size. A baby's genes come from both the mother and father, 4-1. These genes start to control how babies grow and develop before they are even born.

4-1 Even as an infant, this baby resembles his father. Genes are responsible for their physical similarities.
Nancy Konopasek

Pregnancy is the process through which a new human prepares to enter the world. This process begins when a baby is created inside the mother's body. During the nine months of pregnancy,

Conception

A **cell** is the smallest unit of life that is able to reproduce itself. Life begins with the joining of two separate cells—one from the male and one from the female. These cells are called *germ cells* (the cells involved in reproduction). The male germ cell is called the **sperm**. The female germ cell is the **ovum** (often called the *egg*). The joining of these two cells is called **conception**. At conception, ovum and sperm combine to form a single cell called a **zygote**. Another name for the zygote is a fertilized egg.

How do these two types of germ cells form and unite to create new life? Ovum are produced and stored by the woman's ovaries. Inside the ovary, the ovum is stored in a small sac called a *follicle*. Hormones cause some follicles to grow and fill with fluid each month. Around the middle of the menstrual cycle, one ovum is released from the follicle, and the other follicles that were growing become inactive. (Sometimes more than one ovum is released.) The release of the ovum from the ovary is called *ovulation*.

When the egg is released, it travels toward the **fallopian tubes**. These are two hollow tubes that extend from the right and left sides of the uterus. The **uterus** is the organ in which the baby develops and is protected until birth. One end of each fallopian tube is connected to the uterus. The other end of each tube has fingerlike projections. These projections lie near, but are not attached to, the ovary. The projections from the fallopian tube help gather the ovum as it emerges from the ovary. Once inside the fallopian tube, the ovum moves very slowly down the tube. Here, the ovum is ready and available to be joined by a sperm.

At the time the egg is released, hormones help the fallopian tube move to gather the egg. These hormones also prepare the uterus to receive and support a baby if conception occurs.

Semen, which includes over 100 million sperm, enters the woman's body during intercourse. These sperm begin a journey to the ovum that lasts only minutes. Many sperm do not survive. Only a few hundred reach the fallopian tube.

Sperm may meet the ovum at any point. Conception usually happens when the ovum is less than one-third of the way down the fallopian tube. After that point, conception is unlikely because the ovum has a short life span. It lives only about 24 hours after ovulation.

About a dozen sperm approach the ovum and try to break through its surface. Only one sperm successfully enters, or fertilizes the egg. Once one sperm is accepted, no other sperm can enter the ovum. Conception has occurred, and the zygote forms.

Genetic Factors and the Unborn Baby

In chapter 1, you learned that genetics is the study of heredity. A person's inherited traits are passed to him or her at conception. The total heredity is received at this one time— no new genes will be inherited.

Genetic factors are the traits passed through the genes. These factors affect all stages of growth and development. In many ways, genetic factors influence the prenatal stage more than any other stage of life. Following certain rules, each parent's genes combine to make a blueprint for the unborn child's growth and development. During pregnancy, this blueprint guides growth and development as the baby changes from a zygote to a baby ready to be born. The unborn baby will come to look much like other members of the family. He or she will likely have abilities, interests, and personality traits that are similar to those of family members, too.

During the prenatal period, the genetic blueprint also gives the cells instructions for family-like traits that will unfold throughout life. For example, during the prenatal period a baby boy's cells receive instructions on whether he will be bald later in life, what the pattern of hair loss will be, and when hair loss will occur. Some people's genes lead them to lose hair, while others have genes that promote keeping a full head of hair.

What causes each person to be so different? Heredity does, and it works in complex ways. You may understand heredity better by reading about Steve.

Heredity and Steve

Steve is a five-year-old boy. Like many children his age, Steve asks many questions, enjoys pretend games, and shows interest in letters and numbers. Although Steve shares many traits with other five-year-olds, he is uniquely Steve—not Kate, Peter, Susan, or even his older brother, Chris. How did Steve become the person he is?

Like all people, Steve began life as a single-celled zygote. The *nucleus*, or center, of this cell contains a set of instructions to build a living being.

 cell. The smallest unit of life that is able to reproduce itself.

sperm. The male sex cell.

ovum. The female sex cell; also called the *egg*.

conception. The union of the ovum and sperm cells.

zygote. The single cell formed at conception; also called a *fertilized egg*.

fallopian tubes. Two hollow tubes that connect to the uterus and have fingerlike projections that reach toward each ovary.

uterus. The organ in which the baby develops and is protected until birth.

genetic factors. Traits that are passed through the genes.

These directions tell the body whether a being will be a person, an animal, or a plant. The instructions are written in what scientists call a *genetic code*.

Where does nature keep this important genetic code? The genetic code is stored in DNA (deoxyribonucleic acid). DNA is a chemical compound that is found in threadlike structures called **chromosomes**. The chromosomes carry genes in living cells. Chromosomes contain the information nature needs to make Steve a human.

Chromosomes and Genes

All living organisms have a certain number of chromosomes. Each human baby receives a total of 46 chromosomes, which form 23 pairs. Half of these chromosomes come from the mother and half come from the father. Each sperm contains 23 chromosomes, as does each ovum, 4-2.

Each chromosome contains about 20,000 genes. These genes determine the individual traits the person will have. Human cells contain about a

Ties with Family & Community

Because blood relatives share ancestors, they have some genes in common. These genes can cause family members to share common traits. Make a list of the traits of someone you know well. Include physical, mental, and personality traits as well as interests and talents. Beside each trait, write the relative(s) with whom the person shares a trait.

million genes. Sometimes one gene determines a trait. Other times, a group of genes decides a trait.

Steve's genes have determined he has blue eyes; light brown hair with a reddish tinge; and fair, freckled skin. His genes give him Rh positive blood, type O. They also carry a better-than-average chance of having high blood pressure. Because of his genes, Steve learns quickly. These qualities are only part of Steve's genetic information. The sum of Steve's genes, along with his environment, makes him Steve and no one else.

Steve's appearance is unique; he doesn't look exactly like anyone in his family. He looks like his father in some

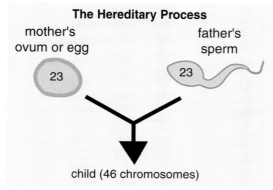

The Hereditary Process

mother's ovum or egg   father's sperm

23   23

child (46 chromosomes)

4-2 Every child inherits 23 chromosomes from the mother's ovum and 23 chromosomes from the father's sperm.

ways and his mother in other ways. Some of Steve's features don't look like either of his parents' features. Steve's hair is the same color as his mother's, but his body is built like his father's. Even though both of Steve's parents have brown eyes, his eyes are blue.

Steve's traits were passed to him through his parents' germ cells (ovum and sperm). Of the 46 total chromosomes a parent has, only half (23) will be present in his or her germ cell. Chance determines which chromosomes these will be. The baby inherits a set of 23 chromosomes from each parent. It is the final combination of these two sets of chromosomes that makes each person unique.

Dominant and Recessive Traits

In each chromosome, the genes occur in pairs. In each gene pair, one gene originates from the father and the other is from the mother. The genes from each parent work together to determine the appearance of each trait in a child.

In the case of Steve, his genes give him blue eyes but both his parents are brown-eyed. You may wonder how Steve's parents could pass on this trait even though neither of them has blue eyes. This is an example of how heredity can be complex.

People can pass on traits that don't show up in them. This is because some traits are dominant and some are recessive. **Dominant traits** are those that always show in a person even if only one gene of the pair is inherited

for that trait. **Recessive traits** typically do not show in a person unless both genes for the trait are inherited (one from each parent). In a few cases, a boy can inherit recessive traits by receiving a single a recessive gene from his mother. Examples are color blindness and hemophilia. Most often, however, it takes two recessive genes for a recessive trait to show. A person who inherits only one recessive gene for a trait becomes a *carrier* of that trait making it possible for the trait to show up in later generations.

People have both dominant and recessive genes for height. Tallness is dominant and shortness is recessive, 4-3. There were both tall and short relatives in Steve's mother's family— possibly even several generations back. Because of this, Steve's mother inherited one gene for tallness and one for shortness, so she is tall. Steve's father also had tall and short relatives. He is a tall man but also has one gene for tallness and one for shortness. Some of the ova from Steve's mother were for

chromosomes. Threadlike structures that carry genes in living cells.

dominant traits. Traits that always show in a person even if only one gene of the pair is inherited for that trait.

recessive traits. Traits that typically do not show in a person unless both genes for the trait are inherited.

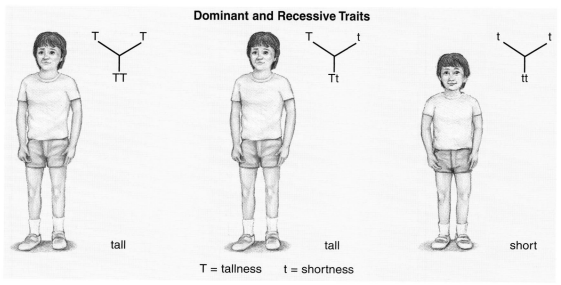

4-3 A dominant trait shows if either gene (or both genes) in the pair is for that trait. Recessive traits only show when both genes are for that trait.

tallness and some for shortness. In like manner, some sperm from Steve's father were for tallness and some for shortness. Steve received both an ovum and a sperm for shortness (just like the child on the right in 4-3). Because he has two recessive genes, Steve shows the recessive trait of shortness. Steve's brothers and sisters could be short like Steve or tall like the other child in 4-3.

Sex Chromosomes

Of the 23 pairs of chromosomes, 22 are alike in both males and females. These 22 pairs provide genetic information for both males and females, such as height and eye color. The chromosomes that make up the twenty-third pair are different for females and males. This pair is called the *sex chromosomes*. Height and eye color are determined by a few gene

pairs within the chromosome. The sex of a child, however, is determined by the entire chromosome pair.

Females have the chromosome pair called *XX* (because when viewed with a microscope, the pair looks somewhat like the letters *X* and *X*). When a female's chromosome pair splits to form germ cells (ova), all ova will be X because each chromosome pair was XX.

Males have the chromosome pair called *XY* (because when viewed with a microscope, the pair looks somewhat like the letters *X* and *Y*). When a male's chromosome pair splits to form germ cells (sperm), some will be X and some will be Y. This is because each chromosome pair was XY.

All the mother's egg cells will carry the X chromosome. If fertilized by a sperm carrying an X chromosome, the child will be female (XX). If the sperm cell carries the Y chromosome, the child will be male (XY). Because the father's sex chromosome is the one that can vary, it is the father's sperm that always determines the sex of the child, 4-4.

Multiple Pregnancy

Sometimes two or more babies develop in the same pregnancy. This is called a **multiple pregnancy**. Multiple pregnancies are far less common than single pregnancies. Likewise, twins are more common than triplets, and triplets are more common than quadruplets. In very rare cases, as many as seven or eight babies can be conceived in the same pregnancy.

Multiple pregnancies have become more common. This is because more women are using fertility drugs to help them become pregnant. Many of these drugs increase the chances of multiple pregnancy. An increase in

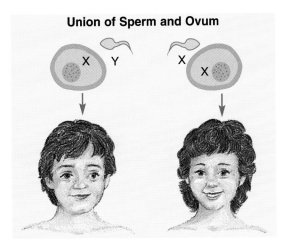

Union of Sperm and Ovum

4-4 The sex chromosome in the father's sperm determines whether a child will be a boy or a girl.

multiple pregnancies is also due to older women having children.

In the United States, the frequency of twins is about 1 in 35 births. The likelihood of having three or more babies in the same pregnancy is about 1 in 540 births. The number of twin births continues to rise. Multiple births of three or more children are declining somewhat after an enormous rise in the 1990s. Improvements in fertility treatments are the main reason for the decline. These improved treatments are less likely to result in multiple births.

Doctors are often concerned about the health of multiple births with three or more babies. Most babies in these births are born early and have low birthweights (under 3.3 pounds for multiple births). This puts them at risk for severe vision, hearing, mental, and developmental disabilities. Twins are also almost 5 times (triplets almost 10 times) more likely to die in their first year than single-birth children.

A common multiple pregnancy occurs when twins develop. There are two types of twins—fraternal and identical.

Fraternal Births

The most common multiple pregnancy is caused when multiple babies develop from two or more ova. Each

 multiple pregnancy. Pregnancy in which two or more babies develop.

ova is fertilized with a different sperm, 4-5. This means each child has a different genetic makeup. These babies are as much alike and different as any other brothers and sisters, 4-6. Children born in these multiple births are called **fraternal** children. They can be twins, triplets, or higher multiple births. (*Fraternal* comes from a Latin word meaning *brother*.)

Fraternal children may or may not be the same gender. They look different at birth and show greater differences as they mature. Each child in a fraternal birth has his or her own chorion, 4-7. The **chorion** is a membrane that surrounds the baby in the uterus.

Identical Births

In identical births, children develop from a single ovum that was fertilized by a single sperm. During the early days of the pregnancy, the ovum splits to produce two or more children, 4-8. Scientists do not know why the ovum splits.

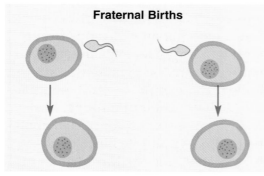

Fraternal Births

4-5 Fraternal twins grow from two separate zygotes. Each zygote carries a different genetic code from the same parents.

4-6 One of these fraternal twins looks more like his older brother than like his twin.
©John Shaw

Fraternal Twins

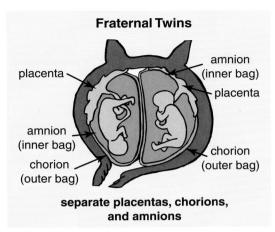

placenta

amnion (inner bag)

placenta

amnion (inner bag)

chorion (outer bag)

chorion (outer bag)

separate placentas, chorions, and amnions

4-7 All fraternal twins have separate chorions.

Identical Twins

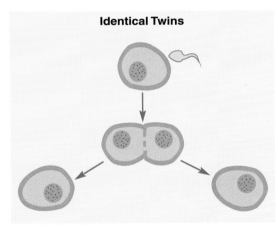

4-8 Identical twins grow from a single zygote that splits into two cells carrying the same genetic code.

If the ovum does not completely split, the babies will be *conjoined twins*. The bodies of these twins are joined in one or more places. Some conjoined twins even share internal organs, such as a stomach.

Babies from an identical birth have the same genetic makeup. This is because they came from one fertilized ovum. These babies are called **identical**. Identical children can be twins, triplets, or higher multiple births.

Identical children are very similar in appearance. People often confuse which child is which. Even family members may confuse them, 4-9. However, except for their genes, identical children are not exactly alike. Their fingerprints, palm prints, and footprints are similar but not exactly the same. Also, environment makes identical children different. For example, one child may be larger because of better nourishment, even before birth.

Some identical twins are *mirror twins*. They look the way you and your mirror image would appear. For instance, one may have a birthmark on the right shoulder and the other may have one on the left shoulder. One may be right-handed and the other left-handed.

Sometimes it is difficult to tell whether children are identical. At

fraternal. Term describing children from multiple pregnancies who develop from two ova and differ in genetic makeup.

chorion. Membrane that surrounds the baby in the uterus.

identical. Term describing children from multiple pregnancies who develop from one fertilized ovum and have the same genetic makeup.

4-9 Identical twins have the same genetic makeup.

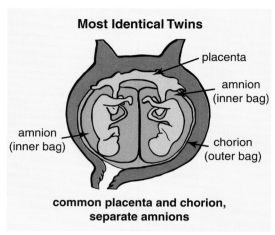

Most Identical Twins

placenta

amnion (inner bag)

amnion (inner bag)

chorion (outer bag)

common placenta and chorion, separate amnions

4-10 Twins who share a common chorion are always identical. In some cases, identical twins have separate chorions, however.

birth, the delivering physician may be able to tell. If not, blood tests or skin grafting can be used for proof. Identical children are always of the same gender. Unlike fraternal children, they usually share one chorion, 4-10. However, it is possible for each identical child to have a separate chorion.

Mixed Types

Multiple pregnancies may be both identical and fraternal if three or more children are born. In mixed types of pregnancies, separate sperm fertilize two or more eggs (fraternal). Then, one or more of the fertilized ova may split (identical).

If all children are identical or all are fraternal, this is not a mixed pregnancy. However, triplets are often from a mixed pregnancy, with two children identical and one fraternal, 4-11.

In like manner, quadruplets also may be all identical or all fraternal. However, quadruplets often are a mixed pregnancy type. With quadruplets, there could be several combinations. Three children could be identical and one fraternal, or two could be identical with the other two fraternal. There could even be two identical pairs, but such a case has not been known.

Production of Triplets

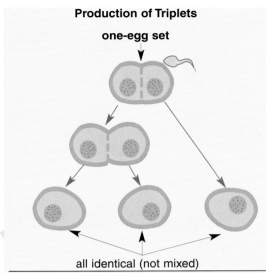

one-egg set

all identical (not mixed)

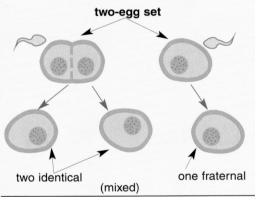

two-egg set

two identical

(mixed)

one fraternal

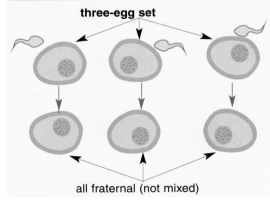

three-egg set

all fraternal (not mixed)

4-11 Depending on the number of zygotes, triplets may be identical, mixed types, or fraternal.

Stages in Prenatal Development

Many changes happen between conception and birth. The development that takes place during this time is called **prenatal development**. Prenatal development is divided into the germinal, embryonic, and fetal stages. See 4-12.

Germinal Stage

The first stage of prenatal development is the **germinal stage**. Conception marks the beginning of the germinal stage. This stage covers about the first two weeks of the pregnancy.

The fertilized egg (zygote) remains a single cell for about a day and a half. Then it starts to divide. On the third day, it has formed a hollow ball of 32 cells. This ball of cells enters the uterus, where it continues dividing rapidly for about three more days. During this time, the ball of cells floats freely in the uterus.

About 10 to 12 days after conception, the ball of cells begins to embed in the wall of the uterus. The cells

prenatal development. The development that takes place between conception and birth.

germinal stage. The first stage of prenatal development, which lasts about two weeks after conception.

Prenatal Development by Week

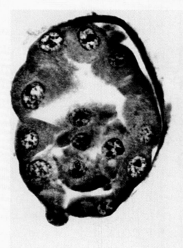

Carnegie Institute of Washington, Dept. of
Embryology, Davis Div.

4-day-old zygote

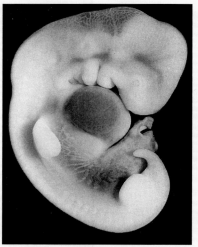

Carnegie Institute of Washington, Dept. of
Embryology, Davis Div.

4½-week-old embryo

The Germinal Stage

Conception through 2 weeks
- ❖ cell divisions occurring
- ❖ fertilized egg embedding in the wall of the uterus
- ❖ amnion, placenta, and umbilical cord beginning to form

The Embryonic Stage

2 weeks through 8 weeks
- ❖ internal organs (heart, liver, digestive system, brain, and lungs) developing
- ❖ tissue segments (future vertebrae) in a spinal column forming
- ❖ limb buds (future arms and legs) appearing
- ❖ ears and eyes beginning to form

4-12 Cell division results in the beginnings of a baby and a life-support system between mother and baby. The amnion, chorion, and placenta develop at the end of the germinal stage. They protect and nourish the baby until birth.

Prenatal Development by Week

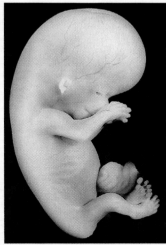

Carnegie Institute of Washington, Dept. of Embryology, Davis Div.

9-week-old fetus

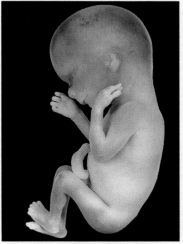

Carnegie Institute of Washington, Dept. of Embryology, Davis Div.

12-week-old fetus

The Fetal Stage

9 weeks
- ❖ facial features forming
- ❖ limbs, hands, feet, fingers, and toes developing

12 weeks
- ❖ 3″ long; weight 1 oz.
- ❖ muscles forming
- ❖ teeth and vocal cords developing
- ❖ eyelids and nails appearing

16 weeks
- ❖ 6-8″ long; weight 5-6 oz.
- ❖ lanugo (cottony growth) appearing
- ❖ heartbeat audible by stethoscope
- ❖ eyebrows and eyelashes growing

20 weeks
- ❖ 10-12″ long; weight 1 lb.
- ❖ sweat glands forming
- ❖ head hair appearing
- ❖ vernix caseosa (cheesy material) covering body
- ❖ skin developing

24 weeks
- ❖ 14″ long; weight 2 lbs.
- ❖ eyes maturing
- ❖ taste buds developing

28-40 weeks
- ❖ growing rapidly
- ❖ lanugo disappearing
- ❖ fatty tissue forming under skin
- ❖ body organs maturing

continue to divide. The chorion and **amnion** (a fluid-filled sac) begin to form. They surround the cells and protect the baby until birth. The **placenta**, an organ filled with blood vessels, begins to develop against the wall of the uterus. The umbilical cord grows out from the developing child, at the site of the future navel, and connects with the placenta, 4-13. The **umbilical cord** contains three blood vessels that connect the child with the placenta. As the placenta develops, it will begin to nourish the baby, remove the baby's wastes, exchange gases between mother and baby, and provide the baby with needed hormones. When the baby can receive nourishment from the mother, the germinal stage has ended.

Embryonic Stage

The second stage of prenatal development is the **embryonic stage**. Experts say this is the most critical stage of pregnancy. That is because almost all body systems develop during this stage. The embryonic stage lasts about six weeks. During this stage, the baby is called an **embryo**.

Changes happen so quickly that, when this stage ends, the embryo looks like a small human being. The embryo has tiny arms, legs, fingers, toes, and a face. All the major organs, such as the heart, brain, and lungs, are present. The heart begins beating in this stage. The embryo's body does not yet have solid bones but is supported by cartilage. **Cartilage** is soft, elastic, flexible tissue that

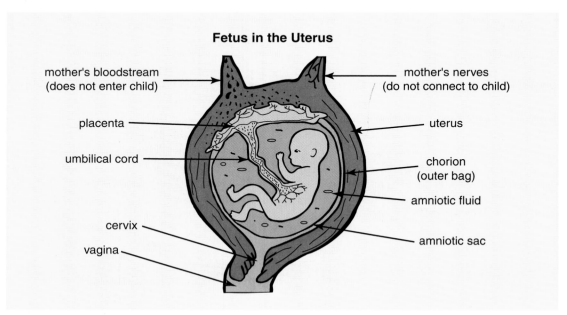

Fetus in the Uterus

mother's bloodstream (does not enter child)

mother's nerves (do not connect to child)

placenta

uterus

umbilical cord

chorion (outer bag)

amniotic fluid

cervix

amniotic sac

vagina

4-13 Prenatal development occurs throughout three major stages.

provides structure for the body. Cartilage is the tissue found in the tip of your nose.

The baby now receives both good and harmful substances from the mother's placenta through the umbilical cord. Because the baby's body parts are developing so quickly, passing harmful substances to the child can affect him or her for life. That is why the mother's health habits become very important during this stage. She should eat healthful foods so her baby receives the needed nutrients. She should also avoid substances like alcohol, drugs, excess caffeine, smoke, and X rays that may harm the baby. By taking care of herself, a woman does her part to help her baby be born healthy.

Fetal Stage

When bone cells start to replace cartilage, the baby enters the fetal stage of development. This stage begins about nine weeks after conception. From this point until birth, a baby is known medically as a fetus.

During the fetal stage, all parts of the body mature, and overall size increases quickly. Major changes happen in the fetus. By the fourth month, the fetus has usually grown enough to give the mother's growing abdomen a pregnant look.

Two milestones happen during the fetal stage. In the third month of pregnancy, parents-to-be may be able to hear their baby's heartbeat for the first time. They can do this at their doctor's office with the use of a special listening device. In the past, parents-to-be had to wait until much later in the pregnancy when the heartbeat could be picked up by the doctor's stethoscope.

Between the fourth and fifth months, a mother will begin to feel her baby move. Amazingly, the baby can turn, swallow, and even suck its thumb. The fetus also can move its head and push with the hands, feet, and limbs. When the mother feels these movements,

amnion. A fluid-filled sac that surrounds the baby in the uterus.

placenta. An organ filled with blood vessels that nourishes the baby in the uterus.

umbilical cord. The cord that connects the baby to the placenta.

embryonic stage. The second stage of prenatal development, which lasts about six weeks.

embryo. Term used to describe a baby in the embryonic stage of development.

cartilage. Soft, elastic, flexible tissue that provides structure for the body.

fetal stage. The third stage of pregnancy, lasting from about nine weeks after conception until birth.

fetus. Term used to describe a baby in the fetal stage of development.

it is called **quickening**. The mother should tell her doctor when she first feels movement.

A second milestone is reached when the fetus is seven months (28 weeks) old. This is the age at which most babies could survive if they were born. It is called the **age of viability**. By this time, the baby's brain has more control over body systems than before. However, most babies born at this time would need some intensive care in hospitals. With recent advances in medicine, more babies born before seven months have survived with special care.

Although a baby born at seven months can survive, the chance of surviving improves with each week closer to nine months. (This is true unless earlier delivery is needed for medical reasons.) In the last two months of pregnancy, the baby's lungs become stronger and the baby becomes larger.

In the ninth month of pregnancy, the fetus receives immunities from the mother. These help prevent the baby from catching some diseases after birth. In most cases, the baby also turns to a head-down position to prepare for birth.

quickening. Movements of the fetus that can be felt by the mother.

age of viability. The age at which most babies could survive if they were born (28th week of pregnancy).

Summing It Up

The nine-month pregnancy process begins with conception. At this moment, ovum and sperm unite and combine to form a single cell.

In this one cell is all the genetic information the child will receive from each parent. These genetic factors will influence all stages of life, especially the prenatal period. Genetic factors provide a blueprint for the future unfolding of family traits.

The zygote's nucleus stores this blueprint within DNA molecules, which are part of the chromosomes. Humans have 23 pairs of chromosomes—an equal number of which are received from the mother and father. Genes within each chromosome can determine some of an individual's traits. How genes from the parents interact can also determine traits. Two types of traits are dominant and recessive. Gender of the child is controlled by whether an X or Y sex chromosome is received from the father's sperm.

Multiple pregnancies occur when one or more eggs are fertilized by one or more sperm. Two types of multiple births are fraternal and identical. Each type forms differently from the other. While fraternal twins differ genetically, identical twins share the same genetic makeup. Multiple pregnancies may include combinations of identical and fraternal children.

Prenatal development is divided into the germinal, embryonic, and fetal stages. In the germinal stage, the dividing cells of the zygote travel toward the uterus, float freely, and then embed in the wall of the uterus. Almost all body systems develop during the embryonic stage. The fetal stage lasts from about nine weeks until birth. During this stage, the fetus grows and its body systems mature. At the end of the ninth month, the baby is ready to be born.

Reviewing Key Concepts

Write your answers on a separate sheet of paper.

1. Describe briefly what happens during conception.
2. Each sperm contains _____ (23, 46) chromosomes; each ovum contains _____ (23, 46) chromosomes.
3. Explain what determines an unborn baby's gender.
4. Paul and Emily both have blue eyes, a recessive trait. They are expecting a baby. Their baby's eyes will be
   A. brown, because both of Emily's parents and Paul's father have brown eyes.
   B. blue, because neither Paul nor Emily carry traits for brown eyes.
   C. blue or brown, because Emily inherited a trait for brown eyes from her mother.
5. List the three different kinds of multiple pregnancies.
6. Patty and Patrick—who look almost alike in size, coloring, and facial features—are _____ (identical, fraternal) twins.
7. True or false. In the germinal stage, the zygote receives nutrients through the placenta.
8. In which stage do the baby's body systems and organs start to form?
9. True or false. The mother's nutrition doesn't matter during the embryonic stage because the baby has not developed enough.
10. During the fetal stage, the baby's limbs are supported by _____ (cartilage, bones).
11. By the fourth or fifth month of pregnancy, the baby begins to
    A. develop vital organs.
    B. receive nutrients from the mother.
    C. make movements the mother can feel.

Using Your Knowledge

1. **Technology/Science.** Go online to research genetic counseling. What job duties do professionals in this field have, and what technologies do they use to investigate which genes a child might inherit from parents? Use a computer to compose a short report on your findings.
2. **Science.** Collect pictures of identical and fraternal siblings and note how alike or different they are. Try to find various pictures of the same people taken over several years.
3. **Art.** Design a poster showing how quadruplets can be all identical, three identical and one fraternal, two identical and two fraternal, two identical pairs, and all four fraternal.
4. **Science.** Record the color of your eyes and those of each of your parents. (If you wish, record the eye colors of another person and his or her parents instead.) Based on what you have learned about

dominant and recessive traits, try to determine the following:

a. what gene combinations are possible for you, given your eye color

b. what gene combinations are possible for your mother, given her eye color and yours

c. what gene combinations are possible for your father, given his eye color and yours

5. **Language Arts.** Write a story about prenatal development from the unborn baby's point of view. Use your creativity to explore what life might be like for the baby as new developments occur before birth. Refer to Figure 4-13 to gather ideas as you write.

Making Observations

1. Observe your physical features. Which features seem to come from your mother's family and which from your father's family? Which features do you share with other relatives?

2. Observe brothers and sisters. Which characteristics do they share? How are they different?

3. If possible, observe identical twins. Which of their characteristics are most alike? Which are similar but somewhat different? Which are dissimilar?

Thinking Further

1. Conception is sometimes referred to as the "miracle of life." Biologically, why can conception indeed be thought of as a miracle?

2. How do the stages in prenatal development follow the principles of growth and development (that is, growth and development are constant, happen in sequenced steps, happen at different rates, and have interrelated parts)? Give specific examples as part of your explanation.

3. Identical births have exactly the same heredity. What are some of the biological advantages of having an identical sibling? Are there disadvantages, too?

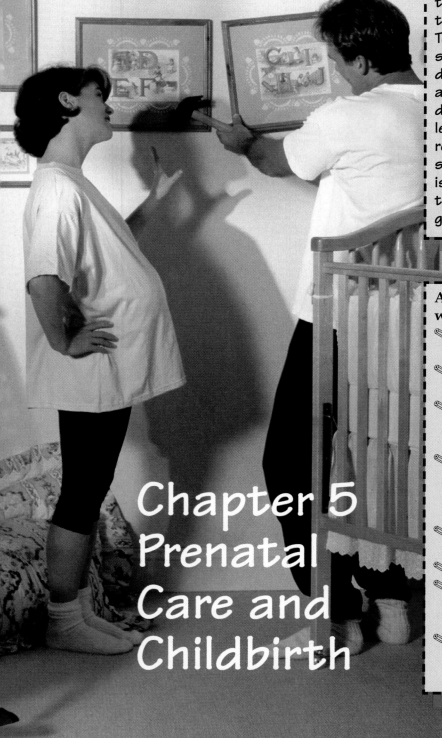

Derek and Lewauna discover there is a 30-minute wait for a table at their favorite restaurant. To pass the time, they decide to sit in the bar and order some soft drinks. Derek and Lewauna notice a couple sitting in the corner and drinking wine. When the woman leaves the table to go to the restroom, Derek and Lewauna notice she is pregnant. Before their table is ready, Derek and Lewauna watch the woman drink three more glasses of wine.

Chapter 5
Prenatal
Care and
Childbirth

After studying this chapter, you will be able to

- describe the early signs of pregnancy.
- explain the role of the environment on prenatal development.
- explain the relationship between the health of the mother and the health of the baby.
- describe how diseases, drugs, radiation, environmental pollutants, and congenital problems can harm the fetus.
- list ways family members can be involved during pregnancy.
- describe the birth process.
- describe the birth process and some of the possible complications of delivery.
- describe physical and emotional changes in the mother during the postpartum period.

Define...

obstetricians
environmental factors
premature
low birthweight
Rh factor
diabetes
pregnancy-induced hypertension
   (PIH)
sexually transmitted diseases
   (STDs)
acquired immunodeficiency
   syndrome (AIDS)
fetal alcohol syndrome (FAS)
congenital problem
miscarriage
stillbirth
ultrasound
chorionic villus sampling (CVS)
amniocentesis
labor
certified nurse-midwives (CNM)
natural childbirth
Lamaze method
Leboyer method
lightening
breech birth position
dilation
episiotomy
forceps
vacuum extraction
caesarean section
bonding
postpartum care
baby blues
postpartum depression (PPD)
postpartum psychosis (PPP)

At no other time are two people closer than a mother and baby during the prenatal period. Even before the mother knows she is pregnant, the baby affects her life. The mother's body changes to prepare for nine months of growth. The baby continues to affect the mother's body through delivery.

As you read in Chapter 1, the environment influences growth and development. The unborn's first environment is the mother's body. She has a great effect on her baby's development.

The mother gives the baby a safe "home" in her uterus. She eats, breathes, and gets rid of wastes for them both, and her body works to bring the baby into the world.

Before a baby is born, all family members need to be close. Family members should help each other adjust to life with a baby. Couples who are close during the prenatal stage can actually have better marriages. Family closeness also can ensure better parenting through each stage in the child's development.

The March of Dimes urges mothers to "Be good to your baby before it is born." Parents-to-be should take this slogan seriously. Because experts know more about pregnancy, childbirth, and infant care than ever before, parents-to-be can take many steps to keep mother and baby healthy and safe.

Ideally, these steps should begin *before* a woman becomes pregnant. Good health habits throughout the younger years help prepare a woman for childbearing. A couple's doctor can also recommend other ways to prepare for a healthy pregnancy. A complete medical checkup is a good idea. This may detect health problems that can be corrected before pregnancy.

As soon as a woman believes she is pregnant, she should seek prenatal care. This medical care is important, whether it is a first, second, or later pregnancy. Starting good prenatal care early in pregnancy greatly reduces the risk of complications.

Signs of Pregnancy

A woman cannot feel the sperm and egg unite. She cannot feel cells divide as the baby begins to develop. Nevertheless, her body immediately begins to nourish and protect the new life. Hormones trigger changes in some of the woman's organs. The signs of pregnancy help a woman recognize these changes.

The signs of pregnancy are not signs of an illness. Pregnancy is a normal process. If a woman is healthy and happy about having a child, she may even feel better than before she became pregnant. The signs of pregnancy are divided into presumptive and positive signs, 5-1. The *presumptive signs* could be signs of pregnancy or something else. Doctors must determine their cause. However, doctors identify positive signs as definitely being caused by pregnancy.

Medical Care

Medical care is the best way to make childbearing safe and successful. If a woman believes she is pregnant, she should make an appointment with a doctor as soon as possible. Many pregnant women choose to visit obstetricians, or doctors who specialize in pregnancy and birth.

The First Appointment

The first prenatal appointment sets a foundation for medical care throughout the pregnancy. It's a good idea for the couple to go to this visit together. They can share important information with the doctor and learn much about what to expect in the months ahead.

First, the doctor will gather general information, such as the age and health history of each parent. Next, the doctor will ask details about the woman's menstrual cycle and any past pregnancies. The doctor will also answer any questions the couple has about the pregnancy. First-time parents often have more questions than those who have given birth before.

The visit continues with a complete physical exam for the mother-to-be. The doctor will weigh the woman and take her pulse, blood pressure, and respiration rates, 5-2. He or she will check the woman's breasts and perform a pelvic exam. The doctor may measure the woman's pelvis to be sure it is large enough to allow the baby's head through during delivery. Urine tests

Signs of Pregnancy

Presumptive Signs

❖ Amenorrhea (menstruation stops)—If the woman is usually regular in her menstrual cycle, a delay of 10 or more days is a sign.

❖ Nausea—Nausea is present in about ½ to ⅔ of all pregnancies. Because it often occurs in the morning hours, it is called *morning sickness*. Nausea may happen at any time of the day. Nausea occurring at the same time daily from weeks 4 to 12 is a sign.

❖ Tiredness—Many women feel tired during the first few months of pregnancy.

❖ Frequency of urination—The growing uterus puts pressure on the bladder. Hormones may also cause more frequent urination.

❖ Swelling and tenderness of the breasts—This is often the first sign women note.

❖ Skin discoloration—Stretch marks may be seen as the breasts and abdomen enlarge. Darkening of skin may occur on the face and nipples.

❖ Internal changes—Doctors often note softening of the cervix (Goodell's sign). There also may be a softening of the lower part of the uterus (Hegar's sign) and a bluish tinge to the vagina and cervix due to circulatory congestion (Chadwick's sign). The uterus is also enlarged with irregular areas of firmness and softness (Piskacek's sign).

❖ Other signs—Other symptoms include backache, groin pains, dizziness, abdominal swelling, leg cramps, varicose veins, and indigestion.

Positive Signs

❖ HCG (Human Chorionic Gonadatrophin)—HCG is a hormone found in the blood and urine of pregnant women. Lab tests may detect the hormone's presence as early as the first two weeks of pregnancy.

❖ Fetal heartbeat—This can be heard through a special device at 12 weeks and through a stethoscope at 16 weeks.

❖ Fetal movement—Spontaneous movement begins at 11 weeks but is not felt until 16 to 18 weeks.

❖ Fetal image—This may be seen with ultrasound scanning.

❖ Fetal shape—The baby's shape may be felt through the abdominal wall.

❖ Uterine contractions—A doctor may note these painless contractions.

5-1 Presumptive signs could be signs of pregnancy, or they might be signs of other conditions. Positive signs, however, are definitely caused by pregnancy.

and blood tests will be done. The blood tests check for blood type, *anemia* (a condition caused by lack of iron), and diseases that can harm an unborn child. In some women, a test will be done for blood sugar level at this time.

obstetricians. Doctors who specialize in pregnancy and birth.

5-2 Checking weight is a routine part of a prenatal checkup.
© John Shaw

The doctor will advise the couple on health habits to follow in pregnancy. Most of these pertain to the mother, but the father can be involved, too. For example, the couple could work together to quit smoking. This will protect their baby's health, as well as their own. The father-to-be can also encourage his partner to eat right, be active, and get enough rest. He can join her in following these healthful habits.

At the end of the checkup, the obstetrician estimates the *due date* for the baby's birth (which is now given as the expected week of birth). Babies are usually born about 40 weeks after the beginning of the last menstrual period.

Couples then set the date for the next appointment. Usually the doctor sees a pregnant woman once a month during the first six months of pregnancy. Visits increase to twice a month during the seventh and eighth months. During the ninth month, visits increase to once a week or more. Going to each of these appointments is important. Having a doctor monitor the pregnancy increases the chance of delivering a healthy baby.

The Unborn Baby's Environment

At the moment the sperm enters the egg, the baby begins to form traits from both the mother and father. These inherited traits, or genetic factors, are merged into a unique new person. They will influence the child's growth and development throughout life. Development is not determined solely by genetic factors, however.

Immediately after conception, the environment begins to exert an influence on the unborn's traits. Environmental factors are those factors caused by a person's surroundings. The prenatal environment is the mother's body, 5-3. Thus, the mother's age, weight, health habits, and hazards she encounters are environmental factors that affect the baby.

5-3 Taking time to relax and reduce stress is critical for mothers-to-be. A high stress level during pregnancy can affect the unborn in negative ways.
© John Shaw

Factors That Affect the Baby's Health

An unborn baby depends on the mother for a healthy start. Women with good health habits before pregnancy most often have healthy babies. Some women are often called *high-risk mothers-to-be*. This describes a pregnant woman with environmental factors that do not promote a healthy pregnancy. These factors include age, physical health, Rh factor, and emotional stability. These are only some of the environmental factors that affect prenatal development.

Mother's Age

In regards to health, the ideal time for a woman to have a baby is between ages 21 and 28 years. Teens and women over 36 are high-risk mothers-to-be. Because pregnant teens are still growing themselves, their bodies cannot always meet the needs of babies. Very young teens tend to have babies who are **premature** (born too soon), have **low birthweights** (weigh less than 5½ pounds at birth), have disabilities, or are born dead. Women over age 36 tend to give birth to more babies with health problems, disabilities, and disorders.

Mother's Physical Health

The mother's prepregnancy health greatly affects the outcome of pregnancy. Women who are in excellent

environmental factors. Those factors caused by a person's surroundings.

premature. Term that describes babies who are born too soon.

low birthweight. Term that describes babies who weigh less than 5½ pounds at birth.

health before pregnancy are the most likely to have healthy pregnancies. Those with poor prepregnancy health are more likely to have health problems in pregnancy. Their babies may have health problems before and after birth, too.

Any health problems a woman has may play a role in pregnancy. Women should ask their doctors (before pregnancy, if possible) how these problems might affect the pregnancy. In many cases, steps can be taken to protect the unborn. The doctor will want to monitor health problems more closely during pregnancy. Special testing might be done, and medications or treatments might need to be adjusted for the safety of the unborn. With good health care during pregnancy, women can overcome many health problems.

It is also important for a woman to enter pregnancy at a healthy weight for her age, height, and body type. Being underweight or overweight before pregnancy can lead to serious health problems for mother and baby.

Women who start pregnancy at 15 percent or more under healthy weight more often have low-birthweight infants than women of healthy weight. Being underweight can also lead to other problems that endanger the health of both mother and baby. Women who start pregnancy at over 20 percent more than healthy weight have more complications, too. They experience more fatigue, high blood pressure, heart strain, and blood sugar problems.

If a woman is unsure what a healthy weight is, she should ask her doctor. Reaching a healthy weight before becoming pregnant should be the goal. This will increase the chance of a healthy pregnancy. However, women who are already pregnant should discuss their weight with a doctor or dietitian. Large or sudden weight changes are not advised in pregnancy. These could jeopardize the health of both mother and baby.

Closely related to healthy weight are nutrition and activity level. Women who have good eating habits and engage in regular physical activity are more likely to have healthy pregnancies. Women who are inactive or have poor eating habits may face more problems during pregnancy.

Rh Factor

The **Rh factor** is a protein substance found in the red blood cells of about 85 percent of the population. (The substance was discovered and first tested in the Rhesus monkey. This is why it is named *Rh factor*.) People who have the substance are called *Rh positive* (Rh+), and those who do not are called *Rh negative* (Rh–).

The only time this factor can cause the baby a problem is when the father is Rh+ and the mother is Rh–. This combination occurs in 12 percent of all marriages. If the baby inherits the Rh+ blood type from the father, the baby may develop *Rh disease*. Rh disease is a type of anemia that destroys the baby's red blood cells.

Rh disease does not affect the first Rh+ unborn. However, during any pregnancy, some of the baby's Rh+ cells may enter the mother's bloodstream during birth. This happens in about four percent of cases. These cells are foreign to the mother's Rh– system. Her body fights these Rh+ cells by making antibodies. This then makes the mother immune to the blood cells of future Rh+ babies. In the next pregnancy, these antibodies cross the placenta. If the baby has Rh+ blood, the antibodies destroy the baby's red blood cells.

In 1968, a vaccine called *anti-Rh-immune globulin* was approved to greatly reduce the danger of Rh disease. An Rh– mother receives the vaccine within 72 hours after the birth of each Rh+ baby. The vaccine blocks the growth of antibodies in her body. The vaccine is given after miscarriage or abortion of an Rh+ baby, too. An Rh– female should also receive the vaccine after a transfusion of Rh+ blood anytime during her life. The vaccine is almost 100 percent effective unless the woman's body has already made antibodies to Rh+ cells.

Mother's Emotional Health

Positive thoughts and feelings are important for a woman to have a healthy baby. Negative feelings can stimulate the nervous system and the flow of adrenaline. *Adrenaline* is a hormone that prepares the body to cope with stress. It can make a person feel more energetic. Both the nervous system and adrenaline control heart rate, breathing, and muscle tension.

When a mother is happy and relaxed, her adrenaline level is low, her heartbeat and breathing are slow, and her muscles are relaxed, 5-4. When the mother is under stress, adrenaline crosses the placenta to the baby, carrying stress signals. The mother's stress increases her heartbeat and muscle tension as well as the baby's. Later in the pregnancy, the baby not only receives the adrenaline signal but also hears changes in the mother's heartbeat and breathing.

Can stress harm the unborn baby? The unborn baby can handle some stress. However, if the stress is long-lasting, severe, or frequent, the mother may have a more difficult delivery. The baby may be smaller, fussy, or quite active. Thus, emotional support during pregnancy is good for both mother and baby.

 Rh factor. A protein substance found in the red blood cells of about 85 percent of the population.

5-4 During the prenatal stage, the mother's body serves as the baby's environment. The mother should work to make this the best possible environment for her growing baby.
Adrian Demery

Health Habits During Pregnancy

Good health habits are always important. Health habits for pregnant women are similar to good health habits for all people. However, when a woman is pregnant, health habits have an even greater effect on her health and her baby's health. In sum, there are major environmental factors affecting the unborn baby.

During pregnancy, certain health habits do change. A pregnant woman may have to eat more of some foods. She may have to take vitamins. A mother-to-be may also need to be more cautious about her physical activities. She may need to give up active sports, such as volleyball. Every pregnant woman should take care of herself. Because each pregnancy differs, the mother-to-be should ask her doctor for health guidelines to follow.

Nutrition

The old saying that mothers-to-be are *eating for two* (or maybe more) is correct. During the first week, the baby is fed entirely on the contents of the ovum's yolk sac. After embedding, the fertilized egg feeds on mucous tissues that line the womb. By the 12th week, the contents of the yolk sac have been used, so the baby completely depends on the mother for food.

Eating for two does not mean a woman should double or greatly increase the number of calories she eats. After all, the unborn baby is tiny. The mother may need to change her food choices to include more nutritious foods than usual. These foods will help the baby grow.

Scientists now feel a woman needs essential nutrients throughout her life to prepare for pregnancy. Providing for her own needs and those of her baby may put a nutritional strain on the woman's body. If she had good nutrition before pregnancy, she will have built nutrient stores in her body that will help meet these needs. Pregnant teens under 17 years of age have more nutritional problems because they are still growing. Their bodies have not had time to build these stores.

Good nutrition during pregnancy is vital. There is a direct link between what a pregnant woman eats and the following factors:

❖ her weight gain
❖ the unborn's weight gain
❖ the infant's growth
❖ the infant's mental capacity
❖ the infant's physical performance

Thus, a nutritious diet is essential. Cells need proteins, fats, carbohydrates, minerals, and vitamins to help them grow. A healthful pregnancy diet includes foods rich in these nutrients. Like all Americans, pregnant women should follow the *Food Guide*. This is a guide for healthful eating developed by the USDA, 5-5. While this is a good basic guide, the need for some nutrients does increase during pregnancy. A pregnant woman's doctor or dietitian can advise her what specific diet changes to should make during pregnancy. Following these recommendations will help her nourish both herself and her unborn baby.

Diets for pregnant and nursing mothers provide more calcium, iron, folic acid, and protein than diets for nonpregnant women. Pregnant women should have eight 8-ounce glasses of water daily. Because the effects of caffeine on the unborn baby are not clear, its use should be limited during pregnancy. Daily intake of caffeine from all sources (including coffee, tea, soft drinks, and chocolate) should not exceed the amount of caffeine found in one cup of coffee.

Weight Gain

Mothers-to-be and their doctors are concerned about weight gain. Experts suggest women gain between 25 and 35 pounds in pregnancy. The exact amount depends on the woman's height and prepregnancy weight. Women who enter pregnancy underweight may be advised to gain more. Overweight women may be advised to gain less than this amount.

To meet the nutrient needs of themselves and their babies, pregnant women need to eat 300 extra calories per day, starting in the fourth month. Weight gain during pregnancy is not all stored as fat, 5-6. Much of the weight gain goes to the growing baby and the tissues that support it.

Doctors carefully watch how much weight pregnant women gain. Gaining too much puts extra strain on the heart and makes the woman uncomfortable. Doctors also watch for sudden weight gain and unusual swelling. These conditions are serious and require prompt medical attention. Gaining too little weight is not good for the developing baby, either. This can signal the baby is not growing properly or receiving enough nutrients.

Basic Daily Diet for Pregnant Women

Food Group	Number of Servings	Typical Servings	Special Notes
Bread, Cereal, Rice, and Pasta Group	6 to 10	1 slice bread 1 biscuit, muffin, or roll 1 ounce ready-to-eat cereal ½ to ¾ cup cooked cereal, grits, rice, or pasta	Look for whole grain or enriched breads and cereals. At least 3 servings should be whole grain.
Vegetable Group	5 to 8	½ cup vegetables, cooked, or chopped, raw 1 cup of raw, leafy vegetables ¾ cup vegetable juice	Eat at least one good source of vitamin A and vitamin C daily. Good sources of vitamin A include dark green and deep yellow vegetables and fruits, such as spinach, carrots, sweet potatoes, and cantaloupe. Good sources of vitamin C include citrus fruits, tomatoes, strawberries, broccoli, and brussel sprouts.
Fruit Group	4 to 5	½ cup fruit ¾ cup juice ½ large grapefruit 1 medium fruit (apple, orange, banana) ½ cup chopped, cooked, or canned fruit	

Milk, Yogurt, and Cheese Group	4 to 6	1 cup whole, reduced fat, or fat free milk
		To equal the calcium content of 1 cup of milk, it would take
		    1 cup plain yogurt
		    3-inch cube Cheddar cheese
		    1½ slices American process cheese
		    2 cups cottage cheese
		    1¾ cups ice cream
			Remember that 1¾ cups of ice cream have the same amount of calcium as 1 cup of milk, but the ice cream has many more calories.

Meat, Poultry, Fish, Dry Beans, Eggs and Nuts Group	2 to 3	2 to 3 ounces of cooked, lean meat, poultry, or fish
		The following count as 1 ounce of lean meat:
		    ½ cup cooked dry beans
		    1 egg
		    2 tablespoons peanut butter
			Eat a variety of protein foods from both animal and vegetable sources.

5-5 This chart shows the number of servings people need to eat a day from each group. Nutritional needs differ slightly during pregnancy, so women should consult their doctors or dietitians about what to eat during pregnancy.

Weight Gained During Pregnancy

Portion of Added Weight	Weight Gain in Pounds
Baby	7.5
Uterus	2.0
Placenta	1.5
Amniotic fluid	2.0
Increased maternal blood volume	3.5
Increased maternal breast mass	1.5
Increased maternal stored fat and protein	4.0
Increased maternal fluid retention	4.0
Total weight gain	26.0

5-6 Weight gain is a necessary part of pregnancy, but this weight gain has many causes.

A woman should steadily gain a healthy amount of weight throughout her pregnancy. The following amounts are common:

- ❖ during the first three months— about five pounds total
- ❖ from four to eight months—about two to three pounds per month
- ❖ during the ninth month—about one pound per week

Hygiene Practices

Women should continue their normal grooming and body care habits during pregnancy. Paying attention to appearance may help the mother-to-be

5-7 Physical activity has many benefits for pregnant women.

feel better during physical discomfort or emotional stress, 5-7.

Many doctors suggest pregnant women do the following:

- ❖ Have a dental checkup. (Recent studies show a link between gum disease in pregnancy and premature delivery.)
- ❖ Avoid very cold or very hot baths.
- ❖ Replace tub baths with showers or sponge baths during the last four to six weeks of pregnancy. (This helps to prevent internal infection. It also helps to prevent possible falls due to the woman's larger body size.)

Rest and Sleep

A mother-to-be needs much rest and sleep. Many doctors advise eight to nine hours of sleep a night. In addition, pregnant women need at least one 15- to 30-minute rest (with or without sleep) during the day. Many women feel the most tired during the first few months and last weeks of pregnancy. Exhaustion is never good, especially in pregnancy. However, a sleepless night is not dangerous. If a woman has frequent sleep problems, she should talk with her doctor. She should never take drugs (even over-the-counter medicines) unless her doctor prescribes them.

Physical Activity and Exercise

Unless advised by her doctor to limit physical activity, a pregnant woman can and should be active. Activity helps keep weight within normal limits, strengthens muscles women use in delivery, increases energy, and relieves tension, 5-7.

Many doctors advise mothers-to-be to avoid contact sports, activities that jolt the pelvic region, and activities that could result in falls. On the other hand, doctors often advise women to walk during pregnancy. Some women take special exercise classes for pregnant women.

In childbirth classes, women may learn conditioning exercises to relieve back and leg strain of later pregnancy. They can also learn exercises that prepare the muscles for delivery.

Health Hazards to Avoid

Many health problems in the unborn can be prevented if the mother protects herself before and during pregnancy. Only about 20 percent of disabilities present at birth are caused by genetic factors. Most are caused by environmental factors. These include diseases, drugs, radiation, and pollutants. Experts may add other items to this list as research continues.

Harmful substances can enter the mother's body, pass through the placenta, and enter the baby's body. Some substances can pass from mother to baby during the birth process. Any substance may be harmful if passed to an unborn child at a critical time during growth. In most cases, the strength of the substance may be less important than the time when it reaches the baby. Other substances are equally dangerous throughout pregnancy.

Diseases or Illnesses in the Mother

Maternal illnesses may exist prior to pregnancy. They may also develop during pregnancy. Some illnesses have few effects on the fetus, while others affect the baby severely.

Diabetes

Diabetes is a disorder caused by the body's inability to use sugar properly. In diabetes, the body does not produce or use the hormone insulin properly. Some women might have diabetes before they become pregnant. If so, they should talk to their doctors about how to manage the disorder during pregnancy.

Another kind of diabetes can occur during pregnancy. It is called *gestational diabetes*, and it appears in women who did not have diabetes before pregnancy.

Soon after pregnancy ends, gestational diabetes usually goes away.

Women with gestational diabetes usually have larger babies, often weighing 10 to 12 pounds at birth. A large baby is a risk to the mother during delivery. In addition, these babies are at risk for high blood pressure, congenital problems, heart problems, and infant death.

Careful balance of diet, physical activity, and medication (if needed) will keep both types of diabetes under control. Pregnant women with this condition should work closely with their doctors and dietitians to plan for a healthy pregnancy.

Pregnancy-Induced Hypertension (PIH)

Pregnancy-induced hypertension (PIH) is the name for high blood pressure caused by pregnancy. This dangerous condition has also been called *preeclampsia* or *toxemia*. It includes a sudden increase in blood pressure, protein in the urine, and swelling. PIH appears late in pregnancy, but its cause is unknown. If untreated, PIH can lead to damage or death of the mother, baby, or both. Early treatment can help both mother and baby avoid serious health problems. This may include bed rest, medicine, and perhaps early delivery of the baby.

Rubella and Other Infections

Rubella (formerly called *German measles*) is a virus that can cross the placenta and affect the baby during the first three months of pregnancy. For the mother, this disease is mild. Infected babies, however, may be born blind, deaf, mentally disabled, or with heart problems.

Doctors are also concerned about exposing the unborn to chicken pox, mumps, and measles. The only way to protect babies is to prevent their mothers from catching these diseases. Mothers should have received vaccinations for all these during childhood, except chicken pox. Many adults have a natural immunity to chicken pox, which they developed by having the disease as children. (A vaccine for chicken pox called the varicella vaccine is now available.) A pregnant woman should avoid exposure to anyone she knows that has any of these diseases.

Many other infections can be dangerous during pregnancy. One of these is *toxoplasmosis*, which is caused by a parasite that primarily infects cats. Because this infection can damage an unborn's nervous system, pregnant women should avoid contact with cats. They should not garden without rubber gloves, be near soil used by cats, or change the cat's litter box.

diabetes. A disorder caused by the body's inability to use sugar properly.

pregnancy-induced hypertension (PIH). The name for high blood pressure caused by pregnancy.

Sexually Transmitted Diseases (STDs)

Sexually transmitted diseases (STDs) are infectious illnesses that are passed primarily through sexual intercourse. Some STDs can enter the bloodstream of the mother and cross the placenta to reach the unborn. Others infect the mother's reproductive tract and can pass to the baby during delivery. Still other STDs can be passed from mother to infant during breast-feeding.

STDs and Their Effects on the Unborn/Newborn		
STD	**Transmission**	**Effects on Baby**
Syphilis	Contracted by mother through sexual activity. Crosses the placenta beginning in the eighteenth week of pregnancy.	Effects prevented if treated before the sixteenth week. Untreated infection causes deafness, brain damage, skin lesions, bone and facial deformities, and fetal death.
Cytomegalo-virus (CMV	Transmitted by respiratory contact or sexual activity. CMV crosses the placenta.	Fatal for embryo or young fetus. In older fetuses, causes brain, liver, and blood problems. No treatment or means of prevention.
Herpes Simplex (herpes)	Contracted primarily by sexual relations. Transmitted to baby at or shortly before delivery by baby's contact with infected secretions.	Newborns develop skin lesions and brain damage, and 50 percent die. No treatment available. C-sections may prevent contact with secretions.
Gonorrhea	Contracted by sexual relations. Transmitted to baby at or shortly before delivery by baby's contact with reproductive tract infection.	Blindness if untreated. Treatment includes placing silver nitrate in the infant's eyes and treating baby with antibiotics.
Chlamydia	Transmitted through sexual relations. (Twice as common as gonorrhea.) Women rarely experience symptoms. May lead to sterility.	Miscarriage, low birthweight, and death of infants due to lung disorders.
Acquired Immuno-deficiency Syndrome (AIDS)	Acquired by mother through sexual relations or contact with infected blood or body fluids. Infected mothers transmit the virus in 25 percent of births. (Women who are pregnant usually have HIV only with full-blown AIDS following pregnancy.)	Illness and perhaps very early death of child. Treatment of symptoms. No cure.

5-8 STDs can have serious effects on the unborn baby.

All STDs are dangerous to unborn babies, 5-8. None is more dangerous, however, than **acquired immunodeficiency syndrome (AIDS)**. This disease is caused by the *human immunodeficiency virus (HIV),* which attacks the body's immune system and leaves it unable to fight illness. HIV is spread through sexual relations or by contact with contaminated blood and bodily fluids. It can also pass from mother to unborn baby during pregnancy, childbirth, or breast-feeding. Among babies born to mothers with HIV, about one in four also have the virus. Scientists continue to work on a cure for AIDS. Prevention, however, is the best way to keep unborn babies safe from this disease.

Drugs

The term *drugs* includes medications, alcohol, nicotine (from cigarettes), and illegal drugs. Each of these drugs can cross the placenta and reach an unborn baby. Some drugs harm the baby in the early months of pregnancy, and many harm the baby throughout pregnancy. Other drugs, such as aspirin, are most hazardous near delivery.

Medications

Only a few medications have been proven safe for use during pregnancy. Some have been proven unsafe for unborn babies. These should not be used in pregnancy. Out of possible risk to the babies, medication studies rarely include pregnant women. For this reason, the effects of most medications on unborn babies are not known.

To be safe, a pregnant woman should not take any medication without consulting her doctor. This includes prescription and over-the-counter medicines. A woman's doctor can find out what risks have been identified. He or she can then weigh this risk against the woman's need for the medicine. In some cases, a severely ill mother may be given medicines because the benefits outweigh the risks. This is best decided by the woman's doctor on a case-by-case basis.

Alcohol

Doctors advise women never to drink alcohol during pregnancy. Any alcoholic drink, whether beer, wine, or hard liquor, can harm an unborn baby. Taking even one drink may cause the baby to be abnormal.

Almost three babies in 1,000 are born with a condition called **fetal alcohol syndrome (FAS)**. This happens when mothers drink heavily

sexually transmitted diseases (STDs). Infectious illnesses that are passed primarily through sexual intercourse.

acquired immunodeficiency syndrome (AIDS). A disease caused by the HIV virus, which attacks the body's immune system.

fetal alcohol syndrome (FAS). A condition in infants that occurs when mothers drink heavily during pregnancy.

during pregnancy. Babies with FAS are shorter and weigh less than other babies. Their growth and development is slow. These babies have small heads, unusual facial features, heart defects, poor motor development, and disabilities. *Fetal alcohol effect (FAE)*, a term used to describe less severe damage, causes children to have serious learning problems.

Nicotine

When a pregnant woman smokes, her baby feels the effects. Babies of smokers are usually smaller than average or premature. Nicotine raises the mother's heart rate, blood pressure, and breathing rate and reduces the flow of blood. While a mother is smoking, the baby's oxygen is greatly reduced. Babies need oxygen as they grow, especially during the prenatal period. Smoking, especially after 16 weeks of pregnancy, is very risky because it raises a woman's chance to miscarry.

Smoking can also cause a baby's brain to develop abnormally. This can lead to learning problems, hyperactivity, and poor attention spans. Ear infections and breathing problems are also more common among babies exposed to smoke during pregnancy. Secondhand smoke affects an unborn baby's health in similar ways.

Illegal Drugs

Illegal drugs, such as cocaine, crack, heroin, and marijuana, all cross the placenta quickly and reach the baby. If a woman is addicted to drugs, chances

are her baby is, too. In large urban areas, up to 10 percent of babies have been exposed to cocaine before birth.

Pregnant women who use drugs often have low-birthweight and premature babies. One of the greatest problems for these babies happens after they are born. Because they no longer are receiving the drugs (as they cross the placenta), their bodies go through withdrawal. This causes the baby great stress. Symptoms of the baby's withdrawal include a high-pitched cry, shaking, poor feeding, and fever.

Babies affected by cocaine grow slowly. They may have malformed urinary and intestinal tracts and poor attention spans. By the first month, these babies' behaviors worsen rather than improve.

Pregnant women who use illegal drugs also often neglect their own health. In many cases, these women eat poorly, smoke, or abuse alcohol. Some never see a doctor during pregnancy. For these reasons, babies whose mothers use illegal drugs have a slim chance of living a healthy life.

Radiation Exposure

During pregnancy, X rays should be avoided if possible. This is because X rays aimed toward the fetus increase the likelihood of childhood cancer. Some studies also link the use of X rays in pregnancy to congenital disabilities in the fetus.

Pregnant women should always inform their doctors or dentists of possible or known pregnancy before X rays are performed. Women should not work near X-ray machines or stay in the room when an X ray is being taken.

If an X ray is necessary before delivery, it must be low in intensity, taken away from the fetus, and done only when the abdomen is shielded by a lead safety drape.

Environmental Pollution

Parents should determine whether their home and workplace are safe. Lead, chemicals, pesticides, and herbicides all pose risks to the unborn baby. Pregnant women should check to be sure their environments do not harm their babies.

Complications of Pregnancy

Pregnant women can greatly reduce the chance of problems in their pregnancies by receiving prenatal care, following their doctors' advice, and practicing good health habits. However, complications (problems) can occur in any pregnancy. The major complications of pregnancy are described in 5-9. Complications can damage the mother's health. Some can result in congenital problems or the loss of the baby before birth. Doctors must treat complications immediately. Prenatal care helps doctors note problems early, which allows them to treat these right away.

Congenital Problems

A **congenital problem** is a physical or biochemical problem in a baby that is present at birth. It may be inherited or caused by environmental factors. These disabilities and diseases occur with varying degrees of severity. Figure 5-10 describes the most common congenital problems.

Miscarriage

A **miscarriage** is the expulsion (forcing out) of the baby from the mother's body before week 20 of pregnancy. The medical term for miscarriage is *spontaneous abortion*. **Stillbirth** is the loss of the fetus after 20 weeks of pregnancy. In a stillbirth, the baby is born dead.

About one-third of all pregnancies end in the loss of the baby. Miscarriage is most common in the first three months but it can occur later. Some miscarriages occur even before the couple is aware of the pregnancy.

congenital problem. A physical or biochemical problem that is present at birth and may be caused by genetic or environmental factors.

miscarriage. The expulsion of a baby from the mother's body before week 20 of pregnancy.

stillbirth. Loss of a fetus after 20 weeks of pregnancy.

Complications in Pregnancy

Problem	Cause	Symptoms
Ectopic pregnancy (development of fetus outside of uterus)	Blocked fallopian tube	Spotting and cramping; uterus does not enlarge as it should; rupture of fallopian tube
Too much amniotic fluid	Uncontrolled diabetes; multiple pregnancy; incompatible blood types; congenital problems	Excessive pressure on mother's body; breathing problems, congenital problems in the newborn
Too little amniotic fluid	Congenital problems, growth problems, death of fetus	Fetal movement slows or stops
Bleeding in late pregnancy	Abrupto placentae; placenta previa; vaginal or cervical infection	Bleeding—often heavy
Abrupto placentae (placenta becomes detached from the uterine wall before it should)	Unknown Occurs more in women who smoke, have high blood pressure, and have had previous children or a history of detached placentas	Bleeding, cramping, abdominal tenderness
Placenta previa (placenta attaches itself to the uterus near or covering the cervix rather than in the upper half of the uterus)	Scarring of the uterine wall from a prior pregnancy; tumors of the uterus; surgery of the uterus	Bright red bleeding without pain or tenderness of the abdomen
Pregnancy-Induced Hypertension (also called toxemia or preeclampsia)	Multiple fetuses; teen pregnancy or pregnancy of woman over 40 years of age; high blood pressure; kidney disease	Sudden swelling of hands and face; high blood pressure; headache; dizziness; fever; irritability; protein in urine; abdominal pain; blurred vision; seizures

5-9 Complications in pregnancy require immediate medical treatment to protect the health of mother and baby.

Congenital Problems

Problem	Symptoms	Cause	Treatment
Cleft lip/palate	Noticeable at birth. A cleft lip occurs when the two sides of the upper lip fail to grow together properly. A cleft palate occurs when an opening remains in the roof of the mouth. This creates problems in breathing, talking, hearing, and eating.	Variable; often caused by a number of factors working together.	Corrective surgery and speech therapy.
Cystic fibrosis	A chemical failure affects lungs and pancreas. Thick sticky mucus forms in the lungs, causing breathing problems. Reduced amounts of digestive juices cause poor digestion of food. An excess amount of salt is excreted in perspiration.	Recessive gene.	Physical therapy, synthetic digestive enzymes, salt tablets, and antibodies can lessen the effect of the symptoms. However, there is no known cure. People with cystic fibrosis usually have shorter-than-normal life spans because they are highly susceptible to respiratory diseases.
Diabetes	Metabolic disorders cause high blood sugar. The person feels thirsty, hungry, and weak and usually loses weight.	A number of factors working together.	The disease can be controlled by insulin injections and careful diet and exercise. It cannot be cured.
Down syndrome	Distinct physical features are evident. Slanting eyes; large, misshapen forehead; oversized tongue; single crease across palm of each hand; and varying degrees of mental retardation are typical.	Chromosome abnormality. More likely to occur when mother is over age 35.	Special education. Life span may be nearly normal.
Huntington's chorea	The brain and central nervous system gradually deteriorate when the person is between 30 and 40 years old. This causes involuntary jerking, loss of mental abilities, insanity, depression, and finally death.	Dominant gene.	None.

(Continued)

5-10 Congenital problems have various symptoms, causes, and treatments.

Congenital Problems (Continued)

Problem	Symptoms	Cause	Treatment
Hydrocephalus	Extra fluid is trapped in the brain. The person's head is larger than normal.	A number of factors working together.	Surgical removal of excess fluid. Without treatment, children rarely survive.
Muscular dystrophy	A group of disorders which damage muscles. They cause progressive weakness and finally death.	Often sex-linked.	There is no cure, but therapy and braces offer some relief.
Phenylketonuria (PKU)	An enzyme deficiency makes the person unable to digest a certain amino acid. The baby appears normal at birth, but slowly develops mental retardation because the amino acid builds up in the body and causes brain damage.	Recessive gene.	A carefully prescribed diet that balances the enzyme deficiency. The effects of the disease can usually be avoided if treatment begins within the first six weeks of birth.
Sickle-cell anemia	Red blood cells are sickle-shaped rather than round. They cannot carry oxygen efficiently throughout the body. People become pale, tired, and short of breath. They have occasional pains and low resistance to infection. Their life span is often shorter than normal.	Recessive gene.	There is no cure. Various treatments relieve some symptoms, and blood transfusions are needed occasionally.
Spina bifida	A condition that causes partial paralysis due to an incompletely formed spinal cord.	Heredity and environmental factors.	Corrective surgery and physical therapy.
Tay-Sachs Disease	A lack of a specific chemical in the blood resulting in an inability to process and use fats. Leads to severe brain damage and death, often by age two or three years.	Recessive gene.	None.

Losses frequently occur for unknown reasons. Most miscarriages result from congenital problems of the fetus. Miscarriages also occur more often with pregnancy complications and certain diseases. Habits of the mother, such as smoking, drinking, or using drugs can also lead to fetal loss.

Having a miscarriage does not mean a couple will never have a baby. Their risk of a second miscarriage is higher than that of couples who have never miscarried. However, with good medical care, many couples can conceive again and deliver healthy babies after having a miscarriage.

Monitoring the Baby's Development

Monitoring the baby helps doctors determine the baby's health and exact age. Monitoring also indicates the size and gender of the baby. It will show if there is one or more than one baby in the mother's uterus. It will also indicate the baby's position before delivery.

Ultrasound

One test that is done to monitor an unborn baby is **ultrasound**. This is a test in which sound waves bounce off the fetus to produce an image of the fetus inside the womb. The picture of the fetus the ultrasound produces is called a *sonogram*.

The technician holds a *transducer* over the mother's abdomen. The transducer emits sound waves. The waves are deflected or absorbed at different rates, depending on whether they hit bone, organ tissue, blood, or water. These differences are changed into electrical impulses. This produces a visual image of the fetus on a computer monitor, 5-11. From this image, the doctor can see whether the baby seems to be developing correctly.

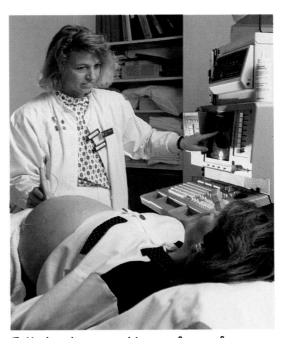

5-11 An ultrasound is a safe way for obstetricians to check on fetal health.
"Child development: Prenatal to Birth," Meridian Education Corp.

 ultrasound. A prenatal test in which sound waves bounce off the fetus to produce an image of the fetus inside the womb.

Because ultrasounds are considered safe, they are used fairly routinely. Ultrasounds provide information much like X rays but without radiation risks.

Chorionic Villus Sampling

Chorionic villus sampling (CVS) is a procedure for finding abnormalities in the unborn by testing a small sample of the chorion, which will later develop into the fetal part of the placenta. CVS is used between weeks 8 and 12 of pregnancy. This test can detect serious problems with the fetus early in the pregnancy.

A hollow tube is inserted through the vagina into the uterus and guided to the chorion. Chorionic villi projections from the chorion transport nutrients to, and wastes from, the unborn. A small section of the villi is painlessly suctioned off and analyzed for congenital problems. CVS has a slight risk of infection, which can result in a miscarriage.

Amniocentesis

Amniocentesis is a prenatal test used to check for the presence of over 100 congenital problems. Usually it checks for problems such as Down syndrome, Tay-Sachs disease, and sickle-cell anemia.

To perform the test, a medical specialist inserts a needle through the abdominal wall into the uterus. Ultrasound is done at the same time to position the needle. The specialist draws a small amount of fluid from the amniotic sac.

Why does this fluid give so much information? Cells cast off by the fetus float in the fluid. These cells are cultivated in a lab for three to five weeks and are then checked for congenital problems.

Amniocentesis cannot be done until the fetus is 14 to 16 weeks old. At this time, there is enough amniotic fluid for the test. Due to the lab time required, the woman will be 20 to 21 weeks pregnant when she learns the results.

Amniocentesis is a safe procedure in 99 percent of cases. However, miscarriage or premature birth may result in a few cases. For this reason, amniocentesis is not a routine procedure. It is used only when problems are suspected or the mother-to-be is older.

The Role of the Family

Pregnancy should be a family affair. Studies show that fathers-to-be who become involved with pregnancy and childbirth later become more involved in parenting. Children enjoy preparing for the new arrival. This helps them lessen their jealousy of the new sister or brother.

Family Involvement

Long ago, when mothers delivered their babies at home, some fathers became involved. However, women relatives and friends usually helped the new mother. When hospital deliveries became common, fathers were further detached from the birthing process. It was the father's duty to call the doctor and bring his wife to the hospital. Once in the hospital, he was sent to the "pacing room" to pace the floor, nap, compare notes with other fathers, and watch the clock. When the baby was born, the father handed out cigars and smiled at his baby through the nursery window.

Today's Fathers-to-Be

Today, most fathers-to-be take a more active role during pregnancy and delivery. Their role changes throughout pregnancy and birth. During the first few months, many mothers are concerned about their health and that of their babies. Husbands need to reassure their wives. Husbands can also help select a doctor and decide other aspects about delivery.

The middle part of pregnancy is often the most pleasant for the entire family. Mothers-to-be often feel their best. Husbands and family members are more aware of the baby because they can see the mother's abdomen grow. They can also feel the baby move. The couple may decorate a nursery and gather items needed for the baby. At this time, young children are often told about the baby. Parents should include them in baby preparations as much as possible.

The final months are an exciting and trying period. Mothers-to-be are often concerned about their health and safety in delivery. They may also feel more tired as the due date approaches. Husbands should support their wives. Couples often become educated about childbirth by reading books and attending classes, 5-12.

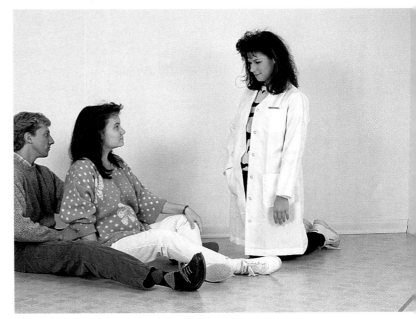

5-12 Husbands can support their wives through pregnancy by attending childbirth classes.
© John Shaw

chorionic villus sampling (CVS). A prenatal procedure for finding abnormalities in the unborn by testing a small sample of the chorion.

amniocentesis. A prenatal test in which a needle is inserted through the woman's abdomen into the amniotic sac and a sample of the fluid is removed for cell study.

Today, many fathers see their babies being born. When fathers are involved in childbirth, there are many benefits. Some research shows that it is good for mothers to have helpers during labor. (**Labor** is the process that moves the baby out of the mother's body.) Mothers with helpers have shorter and more enjoyable labors. Helpers tend to calm mothers and reduce their feelings of anxiety. Anxiety can be a problem in labor because it causes changes in the blood chemistry. These changes

❖ decrease the flow of blood to the baby, which can harm the baby

❖ slow contractions, which results in a longer labor

A final benefit of fathers as labor and delivery helpers is the bonding it provides for the fathers. Fathers who participate in labor and delivery often have closer relationships with their children than those who do not.

Family Decisions Concerning Childbirth

Parents have many decisions to make before the baby is born. They must choose where the birth will take place (a hospital or at home). Parents also need to choose a method of delivering the baby. The delivery method should mainly depend on the condition of the mother and baby. Parents should base their choices on their doctor's advice as well as their own preferences.

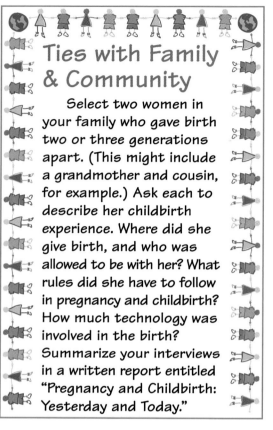

Ties with Family & Community

Select two women in your family who gave birth two or three generations apart. (This might include a grandmother and cousin, for example.) Ask each to describe her childbirth experience. Where did she give birth, and who was allowed to be with her? What rules did she have to follow in pregnancy and childbirth? How much technology was involved in the birth? Summarize your interviews in a written report entitled "Pregnancy and Childbirth: Yesterday and Today."

Home or Hospital Delivery

For most of history, home deliveries were the norm. Then, hospital deliveries started becoming more common. Women wanted relief from pain and safer conditions, which hospitals provided. For the last 60 to 70 years, most babies in the U.S. have been delivered at hospitals. In recent years, however, home births have begun to increase in popularity again. This leads many parents-to-be to choose between home and hospital deliveries for their babies.

With today's technology, the number of deaths (of mothers and infants) during childbirth has declined. At least 10 to 15 percent of deliveries need special medical help. This type of help is often unavailable in home births. These births pose much risk to the mother and baby in cases of emergency. The infant death rate is higher for home births than for hospital births.

For these reasons, many doctors have taken a stand against home births. These doctors will not perform deliveries in homes. Some states have also made home births illegal.

Those who favor home births believe parents should have more control over their children's births. To them, hospital deliveries treat childbirth as an illness rather than a natural process. They think hospitals lack family warmth and support. To make home births safer, some parents use **certified nurse-midwives (CNM)**. These nurses have special training in delivering babies during normal pregnancies. CNMs do not handle high-risk pregnancies. Many CNMs work out of hospitals where they can call for help if an emergency arises.

Many hospitals now offer parents the choice of a homelike birthing room rather than a standard delivery room. The *birthing room* is furnished like a bedroom. It is used for labor, delivery, and recovery. Family members and/or a few close friends stay with the mother-to-be throughout labor and delivery. In most hospitals, a nurse attends the labor. This nurse checks on the laboring woman often and calls the doctor just before delivery. The birthing room provides a homelike setting with family support and hospital safety.

Choosing a Method of Delivery

Parents may be able to choose which method of delivery they would like to use. They should discuss this decision with their doctor. All methods try to make labor and delivery safer and more comfortable for the mother and baby. Labor is hard work. It requires the use of many muscles. Some of these muscles are seldom used except during labor. Pain is a part of labor, but if muscles are tense, the mother has even more pain.

For any given delivery, the amount of pain cannot be known in advance. Labor may range from quick and easy to long and painful. People also feel and react to pain differently. Once a woman knows her options, she should discuss these with her doctor. She should also know options may change during labor. For example, a woman may begin labor without

labor. The process that moves the baby out of the mother's body.

certified nurse midwives (CNM). Nurses who have special training in delivering babies during normal pregnancies.

drugs but ask for pain relief as the birth nears if problems arise or labor is just too painful. The doctor, too, may opt for the use of a drug for pain relief.

Some mothers hope to be totally alert through delivery. They cope with pain by using breathing and relaxation techniques. Since the mid 1900s, doctors have moved away from using more drugs than necessary. Any drugs used can cross the placenta and affect the baby. These drugs can make the baby sluggish. In addition, most doctors like the mother to stay alert through delivery so she can help bring her baby into the world.

Even women who opt for delivery without drugs should prepare for the possibility of needing them. In some cases, drugs are needed if complications arise. These might also be used if the pain becomes more than the mother can handle. Learning about medication options in advance helps the mother know what to expect if the need arises. When she is in labor, she may be in too much pain to understand an explanation about the benefits or risks of a drug.

Types of drugs often used for pain relief are described in 5-13. To make sure the drug is safe for mother and baby, the doctor must know the mother's health history, her current health status; and any food or drink intake during the last several hours.

Different methods of childbirth differ in how the laboring mother is expected to handle the pain of labor. In some methods, using no drugs is the goal. In others, the use of pain relief drugs is seen as acceptable.

Natural Childbirth

One method of delivery without drugs is called **natural childbirth**. Dr. Grantly Dick-Read, an English physician, developed this method in the 1930s. Dr. Dick-Read questioned the regular use of drugs when one of his patients chose not to use them. The woman felt little pain during labor. The case made Dr. Dick-Read decide part of the pain from labor was due to fear.

In natural childbirth, the woman learns about the birth process so she knows what to expect. She is also trained to breathe and relax in a way that helps the birth process. With this training, the woman can deliver without drugs. The father usually plays an active role in prenatal study and delivery with this method.

Lamaze Method

Another method is called the **Lamaze method**. It is named for Dr. Fernand Lamaze, the French doctor who made the approach popular. The idea behind the Lamaze method is that women are conditioned to fear childbirth. In Lamaze training, the mother is taught to focus on something other than pain. This is like an injured athlete who thinks about the competition rather than a painful injury.

In this type of delivery, the mother uses breathing patterns (such as deep breathing or panting) to keep her mind off the pain. The pregnant

Commonly Used Drugs for Labor and Delivery

Drug	Comment
Sedation	Drug given by injection or intravenously (IV) to help reduce pain and ease anxiety.
Local Anesthesia	Drug injected to numb the vaginal area with birth is near, an incision will be made, or stitches are needed.
Regional Anesthesia	Drug injected to numb one area (region) of the body.
Epidural	Drug given through a tiny tube (catheter) placed in the small of the back, just outside the spinal canal. Mothers feel touch and pressure but not pain. Usually the epidural is given when the cervix has dilated more than 4 cm, but less than 8 cm. Although safe for most deliveries when given by a doctor trained in epidurals, there can be side effects for both the baby and the mother.
Spinal	Drug administered into spinal canal. Side effects are similar to those of epidural but may be more dangerous. Epidural has almost replaced the spinal.
General Anesthesia	Drug given intravenously (by IV) or by breathing a gas that puts the mother to sleep. General anesthesia is reserved for when complications arise, such as when an emergency C-section must be done. General anesthesia has side effects for both mother and baby than other types of anesthesia.

5-13 Many drugs are available to ease the pain of labor and delivery.

woman and her coach, usually the father, attend Lamaze preparation classes. The classes prepare her mentally and physically, using instruction and practice. The following features describe the Lamaze method:

❖ The woman's coach—the father or another person—learns the breathing patterns and helps the mother-to-be through labor.

natural childbirth. A delivery method in which the pregnant woman learns about the birth process and uses breathing and relaxation techniques to reduce fear and pain.

Lamaze method. A delivery method in which the pregnant woman is trained to use breathing patterns to keep her mind off pain.

❖ The woman receives medication when necessary. Not all women can deliver without drugs, even when they are informed about childbirth. Women usually need drugs when there are complications. A woman may also use drugs if she becomes too afraid.

❖ Training in childbirth is given in small classes—usually no more than 10 women and their coaches. Classes are held weekly for 8 to 12 weeks before the delivery date. The instructor provides factual information about childbirth. He or she teaches physical exercises to tone the body for delivery. The instructor also teaches breathing patterns to use in labor and delivery and encourages couples to talk about their feelings.

Many parents who have used this approach say childbirth was rewarding. Mothers were more alert and felt better by using breathing and relaxation to help them avoid or postpone the use of drugs. Through this method, the mother and father shared the experience. Both parents were ready to welcome their newborn, 5-14.

Leboyer Method

Frederick Leboyer, a French doctor, developed the **Leboyer method** of delivery. This method focuses on the comfort of the baby during delivery as well as the safety of the baby and mother. The Leboyer method assumes that delivery is painful for the baby as well as the mother. This method uses

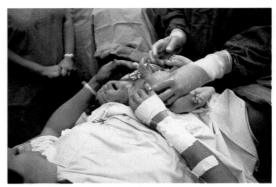

A

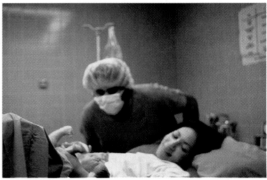

B

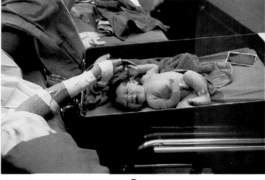

C

5-14 Childbirth is a shared experience for this family. As the awake mother holds her newborn (A), the father proudly shares his daughter's birth (B), and the baby gazes at her parents (C).
Adrian Demery

low lights rather than bright lights in the delivery room. Noise is kept low, because everyone in the delivery room talks in quiet tones. The doctor supports the baby after the head appears. These techniques are thought to add to the baby's comfort.

After birth, the baby rests on the mother's body as she cuddles her newborn. The umbilical cord is cut only after it stops functioning. A few minutes after birth, the baby is lowered into water that is near body temperature. The supported baby can kick and move about in a way similar to that before birth. Finally, the baby is dressed and wrapped in a warm blanket.

Time to Be Born

The months of waiting and excitement during pregnancy come to an end sooner than expected. Friends and relatives often give celebrations like baby showers. Parents may put the final touches on the nursery. Names are often chosen. If parents are planning a hospital delivery, they pack a suitcase for the hospital. Arrangements with employers are made. Babysitters are secured for young children.

Final natural preparations are taking place, too. The mother's body makes the hormonal changes needed for labor to begin. The baby is moving into position for birth. The doctor checks these preparations and keeps the parents informed.

Labor takes most parents by surprise. It may begin any time and any place—even in the middle of sleep. The first contractions are usually so mild that many parents still wonder if the time has really come. Once begun, labor and delivery are completed within hours. Following childbirth, there is a period of readjustment for the mother to a nonpregnant condition. The baby adjusts to life outside the mother's body. The family adjusts to the changes a new baby brings.

The Last Weeks of Pregnancy

Birth occurs about 270 days after conception. How does this baby enter the world? A series of contractions in the uterine muscles move the baby out of the mother's body. These contractions are involuntary. In other words, the mother cannot make these contractions happen. Natural signals from the body control when they begin, how long they last, and how strong they are. Contractions happen in intervals. They are separated by periods that allow the mother's muscles to relax.

Contractions

The nature of contractions changes throughout labor. In early labor,

Leboyer method. A delivery method that focuses on making the baby as comfortable as possible during and immediately after delivery.

contractions may last about 30 seconds. Gradually, their length increases to 1 minute. The strength of the contractions increases until the baby is born. The intervals of relaxation begin at 15 to 20 minutes and decrease to about 2 minutes.

During the last few weeks of pregnancy, the mother experiences lightening. This is especially true for a first pregnancy. **Lightening** is a change in the baby's position. The uterus settles downward and forward, and the baby descends lower into the pelvis. In most cases, the baby's body rotates so the head is toward the birth canal. In about two percent of the cases, the baby takes a buttocks-first position. This is called **breech birth position**. When lightening happens, the mother can breathe easier. However, she may have leg cramps and may need to urinate more often due to the increased pressure on her bladder.

Because her body is preparing for labor during lightening, the mother may have a few irregular contractions. These irregular contractions are known as *false labor*. The contractions are real, but true labor has not begun. Some parents-to-be have gone to the hospital only to find out the contractions were false labor. (Most doctors prefer the mother go to the hospital if she is not sure. They don't want a mother who planned a hospital delivery to end up having the baby at home.) Parents should carefully time the intervals between contractions to tell whether she is really in labor.

Other Signs of Labor

Besides regular contractions, there are several other signs of the coming labor. One sign is the mother may feel a burst of energy due to increased adrenaline. Mothers shouldn't use the energy to do strenuous tasks. They should save the energy for labor.

Another sign is the mucous plug in the cervix will become loose. The small amount of blood in the mucous is called *the show*. It means labor should start within 24 hours.

A third sign is that part of the amniotic sac (sometimes called the *bag of waters*) may break before labor begins. (Often the sac breaks after labor begins.) If the mucous plug becomes dislodged or the amniotic sac breaks, the mother should not bathe. Once contractions begin, the mother should not eat food or drink liquids unless advised by her doctor to do so.

Stages of Labor

In medical terms, labor is divided into these three stages: (1) **dilation**, or opening, of the cervix; (2) delivery of the baby; and (3) delivery of the placenta, 5-15.

Stage One—Dilation of the Cervix

In the early part of labor, contractions come every 15 or 20 minutes and last about 30 seconds. The uterus narrows. This straightens the baby's body and presses the baby's head (or buttocks) against the cervix. As the

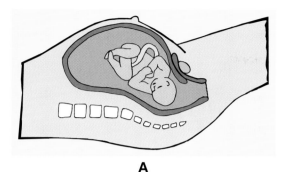

A

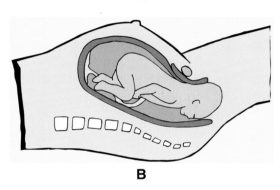

B

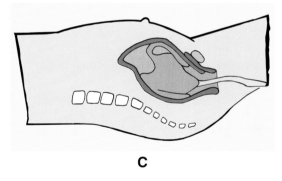

C

5-15 The three stages of labor are (A) dilation of the cervix, (B) delivery of the baby, and (C) delivery of the placenta.

baby pushes against the cervix, the cervix flattens and opens (dilates).

If the amniotic sac has not broken, the doctor will break it when the cervix is fully dilated. Full dilation of the cervix will measure about 4 inches (10 centimeters) in width. This is the size of a small grapefruit. When the cervix is completely open, the first stage of labor ends. The length of time for this stage varies a great deal, but the average length is eight hours for a first pregnancy (less for later pregnancies).

Stage Two—Delivery of the Baby

During the delivery stage, the baby's head enters the birth canal. The mother's muscles push to move the baby down. The walls of the upper part of the birth canal are elastic. However, the arrangement of muscles in the lower part of the canal causes resistance. The resistance causes the mother pain.

The doctor may have the mother use natural techniques, such as breathing, to reduce pain. Often, an incision, called an **episiotomy,** is made to widen the birth canal and prevent tearing. After delivery, the doctor closes the incision with sutures.

lightening. A change in the baby's position in which the uterus settles downward and forward and the baby descends lower into the pelvis.

breech birth position. The buttocks-first position in which some babies enter the birth canal.

dilation. The first stage of labor, during which the cervix opens.

episiotomy. An incision made to widen the birth canal and prevent tearing.

The baby changes position during birth. The baby faces downward as the head emerges. Then the head rotates to the side. The shoulders, abdomen, and legs follow. The remaining fluid from the amniotic sac is expelled. The doctor helps the baby by holding and turning the baby as needed. The doctor uses instruments to suck fluid from the baby's mouth. This helps the baby take his or her first breath.

The second stage ends when the baby is free of the mother's body. The time of birth is noted. The second stage usually lasts from 30 to 90 minutes for a first pregnancy. The doctor cuts the umbilical cord before the third stage begins.

Stage Three—Delivery of the Placenta

About 20 minutes after birth, the mother has a few irregular contractions. These cause the placenta to completely detach from the uterus and descend. The placenta and fetal membrane that are expelled following the birth of a baby are called the *afterbirth*. As the third stage ends, mothers feel a little cold and physically tired. They also feel emotionally relieved and overjoyed.

Complications of Delivery

Years ago, many mothers and babies died in childbirth. Due to modern medicine, childbirth is now much safer, especially for women who have prenatal care. Most deliveries occur without complications. The rate of death is low for newborns and even lower for mothers. Still, complications may occur during or after childbirth, even in pregnancies without obvious problems. The most common complications are described in 5-16.

When complications occur, special medical care is needed to protect the health of mother and baby. This care may involve the use of delivery-aid techniques. Which technique is used depends on the nature of the problem. Each technique poses risks but has important advantages. A woman's doctor should explain to her any technique, risks, and advantages. The woman can then decide whether to have the procedure. The most common techniques used to aid delivery include the following:

❖ *version*, or manually rotating the unborn baby into the correct position for delivery
❖ the drug *oxytocin*, which can speed up labor by causing contractions to start or strengthen
❖ forceps, a curved instrument that fits around the sides of a baby's head, which the doctor can use to ease the baby down the birth canal during a contraction

forceps. A curved instrument that fits around the sides of a baby's head and is used to help the doctor ease the baby down the birth canal during a contraction.

Complications of Childbirth

Complication	Comment
Premature delivery	Baby may not be mature enough to survive. Baby is often not in the correct position for delivery.
Premature rupture of membranes (PROM)	The amniotic sac breaks, but labor does not begin. Infection is a danger. Babies who are mature will be delivered. With immature babies, drugs are given to prevent infection until delivery.
Prolonged delivery	Both mother and baby are at risk for other complications.
Abnormal position for delivery	Babies may be injured and uterus may rupture. Sometimes the position may be corrected; if not, the baby must be surgically removed.
Cephalopelvic disproportion (baby's head is too large to pass through mother's pelvic bones)	Baby is often surgically removed.
Umbilical cord problems compression (hollow cord is wrapped around the baby's body) or prolapse (cord slips into the birth canal and is trapped between baby and canal)	Cord supplies oxygen. If the cord cannot be returned to the proper position, the baby is surgically removed.
Asphyxia	Oxygen supply is cut off due to problems with the placenta or umbilical cord. This can cause brain damage or death. (After birth, breathing problems may result if lungs contain fluid or waste materials. Chest massage, drugs, and respirators can be used to stimulate breathing.)
Postpartum bleeding	The uterus should contract and squeeze shut the blood vessels that supplied it during pregnancy. Massage and hormones are given to help the uterus return to its original size. In rare cases, surgery may be needed to close the blood vessels and stop bleeding.

5-16 Complications may occur in childbirth and can put mother and baby at risk.

❖ **vacuum extraction**, in which suction is used to attach a cuplike device around the top of the baby's head so the doctor can gently pull the baby down the birth canal as the mother pushes

Cesarean Births

In some cases, the traditional methods of delivery would be unsafe or unwise. About 27 percent of children born in the United States are born by the cesarean section (or C-section) method. In the **cesarean section**, the mother's abdomen and uterus are surgically opened and the baby is removed. The incisions are then closed as with any other surgery. (The method was named for Emperor Julius Caesar who, it has been incorrectly said, was born that way.) Doctors use C-section deliveries for the following reasons:

❖ The mother's pelvis is small or not shaped correctly for an easy birth.
❖ The baby or mother is at medical risk.
❖ The baby's head is large.
❖ Contractions are weak or absent.
❖ The baby is in an incorrect position for birth.
❖ The doctor feels that previous cesarean scar(s) could rupture during labor (one cesarean birth does not mean that all later births must be C-sections, too).

Some couples have planned for a Lamaze method of delivery but found that a C-section was necessary. To help these couples share the childbirth experience, some hospitals use drugs that permit the mother to be awake but feel no pain during the surgery. They allow the father in the room. These couples are able to experience the same benefits and joys as couples who used the Lamaze method.

Hospital Care

After the birth of a baby, both mother and baby can expect to remain in the hospital 24 to 48 hours. The stay will be longer for a complicated or C-section delivery. Medical care is given to ensure their health and safety. The mother's body must recover from the exhausting delivery. She will be closely watched to see whether she is recovering as she should. The baby must be monitored for health problems and his or her adjustment to life outside the mother's body.

The specifics of care vary from one hospital to the next. In some hospitals, much of the infant's stay will be in the nursery. Nurses are on duty in the nursery at all times. Hospital employees may rock and feed the babies in the nursery. Visitors may be allowed to see the baby only through the nursery window and only during certain hours. Young children, including brothers and sisters, may not be able to visit the hospital at all. Restrictions such as these were most common in the past, but some of today's hospitals may still operate in these ways.

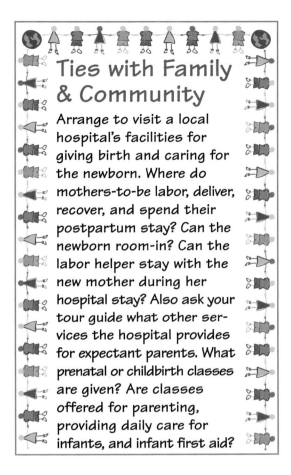
cot or bed might be provided for use during the stay. Visitors may be able to come to the mother's room to see, perhaps even hold, the newborn. Brothers and sisters are usually the only young children allowed in the room, 5-17. Visits are limited to certain hours and only a few visitors may be allowed in the room at one

5-17 Many hospitals encourage the whole family to spend time together with the new baby.
© John Shaw

vacuum extraction. Technique that uses suction to help the doctor move the baby down the birth canal as the mother pushes.

cesarean section. A delivery method in which the mother's abdomen and uterus are surgically opened and the baby is removed.

Most of today's hospitals have a more open, family-centered view of childbirth. These hospitals encourage mothers to use a *rooming-in* arrangement. This means if the baby is healthy, he or she is placed in a bassinet in the room with the mother. The medical care of the baby can be given right there in the mother's room. Nurses will still be available to help the new mother.

In these hospitals, the father or labor helper can often stay with mother and baby at all times. An extra time. Many hospitals have security measures to keep unauthorized people out of the part of the hospital used for mothers and newborns.

Bonding

Bonding, or developing a feeling of affection, is important for parents and their baby. The first hour after birth is perhaps the most sensitive bonding time. The newborn will watch, hear, and respond to the body movements, voice, and touch of the mother and father. Bonding continues during the next few weeks as parents become more and more attached to their babies, 5-18.

Benefits of Bonding

To Infant

❖ increased chance of survival
❖ better weight gain
❖ less crying, more smiles and laughter
❖ fewer infections
❖ possibly higher IQ
❖ better language development

To Parents

❖ less incidence of child abuse
❖ faster recovery from delivery
❖ longer breast-feeding
❖ more self-confidence as a parent
❖ less depression after delivery

5-19 Bonding helps both infants and parents. It is the first step toward a healthy parent-child relationship.

Bonding helps both infants and parents, 5-19. Because bonding is so helpful, many hospitals have changed their rules regarding premature or ill infants. These new policies allow parents to visit the intensive care nursery and feed, touch, talk, and sing to their babies.

5-18 Both parents and baby have much to gain from bonding in the early days after birth.

Postpartum Care

Postpartum care is the care the mother receives during the six to eight weeks following the birth of her baby. In this six- to eight-week period, the mother's body returns to its prepregnancy state. For nursing mothers, the body's complete return to normal requires more time.

The first hour after birth is a critical time for restoring body stability. Vital signs (pulse, respiration, and other body functions) are measured every few minutes just as they would be following surgery. Doctors want to make sure the uterus contracts properly.

In order to regain their strength and avoid health problems, women are encouraged to get out of bed within 24 hours of delivery. Many women walk much sooner.

After a few days, the doctor might allow a new mother to begin certain exercises that will help tone the abdominal muscles. These exercises are done slowly and gradually for safety. Most mothers also want to lose some of the extra weight from pregnancy. On the average, a woman loses 11 pounds during birth and another 7 pounds during the few weeks after birth. The remaining weight must be lost through diet and/or exercise.

A woman should check with her doctor about dieting. A nutritious diet is essential for a new mother as her body returns to normal. For nursing mothers, the final pounds are usually shed after weaning. A nursing mother should not diet to lose weight. Her body needs many nutrients and much energy to create the breast milk that will sustain her baby.

Rest is also important. For a few days after delivery, many mothers need a great deal of sleep. Doctors often advise mothers to sleep when their babies sleep for the first few days. Because the baby will wake often throughout the night for feedings, new mothers will have to plan ways to get the sleep they need. They can do this by lessening their workload. The following timesaving steps can help:

❖ Ask a friend to watch the baby so the mother can take a nap.
❖ Pack away nonessential items that add to housekeeping time.
❖ Prepare and freeze meals before baby comes to use after the baby is born.
❖ Use disposable dishes and plastic utensils for a few days or weeks.

If the mother must return to work before the end of the postpartum period, she should get special guidance from nurses and doctors. The key to complete recovery, whether the mother is at home or on the job, is to go slow with activity. Too much activity slows the reversal process.

Postpartum Mood Disorders

Closely linked to physical changes are emotional changes. Certainly, mood disorders are very common,

bonding. Developing a feeling of affection.

postpartum care. The care the mother receives during the six to eight weeks following the birth of her baby.

affecting 15 to 25 percent of all people. Mood disorders are twice as common in women as in men. These disorders occur far more often in women during the childbearing years.

Many women are aware of mood changes that occur with each menstrual cycle. In addition, mood disorders peak during the postpartum period. Although the exact causes are not known, scientists believe the problem may be due to the following:

❖ an inherited tendency for mood disorders
❖ dramatic changes in the body chemistry after giving birth that affects the brain
❖ stress caused by caring for a new baby while recovering from pregnancy and delivery

All women in the postpartum period are at risk. However, some women are at a heightened risk of having a postpartum mood disorder. Women with the following factors have an increased risk:

❖ being a teen or over 40 years old
❖ family history of mood disorders
❖ family history of thyroid problems
❖ mood swings during the menstrual cycle—often called PMS
❖ migraine headaches when taking hormones (including birth control pills)

❖ fertility problems
❖ severe family stress
❖ lack of support from family and friends
❖ previous postpartum mood disorder

Mood disorders range from mild to severe as described in 5-20. Each has its own symptoms. **Baby blues** is a mild postpartum mood disorder that goes away on its own. It is by far the most common. **Postpartum depression (PPD)** is a serious form of depression. **Postpartum psychosis (PPP)** is an extremely severe mental illness. (*Psychosis* means *mental illness.*) PPD and PPP need immediate medical treatment.

If a new mother has intense or prolonged feelings of depression after the birth of her child, she should discuss the problem with a doctor. Her doctor can help her get the treatment she needs to overcome her mood disorder.

baby blues. A mild postpartum mood disorder that goes away on its own.

postpartum depression (PPD). A less frequent, but serious form of depression that may occur after giving birth.

postpartum psychosis (PPP). A rare and extremely severe mental illness that may result after giving birth.

Postpartum Mood Disorders

Name	Incidence	Symptoms	Appearance and Duration
Baby Blues	40 to 85% of all deliveries	Irritability; anxious spells; sleep and appetite problems; weeping; feeling tired	Peaks between three and five days postpartum. Often resolves itself with a few days.
Postpartum Depression (PPD)	10 to 15% of all deliveries (26 to 32% of teen deliveries)	Restlessness; exhaustion; inability to concentrate; memory loss; uncontrollable crying; trouble making decisions; lack of interest in pleasurable activities; appetite and sleep problems; overconcern or lack of interest in baby; fear of harming self or baby; guilt	Occurs within first 6 weeks postpartum. If untreated, may last a year or longer. Often happens again in future deliveries
Postpartum Psychosis (PPP)	0.1% of all deliveries (1 in 1,000)	Severe mental illness; includes delusions that often focus on the infant dying; sees the infant as either perfect or defective; desires to kill self or infant	Occurs between 1 and 3 months postpartum with a second peak at 18 to 24 months postpartum. Continues until treated

5-20 Postpartum mood disorders may be mild or serious. In serious or prolonged cases, medical help should be sought.

Soon after birth, the newborn's skin is still thin and may peel somewhat.

Summing It Up

Environmental factors begin to interact with genetic traits the moment after conception. The first environment for the baby is the mother's body. The condition of her body and her daily health habits have a great effect on her baby's development.

As soon as the signs of pregnancy are detected, a woman should seek medical care. The health of the baby depends on the health of the mother.

Good health habits need to be practiced during pregnancy. Doctors recommend most women gain between 25 to 35 pounds. Mothers-to-be should rest when they feel tired. They also should remain active during pregnancy.

Many diseases or illnesses in the mother can harm the baby. The health of the fetus is also endangered through drug use. Radiation exposure and environmental pollution can create possible harmful effects. Congenital problems can occur for various reasons and occur in varying levels of severity.

A miscarriage may occur if a pregnancy has complications. This can result because the mother smokes, drinks, uses drugs, or has certain diseases. It can also occur if the baby has congenital problems. Ultrasound, CVS, and amniocentesis are tests that monitor the health of the fetus.

Family decisions to be made before birth include where the baby will be born and which method of delivery will be used. When delivery nears, the mother-to-be will go into labor. If complications occur during or after childbirth, special medical attention will be needed. When a vaginal birth is not safe for mother, baby, or both, the doctor may perform a C-section.

During the postpartum period, the mother's body returns to normal. She will need to rest, get physical activity, and eat nutritious meals. Having postpartum mood disorders is common. These disorders are mainly due to hormone changes in the body that, in turn, affect the brain. The more severe forms (PPD and PPP) require medical treatment.

Reviewing Key Concepts

Write your answers on a separate sheet of paper.

1. Which is not a sign of pregnancy?
   A. enlarged and sore breasts
   B. cravings for pickles and ice cream
   C. missed menstrual cycle
   D. morning sickness
2. In terms of health, between which ages is it safest for women to become pregnant?
3. True or false. Most doctors advise women to gain as little weight as possible during pregnancy regardless of prepregnancy weight.
4. True or false. During pregnancy it is safe to take over-the-counter drugs like cough medicine and aspirin.
5. True or false. It is quite normal for women to cry and feel sad during the first few days after giving birth.
6. Name the statement that is most true about a low-risk pregnancy.
   A. Pregnant women should limit physical activity to protect the baby.
   B. Most women feel tired and uncomfortable during the entire pregnancy.
   C. After they have a baby, women usually do not return to their prepregnant weight.
   D. Good health practices are much the same during pregnancy as they were before pregnancy.
7. List two ways a father can take an active role during pregnancy and childbirth.
8. Place the following steps of labor in proper order:
   A. birth of the baby
   B. the show
   C. dilation of the cervix
   D. delivery of the placenta
   E. cutting of the umbilical cord

9. True or false. False labor pains do not really cause pain. The mother imagines them.
10. Which of the following is the most accurate statement about delivery?
    A. The delivery method should mainly depend upon the condition of the mother and her baby.
    B. Natural childbirth is best because childbirth isn't that painful.
    C. Cesarean sections are best because childbirth should be quick and easy.
    D. If a woman is really fearful, it is best to put her to sleep by using general anesthesia during delivery.
11. True or false. Birthing rooms and rooming-in arrangements are designed to provide the best of both home and hospital experiences.
12. _____ care is essential for a healthy return to a nonpregnant state.

Using Your Knowledge

1. **Technology/Teamwork.** As a group project, use the computer to create a fill-in booklet for pregnant women. Include sheets of information a pregnant woman would need to give her doctor. Also list questions she needs to ask her doctor. Use these suggested topics to start.
   A. Information the doctor needs–family health history; history of the woman's menstrual cycle and date of last menstrual period; history of any serious or chronic diseases or conditions; history of woman's past pregnancies; current use of drugs, including prescription and over-the-counter drugs.
   B. Information the mother-to-be needs–due date; present weight and recommended amount of weight to gain during pregnancy;

recommendations regarding nutrition, physical activity, and rest; changes in the treatment of any disease or condition; information on giving birth (place, types of delivery, and arrangement for care of newborn); fees and insurance; appointment dates and how to contact doctor in an emergency.

Placing the booklet in a folder with pockets is often helpful, because many doctors give their patients charts and pamphlets.

2. **Interviewing/Communication.** Interview a certified nurse-midwife (CNM) to discuss the advantages of a home delivery, the type of training required of a CNM, the type of deliveries the CNM handles, and what happens in an emergency if the woman is delivering her baby at home. Share your findings with the class in an oral report.

3. **Art.** Design a poster on the theme, "Be Good to Your Baby Before He or She Is Born."

4. **Art/Nutrition.** Create a bulletin board called "Eating for Two Requires Careful Planning." Include sample menus for a pregnant woman for one week. You might also include pictures or a list of some fattening, nonessential foods she should avoid.

5. **Technology.** Use the Internet to research a congenital problem. Compose a report on this problem using a word-processing program on the computer.

6. **Language Arts/Emotional Development.** Write a paragraph on the importance of bonding for both the infant and the parents.

Making Observations

1. Observe pregnant women in informal settings. What healthful activities or behaviors do you see these women use? Do you identify any activities or behaviors they use that are not healthful during pregnancy?

2. Observe advertisements by local hospitals or health programs. What services do they offer for prenatal care, preparation for delivery, and labor and delivery? What options are there in your community (delivery versus birthing room, delivery by obstetrician or certified nurse-midwife)?

3. Observe a family that is preparing for a new baby. How does each family member help with this preparation? How do older children react to the upcoming birth?

4. Observe a sonogram photo. Which features of the baby can you see?

Thinking Further

1. Some of the most severe congenital problems are caused by recessive traits. Based on this statement, why is it biologically better for closely related blood relatives not to marry? Explain your answer.

2. At one time, pregnancy and childbirth were considered a "woman's affair." Now this event is thought of as a family affair. List ways family members can be involved.

3. Years ago, pregnancy could not be confirmed for several weeks. Today's tests can confirm pregnancy within days of conception. What advantages occur as a result of early confirmation?

4. Imagine a couple with a premature baby who will likely remain hospitalized for several weeks. What challenges might the couple face in terms of bonding? What can family and friends do to help the couple bond with the baby?

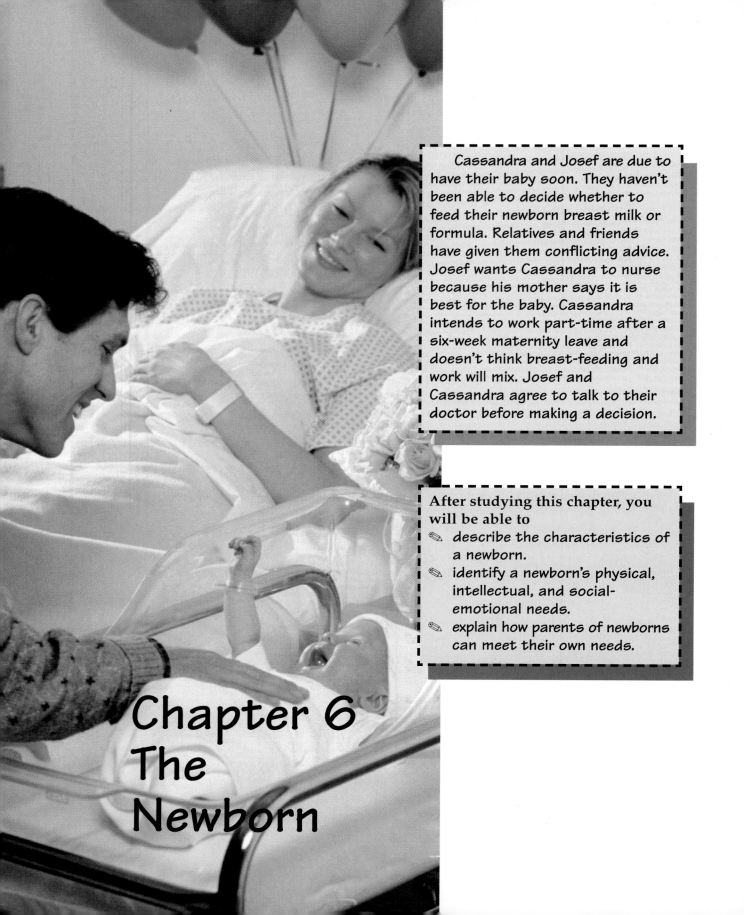

Cassandra and Josef are due to have their baby soon. They haven't been able to decide whether to feed their newborn breast milk or formula. Relatives and friends have given them conflicting advice. Josef wants Cassandra to nurse because his mother says it is best for the baby. Cassandra intends to work part-time after a six-week maternity leave and doesn't think breast-feeding and work will mix. Josef and Cassandra agree to talk to their doctor before making a decision.

After studying this chapter, you will be able to
- describe the characteristics of a newborn.
- identify a newborn's physical, intellectual, and social-emotional needs.
- explain how parents of newborns can meet their own needs.

Chapter 6
The
Newborn

When the doctor cuts the umbilical cord, a baby's life on his or her own begins. The official time of birth happens when the baby is clear of the mother's body. From birth to age one month, the baby is medically known as a **neonate**. (Neonate is from the Latin words *neo*, meaning new, and *natus*, meaning born.)

Great changes happen in the *neonatal* (or newborn) period of growth and development. Newborns come from a world that was dark and quiet. They lived in a home of warm, comfortable fluid. They received food and oxygen easily and without waiting. The support of the amniotic fluid helped them move easily and cushioned them from shock.

At birth, babies enter a more exciting world. They are exposed to light and noise. The newborn's life support system—the placenta and umbilical cord—stops functioning minutes after birth. The newborn's air passage is drained of water. The lungs expand and the baby takes his or her first breath. Now the baby must search for a nipple and suck when hungry. The baby's body feels different because gravity hinders movement. Suddenly the head and trunk seem heavy to the baby. This new world is different and sometimes frustrating.

The birth also turns a man and woman into parents. They must adjust to a different world, too. Parents can enjoy this time of adjustment if they do the following:

❖ Plan carefully.
❖ Accept the responsibility of parenthood.
❖ Love and communicate with each other.
❖ Live one day at a time.
❖ Realize that, in time, frustrations such as sleepless nights will decrease and the joys of parenthood will increase.

neonate. Medical term for the baby from birth to one month of age.

Medical Care and Testing

Good prenatal care gives the baby the best chance for a healthy start. All newborns also need medical care for healthy development. Of course, a sick or tiny newborn needs extra medical care. However, healthy newborns must also go through a few simple procedures.

In hospitals, doctors and nurses provide medical care for the baby that begins at birth. After delivery, the baby is often held head downward. Then the doctor suctions fluid from the nostrils and mouth. The mother may hold the baby on her abdomen until the cord is clamped and cut. The nurse then takes the baby to a special table with a heater above it. The nurse dries the newborn with warm towels, 6-1.

Care for Premature Babies

Some babies are born too small or too soon. Some are born with congenital problems involving the heart, digestive tract, spine, or brain. These babies need immediate, intensive care. They are often placed in an **intensive care nursery (ICN)**. The ICN can save these newborns' lives or prevent further damage, 6-2. Newborns who need intensive care live in **neonatal intensive care units (NICUs)**. NICUs are heated, completely enclosed beds. They have two doors (which are slightly larger than an arm) that open and close to permit care. NICUs are equipped with devices for giving oxygen and monitoring breathing and heart rate. The doctors and nurses who work in ICNs have special training in neonatology. **Neonatology** is a branch of

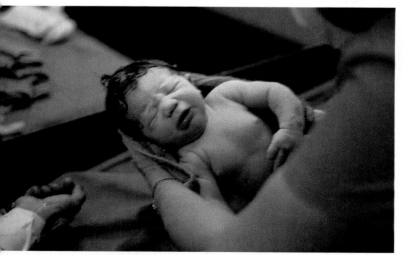

6-1 This healthy newborn is being wiped dry with a warm towel.
Adrian Demery

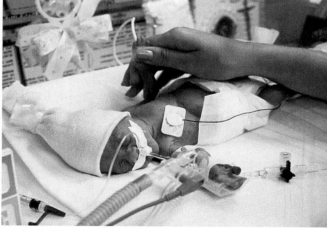

6-2 The neonatal intensive care unit (NICU) protects babies who were born too soon or too small.
National March of Dimes Birth Defects Foundation

Apgar Test			
	Scores		
Sign	0	1	2
Heart rate	Absent.	Slow; fewer than 100 beats per minute.	More than 100 beats per minute.
Respiratory effort	Absent.	Weak cry; hyperventilation.	Good; strong cry.
Muscle tone	Limp.	Some flexing and bending of extremities.	Well flexed.
Reflex irritability	No response.	Some motion.	Cry.
Color	Blue; pale.	Body pink; extremities blue.	Completely pink.

6-3 A newborn's condition may be quickly determined by the Apgar test.

medicine concerned with the care, development, and diseases of newborns.

The Apgar Test

In most hospitals, the newborn's physical conditon is checked using the Apgar test. This test checks the baby's chance of survival. The baby scores a 0, 1, or 2 in each of five areas, 6-3. The best total score possible is a 10.

The Apgar test checks the baby's pulse, breathing, muscle tone, responsiveness, and skin color. The baby's heart rate and breathing are most important. Skin color, which is a sign of circulation, is least important. The test is given one minute and five minutes after delivery. (For the first scoring, the umbilical cord usually has not been cut. It usually has for the second.) The five-minute score should be higher.

intensive care nursery (ICN). Special nursery that can provide immediate intensive care just after birth for babies who need it.

neonatal intensive care units (NICU). Heated, completely enclosed beds for newborns who need intensive care.

neonatology. A branch of medicine concerned with the care, development, and diseases of newborns.

Apgar test. A test that checks the baby's chance of survival.

Most healthy babies score 6 or 7 at 1 minute, then 8 to 10 at 5 minutes. If a baby scores 7 or less at 5 minutes, he or she is tested again at 10 minutes after birth. A low score means the baby needs special medical care.

After the first test, the baby is weighed and measured. Drops of silver nitrate are put into the eyes to prevent infection. Before the baby is taken from the delivery room, footprints are made. Name bands are placed around the baby's wrists and/or ankles for identification purposes, 6-4.

The Neonatal Assessment Scales

Some doctors use the *Neonatal Behavioral Assessment Scales*. This test is commonly called the **Brazelton scale**. It helps doctors spot any problems as early as possible. (This differs from the Apgar test, which predicts the chances of survival and signals the need for emergency medical care.)

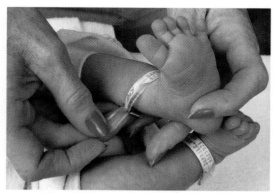

6-4 Bands on the wrists and/or ankles, labeled with the family name, help identify the baby.

The Brazelton scale tests the baby in the following four areas:
- ❖ interaction with the environment—the baby's alertness; attention to sound, light, and other factors; and cuddliness
- ❖ motor processes—the baby's general activity level and reflex behavior
- ❖ control of physical state—self-quieting behaviors and levels of excitement and irritability
- ❖ response to stress—the newborn's response to stress (startle reactions and trembling)

Other Hospital Care

Pediatricians run other tests to determine the newborn's health. A **pediatrician** is a doctor who cares for infants and children. Blood tests are run to rule out anemia. **Anemia** is a low level of oxygen-carrying substances in the blood. Tests also check the presence of **phenylketonuria (PKU)**, which is a disease that can cause mental retardation if untreated by diet.

Another condition that requires special care is jaundice. **Jaundice** is a condition that occurs in newborns that makes their skin, tissues, and body fluids look yellow. Jaundice happens because some babies' livers are immature. Doctors treat jaundice by placing the baby under bright lights, 6-5.

Well-Baby Checkup

Before the newborn leaves the hospital, the pediatrician will ask the parents to make an appointment for a

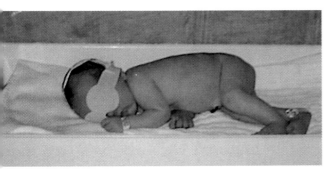

6-5 Jaundice is a common problem with newborns. Placing the baby under special lights helps to reduce the skin's yellow color. A blindfold protects this baby's eyes.
© Nancy P. Alexander

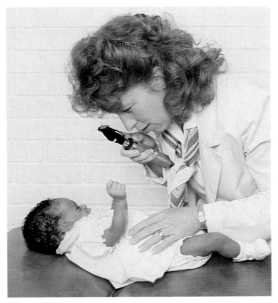

6-6 This pediatrician enjoys examining the newborn in a well-baby checkup.
© John Shaw

well-baby checkup. A **well-baby checkup** is a routine medical visit in which the doctor examines a baby for signs of good health and proper growth. The first well-baby checkup occurs within the first few weeks (sooner if the baby is small or sick). During this checkup, the pediatrician will examine the baby, answer questions, and make recommendations, 6-6. The pediatrician will ask for the family health history. The nurse will weigh the baby and measure the length, head, and chest. Parents then schedule their baby's next checkup.

Physical Traits of a Newborn

The songwriter who said, "You must have been a beautiful baby," was not talking about newborns. The plump, cute babies you see in advertisements are usually several

Brazelton scale. A test used to determine whether a baby has problems interacting with the environment, handling motor processes, controlling his or her physical state, or responding to stress.

pediatrician. A doctor who cares for infants and children.

anemia. A low level of oxygen-carrying substances in the blood.

phenylketonuria (PKU). A disease that can cause mental retardation if left untreated by diet.

jaundice. A liver condition that can make the skin, tissues, and body fluids look yellow.

well-baby checkup. A routine medical visit in which the doctor examines a baby for signs of good health and proper growth.

months old. What does a newborn look like? Their physical traits are described in 6-7.

Newborns possess other physical traits that sometimes worry parents. They cough and sneeze to clear mucus from their air passages and lungs. They breathe unevenly, about 46 times per minute, from the diaphragm in the abdominal area. (Adults breathe about 18 times per minute, usually from the chest.) Newborns' heart rates are often between 120 and 150 beats per minute. (Adults' heart rates are about 70 beats per minute.)

Reflexes

All people have built-in behaviors they did not learn. For instance, your knee jerks when tapped with a mallet. These automatic, unlearned behaviors are called **reflexes**. Newborns enter the world with many reflexes. Some are triggered by an outside stimuli (light, touch, sound) that are directed to a body area (hands, feet, cheeks, eyes, and ears).

For newborns, reflexes are important.

❖ Reflexes are a clue to the health and maturity of the nervous system. The absence or weakness of a reflex may result from prematurity or a congenital problem. For example, newborns jerk or withdraw their legs when the soles of their feet are pricked. This reaction is called the *withdrawal reflex*. The reflex continues throughout life, and its absence may be a sign of brain damage. However, some reflexes should disappear at a certain time. If these reflexes do not disappear, this may signal a problem.

❖ Babies need some reflexes for survival. When you touch a

Ties with Family & Community

Search parenting magazines for pictures of babies. For each picture, examine the baby's physical appearance to identify whether the baby is a newborn or an older baby. First, do you see any of the features of a newborn as listed in Figure 6-7? Also, do the babies pictured show any motor developments? If so, at what ages might they achieve these skills? Based on this evidence, can you estimate the age of the infants pictured?

---

reflexes. Automatic, unlearned behaviors.

What Do Newborns Look Like?

Feature	Description
Size	❖ Most full-term babies weigh slightly over seven pounds and are about 20 inches long. Boys are slightly larger than girls. ❖ Newborns will lose weight after birth, then regain birth weight within 10 days. ❖ They will grow about 1½ pounds and one inch during the first month. ❖ Newborns look thin because they have little body fat.
Body Proportion	❖ Newborns look out of proportion as compared to adults. The head is ¼ of total length. An adult's head is ⅒ of total length. ❖ The chest is rounded. ❖ The stomach protrudes, and the pelvis and hips are narrow. ❖ The legs are drawn up and appear to bow because of their position before birth. ❖ The legs are short compared to the arms. ❖ Newborns have almost no neck.
Face	❖ Newborns have a broad, flat nose. ❖ They have a tiny jaw and chin. ❖ These features help them suck more easily.
Cranium	❖ Newborns have *fontanels* (called soft spots) where the skull is not closed. Fontanels allow the skull and brain to grow. ❖ The fontanels fill with bone as the skull grows. The skull completely closes between one and two years of age, when brain growth has slowed. ❖ The membrane that covers the fontanels moves in and out as the baby breathes. This may be seen in a baby with little hair. ❖ The bones of the skull are soft and may be molded into an egg shape during birth. This makes birth easier. The molded shape of the head will disappear in a couple of weeks.
Skin	❖ Newborns have thin, dry skin. ❖ The skin may look blotchy and ruddy. You may see the blood vessels. ❖ The skin of the feet is loose and wrinkly. ❖ The wrists have deep, bracelet-like creases. ❖ The scalp skin is also loose. ❖ At birth, newborns have a protective, cheese-like covering called the *vernix caseosa*. ❖ Down (called *languno*) on the ears, shoulders, back, forehead, and cheeks frequently is present, especially on premature babies. ❖ Babies often develop a rash one or two days after birth. This should disappear in one week.

(Continued)

6-7 A newborn looks different from older children or adults.

What Do Newborns Look Like? *(Continued)*

Feature	Description
Skin *(continued)* 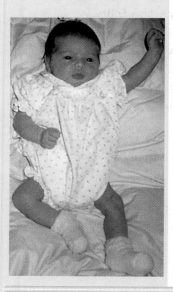	❖ A newborn may have pinkish marks on the forehead, eyelids, and the back of the neck. These are called stork bites. They fade within a year. The name comes from the mythical stork who delivered babies. However, the blotches are caused by a collection of small blood vessels. ❖ Newborns of African, Mediterranean, and Asian decent may have greenish-blue spots on their backs. These are called *Mongolian spots.* ❖ Many newborns look yellow because of jaundice. 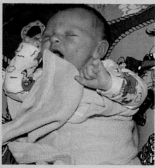 Stork bites
Eyes	❖ Newborns' eyes appear small. ❖ Their eye color is usually a dull gray-blue due to lack of pigmentation. Eye color develops around six months of age. ❖ Red spots may appear in the whites of the eyes. ❖ Babies do not produce tears until three months. Their eyes may drain from the side effect of silver nitrate, however. ❖ A newborn's eyes may cross at times. Eyes usually begin to work together at about six months.
Mouth	❖ Newborns have puffy cheeks. This is because they have sucking pads on the inside of the cheeks. ❖ The tongue is short and cannot be extended beyond the gums. ❖ The lining of the lips may peel. ❖ Most newborns are toothless, but some are born with one or more teeth.

newborn's cheeks, lips, or skin around the mouth, the baby searches for food. The head turns and the mouth moves. This is called the rooting reflex. After finding an object with the mouth, the baby begins to suck. This reflex should vanish in three to four months.

❖ Some reflexes lead to voluntary, learned behaviors. The knee jerk does not lead to a learned behavior. It always remains the same. On the other hand, the sucking reflex leads to learned sucking. The newborn learns to vary sucking strength with the softness of the object.

❖ Using reflexes may give the newborn the practice needed to develop voluntary behaviors such as sitting, walking, and climbing. These behaviors are essential for development.

There are many reflexes, and researchers are observing and describing more. Several are illustrated in 6-8.

Meeting the Newborn's Physical Needs

Newborns are completely helpless. They depend on adults to meet their physical needs. They even look small and helpless. Because newborns are so dependent and fragile, it's no wonder parents are often nervous to take care of them at first.

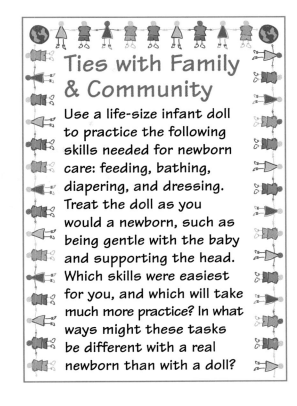

Ties with Family & Community

Use a life-size infant doll to practice the following skills needed for newborn care: feeding, bathing, diapering, and dressing. Treat the doll as you would a newborn, such as being gentle with the baby and supporting the head. Which skills were easiest for you, and which will take much more practice? In what ways might these tasks be different with a real newborn than with a doll?

Feeding

People need nutrients to grow and stay healthy. Because newborns grow quickly, their nutritional needs are especially important. Although parents can meet these needs by either breast-feeding or formula-feeding, breast-feeding is preferred. The best first food for babies is breast

rooting reflex. Reflex that helps babies search for food by turning the head and moving the mouth in response to a touch on the cheeks or mouth.

milk. The American Academy of Pediatrics recommends breast-feeding for at least the first 12 months of life. This option has advantages for baby, mother, and the family, 6-9.

Breast-Feeding

Mothers who breast-feed their babies should do the following:

❖ Eat a balanced diet. The quality of breast milk varies only slightly

 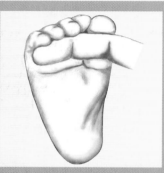 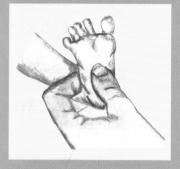

Palmar (grasping) Reflex
Newborns' fingers tighten around any object placed in the palm. Grasp is strong enough to lift them into a sitting position.

Plantar (grasping) Reflex
Newborns' toes tighten around any object when the ball of the foot is stroked. This reflex disappears between 8 and 15 months of age.

Babinski Reflex
Newborns' toes fan out if the outside of the sole is stroked from heel to toe. Reflex ends at about one year of age.

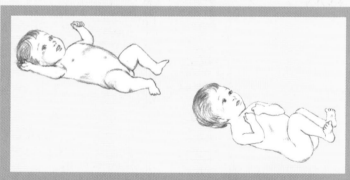 

Moro (startle) Reflex
The reflex consists of two movements. Newborns fling arms and legs out (A) and pull them back again (B) when they are startled.

Walking Reflex
When babies' feet touch a solid surface, alternating steps are taken as in walking. This reflex disappears in three or four months.

6-8 Some major reflexes help infants survive and learn.
Thomas J. Roberts

Advantages of Breast-Feeding

For Babies	For Mothers and Family
Breast milk contains the right proportions of proteins, carbohydrates, fats, vitamins, minerals, and water. This makes it easier to digest than formula.	Breast-feeding helps mother rest during the day and makes night feeding easier.
Mother's immunities to certain diseases are passed to the baby. Breast-fed babies have low rates of: ❖ diarrhea and constipation ❖ rashes ❖ allergies ❖ ear and respiratory infections ❖ urinary tract infections ❖ bacterial infections and possibly lower rates of; ❖ sudden infant death syndrome (SIDS) ❖ childhood diabetes ❖ intestinal tract diseases as adults ❖ lymphoma (cancer).	Breast-feeding has health benefits for mother, such as: ❖ causes uterus to contract to original size ❖ reduces postpartum bleeding ❖ reduces menstrual blood loss ❖ helps bones regain minerals ❖ reduces risk of breast cancer, especially during childbearing years ❖ reduces risk of ovarian cancer Breast-feeding can save the family money on formula, bottles, and nipples. Breast-feeding saves time in formula and bottle preparation.
Breast milk is always sterile (unless put in a bottle) and is ready immediately.	Due to healthier breast-fed babies, families may save money on medical bills and loss of money from wages and salary.
Breast-fed babies are usually the right weight because the milk content is perfect for baby's needs and mother doesn't overfeed the baby.	Parents often miss less work if the mother breast-feeds. This benefits employer and employee.
Vigorous sucking required for breast-feeding satisfies the need for sucking and promotes good development of facial structures and healthier, straighter teeth. Babies rarely choke for they can control the flow of milk.	Breast-feeding women can offer their baby the most nutritional food, even while returning to their careers. (Mothers who work can pump the milk several times during the day and refrigerate or freeze it. The baby takes this milk in a bottle while mother is away.)
Mother and baby develop a warm relationship because of touch and eye contact.	

6-9 Breast-feeding has many advantages for the baby, mother, and family.

from mother to mother. Even malnourished women can provide high-quality milk, but their own bodies suffer. During the first six weeks of nursing, most mothers stay on the same diet they followed while pregnant. After six weeks, they will need about 500 extra calories to produce the amount of milk needed for the growing baby.

❖ Drink at least eight 8-ounce glasses of fluid per day. The best choices are water, milk, and fruit or vegetable juices. Sugary drinks and those with caffeine should be limited.

❖ Check with a pediatrician about giving the baby a supplementary source of iron, fluoride, and vitamin D.

❖ Realize that certain foods may upset the baby. For some mothers, these include coffee, tea, chocolate, cola, cocoa, herbal teas, and artificial sweeteners. The baby's intestinal tract may be irritated by foods the mother has eaten such as broccoli, asparagus, eggplant, onions, tomatoes, garlic, and spices. If the mother notices her baby is bothered by a food she has eaten, she may need to stop eating this food until she weans her baby from breast milk.

❖ Tell doctors and dentists when nursing. Also, the mother should talk to her doctor before taking over-the-counter drugs. Any drug could affect her milk and the baby.

❖ Rest and avoid stress. Milk supply decreases when mothers are tired or under stress.

❖ Consult with a doctor, nurse, or breast-feeding expert for help with breast-feeding.

❖ Use breast-feeding time to bond with the baby. As they breast-feed, mothers should smile at, sing to, talk with, and cuddle their newborns, 6-10.

Formula-Feeding

Although most mothers can breast-feed, a few cannot, 6-11. Even when mothers can breast-feed, sometimes they choose not to do so. If

6-10 Breast-feeding helps a mother and baby bond.
Gerber Products

Formula-Feeding Is Sometimes Necessary

Adoptive and foster mothers usually formula-feed.

Some infant diseases prevent babies from breast-feeding.

Formula-feeding is recommended if mothers have the following:
* tuberculosis (TB)
* HIV
* herpes
* hepatitis
* certain strep infections
* silicone breast implants (in some cases)

Formula-feeding is recommended for mothers taking certain drugs for:
* cancer
* Parkinson's disease
* migraine headaches
* mood disorders (depression)
* arthritis

The use of illegal drugs, smoking, or radiation treatments may make formula-feeding the better choice.

Breast disease may make nursing impossible.

6-11 In some cases, formula-feeding is necessary. Mothers should seek medical advice if they have questions about which method is safest to use.

parents choose formula-feeding, they should do the following:
* Consult with a doctor about the type of formula to use. Most formulas are based on cow's milk, but some are soy-based. Soy formulas are often used for babies who have problems digesting milk-based formulas.

* Report any digestive upsets or rash to the baby's doctor. These might indicate a problem with the baby's formula.
* Formulas are available in powdered, liquid concentrate, or ready-to-feed forms. When using powdered and liquid concentrate forms, any water added (including bottled water) should be first be boiled for one to two minutes and then cooled.
* Do not make your own formula. Commercially-prepared formulas are regulated by the Food and Drug Administration. Milk products used in purchased formulas are specially processed to make it easier for the baby to digest. Do not feed the baby cow's milk before the baby is a year old.
* Feed newborns the right amount of milk as recommended by the baby's doctor. Two to 2½ ounces per pound of body weight in a 24-hour period is a good general rule.
* Keep utensils, bottles, and nipples completely clean.
* Keep mixed and ready-to-use formula refrigerated. Bacteria can grow quickly in unrefrigerated milk.
* Check nipples. Large or clogged holes cause feeding problems. Torn or worn nipples could cause the baby to choke.
* Babies do not always finish their bottles. Throw away all unfinished formula. Bacteria grow quickly in the unfinished milk because this milk contains some of the baby's saliva.

❖ Hold and cuddle the baby during feeding. Parents may want to take turns feeding the baby. This helps both of them bond with the baby, 6-12.

❖ Do not prop the bottle. Babies can choke while feeding. (If a baby chokes, parents should turn the baby on his or her side or abdomen, then pat on the back.)

Burping the Baby

Whether breast- or formula-fed, babies must be burped. This is because they swallow air while sucking or crying. Burping rids the body of this air. To burp a newborn, do the following:

❖ Place the baby in a sitting position with a hand on the collarbone and under the chin.

❖ Laying the baby face down across your lap is another way to burp him or her. (You may burp a newborn on your shoulder, but the shoulder position is easier when the baby is larger.)

❖ Lightly pat the baby's back once he or she is in position. Pat the baby below the ribs for two or three minutes unless the baby burps sooner.

❖ Burp a baby before, midway, and/or after feeding.

Clothing and Dressing

Babies' clothing should be comfortable, easy to put on and take off, suitable for weather and temperature, and safe. What clothes do babies find comfortable? Loose-fitting clothes are easy to move in, and clothes without too many ties, buttons, or snaps are also good choices. Be sure that clothes are flame-retardant and that fasteners and decorative items are secure. Because babies kick off their blankets, they need warm clothes. However, do not overdress them.

Because baby clothes are so cute, it is easy to make unwise choices. Babies outgrow their clothes quickly, so they don't need too many. Parents can stay within their clothing budget by watching for sales. They can also save

6-12 Bottle-feeding helps a father develop a good relationship with his baby.
© John Shaw

Basic Clothing Needs for the Newborn

- ❖ 3 to 4 cotton knit nightgowns or kimonos
- ❖ 3 to 4 cotton knit shirts
- ❖ 2 to 3 sweaters or sweatshirts
- ❖ 1 knit cap
- ❖ 3 to 6 dozen cloth diapers or several boxes of disposal diapers
- ❖ 1 dozen cloth diapers (for burping, protection of bedding, etc.)
- ❖ 3 plastic pants, if using cloth diapers
- ❖ 3 to 4 pairs of socks
- ❖ 4 to 6 bibs
- ❖ 1 dressy outfit for outings and pictures

6-13 Parents usually receive many baby clothes as gifts shortly before and after their baby is born.

money by borrowing baby clothes from friends and relatives. Choosing clothes suitable for either boys or girls (and storing for the next child) is smart, too. Another smart idea is for parents to buy or make clothes the baby can grow into. Clothes should be easy to launder, also. Clothes that must be hand-washed or dry-cleaned are not practical. See 6-13 for a newborn's basic clothing needs.

Remember, dressing time is a chance to talk with newborns. Newborns talk with their body movements, eyes, and sounds. Tell babies what you're doing as you dress them. ("I'm snapping your shirt. Snap...snap...snap.")

Newborns are easier to dress than older babies because they do not squirm as much. The following suggestions should make dressing easy and safe.

- ❖ Put out the baby's clothes before you begin. Undo any buttons or snaps before you get the baby.
- ❖ Support the baby's head as you lift him or her.
- ❖ Pull the baby's arms and legs through the openings. Newborns can't push.
- ❖ Cuddle fretful babies before continuing to dress them.

Diapering

Parents can use either disposable or cloth diapers for babies. There are many different brands and sizes of disposable diapers. They all have waterproof outer layers and are easy and convenient to use. Some babies wear cloth diapers with plastic pants over them most of the time. When traveling, they use disposable ones. See 6-14 on how to diaper a baby.

Both cloth and disposable diapers have advantages and disadvantages. Parents must consider cost and convenience. If the baby will attend child care, it is likely disposable diapers will be required. Parents must also consider how much time they have to wash diapers. In some places, parents have the option of using a diaper service that picks up soiled diapers and delivers sterilized cloth ones. This service may be costly, however.

How to Diaper a Baby

1. Gather diapering materials before you get the baby.
2. Place the baby on a safe, firm surface. Unfasten and remove soiled diaper.
3. Clean the diaper area thoroughly. Be sure to wipe from front to back.
4. With one hand, grasp the baby's ankles and slide a fresh diaper under the baby's bottom. Then pull the front of the diaper up between the baby's legs.
5. When using disposable diapers, the tape fastens from the front to the back. With cloth diapers, protect the baby from the pin by slipping two of your fingers between the baby and the diaper. (Diaper pins that have been pushed into a bar of soap will slide easily through a cloth diaper.)

6-14 If you unfasten a diaper and find the baby does not need to be changed, refasten the diaper with tape or diaper pins.

Parents can prevent most diaper rashes by changing the baby's diapers regularly. Diaper rashes may develop from the constant use of plastic pants or from the outer layer of disposable diapers. In a diaper rash, bacteria grow rapidly on the warm, moist, and air-free skin. Most babies develop diaper rash at one time or another. The most common treatment is to wash the area with soap and water after each change, expose the area to air, and use petroleum jelly or a rash ointment before diapering. If the rash persists following several days of treatment, parents should consult a pediatrician.

Bathing

Newborns don't get too dirty except for their faces, necks, and diaper areas. These areas must be kept clean.

Sponge baths are recommended until the navel has completely healed—up to three weeks after birth. (Leave the cord alone until it becomes dry and loose. Then wipe with a cotton swab dipped in 70 percent rubbing alcohol four or five times per day.) See 6-15 on how to give a sponge bath.

Sleeping

Newborns average about 17 hours of sleep per day. (Some sleep as few as 11 hours daily, while others sleep as many as 23 hours per day). Because newborns are growing so rapidly, their tiny bodies need lots of rest.

Newborns do not sleep quietly between feedings. They usually take seven or eight naps in which they suck, wheeze, and gurgle. This pattern of light sleep continues for the first half year. Newborns adjust to regular household sounds, so it isn't necessary to whisper or tiptoe while they sleep.

Place the baby on a firm mattress in a bed with sides that will prevent the baby from falling. Pillows and stuffed toys should only be used after the baby is a year of age. Until a baby can change sleep positions easily, a

How to Give a Baby a Sponge Bath

1. Collect all supplies. You will need the following:
   - ❖ towel or sponge for baby to lie on
   - ❖ baby soap
   - ❖ cotton balls
   - ❖ washcloth, towel, and wrapper (a hooded cape or a hooded, front-opening "robe" to wrap around baby), or another large towel
   - ❖ bath oil and lotion
   - ❖ manicure scissors (made for babies)
   - ❖ hair brush and comb (made for babies)
2. Place supplies within the adult's reach but out of the baby's reach.
3. Place the baby on a towel or a baby-sized sponge placed on a cabinet or bathing table. Never leave the baby unattended—even for a second!
4. Wash the baby's face with a washcloth dipped in clear water and squeezed out.
5. Clean eyes, ears, and nose with fresh cotton balls dipped in clear water and squeezed out.
6. Lightly soap the rest of the baby's body and rinse with a wet washcloth. Pat the baby dry as you wash each area. Keep the baby covered with a wrapper or an extra towel.
7. Moisten the baby's skin with baby oil or lotion.
8. Shampoo the scalp once or twice a week with soap to prevent scaling, called *cradle cap*.
9. Brush and comb hair after you have dressed the baby.
10. Cut the baby's nails when necessary.

6-15 Gather and organize all bath supplies before placing the baby on a towel.

pillow or stuffed toy could hamper breathing. It may be best never to place pillows and stuffed toys in a baby's bed. Once he or she can stand on these items, the baby can climb over the railing.

Until age one year, babies should be placed on their backs for sleeping. This greatly reduces the risk of **sudden infant death syndrome (SIDS)**. This is a syndrome in which a baby dies without warning while sleeping. Lying face-down on soft, fluffy bedding is a risk. For this reason, babies should not be placed on their stomachs for sleeping. Side positions aren't good, either, because a baby might roll onto the stomach. Allowing the baby to become too hot has also been linked to SIDS. For this reason, it is best not to overdress the baby for sleep or cover the baby in heavy blankets.

Bedding equipment and supplies are simple for newborns. The basic items needed are listed in 6-16.

Exercising

Movement is a large part of life—before birth and in the newborn stage. Watch the constant movement of newborns lying awake on their backs. Exercise is important for muscle

sudden infant death syndrome (SIDS). A syndrome in which a baby dies without warning in his or her sleep.

Bedding Equipment and Supplies

Bed

❖ Bassinets, cradles, or cribs are all fine beds.

❖ A baby bed should be high and stable enough to prevent young children or pets from tipping it over.

❖ If a cradle or bed with slats is used, the slats should be no further apart than 2⅜ inches. This prevents babies from wiggling feet first through the slats until their heads are caught. This could cause serious injury or death.

Bumper pads

❖ Use bumper pads in cradles or beds with slats. Bumper pads should tie securely in a least six places.

❖ Do not use bumper pads until babies can lift their heads. This prevents suffocation.

❖ Remove bumper pads when the baby can stand. This prevents the baby from using them as climbing devices.

Large pieces of flannelette sheeting

❖ Cover the mattress or pad with two or three pieces of 25 by 30 inch waterproof flannelette sheeting.

❖ Put the sheet over these pieces. (Large pieces are important once the baby begins to move around in bed.)

❖ Use the sheeting until the child remains dry at night without diapers.

Small pieces of flannelette sheeting

❖ Place four to six 18-inch squares of waterproof flannelette sheeting on top of the baby's sheet.

❖ Use the sheeting to catch spit up or overflows from a diaper.

Sheets

❖ Three or four sheets are needed for frequent middle-of-the-night changes. Sheets come in various sizes to fit bassinets, cradles, portable cribs, and standard cribs. Parents should choose the size that matches their baby's bed and has fitted edges for a tight and smooth fit. If sheets don't fit properly, they can come off the bed easily and present a safety risk. The fabric can tangle around the baby and smother or strangle him or her. Look for crib sheets approved as safe by the *Good Housekeeping Institute* and the *American Society of Testing and Materials*.

Blankets

❖ Three or four cotton flannel blankets may be needed.

❖ Receiving blankets (about 30 by 40 inches) are often used.

❖ Crib blankets (36 by 50 inches) may be more economical. Babies soon outgrow the smaller blankets.

❖ Sleepwear that keeps the baby warm is essential. Babies kick off their blankets while they sleep. Warm sleepwear for newborns has bottoms and cuffs that convert to mittens.

❖ Sleepwear includes elastic-bottom gowns and sleepers.

6-16 The bedding needs of newborns are simple.

development, coordination, and even relaxation. Helping newborns exercise will not cause them to crawl or walk sooner. It may help the general development of the muscles, however. To help the baby exercise, see 6-17.

Suggestions for Helping Babies Exercise

❖ Place the baby on a foam pad or bed where he or she is comfortable and safe.
❖ The baby should wear nonrestrictive clothing while exercising so he or she can move easily.
❖ Select a good time. The baby should exercise for 10 to 15 minutes. Choose a time when the baby is alert but not fussy. Watch a baby's schedule for several days before selecting a time. (Just before or after a feeding time is not a good time.)
❖ Move the baby gently. If the baby shows resistance, stop.
❖ Talk or sing to the baby during exercise.
❖ Try the following exercises for a newborn. Be creative and use others, too.
   a. With the baby on his or her back, lift arms above the head, straighten them from the shoulders (in the form of a cross), and down to the sides.
   b. Draw the palms of the hands together as in clapping.
   c. Alternately move one knee up to the chest and then the other.
   d. Straighten the knees by holding the legs together with one hand under the calves and the other hand gently pushing the knees flat.

6-17 Exercising is good for the baby. It also gives the parents and baby time to "talk."

Helping the baby exercise has added bonuses. Exercising, if started early in life, may become a daily, life-long habit. Daily exercise is also a way to have fun with babies and develop a warm relationship. Many families find that doing physical activities together is great family fun.

Scheduling

Babies don't come into the world knowing anything about a schedule. The following is an age-old question:

Q *Should parents try to figure out when their baby "tells them" he or she is hungry or sleepy, or should parents try to teach babies to adopt a schedule for eating or sleeping?*

A Doctors now suggest that newborns feed on demand and that mothers watch for clues of hunger (baby is alert, mouthing, and rooting). Newborns nurse about every two hours; that is, 8 to 12 times in 24 hours. They breast-feed until *satiety* (being full), which takes at least 15 minutes per breast. Sleeping should be done on the newborn's schedule, too. Doctors suggest arousing a sleeping newborn every three or four hours for feedings, however. This keeps the baby from becoming too hungry or lacking for needed nutrients.

In a few weeks, most babies begin to develop eating-sleeping patterns. These patterns change, however, as the baby's needs change. The length of time between feedings will increase, which results in fewer feedings per day. The many short daytime and nighttime naps will gradually be replaced by fewer but longer daytime naps and longer periods of sleep at night. These changes lead the baby to spend more time awake, too.

Meeting babies' needs helps them learn to trust the world (and show less fear and anxiety). In the long run, parents who work to meet their babies' needs promptly are rewarded with happier, less fussy babies.

Meeting the Newborn's Intellectual Needs

For years, people thought newborns were sleepy, helpless, and unable to understand the world around them. The more people study children's learning, the more they realize that learning begins right after birth. In fact, the brain and some of the senses are active before birth. Because learning begins so early, parents are a child's first teachers.

What Brain Research Says About Newborns

As you learned in chapter 1, brain research shows the importance of early experiences. During the prenatal period, genetic factors and the environment of the unborn wired the brain stem. The brain stem regulates heartbeat, breathing, and reflexes. In short, neonates are wired to live in the world.

They are also wired to learn, but these connections are weak. Much wiring remains to be done.

The *sense organs* (eyes, ears, nose, skin, tongue) transmit information from the environment to the brain. All the sense organs can function at birth. Thus, newborns have a great ability for learning.

Brain research indicates newborns need to be touched and cuddled, talked to, and offered sensory experiences. To prevent newborns from becoming overwhelmed, parent talk and other experiences should be slow, quiet, and repeated often. Just as newborns sleep and eat on their schedule, they should receive this important "food for the brain" when they are alert.

What Can Newborns Do?

Newborns can tell the difference between human speech and other sounds. Some studies found that babies in the delivery room responded to human speech by looking in the direction of the sound. The same babies ignored other sounds. At just 12 to 24 hours old, newborns can move their arms and legs rhythmically to human speech.

During the first few hours after birth, babies can tell the difference between a click and a tone sound. They can learn whether to turn their heads right or left for a reward of sugar water. Within a week, newborns become even better at distinguishing sounds. For example, newborns will cry in response to another baby's cry, but not to a fake cry. From birth, babies will turn toward a parent's voice over a stranger's voice.

During the first few weeks of life, babies begin to learn about space. If babies see a moving object approaching them on a collision course, they will turn their heads or pull away as much as possible. If the object is not on a collision course, babies will not defend themselves.

Imitation, or copying the actions of another person, is a common way people learn. Until recently, experts thought babies didn't imitate until they were at least eight months old. Now they know newborns can imitate adults' facial and hand gestures. The baby's ability to imitate develops quickly. Within a year, infants can imitate some child care tasks. For instance, they can give a doll a bottle.

Newborns show they're learning by their behavior. When presented with a stimulus such as your face, an object, or a sound, they respond by becoming quiet and looking. Their heart rate increases. Newborns also show learning because they can remember for a short time. If you show newborns a stuffed dog a few times and show them the same stuffed dog and a stuffed duck, they will look at the duck. Thus, they remembered the older stimulus (the dog) and were more interested in the newer stimulus (the duck).

How Can Parents Help Their Babies Learn?

As you can see, newborns are learners. Just as parents need to meet the newborn's physical needs, they need to meet his or her intellectual needs. Parents must take time to stimulate their newborns.

Most parents ask, "When and how do I stimulate my newborn?" Babies learn in their waking, alert state. Their eyes are open and shiny, and they look around. When they are overstimulated or bored, they either become more active and fretful or go to sleep. (Adults behave in much the same way.) Because newborns can't walk or crawl, experiences must be taken to them. Newborns learn through their senses.

Most of the stimulation comes from being near parents and other caregivers. Newborns are fascinated at seeing faces, hearing sounds, and feeling warm and loved when cuddled, 6-18. Warm and expressive talk stimulates newborns. Newborns love to hear singing (and they are an uncritical audience).

Newborns enjoy looking at objects, 6-19. Because their distance vision is limited for the first three to four weeks, mobiles hung above the beds this early are almost useless. Newborns can see objects in the corners of their bed as they turn their heads left and right. (Because newborns tilt their heads back, they see objects placed in the corners of the bed more

6-18 Babies need to be cuddled.
© John Shaw

easily than those placed on the sides.) Objects should be changed frequently. Newborns get bored, too. Because newborns have very short memories, objects can be rotated. (Well into infancy, babies see rotated objects as "new.")

Grasping objects during the newborn stage is a reflex action. For added safety, objects should be securely fastened, nontoxic, and too large to swallow.

Other ways to stimulate the newborn include using colorful bed bumper pads. A wind chime, music box, or soothing music are other good sensory experiences for newborns.

Newborn Toys

Designs and Patterns	Objects that Move	Circular-Shaped Objects	Other Objects
Newborns like bold, black-and-white patterns. They prefer horizontal and diagonal designs to vertical ones. Babies like spiral patterns and concentric circles more than solid-colored circles.	Helium-inflated mylar balloons and large plastic lids with designs painted on them flutter with the bed's movement.	Newborns enjoy large balls made from aluminum foil and bright-colored yarn. Rings are also a favorite.	Pictures of faces are favorites. Newborns also enjoy bright-colored bows and ribbons, artificial flowers, and mirrors.

6-19 Newborns' first toys are objects to see, and they already prefer certain toys.

Meeting the Newborn's Social-Emotional Needs

Each baby is an individual. Some babies are more active. Some like to be cuddled. Some cry a lot, and others seem happy. This individuality influences the parents' response to the baby, just like a person's personality affects the way you respond to him or her. In this section, you will examine the individuality of babies. You will also learn ways parents can meet their babies' social-emotional needs.

Alertness of Newborns

Babies seem to learn best when they are in the alert, inactive state. At this time, babies are quiet but alert. In this state, babies also seem to develop warm relationships with others. Newborns are not much fun if they are always asleep or fussy. Parents often refer to alert and inactive babies as good babies and fussy babies as difficult ones.

Babies differ in alertness because of their individuality. For example, premature babies are often not as alert. Also, babies differ in the length of time they are alert. There seems to be a general pattern in the development of alertness. Unless affected by drugs used in delivery, newborns are usually alert for a while after their birth. Then newborns tend to sleep a lot during the next few days. With each passing week, newborns spend more time in the alert-inactive stage. They total about 11 hours in the first week and 22 hours in the fourth week.

Parents can work to establish a good relationship early in the newborn's life, even if the baby is sleepy or fussy most of the time. Time takes care of the sleepiness of healthy newborns. Parents should take advantage of their alert states by cuddling and playing with them. Parents can enjoy fussy newborns in their quiet, alert times and attempt to soothe them when fussy.

Soothing a Fussy Baby

All newborns cry. Some babies cry ⅙ to ¼ of each day, even when nothing is wrong. Parents need to understand this crying is not related to their parenting abilities. Some babies just cry more and are harder to soothe than others.

Newborns cry for almost any reason because crying is the way they "talk." They may cry because they are tired, hungry, lonely, or uncomfortable. Babies also cry to relax from tension. Colic is a major reason babies cry, especially during the first three months. Colic is a condition (not a disease) in which the baby has intense abdominal pain. There are many causes of colic, such as allergies, tension, swallowing

colic. A condition in which a baby has intense abdominal pain and cries inconsolably.

air when sucking, and hunger. Medication may be prescribed in severe cases, but soothing often works.

Parents should try to soothe newborns. They will not spoil the baby by answering his or her cries. To soothe a newborn, try to interpret the cry, then respond. Chart 6-20 describes three distinct cries and how to respond to them. Some ways to soothe a baby are the following:

❖ Rock the baby in a vertical (over your shoulder) position. Put your hand behind the baby's head and rock quickly.

❖ Carry the baby around the house or yard.

❖ Sing and play music. Babies like the quiet tones of lullabies or even a steady tone. Dr. Hajime Murooka recorded the sounds a baby hears before birth—the mother's breathing and heartbeat.

He discovered these sounds soothe the newborn. The recording is now sold as "Lullaby from the Womb."

❖ Take the baby for a car ride or a walk in a stroller.

Constant crying causes tension in parents. Relief from tension is good for family relationships. Using a babysitter for an hour or even an entire afternoon may help reduce tension.

Meeting the Parents' Needs

Parenting skills do not come automatically. They are learned. Even experienced parents find they must learn new things with each child. Each parent learns to cope in a different way. Because this learning takes time, the first few weeks are especially difficult ones. This is also

The Meanings of Cries

Cause	Sounds of Cry	Ways to Respond
Pain	Cycle begins with shrill scream, followed by silence, and ends with short gasps. Cycle is repeated.	Respond immediately. Ease pain if possible. Cuddle baby to calm.
Hunger or Boredom	Slow cries that become louder and rhythmic.	Feed if near feeding time. OR Entertain by giving baby a tour of the house or yard.
Upset	Fussy, rather quiet cry. Cry sounds a bit forced.	Cuddle or entertain.

6-20 Newborns communicate with their cries.

the time when parents get the least amount of sleep because the baby awakes to feed often.

Parents shouldn't forget about their own needs while learning to care for newborns. Even though their sleep will be disrupted by demands of their newborn, parents still need to rest. They need to organize their tasks. They need adult companionship.

The Need for Rest

Getting enough rest is always important, and it is even more important for new parents. Newborns can tire parents. This is hard on their physical health. It can also lead to irritability and depression. Thus, it is important for parents to rest when possible. Parents of newborns need to put off unnecessary chores, such as cooking complicated meals or doing extra cleaning. They should sleep or rest while babies sleep. Parents can take turns getting up with the baby at night. Even if the mother is nursing, the father can get the baby, change the baby's diaper, and bring the baby to the mother for feeding. This allows the mother more rest.

Organize Tasks

Parents need to organize their households. Valuable time is wasted looking for misplaced items. New parents need to find a place for baby gear. If parents travel with babies, their vehicle must also be organized. Parents need to be mentally organized, too. A bulletin board used for posting doctors' recommendations, appointments, bills, shopping lists, and other reminders may help.

Time to Be with Adults

Parents need to spend time with other adults—especially each other. Mothers and fathers need attention, too. Spending some time with adults each day restores their energy. Parents should plan for extra time for each other and other adults.

Parents need to get out of the house with and without their newborns, 6-21. Spending too much time in the house often gives parents the feeling they are living in a baby's world. Going out, even for a short walk, restores physical and mental energy. It can make both babies and parents feel better. Parents also need to have competent babysitters for some outings without babies.

New parents can learn much from sharing with other parents. Many first-time parents find it helpful to call close, experienced friends for advice. In fact, studies have shown that many parents who found having children an unhappy experience were isolated from family or friends.

The successful development of newborns depends on the parent-child relationship. With their own needs met, parents are better able to meet their newborn's physical, intellectual, and social-emotional needs. Babies whose needs are met by loving parents are off to a good start, 6-22.

6-21 New parents need to spend time away from their baby to help restore mental energy.

6-22 Babies whose needs are met by loving parents are off to a good start.

Summing It Up

Soon after birth, newborns undergo various tests to assess their health. Among these are the Apgar test, Brazelton scale, and test for PKU.

Newborns are not the plump, pretty babies shown in advertisements. Their bodies look out of proportion to their heads. Their skin may be wrinkled, blotchy, and reddish in color.

Babies have a number of automatic, unlearned behaviors called reflexes. How babies respond to these reflexes reflects the health and maturity of their nervous system.

Although babies can thrive on both breast-milk and commercially prepared formula, breast-feeding is preferred. Breast-feeding has many advantages. Nursing mothers need to eat nutritious diets.

Newborns' clothing should be comfortable, safe, easy to put on and take off. It should also be appropriate for the temperature and easy to launder. Using disposable or cloth diapers is a decision that parents make based on expense and convenience.

Brain research stresses the importance of the newborn period for being loved and cuddled, talked to, and having sensory experiences. Stimulation meets the intellectual needs of newborns. Most of this comes from being near parents and other caregivers. Hearing and seeing others talk and looking at and feeling objects helps their sensory awareness. Parents meet the social-emotional needs of children by enjoying babies' alert quiet times and soothing them when they are fussy.

In addition to meeting their baby's needs, parents must take time to respond to their own needs. Caring for babies is time-consuming and can be exhausting. Time alone and as a couple can help new parents refresh themselves and become happier, more successful parents.

Reviewing Key Concepts

Write your answers on a separate sheet of paper.

1. Which five areas are included in the Apgar test?
2. Explain the difference between reflexes and voluntary movements. Describe two reflexes seen in the newborn.
3. Describe four aspects of a newborn's appearance.
4. List three advantages of breast-feeding for the baby and three for the mother.
5. Chris is a newborn who is formula-fed every 4 hours during a 24-hour period. He weighs 10 pounds. Based on the guideline given in the chapter, calculate how much formula Chris needs at each feeding.
6. True or false. Newborns who cry a lot are just spoiled. The way to stop the crying is to let them cry it out.
7. Explain how parents may meet their own needs for the following:
   A. rest
   B. time spent with each other
   C. organizing their household
   D. getting out of the house

Using Your Knowledge

1. **Consumer Skills.** Work in a small group to make a shopping list of items needed for each of the following:
   A. clothing and diapering
   B. bedding
   C. bathing
   D. traveling
   E. toys for newborns

   Do some comparison shopping (in stores, in catalogs, or online) to find the range of prices for each item. Share your findings with the class.

2. **Technology.** Working with a small group, visit various Web sites hosted by the manufacturers of the leading infant formulas. What types of formula does each offer? What major differences do you note among brands? Use the computer to create a chart showing your findings.

3. **Child Development.** Make some safe, interesting objects for a newborn's crib (see 6-19).

4. **Interviewing.** Interview a pediatrician about the medical care of a newborn and the importance of well-baby checkups. Write a paper summarizing your findings.

5. **Communication/Graphing Skills.** Poll 10 parents by asking each parent what he or she found was the hardest part of life with a newborn. Using your master list of responses, create a graph showing the results of your poll.

Making Observations

1. Observe a newborn. Compare the newborn's physical characteristics with those in 6-7.
2. Observe a newborn's movements. What reflexes did you observe?
3. Observe a parent caring for a newborn. How much time does each task take? Which tasks seem easy? Which tasks seem more difficult?
4. Observe a newborn being dressed. Which clothing features made dressing the baby easy? Which made dressing the baby difficult? Did the clothes look comfortable on the baby? Why or why not?

Thinking Further

1. Some new parents have never been near newborns. How do you think advertisements posing older babies as newborns affect their perceptions of their newborns?
2. Child development experts often advise parents to follow the baby's lead. Brainstorm with classmates how you can follow a baby's lead in meeting his or her needs. Are there times when newborns should follow their parents' lead? Why or why not?
3. Sometimes one spouse becomes unhappy when the other spouse spends so much time with the baby. How can a spouse tell when this is a reasonable complaint? What are some specific ways parents can make time to meet each other's needs?

Part 3
Infants

Infancy is the period of life between two weeks and one year after birth. Children's development during this time is exciting because they grow and learn new skills each day.

By studying **chapter 7**, you will learn how quickly an infant's size and body proportions change. You also will see how motor skills follow growth patterns. This means they proceed, in an organized way, from reflexes to the first wobbly steps.

As you read **chapter 8**, you will learn how babies actively master their worlds. Their well-worked senses are becoming more refined and coordinated. Babies are interested in hearing others speak. This helps them learn, and by the end of their first year, babies reach the stage of beginning speech.

Special bonds are as important for the infant as they are for you. In **chapter 9**, you will see how babies' tools for interaction change throughout the first year. These interactions help babies form secure attachments, develop self-awareness, and become more independent.

Chapter 10 will teach you how to care for babies during their first year. Babies depend on adults for physical care. In addition, they need support for their intellectual and social development.

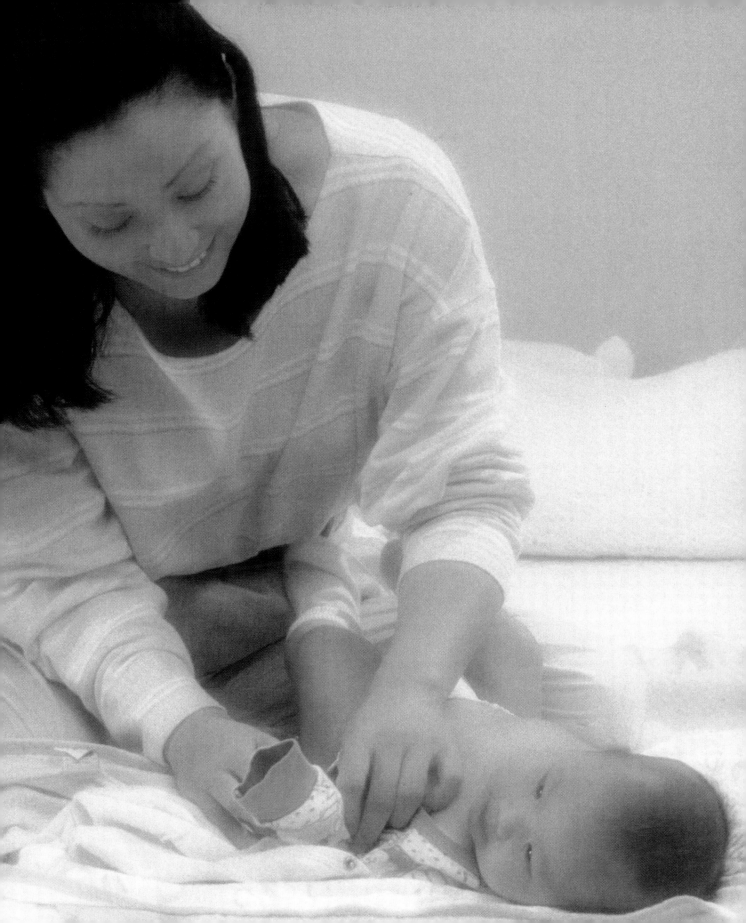

Chapter 7
Physical
Development
of the Infant

Mason is 10 months old. Although he is large for his age, his motor skills lag far behind those of other children his age. For example, Mason has trouble sitting unassisted. How can Mason's parents encourage his motor development? What activities would you suggest? Would you be concerned? What types of professional help, if any, would you advise his parents to seek? If you were Mason's caregiver at a child care center, how would you discuss his development with his parents?

After studying this chapter, you will be able to

✍ describe how an infant develops physically during the first year.

✍ describe the order in which an infant's motor skills develop.

Define...

skeletal system
failure to thrive
body proportions
ossification
deciduous teeth
motor development
gross-motor skills
fine-motor skills
age norm
crawl
creeping
cruising
voluntary grasping

With the help and care of others, babies develop physically during the first year. A human's physical growth is completed at 20 or 21 years. This growth period is longer than that of any living creature. During much of this time, others must care for the human.

Just as babies grow quickly during the prenatal and neonatal stages, they grow quickly during their first year of life. It is fun to watch a tiny newborn grow into a more chubby-looking infant. Good physical development is important during this time. A healthy baby keeps growing and developing in all areas.

Skeletal Growth

The **skeletal system** is made of bones and teeth. *Skeletal growth* refers to the changes in length, weight, and the appearance of teeth.

Length and Weight

The baby's length and weight changes quickly during the first year. (The term *length* is used for the first year because the baby does not stand. After the first year, the term *height* is used.) Changes happen so quickly that even people who see the baby daily are amazed at how fast he or she grows. They can see the baby change.

All children grow at their own rates. The average length of a baby at birth, however, is 20 to 21 inches. Most infants reach 1 ½ times their birth lengths (adding 9 to 10 inches) during the first year, 7-1. Babies usually double their birthweights in four or five months and triple their birthweights by one year. Usually boys are slightly longer and heavier than girls (by about ¾ of an inch and 1 ½ pounds).

By about nine months, the infant becomes chubbier. This change happens because fat tissues under the skin have increased. After this time, fat tissues begin to decrease. Even at this early age,

skeletal system. The body system that includes the bones and teeth.

Average Length and Weight During First Year

Age in Months	Length in Inches	Weight in Pounds
Birth	20	7½
3	23¾	12½
6	26	16¾
9	28	20
12	29½	22¼

7-1 A baby's length and weight increase quickly during the first year.

boys have more muscle length and thickness, while girls have more fat.

The rate of growth is more important than the actual length and weight. The baby's doctor will use a growth chart to record the baby's growth at each checkup. This growth chart shows the average growth for babies as well as the measurements for this baby. The doctor will compare the baby's actual measurements to these averages. As long as growth seems to continue at a constant rate, the doctor will not likely be concerned.

Sometimes, however, babies experience a **failure to thrive**. This means their rates of growth slow considerably over time. This may indicate a health problem exists. In this case, the growth chart would show the baby was growing at a steady rate and then showed a decline. Possible causes of failure to thrive include the following:

❖ diseases that prevent all or some nutrients from being absorbed or that cause nutrients to be quickly expelled from the body
❖ the baby's food is not providing enough nutrients (diluted formula or breast milk affected by mother's malnutrition)
❖ feedings are offered too infrequently or last too short a time
❖ the baby is abused or neglected

With the proper care and attention, the baby's health can often be restored. The length of time this will take depends on how severe the problem was and how long it lasted.

Body Proportions

Infants do not look like small adults. Their **body proportions** (relative size of body parts) differ from those of adults. For example, an infant's head is about one-fourth his or her total length, while an adult's head is one-tenth of his or her total height. Unlike adults, the forehead of an infant is wider than the chin. The jaw is smaller and slopes backward. This is commonly called the "baby look."

From birth until six months, the infant's head is larger than the chest. In most six-month-old children, the chest becomes larger. The difference in the distance around the chest as compared to distance around the head continues to increase with age.

Besides having a large head, an infant has a long trunk, a "pot-bellied" abdomen, and short legs. The gain in length during the first year is because the trunk grows. The legs do not grow much longer at this time. The abdomen sticks out because the internal organs are large for the baby's small body. Because the center of gravity is high on the baby's body, the result is poor balance. No wonder babies toddle rather than walk!

Bones and Teeth

The infant skeleton is mainly made of cartilage. That is why infants' bones do not break easily. There are large spaces between their "bones" to help the joints bend easily without breaking. Young babies can suck their toes with no trouble, but sitting and standing are impossible because their skeletons are not sturdy. Due to their softness, an infant's bones can easily become misshapen. Lying in one position all the time can flatten the baby's head in one place. This has become more common in recent years with the recommendation for babies to sleep on their backs. (This position for sleeping greatly reduces the risk of SIDS.)

Changing a baby's position during waking hours can keep the head from flattening. Many doctors now recommend "tummy time" for babies. Once babies can hold their heads up (at two to four months), they should spend time on their stomachs while alert.

This encourages the development of motor skills, such as rolling over, reaching, and crawling. It also aids bone growth. During tummy time, caregivers should stay close and offer the baby toys to see, reach, and grasp. This stimulates the baby's brain.

During the first year, three changes occur in a baby's bones.

- ❖ First, the length of the bones increases.
- ❖ Second, **ossification** (depositing of the minerals calcium and phosphorus) begins. Ossification helps the skeletal frame become sturdy. This helps the infant sit and eventually walk.
- ❖ Third, the number of bones changes. For example, the hand and wrist of a one-year-old infant has only three bones, but there are 28 bones in the adult's hand and wrist. Also, ossification in the skull results in several bones becoming one skull bone. This growth is completed in about two years.

failure to thrive. A condition in which a child fails to grow at a healthy rate.

body proportions. The relative size of body parts.

ossification. Hardening of bones caused by the depositing of the minerals calcium and phosphorus.

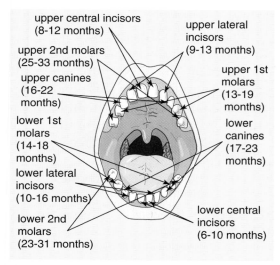

upper central incisors
(8-12 months)

upper lateral
incisors
(9-13 months)

upper 2nd molars
(25-33 months)

upper canines
(16-22
months)

upper 1st
molars
(13-19
months)

lower 1st
molars
(14-18
months)

lower
canines
(17-23
months)

lower lateral
incisors
(10-16 months)

lower 2nd
molars
(23-31 months)

lower central
incisors
(6-10 months)

7-2 Deciduous (nonpermanent) teeth appear in a predictable pattern.

Teeth, a part of the skeletal system, begin forming in the sixth week of prenatal life. By birth, all 20 **deciduous teeth** (nonpermanent teeth) and a few permanent teeth are developing deep in the jaw. Most babies begin cutting teeth during the second half of the first year, 7-2. The *sequence* (order) of teething is easier to predict than *when* teeth will appear (timing). In fact, a few babies are born with one or more teeth. Other children are more than a year old when their first teeth appear.

Motor Development

Motor development is the use and control of muscles that direct body movements. Learning to use and control large muscles (such as the trunk, arms, and legs) helps babies crawl and walk. These abilities are called **gross-motor skills**. Being able to control the small muscles, such as the hands and fingers, leads the baby to develop **fine-motor skills**. Having control over the body is a sign of babies' growth and development.

The baby's motor skills develop in three main patterns. This order of motor development builds upon the order of brain development. The following list shows the pattern of motor development:

1. Babies move slowly because they must think as they move.
2. Babies' reactions develop from general to specific. At first, babies show general reactions to what they see and hear. Later in the first year, babies give more specific reactions. For example, if young infants see something they want, they wiggle all over. Older infants smile and reach for the object.
3. Motor development occurs in two directions. The first is from the head to the foot. The second is from the center of the body out to the extremities (from the trunk to the hands and feet).

Head-to-Foot Development

Head-to-foot development begins before birth. The unborn baby develops a head, then arm buds, and then leg buds. At birth, babies have well-developed facial muscles but less well-developed leg muscles. This is why babies can suck but cannot walk.

Drawing 7-3 shows the sequence in which babies can control their head, neck, and trunk muscles. These are called *milestones* in the infant's motor development. Milestones are sequenced steps, and the order of these steps is more constant than their timing. How do experts calculate the timing of these steps? Some babies develop when they are older, others when they are younger. Experts use the average of this range of ages, called an **age norm**, to predict when babies will develop certain skills.

Head and Neck Control

Newborns need to have their heads supported continually. Their muscles are not strong enough to hold their heads steady themselves. Some babies can raise their unsteady heads briefly when lying on their stomach. By two months, most babies spend a great deal of time with their heads and chests raised. Between three and four months, eye muscles are well developed, permitting babies to focus on objects in any direction. They can smile when they want to and make some sounds with the lips. Head control is almost complete when babies are about six months old. By this time, babies can raise their heads while lying on their backs. They can also hold their heads steady while sitting.

Trunk Control

Control of the trunk develops more slowly than control of the head. Babies placed on their stomachs can lift their heads before they can lift both their heads and chests, 7-4. Trunk control permits babies to achieve two major milestones in motor control—rolling over and sitting.

Rolling Over

Often between the second and fifth month, babies learn to roll over. Usually they first roll from front to back. A month later, they usually roll from back to front. It is easier for a baby to lift the head and trunk when on the abdomen than when on the back.

deciduous teeth. The first set of teeth, which will later be replaced by permanent teeth. Also called nonpermanent or baby teeth.

motor development. The use and control of muscles that direct body movements.

gross-motor skills. Being able to use the large muscles to roll over, sit, crawl, stand, and walk.

fine-motor skills. Being able to use and control the small muscles, especially those in the fingers and hands.

age norm. A range of ages at which average children reach developmental milestones.

Sitting

Learning to sit takes several months. The baby first must gain strength in the neck and back. The baby must also be able to control the head.

Babies can sit briefly with support (being held or with pillows placed at their backs) at three or four months of age. By age seven months, most can sit for a short time without support. For longer periods of sitting, they often

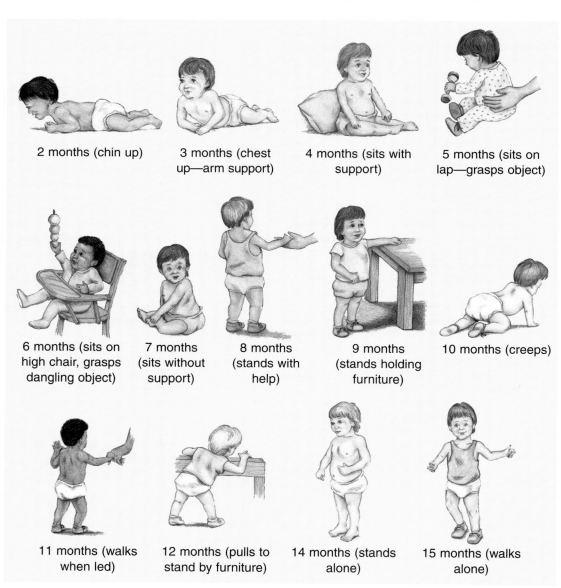

2 months (chin up)

3 months (chest up—arm support)

4 months (sits with support)

5 months (sits on lap—grasps object)

6 months (sits on high chair, grasps dangling object)

7 months (sits without support)

8 months (stands with help)

9 months (stands holding furniture)

10 months (creeps)

11 months (walks when led)

12 months (pulls to stand by furniture)

14 months (stands alone)

15 months (walks alone)

7-3 A baby gains control over the head and neck before the leg muscles.

lean forward and support themselves with their arms and legs, 7-5. They may even topple over if distracted. Progress in sitting is rapid in the next few months. By nine months, most babies can sit without support.

Leg Control

Leg control is the last phase of head-to-foot development. With leg control, locomotion really begins. (*Locomotion* is the ability to move from place to place.) Babies usually go through the stages of crawling, creeping, standing, and walking.

7-4 This baby can raise his head and chest high for rather long periods of time.
Used with permission of Lakeshore Learning Materials, Carson, CA

Ties with Family & Community

Visit a child care program that serves infants of various ages. Choose four or five babies who represent different ages. Watch the babies closely and record your observations. Compare the babies' abilities to sit, move about, and grasp objects. Share your findings with the class. What do your observations tell you about the way in which infants grow and develop?

7-5 Until back muscles are strong, leaning forward helps babies to sit unaided.
American Guidance Service, Inc.

Crawling

How can you tell when a baby is gaining leg control? When the hands and feet work together smoothly, this shows leg control. Babies play with their own feet and toes at about seven months. They begin to crawl at the same time, 7-6. Babies **crawl** by pulling with the arms. They do not lift their abdomens from the floor.

Creeping

Babies may begin **creeping** between six and eight months. Creeping means to move by using the hands and knees or hands and feet. Babies begin to creep by lifting their abdomens and hips off the floor alternately. The movement may become a rhythmical, rocking motion. Within a couple of months, many babies can move forward or backward on hands and knees (or on hands and feet) with their abdomens off the floor, 7-7.

Standing and Walking

Six-month-old babies enjoy standing when supported under the arms. They push with their feet and bounce on adults' laps. A few months later, babies can pull to a standing position. When babies stand alone, they often enjoy **cruising**, or walking by holding something for support.

At first babies stand with support, holding on to a stable object. As they develop, babies stand further away from objects. They use large objects for balance by holding on with only one of their hands. They also take a few cautious steps between objects and people, 7-8. Most babies first

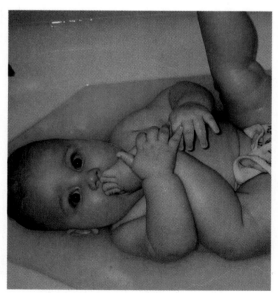

7-6 Playing with toes is a sign of the leg control needed for crawling.

7-7 To creep, this baby must raise the trunk of her body and coordinate the movements of her arms and legs.
© John Shaw

7-8 With adults ready to "catch," a baby who is almost ready to walk will take a few steps.
© John Shaw

stand alone at between 12 and 14 months and begin walking a few weeks later.

Center-to-Extremities Development

In center-to-extremities development, control begins with the trunk, then arms, hands, and fingers. This control extends to the hips, then legs, feet, and toes. Children can use their arms and hands to crawl and lift objects before they can use the hand and finger control needed to stack blocks. As you can see, the ability to control the body begins with the center of the body and moves outward.

Control of the arms, hands, and fingers develops in stages, 7-9. As you read earlier, the baby comes into the world with a grasping reflex called the *Palmar reflex*. With this reflex, the baby will automatically grasp whatever is placed in the hand. At two

crawl. To move by pulling with the arms but not lifting the abdomen from the floor.

creeping. Moving by using the hands and knees or the hands and feet with the abdomen off the floor.

cruising. Walking by holding something for support.

Grasping Ability

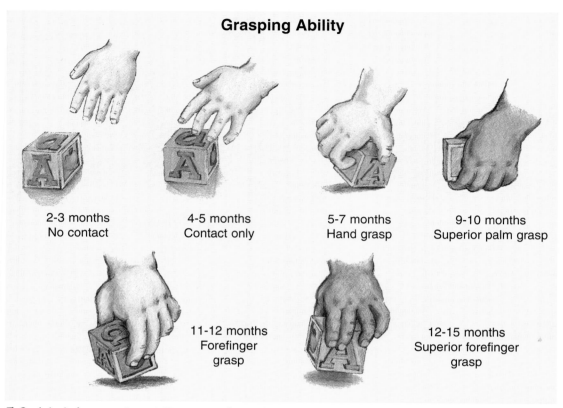

2-3 months
No contact

4-5 months
Contact only

5-7 months
Hand grasp

9-10 months
Superior palm grasp

11-12 months
Forefinger
grasp

12-15 months
Superior forefinger
grasp

7-9 A baby's grasping ability goes through stages. In the beginning, a baby has a rather clumsy grasp, using the fingers to press an object to the palm. Later the baby can grasp precisely, using the index finger and thumb.
Thomas J. Roberts

months, babies begin to swipe at objects in an attempt to grasp them.

When the baby is about four months, the grasping reflex is replaced by **voluntary grasping** (the intentional act of grasping of an object). The first grasps are rather crude, but with practice, the baby refines his or her skills. Voluntary grasping is well developed between ages five to six months. At this time, a baby can grasp one object that is handed to him or her.

Six- and seven-month olds usually bring any grasped item directly to the mouth to explore it. At seven months, babies can accept two objects handed to them. A month or two later, babies can use the thumb in opposition to the forefingers to pick up an object. This is the most complex grasp the baby will learn. It is called the *pincer grasp*. Ten-month-olds can often accept three objects handed to them.

Differences in Physical Development

With few exceptions, the order of physical development is the same for every child. However, each child develops at his or her own rate. The rate is affected by heredity, nutrition, illnesses, and activity. Whether a child is praised and encouraged (environment) can also make a difference. Some infants develop more quickly than the age norm; others lag behind.

A particular infant may also develop quickly in one area but more slowly in another.

If development seems to be much slower than the norms, parents should talk to a doctor. Regular medical care is the best way to find and treat problems that may exist. A doctor, parent educator, or other child development professional might also advise the parents how to best encourage this area of the child's development.

voluntary grasping. The intentional grasping of objects.

Summing It Up

A baby's physical development is rapid during the first year. Length and weight increase quickly. The baby's body proportions soon change. The bones begin to develop. Teeth begin to appear in a certain order.

Motor development is the ability to control the large and small muscles. Movements using these muscles are called motor skills. Examples include walking; crawling; and using the arms, hands, and fingers. Motor development occurs rapidly in the first year.

Control over the body comes in a slow, predictable pattern. Babies' reactions to what they see and hear are general at first and then become more specific. Control of the body begins from head to foot and also goes from the trunk outward. There is a sequence to babies' motor development.

All children develop physically in much the same way. The rate of development may vary because it can be affected by heredity, environment, nutrition, illnesses, and activity. Parents who have concerns about the rate of their child's development should seek a doctor's advice.

Reviewing Key Concepts

Write your answers on a separate sheet of paper.

1. Most babies (add half, double, triple) their birthweights during the first year.
2. True or false. The rate of growth over the months is more important than the measurement of total growth.
3. True or false. In the first year, the baby gets longer because the legs grow.
4. What are three changes that occur in the bones during development?
5. True or false. Motor development is the way children learn how to play with others and share their toys.
6. True or false. There is a pattern to children's physical development.
7. Which best describes the motor skill development of infants?
    A. Infants develop the same motor skills at the same time.
    B. Infants develop rapidly and slowly in the same areas.
    C. Infants learn at the same rate but the sequence of skills varies.
    D. Infants learn in the same sequence but the rate varies.
8. The baby gains body control in a certain order. Number the following motor skills in order of occurrence.
    _____ sits without support with back straight
    _____ raises the head while on abdomen
    _____ creeps
    _____ walks
    _____ rolls over from front to back
    _____ stands without help
    _____ picks up object with thumb used in opposition to finger
9. Reflexes are _____ (learned, unlearned). Voluntary movements are _____ (learned, unlearned).

Using Your Knowledge

1. **Mathematics.** Interview 4 to 6 parents of young children. Ask each parent what the baby's weight and height were at birth, six months, and one year. Record these figures in a master list. Showing your work, figure the average weight and height for this group of babies at each age. How do these figures compare to those given in Figure 7-1?
2. **Art.** Draw a cartoon featuring an infant who is learning a new fine- or gross-motor skill. Show what the baby might think about gaining this skill and how parents might respond.
3. **Child Development/ Communication.** As a group or class project, write a one- or two-page brochure that explains at what ages parents can expect their children to learn certain motor skills. You may also find pictures or drawings to illustrate the various skills. The brochure could be checked by a physician before making copies. Find out whether copies could be given to new parents at the hospital, posted in medical offices, or printed in a local newspaper.

4. **Child Development/Parenting.** Create a homemade toy that would encourage an infant to develop a fine- or gross-motor skill. You can use household items to create the toy, but make sure the toy will be safe and appropriate for use by infants. Demonstrate your toy to the class and explain what skill it would promote.

5. **Technology.** Work with a partner to visit a Web site designed for parents. Search for information that would help the parents of infants understand their child's physical development in the first year. With your teacher's approval, print out the information. Use the computer to write a review of this information. Based on what you have learned in the chapter, does the advice seem sound to you? Why or why not?

Making Observations

1. Observe a doctor giving a well-baby exam. Ask the doctor to explain each procedure. Note weight and length as well as head and chest measurements. Also note heart and breathing rates and reflexive and voluntary movement. How does the baby's progress compare to age norms? What progress has the baby made since the last checkup?

2. Visit a child care program that serves infants of various ages. Choose four or five babies who represent different ages. Watch the babies closely and record your observations. Compare the babies' abilities to sit, move about, and grasp objects.

3. Observe two infants who are the same age. How do they differ in their physical maturity? How do they differ in their motor skills? Does one infant have a lag in maturity or skills? If so, did the parent say anything that explains the lag, such as low birthweight or serious illness?

4. Observe how several babies move toward a toy. Describe exactly how each baby moves toward the toy. (Often babies use more than one motor skill to reach a toy.)

Thinking Further

1. Some people believe babies should be fat. Why do some people have this perception? Can such a perception lead to problems?

2. Parents sometimes push their babies to walk early. Can this be harmful to babies? Why or why not?

3. As you read, the grasping reflex is not highly developed until almost one year of age. Does this mean parents can assume their baby is not able to grasp small objects on the floor and insert them into his or her mouth, nose, or ears? Why or why not?

Chapter 8
Intellectual Development of the Infant

After studying this chapter, you will be able to
- describe how and what infants learn.
- explain how infants express what they know through language.
- identify the order in which infants learn.

Eleven-month-old Gregory doesn't say much. He points to objects he wants instead of using words. Gregory's cousin Keisha is also eleven months old. She "talks" constantly and says many single words. She calls her parents by name and uses words like *hi, bye, eat,* and *no* to express what she wants. Her language skills make Keisha seem older and smarter than Gregory. Gregory's parents are beginning to wonder whether his language development is slow. They also fear this might be a sign of problems with his intellectual development.

Intellectual development is how people learn, what they learn, and how they express what they know through language. (It is also called *mental* or *cognitive development*.) During the baby's first year, intellectual development happens as quickly as physical development.

Babies come into the world using all their sense organs. They react to **stimuli** (sound, light, and others) with certain reflexes. Within 12 months, infants have highly developed sense organs and motor skills. They use these to learn about people, objects, places, and events in their world. At birth, the main sound babies make is crying. By the end of the first year, they know many words. Some can even say a few words.

How Infants Learn

For many years people have wondered how infants learn. Learning involves more than physical development. Most researchers in child development believe babies *want* to learn. Each month babies exert more and more effort to explore their world, 8-1.

Brain Development Supports Learning

As you read in chapter 1, the complex building process of the brain does not occur all at once. Different parts of the brain get priority at different times. At given times, certain experiences are especially helpful to brain development. These times are called windows of opportunity.

 intellectual development. How people learn, what they learn, and how they express what they know through language.

stimuli. An agent, such as light or sound, that directly influences the activity of the sense organs.

8-1 Each month, infants exert more and more effort to explore their world.

Experiences that are repeated or like others reinforce a baby's learning. New experiences expand a baby's knowledge.

Brain development research suggests the following three factors affect the rate of mental development:

❖ the baby's physical development (mainly brain growth)
❖ the baby's environment
❖ the interaction of the first two factors; that is, using the windows of opportunity

A baby's brain and sense organs mature a lot during the first year. This helps babies learn. As motor skills develop, infants are able to move toward many sights, sounds, and other learning experiences. Research provides support for areas of brain development that have long been recognized as major mental learnings of infancy. For example, brain research has noted much activity in the motor and vision centers of the brain.

Motor Center

As reflexes wane, much activity occurs in the motor center. Wiring here begins at two months. At this time, babies begin the multi-year process of learning voluntary gross-motor movements. Wiring for fine-motor movements begins at two or three months. This is when babies make their first attempts to grasp objects.

Vision Center

Vision is needed quite early in life. For this reason, the vision center is very active in early infancy. Their maturing eyes and brain wiring helps them look at people's faces and objects. Infants need many chances to see interesting objects.

First to mature is the ability of the baby to see through each eye clearly. Although they do not have the acuity (ability to see objects sharply) of adults, by to two three months, infants can see objects at many distances very clearly.

Between one and three months of age, babies begin to look at objects with both eyes. Watching a young infant, the adult may notice the baby's eyes do not seem to work together. Often, one eye drifts off focus. At first the baby's brain "sees" two slightly separated images of the same object. Around three months, the baby's brain can fuse the image, or see it as one object using both eyes. To fuse an image requires the eyes to stay focused together on the object. The window of opportunity for fusing images is very short. (Fusing images should happen naturally unless the baby has weak eye muscles.)

Once the baby can fuse images, he or she has what is called binocular vision. **Binocular vision** is necessary recognizing how far away an object is. Thus, the eyes guide the hand in knowing how the arm must extend before grasping. The eyes also guide the feet in knowing how far down the next step will be.

Vision is highly important to learning other things, too. Activity in the vision center of the brain peaks at eight months. At this time, the baby begins inspecting everything—the details of their world and thus adding to mental learnings.

Thinking and Memory Centers

Instead of just seeing, hearing, and touching, babies try to make sense of people, objects, sounds, and events. Babies don't just try to figure out what is happening, however. They also try to cause things to happen, such as making their cradle gym bounce or

making a ball roll. Babies like to repeat and vary these events, too. Brain development research suggests that wiring in the thinking and memory centers of the brain begins at 6 months. Because thinking and memory are so complex, wiring in these centers continues for about 10 years.

Just as an infant needs good nutrition for physical growth, he or she also needs a good mental diet. Interesting things to see, hear, and touch are "food for thought." Because the world is new to the infant, common objects and experiences provide a rich mental diet. The adult's face, a cardboard box, some pans and spoons, or a trip in the yard can provide good learning experiences, 8-2.

Perception

Perception involves organizing information that comes through the senses. This is a major step in learning. People perceive by noting how things are alike and different in size, color, shape, and texture. Perceptions come through the senses about form, space, weight, and numbers.

binocular vision. Type of vision that involves fusing an image so it appears as one image using both eyes.

perception. Organizing information that comes through the senses.

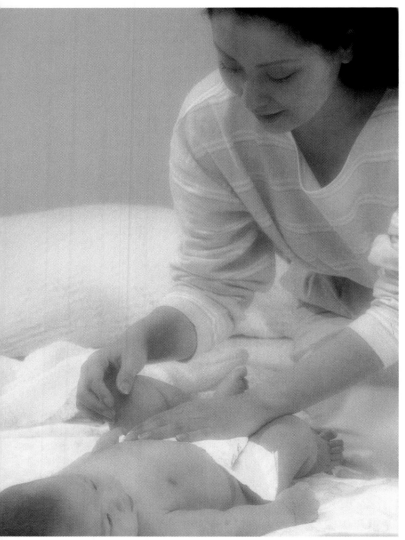

8-2 Common experiences, such as interacting with a parent during daily routines, provide a rich mental diet for the infant.

Perception also involves how fast the brain organizes information. For example, a mature reader can tell the difference between *b* and *d* faster than a beginning reader.

Finally, perception involves the way a person reacts to different sensory experiences. As an example, a child in a room crowded with strangers may run to his or her mother. However, if the child is alone with the mother, he or she may play with a toy on the floor rather than in the mother's lap.

Perceptual Learning

The process of developing perception is called **perceptual learning**. Perceptual learning happens because the sense organs mature and preferences for certain stimuli change.

The sense organs develop at rapid rates. At birth, infants can hear differences between high- and low-pitched sounds. They can move their bodies to the rhythm of adult speech. By three months, babies can tell the difference in the sounds of words like *daddy* and *mama*. Their vision improves as their eye muscles become strong enough to focus on objects.

Changes in Preferences

From the time of birth, babies are bombarded with all types of stimuli. In order to learn, infants must choose from among these stimuli. See 8-3 through 8-6 to learn why babies tend to choose some objects over others.

 perceptual learning. The process of developing perception.

Babies Choose One Object over Another

Babies have certain preferences. They prefer to play or interact more with one object than another. Researchers believe infants have inborn abilities to choose the stimuli that will most help them learn. Studies show the following changes in preferences, or choices, they make:

❖ Preferences change from parts of objects to complete objects.

At first, infants react to, or study, parts of objects. Later, they pay more attention to the entire object. For instance, at two months they smile at eyes drawn on a blank background. At three months, they study a picture that has eyes and a nose. By five months they smile only at the picture of the full face. They prefer the complete objects rather than parts of objects.

❖ Preferences change from simple to complex objects.

Until babies are almost two months old, they do not prefer one object over another. After that, babies prefer more complex objects. For example, babies prefer 3-D objects over 2-D pictures. They prefer patterned or textured cards over plain white or solid-colored cards. Babies also prefer a drawn human face over any other drawn pattern or solid-colored card. Other preferences include slow-moving objects over nonmoving objects and curved lines over straight lines. They may show little or no reaction to complex stimuli because they can not understand them.

❖ Preferences change from familiar to new objects.

After two months of age, babies begin to explore things that are new to them. They ignore objects that are too different because they may not understand them.

8-3 Infants change their preferences for certain objects.

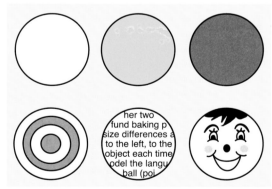

8-4 When shown each of these figures, babies' preferences (from most to least liked) were—circle with face, circle with words, concentric circles, red circle, yellow circle, and white circle. (Frantz's study.)

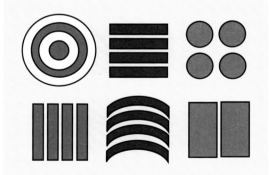

8-5 When shown each of these pairs of lines, infants liked the curved lines more than the straight lines. (Frantz's study.)

Infants' Preferences for Experiences

Approximate Age	Seeing	Hearing	Touching
Birth to 3 months	❖ Follows slow-moving objects with eyes. ❖ Looks when held to shoulder. ❖ Looks at hairline part of face at 1 month. ❖ Looks at eyes, nose, and mouth at 2 months. Often smiles. ❖ Prefers patterns to solids. ❖ Follows the gaze of an adult to look where the adult is looking at 2 months.	❖ Reacts physically to sounds by opening eyes widely, startling, or making other movements. ❖ Is calmed by gentle voice. ❖ Connects voices with faces at 1 month.	❖ Lessens reflexive grasping and begins voluntary grasping between 6 weeks and 3 months. ❖ Holds objects less than 1 minute. ❖ Swipes at objects suspended overhead at 2 to 3 months.
3–6 months	❖ Prefers red and blue to green and yellow. ❖ Enjoys mirrors but does not know his or her own image until after 1 year of age. ❖ Grasps what is seen. ❖ Enjoys small objects. ❖ Imitates facial expressions.	❖ Learns the meaning of familiar sounds, such as making food and a nearby parent. ❖ Reacts to differences in tones of voices. ❖ Tries to locate source of sounds. ❖ Repeats own sounds. ❖ Tells differences in sounds, such as *ba* and *pa*.	❖ Grasps with both hands and often clasps hands when object is out of reach at 3 to 4 months. ❖ Takes 1 object at a time. ❖ Plays with hands at 4 months. ❖ Plays with toes at 5 to 6 months. ❖ Mouths all objects; opens mouth well in advance of approaching objects. ❖ Opens hands wider for larger objects than for smaller objects.

(Continued)

8-6 Babies change their seeing, hearing, and touching preferences as they try to learn about their new worlds.

Infants' Preferences for Experiences (Continued)

Approximate Age	Seeing	Hearing	Touching
6 to 9 months	❖ Examines objects with eyes and hands. ❖ Recognizes drop-offs (but is not safe from falls). ❖ Looks for hidden (covered) toys.	❖ Learns noises different toys make. ❖ Notes differences between questions and statements by changes in pitch. ❖ Enjoys hearing singing and tries to sing along.	❖ Handles objects by turning, shaking, and banging. ❖ Enjoys toys with moving parts such as dials and wheels. ❖ Holds own bottle. ❖ Uses one object to work another, such as hitting a drum with a stick. ❖ Transfers objects from one hand to the other.
9 to 12 months	❖ Shows less interest in faces except to quickly identify the familiar face and the strange face. ❖ Looks where crawling. ❖ Watches dropped objects with interest to see whether they roll, break, or bounce ❖ Enjoys hiding games, such as hide and seek.	❖ Imitates sounds. ❖ Enjoys hearing own name. ❖ May make sounds of some animals. ❖ Knows meaning of many words and may respond to requests.	❖ Predicts weight of objects with correct arm tension. ❖ Enjoys self-feeding. ❖ Shows held objects to others. ❖ Enjoys dropping objects into pails and boxes. ❖ Enjoys stacking blocks and knocking them down. ❖ Takes lids off objects. Pulls and pushes roll toys. ❖ Turns knobs and switches. ❖ Nests (puts smaller into larger) objects.

Cognition

Cognition is the act or process of knowing or understanding. Cognition gives meaning to perceptions. The baby's brain begins to piece together perceptions to form a picture in the mind.

Jean Piaget, a Swiss psychologist, described how humans learn. He believed people learn by exploring on their own in a stimulating environment. Because of reflexes such as sucking and grasping, people begin to explore the world from birth. As reflexes disappear, voluntary movement and sensory perceptions help infants explore.

The Sensorimotor Stage

Because infants explore with their senses and motor actions, Piaget called the first stage of mental development the **sensorimotor stage**. This stage begins at birth, and most children complete it in two years. During this stage, infants use their senses and motor skills to learn and communicate. Learning at this time is important. This time is the basis for all future mental development.

Piaget described the learnings of the sensorimotor stage through a series of processes that become more and more complex. He found that children solved problems by working through a certain order, 8-7.

Practicing Reflexes and Repeating New Learnings

Piaget observed how infants go from the stage of practicing reflexes they already know, such as sucking,

Piaget's Stages of Cognitive Development

Stage 1: Sensorimotor Stage (Birth to 2 years)
  a. Substage I: Practicing Reflexes (birth to 1 month)
  b. Substage II: Repeating New Learnings (1 to 4 months)
  c. Substage III: Beginning to Control Their World (4 to 8 months)
  d. Substage IV: Applying Learnings to Solve Complex Problems (8 to 12 months)
  e. Substage V: Discovering New Ways to Solve Problems (12 to 18 months)
  f. Substage VI: Beginning of Thought (18 months to 2 years)
Stage 2: Preoperational Stage (2 to 7 years)
Stage 3: Concrete Operations Stage (7 to 11 years)
Stage 4: Formal Operations Stage (11 years on)

8-7 Piaget described how infants use their senses and motor skills to learn. Infants are in the sensorimotor stage.

grasping, and crying, to changing some of their reflex skills. For example, they may suck their thumbs or open and close their hands. They repeat these actions often.

Beginning to Control

Infants then begin to control their world by making a mental connection between what they do and what happens. If they kick the cradle gym, the bells ring and the characters move. When they cry, a parent comes to see what they want. Infants try many new actions during this time. They also realize that objects exist even when they cannot see them. For example, they look to see where something has been dropped.

Solving Problems

Piaget believed that by age one year, babies apply all their learnings to solve other kinds of problems. They may mouth an object like a teething ring. Infants may squeeze, hit, turn, and shake an object to see what it will do. By combining several actions, they discover new ways to solve problems. For example, a baby may push away a box in order to grasp a toy.

Imitating

Children learn by **imitating**, or doing what they have seen others do. This is an important way to learn for many years. Babies begin by imitating simple actions. For example, they might bang their hands on a table after seeing an adult do this action. As they mature, babies can imitate more complex actions, such as a short series of actions.

What Infants Learn

As babies explore their world, they learn many concepts. A **concept** is an idea formed by combining what is known about a person, object, place, quality, or event. Thinking is organized through concepts. For example, if you see an animal you believe is a cat, you immediately think of all you know about cats. Then you note how this animal is like or unlike other cats you recall. Children must learn to understand the ideas of cats, then animals, and finally living creatures, 8-8.

Concepts change as the child's brain matures and experiences increase. Concepts change from simple to complex. A child understands the word *chair* before knowing about the many types of chairs. Concepts also change from concrete to abstract. For example, children can draw themselves and their parents (concrete) before they can draw other people (more abstract).

As children grow, their concepts change from incorrect to correct. First, a child may call all men *Daddy*. Later, they understand the concept of *men*.

Concepts are different for each person, too. No two people have

cognition. The act or process of knowing or understanding.

sensorimotor stage. The first of Piaget's stages of cognitive (intellectual) development in which children use their senses and motor skills to learn and communicate with others.

imitating. Copying the actions of someone else.

concept. An idea formed by combining what is known about a person, object, place, quality, or event.

8-8 Children must learn to understand the concepts of cats, then animals, and finally living creatures.

exactly the same experiences. Not only do experiences differ, but also many concepts involve emotions. For example, the concept of school may be pleasant for one person but unpleasant for another.

During the first year, infants form many concepts. These concepts help infants make sense of their world. The concepts learned further their mental development.

8-9 Babies begin to make order out of what they see, hear, smell, taste, and touch.

Perceptual Concepts

Information comes to infants through their senses. At this time, babies begin to make order of what they see, hear, smell, taste, and touch, 8-9. They begin to mentally organize this information. The following sections describe major perceptual concepts children learn in the first year.

Object Constancy or Sameness

Object constancy is knowing that objects remain the same even if they appear different. For example, a child may see a big airplane with bright colors take off and then look small and gray in the distant sky. Children learn that, although it may look

| A | B | C | D |

8-10 Seeing a chair from different views while crawling (A and B) and later while walking (C and D) helps a baby learn object constancy.

different in size, shape, or color, it is still the same plane, 8-10. Object constancy begins during the first year. It is not fully developed until the second or third year.

Object Concept

Object concept is the understanding the world of objects, people, and events are separate from one's interactions with them. Parents are often the first "objects" with whom babies relate. Although they relate to them, they come to see they are separate from themselves. This understanding must happen before they can develop object concept about all people and objects in a general sense.

Object concept has two parts—object identity and object permanence. A child who has object identity knows that an object stays the same from one time to the next. For example, a toy bear is the same bear each time the child sees it, and Daddy is the same Daddy although perhaps

he is dressed differently and doing different tasks from time to time.

Object permanence is knowing that people, objects, and places still exist even when they are no longer seen, felt, or heard. For example, a baby may know mother is in the house, even though she is not in the

object constancy. The ability to learn that objects remain the same even if they appear different.

object concept. The ability to understand that an object, person, or event is separate from one's interaction with it.

object identity. The ability to learn that an object stays the same from one time to the next.

object permanence. The ability to learn that people, objects, and places still exist even when they are no longer seen, felt, or heard.

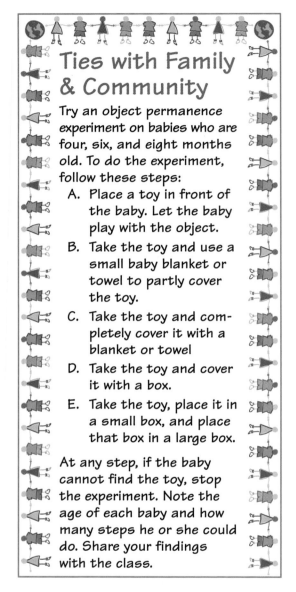

Ties with Family & Community

Try an object permanence experiment on babies who are four, six, and eight months old. To do the experiment, follow these steps:

A. Place a toy in front of the baby. Let the baby play with the object.

B. Take the toy and use a small baby blanket or towel to partly cover the toy.

C. Take the toy and completely cover it with a blanket or towel

D. Take the toy and cover it with a box.

E. Take the toy, place it in a small box, and place that box in a large box.

At any step, if the baby cannot find the toy, stop the experiment. Note the age of each baby and how many steps he or she could do. Share your findings with the class.

room. Like most concepts, object permanence develops with many experiences over time. The concept begins to develop as early as a month or two of age. At this time, the baby will stare for a second in the place where an object or person was just seen but has disappeared. A few months later, the baby will gleefully recover an object partially hidden. Toward the end of infancy, babies will watch an adult completely hide an object and will then "search" for it.

Depth Perception

Depth perception is the ability to tell how far away something is. It requires the development of binocular vision. Depth perception is needed for safety purposes. It keeps a person from stepping off an object far from the ground. People also use this skill to judge how far something is so they can reach it. Depth perception is rather well developed by seven to nine months of age. However, children are not safe from falls for many years.

Beginnings of Language: Brain Development Research

Language is closely related to mental development. Brain development research shows language wiring begins at birth, if not before, 8-11. The first wiring has to do with the sounds of language, for these are needed to understand speech and to speak. The wiring follows this sequence:

❖ During the first half-year, babies distinguish small differences in sounds. They are prepared to learn any language.

8-11 Even before birth, this baby's brain was busy being wired to create sounds and understand language.

❖ Because there are so many connections, pruning begins at six months of age. Babies come to notice only major differences in sounds in the languages they hear from caring adults. (Brain development research says they ignore language from the radio or television.) Even in adults, the brain detects small differences in sound through context clues; that is, through hearing the entire word or the word used in a phrase. For this reason, spelling words are often pronounced and then used in sentences.

❖ By 12 months of age, babies complete the auditory maps needed for their own language. Learning to speak another language without "an accent" becomes much more difficult as the wiring for the sounds of other languages begins to be pruned away.

Not only is wiring for language sounds begun early, between 9 and 12 months, the brain's speech center begins the wiring process.

Language relates to mental growth in other ways, too. As people understand more concepts, their vocabularies tend to grow. A person's **vocabulary** consists of the words he or she understands and uses.

Because language and mental growth are closely related, vocabulary words are often thought to measure mental growth. However, this is not always true. People can do and understand more than they can explain. This is especially true for infants. Their speaking vocabularies lag behind what they understand. In addition, people sometimes use words they don't understand.

depth perception. The ability to tell how far away something is.

vocabulary. The words a person understands and uses.

There is a relationship between language and social and emotional growth. Language is used to express feelings or emotions. Before infants develop language, they show feelings by crying, laughing, clinging, and other physical signs. Even young children express many of their feelings physically. They show these feelings with temper tantrums, snatching toys from others, and hitting. As children grow older, they learn to express more of their feelings in words. Through language, children learn to make friends and get along with others.

How Babies Communicate

From the time infants are born, they are communicating. Through the sounds they make, others learn to understand their language.

Crying and Cooing

Newborns do not have control over the sounds they make. They make many noises while eating and sleeping. They swallow, smack, burp, yawn, and sigh. During the first month, babies communicate by crying. Parents can quickly learn what their baby's cries mean.

Between the sixth and eighth week, most babies begin to **coo**, making light, happy sounds. Babies coo more when others talk to, smile at, and touch them.

Babbling

Between the fourth and fifth month, babies begin to babble. Babies **babble** by making a series of vowel sounds with consonant sounds slowly added to form syllables, such as *ba*, *da*, and *gi*.

Babbling is an important pretalking skill. When babbling begins, babies practice all the sounds of all the world's languages. Babies are ready to learn any language or languages they hear, 8-12. Around one year, however, they make only the sounds needed to speak the languages they hear. This is because the brain has pruned away the connections needed to make sounds from other languages.

Babbling is not **monotone** (at a single pitch). Babies babble with **inflections** (changes of pitch) to express happiness, requests, commands, and questions. Often a baby babbles with so much feeling you can almost guess what he or she is saying!

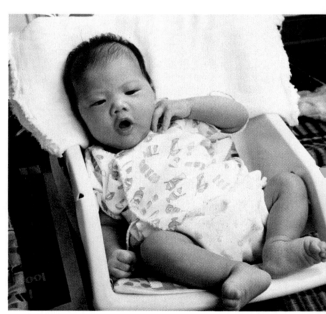

8-12 A baby babbles all the sounds of all languages.

First Words

Babies may begin talking during the last three months of the first year. Many start talking later. Most experts state that in order to count sounds as a word, the same sounds must be used each time to refer to a specific person, object, place, or event.

No wonder many babies do not talk during the first year! Before talking, babies must do the following:

❖ understand object permanence
❖ understand that people, objects, places, and events have names
❖ remember words that go with people, objects, places, and events
❖ have the ability to make the sounds
❖ realize that talking is important

Reduplication Babbling

Often, first words come from babbling. Babies do **reduplication babbling**. They repeat the same syllable over and over, such as *da-da-da-da*. An adult who hears *da-da-da-da* may say, "That's right, *Dada*." The adult may point to Daddy. Daddy may pick up the baby, smile, nod, and call himself *Dada*. With practice, the baby connects the sound, which was already mastered, to the person.

The number of words babies learn varies a great deal. Studies show that most babies say about three words by the end of the first year. Spoken vocabulary does not begin to increase quickly until later in the second year.

Passive Versus Active Vocabulary

Although babies can say only a few words, they understand many, many more. The words people understand but don't say are called their **passive vocabulary**. In contrast, **active vocabulary** includes the words used in talking or writing.

Babies' passive vocabulary far exceeds their active vocabulary. Once babies get the idea that objects in their world have names, they learn these names quickly. They even understand sentences that refer to part of their daily routines such as, "Time for breakfast." Soon their favorite spoken word may be *whaddat* (What is that?) as they begin to learn language.

coo. A light, happy sound babies begin to use to communicate between six and eight weeks after birth.

babble. To make a series of vowel sounds with consonant sounds slowly added to form syllables.

monotone. Sounds all in a single pitch.

inflections. Changes of pitch.

reduplication babbling. Repeating the same syllable over and over again.

passive vocabulary. The words a person understands but does not say.

active vocabulary. The words a person uses in talking or writing.

Babies begin to communicate their feelings by making sounds.

Summing It Up

Intellectual development includes how babies learn, what they learn, and how they communicate. The rate of development is affected by the child's physical development and the environment.

Organizing information that comes through the senses is a major step in infant learning. Babies perceive whether things are alike or different in size, color, shape, and texture. They develop perceptions of form, space, weight, and number. They begin to piece this information together and give meaning to their perceptions.

In addition to the senses, children use their motor skills to know and understand their world. As their newborn reflexes give way to voluntary movement and sensory perceptions, children begin to learn. Piaget called this first stage of mental development the sensorimotor stage. He found that children go through a series of more difficult processes before they discover new ways to solve problems.

Through children's early experiences, they form ideas, or concepts, about the world around them. As their brain matures and experiences increase, they learn various perceptual concepts. These include object constancy or sameness, object identity and permanence, and depth perception.

Language and mental development are closely related. Brain research shows that major wiring occurs in the brain's ability to distinguish the sounds of language. Toward the end of the first year, the speech center of the baby's brain becomes very active. Vocabulary tends to increase as more concepts are understood. Learning to express themselves promotes children's social and emotional development.

Crying is the baby's first communication method. Before first words are said, cooing and babbling occur. Babies have a much more extensive passive vocabulary than active vocabulary. At age one year, many babies have an active vocabulary of three words.

Reviewing Key Concepts

Write your answers on a separate sheet of paper.

1. True or false. A baby's intellectual development is slow compared to physical development during the first year.
2. What are two factors that affect the rate of intellectual development?
3. Which of the following is an example of perception?
   A. tasting a sugar cube
   B. telling the difference between a mother's face and the faces of other women
   C. calling mother *mama*
4. Which member of each pair do infants like better?
   A. 2-D pictures or 3-D objects
   B. plain white cards or solid-colored cards
   C. patterned cards or solid-colored cards
   D. human face or other patterns
   E. straight lines or curved lines
   F. new objects or familiar objects
5. True or false. Babies first study parts of an object before paying attention to the object as a whole.
6. True or false. Babies would rather play with a familiar toy than try a new toy.
7. True or false. Babies can make all the sounds needed to speak any language.
8. Which statement would Piaget support?
   A. Children learn more by exploring on their own in a stimulating environment.
   B. Children learn more when adults sit down and teach them.
   C. Children learn to the same degree whether they explore on their own or are taught by adults.
9. According to Piaget, the baby gains knowledge in a certain order. Number the following intellectual skills in order of their occurrence:
   A. _____ Babies change some of their reflex skills, such as opening and closing their hands.
   B. _____ Babies hit their hands on the high chair tray and realize they made the sound.
   C. _____ Babies exercise inborn reflexes.
   D. _____ Babies can pick up a rubber duck, place it in the water, and give it a big push.
   E. _____ Babies look for objects they have dropped.
10. Match the incidents with the perceptual concepts.
    A. depth perception
    B. object permanence
    C. object constancy
    _____ Maria is looking from the back door and sees her mother in the garden. She happily exclaims, "Mama!"
    _____ Joe is being carried in a department store by his father, who is shopping. When the father stops at one counter, Joe quickly picks up a toy car without knocking over a sign in front of the toys.
    _____ Tyrone wakes up and looks around. His mother is not in the room. He begins to cry loudly so his mother will know he is awake.

11. Pretalking skills begin at birth. Number the following skills in the order of their occurrence.

_____ cooing

_____ crying

_____ reduplication babbling

_____ babbling

_____ first words

Using Your Knowledge

1. **Technology.** Use the Internet to research brain development in the first year. Then, use the computer to write a report on your findings.
2. **Science.** Have your teacher or one student give a common word such as *blue, school, music,* or *food.* Each student should write a few phrases about what they think when they hear the word. Compare the perceptions of class members. Discuss your experiences and emotions associated with your perceptions of each word.
3. **Art.** Make a poster using words and/or drawings to describe the baby's learnings during the first year as stated by Piaget.
4. **Child Development.** Listen to a recording of the sounds of babies who are 2, 4, 6, 8, 10, and 12 months old. Try to distinguish cooing from babbling. Listen for babbling sounds that are similar to words.
5. **Communication.** Interview the parents of young children about the first words their babies said and the age the babies began to talk. Share your findings with the class, then compare them. Note the similarities and differences in the beginning of spoken language.

Making Observations

1. For one week, observe an infant exploring his or her world for 30 minutes per day. Record what the baby does during this time. What senses were used? What concepts and skills might the baby have been learning?
2. Observe infants as they see, hear, or touch objects in their environments. Compare your observations with information given in Chart 8-5.
3. Get down to observe objects from a baby's walking and crawling heights. Describe how the objects look from each of these views.
4. Observe a baby trying to talk. Identify the baby's sounds as coos or babbles. What might the baby have been saying with his or her sounds?

Thinking Further

1. Bring in several toys designed for infants. What do you think would be appealing about each toy? Make a list. What suggestions would you make to improve the appeal?
2. Hold up a given object (such as a colored cube or cylinder). How could that object look different in size? color? shape? Be specific in your explanation.
3. Suppose a friend told you it isn't important for adults to talk to babies until babies begin to talk. Do you agree or disagree? Why? What should parents do?

Your best friend has a child, Isaac, who is nine months old—the same age as your son Raul. Raul is active and assertive. He interacts well with people in his environment. Isaac is quieter and prefers to be with his parents. He cries when people talk to him. The differences between Isaac and Raul are most obvious when your family and your friend's family go places together. Your friends tell you they want Isaac to be more sociable, like Raul. They are worried about him.

After studying this chapter, you will be able to

- identify temperamental differences in babies.
- describe the infant's major first-year social tasks.
- explain the roots of four emotions—love, fear, anxiety, and anger.

Chapter 9
Social-Emotional Development of the Infant

Social-emotional development is an important type of development. It has three main parts. The first part is a person's **disposition** or mood. Some people have a more cheerful disposition, and others are more moody. The second part is learning to interact with people and social groups. These may include family members, schools, and clubs. The third part includes the ways people show feelings through emotions of love, fear, anxiety, and anger.

Social-emotional development happens as quickly during the first year as physical and intellectual development. A baby enters the world with some unique traits. These traits are the root of the child's later personality. By the end of the first year, personality traits show even more. As a baby's social world expands, the infant forms ideas about whether the world is a friendly place. The baby begins to express feelings with different emotions.

Temperamental Differences in Infants

Temperament is the tendency to react in a certain way, such as in a cheery or grumpy way. Sometimes the word *disposition* also defines the ways people react. Experts think temperament is partly inherited. They also think a person's temperament may be due to prenatal conditions and ease of birth. These factors, along with environment, shape a person's personality. A baby's temperament often shows by two or three months. In many children, but not all, temperament stays the same for years.

Some experts rate characteristics of a baby's temperament. These ratings place most babies in one of three groups. These groups are called *easy, slow to warm up,* and *difficult*.

social-emotional development. Type of development involving a person's disposition, interaction with people and social groups, and emotions.

disposition. A person's general mood.

temperament. The tendency to react in a certain way to events.

❖ Easy—Easy babies have regular habits (eating, sleeping, and others). They respond quickly to a new situation. They are cheerful.
❖ Slow to warm up—These babies take more time to adapt to new situations.
❖ Difficult—Difficult babies are irregular in their habits. They often withdraw or protest—even scream—when facing new situations.

Researchers found that 4 in 10 babies are easy. One in 10 babies are slow to warm up, and 1 in 10 are difficult. A few babies cannot be grouped because their temperaments vary from day to day.

Easy babies usually get off to a good start with their parents. Difficult babies often have a rough start. This may be because many parents feel they are doing something wrong because the baby is unhappy. If the parents are stressed, this may cause increased stress in the child. Good, constant care of difficult babies may make them happier. This supportive care includes extra holding, cuddling, and soothing. Easing these babies into new situations and alerting them to upcoming changes is also helpful.

The Infant's Growing Social World

Infants are not truly social at birth. *Social* refers to a relationship between two or more people. Social development is shaped by how other people affect the baby and how the baby affects other people. By the end of the first year,

Ties with Family & Community

Interview two parents about the expanding social world of their babies. Prepare your list of interview questions in advance. Use the following for starters:

❖ Who were the first people (not including hospital staff) to see your baby? hold your baby? feed, dress, and change your baby?
❖ Besides parents, who are other important people in your baby's life?
❖ How did your baby react to siblings and other children? How did siblings and other children react to your baby?
❖ Did your baby become attached to an object? What object?

What do the responses of the parents tell you about the differences in the social-emotional development of their babies? Report your findings to the class in an oral report.

social development is well underway. This section will focus on three aspects of social development in the first year. These three aspects are (A) interacting with others, (B) learning to trust, and (C) showing attachment.

Interacting with Others

Babies are born with tools for social development. At birth, babies can turn in the direction of the human voice. They move their bodies in the rhythm of human speech. They like to look at people's faces.

Babies understand social messages by the way others talk to, look at, or hold them. Babies send signals to others through their cries, coos, and smiles. These communications begin as early as two weeks after birth. Smiles with expressive eyes begin around the fifth or sixth week.

From the third to sixth months, babies become even better at understanding and sending social signals. They also begin to distinguish between those who care for them and strangers.

Once babies are able to creep easily and have better arm and hand control, they **initiate** (begin) social contact. For example, they may follow others around the house. They reach with their arms to signal they want to be held.

Interacting with Adults

Babies thrive most when they are held, talked to, cuddled, and comforted, 9-1. They are often happier babies, crying less than those who receive

9-1 Loving parents provide babies with their first social interactions.

little attention. Parents and caregivers help their baby's mental development as well as social development by providing lots of loving care.

Grandparents, friends, babysitters, and others are helpful to babies' total development. When these people care for and show an interest in them, babies learn to understand and trust others. This helps expand babies' social environment.

Interacting with Other Children

Babies enjoy being around **siblings** (brothers and sisters) and other children. Babies tend to watch

initiate. To begin.

siblings. Brothers and sisters.

9-2 Babies and their older brothers and sisters learn from each other.
© John Shaw

Erikson's Stages of Personality Development

Basic trust versus basic mistrust (first year of life)

Consistency in having needs met and sameness in environment leads to a feeling the world is reliable The baby develops a sense of basic trust. If the world is not seen as a reliable place, the baby develops a sense of basic mistrust.

Autonomy versus shame and doubt (second year of life)

Initiative versus guilt (preschool years)

Industry versus inferiority (middle childhood)

9-3 Learning to trust while avoiding mistrust is the social-emotional task of infancy.

and follow children. They like to play with the toys of older children. Infants learn from older children. From infants, older children learn lessons in loving and caring for others. All children benefit in these relationships, 9-2.

Learning to Trust

Trust is a key part of social development. How much a person trusts or doesn't trust other people affects how he or she interacts with them.

Many experts have researched the development of trust in infants. One of the most famous was psychologist Erik Erikson. He studied trust as one aspect of personality development, 9-3.

Erikson viewed personality as ever-changing from birth through old age. He saw the family and other factors as major influences on personality. Erikson believed personality could develop in healthy or unhealthy ways.

Erikson described personality in eight stages that cover a person's *life span* (from birth throughout life). Each stage presents a specific developmental change for the person. The stages unfold one after another throughout a person's life. During each stage, the person faces an important task that must be met. This task can have either a positive or negative outcome. No one is completely successful in any stage, but the more one is successful, the healthier the personality will be. If unsuccessful, the personality is more vulnerable during other stages. Erikson believed a person can overcome unsuccessful past tasks, but positive changes later in life are more difficult.

Each of Erikson's stages has a descriptive title that shows both outcomes of the task. For infants, the first stage is called *trust versus mistrust*. In this stage, infants learn whether to trust others or mistrust them. **Mistrust** is the most serious form of not trusting for it includes a lack of trust and feelings of suspicion.

Erikson stated that two key factors are essential in whether infants learn to trust. First, infants learn to trust by having a consistent environment. This is an environment that includes sameness in routines, caregivers, and surroundings. Second, infants learn to trust by having their basic needs met promptly each time. Babies' basic needs include food, clothing, warmth, sleep, cleanliness, cuddling, playing, and communicating with others.

According to Erikson, if a baby's basic needs are met and with consistency, then babies feel the world is a good and happy place. This helps them learn to trust others and adapt to their world. If basic needs go unmet or partly met and the surroundings are less than stable, then babies feel helpless and confused. They develop mistrust.

Erikson also believed that feelings of trust or mistrust are the basis for later feelings toward others. Adults can either be trusting or mistrusting persons. Figure 9-4 shows the cycle of how parents affect babies and babies, in turn, affect parents. The cycle shows that meeting babies' needs is helpful to adults as well as babies.

Showing Attachment

Attachment is closeness between people that remains over time. In chapter 5, you learned about a special type of attachment called bonding. *Bonding* is the feeling of love parents have for their baby that often begins soon after birth. During the first year, babies come to care for their parents, too. This is called attachment, 9-5.

Brain development research indicates that healthy brain development depends on attachment. Overcoming stress throughout life is easier for those babies who formed strong attachments early in infancy.

Babies develop an attachment to those who care for them. They show

 mistrust. The most serious form of not trusting, which includes a lack of trust and feelings of suspicion.

attachment. Closeness between people that remains over time.

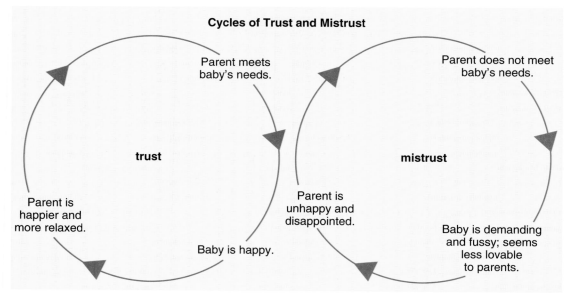

Cycles of Trust and Mistrust

Parent meets baby's needs.

trust

Baby is happy.

Parent is happier and more relaxed.

Parent is unhappy and disappointed.

Parent does not meet baby's needs.

mistrust

Baby is demanding and fussy; seems less lovable to parents.

9-4 When a baby's needs are met, both baby and parent are happy.

this in a number of ways. **Attachment behaviors** are actions one person demonstrates to another to show closeness to that person. Attachment behaviors include trying to stay close to, following, or clinging to the adult. Smiling, crying, or calling are other attachment behaviors. However, babies who cry the loudest are not always the ones with the strongest attachment. For example, a strongly attached baby who is sure of the parent's return may not cry much when left. Attachment is developmental; thus attachment behaviors often occur in a set order, 9-6.

Attachment is closely related to fear of strangers and fear of being left alone. These emotions are described in the next section.

Attachment can be good. For healthy social-emotional development, attachment is important. Everyone needs to love and be loved. Attachment also helps mental development.

Bonding and Attachment

Relationship	Term Used
Parents come to love their babies soon after birth. Parents ⟶ Baby	Bonding
Babies whose needs are met come to love their parents. Children realize this tie after six months of age. Baby ⟶ Parents	Attachment

9-5 Bonding and attachment are terms used for two loving relationships between parents and babies.

Development of Attachment Behaviors

Approximate Age	Attachment Behaviors
1 month	Baby can recognize familiar and unfamiliar voices.
2 weeks to 2 months	Baby smiles.
3 months	Baby gives joyful movements, such as kicks, coos, and gurgles. Baby may even laugh.
4 to 5 months	Baby becomes still and breathing becomes shallow when unknown people are close.
7 to 8 months	Baby cries when a stranger is nearby or when the baby is left alone.

9-6 Attachment behaviors are closely related to the baby's mental development.

Attached babies tend to explore their worlds through play more than babies who are not attached to others.

Infants Express Emotions

Long before feelings are expressed, the emotion center of the brain becomes active. Brain development research shows that by two months, babies begin to construct emotions. Babies first get visual cues of emotions in others at this age. Feelings are

complex and they are tied to thinking, memory, and even language. For this reason, emotions are wired over a rather long period.

During the first three or four months, babies have two basic responses to their worlds. The first is distress, shown by crying and muscle tension. The second is excitement, shown by smiling, cooing, and wiggling the body. By the end of the first year, babies can express love, fear, anxiety, anger, jealousy, joy, and sadness. Babies who express a range of emotions, from happy to unhappy, show healthy development.

Emotions are thoughts that lead to feelings and cause changes in the body. For example, if you are upset at someone or something (a thought), you may become angry (a feeling). Your anger may increase your heart rate (change in your body).

Because thinking changes, the situations that cause emotions change over the years. Four-year-olds may fear monsters in their rooms at night, but older children do not. As people mature, the way they respond to their emotions changes, too. For example, a

attachment behaviors. Actions one person demonstrates to another person to show closeness to that person.

emotions. Thoughts that lead to feelings and cause changes in the body.

two-year-old may throw a temper tantrum when angry. Adults show their anger in more mature ways. When people act their age, they use **age-appropriate behaviors**. These are proper or expected ways to express emotions at certain ages.

Love

Before love can develop, babies must realize they are separate from caregivers and others. (This is an example of object concept, which was described in chapter 8.) Over time, babies come to know that other people make them feel full, clean, and comforted. As babies associate these feelings with their caregivers, they become attached to these adults. They begin to feel and show love and affection, 9-7. Babies show love not only to important adults but also to children who keep them company.

Besides loving people, babies become attached to objects, including pacifiers, stuffed toys, and even blankets. Babies seem to need these objects even more when they are upset or afraid. They also seem to need them when routines change. Sometimes adults worry about children's love for these objects. However, such attachments

9-7 Babies come to love those who care for them.

tend to give babies security and are important to them. Children will give up these objects in time.

Fear

At birth, babies react with the startle reflex when they hear loud sounds or do not have support for their bodies. Babies are not showing true fear with this reflex. This is because the change in their bodies is caused by reflex rather than by a feeling, which would be driven by a thought (emotion). However, certain fears are thought to have their roots in the startle reflex. By four or five months, some babies fear adult strangers. They may even fear adults they know who have new hairstyles, hats, sunglasses, or other such changes. Babies do not seem to fear young children they do not know.

Fear as an emotion occurs at around six months. To be fearful, babies must know they can be hurt. The following are the two kinds of fear:

❖ Fear of the unknown. Infants fear adult strangers, a new bed, or a sudden movement. They also fear different sounds, such as the crack of thunder or a screaming siren.

❖ Fear learned from direct experiences or teachings. Infants may fear getting soap in their eyes, a doctor's office, or a snapping dog because of a negative past experience. They also fear hot stoves and bad dogs because of an adult's constant warning.

What adults say and how they act affect babies' fears. Adults who act or look fearful in a storm, for example, will cause children to be fearful. Adults who tell babies that many situations can hurt them teach children to fear. Of course, some fear is good. However, too much fear is not healthy. Fear affects motor and mental development because fearful babies often will not welcome new experiences.

Anxiety

Anxiety is fear of a possible future event. Sometimes the words *worry* or *concern* are used to describe anxiety.

Anxiety is seen in babies most often between 10 and 12 months. Before this time, babies cannot anticipate a future event. The first anxiety of an infant is called **separation anxiety**, 9-8. During this time, babies become anxious when the adults they love must leave them for a time. This is common when a parent goes to work or leaves the house on an errand. The anxiety begins when the baby sees clues of

age-appropriate behaviors. Proper or expected ways to express emotions at certain ages.

anxiety. Fear of a possible future event.

separation anxiety. Anxiety common in babies caused by the fear that loved ones who leave them will not return.

9-8 Older babies may find it hard to separate from their parents, even at bedtime.

the upcoming separation, such as a parent picking up car keys or telling the baby good-bye. Separation anxiety is more intense when strangers, such as new babysitters, are near.

Most two-year-olds show less separation anxiety than younger babies do. Separation anxiety in babies younger than two years may be due to the following:

❖ Babies younger than two years of age cannot understand why parents must leave.
❖ Unlike two-year-olds, who remember their parents have returned after each separation, babies do not have the memory of past events.
❖ During the first year, babies need someone to fulfill their needs. (Relying on someone else to meet your needs is called **dependence**.) Two-year-olds are more **independent** (want to do things for themselves).
❖ Two-year-olds can express their needs better. Young babies cannot express their needs to others well, especially to those adults they do not know. Being unable to express themselves can lead to anxiety.

Anger

Almost from birth babies show what is called *infant rage*. Infant rage occurs when the baby is distressed. When they feel infant rage, babies may swing their arms and legs excitedly, turn red, and cry loudly, 9-9. Infant rage is not anger, for there is no thought.

By 8 to 10 months, babies begin to develop true anger. At this age, infants direct their anger toward a certain person or object. Babies may express anger in physical ways, such

9-9 When parents soothe an angry baby, the baby learns to trust the parents to meet his or her needs.

as trying to get away from the person holding them. They also may grab, shake, or hit an object. Babies often show anger when

❖ they are held against their will. They may be angered if held when they want to be down. They also may be angered if being diapered or dressed when they don't want to be. In addition, being left in a crib when they want to be out makes them angry, too.

❖ toys are taken from them. Babies show anger when they cannot reach a toy they want.

❖ they are being distracted when they want their needs met. For example, showing a crying, hungry baby a toy may cause the baby to cry louder and push the toy away.

All babies express their anger in physical ways because they lack language skills. Babies vary in their amount and strength of anger. Some babies with calm dispositions seem to show little anger during the first year. Babies whose moods are more negative may show much more anger. Meeting the baby's needs quickly often prevents anger. Staying calm by talking in a quiet voice and not looking upset helps children see how to control their anger. Parents can sometimes reduce a baby's anger by holding him or her close for a short time.

dependence. Reliance of one person on another to meet his or her needs.

independent. Wanting to do things for oneself.

Babies and parents spend much of the first year learning to interact with each other.

Summing It Up

Social-emotional development involves a person's basic disposition, the way they interact with others, and how they show their feelings. Babies vary in their temperaments. Some are easy, others are slow to warm up, and still others are difficult. Temperaments, along with the environment, helps shape personality.

An infant's social development is affected by interacting with others, learning to trust, and showing attachment. Babies interact with others at an early age through crying, cooing, and smiling. They need the loving care provided by parents and other caregivers. These people give babies attention they need.

Babies learn trust by having their basic needs met and living in a consistent environment. These basic needs include physical needs of food, clothing, warmth, sleep, and cleanliness. Psychological needs such as cuddling, loving, playing, and being talked to are also important in their development. Having the baby's needs met makes the baby happier, which makes parents happier, too.

Many babies develop an attachment for their parents and others who are close to them. These attachments are important for healthy development, including brain development. Babies who form attachments tend to reach out and want to explore their world.

The emotional center of the brain begins to be wired at two months of age when babies see emotions in others. Emotional development is complex and depends on brain development in other areas such as thinking, memory, and language. Thus, emotions are slow to develop.

Emotions of love, fear, anxiety, and anger arise in all children. These emotions consist of thoughts that lead to feelings and, in turn, cause changes in the body. It is healthy for babies to express a wide range of emotions, from unhappy to happy. Emotions are handled differently throughout life.

Reviewing Key Concepts

Write your answers on a separate sheet of paper.

1. True or false. Babies enter the world with unique traits.
2. Name two factors that affect a baby's temperament.
3. What are three pretalking social signals babies can send to the parents?
4. True or false. Giving babies love and care helps their mental and social development.
5. True or false. Meeting an unhappy baby's needs by soothing his or her cries will spoil the child.
6. Adults can help a baby develop trust by
   A. meeting the baby's needs as soon as possible
   B. changing all the baby's toys once a week so the baby doesn't get bored
   C. keeping daily routines as consistent as possible
   D. both A and B
   E. both A and C
7. Give two examples of attachment behaviors.
8. True or false. Babies who cry loudly when parents leave them are more strongly attached to their parents than babies who do not.

9. Which statements about emotions are true?
   A. Feelings occur before thoughts.
   B. Over the years, the causes of emotions remain the same.
   C. Over the years, the ways a person expresses emotions remain the same.
   D. Over the years, causes and expressions of emotions both change.
10. True or false. Babies are as afraid of unknown young children as they are of adult strangers.
11. Identify the emotion that completes each sentence.
    A. Love
    B. Fear
    C. Anxiety
    D. Anger
    _____ comes from good physical care.
    _____ is often taught by hearing adults say, "No! That will hurt you!"
    _____ is seen as a reaction to being held against their will.
    _____ is similar to attachment.
    _____ in its early form may be the startle reflex.
    _____ is not seen as a response to young unknown children.
    _____ is closely related to fear.
    _____ may be a reaction to an adult trying to distract a hungry or tired baby.

Using Your Knowledge

1. **Language Arts/Child Development.** Write a one- or two-page brochure about the importance of trust in the infant's life. Explain how adults can promote trust in the infant.
2. **Interviewing.** Interview a child care provider. Ask the provider about his or her experience with separation anxiety among the children in his or her care. At what ages has the provider seen this anxiety the most? What techniques proved successful and unsuccessful at comforting children in these situations? Share your findings with the class.
3. **Technology.** Visit a parenting Web site in search of information about social and emotional development in the first year. If approved by your teacher, print the information you find. Share your findings with the class.
4. **Group Discussion.** Have a class discussion on how emotions are useful. Compare the usefulness of emotions to those emotions that can hinder abilities to work and play to the fullest.
5. **Emotional Development.** People's expression of emotions should change as they mature. Each stage of life has age-appropriate behaviors. List behaviors that would be considered mature for an infant but immature for a high school student.

Making Observations

1. Observe a group of infants. Note differences in temperament. Do some infants seem easygoing? Do other infants seem more difficult?
2. Observe an infant with a parent or regular caregiver. How does the baby show attachment? How does the adult encourage attachment (for example, by soothing the baby or showing affection)?
3. Observe a baby showing fear, anxiety, or anger. What seemed to trigger the infant's reactions?

Thinking Further

1. Babies' temperaments seem to shape their personalities. How would you describe your temperament? Have you had these characteristics for a long time? Do others in your family (such as a grandparent, parent, or cousin) have the same temperament?
2. Some parents believe babies can be spoiled if people hold them when they do not have physical needs. Do you agree with this idea? Why or why not?
3. Your friend has a cute baby you'd like to hold. As you approach the baby, you see obvious signs of stranger anxiety. What are some things you can do to lessen the baby's anxiety?

Sophia works part-time in the infant room of a child care center. The director has asked her to spend a few minutes each day talking with each parent about his or her child. Sophia dreads talking to the parents. She doesn't know what to say that is both truthful and positive. Homer is 8 months old and shows extreme separation anxiety. Maria is 11 months old and afraid of all new experiences. Curtis is very demanding. He cries constantly unless he is held.

After studying this chapter, you will be able to
- plan ways to meet the developmental needs of babies in their first year.
- demonstrate skills that meet babies' physical needs.
- stimulate babies' mental development.
- enhance babies' growing awareness of themselves.

Chapter 10
Providing for the Infant's Developmental Needs

Define...

nutrients
solids
intolerance
stimulants
depressants
weaning
finger foods
enriched environment
sensory stimulation
coordination
self-awareness

Because babies develop so quickly in the first year, they have many needs. To meet their physical needs, adults must understand babies and respond to their signals. To meet their social-emotional needs, parents must touch, hold, and look at babies lovingly. Adults also must meet baby's mental needs with activities that help infants learn and develop.

Babies develop best when they feel the love and joy of their caregivers. By meeting a baby's needs promptly, adults help the baby develop trust. From learning to trust others, the baby becomes more aware of his or her own abilities.

Physical Needs

Babies need others to meet all their physical needs. *Physical needs* are the most basic needs of humans.

These include the needs for food and sleep. Babies who are hungry, tired, or sick suffer in physical, mental, social, and emotional ways. For example, a baby who is fed late may not want to play and explore. The baby may also act fussy.

Feeding

The need for food is the baby's most basic physical need. This is because a baby's body grows so quickly in the first year. In fact, the body grows three times faster in the first year than in the second or third years. The baby is also busy exploring and developing, 10-1. A healthful diet provides the nutrients the baby needs to grow, explore, and develop. **Nutrients** are the substances in food that give babies energy and help them grow.

Meeting a baby's food needs quickly alleviates hunger. Some studies indicate that, for very young babies, the sensation of hunger may be physically painful. A hungry baby may cry until fed. This cry of hunger differs from other cries, which makes it easy for parents to recognize. Responding promptly to the baby's need for food teaches the infant his or her needs will be met. Erikson calls this learning a sense of *basic trust*.

nutrients. Substances in food that give people energy and help them grow.

10-1 A variety of nutritious food is essential for meeting the physical needs of the baby's body as he or she grows, develops, and explores.

Feeding times can also be comforting for babies. As adults feed a baby, they should show warmth and concern. This helps deepen their relationship with the baby. Being cared for by gentle, loving adults promotes a baby's social and emotional development.

Feeding During the First Year

How much food does a baby need? It all depends because each baby has unique needs. These needs depend on the baby's size and how fast he or she is growing. The baby's health, heredity, and level of activity also affect his or her food needs. A pediatrician or dietitian can help parents learn what and how much to feed a baby.

First Foods

Most babies begin "eating" an all-liquid diet of milk (either breast milk or formula). Between six months and one year, the baby begins to eat fruits, vegetables, meats, and breads. These foods are called solids. Solid foods for infant feeding are semi-liquid, mushy foods, including commercially prepared baby foods and table foods that have been mashed, pureed, or strained. Many doctors advise parents to wait until their baby is at least six months old before starting solids. (See chart 10-2 for a basic first-year feeding plan.) Doctors do not suggest solids for the first six months for the following reasons:

❖ Babies are not born with the ability to swallow solids. Their jaw and throat muscles must develop before swallowing is easy and safe.
❖ In the first six months, babies do not need solids for nutritional reasons. Their immature digestive systems cannot process the complex nutrients found in solids.
❖ Starting solids too early may cause allergy or intolerance problems.
❖ Some solids have too much sodium. This may increase the baby's chance of high blood pressure as an adult.
❖ Solids may be too high in calories. This may make the baby gain weight too quickly.

Basic Feeding Plan for Baby's First Year

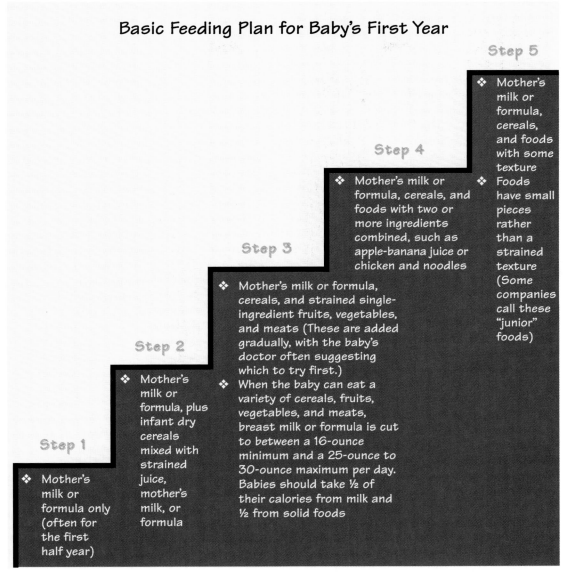

Step 1

❖ Mother's milk or formula only (often for the first half year)

Step 2

❖ Mother's milk or formula, plus infant dry cereals mixed with strained juice, mother's milk, or formula

Step 3

❖ Mother's milk or formula, cereals, and strained single-ingredient fruits, vegetables, and meats (These are added gradually, with the baby's doctor often suggesting which to try first.)
❖ When the baby can eat a variety of cereals, fruits, vegetables, and meats, breast milk or formula is cut to between a 16-ounce minimum and a 25-ounce to 30-ounce maximum per day. Babies should take ½ of their calories from milk and ½ from solid foods

Step 4

❖ Mother's milk or formula, cereals, and foods with two or more ingredients combined, such as apple-banana juice or chicken and noodles

Step 5

❖ Mother's milk or formula, cereals, and foods with some texture
❖ Foods have small pieces rather than a strained texture (Some companies call these "junior" foods)

10-2 Babies begin with a liquid diet and advance gradually in a step-by-step pattern to eating more solids.

❖ Holding a baby close while formula- or breast-feeding gives the baby a warm feeling of physical closeness. Spoon-feeding does not do the same.

 solids. Foods that are semi-liquid and mushy for feeding an infant by spoon.

10-3 When babies are ready for solid foods, caregivers should introduce these foods one at a time.
Fisher-Price

Introducing New Foods

When babies are ready for solids, parents should introduce one food at a time, 10-3. They should feed the new food in small amounts, such as a bite or two.

Parents should not add another new food for at least four or five days. This helps the parent see whether the baby has an intolerance for the food. **Intolerance** is a negative physical reaction that eating a certain food can cause. A food may cause fussiness, a rash, or an upset stomach. If the baby's stools become looser, more watery, or contain mucous, parents should inform the baby's doctor.

Food intolerance among infants often shows in one to four days. Many doctors suggest waiting until after the first birthday to try an offending food again. If babies react to many foods, doctors can test the baby and give him or her a special diet.

Foods to Avoid

Babies should not eat some foods, 10-4. For example, small or hard foods may cause the baby to choke. Foods like cake, crackers, and soft drinks may have too much sugar, sodium, or artificial flavors. Unpasteurized yogurt and foods that contain yeast are hard for babies to digest. Substances called stimulants and depressants are harmful for babies. **Stimulants** (such as caffeine) speed up the functions of organs, such as the heart, and the nervous system. **Depressants** (found in alcohol) slow the functions of organs and the nervous system.

The Feeding Schedule

The daily feeding schedule should fit the baby's needs. Some babies like smaller, more frequent meals. Others eat more food less often. When the baby's growth rate slows toward the end of the first year, his or her appetite will decrease, 10-5. Most babies will establish an eating pattern, but some days they will be hungrier than others.

Homemade Versus Store-Bought Baby Foods

Parents today can choose from a variety of commercially prepared baby foods in the grocery store. Still,

Foods Babies Should Not Eat

choking
- berries
- small candy
- raw carrots
- whole kernel corn
- grapes and raisins
- hot dogs sliced in rounds (rounds should be quartered)
- pretzels
- nuts and peanut butter
- whole kernel cooked corn and popcorn

too much sugar
- cake, in excess
- candy, in excess
- cookies, in excess

too much sodium
- saltine crackers, in excess

little or no nutritional value
- artificially flavored fruit drinks
- soft drinks

hard to digest
- yeast or unpasteurized yogurt

stimulants
- coffee
- tea
- soft drinks with caffeine
- cocoa

depressant
- alcohol

10-4 Some foods are not good for a baby's health.

First-Year Daily Feeding Schedule

Months	Hours Between Feedings
1 to 3*	3 to 4
3 to 5	5**
6	6**

*Often sleeps through the night in about 3 months. Babies are given a late evening feeding (about 11:00 p.m.). They sleep until early morning (5:30 or 6:00 a.m.).

**Nutritious snacks of regular baby food (fruit juice, fruit, etc.) or milk and water should be offered about halfway between feedings (2½ to 3 hours after each feeding) if the baby is awake.

10-5 A baby's feeding schedule changes during the first year.

When buying commercially prepared baby food, check for freshness. Check the *sell-by date* on the cap or the side of the container. This date is the last date the store should sell the product. (You can still safely use the food for a few days after this

intolerance. A negative physical reaction caused by eating a food.

stimulants. Substances that speed up the functions of organs such as the heart and nervous system.

depressants. Substances that slow the functions of organs and the nervous system.

many prefer to make the baby's food at home for health or economic reasons. See 10-6 and 10-7 for advantages to both methods.

Advantages of Commercially Prepared Baby Food

❖ Food is easy to buy and use. In fact, commercially prepared foods were first introduced as "convenience foods."

❖ The food may be more economical than homemade food if the cost of ingredients, gas or electricity, and time used to prepare the food are considered.

❖ Many foods are available in all four seasons. (Some fruits and vegetables may not be available year-round for preparing homemade foods.)

❖ Foods can be bought with the right texture for the baby's age.

❖ Foods are sterile until opened.

❖ Unopened foods can be stored without refrigeration for a long time before they lose quality.

❖ Foods, except dry cereals, are packaged in small amounts for one or two servings.

❖ Possibly harmful additives have been removed or reduced.

10-6 Commercially prepared baby foods may have many advantages.

Advantages of Homemade Baby Food

❖ Possibly harmful additives are not used.

❖ Food is usually less expensive to prepare.

❖ Food can be prepared while making foods for other family members.

❖ No special appliances are needed to prepare baby food.

❖ Making your own food saves storage space required for baby food products.

❖ If the baby has allergies, it may be necessary to prepare special food.

❖ Recipe books are available with many tasty recipes.

❖ A creative cook is not limited to commercially prepared foods.

❖ Making food brings a sense of satisfaction to those who like to cook.

10-7 Parents may choose to make their own baby food for many reasons.

date.) Make sure food containers are sealed properly and have not been opened. Check to see whether the safety button on unopened jars has risen. If so, the food is unsafe to eat. It may have been tampered with or spoiled.

When you are giving the baby store-bought food, spoon out the amount of food you need. Do not feed the baby from the jar. Bacteria in the saliva from the baby's spoon can spoil the food. Most babies like food at room temperature. If the food needs to be heated, test the temperature by putting a small drop on your wrist before serving. After baby food jars have been opened, store them in the refrigerator. Use the leftover baby food within two days.

Weaning

Weaning is the process of taking a baby off the bottle or breast. The process should be gradual because the baby must learn a new way to drink. The process also takes time. Allow the baby to get used to this change.

When do you start to wean a baby? Age at weaning will depend on whether the baby is fed breast milk or formula. Parents should also consult their baby's doctor about what age he or she recommends for weaning.

Weaning from the Breast

The American Academy of Pediatrics recommends mothers breast-feed their babies for at least 12 months. Mothers may nurse longer, however. Often the baby is completely weaned from the breast by 18 to 24 months.

Age at weaning will determine which fluid is offered. If weaned before one year of age, babies should receive iron-fortified infant formula for the remainder of the first year. Babies weaned after one year should be offered whole cow's milk. Children between one and two years of age should drink only whole milk rather than milk with reduced quantities of fat. Formulas designed for toddlers are not better for children than cow's milk after age one year.

Whether the baby is weaned to a bottle or directly to a cup will also depend on age. Babies who are weaned before they are skilled enough to use a cup will be weaned from the breast to the bottle. Older babies can be weaned directly to a cup.

Weaning from the breast cannot be abrupt either for the baby or the mother. Abrupt weaning for the baby is stressful. For the mother, abrupt weaning can cause blockage of the milk ducts and possible depression. A woman may need to consult her doctor during the weaning process.

When weaning begins, parents should offer the new liquid (formula or whole milk, depending on age) as part of one feeding. (The early evening feeding is usually best, because there is less breast milk then.) Increase the amount of liquid offered at this feeding until the baby has taken an entire feeding by bottle or cup for several days.

Parents should wait at least three days before replacing another feeding with the bottle or cup. Then apply the same steps to another feeding until the baby is weaned. (The early morning feeding is often the last one to stop.) Often, breast-fed babies accept a cup sooner than bottle-fed babies.

Weaning to a Cup

For formula-fed babies, weaning from a bottle to a cup may begin as early as the child can use the cup and shows interest in doing so. Although this may be as early as 9 months of age, a recommended age to start weaning from the bottle to a cup is 12 months. At this time, cow's milk can be given instead of formula. This process should often be complete by age 18 months.

Parents often teach babies to drink from a cup in the following ways:

❖ Give the baby a special baby cup. The cup may have two handles and be weighted to keep it from tipping. Some cups also offer special features that make liquid less likely to spill.

 weaning. The gradual process of taking a baby off the bottle or breast.

❖ Praise the baby when he or she tries to handle the cup. Parents should not expect this to be an easy task for several months. Even after that age, many accidents will occur.

❖ Give the baby a few sips of liquid (about one tablespoon in the bottom of a cup) at about six months. The small amount is less scary if it splashes against the baby's nose. It also is less messy if spilled.

❖ Let the baby drink small amounts of milk at one feeding. If the baby already drinks small amounts of juice or water during a feeding, choose that feeding for putting milk in the cup. A baby should work up to at least four ounces of milk from the cup at one feeding.

❖ Gradually replace other bottle feedings in the same way. The last bottle of the day is often the last to be replaced.

Spoon Feeding

Parents are often eager to see their babies eat solids. Why? Parents probably see this as a transition to a more grown-up stage of eating. Like many other skills, eating from a spoon is developmental. Most pediatricians recommend the baby be six months old before being introduced to solids, 10-8. This is the time when most babies are developmentally ready to begin learning to eat with a spoon and just before solids are nutritionally needed. The closer the baby is to six months old, the better he or she will

10-8 In the second half of the first year, babies begin to experiment with feeding themselves.

do with this developmental task. This is true for the following reasons:

❖ Until babies are 16 to 18 weeks old, they have an extrusion reflex (the tongue thrusts forward when it is touched by an object). Also, babies won't open their mouths when they see food until they are about five months old. If solids are not introduced before eight or nine months, however, the baby may reject them.

❖ Babies do not need more nutrition than breast milk or formula until they reach 13 to 15 pounds.

❖ Before six months of age, babies do not have the needed enzymes (special proteins that aid digestion) or saliva for digesting solid foods.

The American Academy of Pediatrics recommends as the first solid food a commercial iron-enriched rice cereal. For the first feedings, the cereal should contain so much liquid that it "pours" from the spoon. To get this consistency, use about one teaspoon of rice cereal mixed with two tablespoons of breast milk or formula. Although water could be used, breast milk or formula will be more nutritious and offers a familiar taste. Very gradually make the cereal thicker at each feeding as the baby learns to use his or her tongue and tolerate the texture. The baby's pediatrician will recommend when to introduce other solids. As cereal and other solids are introduced, the baby will need water for proper kidney action. The baby's doctor can advise how much water to offer each day.

Solids are always fed from a spoon. Solids should not be diluted with liquid and fed using a bottle with a large hole in the nipple or an "infant feeder." These practices defeat the purpose of having a baby learn to use his or her tongue and throat muscles to chew, swallow, and breathe. Nonspoon methods present a risk of choking, too.

For the first spoon feeding, the baby should be held in the adult's lap in an almost upright position. Later, parents can feed babies from infant seats or high chairs. Use a small spoon with a long handle to make feeding easier. A plastic-coated baby spoon is better for the baby's sensitive gums than a metal spoon. Place a small amount of food on the tip of the spoon. A few bites are enough for the first feedings.

Parents should start these early feedings at times when the baby shows signs of hunger, but is not too hungry. Waiting too long can make a baby too upset to learn something new. Parents often try feeding the baby a few bites of cereal about halfway through the milk or formula feeding. They should give the baby a sip or two of water after the cereal but before resuming the feeding of breast milk or formula. Thus, the baby's meal begins and ends with the familiar taste of breast milk or formula.

Most doctors recommend offering the baby new solids early in the day and no later than early afternoon. They advise this because babies are more apt to have colic in the evening hours. Also an allergic reaction following a night feeding would occur in the wee hours of the morning rather than during the early evening.

During the first spoon feedings, babies often thrust their tongues forward, pushing the spoon and food out of their mouths. This is a reflexive response to having strange objects in the mouth. This does not mean the baby doesn't want the food or is being stubborn. Thus, parents can continue to offer a bite or two as long as their babies continue to cooperate. Once babies turn their heads or close their mouths, parents should stop feeding the solids and resume feeding from the breast or bottle. Waiting a day or two before trying solids again is often best. Frustrated babies are not good learners. During the developmental process, parents must remain calm and pleasant. Babies should see eating solids as loving as drinking from the bottle or breast. Soon the baby will be eating easily from the spoon.

Self-Feeding

Babies begin self-feeding by eating finger foods. **Finger foods** are foods a baby can self-feed using the fingers. Near the end of the first year, babies often develop the skill of self-feeding finger foods at the same time they develop the pincer grasp. Some babies, however, will simply rake the food into their mouths. Finger foods aid the baby's growing independence as well as grasping and chewing skills.

Eating finger foods is fun, but it can also be hazardous. As babies are learning to eat these foods, they may choke or gag at the new textures. For this reason, adults should keep their babies in full view when they are eating. Adults should also offer only "safer" foods. These foods include small pieces of melba toast; crispy, unsalted crackers; bagels; zwieback;

and fruits and vegetables that have been cooked and diced. (Adults should choose from the foods they know their babies already tolerate.)

Self-feeding with a spoon begins in the second year. Younger babies may want to help adults by grabbing the spoon during a feeding. Adults can often solve this problem by giving the baby a spoon to hold as they feed. Babies may even hold a spoon in each hand. Some parents then let the baby use the spoon on the last few bites. The spoon rarely reaches the mouth, but this is good practice for later self-feeding.

Mealtimes should be pleasant for the baby. Caregivers should try to stay calm regardless of what or how much the baby accepts or rejects. If the adult is unpleasant when the baby rejects a food, the baby is more likely to refuse the same food next time. Kindness makes new foods easier to accept.

Clothing

Infants grow quickly and outgrow their clothing several times in the first year. Because babies grow at different rates, infant clothing should be bought by length and weight rather than by age. (Sewing patterns should be bought by length and weight, also.) Companies use different sizes; thus, it is important to read the hangtags carefully before buying to select the right size for the baby. Chart 10-9 shows examples of clothing sizes.

From three months to the end of the first year, babies move more with each passing week, 10-10. Clothing

Typical First-Year Clothing Sizes

Sizes of Clothes Other Than Sleepwear

Size	Newborn	0 to 3 mo.	6 to 9 mo.	12 mo.
Length (inches)	20 to 22	22½ to 24	24½ to 28½	29 to 30½
Weight (pounds)	5½ to 8½	9 to 12	12½ to 19	19½ to 20½

Sizes for Sleepwear

Size	XS/S	M	L
Age	0 to 3 mo.	3 to 6 mo.	6 to 9 mo.
Weight (pounds)	0 to 11	12 to 15	16 to 19

10-9 Length and weight are better indicators of clothing size than age.

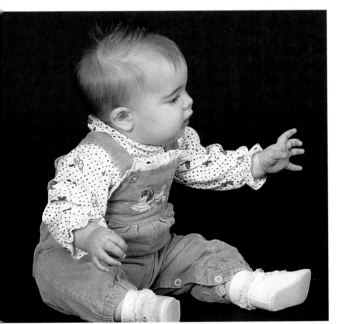

10-10 Because babies move more with each passing week, their clothing should make moving easy.
© John Shaw

should be easy to move in. The basic points given in 10-11 can be used to select baby clothing.

Style and Color

The style and color of baby clothes is a personal choice. Almost any style has advantages and disadvantages. For example, two-piece outfits (tops and bottoms) often can be worn longer because they do not get as tight in the crotch as one-piece outfits. Two-piece outfits make changing the diaper easy, too. One-piece outfits, such as jumpsuits and overalls, look neater on

finger foods. Foods a baby can self-feed using the fingers.

Points to Consider When Choosing Baby Clothes

Feature	Examples
Safety	❖ fire retardant ❖ not tight or binding ❖ no loose buttons or other fasteners ❖ no loose trim ❖ no drawstrings
Comfort	❖ soft (made of knitted fabric) ❖ nonirritating clothes (flat seams and fasteners) ❖ garments without too much extra fabric, so that baby does not rest on the bulk ❖ no fuzzy trims that tickle ❖ neck openings large enough for easy dressing ❖ right weight for needed warmth (Several layers of lightweight clothes, such as an undershirt, a T-shirt, and a sweater are warmer and more comfortable in warm weather than one heavy garment.) ❖ roomy for active body movements ❖ antistatic ❖ absorbent (manufactured fibers, such as polyester or nylon, should be blended with cotton to increase absorbency)
Easy Care	❖ machine washable ❖ can be washed with other clothes ❖ soil-release finish (to make stain removal easier) ❖ shrinkage control ❖ little or no ironing needed ❖ easy to mend

10-11 Babies need clothing that meets their special needs.

crawlers because they do not separate. These outfits are warmer, too.

Shoes

Shoes are not needed until a baby begins to walk outdoors. Shoes protect and cushion the feet from outside dangers. Indoors, babies should walk without shoes to prevent flat-footed walking. Most shoes worn in the first year are for decoration. These shoes have soft, cloth soles. Babies need to wear socks or footed clothing in cool weather to keep their feet warm.

Good Consumer Sense

Because babies quickly outgrow clothing, good consumer sense is important. Adults should shop for quality and compare prices. They should follow these tips:

* Look for built-in growth features. These include a double row of snaps or buttons at the waistline to lengthen the garment from shoulder to crotch. Two buttons on straps used for lengthening is a good feature. Also look for stretch waists and stretch leg and arm openings.
* Choose more stretch knit garments than woven garments. Babies can wear these longer.
* Look for flame-retardant finishes on clothing.
* Look for ease-of-care labels.

Caring for Baby Clothes

Parents can care for baby clothes properly by following these practices:

* Before cleaning clothes, read labels and tags. Follow directions. Pretreat stains before washing clothes to prevent the stains from setting. Also, mend tears before washing to prevent them from getting larger.
* Infants' and children's clothes often need to go through more rinses than other clothing. Extra rinses help remove detergent from clothes. Babies' skin is more sensitive than adults', and detergent residue may cause skin rashes. Parents might also want to choose a gentle detergent designed for infant clothes.
* When washing baby sleepwear, do not add fabric softener to the load.

The chemicals in fabric softeners can reduce the flame-retardant qualities of the clothing.

* Many parents store baby clothes for future children or as keepsakes. Before storing, clean the clothes. Soiled spots change over time, and then stains cannot be removed. When clothes are clean and dry, they are ready to be stored. Do not use plastic bags. Fabrics need air to maintain their strength and oils. Store light and dark clothes separately to prevent the transfer of dyes. All clothing should be stored away from damp areas. Dampness promotes mildew and insect damage.

Diapering a Baby

Babies require frequent diaper changes throughout the first year. This is a skill parents will soon perfect. (You may want to refer to chapter 6 to review the steps used in diapering.) When using disposable diapers, the baby will change sizes as he or she grows. Cloth diapers can be folded differently to accommodate older babies.

Older babies wiggle more and may protest when diapered. This makes the task harder for adults. To keep a baby's interest, it is a good idea to talk, sing, and play with the baby during diaper changes. Offering the baby a toy may also help the baby keep still during the change.

Adults must keep diaper-changing areas very clean! This is crucial to prevent the spread of germs.

Caregivers should also wash their hands (and the baby's hands) after each diaper change.

Tub Bathing

Tub bathing can begin as soon as the baby's navel has healed. When preparing for a tub bath, the steps are the same as those used for sponge bathing listed in chapter 6. The only difference is that a small tub is filled with about three inches of water. The water should be comfortably warm. You can test the water's temperature by dipping your wrist or elbow into the water. See the steps for tub bathing listed in 10-12.

Like diapering, bathing is a good time to play with babies. As babies are bathed, they enjoy parents who talk, sing, cuddle, and smile, 10-13. Babies often respond well because warm water is relaxing. As babies get older, they enjoy kicking and splashing in the water as their parents hold them. Water play is good for baby's developing motor skills as well as being lots of fun.

Establishing Routines

A routine helps children feel secure because it teaches them what to expect. Routines, like having one's physical needs met promptly, help infants develop basic trust. Although babies do not know clock time, they do develop a sense of rhythm in their lives formed around routine care. Schedules also help adults get their baby-care tasks done with greater

ease. A schedule is important, but remember to adjust it as needed.

Routines should fit babies' and adults' needs. Schedules also should change as babies mature. For older babies, feedings are more widely spaced, daytime naps grow shorter, and more playtime is needed.

Rest and Sleep

Rest and sleep are important to a baby's health. Like others, babies vary in the amount of rest and sleep they need. Many babies begin sleeping through the night at twelve weeks, but some sleep fewer hours for many months. Adults whose baby does not sleep well at night might try rearranging their babies' schedules. Awakening babies after four hours of daytime sleep should help the baby sleep longer at night. (If a baby sleeps well at night, parents should not interfere with daytime naps.)

Some babies who have slept through the night may begin to awaken and cry during the night. This often happens between five and eight months. Hunger often is not the reason for this awakening. As babies awaken, they may feel lonely and long to have a parent near. Parents should check on their crying babies, comfort them for a few minutes, and then put them down again. Playing with a baby during the night is not a good habit to form.

Many babies take long naps in both the morning and afternoon until five or six months. At this age, babies

How to Give a Tub Bath

How to Give a Tub Bath
Doctors usually recommend tub baths as soon as the baby's navel and circumcision are healed. Fill the tub (often a large dishpan) with about three inches of comfortable warm water. Test the water temperature with your elbow or wrist. Also, place a towel on the bottom of the tub to keep the baby from slipping.

Step 1: On the Table
Undress the baby, except for the diaper. Cleanse the eyes, nose, ears, and face as you would in a sponge bath. Apply liquid baby bath to head with hand, or use washcloth after about first two months. Note: When the baby is older and has more hair, use a liquid baby shampoo that will not irritate the eyes.

Step 3: Bathing the Body
Soap the front of the baby's body, being careful to wash inside all the skin folds and creases, then rinse. Reverse your hold to soap and rinse the baby's back. It is not necessary to turn the baby over. Clean the genital area during the bath, just like the rest of the baby. In the external folds of a baby girl, a white substance may gather. If it remains after bathing, gently wipe it away with a washcloth or with a cotton ball dipped in baby oil. Be sure to wipe from front to back. When cleansing a baby boy who has not been circumcised, do not push back the foreskin unless your doctor tells you to. If your baby has been circumcised, he may be immersed in a tub as soon as the area has healed, or sooner, on your doctor's advice.

Step 5: Diaper Area Care
To keep the diaper area dry, use baby cornstarch to help prevent irritation and redness.

Step 2: Into the Tub
After removing the baby's diaper, you can place the child in the tub. Use a safety hold—slip your right hand under the baby's shoulders. Place your thumb over the right shoulder and your fingers under the right armpit. Support the buttocks with your left hand, grasping the right thigh with your thumb and fingers. Lower the baby into the tub feet first, keeping the head out of the water. With your left hand, rinse the head, letting water run back into the tub.

Step 4: Out of the Tub
Use the same safety hold to lift your baby onto a warm, dry surface. Cover the baby with a towel and pat dry, paying special attention to folds and creases.

Step 6: General Skin Care
Moisten fingers on a cotton ball dipped in baby oil or baby lotion. Apply it to all tiny creases, such as around the neck, armpits, arms, hands, legs, and feet. Use a little baby oil on a cotton ball to help remove cradle cap. Apply baby cream to any irritated part. Sprinkle baby powder on your hand and pat lightly over large areas of the body.

10-12 Tub baths should be given carefully and quickly for the baby's comfort and safety.
Johnson & Johnson Baby Products Co.

10-13 When babies are bathed, they like parents to talk to and smile at them.

often take a short morning nap and a long afternoon nap. Most babies drop the morning nap between 9 and 15 months. They may continue to take an afternoon nap until three to five years of age. This nap may gradually shorten as a child grows.

Sudden Infant Death Syndrome

Sudden infant death syndrome (SIDS) kills many infants during their first year of life. Like the name suggests, this syndrome suddenly strikes seemingly healthy babies in their sleep. In many cases infants simply stop breathing. SIDS is the third leading cause of deaths in infants from age one week to 12 months. The most common age for SIDS to strike is between one and four months. In the United States thousands of infants die of SIDS each year.

The cause of SIDS is unknown. Unlike most diseases that are diagnosed by the presence of specific symptoms, SIDS is diagnosed only after all other possible causes of death are ruled out. There are many theories about the cause of SIDS. Some experts think the cause may be a virus that attacks the brain stem (where breathing is controlled) before or shortly after birth.

Although the exact cause of SIDS is still unknown, some risk factors are known, 10-14. For example, studies have noted a danger in babies who sleep on their stomachs. Stomach-sleeping may put pressure on the baby's jaw and thus narrow the airway. It also increases the risk of the infant rebreathing exhaled air. This exhaled air (which contains carbon dioxide rather than oxygen) might become trapped in a pocket around the baby's mouth by a soft mattress, fluffy blanket, stuffed toy, or pillow near the face. The pocket holds the exhaled carbon dioxide, which the baby then breathes back into the lungs. Many babies and older children would awaken if they lacked oxygen. However, SIDS babies may have a brain abnormality or immaturity that prevents them from awakening and moving. Furthermore,

Risk Factors for Sudden Infant Death Syndrome (SIDS)

Caregivers should discuss with their doctors ways to protect infants who are at high risk for SIDS. These are infants who meet any of the following conditions:

- ❖ being born to a teen mother
- ❖ lacking prenatal care
- ❖ being exposed to tobacco, alcohol, or illegal drugs (especially cocaine) before birth
- ❖ being born more than two weeks before due date
- ❖ being born at a low birthweight (less than five and one-half pounds)
- ❖ being part of a multiple birth (especially if weighing less than 3.3 pounds)
- ❖ being exposed to cigarette smoke after birth
- ❖ having an older sibling who died of SIDS
- ❖ being male and having other risk factors listed above

10-14 Certain conditions put infants at a higher risk for SIDS.

some very young babies may not be able to raise their heads, leaving them trapped to rebreathe the exhaled air.

Research continues for the cause and prevention of SIDS. Until a prevention is found, parents can take some positive steps to protect their infants:

- ❖ Avoid as many of the risk factors as possible both before and after the baby is born.
- ❖ Place baby on a firm mattress.
- ❖ Do not use fluffy blankets, comforters, throws, stuffed toys, or pillows in the bed. (Display

these baby gifts or purchases somewhere else in the room.)

- ❖ Make sure the baby does not get too warm while sleeping. (Babies who become very warm may go into a deeper sleep and thus find it more difficult to awaken.)
- ❖ Have regular well-baby checkups.
- ❖ Breast-feed the baby for at least seven months and preferably for one year.
- ❖ Use a breathing monitor and alarm if recommended by your doctor.
- ❖ Place baby on his or her back to sleep. If you see a baby roll onto the stomach, turn the baby to his or her back. (Since the American Academy of Pediatrics recommended back sleeping, SIDS has decreased almost 40 percent. The rate would likely decrease more if all parents and caregivers followed the recommendation. It is easy to remember—"back to sleep.")

Places for Sleep and Play

Where do babies sleep and play? Space for sleep and play is based on a family's lifestyle and housing. However, a few guidelines are important.

Babies should sleep away from major activities. Parents might use a screen to section off part of their bedroom to make a private sleeping area for the baby. Others have babies share space with an older sibling. Another option for some parents is providing the baby his or her own bedroom or bedroom/playroom.

The sleeping area should be large enough for a full-size crib and other furnishings. Children often sleep in a crib until they are three years old or 35 inches tall. Many parents like to have a dressing table. Dressing tables can be purchased. You may also make one by attaching a vinyl-covered pad and safety belt to a dresser. An adult-size rocker is convenient for the baby's sleeping area. Parents also need storage space for clothing and baby products.

If adults plan a playroom, they should not expect a baby to stay there all the time. Children like to be near others. During the first year, babies need places to play and toys in several rooms where household activities take place. A playyard may be used for short periods of time, especially when babies need a safe place to play. Parents should limit total time spent in a playyard to no more than two hours per day, however. Babies need to be able to move and explore freely in order to develop crawling, creeping, and walking skills.

When choosing play spaces for babies, adults should keep the following points in mind:

❖ Babies are messy by adult standards. Spaces for children should be washable.

❖ All spaces must be safe. A house must be childproofed by the time a baby can crawl. (Childproofing and safety measures are described in chapter 21.)

❖ Decorate children's rooms with their tastes in mind. Rooms should be bright and cheerful. Place pictures and wall hangings at the child's eye level. Floor coverings should allow play with blocks and wheeled toys.

❖ Babies grow quickly. Spaces should be planned for easy and economical changes as babies' needs change.

Intellectual Needs

Babies need more than physical care to help them grow. Experts know that babies are born with the ability to learn. They also know babies need an environment that offers them chances to learn. This is called an **enriched environment**, 10-15. One study found that babies whose caregivers expected them to learn at an early age developed more quickly than other babies. This may be because adults who expect more provide more activities to help babies learn.

Adults can provide learning experiences for babies soon after birth. In fact, the sooner adults provide activities, the more babies want to learn. Adults shouldn't forget, however, that babies learn at different rates. The rate of learning cannot be increased with lots of activities and toys. Babies can take in only so much. Too many activities and toys can confuse or bore the baby.

Weave activities into daily routines like feeding, bathing, and diapering. Adults do not need to have

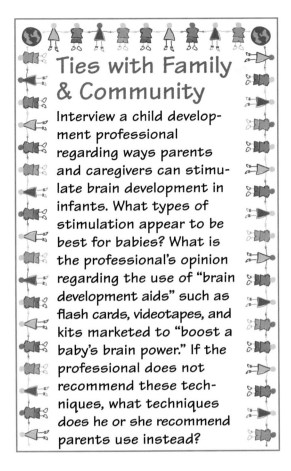

Ties with Family & Community

Interview a child development professional regarding ways parents and caregivers can stimulate brain development in infants. What types of stimulation appear to be best for babies? What is the professional's opinion regarding the use of "brain development aids" such as flash cards, videotapes, and kits marketed to "boost a baby's brain power." If the professional does not recommend these techniques, what techniques does he or she recommend parents use instead?

10-15 In an enriched environment, babies are eager to explore the age-appropriate toys offered to them.

a set schedule of daily games. The number and types of games are not as important as the warmth and caring that adults show for babies.

A skillful caregiver knows how to use activities to meet babies' intellectual needs. Adults can use the following methods:

❖ Watch for signs of the baby's interest in certain experiences. To check for interest, show the baby how to use a toy, and then give him or her a turn. Repeat several times. If there is little or no interest,

the toy or game is probably too advanced for the baby. Try it again in a few days or weeks.

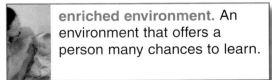

enriched environment. An environment that offers a person many chances to learn.

❖ Let the baby begin most activities, then expand on them. For example, the baby may be patting a high chair tray. Expand the activity by patting a different object (that makes a different sound). You may also pat the tray harder, softer, faster, or slower than the baby.

❖ Repeat games many times. Using games over many months helps the baby retain the skills each game helps build.

❖ Let babies try things on their own. This helps them learn to solve problems.

Activities to Stimulate the Senses

Sensory stimulation involves using the senses to learn about the environment. According to Piaget, babies use their senses as a major way of learning. Infants use their senses to explore objects offered to them and discover how objects operate.

For the baby to develop fully, all five senses (sight, hearing, touch, taste, and smell) must be stimulated. One example of a sensory stimulation activity is to let the baby touch a number of safe objects. This can be done while walking around the room or outdoors. For example, letting the baby touch the bark of a tree helps improve sensory development. See 10-16 for other ways to help children stimulate their sensory learning.

Ties with Family & Community

Imagine you are a parent of an infant and you have $150 allotted in your budget for first-year toys. Use a catalog, shop online, or visit local stores that carry infant toys. List the items you would purchase, giving a description of each item and listing its price. Consider the various areas of development and ability levels of infants in the first year. Present your list to the class and explain the reasons behind your choices.

Problem-Solving Activities

As babies use their senses to observe their world, they try to make sense of what they see, hear, smell, touch, and taste. In an enriched environment, babies learn how their world works as they begin to explore.

A number of games and activities can help babies begin to organize and understand their world. Peek-a-boo is one of the first games babies love to play. To play this game, cover your eyes, or go out of sight, saying, "Where did (baby's name) go?" The baby will

Sensory Stimulation Activities

Activity	Sense
Mobiles ❖ Place mobiles on crib and playpen. Keep them out of the baby's reach. Change the objects on the mobile often. Try to visualize them from the baby's point of view.	Sight
Tracking Objects ❖ Hold an object like a yarn ball, small flashlight, or rattle about 12 inches from the baby's eyes. Move it in a short arc and gradually extend the arc to a half circle. The baby's eyes should track or follow the object.	Sight
Wind Chimes ❖ Hold the baby near wind chimes blowing outdoors. Hearing wind chimes and seeing them move is interesting for babies.	Hearing & Sight
Face Hoop ❖ Draw a face by decorating fabric with fabric scraps or paint. Insert the fabric between round embroidery hoops. Hang the face down or hold it for the baby to see. (The face hoop is not safe for the baby to mouth.)	Sight
Sound Can ❖ Place some large wooden beads or large spools of thread in a juice can. Tape on the lid. The baby can hear the objects move inside the can. Other baby-safe objects can be used, too.	Hearing

© John Shaw

© John Shaw

© John Shaw

10-16 Sensory stimulation activities help babies learn about their environment.

wait expectantly for you to uncover your eyes or come out of hiding and say, "Peek-a-boo, I see you!" Through this game, babies learn to understand a person is still there even though he or she can't be seen. This is an example of an object permanence activity.

Babies need to repeat games with many objects and with some changes in order to test how something works. There are many kinds of problem-solving activities. More activities are found in 10-17.

sensory stimulation. Using the five senses to learn about the environment.

Problem-Solving Activities

Stacking

© John Shaw

Spatial Relationship Activities

❖ **Stacking and Nesting**

Find or purchase three cans or boxes that are different sizes. They must fit inside each other. These can be stacked by placing one on top of the other. They can also be nested by placing one inside the other. Show the baby how to stack and how to nest. (For young babies, the boxes should differ greatly in size. If there are many pieces, start with only the smallest, the middle-size, and the large pieces. After the baby can work with three pieces well, add others one at a time.)

❖ **Far and Near**

Hold a toy close to the baby's eyes. Move it back slowly and say, "There it goes." Move it forward slowly and say, "Here it comes." The game helps babies see size differences in near and far objects.

Stacking

© John Shaw

Other Performance Activities

❖ **Where's the Object?**

Hide a favorite toy, starting with simple ways of hiding and moving. Advance to more complex ways as the baby masters each. During each game, let the baby watch you hide the toy. If the baby finds the toy, move on to the next step. (1) Partially hide the toy under a blanket. (2) Next, totally hide the toy under the blanket. (3) Wrap the toy in paper so that the shape of the object shows. (4) Place the toy in or under a box. (5) Place the toy in a box that is in another box.

❖ **Hide and Seek**

Hide from the baby, leaving some part of yourself visible. Let the baby find you. Once found, make the reunion happy, with lots of hugs and kisses. (This helps the baby overcome anxiety when left with others.) After partially hiding yourself during many games, hide yourself completely. Choose a hiding spot where the baby can find you easily.

Nesting

© John Shaw

Activities Using Objects as Tools

❖ **Pulling Strings**

Babies can learn to get an object by pulling a string in many ways. You may buy toys that are pulled on a string. You also may attach any toy or safe household object to a string for the baby to pull.

❖ **Making Sounds with Objects**

By hitting objects together, babies can learn to make different sounds. They will learn to vary the sounds by hitting softer or harder, or by changing the objects. Different objects to use include a pan with a spoon, a box with a spoon, a drum with a stick, and a block with a block.

10-17 Problem-solving activities help babies understand their world.

Motor Activities

Movement is important for infants. Babies begin moving even before birth. Although motor nerves are not fully developed for four or five years, coordination improves quickly after birth. Coordination is the working together of muscles in movements such as walking. As infants explore, motor activity helps their coordination and mental development. As motor skills improve, babies feel better about their abilities, which boosts social and emotional development.

If they are free to move, babies will engage in many motor activities on their own. However, they need some encouragement from caregivers. Babies use their large muscles as they perform gross-motor skills, such as rolling over, sitting, crawling, standing, and walking. An example of an activity that encourages gross-motor skills is crawling in and out of boxes or cartons. Coordination in the small muscles, especially those in the fingers and hands, is evident in the use of fine-motor skills, 10-18. Playing with blocks is a fine-motor skill that requires coordination of the small muscles. See 10-19 for other activities for gross-motor and fine-motor games.

Language Activities

Hearing spoken words is important for the child's language development. Babies learn language by hearing people talk. This is best done during baby's routine care. Adults can

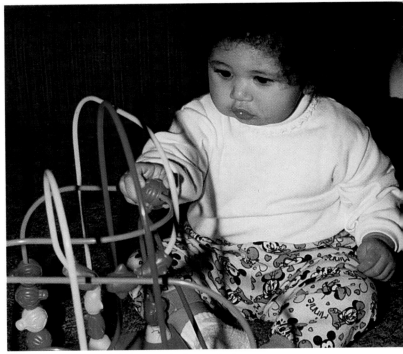

10-18 Using activity toys helps a baby improve fine-motor skills.

talk about the foods, toys, people, and routines that are part of the baby's world. Exact words are not as important to the infant as hearing language. While dressing a baby, the adult could make any of the following statements:

- ❖ "I'm putting on your green shirt."
- ❖ "Isn't this a pretty shirt?"
- ❖ "Are you ready for the shirt to go over your head?"

 coordination. The working together of muscles to form movements.

❖ "Here's a button, here's a button, and here's one."

❖ "Do you like green?"

Although it does not matter exactly which words parents use, words should be pronounced correctly.

Gross-Motor and Fine-Motor Games

Gross-Motor Games

❖ **Knock the Toy**
When a baby can stand by holding a playpen or crib railing, place a stuffed toy on the railing. Tell the baby to hold the railing with one hand and to knock the toy off with the other.

❖ **Cartons or Boxes**
Place a large carton or box on its side so the baby can crawl into it. Let the baby crawl in and out of the carton.

❖ **Dance to the Music**
Tell the baby to dance to the music. You may want to dance with the baby.

Fine-Motor Games

❖ **Cups**
A baby can improve fine-motor skills by playing with a plastic infant cup. When the baby can handle the hand-to-mouth movement, add a teaspoon of water to the cup. As the baby becomes more skilled, add more water.

❖ **Blocks**
Show the baby how to use blocks in different ways. Then let the baby try. Blocks can be stacked, hit together, or placed in a line and moved by pushing the last block.

10-19 Gross-motor and fine-motor games help babies' coordination and mental development.

Changing pitch or singing also varies the sound and adds interest.

Adults can encourage babies to talk, too. Often, the baby will babble in response. When the baby babbles, encouragement should be given such as, "That's right!"

Reading to infants daily exposes them to new words and ideas. Even babies who can't comprehend the words benefit from being read books, magazines, and newspapers. Time spent reading and hearing words is important at all ages.

Language games can be worked into daily routines. These routines can include a special time of sharing for babies and adults, 10-20. Perhaps one of the earliest language action games babies enjoy is pat-a-cake. See 10-21 for this and other language games.

10-20 Language games can be part of fun times shared by babies and adults.
© Nancy P. Alexander

Language Games

❖ **Verbal Imitation**
   Imitation of verbal (and even nonverbal) signals helps language development. Two stages are used during the baby's first year.
   Stage 1 (0-6 months)—Imitate the baby's gestures and babbling. If you see a gesture or hear a sound, repeat it with a smile or laugh. See whether the baby repeats it. If the baby has not repeated the gesture or sound in return, repeat the sound. Once the baby catches on, the baby will imitate sounds after you.
   Stage 2 (6-12 months)—In this stage, you can begin by making a gesture or sound. See whether the baby imitates it. If the baby has not repeated the gesture or sound in return, make the same gesture or sound again. The baby should catch on quickly.

❖ **Books**
   Begin looking at books while the baby is still young. At first, talk about the pictures. As you talk, point to the pictures. Later, begin to read if the story is short. Go on to the next page as the baby loses interest in one page. Between 9 and 12 months, you can ask the baby to find certain pictures, such as cars, pets, or people.

❖ **Puppets**
   You can make or buy a puppet to talk to the baby. At first, the baby will just look and listen. Later, he or she will talk to the puppet.

❖ **Action Rhymes**
   Children can enjoy action rhymes toward the end of the first year. Action rhymes combine the rhythm of language with a few motor actions. An example follows:

Pat-a-Cake
Pat-a-cake, pat-a-cake, baker's man.
(Help baby clap hands on the words "pat-a-cake")
Bake me a cake as fast as you can.
Roll it, and pat it, and mark it with a "B."
(Help baby roll hands on the word "roll.")
Put it in the oven for baby and me.

10-21 Language games expose babies to words.

Social-Emotional Needs

Babies have needs that must be met for healthy social-emotional development. During the first year, social and emotional development seems to center on the baby-adult interaction, the baby's developing self-awareness, and adults' ways of handling special problems.

Baby-Adult Interaction

Each baby comes into the world with a unique temperament. Adults may respond positively or negatively toward the baby's temperament. Adults' feelings are conveyed mainly through the way they hold, touch, and look at the baby. The baby reacts to adults' feelings and actions. For example, if adults are tense or the baby's needs are unmet, the baby becomes fussy and difficult. On the other hand, when adults are relaxed and the baby's needs are promptly met, the baby is more often quiet and cooperative.

Adults who have good relationships with babies seem to respect their temperaments. For example, active babies often get into places they don't belong. They require more watching than less active children. These parents should adjust their own behaviors to provide this extra level of care.

Babies feel love through physical contact with the adult, 10-22. Physical messages shape feelings between adults and babies. A single or seldom-sent message does not determine the relationship. The quality of the relationship is influenced more by the total number of messages and the strength of these messages. Even the most loving adults can be hurried and tense at times. In a healthy relationship, the balance must be on the positive side.

10-22 The feeling of love and joy between a baby and an adult can be shared through physical contact.

Adults should realize that relationships with children are rather one-sided for many years. Babies may give some smiles and hugs, but adults must do most of the giving. This giving is important, though, because the feelings adults show for babies help to shape babies' self-concepts. Fostering good feelings in babies seems to increase the joy and love between babies and their caregivers.

Helping Babies Develop Self-Awareness

In the first year, a baby begins to develop self-awareness, or an understanding of himself or herself as a unique person. As babies develop self-awareness, they form a mental picture of themselves. They form an idea of who they are and what they can do.

Babies gaze at their hands for hours, making slight movements. As their brains process the sight and sensation of these moving hands, babies learn these hands are a part of them. This discovery helps babies become more aware of their bodies.

Infants also learn how their movements can affect other objects. For example, a baby might move a hand, bat a toy on a cradle gym, and make the toy turn. This discovery teaches the baby which objects are part of himself or herself (the hand) and which are not (the toy and the cradle gym). When a baby crawls to get a toy, the baby learns his or her actions can make things happen.

At eight or nine months of age, babies start to learn they are individuals separate from others (known as *object concept*). They begin to realize they are not just extensions of their parents. Feeling separate leads babies to express anxiety when caregivers leave them.

Adults can promote self-awareness by using the baby's name as much as possible. Calling the baby by name during happy times gives the baby positive feelings about his or her name. Happy times include reunions between adult and baby, such as after a nap or when the adult returns from work. Parents can also call the baby by name when talking to him or her during child care tasks or games.

Looking in mirrors also increases self-awareness. Babies enjoy seeing themselves in mirrors even before they know the images they see are their own. Calling the baby's image by name is helpful. Adults may also place babies in front of mirrors so they can watch themselves eat, dress, and move. Babies also enjoy having nonbreakable play mirrors as toys, 10-23. They like to point to their eyes, ears, nose, mouth, and toes. They also like finding these body parts in the mirror.

Toward the end of the first year, babies become possessive about some objects. This should be encouraged, because babies' understanding that some objects belong to them is part of self-awareness. Also, babies must possess things before they can learn to share in a few years. Adults can help

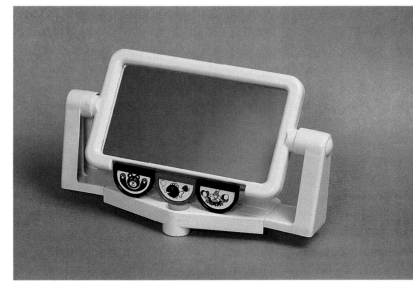

10-23 A nonbreakable mirror helps babies see themselves and begin to learn self-awareness.
© John Shaw

teach possession by making statements like "Here's Barbara's dress," or "Where are Keith's blocks?"

Handling Special Problems

All babies have some problems. These may include feeding and sleeping problems, fear of strangers, or lots of crying. When problems arise, these tips may help.

❖ Decide if the problem is temporary. Wait a few days, unless the baby seems ill. Babies do have mood

self-awareness. The understanding a person has about himself or herself as a person.

changes. Also, the problem may be because of a hurried or tense caregiver. In these cases, the problem will likely end as soon as the adult slows down or relaxes.

❖ If the problem continues, talk to an expert. Start with your pediatrician or a family doctor.

❖ Get help when needed. For example, parents who have a fussy baby may need to use babysitters to give them time to rest or leave home for a few hours.

❖ Give in to a baby's demands sometimes, if the results are not serious. Even babies have wills of their own, and letting them have their way sometimes isn't going to spoil or harm them. For example, if a baby refuses to eat peas, try other vegetables with similar nutrients.

❖ Remain calm. This helps the baby and the adult.

Experienced caregivers tend to almost ignore many common, not-too-serious problems. Experience teaches that all babies are different and many problems solve themselves in time.

Recognizing Developmental Delays

As you read in chapter 1, a developmental delay simply means a child's development falls far behind typical children of his or her age in one or more areas. A larger gap indicates a more serious delay. Infancy is the best time to begin watching for delays and treating problems. Seeking help early can keep some problems from worsening. If an infant's development seems to be much slower than the norms, parents should consult a doctor. Knowing some typical infant behaviors may help parents to recognize delays, 10-24.

Typical Infant Behaviors

One Month
- raises head slightly when lying on stomach
- can hold head up for a second or two when supported
- briefly watches and follows moving person or object with eyes
- makes throaty sounds

Two Months
- holds head erect but bobbing when supported in sitting position
- responds to smiles with an occasional smile
- vocalizes

Three Months
- lifts head and chest when lying on stomach
- has strong body movements
- has good head control—less bobbing—when supported in sitting position
- recognizes bottle or breast (knows it is feeding time)
- coos
- chuckles

Four Months
- rolls from side to side
- grasps objects held near hand and may reach for objects
- follows moving objects with eyes easily from a sitting position
- laughs aloud
- plays

Six Months
- sits with very little support
- rolls from back to stomach
- transfers objects from mouth to hand and from hand to hand
- babbles three or more sounds (*ma, pa,* and *ba*)

Nine Months
- sits without support and can change position without falling
- plays with two objects at a time
- can unwrap a block placed in an piece of cloth
- repeats same babbling sounds (*ma-ma* and *ba-ba*)

One Year
- pulls to standing and may take a step or two with support from an adult's hand or an object.
- picks things up with thumb and one finger
- stacks two blocks
- gives toy when asked
- shows affection ("asking" to be picked up by holding arms up, kissing)
- may say two or three words

10-24 Knowing what typical infant behaviors are can help to recognize developmental delays.

A parent provides for the developmental needs of a baby.

Summing It Up

With the rapid development during the first year, the baby has many needs. Adults must meet their physical, intellectual, and social-emotional needs.

Only breast milk or formula is recommended for the first six months. After that, adults can introduce solid baby foods one at a time. Learning to drink from a cup, eat finger foods, and use a spoon takes time. These tasks require the child to use a different set of throat and tongue muscles and develop coordination.

Babies outgrow their clothing quickly. Good consumer sense is important when buying baby clothes. Parents should read labels for care instructions and check for flame retardant and anti-static finishes. Clothing must be clean and free of detergent residue before wearing.

Other needs include bathing, sleeping, and playing. When giving a tub bath, make sure the water is comfortably warm and the child is safe from slipping. Children should have their own sleep area away from distracting noises. Keep the child's bed free of soft, fluffy products, and put all infants on their backs to sleep. All play spaces for babies and young children should be safe, yet provide stimulating play.

To develop intellectually, children need an enriched environment. They need activities that will stimulate all the senses. Problem-solving activities help them learn about the world around them. Activities that develop motor skills are encouraged. For language development to take place, it is important to talk to children and encourage them to make sounds and words.

Babies' social-emotional needs center on their interaction with others and their growing self-awareness. Adults and those around them help babies develop their self-identity.

Different problems in feeding, sleeping, and crying may develop. Parents and caregivers need to try a number of methods to handle these problems calmly, yet effectively. If a problem persists, or a delay is suspected, parents should contact the child's doctor for advice.

Reviewing Key Concepts

Write your answers on a separate sheet of paper.

1. Babies' most basic needs are in the _____ (physical, intellectual, social) area.
2. Give three reasons for not starting solids before babies are six months of age unless advised by a baby's doctor.
3. Which statements about the weaning process are true?
   A. Weaning is best done gradually.
   B. Complete weaning prior to nine months has no harmful effects on the baby.
   C. Weaning is a physical and social-emotional process.
4. True or false. Generally, SIDS occurs in babies between 10 and 12 months of age.
5. List three suggestions in planning sleep and play spaces for a baby.
6. True or false. Activities and games should be woven into child care routines.
7. For each lettered item below, indicate which of the two phrases describes the caregiver action that would best help babies learn.
   A. checking age charts and doing an activity when it's time OR watching for signs of each baby's interest in certain experiences
   B. repeating games many times over several months OR not repeating games because babies get bored with them
   C. showing babies exactly how to do activities so that babies will not become confused OR letting babies try things for themselves
8. True or false. Learning to sit is an example of a fine-motor skill.
9. True or false. Babies learn language by hearing people talk.
10. List two ways to help a baby learn to talk and understand words.
11. How can parents help their child develop self-awareness? List three ways.

Using Your Knowledge

1. **Consumer Skills/Creative Skills.** Examine five articles of baby clothing and list the good features noted in each piece. Create a hangtag for each item that lists its best features. Show each piece to the class as you read its hangtag aloud.
2. **Child Care Skills.** After viewing a demonstration of tub bathing for infants, practice the steps using a doll. Remember to talk and play with the baby as you give the bath.
3. **Technology.** Conduct Internet research of at least three Web sites that provide information about sudden infant death syndrome (SIDS). Use the computer to compose a two-page report based on your findings.
4. **Child Development/Creative Skills.** Create a pamphlet for parents listing activities they can do with their infants to promote the development of fine- and gross-motor skills.

5. **Interviewing Skills.** Ask a pediatrician or child development expert to identify various signs that would indicate a child might have a developmental delay that requires professional help. Ask the expert to explain why seeking help early is important. What experiences has the expert had in working with infants who have developmental delays? Do delays in infancy always guarantee lifelong delays? If possible, record the interview on audio- or videotape to share with the class.

Making Observations

1. Observe a baby trying to drink from a cup or handle a spoon. What problems does the baby experience? How are these problems related to messiness?
2. Observe several babies wearing different types of outfits. Describe the outfits and list the advantages or disadvantages of each.
3. Visit the home of a 6- to 12-month-old. Observe the places designed for the baby's sleep and play. Ask the parent whether he or she likes these arrangements, and why. Describe your findings to the class.
4. Observe a baby playing. What senses are being stimulated? Which motor and language skills are being developed?
5. Observe an infant and parent playing. How does the adult encourage a positive relationship?

Thinking Further

1. Some parents believe that feeding babies solids early is the best way to ensure they sleep throughout the night. How can this belief be harmful to babies?
2. In the text, peek-a-boo is described as a good game for developing object permanence in babies. What other games besides peek-a-boo promote object permanence?
3. Adults need to respect babies' temperaments. What are some ways parents can respect the temperament of a happy baby? a shy baby? a fussy baby? an active baby? a quiet baby?

Part 4
Toddlers

Children between ages one and three years are called toddlers. This name fits them, because toddlers toddle during almost all their waking minutes as they explore the world around them.

You will see how the chubby one-year-old develops into a slender three-year-old in **chapter 11**. During this time, toddlers become sure-footed as they practice jumping, hopping, throwing, and catching. Small-motor coordination improves some, also.

In **chapter 12**, you will see that toddlers truly begin to understand their environment. They learn about the properties of objects and what happens when they manipulate them. Because they learn to think before acting, toddlers plan new ways to achieve goals. Toddlers also become able communicators as they learn new words and speak in short sentences.

Chapter 13 discusses the other traits of toddlers—their desire for independence and sometimes negative expression of self-will. Although toddlers express their emotions in intense ways, their self-esteem is fragile and adults must protect it.

Chapter 14 will give examples of ways to assist toddlers' development. Adults need to help toddlers begin to think independently and practice self-care. They need to help children find a balance between their own will and the limits to self-will society expects.

Tarik just celebrated his first birthday. He is already walking, although he doesn't have much coordination. Tarik is adventurous and eager to try new movements. His mother says he is fearless, although sometimes his stunts make her nervous! At times, Tarik seems frustrated that his body can't do all he wants it to. Tarik is better with gross-motor skills, such as standing and walking, than he is at fine-motor skills, such as stacking blocks and nesting cups. In fact, Tarik is on the move so much, he rarely seems interested in toys that build these fine-motor skills.

Chapter 11
Physical Development of the Toddler

After studying this chapter, you will be able to
- describe the physical changes that occur between the first and third years of life.
- identify the toddler's major gross-motor and fine-motor skills.

As toddlers develop physically, their bodies mature. This helps them handle more complex tasks. Although toddlers do not grow as quickly as infants, they go through many important physical changes.

Babies do not have much control over their muscles when they are born. By the end of their first year, infants are just learning to control voluntary muscle movements. Both the gross-motor and fine-motor skills of toddlers improve. These skills improve so much that, by the end of their second year, toddlers can run, jump, throw, and feed themselves, 11-1.

Body Growth and Development

After the first year, babies continue to grow quickly. Their organ systems continue to mature, too. However, they do not grow as quickly as they did during their first year.

11-1 Improving motor skills allow toddlers to feed themselves.
Fisher Price

Height and Weight

Toddlers grow at different rates. This is due to environment and heredity. What does heredity affect? Heredity affects a baby's height. It affects how fast the baby grows taller, too. Because genes determine height, they also influence weight. (Taller people usually weigh more than shorter people.) However, the environment (diet, exercise, health, and even emotions) affects a person's weight more than genes. Because of these factors, toddlers sometimes grow at different rates than norms predict for their age.

Years One and Two

Body growth begins to slow after the first year. Babies grow about half as much in height during the second year as compared with the first year. Most babies triple their birthweight during the first year, then gain only one-fourth of that amount during the second, 11-2. Some babies grow a little faster than these norms in their second year. (They may be "catching up" to norms after a premature birth or first-year illness.) Most girls reach 53 percent of their adult height by age two. Boys usually reach 50 percent of their adult height by age two, 11-3. Thus, it is often true that a tall two-year-old will be a tall adult. Likewise, a short two-year-old may be a short adult.

After Year Two

After 24 months, children grow at a slower but steadier rate. They tend to gain two to three inches and about six pounds per year throughout childhood. (This rate of growth continues until about 11 years for girls and 13 years for boys.) Chart 11-4 shows the height and weight norms from 12 to 36 months.

Other Body Changes

The body proportions of a two-year-old still differ from those of an adult. At 24 months, the head is one-fourth of the total height. An adult's head is one-tenth of his or her height. A 24-month-old's chest and abdomen are about the same size. By 30

Growth from Birth to Age Two Years

Let's suppose Sarah was 20.5 inches and weighed seven pounds at birth. She is growing exactly by the norms. Based on her birth length and weight, we would calculate her two-year growth the following way:

First Year

Length/Height	Birth	20.5"
	Add 9"	
	(based on norms) +	9.0"
	Total Length	29.5"
	A 9" increase	
Weight	Birth	7 lbs.
	Triple birthweight	× 3
	Total	21 lbs.
	A 14 lb. gain	

Second Year

Length/Height	12 months	29.5"
	Add ½ of 9"	+ 4.5"
	Total height	34.0"
	A 4.5" increase	
Weight	12 months	21 lbs.
	Add ¼ of total weight at	
	12 months	+ 5.25 lbs.
	Total weight	26.25 lbs.
	A 5 lb. increase	

11-2 Growth slows after the first year.

11-3 By age two, most boys reach 50 percent of their adult height. At this same age, most girls reach 53 percent of their adult height.

months, the chest is larger than the abdomen. As the child matures, the difference between chest and abdomen size will become even greater. The child's body-build type will become apparent during the toddler years.

Bones and Teeth

As toddlers grow, their bones continue to become harder. The degree of ossification is not the same throughout the body, however. Due to the cartilage, the toddler's bones are

Average Height and Weight from One to Three Years

Age in Months	Height	Weight
12	30 in.	21 lbs.
18	32 in.	24.5 lbs.
24	34 in.	27 lbs.
30	36 in.	30 lbs.
36	38 in.	32 lbs.

11-4 Children's height and weight increases steadily from ages one year to three years.

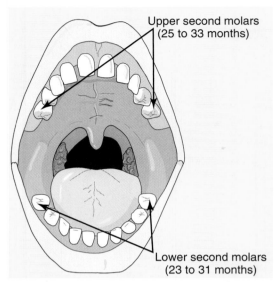

Upper second molars
(25 to 33 months)

Lower second molars
(23 to 31 months)

11-5 Before the third birthday, a toddler's set of deciduous teeth in completed.

11-6 The toddler will slowly become slender because fat deposits under the skin are decreasing.
© John Shaw

more flexible and less likely to break than an adult's. However, the softer bones are more prone to disease or deformation. The toddlers' *fontanels* (gaps between the skull bones, also called *soft spots*) are closed or almost closed. The toddler's spine becomes S-shaped rather than C-shaped like the adult's, allowing the posture to become straighter and more upright. This makes standing and walking easier. Shortly after two years, a child has the full set of deciduous teeth (often called *baby teeth*), 11-5.

The Brain

By the end of the second year, the brain is four-fifths of its adult weight. The brain now is closer to maturity than any other organ. The other body organs continue to mature, but they do so at a slower rate than the brain. (This is an example of the head-to-foot principle—development is completed from the brain down the spine.)

Fat and Muscle Tissue

Fat deposits under the skin decrease rapidly between 9 and 30 months. The chubby baby becomes a slender child, 11-6. **Muscle development** (the lengthening and thickening of muscles) is slow during the toddler stage.

Motor Development

Toddlers improve the motor skills they developed as infants. However, they also learn many new skills. Motor skills develop as the child grows and develops. As the child practices new skills, motor development improves even more.

Large-Muscle Development

Large-muscle development refers to the development of the trunk and arm and leg muscles. Movements such as crawling, walking, jumping, and running depend mainly on these large muscles. (These movements are examples of gross-motor skills.) During the first year, most babies developed these muscles at least to the point of standing and walking with support. After one year, babies master walking and begin learning other motor skills. Toddlers love to run, jump, and use other large muscles. When they are held in one place too long, they begin squirming, as if to say, "I want down!" (Squirming is an example of a large-muscle movement.)

Walking

Most toddlers begin to walk without support within two or three months before or after the first birthday. Why do babies begin to walk at different ages? Some children are frustrated or even fearful when they fall when trying to walk. Others who creep quickly may not walk early because creeping gets them where they want to go. Often, girls begin to walk before boys. Also, lighter babies may walk earlier than heavier babies.

Although some conditions are helpful, babies learn to walk in their own time and way. To do so, they need warm adult support, a positive reaction to the baby's attempts, and a safe area. Pushing a baby to walk early will not help. It may even delay walking and will surely frustrate both the baby and adult.

Beginning Walkers

Regardless of age, all beginning walkers share some common traits. They stand with their feet wide apart, which gives them a wider base of support. They turn their feet outward and slightly flex their knees, 11-7. Some children walk on their tiptoes. This is not because they want to stand taller (which they learn to do). Babies stand on their tiptoes because they have not learned to lower their heels yet. A baby's first steps often seem like staggers. The baby may step to the side or backward. He or she may also take irregular steps, lurch forward, and weave. Arms are often

 muscle development. The lengthening and thickening of muscles.

large-muscle development. The development of the trunk and arm and leg muscles.

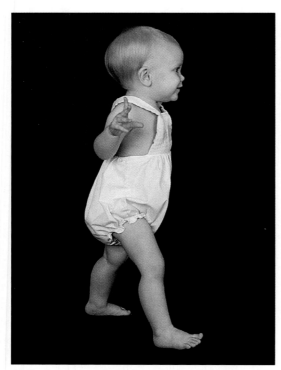

11-7 To maintain balance, toddlers first walk with a wide stance and knees flexed.
© John Shaw

held up or out and do not swing alternately with foot movement. Because it is hard for babies to balance their large heads, they fall often.

A flat spine causes the toddler to tilt forward slightly when walking. As the toddler grows, this walking posture changes as the lower back curve takes on the S-shape, or *lumbar curve*, as it is called, 11-8. As it does, the walk becomes more upright. This, plus improved ability to balance, helps the toddler to walk steadily. The toddler's stance also becomes narrower, the feet are positioned straighter, and the knees are less flexed.

Walking at Two Years

At two years, a child's walk may look like a run, but it is not a run. Toddlers take about 170 steps per minute. Their stride is half the length

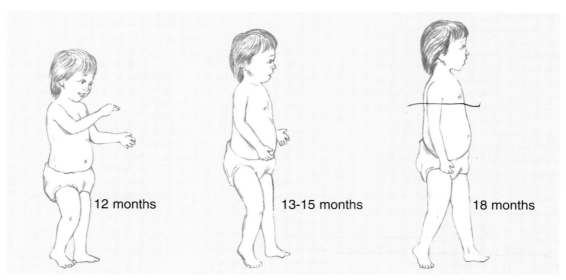

11-8 Toddlers walk in a more upright way between 12 and 18 months of age.
Thomas J. Roberts

of an adult's stride. Can you imagine doubling your steps, taking 170 steps per minute, and having someone hold onto your hand above your head? Yet, this is how many toddlers walk with adults. No wonder walking tires young children before it tires adults.

Toddlers rarely go around small obstacles on the floor, such as a toy or book. They simply walk over these objects, which increases their chances of falling. Toddlers must watch their foot placement while walking until almost three years of age. They must watch each step the same way you would if you were walking on stones across a creek. Being distracted is another reason toddlers fall.

Running

True running (not just a hurried walk) begins around two years of age. Two-year-olds are not skillful runners. This is due to their arm placement. They tend to hold their arms up or out as they run. Running is also awkward because toddlers cannot start or stop quickly.

Jumping

Stepping off low objects at about 18 months is the way children learn to jump. Before two years of age, children may step off a low object and remain suspended in air for a brief moment. At two years, children can jump off low objects with two feet. However, they move their arms backward instead of helping the jump by swinging their arms forward, 11-9.

11-9 At first, toddlers "jump" by stepping off low objects. Then they jump with both feet while pulling their arms back instead of swinging them forward.
Thomas J. Roberts

Climbing

Babies may begin to climb as soon as they can crawl or creep. Between 15 and 18 months, babies will climb onto furniture. They will walk up and down stairs with help. They often hold onto the stair railing and the adult's hand, or turn to the side and hold the railing with both hands. For toddlers, going up stairs is easier than coming down stairs. Toddlers do not change feet while climbing until after the second birthday.

When does climbing begin? There really isn't a set time. Climbing ability relates to the kinds of stairs and other objects the baby has nearby. Babies can climb more easily if stairs are enclosed and not too steep. Climbing

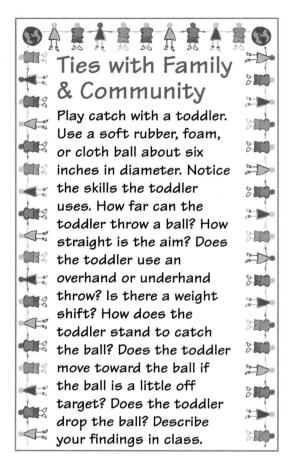

Ties with Family & Community

Play catch with a toddler. Use a soft rubber, foam, or cloth ball about six inches in diameter. Notice the skills the toddler uses. How far can the toddler throw a ball? How straight is the aim? Does the toddler use an overhand or underhand throw? Is there a weight shift? How does the toddler stand to catch the ball? Does the toddler move toward the ball if the ball is a little off target? Does the toddler drop the ball? Describe your findings in class.

also relates to courage. A courageous baby is likely to try climbing sooner than a timid baby.

Throwing and Catching

Infants begin throwing by accident. They forget to hold onto an object while swinging their arms. They enjoy seeing the object move and hearing the sound it makes when it lands. Then, babies start to throw on purpose. Planned throwing begins around one year of age.

Year-old babies usually throw from a sitting position, such as from the high chair. After babies feel secure standing or walking, they throw from standing positions. Children under three years are not very skillful throwers. These children usually use a rigid throw and do not shift their weight. In fact, when throwing with one hand, they often step with the same-side foot. They also cannot release the ball at the right time, which sends the ball in almost any direction.

For almost a year after children begin to walk, they "catch" an object by squatting and picking it up, 11-10. Around two years of age, the child will bend at the waist to pick up the thrown object. Two- and three-year-olds may try to catch by standing in

11-10 Toddlers squat to pick up thrown objects until they are about two years old.
Courtesy of PlayDesigns

one position with arms extended and elbows stiff. For the child to catch a ball, it must be exactly on target. The child does not move toward the ball. In fact, many children close their eyes as the ball comes toward them.

Small-Muscle Development

Small-muscle development refers to the development of small muscles, especially those in the hands and fingers. The movements that depend on these muscles are called fine-motor skills. Fine-motor skills also depend on a child's level of eye-hand coordination. To have **eye-hand coordination**, children must coordinate what they see with the way they move their hands. As eye-hand coordination and small muscles improve, toddlers can handle more complex fine-motor skills, 11-11. With time and experience, clumsy and difficult movements become more smooth and require less effort.

By the end of the first year, babies can hold objects between the thumb and index finger. This helps them learn many new fine-motor skills. Between 12 and 18 months, toddlers

 small-muscle development. The development of small muscles, especially those in the hands and fingers.

eye-hand coordination. The ability to coordinate what a person sees with the way the person moves his or her hands.

11-11 As toddlers gain motor skills, they can use more complicated small-motor movements, such as holding a paintbrush.

can hold spoons in their fists. They can feed themselves and drink from cups. They may miss their mouths often and spill food at first. With practice and better eye-hand coordination, however, toddlers become better at feeding themselves. By 15 months, they can fill and empty containers. They can also make marks on paper by holding a pencil or crayon in their fists. At this age, the toddler can do the following:

❖ remove a hat and socks
❖ insert rather large objects into holes
❖ turn pages of a book several at a time
❖ begin to fit objects together
❖ build a tower of two to three soft blocks

Between 18 months and 2 years, fine-motor skills improve even more. By this stage, toddlers can string large beads on cords. They can turn the pages of books one at a time. They can open doors by turning knobs. Most two-year-olds can hit pegs with a hammer. After two years, many children hold crayons or pencils with the thumb on one side and fingers on the other side, 11-12. They still cannot hold or write with a crayon or pencil the way an adult can.

11-12 A toddler can hold crayons with the thumb and fingers, but the grasp is much more awkward than a mature grasp.
Thomas J. Roberts

By two years, most children show a definite hand preference. They still switch hands a lot. Their right hand tends to be used for drawing or throwing a ball and the left hand for holding a cup and eating. With each passing year until age seven or eight, more and more children use the right hand for most activities. At that time, 95 percent of all children are right-handed. (This is the same percentage as found among adults.)

Summing It Up

Children tend to grow more slowly after their first year. Individual differences are due to heredity and environment. A toddler's bones continue to harden. Fat deposits under the skin decrease, making the toddler more slender. Body build becomes more apparent. The brain matures at a faster rate than other body organs. A full set of baby teeth may be present shortly after age two years.

Toddlers refine gross-motor skills, such as walking, climbing, and throwing. Many new skills are emerging, such as running, jumping off objects, and catching objects. Fine-motor skills depend on the child's level of eye-hand coordination. Most children begin to show a definite hand preference by their second year.

Toddlers refine many physical skills, such as standing and grasping.

Reviewing Key Concepts

Write your answers on a separate sheet of paper.

1. A person's height and the rate of increase in height is mainly due to (heredity, environment). A person's weight and the rate of increase in weight are mainly due to (heredity, environment).
2. True or false. A baby's rate of growth slows after 12 months.
3. True or false. Between 12 and 24 months, a toddler will gain only about one-fourth of his or her total weight.
4. The fastest organ to develop is the
   A. heart
   B. brain
   C. liver
   D. lungs
5. True or false. Children are usually chubbier after their first year than before.
6. Give two possible reasons babies might begin to walk at different ages.
7. Explain why toddlers may fall if they do not think about what they are doing as they walk.
8. Match the toddler's skills to the motor actions by putting the correct letter before the skill.
   Skills—
   _____ walking
   _____ running
   _____ jumping
   _____ climbing
   _____ throwing
   _____ catching

Motor Actions—
A. moves arms toward the back
B. uses improper arm actions and cannot stop or start quickly
C. stands without moving with arms extended stiffly
D. begins each movement with the same foot rather than alternating feet
E. shows little or no weight shift
F. steps forward, backward, and to either side

9. True or false. One-year-olds have well-developed eye-hand coordination.
10. True or false. Year-old babies can grasp objects between the thumb and index finger, so they hold flatware and crayons the same way adults hold them.

Using Your Knowledge

1. **Child Development/Mathematics.** Use the formula given in Figure 11-2 to calculate expected growth at one year and two years for Marcus if he grows according to the norms. At birth, Marcus was 18 inches long and weighed 6.5 pounds.
2. **Child Development/Teamwork/ Communication.** As a group or class project, write a one- or two-page brochure explaining toddlers' motor skills. Include information on the order (and approximate age) when toddlers learn motor skills. Also explain the motor actions used when walking, running, jumping, climbing, throwing, and catching. (Illustrations may help.) Have the teacher check your brochure, then

make copies. Give copies to parents and adults at a program that serves toddlers, such as a child care program or preschool.

3. **Child Development.** The text indicates toddlers walk at a rate of about 170 steps per minute. Walk quickly for one minute as you have a partner time you. Next, time your partner for one minute as he or she walks quickly. How do your results compare with your partner's and with the average rate for toddlers? What conclusions can you draw from this experiment?

4. **Technology.** Visit Web sites of manufacturers of toddler play equipment. What kinds of equipment can you find that provides safe opportunity for toddlers to climb both indoors and outdoors? If approved by your teacher, print any product information and photos and share with the class.

5. **Interview.** Ask a pediatrician or child development expert to explain whether it is desirable for parents to push toddlers to use a particular hand or if they should let the child's natural preference determine hand use. Write a brief report on your findings.

Making Observations

1. Observe infants and toddlers. Describe how children from the two age groups differ in appearance.
2. Observe several 24-month-olds with their parents. Do the taller toddlers have taller parents? Do the shorter toddlers have shorter parents?
3. Observe two toddlers—a new walker and an experienced walker. How do their posture and walking skills and style differ?
4. Observe the gross- and fine-motor skills of toddlers between 12 and 36 months of age. Note the kinds of movements they make and how they compare to adult movements. Share your findings with the class.
5. Observe toddlers with materials that require fine-motor skills. How do they grip pencils, crayons, or markers? How messy is their self-feeding? Are large beads and puzzle pieces hard to manage?

Thinking Further

1. Two-year-old Sarah has a shorter-than-average mother and a taller-than-average father. Her parents wonder whether Sarah will be a tall, average, or short adult. Can they predict her height? If so, how? Do you think such a prediction will be very accurate? Why or why not?
2. When toddlers walk or run, they usually hold their arms out. Why? In what situations might adults do this?
3. Why is coloring within the lines an impossible skill for toddlers?

Chapter 12
Intellectual Development of the Toddler

After studying this chapter, you will be able to:
- describe how and what toddlers learn.
- describe the sequence of language development.

Two-year-old Ling talks constantly! Ling's parents encourage her to ask for what she needs rather than pointing or grunting. They rotate Ling's toys to give her more variety. Unlike Ling, her two-year-old cousin Ming has been slow to talk. He's very active, but doesn't have many toys. Although Ming says a few words, his parents often use his gestures and sounds to figure out what he wants. They wonder if Ming's slow speech is a sign of a developmental delay.

Define...

deferred imitation
attributes
language
parentese
articulation
communication
grammar

In previous chapters, you have read about how babies learn. Much of what babies learn begins in the neonatal period. By the end of infancy, learning becomes much more advanced. All areas of development are closely linked. During the first two years, motor skills are highly linked to mental skills because very young children act upon objects within their environment. Also, walking and other motor skills expand the child's physical and social worlds.

Toddlers are eager to learn. They are curious about everyone and everything, 12-1. They may not always be interested in learning what adults want them to learn. However, when working at a task they choose, toddlers will stay with the task until they are satisfied with the results.

12-1 Toddlers explore everything. Even a stick can be interesting.

How and What Toddlers Learn

Through stages of development, Piaget has described how children's thinking changes as they mature. He called the first stage the sensorimotor stage. It includes children from birth to two years of age. As you read in chapter 8, children in this stage learn through their senses and motor actions, 12-2. From about 12 to 18 months, says

12-2 This toddler uses her senses and motor actions to explore the world around her.

Piaget, children learn by discovering new ways to solve problems. Piaget states that the beginning of thought occurs from 18 to 24 months.

Discovering New Ways to Solve Problems

From 12 to 18 months, children are busy exploring. They show lots of interest in new actions. Toddlers are active explorers and experimenters.

Piaget called them "the little scientists." They seem to get into everything. After discovering one way they can use an object, toddlers seem to want to know what else they can do with the same object. They also enjoy repeating their actions. Repeating actions helps them verify their observations in much the same way that scientific findings are verified through additional research.

Working Toward a Goal

In this stage, children's actions involve reaching a goal. The goal may be obvious to an adult. For example, a child may pull an object by its string in order to grasp it. Sometimes the goal may not be obvious. It may seem as if the child is only playing with or throwing objects. However, children play with objects to see how they work, 12-3. They want to know what happens to objects when they are rolled, shaken, thrown, or moved in other ways. Children are looking for the best ways to reach their goals. This is why children repeat actions many times with slight variations.

Toddlers can begin to solve common problems themselves. As they learn more about objects their thinking skills improve. Toddlers learn how to feed and dress themselves, 12-4. They discover how to open doors and put objects in containers. They can find ways to grab out-of-reach objects. They solve their problems the best way they

12-3 Children learn by playing with different objects.

12-4 Toddlers feel proud when they dress themselves. Elastic waists and wide neck holes make their task easier.

know how but do not think about the consequences of their actions. To snatch a cookie on the kitchen table, a toddler may pull on the tablecloth until the cookie falls (along with other items on the table).

Beginning of Thought

Around 18 to 24 months, most children think about what they do before they do it. When you see toddlers pause in mid-action, they are probably thinking. Unlike younger children who have not developed thought processes, these children will "figure things out" mentally instead of actually testing them out physically. For example, the two-year-old will discover in thought that a large object will not fit through a small opening in a container. On the other hand, a one-year-old would try to push the object through the opening to realize that it would not fit. Although these older toddlers think, their thinking is not mature yet. For this reason, they think mainly in terms of actions. In the example you just read, the two-year-old would mentally see himself or herself trying to put the object through the opening before concluding it was too big to fit. These older toddlers even identify objects in terms of actions. For example, a 30-month-old may answer the question, "What is a ball?" with the reply, "To play with," or "To roll."

12-5 Feeding a doll the way adults feed babies is an example of deferred imitation.
© John Shaw

Thinking and Imitation

Children also show they can think by imitating what someone else has done at an earlier time. The ability to recall an observed behavior and later imitate it is called **deferred imitation**, 12-5. (*Deferred* means postponed.) Deferred imitation is used in both pretend play and language.

Thinking and Goals

Thinking also shows in the child's way of reaching goals, 12-6. A child may want to reach a toy on a high playroom shelf (goal). He or she may have used a stepstool in the bathroom but not in the playroom. The child thinks about the stool and how it works in the bathroom. Then the child gets the stool to reach the object. If the

12-6 Thinking is evident as this toddler moves wooden beads along the brightly colored tracks of this toy.

child cannot bring the stool into the playroom, he or she may use another object as a stool. The child has thought through how to reach the goal.

Thinking and Hiding Games

Thinking is evident in hiding games, too. Children at this stage will search for objects they have not seen someone hide. This might happen when the adult pretends to hide a toy in one place but really hides it in another. The child knows the object still exists (object permanence) and thinks about where the adult could have hidden it. To find hidden objects, the child must also think in terms of spatial concepts. For example, the child must consider which objects would be large enough to conceal the hidden toy.

Thinking and Shape, Size, Color, and Texture

Toddlers continue to use their senses to learn about their world. They are learning about the **attributes** of objects, such as their shape, size, color, and texture. A toddler might often refer to these attributes when talking about a red ball or a big dog, for example.

Toddlers begin to perceive differences in shape, size, color, and texture. Noting these differences is a thinking skill, for it requires comparison. This perceptual and thinking skill is needed for the identification of objects. Children must be able to mentally compare differences before they can successfully use terms such as *ducks* and *geese* or *red* and *pink*. Although toddlers sometimes use the wrong word for an attribute, they do note the differences among objects.

Thinking and Object Exploration

Toddlers also learn more about what will happen as they handle objects. They learn by throwing, rolling, shaking, or moving objects, 12-7. Toddlers learn that round objects

12-7 Toddlers use their motor skills to explore playthings. They learn important concepts as they stack, nest, hit, bang, and manipulate these objects.
© John Shaw

roll and flat objects slide. They also learn that hard objects will make a loud noise when hit together but soft objects will not.

> **deferred imitation.** The ability to recall someone's behavior and later imitate it.
>
> **attributes.** Distinctive characteristics of an object, such as size, shape, color, and texture.

A toddler often knows the attributes of new objects based on prior experience. He or she uses this knowledge in play. Suppose a child has already been exposed to the noise made by metal objects and the lack of noise made by soft objects. He or she will use this knowledge when given new objects for play. The child would immediately bang metal pans together but would not bang together two balls of yarn. This is a very valuable thinking skill.

Thinking and Language

Finally, the way children think is observed through their use of language. Language is a symbol system in which words are used as labels for people, objects, and ideas. Unlike other symbol systems, such as pictures, words do not sound or look like the people and objects they represent.

In order to learn language, children use two thinking skills. First, they must associate the word with the person or object to which it refers. For example, toddlers must understand the word *milk* refers to a certain liquid, not water or juice. Second, children must recall the word and its meaning when they hear the word or want to say it. Language requires high-level thinking skills.

Language Abilities

As you read in chapter 8, babies begin to learn language as infants. Newborns will turn toward the sound of human speech just minutes after delivery. Babies react to differences in sounds during the first couple of months. Then they begin to babble these sounds at about six months. Toward the end of the first year, they understand many words and sentences. They may also say a few words.

Language is often used to distinguish infants from toddlers. Learning language is important for children's mental and social development.

Research emphasizes the importance of parents as the first language teachers. Parents speak in a high-pitched style known as **parentese**. While speaking, parents put their faces closer to children, use shorter sentences, and speak in a singsong fashion. As a way to help toddlers learn the meanings of words, parents who use parentese look at objects they are describing more than other parents.

Learning Spoken Language

Spoken language develops at a faster rate between one and three years than at any other time in a person's life. However, learning to talk takes time and effort. This is because speaking involves **articulation** (making the sounds of language) and learning the meanings of words.

Learning to Articulate

Babies can make all the sounds of any language. They learn the words and language of those around them through imitation. Learning to control the tongue, lip muscles, and vocal chords to form words takes practice. Babies do not pronounce sounds accurately each time.

Children who cannot make one sound will substitute another. For example, they may use *d* for *th*. A toddler may say *dat* instead of *that*. Sometimes children can articulate the right sound in one place in a word but not in another. A toddler may have no problem with *m* at the beginning of a word such as *milk*. However, the toddler may have trouble making the *m* sound in the middle of *hammer* or at the end of *broom*.

Toddlers may also change the sound order of a word. They may say *perslip* to mean *slipper*. They even may change an entire word, such as say *book* and mean *bird*. Sometimes toddlers will drop a sound if they can't pronounce it. For example, they may say *seepy* instead of *sleepy*.

A few children articulate most sounds correctly from the beginning. Most children make substitutions. They tend to correct themselves in time. Adults should pronounce words correctly, even if the toddler's way of saying words sounds cute. Children need good examples to follow. In time, the child will learn from listening. Forcing children to repeat a word again and again is not a recommended way to correct pronunciation, because it may cause the child stress.

Learning Meanings: A Major Brain Development Activity

Many studies support recent research in brain development. Wiring for language is very active in the toddler years. Studies support the window of opportunity for language

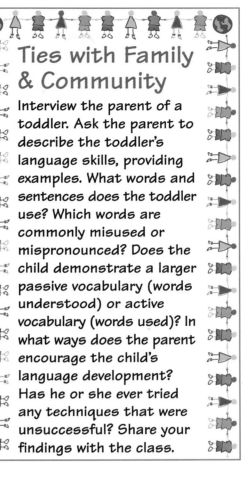

Ties with Family & Community

Interview the parent of a toddler. Ask the parent to describe the toddler's language skills, providing examples. What words and sentences does the toddler use? Which words are commonly misused or mispronounced? Does the child demonstrate a larger passive vocabulary (words understood) or active vocabulary (words used)? In what ways does the parent encourage the child's language development? Has he or she ever tried any techniques that were unsuccessful? Share your findings with the class.

language. A symbol system in which words are used as labels for people, objects, and ideas.

parentese. High-pitched style in which parents speak to their children.

articulation. Making the sounds of a language.

learning. How many words a child understands or speaks is related to how much parents and other caregivers talk to him or her. The most important thing for word growth is the number of times a child hears given words. At age 20 months, toddlers of chatty mothers or caregivers knew more words than children of less talkative ones. By 24 months, the gap had doubled in favor of talkative adults. The same results held for grammar. Mothers and caregivers who use complex sentences have children who use them, too.

Learning the meanings of words is hard. To do so, the child must link certain features with a name. This is difficult because many objects with different names share common features. For example, both lambs and ponies run outside and have four legs.

Sometimes children confuse the meanings of words they hear. They may use a wrong name for an object, such as call a cow a *moo* or a stove *hot*. Without meanings attached to spoken sounds, there would be no language. These meanings give the child two new tools—communication and a new way to think.

Communication is the skill needed to understand others and be understood by them. Already, toddlers can understand many words and sentences. When they begin to say words, they want to be understood. Toddlers often use their communication to achieve three goals, 12-8.

As you read, language is part of the thinking process. In other words, people learn to think in words. As the child learns to talk, words go with actions. For example, the toddler will

The Tool of Communication

Reasons to Communicate	Examples of Communication
To achieve a goal	"Want cookie." (I want a cookie.) "Go bye-bye." (I want to ride in the car.) "No!" (I don't want _____.)
To identify an object	"See doggie." (I see a dog.) "Big!" (That is big.) "What dat?" (What is that?
To create a bond with another person	"Mommy?" (Where are you mommy? I want you.) "Kiss." (I love you) "Hurt." (Please help me.)

12-8 Reading to toddlers helps them learn about the usage and meaning of words. It also provides a special time for parents and toddlers to share a quiet closeness.

say *goodbye* while waving. Later, children talk to themselves as they play or lie in bed. They then often whisper words. Finally, they think about words without saying them.

Young children develop both vocabulary and grammar. As children learn language, they attach meanings to words and to the order of words. This process is gradual, however.

Vocabulary

Most children's vocabularies grow slowly until 18 months to two years of age. The fastest growth occurs around 30 months of age.

Toddlers will vary in the number of words their vocabularies include at different ages. This can also depend on whether all spoken words or only those used correctly are counted as part of the vocabulary. Children may use words for a while, drop them, and pick them up again months later. The size of the vocabulary can be measured most easily in children three years of age and older.

Grammar

Grammar is the study of the preferred word usage and order in a given language. Each language has grammar rules. Children begin to learn these rules in the toddler period. This learning begins with single-word "sentences" and will often progress to simple sentences of a few words during the toddler years. Within six months of saying their first words, toddlers usually begin to put words together. Combining words is an advanced skill because word order affects the meanings of sentences. By listening to adults and having good books read to them, toddlers learn the basic rules for the language they hear and apply these rules to their own phrases and sentences.

Single Words

From 12 to 18 months of age, toddlers use sentences of only one word. This single word is often used by the toddler to mean different ideas at different times. A child may say *bye-bye* both to identify a moving object (a car) and to make a request ("Let's go!") To understand these meanings, the caregiver must note how the child says the word, what gestures he or she uses, and what is happening at the time.

Children use words that represent the actions they see and the people and objects they know. First words are usually nouns and simple action verbs. Nouns may include words like *mama*, *daddy*, and *kitty*. For toddlers, action verbs may include *hi, bye-bye, run,* and *fly.* Next, the child learns descriptive words (adjectives and adverbs), such as *big, hot, pretty, loud,* and *fast.* Young

communication. The skill needed to understand others and to be understood by them.

grammar. The study of the preferred word usage and order in a given language.

children quickly learn words for love and affection, too, such as *hug*.

Two or More Words

After 19 months, many children begin combining two or more words to form sentences. At the early stage of combining words, toddlers use only the most necessary words. By 24 to 30 months, many toddlers begin using three or more words in their sentences. When the child begins to use these multi-word sentences, the words that are added fill in the gaps. *All gone milk* becomes *Milk is gone*. By the time the child uses three-word sentences, word order is often used correctly. The child may say, "Bird is flying," instead of saying, "Fly bird."

Different Rates of Learning to Talk

The rate at which toddlers learn to talk can vary by several months. Many adults worry about a slow talker, only to see the toddler become a nonstop talker a few months later. These toddlers are hearing sounds and learning meanings all along. When they begin to talk, they progress quickly.

A number of factors can affect language development. Learning to talk depends on the following:

❖ hearing—A child must hear human speech clearly in order to learn to talk without special training. Even ear infections can delay speech in toddlers.

❖ interest—Some active toddlers are more interested in motor skills than in talking. Within a few months, they often catch up to earlier talkers.

❖ mental abilities—Because language is so closely related to thinking, a child with a mental disability is often slower to talk. On the other hand, early talking does not mean a child is bright. Children of average and even below average mental abilities may talk at a young age simply by repeating what they hear.

❖ gender—From the first year of life, girls tend to excel in verbal skills more than boys. Researchers do not know whether this is due to heredity or the environment. (For example, adults may talk to girls more than to boys.)

❖ need for speech—Some children get what they need without saying anything. For example, if a toddler receives milk by pointing, holding a cup, or crying, there is no need to learn to say, "I want milk."

❖ interesting environment—Just as adults have more to say when they have new experiences, so do toddlers, 12-9.

12-9 Toddlers can communicate their needs.

In some cases, the rate of language development may lag far behind the norms. In these situations, the child should receive professional help. Each child needs the best opportunity to develop language because language is essential to healthy mental and social-emotional development.

Summing It Up

As toddlers explore and learn more about the world, they discover many new ways to solve problems. Through their actions, they find out what and how things work. You can see children begin to think by the way they work through problems to reach goals. Their language development is a good indication of the way toddlers think.

Language is one of the most difficult skills children must learn. Articulating sounds and learning meanings of words takes time and practice. The peak age of language development occurs between one and three years of age. Recent brain research supports this concept. Toddlers need many experiences in hearing words and sentences, especially from parents who use parentese. Children first use single words of familiar people, objects, and actions before joining words to form sentences.

A number of conditions can affect language development. These include hearing problems, interest in talking, and mental abilities. Girls tend to talk sooner than boys. Having a need for speech and an interesting environment also affect when and how toddlers learn to talk.

Reviewing Key Concepts

Write your answers on a separate sheet of paper.

1. Which of the following statements describes toddlers' learnings?
   A. Toddlers have a real desire to learn about their world.
   B. Toddlers prefer to solve their own tasks, not the tasks adults plan for them.
   C. Toddlers will often try many times to solve their tasks.
   D. Toddlers use their past learnings and increased motor skills to help them learn.
   E. All of the above statements are true.
2. True or false. Trying to see how something works helps toddlers develop intellectually.
3. According to Piaget's developmental stages, problem solving is achieved by
   A. thinking on an abstract level
   B. trying out all possible answers physically
   C. thinking in terms of physical actions
   D. watching an adult and copying the adult's action
4. True or false. Learning to talk is a high-level thinking skill.
5. Give two reasons language development is one of the most difficult skills toddlers learn.
6. Describe what the term *articulation* means.
7. Replacing one sound with another sound, such as saying *wed wabbit* instead of *red rabbit,* is (common, uncommon) among toddlers.
8. True or false. Good language development is reinforced when adults repeat and encourage children's cute sayings, even when they are wrong.
9. In the following groups of words, which would the toddler probably learn to say first?
   A. happy or daddy
   B. bye-bye or empty
   C. kitty or pretty
10. Describe three reasons children may be late talkers.

Using Your Knowledge

1. **Art.** Make a poster describing in words and/or drawings the toddler's learnings between 12 and 24 months.
2. **Creative Writing.** Write a story from a toddler's point of view in which the language used shows typically toddler language development as described in the text. Share your story with the class.
3. **Role-play/Teamwork.** Work with a partner to role-play both positive and negative ways parents can respond to their toddler's language usage errors. Show how toddlers might react to each of these responses.
4. **Interview/Public Speaking Skills.** Interview a speech professional. Ask this person to explain both average language skills of a toddler and signs that professional assistance should be sought. Share your findings with the class in an oral report.

Making Observations

1. Observe a toddler playing with an object. Which senses did the toddler use? How did the toddler handle the object (shake, hit, or squeeze it)? What might have the toddler learned about the object (color, texture, rolls when dropped, soft when squeezed)?

2. Observe a toddler talking. List words the toddler says. Did the toddler seem to understand each word's meaning or incorrectly name some items? What type of words did the toddler mainly use (nouns, verbs, adjectives)?

3. Observe two or more toddlers of the same age. After listening to them talk, compare their vocabularies, articulation skills, and abilities to speak in sentences (versus words or phrases).

4. Observe a toddler exploring his or her world for 30 minutes. Record your observations. Especially note answers to the following questions: What senses were used? What activities interested the toddler most? How did the child try to solve problems? What were some possible learnings?

Thinking Further

1. Parents often think their toddlers throw objects to see how often they'll pick them up. Do you agree with this idea? Why or why not? What might a toddler learn from throwing objects?

2. Why is imitation an important mental skill? What things do toddlers learn by imitation? What are some things you've learned by imitation? Why is deferred imitation a more advanced mental ability than imitating while seeing an action performed?

3. Why is it important for adults who talk to toddlers to pronounce words correctly, as opposed to "baby talking" to them?

As she has become a toddler, Emily has begun to prefer her family members over strangers. She is quite attached to her yellow, fuzzy blanket, too. Emily wants to cuddle with her blanket at naptime when she is tired. Emily's father has found it harder to part from Emily at the child care center each morning. She cries and clings to his leg as he's leaving. The teachers say Emily keeps crying for more than an hour after he leaves. Emily's father is unsure what to do to make mornings easier for her.

Chapter 13
Social-Emotional Development of the Toddler

After studying this chapter, you will be able to
- ✎ describe how toddlers develop self-will.
- ✎ explain the way toddlers extend their social relationships with others.
- ✎ describe how toddlers develop a sense of self-worth.
- ✎ identify how toddlers reveal their emotions.

Most babies begin life surrounded by people who meet all their needs. Babies' needs are rather simple, so caregivers can meet most of them promptly. When their needs are met and their environments are consistent, babies become attached to their caregivers. They then learn to trust their world.

As babies become toddlers, two changes happen. First, toddlers find out more about their world and themselves as individuals. Second, toddlers find the world is not solely devoted to meeting their needs. Toddlers learn that caregivers cannot always give them what they want right away, 13-1. However, if love and trust are established by the end of the first year, toddlers will reach out in this new world. They will learn about themselves and others. Toddlers will begin to meet their needs without always depending on others. They will show emotions to others and learn how people respond to those emotions.

13-1 Toddlers often feel they should receive most, if not all, of a caregiver's attention.
© John Shaw

Self-Awareness

By the first birthday, toddlers have rather highly developed physical and mental skills. They can move around by themselves and reach objects they want. They are beginning to talk, which also helps them express their needs. These fast-growing skills influence the toddlers' relationships with others. In turn, others' reaction to them affects how toddlers see and understand themselves.

The self-awareness that began to develop at birth continues to build throughout life. In the toddler years, self-awareness emerges as a separate, possessing self (concerned about *me* and *mine*) and as a drive for independence. Toddlers become aware of how they look, what belongs (and doesn't belong) to them, and what they can and cannot do (especially physically).

Toddlers are also becoming more aware of others' feelings toward them. They realize they can be praised, thwarted, and hurt emotionally by others whom they love. This lays the foundation for feelings about oneself, such as pride, shame, guilt, and jealousy. Toddlers are more often aware they can affect others, too. Thus, at times they show positive emotions, such as true affection for others. At other times, they show negative emotions, such as defiance when they are angry.

Achieving Autonomy

Erikson stated that social-emotional development begins in infancy when the baby learns to trust or mistrust. As you read in chapter 8, babies whose needs are met and who have consistent environments develop a sense of trust. This sense of trust helps them as they enter the second stage, called *autonomy versus shame and doubt*, 13-2. For most children, this stage begins sometime between 12 and 18 months and is completed at about 3 years of age.

Autonomy is a form of self-control in which a toddler seeks to do his or

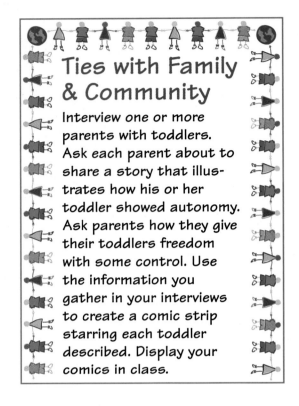

Ties with Family & Community

Interview one or more parents with toddlers. Ask each parent about to share a story that illustrates how his or her toddler showed autonomy. Ask parents how they give their toddlers freedom with some control. Use the information you gather in your interviews to create a comic strip starring each toddler described. Display your comics in class.

her own will. Autonomy builds on the toddler's expanding motor and mental skills. Toddlers are proud of their new skills and want to use them. They have the energy to carry out their goals. Because toddlers have much more "know how" than infants, they feel very independent. The independent feeling comes from the toddlers' increasing self-awareness of their abilities. Thus, Erikson explained autonomy as the toddler's feeling of being able to do some tasks without help from others. He felt that caregivers should recognize toddlers' desire to be more independent and allow them to do what they can at their own pace.

Erikson's Stages of Personality Development

Basic Trust versus Basic Mistrust
(First Year of Life)

Autonomy versus Shame and Doubt
(Second Year of Life)
❖ Toddlers seek some autonomy so they
   can use their new skills and knowledge.
❖ Toddlers seek control over whether to
   rely on others as they see fit.
❖ Autonomy learned at this stage leads
   to self-pride.
❖ Failure to achieve autonomy leads to
   feelings of shame in front of others and
   self-doubt.

Initiative versus Guilt (Preschool
Years)

Industry versus Inferiority (Middle
Childhood)

13-2 Learning to become more independent
while avoiding shame and doubt is the
social-emotional task of toddlerhood.

13-3 A conflict of wills between toddlers
and adults often occurs during daily
routines, such as mealtimes.
© John Shaw

Although toddlers want to be independent, they can misjudge their skills. They also do not understand possible results of some of their actions. For example, they can spill or break objects and harm themselves or others. Thus, adults must set limits on some of their actions. Toddlers often become defiant in response. Sometimes, too, toddlers find limits to their actions through their own failed attempts. This is most frustrating for them, too. Parents and their toddlers may also have conflicts when adults offer to help or take over tasks for toddlers. Because many of the toddler's activities center on routines, many of these conflicts concern eating, sleeping, toileting, and dressing, 13-3.

During this stage, parents may wonder why a child turns negative and yells or kicks when told what to do.

autonomy. A form of self-control in which a person seeks to do his or her will.

When limits need to be set or when things do not go the toddler's way, negative attitudes surface. At these times, toddlers need help to control their negative impulses. Calm controls are helpful and not damaging to the toddler. On the other hand, Erikson says that when impatient caregivers do for toddlers what toddlers can do for themselves, damage occurs. Consistently criticizing or overprotecting toddlers leads them to feel they cannot control themselves and their world. Erikson called this feeling a sense of *shame and doubt*.

Promoting a Toddler's Autonomy

Adults can promote autonomy by giving toddlers safe choices. Caregivers must find creative ways to build toddlers' feelings of independence and allow them to use their new skills. First choices offered should be simple, such as indoor play versus outdoor play. The toddler should be offered two alternatives and allowed to choose.

Before offering the toddler a choice, however, caregivers must be sure they can stand by either option chosen. If they fail to honor the child's choice or try to talk him or her out of it, this can be damaging. It undermines the toddler's sense of autonomy.

Caregivers should also step in and redirect a toddler before he or she engages in a forbidden or unsafe action. This is more helpful than waiting to intervene until the child is already performing the action. It is also more helpful than simply reacting to the consequences.

Adults may find it hard to help toddlers achieve autonomy while keeping them safe and preventing conflicts. Erikson feels adults should firmly reassure the toddler. They do not need to give in to the child's will all the time. However, when they confront a child, they should stay calm. Parents must also assure the child they still love him or her. This protects children from harm without making them feel ashamed or guilty. Chart 13-4 shows how to help the toddler in this stage.

Extending Social Relations

As children get older, their growing motor and mental abilities help them interact with others more. These interactions teach them new skills and attitudes, which help toddlers get along with other people. This process of interacting with others socializes children.

Toddlers with a healthy attachment to caregivers have a safe base from which to meet people, 13-5. Although toddlers continue to look to their main caregivers for social interaction, they now spend more time with other adults. These adults include babysitters, relatives, and neighbors. Having more than one caregiver often helps toddlers adjust to others. This also helps children to expect differences among people. When children have

Ways to Promote Autonomy in Toddlers

❖ Make sure the environment and play space is safe. This will help you avoid having to warn or threaten the toddler constantly.

❖ Set some important limits for the toddler, but don't make everything off limits. Let the toddler know what is off-limits beforehand.

❖ Follow through on limits set for the toddler by making sure the toddler does as told each time in these areas. Avoid inconsistent enforcement of limits.

❖ Allow the toddler to make some minor decisions and abide by the toddler's choices on these matters. Avoid making all the toddler's decisions for him or her.

❖ Let the toddler make mistakes without scolding or being criticized. Avoid making demands that are too rigid for a toddler to follow or correcting the child for every mistake.

❖ Give the toddler the freedom to play in safe places with safe playthings in his or her own way. Avoid directing or interfering with the toddler's safe play.

❖ Praise the toddler for becoming more autonomous. Avoid mixing praise with criticism, however.

13-4 Adults should let toddlers explore and make mistakes within adult-set limits.

13-5 Parents, especially mothers, serve as the secure base from which toddlers can explore new experiences and people.

13-6 The warm relationship between this toddler and his father teaches the child to trust adults.
© John Shaw

positive experiences with many adults, they develop trusting relationships with them, 13-6.

Getting Along with Other Children

During the second year, toddlers tend to interact more with other children.

Their first interactions are brief. They often imitate each other's actions with a toy. Later, they talk as they play.

Toddlers are possessive of their toys and belongings when they play. Between ages 30 and 36 months, toddlers become good at keeping their possessions by holding them firmly or retrieving them from others. Often toddlers are not quite ready to share all the time.

Some studies show that toddlers are not as self-centered as experts once thought. Toddlers can share sometimes. They may return a snatched toy if the owner cries. They praise other children and show concern for someone who is hurt. When toddlers have loving relationships with their caregivers, they seem better able to show concern for other children.

Self-Esteem

Children become more aware of themselves, especially as physical beings, as they approach the first birthday. They enjoy hearing their names and seeing themselves in mirrors. With the help of caring adults, children develop good feelings about themselves. Feeling good about yourself and what you can do is called **self-esteem**. People with high amounts of self-esteem believe they are worthwhile people, 13-7.

As you read in chapter 9, babies sense how others feel about them from the way they are spoken to and held. Toddlers must feel loved, even when they are difficult or make

13-7 When provided with a nurturing environment, toddlers learn to like themselves and feel good about what they can do.
© John Shaw

mistakes. If adults scold toddlers each time they do something wrong, toddlers will feel they are beyond being loved, 13-8.

When toddlers feel good about themselves, they seem to admire themselves and their growing control over their bodies, 13-9. They are confident and like to show off their physical feats for others. They will often clap for themselves and laugh with delight at their new skills.

13-8 Adults need to comfort toddlers who have made mistakes.
© Nancy P. Alexander

13-9 Touching a mirror image is one way that toddlers say to themselves, "I am special."

Toddlers become more aware of their bodies and what their bodies can do. They can name some body parts. Toddlers also know they can see, hear, touch, taste, and smell, but may not know which body part controls each sense. (For example, they may not know that eyes are used for seeing). Toddlers seem to have little awareness of their own weight. Toddlers will run and thrust themselves on the laps of adults. They also may run and cling to standing adults, causing adults to lose their balance. They can feel pain, but do not always know where it is. Unless they can see a cut, scrape, or burn, they cannot tell someone where it hurts. A toddler with a throat infection may even deny having a sore throat. More advanced body concepts develop later.

Emotions

Toddlers' mental abilities seem to result in the following changes in emotions, which are different than those of adults or infants:

❖ Toddlers react to more stimuli than infants. They know more people to love, experience more things and people to fear, have more things to make them anxious, and find more to anger them.

❖ Toddlers can better sense emotions in others. Toddlers can detect fear in adults. They may even sense something is wrong when adults are anxious. Toddlers respond to

 self-esteem. Feeling good about yourself and what you can do.

emotions in other children. They can imitate others' emotions, too.

❖ Toddlers' motor skills allow them more physical responses, 13-10. For example, they can run or hide when fearful, or they can hit or kick when angry. The toddler's ability to talk allows a verbal response. Even the single word *no* shows feelings.

❖ Toddlers' abilities to imagine increase the number of negative emotions, such as fear of the dark and fear of monsters. Toddlers cannot totally separate what's real from what's pretend. Emotions caused by imagination are just as real as the feelings they may have when a prized toy is broken.

Affection

Toddlers are still attached to their caregivers. They express affection for their caregivers by wanting to be near them. They seek caregivers when faced with a strange situation. This attachment seems to help other aspects of social-emotional development. This is because the love a toddler feels for caregivers extends to non-caregiving adults, children, and pets, 13-11.

13-10 Toddlers often cry and cling to their parents when afraid.

13-11 Toddlers begin to show affection for beloved toys as well as people and pets.

Fear

Many fears that began during infancy are evident after the first birthday. Fears increase quickly after age two because toddlers know about more things to fear. They know of more objects and situations that can hurt them. They can also imagine things that do not exist, such as monsters, 13-12. Toddlers also may fear animals, darkness, nightmares, "bad people," injury, gestures, and startling noises.

Instead of talking about their fears, toddlers tend to act them out in play. It is common to see a two-and-a-half-year-old who fears dogs barking and growling in play. Toddlers may imitate bad people seen on television or in books.

Adults should handle these fears in a matter-of-fact way. Never tease toddlers about their fears or push them into scary situations. To decrease toddlers' fears, adults may want to keep them from watching too much television. The American Academy of Pediatrics advises parents to avoid TV viewing for children younger than two years. For children two years and older, parents are advised to limit TV viewing to two hours or less daily.

Anxiety

Separation anxiety continues into the toddler stage and sometimes beyond, 13-13. Many toddlers overcome some of their separation anxiety if they feel a caregiver's love and know the caregiver will return. Increased language skill helps toddlers understand why parents sometimes leave. Parents must make sure their toddler receives good

13-12 Toddlers fear monsters and unnatural creatures that exist in their minds.

13-13 Being separated from caring adults still causes anxiety in the toddler.

and loving care during separations.

Nightmares may begin around two years of age. A nightmare is a way of dealing with an anxiety. Nightmares may stem from fear of being left alone, getting hurt, or angering adults. The details of the nightmare are unreal, often including unknown lands and monsters. If toddlers are content during the day, nightmares do not reveal a problem. These bad dreams are a way of dealing with anxiety. For most children, nightmares decrease in time.

Anger

As you have read, toddlers desire more independence and have a strong will. When thwarted in their goal-seeking behaviors, toddlers react with anger. Sudden emotional outbursts of anger, called **temper tantrums**, often appear during the second year of life. The child may lie on the floor, kick, and scream. Tantrums tend to happen when something does not go a toddler's way. Because this is often the case, temper tantrums are common for toddlers.

Temper tantrums are meant to attract attention. Often they are not directed at anyone. Because tantrums are done to seek attention, ignoring the toddler may cause him or her to stop. After the tantrum is over, give the toddler love and reassurance, 13-14.

13-14 Toddlers often feel alone and even unloved after a temper tantrum.
© Nancy P. Alexander

Remember a child's anger is not purposefully directed toward others until the child is three years old.

temper tantrums. Sudden emotional outbursts of anger commonly displayed by toddlers.

Summing It Up

The second period of social-emotional development begins when children develop wills of their own. Erikson called this period *autonomy versus shame and doubt*. During this time, toddlers become independent. They don't always understand the dangers their actions may cause. Because of this, many conflicts with caregivers occur.

Toddlers begin to interact with others besides their parents and caregivers. Through socialization, they learn to get along with others. Having positive experiences with others helps them develop trusting relationships. Toddlers' interactions with other children are brief. They often imitate each other before they interact by talking. Toddlers are possessive of their toys and belongings, but can show concern for others, too.

The good feeling children develop about themselves is called self-esteem. Toddlers are becoming aware of their bodies but cannot always tell adults where they feel pain.

Toddlers experience a wider range of emotions than infants do. They are still attached to their caregivers but are also beginning to show affection for others. Fears tend to intensify during this period, including the fear of the unreal, such as monsters. Being separated from parents continues to make toddlers anxious. Nightmares are a way toddlers often deal with their anxieties. Anger occurs when events do not go how the toddler wants. These frustrations often result in temper tantrums. Ignoring tantrums may make them end sooner.

Reviewing Key Concepts

Write your answers on a separate sheet of paper.

1. True or false. Toddlers find their world is solely devoted to meeting their needs.
2. True or false. Adults' reactions to toddlers affect how toddlers feel about themselves.
3. True or false. Autonomy means being able to do some things without the help of others.
4. Identify the correct statement in each pair.
   A. Autonomy often happens during new activities./Autonomy often happens during routines.
   B. Autonomy often involves working at the ability level./Autonomy often involves trying to work beyond the ability level.
5. List three ways adults can help the toddler develop autonomy rather than shame and doubt.
6. True or false. Adjusting to others is easier if the child has had only one main caregiver, such as the mother.
7. Which of the following does *not* promote social development?
   A. spending time with others
   B. babysitters and other caregivers
   C. insisting that toddlers play alone more often
   D. letting other children play with the toddler
8. Shaming toddlers for their mistakes _____ (does, does not) affect their self-esteem.
9. Toddlers' sense of self-esteem is centered on their awareness of their _____ (physical, mental) abilities.
10. What four general changes in emotion occur during the toddler stage?
11. List three fears common to toddlers.
12. How should adults react to toddlers' temper tantrums?

Using Your Knowledge

1. **Group Discussion.** Toddlers often admire themselves in mirrors and enjoy their new abilities. Have a class discussion on how adults admire themselves and whether self-admiration is good when expressed by older children and adults.
2. **Language Arts.** Some people refer to the toddler years as the "terrible twos." Write an essay explaining why people use this term to describe toddlers. Also discuss why this term is incorrect.
3. **Child Development.** Use the dictionary to find the definitions of the terms autonomy, shame, and doubt. List common situations that toddlers might experience. Identify whether each experience promotes autonomy or shame and doubt. Compare your list to that of a classmate.
4. **Library Skills.** Visit your local public library and look for three children's books that relate to the social and emotional development of toddlers. List the title, author, publisher, and copyright date of

each book. Then, write a paragraph describing the message of each book. Conclude the paragraph with your opinion of the book.

5. **Role-Play.** Role-play a situation in which a toddler fears the dark and monsters that loom in the closet. Have one student play the toddler and one (or two students) play the parent (or parents) coping with the toddler's fears. Follow the role-play with a class discussion.

Making Observations

1. Observe two or three toddlers of the same age. How do they show their attachments to several people? How do the strengths of these attachments differ for a parent versus a babysitter?

2. Observe several toddlers playing together. Are they possessive about toys? How do they reclaim a special toy from another child? How do they react when a toy is reclaimed from them? How do adults settle toddlers' disputes?

3. Observe several toddlers playing. Describe actions that would show self-esteem. Describe actions that would show the toddler doesn't feel good about him- or herself. What did the adults do to promote positive self-esteem in toddlers?

4. Observe toddlers in a group care situation. Note how toddlers show autonomy. Under what conditions did adults prevent toddlers from carrying through their goals? How did the toddlers react?

5. Observe a toddler showing affection, fear, anxiety, or anger. What seemed to trigger the emotion? Compare what you noted with your text.

Thinking Further

1. A conflict of wills between children and adults often occurs during routine care times such as meals and dressing. How much freedom should parents give toddlers? How much permissiveness might result in spoiled babies?

2. Why is it impossible to explain to toddlers that monsters and other unreal creatures exist only in their dreams or minds?

3. What are various means people use to seek attention? Why do toddlers use temper tantrums to get attention rather than other means?

Chapter 14 Providing for the Toddler's Developmental Needs

After studying this chapter, you will be able to
- ✎ plan ways to meet toddlers' physical needs.
- ✎ stimulate toddlers' growing mental abilities.
- ✎ help toddlers adjust to their first social controls.

Near the end of a shopping outing with his mother Tina, Eddie suddenly started to complain and cry loudly. As the crying escalated, two-year-old Eddie began to run in the aisle, grabbing chips, dip, and whatever else he could. Tina picked Eddie up, realizing he had developed a full-blown tantrum. An elderly man and woman stared at Tina and exclaimed how terrible it was to take a hungry child shopping. The checkout clerk gave Tina an angry look as Eddie kicked, cried, and screamed for candy. At home a few minutes later, Eddie was calm and ate a sandwich hungrily as if nothing had just happened.

Define...

- nutrient density
- registered dietitians
- Food Guide Pyramid for Young Children
- ritual
- toilet learning
- regression
- training pants
- spatial
- transitional stage
- self-restraint
- self-assertion
- obedience
- contrariness

Children continue to develop quickly between their first and third birthdays. Toddlers still depend on adults to provide for their needs. During these years, however, toddlers begin learning some self-care skills, such as self-feeding, self-dressing, and toileting. They will even help with washing their hands and bathing.

At this age, intellectual abilities seem to blossom. Toddlers learn to use language to talk with others and help them think. They learn many concepts through daily routines at home and then practice these concepts in play.

Toddlers have many social-emotional needs. They try to do tasks on their own, but they find some too hard for their immature bodies and minds. Toddlers need loving adults who understand their wills. Adults need to allow some freedom. They need to praise toddlers when they master a new skill. They need to help toddlers when they can't manage a task.

Physical Needs

Caregivers must meet toddlers' physical needs to keep them healthy and safe. Meeting physical needs also keeps toddlers mentally and socially fit. To meet toddlers' physical needs, adults must make sure toddlers are fed,

Ties with Family & Community

Interview two successful caregivers about skills that have helped them overcome some problems with toddlers. Ask the caregivers to recommend tips for helping toddlers with feeding, hygiene, toilet learning, contrariness, temper tantrums, and fears or anxieties. Have each caregiver share with you what he or she finds most rewarding and most challenging about working with toddlers. Share your findings with the class.

clothed, cleaned, and rested. Adults also must guide toddlers' self-care skills, such as self-feeding, self-cleaning, and toileting. As toddlers learn self-care skills, they can meet their physical needs. Self-care skills also help toddlers advance in mental and social-emotional development.

Feeding

During the toddler years, the eating experience changes. Toddlers graduate from a bottle and baby foods to a cup and table foods. They begin to feed themselves. In addition, toddlers often join the family for meals instead of eating at other times.

The Eating Style of Toddlers

The toddler's appetite decreases. This is because the physical rate of growth slows. Infants usually gain about 15 pounds in the first year. In contrast, toddlers gain only about 11 pounds in two years. The energy needs of toddlers are incredibly high, however.

Typically, toddlers are picky eaters. They develop definite food likes and dislikes, just as they do about most things in their world. For example, they may settle on a diet of only a few foods for days or even weeks. Being assertive about foods and eating is part of what it means to be a toddler.

Toddlers' eating patterns are not at all like those of adults. In fact, toddlers seem to have odd eating habits. Erratic eating habits are as normal as toddler mood swings. They may skip a meal or two and then eat as though they are starved a few hours later. These busy explorers often do not like to sit down to a feast. They prefer to eat on the go. Although these habits may concern the adult, the habits should not harm the child. Most toddlers who are offered nutritious meals and snacks will eat enough over time to meet their food needs.

Most toddlers want to feed themselves (*self-feed*), 14-1. They want to control their own eating. Toddlers can

14-1 Young toddlers hold spoons with an overhand palm grasp rather than with the thumb-and-finger grasp of the adult.
Gerber Products

pick up food with fingers and learn to use a spoon. However, a toddler's fine-motor skills are not mature. Therefore, playing with food—including smearing it on the wall or dropping it on the floor—is part of self-feeding, 14-2.

When mishaps occur, parents must remember the toddler is not being naughty. He or she is learning about the texture, color, and qualities of food. Self-feeding also helps the toddler show independence. It boosts the toddler's self-esteem, too.

Providing for Toddlers' Food Needs

Food intake should always meet a child's nutritional needs. Toddlers eat smaller amounts of food than infants or adults. Adults must give toddlers foods that are of high nutrient density. **Nutrient density** is the level of nutrients in a food in relation to the level of calories in the food. High nutrient density foods are high in vitamins and minerals needed for the body's growth and repair. These foods are not high in calories. Foods of low nutrient density mainly provide calories rather than vitamins and minerals. (These foods are said to contain *empty calories* because they are not nutritious.) When children eat foods of low nutrient density, they are often too full to eat nutritious foods. This is unhealthy and may cause the child to gain too much weight now or in the future.

The toddler's pediatrician often makes food recommendations based on height and weight of the toddler, as well as other factors. These factors include history of weight gain, anemia, illnesses, food intolerances and allergies, and physical activity level. Some toddlers have special food needs, too. For these children, a physician or registered dietitian should plan the child's diet. **Registered dietitians** have special training in nutrition and diet. They meet the qualifications of the American Dietetic Association (ADA).

14-2 Toddlers are messy eaters because they are still learning about food.

nutrient density. The level of nutrients in a food in relation to the level of calories in the food.

registered dietitians. People who have special training in nutrition and diet and meet the qualifications of the American Dietetic Association.

Providing for the Needs of One- to Two-Year-Olds

As you read in chapter 10, by the time infants weigh about 15 pounds, they begin to need more nutrition than is provided by breast milk or formula. Solids are called *complementary foods* because they provide the nutrients needed in addition to formula or breast milk. During infancy, the number of calories received from complementary foods is rather low (about 280 calories for the 6- to 8-month-old and about 450 calories for the 9- to 11-month-old).

From 12 to 24 months, toddlers should continue to breast feed or start drinking whole cow's milk. (Toddler formulas or reduced fat cow's milk are not recommended.) After the first birthday, toddlers need about 900 calories a day. This amount gradually increases. By the time the child approaches the second birthday, about 1300 to 1400 calories are needed each day. Although it is not necessary to count calories, complementary foods should provide about half of the calories consumed.

The ADA recommends that toddlers be served about two cups of whole milk each day. They advise against serving fruit juices or drinks in place of milk. This is because these drinks do not provide the calcium and other minerals toddlers need for proper bone growth and ossification. In addition to milk, the ADA recommends offering calcium-rich foods (such as yogurt or cheese) as part of meals and snacks.

Between one and two years of age, a toddler should be able to eat *table foods* (foods prepared for the entire family). In preparing table foods, parents can use the following helpful hints:

❖ Avoid adding salt, sugar, or spices to the food served to toddlers. (Parents can separate the toddler's serving from the dish before adding these for other family members.)
❖ Cook and refrigerate all foods properly.
❖ Continue to introduce new foods at three- or four-day intervals to check for allergies and intolerances.
❖ Mash foods or cut them into bite-sized pieces for the toddler.
❖ Offer the toddler six offerings of food (meals and snacks) per day using a toddler-sized plate to avoid overwhelming the toddler with too much food.

The ADA advises that an appropriate serving size for toddlers is about one measuring teaspoon of food per year of age for cooked fruits, vegetables, cereals, and pasta. Although the ADA gives general guidelines about how many servings to offer, they advise parents to let toddlers eat a variety of nutritious foods until they are full. The exception to this recommendation would be if a toddler has a health concern that merits a special planned diet.

According to the ADA recommendations, younger toddlers should eat the following daily:

* *Four servings of dairy products.* Examples of serving size for this age group are ½ cup whole milk, ½ cup yogurt, or 1 ounce cheese.
* *Six servings of grain products.* Examples of serving size for young toddlers are ½ slice bread, ½ bagel, 1 ounce infant cereal, or 1 to 2 tablespoons cooked rice or pasta.
* *Six servings of fruits and vegetables.* A serving for this age group includes 1 to 2 tablespoons of cooked or fresh fruit or vegetables. At least one serving daily should be rich in vitamin C.
* *Three to four servings of meat and meat alternates.* Examples of serving sizes for young toddlers includes 1 ounce of lean meat, fish, or poultry; 2 ½ ounces of tofu; 1 egg; or ¼ cup cooked dry beans.

Meeting Nutritional Needs of Older Toddlers

Older toddlers (those who are two to three years old) can follow the **Food Guide Pyramid for Young Children** in order to meet their nutritional needs, 14-3. The United States Department of Agriculture (USDA) designed this child-friendly version of Food Guide Pyramid to address the needs of children ages two to six years. It emphasizes food choices, serving numbers and sizes, and physical activity with the young child in mind.

The serving sizes given with the Food Guide Pyramid apply to four- to six-year-olds. The USDA recommends offering smaller serving sizes to two- and three-year olds. This might be one-half to two-thirds the full serving size. (Parents could also follow the ADA recommendation to serve one tablespoon per year of age—two to three tablespoons for older toddlers.) Regardless of the amount offered, an older toddler will likely eat as much as he or she wants and play with the rest.

The Pyramid has five major food groups. Fats and sweets make up the point of the Pyramid because foods in this category should be eaten in limited amounts. The following groups are included in the Food Guide Pyramid for Young Children:

* *Grain Group.* This group includes breads, cereals, rice, and pasta. These foods provide carbohydrates (starches), which are a good source of energy and fiber. They also provide many needed vitamins and minerals. The Pyramid suggests six servings a day. For older toddlers, one serving would include the following: ½ to ⅔ slice of bread;

Food Guide Pyramid for Young Children. A child-friendly version of the Food Guide Pyramid developed by the USDA to address the needs of children ages two to six years for nutritious foods and physical activity.

14-3 For good health, a toddler needs physical activity as well as foods from each group of the Pyramid every day.
USDA Center for Nutrition Policy and Promotion

¼ to ⅓ cup cooked cereal, rice, or pasta; or ½ to ⅔ ounce ready-to-eat cereal or crackers.

❖ *Vegetable Group.* The Pyramid suggests three servings of fresh, frozen, or canned vegetables daily. Foods in this group provide vitamins, folate, minerals, and fiber. For older toddlers, one serving is ¼ to ⅓ cup chopped raw or cooked vegetables or ½ to ⅔ cup raw, leafy vegetables.

❖ *Fruit Group.* Fruits and fruit juices provide needed amounts of potassium and vitamins A and C. The Pyramid recommends two servings from this group daily. The American Academy of Pediatrics advises no more than one of these servings should come from fruit juice. This is because the actual fruits are more nutritious and less likely to cause dental caries than fruit juice. For an older toddler, one serving of fruit equals: ½ to ⅔ piece of fresh fruit; ½ to ⅔ melon wedge, ⅓ to ½ cup juice; about ⅛ cup dried fruit.

❖ *Milk Group.* Foods in the milk group provide protein, vitamins, and minerals. This is the only group in which serving sizes for two- and three-year olds are the same as those of preschoolers. The Pyramid suggests two servings each day. One serving includes the following: 1 cup 2 percent, reduced-fat milk; 1 cup yogurt; 1 ½ slices American process cheese; 3-inch cube of cheese; 1 piece of string cheese; or 2 cups cottage cheese.

❖ *Meat Group.* This group includes meat, poultry, fish, dry beans, eggs, and nuts. (Nuts, however, are a choking hazard, and are not recommended for this age group.) Meat, poultry, and fish provide protein, B vitamins, iron, and zinc. Dry beans and eggs provide protein, vitamins, and minerals. The Pyramid suggests two servings from the meat group daily. A serving for an older toddler is 1 to 2 ounces meat, fish, or poultry (cooked and lean) or ¼ to ⅓ cup cooked, dry beans. One egg is the equivalent of 1 ounce of meat.

❖ *Fats and Sweets.* The tip of the Pyramid includes fats and sweets. Foods in this group supply calories but few nutrients. Oil, butter, and mayonnaise are examples of fats. Sweets include added sugar as well as cookies, cakes, pies, and candy. Older toddlers should be offered very few fats and sweets.

Preventing Feeding Problems

Toddlers need to be carefully watched while they are eating; they can easily choke on foods. Toddlers should sit or stand still while eating. They should not crawl, creep, walk, or run while eating. The ADA recommends that parents avoid certain foods that are choking hazards for this age group. These foods include the following: popcorn; grapes; raisins; nuts; spoonfuls of peanut butter; hot dogs; small, hard candies; and chunks of raw carrot. Softer raw foods may be safer in larger pieces than in finely chopped pieces because they are easier for the older toddler to hold.

Sometimes toddlers develop feeding problems. Most problems stem from the toddler's stage of development—the slowing growth, improving motor and learning skills, and changing social needs. See 14-4 for some common feeding problems and suggestions to solve them. Toddlers work out most feeding problems in time with the help of patient adults.

Clothing

Choosing the right clothes and shoes for toddlers is important. Proper clothing helps toddlers stay active, comfortable, and safe. It also stands up under the strain of constant movement and messy play.

Feeding Problems of Toddlers

Problem—A toddler refuses to eat a meal or takes only a few bites.

Possible Solutions—

- ❖ Keep records of all the foods the toddler eats during the week. (The toddler may be getting enough of the needed foods.)
- ❖ Break meals up by offering part of the meal early and the rest of the meal in two or three hours.
- ❖ Make snacks high in nutritional quality.
- ❖ Eat foods of high nutritional quality. Toddlers imitate adult food habits.
- ❖ Serve small portions and let the toddler ask for seconds. Too much food can be discouraging.
- ❖ Make mealtime pleasant even when the toddler refuses to eat.

Problem—A toddler refuses to eat new foods.

Possible Solutions—

- ❖ Offer a taste or two of new foods on a regular basis to help the toddler to accept them over time.
- ❖ Offer only one new food at a time.
- ❖ Serve a taste or two of a new food on a plate that also has favorite foods.
- ❖ Model proper food attitudes for toddlers. Saying, "Eat your spinach, it's good for you," may give the toddler the idea that spinach is a must but not good tasting.
- ❖ Try a new way of preparing foods. For example, toddlers usually like simple foods more than mixtures (casseroles). Toddlers prefer finger foods to foods eaten with flatware. They like less salty and spicy foods more than highly seasoned foods.
- ❖ Remain pleasant with the toddler. Force-feeding and anger do not work.

Problem—A toddler shows lack of self-feeding skills and plays with food.

Possible Solutions—

- ❖ Give the toddler time to learn how to self-feed. (Most children cannot hold flatware in the mature way until five years of age or older.)
- ❖ Provide a comfortable setting for eating. The correct chair provides support (so the child is not sliding down), is the correct height, and has a place for feet to touch rather than dangle.
- ❖ Provide suitable eating equipment, such as small plates (especially those with sides), small cups (perhaps with handles or spill proof features), and baby or junior flatware (or small spoons and salad forks).
- ❖ Use a high chair or table and chair that can be cleaned easily. (Nearby floor and walls should also be easily cleaned.)
- ❖ Keep cleaning supplies handy during meals.
- ❖ When possible, prepare foods in easy to manage form, such as finger foods. (Runny foods, foods that must be cut, and foods that are hard to pick up will be messy for the toddler.)
- ❖ Praise the toddler for successes. Never laugh at mishaps.
- ❖ Prevent playing with food by staying near the toddler during eating time and removing food once the toddler is playing more than eating.
- ❖ Be firm in saying no when the toddler goes too far with playing. You may even say, "Balls are for throwing, food is for eating," or "I want the kitchen to stay clean; food on the floor is messy." If the toddler does not control the play, remove the food or the toddler. (Toddlers learn quickly when eating rules are fair and consistently enforced.)

14-4 Feeding problems are common for toddlers.

Choosing Garments

Although toddlers grow more slowly than infants, they still outgrow their clothes quickly. Fit is important for the toddler. Clothes that are too tight will bind and restrict movement. Clothes that are too loose will be uncomfortable and perhaps unsafe. To check for fit, let toddlers try on garments.

When it is not possible for the toddler to try on the garment, parents have to choose the garment based on size alone. Sizing can be confusing. Some companies use descriptive terms, such as *small, medium,* and *large* as their sizes. Other companies set sizes by age, such as *18 mo. (1T), 24 mo. (2T), 3T,* and *4T.* The most accurate sizing method is the weight range or weight and height ranges. A few companies provide more than one type of sizing on their labels for easy comparison. Sizes vary from one company to the next, but an example is provided in Figure 14-5.

Quality features include safety, comfortable fabric and construction, growth features, durability, attractive style, and easy care. See chart 14-6 for some examples of each of these features.

Some adults consider self-dressing features when choosing a toddler's clothes. Such features make dressing and undressing without help easier. However, toddlers are better at taking clothes off than putting them on. By 18 months, toddlers will help by extending arms and legs while being dressed. They will also unzip zippers and remove mittens, hats, socks, and untied shoes, 14-7. A few items are designed to teach self-dressing to children under three, 14-8. Adults should accept self-dressing efforts of the toddler even if the results are incorrect.

Toddler Clothing Sizes

Size	Height	Weight	
18 mo./1T	30¾ to 32 inches	22 to 24 pounds	
24 mo./2T	32½ to 35½ inches	24½ to 28 pounds	
3T	36 to 38½ inches	28½ to 32 pounds	
4T	39 to 41 inches	32½ to 36 pounds	
5T	41½ to 43 inches	36½ to 41 pounds	

14-5 When they are given, height and weight ranges provide the more accurate sizing than a size based on age alone.

Important Features in Toddler Clothes

Safety
- ❖ fire retardant (will burn, but smolders slowly rather than flaming when on fire)
- ❖ no drawstrings or loose buttons, fasteners, or trim
- ❖ belts, ties, and sashes fastened to the garment securely to prevent tripping, choking, or strangling
- ❖ bright-colored clothing (increases ability to see toddlers)

Comfort
- ❖ made of lightweight and absorbent fabrics
- ❖ made of stretch fabrics
- ❖ elastic encased or nonbinding
- ❖ fullness in pant legs to permit knee bending and stooping with ease
- ❖ collars and sleeves that do not rub or bind
- ❖ coats. sweaters, and jackets that can fit over clothes without binding
- ❖ underwear that is not binding
- ❖ neck openings large enough for ease of dressing

Growth Features
- ❖ made of stretch fabrics
- ❖ dresses without definite waistlines
- ❖ pants and skirts with elastic or adjustable waistbands
- ❖ adjustable shoulder straps
- ❖ clothes with deep hems, large seams, and pleats or tucks that can be easily let out
- ❖ two-piece outfits

Quality Construction
- ❖ reinforcement at points of strain such as seams, knees, pockets, and pocket edges
- ❖ stitches that are even and not too long
- ❖ seams that are flat, smooth, and finished
- ❖ securely attached fasteners and trims
- ❖ built-in growth features, such as deep hems
- ❖ patterns are matched at seams

Easy Care
- ❖ washable (especially machine washable with other colors)
- ❖ little or no ironing needed
- ❖ easy to mend

14-6 Toddlers' clothes need to have certain features.

Fitting Shoes

Because the bones and muscles of the foot are developing, shoe fit is important for proper growth and comfort. Shoes that fit improperly can cause permanent damage to the child's feet. Toddlers often outgrow their shoes before they wear them out.

14-7 Toddlers master how to remove shoes and clothing before learning to dress themselves.
American Association of Retired Persons W.B. Doner and Company

14-8 Simple dressing aids, such as a mitten and zipper sewn in a cloth book, help teach toddlers self-dressing skills.
© John Shaw

The average rate of foot growth for toddlers is one shoe size every three to four months.

The toddler has flat feet because the arch is relaxed. This flat-footed look disappears around age three years. Going barefooted or wearing socks without shoes is good for the development of the arch. Shoes, even high-top shoes, do not provide support. Parents often choose high-top shoes because they are more difficult for the toddler to remove.

Toddlers need shoes to protect their feet from cold, dampness, and harmful objects. Shoes that fit properly have ½ inch of space between the large toe and shoe when the toddler stands. They also have a flexible sole and snug-fitting heel.

Rest and Sleep

Toddlers often sleep fewer hours and take fewer naps than babies. Chart 14-9 shows the general trend in sleep patterns. The sleep needs of toddlers vary. Toddlers may sleep less when under stress and more than average when recovering from an illness.

How much sleep does a toddler need? Parents should not use age to figure this. Instead, they should awaken toddlers at the same time each morning for about a week and then note when they become sleepy. The amount of time between the average "sleepy time" and the same waking time is close to the amount of sleep needed.

Average Sleep of Toddlers

Age	Night	Naps
9 to 12 months	12 to 14 hours	1 to 4 hours, morning and afternoon
13 to 30 months	10 to 12 hours	1 to 3 hours, afternoon
31 to 36 months	10 to 15 hours	Naps beginning to disappear*

*Two-thirds of two-year-olds take a nap; 10 percent of three-year-olds take a nap.

14-9 A toddler's sleep needs change over time.

Toddlers are more likely than babies to resist rest and sleep, even when they are tired. Bedtime problems stem partly from the toddlers' struggle for autonomy. Often adults become physically tired from coping with toddlers who resist sleep. Adults may even feel stress if bedtime becomes a battle of wills. These ideas may help solve problems.

❖ Accept that adults cannot force toddlers to sleep. Resistance often disappears after the toddler years.

❖ Have a definite hour for bedtime. Use a neutral sign, such as a clock (not a person), to signal the hour.

❖ Set a bedtime ritual or routine. The ritual should last about an hour a night. Include only restful activities, such as a warm bath, drink of water, story, song, and hug. Naptime rituals can be developed, too.

❖ Provide a comfortable place for sleep.

❖ Tell toddlers who do not want to sleep they do not have to sleep, only stay in bed. Toddlers usually accept this.

❖ Comfort fearful toddlers. Tell them where you'll be while they sleep. Provide a night-light in their room. Place a stuffed animal in their bed. Tell fearful toddlers you are there to keep them safe and will check on them every 10 to 15 minutes. (Toddlers are often asleep after two or three check times, 14-10.)

14-10 Checking on toddlers may help them feel secure enough to get the rest and sleep they need.

❖ Comfort toddlers who awaken with nightmares. Do not ask them to tell you about their nightmares. It is best to forget them. (If they want to tell you about their nightmares, listen. Assure them these are just bad dreams.)

❖ Return children who get up to their bed. Meet any real needs, such as a drink for a child who is thirsty, but turn down nonessential requests. Be firm but calm.

❖ Keep the child away from active spots, such as where others are watching TV or talking.

Adults' actions will determine whether toddlers learn the tricks to get what they want or learn that adults will insist on their staying in bed.

Hygiene

One of the most important parts of hygiene for toddlers is bathing. Bathing is fun for most toddlers. Although toddlers can sit and stand easily, they are not safe when left alone while bathing, 14-11. Young toddlers may feel more secure being

ritual. A pattern of activities repeated at a regular time each day, such as a bedtime.

14-11 Keeping children safe in the tub is extremely important. A secure toddler usually enjoys bathing and splashing in the water.
© John Shaw

bathed in a child's tub. This tub can be placed inside the regular bathtub for easy bathing and less messy splashing. Other parents find their toddlers enjoy special bathtub seats designed for toddlers.

Toddlers may want to help bathe themselves. A bath mitt is the easiest for them to use. (You can make one by sewing three edges of two washcloths together or by using a woman's cotton ankelet.) Most toddlers have fun trying to hold slippery soap. Some toddlers enjoy rinsing themselves with a hand-held shower.

Water Play

Toddlers also need some time for water play during baths. They have fun playing in water and learn a great deal, too. From playing in the bathtub, toddlers can learn that
- ❖ some toys float and some sink
- ❖ water power can push toys
- ❖ water can be held for a brief time in the cupped hand
- ❖ water makes all things wet
- ❖ they can make water splash, squirt, and drip
- ❖ the bottom of the tub can be seen through water
- ❖ soap makes bubbles

Many bath toys are sold for toddlers. Toys can be made easily from household objects, too.

Dental Care

Dental care is also important for toddlers. Many dentists recommend a first dental checkup by two years of age. Eating nutritious foods helps teeth stay healthy. However, cleaning teeth regularly is also needed. When the toddler is about 18 months of age, a caregiver can brush the toddler's teeth with a child-sized brush, 14-12. At this age, brushing can replace wiping the teeth. The toddler may begin to "help" brush his or her teeth around 30 months of age. (Adults should supervise and assist with brushing throughout the preschool years.)

Toilet Learning

Toilet learning is one of the most discussed aspects of the toddler years. **Toilet learning** is the process by which adults help children control

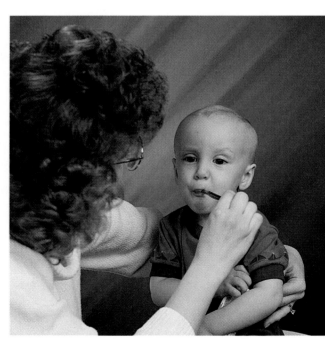

14-12 An adult must brush the toddler's teeth.
© John Shaw

Ties with Family & Community

Visit your public library or a bookstore. Search for two toddler books on toilet learning. Record the title, author, publishing company, and copyright date of each book. Along with this information, provide a brief summary of each book that includes your opinion of the book. Why do you think toddlers would enjoy (or not enjoy) this book? How could parents use the book to help children learn to use the toilet? Does the book provide more information or motivation? Prepare a written report on your findings.

their excretory systems, namely bowel movements and urination. Over the years adults have tried to help children at different ages. They have tried helping children early—before age one. Adults have let the child choose when to learn. They have also tried every age between these extremes.

Experts have found that two things are certain in toilet learning. First, the timing of learning varies from toddler to toddler. Second, many toddlers do not complete the learning process quickly. Learning may take most of the toddler years and perhaps even longer to complete.

Physical and Emotional Factors

Toilet training involves factors like physical development, motor skills, and emotional readiness. The physical and motor skills involved are the following:

❖ Ability to feel a full bowel and bladder. Until about 15 months, children move their bowels and pass urine without knowing in advance or realizing they have done so. Today's disposable diapers and disposable pull-up pants do not help with the feeling of wetness because they are designed to keep the skin drier.

❖ Ability to know what the sensation of needing to eliminate means in time to get to the potty.

❖ Ability to control muscles used for holding in or letting go. These muscles, which are low in the body, are among the last to develop. (This is a good example of the head-to-tail development principle.) Nerves can control these muscles around 18 months of age. Children tend to learn to control bowel movements before they learn to control their bladders.

toilet learning. The process by which adults help children learn to use the toilet to manage their elimination needs.

- ❖ Ability to walk (or often run) to the potty.
- ❖ Ability to remove or push down clothes. Several layers of clothes or a one-piece jumpsuit can be hard for the toddler to manage. Some fasteners make the task impossible.

For toilet learning to work, emotional readiness must occur at the same time the child is physically developed. Toddlers must see the need to use the potty. Busy toddlers often do not want to sit the needed time. Saying no to using the toilet is part of the self-will toddlers want to express. Toddlers also may need to master fears of falling in, the flushing water, and even the stools passed.

Procedure for Toilet Learning

Caregivers have tried many methods for toilet learning. Although many work, certain proven ideas help the toilet learning process. Adults should realize that toilet learning is not a one-way street. Toilet learning is something adults do *with* a child. Adults cannot do the learning for the toddler. Toddlers must be ready.

Toddlers are ready to learn at different ages. Many toddlers are ready to start toilet learning around two years of age. Age three years is often a difficult time to begin for there is a brief, but intense stage of **regression** (going back to an earlier stage) in the child's desire to be independent. A toddler should not begin toilet learning during periods of family or child stress. Furthermore, adults also should accept that toddlers vary in age of complete control. The average age for complete day control is 28 months, but the normal range varies greatly. No relationship exists between being a smart child and learning to use the toilet early. A rule of thumb is that a child must be able to stay dry two or more hours before he or she can begin to learn.

Third, if the toddler is in a group program, toilet learning must be a team effort—child, family, and caregivers. A constant exchange of information between the home and the program is needed. Child care programs are often good places for toilet learning due to the experience of the staff, child-sized bathrooms, and the program focus on helping children develop competence in self-care.

Even before toddlers are ready for toilet learning, adults can help them see what is expected. If an adult notes the child is eliminating, he or she should say something to make the child aware of it. When a diaper gets wet or soiled, the adult should say to the child as he or she changes the diaper, "Try to tell me next time, that way we can use the toilet."

When the Toddler Is Ready

When the toddler is ready for toilet learning, caregivers should borrow or buy a child-sized potty for him or her. Toddlers find regular toilets difficult to use and sometimes scary to toddlers. A potty designed for toddlers is the easiest to use, 14-13.

"Chairs" or potty rings that fit on standard toilet seats are also made for toddlers. Potty rings have some advantages over potty chairs that are placed on the floor. The rings can be carried to places that do not have child-sized toilets. They are also more sanitary and do not require cleaning after each use as the potty chair does.

14-13 Potty chairs are easy for toddlers to use as they learn to manage their toileting needs.
© John Shaw

Because the ring is placed on the toilet seat, it eliminates the extra step of learning to use the regular toilet after using the potty chair.

When standard toilets are used (with or without toddler seats), toddlers will need help. Getting on the standard toilet is difficult for a toddler. Also, his or her legs can hurt after dangling for even a few minutes. Parents or caregivers can build a simple wooden platform for use in front of the toilet. This is easy for the toddler to climb onto and turn around before sitting. It can be pulled away after use or for cleaning. If a platform is not used, adults should choose a step stool with a wide base that is sturdy and will not tip.

Show the child the potty he or she will use. Some toddlers want to sit on the potty first with their clothes on to check it out. Bathroom light switches should be easy to reach. You also may want to use a night-light in the bathroom.

Easy-to-manage clothing is crucial. Many adults wait until warm weather to start the toilet learning process because toddlers can wear fewer clothes. They can also wear elastic-waist shorts or pants, which are easy to manage.

 regression. Going back to an earlier stage of development.

Once Toilet Learning Begins

Once toilet learning begins, adults should encourage the toddler to use the toilet. However, they should not put requests in moral terms like, "Be good and use the potty." Take toddlers to the toilet at set times until they go on their own. Before and after meals, before and after sleep times, and every two hours are good times. Adults must remind children to use the toilet for many years after they learn.

Adults need to accept success and failure in a matter-of-fact way. Toddlers need some praise, but too much praise adds to the pressure to achieve the next time. Adults should not let failures make children feel bad or little. They should stop the learning routine during the illness or if a child shows signs of stress. Using diapers during sleep times, when traveling, or when away from home for long periods makes learning less stressful.

Accidents

No matter how much care is taken, accidents will happen. Being prepared helps prevent accidents from causing too much stress for toddlers or adults. Training pants (pants made of disposable diaper material, pants with a multi-layered cotton fabric crotch, or specially designed ones for wading or swimming pool use) help lessen the mess of accidents. Keep household cleaning products on hand (but safely stored out of the toddler's reach) to clean accidents.

Toilet learning helps children handle their elimination needs the way our society expects—cleanly, without help, and without fuss. Complete learning is a long process.

Indoor and Outdoor Spaces

Toddlers still enjoy being near adults and other children for most of their waking hours. However, between the second and third birthdays many toddlers begin playing more on their own. They need a place where they can rest and sleep without being disturbed. Thus, many families plan indoor and outdoor play spaces and bedrooms for their toddlers.

Bedrooms and play spaces must be safe. (See chapter 21 for safety tips.) If possible, these areas should fit toddlers' needs for play, rest, and learning self-help skills. Open floor and yard spaces make it easy for the toddler to be active. A cozy chair, fuzzy throw rug, corner area, and toddler bed are examples of quiet places. Self-help features include low shelves for toys and low hooks for coats. They also include a sturdy footstool for climbing one step and light switches within reach.

Toddlers like furniture and room decorations chosen especially for them, 14-14. Furniture designed for toddlers is often made smaller than other furniture. It also may be brightly painted. Choose bedspreads, window coverings, wallpaper, floor coverings,

14-14 Bedroom furniture and decorations should be chosen with the toddler in mind.
Seabrook Wallcoverings, Inc.

lamps, and night-lights the toddler will like. Wall hangings and pictures can be chosen with the toddler in mind. Even a few of the toddler's toys or books on display can make the room or area special.

Intellectual Needs

For the most part, toddlers learn during daily activities. They learn as they are eating, bathing, dressing, "helping" with household tasks, and running errands with adults. Adults should use everyday activities to help toddlers learn. Toddlers can learn during meals. They can talk with others at the table (language learnings). They can see, taste, smell, and feel foods of many colors, shapes, sizes, and textures (perceptual learnings). They can make choices about the foods and amounts of each they want (decision making). Toddlers can handle finger foods and flatware (motor skills). They hear comments such as, "Food helps you grow and become strong," (a nutrition lesson). They even join in celebrations involving food, such as eating birthday cake (a social time).

Learning Through Activities

Many other activities help toddlers learn, 14-15. Bathing and dressing provide the means for language, perceptual, health, and motor learnings. Helping with household tasks develops **spatial** (pertaining to space) concepts as toddlers put items in drawers or laundry in a basket. Vocabulary increases as toddlers learn the names of common objects found in the home and yard. Science becomes a part of everyday life as toddlers see how the

training pants. Special underpants or pants made of disposable diaper material that help lessen the mess of accidents during toilet learning.

spatial. Pertaining to space.

14-15 Playing in the rain teaches toddlers about science and their world.

vacuum cleaner picks up dirt, how air dries clothes, and how heat makes dough change into cookies.

Learning Through Play

Toddlers also learn as they play in a safe environment with many objects to explore. Play lets the toddler check and recheck learnings. A toddler may fill a plastic pail with the same toys many times to check how much space the toys need. Adults may play with toddlers sometimes. For the most part, however, they should let toddlers play on their own, stepping in only when toddlers need help or show they desire adult participations. They may show a toddler how to put a piece in a puzzle or introduce new ideas to play.

Adults may need a few ideas for games to enrich a toddler's learnings. They can use adult-planned games when they seem to fit the toddlers' interest and skills. These planned games should never be forced on the child, however. Adults should keep ideas in mind and use them only to enrich toddlers' learnings. This method is the best way to meet their intellectual needs.

Sensory Stimulation Activities

The senses help toddlers learn about the qualities of objects. Through sight, they learn about an object's color and darkness or lightness. Touch teaches them if objects are rough or smooth. They use hearing and touch to find out if objects are hard or soft. Toddlers use taste to learn about sweet, sour, salty, and bitter. Using the senses helps toddlers form concepts about objects. For example, they learn that when peeled, oranges are round, orange colored, sweet smelling, sweet tasting, and juicy.

Games can enrich what toddlers are learning on their own. As toddlers play games, adults should teach them by talking through the activity.

When a caregiver notices a toddler hears a sound, the caregiver should stop briefly and listen. Then say, "Do you hear that? I hear a _____. Do you hear it, too?" Point in the direction of the sound. This helps stimulate the toddler's sense of hearing. As another activity, when cooking a food with a distinct odor, sniff loudly and tell the toddler what you smell. Say, "I smell chicken frying," or "I smell a cake baking." Later, ask the toddler, "What's cooking? What smells so good?" Variations of this include smelling and talking about other odors. Flowers, an outdoor barbecue, and the rain all have distinct smells. See 14-16 for other examples of sensory stimulation activities.

Sensory Stimulation Activities

Activity   ### Sense

Looking at objects   **Sight**

Ask a child to look in a certain area (such as out of a window) and name something he or she sees. When the child points to or names an object, say, "That's right, it's a _____." Then talk about the qualities of the object. You may include color, size, the sound it makes, and what it does. Talk about other times when the toddler has seen the object. Three or four objects at one time are enough for most toddlers.

Animal sounds   **Hearing**

Sing "Old MacDonald Had a Farm" and point to pictures of each animal as you sing. Start with a few of the toddler's favorite animals and gradually add others.

Recognizing objects by touch   **Touch**

Put three or four familiar objects in a paper bag or pillowcase. Pull an object out of the bag. Ask the toddler to name it. Then show the toddler how to feel the object using the fingers. As the toddler feels the object, the adult should describe the texture. For instance, a ball may feel "round and soft." Continue in the same way with the other objects. After feeling all the objects, put them back into the bag. Have the child identify each one by feeling without peeking. *Variations:* (1) Place pictures or identical objects outside the bag. Have the toddler feel an object in the bag and point to the object or picture outside the bag. (2) Describe and name an object and have the toddler find it. You may say, "Put your hand in the bag and see if you can find the comb with all the points."

Recognizing objects by smell   **Smell**

Select three or four familiar objects that have distinct odors. Show the toddler how to smell by sniffing loudly. First, smell and talk about each object's odor. Then have the toddler close his or her eyes and identify each object by smelling it. If the toddler needs help, name two objects from which the toddler can choose. You may say, "Is this soap or a banana?"

Sweet and sour   **Taste**

Give the toddler a sugar cube and refer to it as sweet. Then have the toddler taste lemon juice mixed with water. Refer to it as sour. (Use equal parts of lemon juice and water. Pure lemon juice is too sour and can be hard on teeth.) Sweeten the lemon juice and water with sugar and serve as lemonade. Although the toddler may not understand, explain, "I am making this sour lemon juice sweeter with this sweet sugar. Now we have lemonade. It is sweet." *Variation:* Give the toddler a small amount of salt to taste. Give the toddler a bite of a salty food, such as a salty cracker. Use the term salty to describe both flavors.

© John Shaw

14-16 Sensory stimulation activities help toddlers learn about the qualities of objects.

Problem-Solving Activities

Toddlers can solve many problems by testing their ideas. They are not ready to solve problems just by thinking alone. Many of the best problem-solving games involve motor actions, such as opening and closing containers, finding hidden objects, and watching how objects move.

Simple puzzles are another good problem-solving activity for children. Begin with a few pieces and work up to puzzles with five or six pieces. For toddlers, each puzzle piece should be an entire picture of an object rather than a jigsaw piece. A knob on the puzzle piece helps fine-motor control. See 14-17 for other problem-solving activities.

Problem-Solving Activities

Opening lids

Place a small object in a container with a snap-on lid. Show the toddler how it works. Then let the toddler try to open it. When the toddler has mastered one type of lid, try another. You may use screw-on lids and plugs. (Do not show toddlers or even older preschool children how safety caps work.)

Opening lids

© John Shaw

Stacking

© John Shaw

Stacking and nesting

If the toddler can nest and stack two or three objects as described in chapter 10, add a few more pieces for nesting and stacking. Rings can be sequenced also. The toddler should start with two or three rings. Slowly add the other rings as the toddler masters the game. (If there is very little difference in the size of the objects, the task becomes much more difficult. These objects can be saved for children who are a little older.)

Where am I?

Hide from a toddler who is involved in another activity. Call out. The toddler will look for you. Praise the toddler for finding you. (Of course, do not hide behind locked doors or other places where the toddler cannot search.)

Rolling cars

Place small cars or trucks on a board that is flat on the floor. Chair cushions, sturdy cardboard lids, or trays can be used as the board. Say, "The cars do not go." As you slowly raise the board on one end say, "Here they go." After the toddler has played with the cars in this way many times, ask, "Can you make the car go down the hill fast (slow)?" See if the toddler increases (decreases) the slope of the board.

Through the tunnel

Using a mailing tube with both ends removed, show the toddler how to roll objects through it. The toddler will learn how objects can go in one open end and come out the other open end. After much play, some toddlers may learn to vary the slope of the tube to control the speed of the object's roll.

14-17 Problem-solving activities encourage toddlers to try out their ideas.

Motor Activities

Toddlers develop motor skills quickly. Because most toddlers are always on the go, they need few planned motor activities, 14-18. Some games can improve gross-motor skills whereas others improve fine-motor skills, 14-19.

Riding toys help children develop their large-motor skills. Toys that can be pushed with the feet or ridden help develop gross-motor skills.

Interlocking blocks help fine-finger control while sparking creativity. See 14-20 for other suggestions for gross-motor and fine-motor games.

Language Activities

Parents and caregivers can enhance the toddler's use of language. Early childhood programs that let children explore and play help language learning. Parents can organize their homes to promote language learning, too. Good feelings between the child and caregivers may also increase the child's verbal skills.

Toddlers Need to Hear Language

The toddler's active world needs a background of language. Adults should talk during many games played with

14-18 The toddler develops most gross-motor skills in play.

14-19 Hitting a peg with a hammer develops fine-motor skills and teaches cause and effect. Toddlers learn the force and speed of pounding affects the peg's descent.
© John Shaw

Gross-Motor and Fine-Motor Games

Blocks

© John Shaw

Making a face

Make my face

© John Shaw

Gross-Motor Games

Push and pull

Push and pull toys aid the motor skills of walking and crawling. Push toys seem to be easier because the toddler can see the toy's action without walking backward or looking back over the shoulder.

Fine-Motor Games

Pounding pegs

A hammer and peg set can help the child coordinate what is seen with the action. Toddlers should use both hands on the hammer to prevent getting the fingers hit.

Blocks

Building a tower with three to five blocks and knocking it down is fun for toddlers. As toddlers grow, they will build taller towers. Balancing the blocks in towers requires good fine-motor control. *Variation:* Push three or four blocks in a "train" while saying, "choo choo." Pushing blocks in an train requires much fine-motor control.

Making a face

Putting the eyes, nose, and mouth on a felt face can be much fun. The parts of the face are made out of felt with a hook-and-loop tape backing, such as Velcro. Because the pieces are rather small, the toddler should be supervised during play.
Variation: Many other "pictures" can be made using felt pieces. For instance, the toddler can put wheels on cars or trains. They also can put flowers on stems.

14-20 Gross- and fine-motor games help toddlers improve their skills.

toddlers to improve toddlers' skills. Adults and children should talk during daily routines, too. As adults do things, they should say what they are doing and what the toddler is doing.

Adults can begin talking in a conversational manner even before the child can respond verbally. They can pause as though the child will answer, as in the following example:

Adult—"Aren't you hungry?"

Pause about half a second.

Imagined response from toddler—"Yes."

Pause about half a second.

Adult—"Surely you are. Lunch smells good, doesn't it?"

As adults talk to toddlers, they should use all types of sentences. Using statements, questions, and exclamations helps the toddler hear the rise and fall of the voice. Adults can also help toddlers learn to make different sounds. For example, they can make sounds that go with toys, such as *rrr* for a siren.

Clear and Simple Speech

Speech should be clear and simple. Most adults match their sentences to the child's level. For example, new words are explained using words the child already knows. ("A bus is like a big car.") However, mispronouncing words is harmful, as is talking beneath the child's level. Challenging children slightly helps their development.

Adults should model language for toddlers. However, they should be relaxed about toddlers' language errors. These examples show ways to model language.

❖ Toddler—"My wed (red) sooes (shoes)."

Adult—"Yes, these are your pretty red shoes."

Purpose is to correct pronunciation.

❖ Toddler—"I singed a song."

Adult—"You sang a song about a rainy day."

Purpose is to correct grammar.

❖ Toddler—"See the plane go."

Adult—"The plane flies fast."

Purpose is to introduce a new word.

❖ Toddler—"See the smoke."

Adult—"It does look like smoke." Sniff loudly. "It doesn't smell like smoke, though. We see fog. Fog is a cloud near the ground. Can you say *fog*?"

Purpose is to correct meaning.

In each case, the adult guides by expanding the toddler's sentence. Toddlers (and even older children) often feel defeated when adults only correct errors.

Choosing Books for Toddlers

Reading books and saying poems and rhymes helps toddlers develop language. These activities should begin early in the toddler years. When choosing books, look for the following features:

❖ Pictures must be colorful and simple. Young children's books are called picture books because pictures, rather than words, carry the story. Some picture books do not even have words.

❖ Story lines should focus on toddlers' favorite subjects. Subjects may include animals, toys, fun places to visit, cars and trucks, or home and family.

❖ Books should be durable. They should be sturdy and washable. Books made of cloth, vinyl, and heavy cardboard with a plastic coating are best, 14-21. You can make books by sewing a few plastic kitchen storage bags together. Another option is to use top-loading sheet protectors (available at office-supply stores). Then slip pictures mounted on

14-21 Toddler books must be sturdy and easy to clean.
© John Shaw

14-22 Reading favorite books helps toddlers develop language skills.

heavy paper or cardboard into the bags or sheet protectors. (These books have the added bonus of being able to change the pictures.)
❖ Pages should be easy for the toddler to turn and keep open.

How Toddlers "Read"

Toddlers will not sit still and look at books for a long time. Young toddlers may enjoy glancing at a page and turning it. (Using the motor skill of turning the page is more fun than looking at the pictures.) Later, toddlers look at the pictures for a little longer, but they still may not want to hear the story. Adults can name one object and point to it. Then they can ask toddlers to point to the objects named. As language develops, toddlers can name objects in the pictures and even make some sounds of animals or other objects. A two-year-old often enjoys hearing the whole story, as long as it contains only a short sentence or two for each picture page, 14-22.

Reading to Toddlers

Many older toddlers (and even preschool children) insist on hearing the same story over and over. They often request the same story at bedtime. Routines, including favorite, repeated stories, help the toddler feel secure. The child knows what will happen in the story's beginning, middle, and end. Sometimes children will insist that not even a word be changed. The loving adult who reads daily to a child is likely to bring more security than the story itself.

Singing with Toddlers

Songs that act out the meanings of words are helpful to toddlers. An example is "Here We Go 'Round the Mulberry Bush." This song lets toddlers sing and act out lines, such as, "This is the way we eat our soup," and "This is the way we wash our hands." Toddlers can sing many other verses, too. See 14-23 for other language games that are fun and encourage children to use language.

Language Games

Show Me
Young toddlers enjoy running around and pointing to objects. When an adult names objects for the toddler to touch, the toddler's language skills improve. Make statements like, "Show me the door." As the toddler touches the door, praise him or her with a statement like, "You're right. That's the door."

Follow Directions
Give the toddler simple directions using familiar objects. For example say, "Bring me the ball." Praise the toddler for following directions promptly. You may also play the game "Follow the Leader." Give simple directions such as, "Clap your hands," or "Pat your head."

Telephones
Listening to voices on a phone and talking into a phone can help language develop. Toddlers enjoy play phones. Some types have recorded voices that talk to the toddler. Talking on a real phone with adult supervision also is good language practice.

14-23 Adults and toddlers can enjoy language games.

Social-Emotional Needs

Toddlerhood is like the teen years because the toddler is in a **transitional stage** (passing from one stage to another). Adults cannot treat toddlers as if they are babies or five-year-olds. Toddlers are somewhere in-between. They want to do things for themselves, but this desire exceeds what they are able to do. Toddlers are trying to become separate persons, 14-24. They go back and forth between wanting to be totally independent and wanting to be totally dependent.

These changes in toddlers' wills confuse adults. Most adults find they have to give toddlers freedom at times and be firm at other times. Their actions depend on the toddlers' needs.

Discipline

Toddlers do not have **self-restraint**. In other words, they cannot always control themselves. They also do not know all the rules of acceptable behavior. Adults must set limits

transitional stage. A stage of development in which a person is passing from one stage to another.

self-restraint. The ability to control yourself.

14-24 Toddlers often pull away from their parents because they want to gain independence.

for toddlers. Limits keep toddlers safe and show them how to become more socially acceptable.

Balancing Self-Assertion and Obedience

Adults must help toddlers balance **self-assertion** (doing as one chooses) and **obedience** (acting within the limits set by others). The best way to do so is to meet toddlers' needs, not punish what they do wrong. Although each toddler has his or her own unique needs, some needs are common.

Toddlers Need to Feel Loved

Toddlers need to feel loved by caring adults. They seem to sense love that is shown to them physically and directly. For example, most toddlers respond to cuddling, loving words, and special times each day when attention is focused on them, 14-25. Toddlers do not seem to sense love shown in indirect ways, such as having cooked meals or clean clothes (although these are important).

Toddlers Want to Feel Lovable

When toddlers are always made to feel they are "bad," they may grow to dislike themselves. Adults should

14-25 Special times spent with loving adults help toddlers feel loved.

label incorrect behavior as a mistake. They should not call the child *bad, selfish, naughty,* or *mean.* Harsh punishment may cause toddlers to feel they are bad, too.

Toddlers Need Respect

Toddlers are worthy of the same respect other people receive. Adults should not respond to toddlers' mistakes with hurtful teasing or anger. Respecting toddlers helps them like themselves. It also serves as the model for the growing child's relationships with others.

Toddlers Need Understanding and Patient Guidance

Toddlers need some freedom. Giving toddlers choices allows them to express their tastes. For example, adults can let toddlers choose between two green vegetables for lunch. A toddler also may choose between self-control and adult-control. The adult may say, "You may color on the paper, or I'll have to put the crayons away." Toddlers seem more willing to accept a firm no when given choices at other times. Limits given in one situation will seldom carry over to similar cases. For example, a toddler pulling books from a shelf may be told no as the adult pulls the hand from the books. The toddler may pause a moment, then reach for the books with the other hand. Adults must give limits for each case. They also must repeat limits again and again before they become part of the toddler's life.

Toddlers Need Consistency in Discipline

Consistency helps people feel secure. However, people also need flexible rules at times. Toddlers may need flexible rules when they are ill or when other problems occur. Once the situation is back to normal, rules should become consistent again. Of course, discipline changes as children grow. As they grow, children are often allowed more freedom.

Toddlers have good days and problem days, just like adults. When limits are set and discipline is firm yet kind, the toddler will begin to have good days more often. Good days are a sign that toddlers are getting better at balancing self-assertion and the need to obey, 14-26. Balancing the two is a skill they will need throughout life.

Guidance: Helping Toddlers Control Their Emotions

Understanding toddlers' emotions is the first step in helping toddlers control them. To do so, caregivers must control their emotions, as well. Problems with toddlers often include contrariness, temper tantrums, and fears and anxieties.

self-assertion. Doing as one chooses rather than what others want.

obedience. Acting within the limits set by others.

14-26 Toddlers have many good days.
Mead Johnson Nutritional Division

Contrariness

By 18 months, many toddlers show definite signs of contrariness. They tend to oppose adults and even other toddlers. They replace *yes* with *no*, even when *yes* is what they really mean. *Me want* is replaced with *No want*.

Let the Toddler Choose

Certain methods often reduce contrariness. The simplest way is to let the toddler make some choices. As long as results are not harmful, allowing toddlers some freedom makes obeying easier.

Tell the Toddler in Advance

Telling the toddler about upcoming events, such as lunchtime, a few minutes in advance helps reduce contrariness. This time allows the toddler to prepare emotionally for the change of activities, 14-27. Saying no is often a toddler's response to sudden changes. Once they say no, it is more difficult for them to back down. If toddlers say no when you tell them about a change, ignore the reply until the change happens. If children say no again, express toddlers' feelings. Adults can say, "You are really having fun in the sandbox, but we must eat now." If toddlers still resist, use calm actions, such as picking up toddlers.

14-27 Telling toddlers what will happen next prepares them for a change of events.
© John Shaw

Use Pretend Games

Another way to reduce contrariness is to play a pretend game of obedience. The adult might say, "I'm going to wash my hands before you do." (Of course, after much scrubbing, the toddler wins.) Sometimes pretend games of obedience become rituals, such as a "chase" to the bedroom at naptime.

Temper Tantrums

As toddlers discover the powers of self-assertion, they may have temper tantrums. Many two-year-olds have temper tantrums, but some do not. Toddlers who are lively, under stress (even the stress of being hungry), and cannot talk yet are prone to tantrums. Trying the following ideas may help reduce the number and frequency of tantrums:

❖ Reduce or avoid demands when the toddler is tired, hungry, or ill.
❖ Make requests in a pleasant tone of voice.
❖ Remove toys or play equipment that seems to frustrate the child.
❖ Have enough toys or ideas to prevent boredom.
❖ Offer help when the toddler seems to need it. (Waiting until the child shows frustration is often too late.)
❖ Give in on small demands. (Toddlers need to get their way sometimes.)
❖ Praise the toddler for signs of control.

Once a temper tantrum is underway, allow the tantrum to continue. It is a form of release for the child. Ignoring the child's tantrum may help, because tantrums are often done for attention. Toddlers have been known to follow adults from room to room, throwing the tantrum each time. If a tantrum occurs in public, the adult and child should go to a quiet place for the toddler to become calm.

Comforting the Child

Adults should acknowledge the feelings of toddlers and show comfort. The adult may say, "I know you really wanted to stay outside. I'm sorry you are so upset about coming in the house." After the tantrum, hugs often are helpful. When adults hold back this comfort, toddlers may feel unlovable.

Do not use spankings to punish tantrums. If the adult expresses displeasure (or even anger) in a physical way, he or she is modeling that behavior for the toddler.

Tantrums, when handled calmly, often decrease during the preschool years. Also, adult calmness serves as a model for children of ways to deal with anger.

Fears and Anxieties

Adults should not dismiss children's fears and anxieties as silly. They should not tease children about them, either. They should handle the toddler's feelings in a matter-of-fact way.

contrariness. The tendency to oppose almost everything others do or say.

Reducing Fear and Anxiety

Adults should show differences between real and pretend things in the toddlers' world. For example, adults should explain that dreams are not real. This will help reduce toddlers' fears of pretend things. Toddlers will often ask whether something is real or pretend. They will even ask about the same thing many times just to be certain.

Giving toddlers security also reduces fear, 14-28. Night-lights, toys in bed, and familiar caregivers add

security. Avoid situations that cause much fear or anxiety. However, some situations, such as going to the doctor, cannot be avoided. These should be explained in a simple, honest way. As they are explained, address only fears the toddler has already shown.

Overcoming Fear and Anxiety

For toddlers to overcome fears and anxieties, they need to see and talk about their fear in safe ways. Telling toddlers that other children have the same fear may comfort them. Gradual exposure to a feared subject may also help, 14-29. If the toddler is afraid of dogs, the adult may talk about dogs. Later, the adult may read the child a book about dogs or give the child a toy dog. After some time, the toddler may stand near a friendly puppy or small dog that is behind a

14-28 A toddler's attachment to a well-loved toy can provide relief from fear and anxiety.

14-29 A warm and caring adult can help a child overcome fears.
Brian LaPeter—The Island Packet

fence. This method is better for the toddler than suddenly exposing the child to fearful situations.

Toddlers should be praised for small steps toward overcoming fears. For example, toddlers can be praised for only crying a little or for not running from the puppy behind the fence.

Most of the toddler's fears and anxieties will disappear with age. If parents handle fear and anxieties in understanding ways, toddlers will be better able to cope with present and future fears and anxieties.

Planning Self-Awareness Activities

A person's self-awareness begins at birth and continues throughout life. The roots of self-awareness seem to form in the toddler years. Self-awareness grows mainly out of the toddler's daily contact with his or her world. A few planned activities may enhance self-awareness, 14-30.

Examples of self-awareness activities include placing photographs of the toddler on the refrigerator or another viewing area at the child's height. Keeping a photo album of the child's early years is fun for all family members. The parents and child can sit together and talk about how the child has grown and how important the child is to the family. Measuring

14-30 A "Me Doll" helps toddlers understand they are seeing themselves in a mirror.
© John Shaw

the child's height on a chart and keeping a running tally of his or her height also helps the child gain self-awareness. See 14-31 for other examples of self-awareness activities.

With help from loving adults and their increasing mental abilities, toddlers can smoothly leave babyhood behind. Toddlers emerge as happy, confident young children, 14-32.

Self-Awareness Activities

Name the Parts of the Face
Place the toddler's hands on your face. Name aloud each part of your face as the child feels it. Ask the child to name the parts.

Mirrors
With the toddler on your lap, hold a mirror to reflect the toddler's face. Ask, "Who is that?" If the toddler does not answer say, "That is you." Say the toddler's name.

Dressing Up
Children under age three enjoy dressing up with old purses, hats, necklaces, and large flat shoes. To help the toddler play while dressing up, show the child one object. For example, show the toddler a hat and say, "Look at this pretty hat. I'm going to wear it." Place the hat on your head and talk about how pretty it is. Then say, "Do you want to wear a hat?" Place a hat on the toddler's head, saying how nice it looks. If the toddler enjoys this, try other items.

Pretend
Have a pretend tea party with a toddler. Talk about the pretend foods in much the same way you would talk about real food. If the toddler looks confused say, "How funny! We can pretend to have a party!"

A Book About Me
Take pictures of the toddler's daily activities. Place the pictures in a photo album or in plastic bags that are fastened together with string.

14-31 These activities enhance a toddler's sense of self.

14-32 As toddlers begin to understand their abilities, they become more confident and content.
© John Shaw

Recognizing Developmental Delays

Toddlers with developmental delays may show some of the behaviors of infants as listed in Chapter 10. As you may have noted, infant development is judged mainly by gross-motor skills. During the toddler years, gross-motor skills are still important behaviors to observe, but fine-motor skills and language become more important in indicating healthy signs of development. Knowing some typical toddler behaviors may help parents recognize delays and bring their concerns to the attention of a doctor, 14-33.

Typical Toddler Behaviors

Age	Behavior
15 Months	Fills and empties containers May walk without support Vocalizes with pitch changes (babbling sounds like a sentence) Uses 4 or 5 words Begins self-feeding
18 Months	Walks and may run some Climbs up or down one stair step Plays with pull toys Uses 5 to 10 words Likes being read to Marks with crayon on paper attached to a table (cannot hold paper and mark) Partially feeds self
24 Months	Turns pages (may turn 2 or 3 at a time) Kicks large ball Imitates some household work (feeding baby or washing dishes) Recognizes familiar objects in pictures Uses two or three words together ("juice gone")

14-33 Knowing typical toddler behaviors can help adults recognize developmental delays.

Toddlers begin to meet their needs without depending on caregivers.

Summing It Up

Toddlers practice self-care skills like self-feeding, self-dressing, and toileting. These skills also help them advance in their mental and social-emotional development.

Toddlers eat table food and can feed themselves. Parents should offer toddlers foods that are high in nutrient density. The Food Guide Pyramid for Young Children provides parents with guidance on a healthful diet and physical activity for their toddlers. A number of feeding problems can arise because of the toddlers' growing independence.

Clothing and shoes that fit and allow for growth are important. Other features to consider when purchasing clothing for toddlers include safety, comfort, fabric, attractive style, and ease of care.

The sleep and rest habits of toddlers have changed since infancy. Bedtime problems can develop, but if adults establish quiet nighttime rituals, bedtime is less stressful.

For bathing, place a small tub inside the regular tub. Toddlers help a little in their bathing and use this time for play. Eating nutritious foods and cleaning teeth regularly is part of good dental health. Dental checkups can begin at age two years.

Before children can begin toilet learning, their bodies must be physically ready. They also must see the need to go to the bathroom. This generally occurs sometime after age two years. Children should not be shamed or punished when they have accidents. They need praise and encouragement.

Toddlers' mental abilities are stimulated by using daily routines. Parents should also give toddlers time to check and recheck learnings through play. Adults can enrich their toddler's learning environment by providing appropriate materials and planning a few activities for the toddler. Language development is a key part of mental development in the toddler years.

Parents need to give toddlers some freedom while still setting limits for them. Contrariness and temper tantrums are typical problems at this age. Feelings of fears and anxieties should be handled in understanding ways. As toddlers become more aware of themselves and their abilities, they become more confident.

Reviewing Key Concepts

Write your answers on a separate sheet of paper.

1. True or false. Teaching self-care skills is part of meeting the physical needs of toddlers.
2. Which statements about feeding toddlers are true?
   A. Because toddlers are larger, their appetites increase.
   B. Toddlers want to feed themselves.
   C. Toddlers who play with their food are being naughty.
   D. Empty calorie foods provide energy, which makes them a nutritious choice for toddlers, whose bodies demand high amounts of energy.
   E. Many of the toddler's feeding problems work themselves out in time.
3. Are toddlers better at putting on clothes or taking off clothes?
4. True or false. Shoes help toddlers walk by providing good support.
5. Give four suggestions that may help toddlers go to bed.
6. What is the average age for toddlers to begin feeling the sensation of needing to use the toilet?
7. True or false. Potty chairs do not make toilet learning easier for toddlers.
8. Intellectual needs are best met _____.
   A. through planned activities
   B. when toddlers are involved with household activities on a day-to-day basis
   C. when needed concepts and skills are taught in a drill fashion
   D. when language is not part of most activities
9. Give two ways to reduce contrariness in toddlers.
10. Describe three ways to reduce the number of temper tantrums in toddlers.
11. True or false. Toddlers become less fearful when quickly exposed to the feared situation again.

Using Your Knowledge

1. **Nutrition/Technology.** Plan a one-week menu (meals and snacks) for a two-year-old following the Food Guide Pyramid for Young Children. Use the computer to format and print your menu. Post your menu as part of a classroom display.
2. **Art/Nutrition.** Create a poster or mobile of healthful and safe finger foods for toddlers.
3. **Consumer Skills/Creative Skills.** Borrow three items of toddler clothing and bring these to class. Examine each garment for the features listed on chart 14-6. List the good features included. Compare your list with others in the class. Create a hangtag for each clothing item that lists its best features.
4. **Role-Play.** Select a partner and role-play various scenarios where a parent tries to teach a child a self-care skill. Take turns being the parent and the toddler. After a few of these role-plays, discuss with your partner whether teaching toddlers self-care skills is harder or easier than you had imagined.

5. **Child Development.** Plan one activity that would help promote a toddler's sense of self-awareness. Present your activity to the class, explaining how the activity is done and how it promotes the development of self-awareness.

Making Observations

1. Observe a toddler at home or in a child care setting. How does the toddler show independence? In what ways does the toddler depend on adults?
2. Observe a toddler in his or her bedroom or playroom. What decorations seem to have been chosen with a toddler in mind? What things seem to especially fit this toddler?
3. Observe a toddler playing and identify what types of learnings he or she demonstrates in play (examples are perceptual, problem solving, motor, language, and self-awareness learnings).
4. Observe an adult reading a story to a toddler. Which features of the book did the toddler like? Was there anything about the book that didn't seem fit for toddlers? Explain.
5. Observe adults caring for toddlers who are having a hard day. What adult actions seem to work best? Why? What adult actions do not seem to work? Why?

Thinking Further

1. Examine some items used to teach self-dressing. Although these items teach some skills, how are they different from actual dressing? (Be specific about each item.)
2. Examine several pieces of equipment that can be used for problem solving, such as a puzzle. What specific skills does a child need to have or develop in order to use the materials? (As you answer this question, visualize each step.)
3. What are some of the ways adults fail to respect toddlers? What might be the outcome if adults treated their friends in this way? How can they be respectful to toddlers? (Be specific.)

Part 5
Preschoolers and School-Age Children

Children grow and develop in significant ways between ages 3 and 12 years. The most visible changes are physical. However, the maturation of the brain and broadening of experiences allows children to master new intellectual and social tasks as well.

In **chapter 15**, you will see how striking changes in size and shape begin to occur at age three years. By the end of the preschool period (age five years), children's bodies look much more like those of adults than those of babies. Children's motor skills also improve. This enables them to engage in activities that demand coordination and balance, such as biking. Fine-motor skills are improving, but they still lag behind gross-motor skills.

Chapter 16 will show you why preschoolers' expressions often amuse adults. Although these children use symbols, including language, in a more mature way, they cannot consistently use logic in reasoning.

In **chapter 17**, you will study how preschoolers develop independence as they try new activities and meet new adults and peers. These experiences lead to self-understanding.

Chapter 18 will give you many ideas about assisting preschoolers. You will learn how to help them meet their nutritional needs as they choose the foods they eat. You will read about clothing and furnishings that are pleasing and also foster a child's self-help abilities. You will learn activities to meet intellectual needs and help preschoolers understand their social selves.

In **chapter 19**, you will study school-age children. In these years, physical development slows, and most children's gross-motor skills become graceful and strong. Fine-motor skills improve, too. Intellectually, school-age children are becoming logical and express themselves competently. During these years, children also learn formally in school. They depend less on parents and make more decisions on their own. Friendships and groups become important for their social development.

Chapter 15
Physical Development of the Preschooler

Four-year-old Garrett loves to draw with markers. His parents have difficulty identifying what he draws, because his fine-motor skills are not that developed when it comes to drawing. Sometimes Garrett's parents try giving him a theme for his pictures. Yesterday Garrett's father asked him to draw a truck, but Garrett did not want to draw what his father suggested. Instead, he waited until his picture was complete and announced that it was a firefighter.

After studying this chapter, you will be able to
- describe the physical development that occurs in preschool children.
- describe preschool children's gross-motor and fine-motor skills.

Preschool children are those between the ages of three and five years. As you can imagine, they are becoming grown-up. The bodies of preschoolers continue to mature, which makes them able to handle harder tasks. They are changing in ways that make them more like adults and less like small children.

Toddlers have gained many gross-motor and fine-motor skills. However, they do not have as much control over their movements as they would like. In the preschool years, children improve their skills of walking, running, balancing, and self-dressing.

Body Growth and Development

Preschool children grow even more slowly than toddlers. (If the growth rate did not slow, people would grow to be as big as giants!) Instead of growing much larger, the preschooler's body proportions change and the organ systems mature.

The growth rate slows in almost the same way for all preschool children. This means children who are larger than their peers at age three years likely will be larger at age five years, too.

Height and Weight

Most preschool children grow steadily at about 2 ½ inches to 3 inches each year. On average, girls are shorter than boys, but the difference is ½ inch or less, 15-1.

The rate of weight gain also slows during the preschool years. Preschoolers gain about three to five pounds per year. Seventy-five percent of the weight gained during the preschool years is due to muscle development. Because boys have greater muscle development, even during the preschool years, they are, on average, a pound heavier than girls their age, 15-2.

Other Body Changes

As toddler features begin to disappear, the preschooler's body proportions begin to look more like those of an adult, 15-3. The lower face grows more rapidly than the head. This helps the preschooler's face look more like an adult's. Until age 30 months,

preschool children. Children between the ages of three and five years.

Average Height from Three to Five Years

Age in Years	Boys	Girls
3	38″	37¼″
3½	39¼″	39¼″
4	40¾″	40½″
4½	42″	42″
5	43¼″	43″
5½	45″	44½″

15-1 The height of children from three to five years increases rather steadily. Boys tend to be slightly taller than girls.

Average Weight from Three to Five Years

Age in Years	Boys	Girls
3	32¼ lbs.	31¾ lbs.
3½	34¼ lbs.	34 lbs.
4	36½ lbs.	36¼ lbs.
4½	38½ lbs.	38½ lbs.
5	41½ lbs.	41 lbs.
5½	45½ lbs.	44 lbs.

15-2 The weight of children from three to five years increases rather steadily. Boys tend to be slightly heavier than girls.

15-3 These preschool boys have body proportions more like those of adults than those of babies.

the waist, hips, and chest measure almost the same. By age five years, the waist is smaller than the shoulders and hips. The trunk grows to allow more space for the internal organs (heart, lungs, liver, and others). As the trunk grows, the abdomen protrudes less. The legs grow rapidly, too. By 5 ½ years, most children's legs are about half the length of the body. This is the same as the adult's leg-to-body proportions.

Bones and Teeth

The bones continue to ossify and grow larger and longer. Deciduous (baby) teeth begin to fall out between ages four and five years. Although permanent teeth may not erupt until the early school-age years, they are growing under the gums. Bone and teeth development can be harmed by malnutrition and other health problems during the preschool years. Bones, muscles, and joints are more prone to injury in preschool children than in older children.

Organs

Other organs are maturing, too. The heart rate slows and becomes steady. Blood pressure increases. Breathing slows and is deeper. Although the digestive tract is maturing, it lags behind the maturity of other organs. Therefore, the preschooler's digestive tract is more irritated by high-fiber foods and seasonings than the adult's. The preschooler's brain continues to grow, too, but at a slower rate than before.

Fat and Muscle Tissues

The ratio of fat to muscle tissue continues to decrease slowly. Boys lose baby fat more quickly than girls. With good nutrition and physical activity, most of the baby fat will have disappeared by the first day of kindergarten. At age 5 ½ years, the preschooler's fat deposits are less than half as thick as they were at age one year.

The tall, lean body of the preschooler is strengthened. This is due to the *skeletal muscles* (muscles attached to the bones) and bones that are made stronger by ossification. Muscle fiber, which was to a great extent water, is now being replaced with more protein. Preschoolers' activity level also affects muscle development. Besides content changes in muscle tissue, the fiber size of muscles responds to physical activity. Thus, a three-year-old's skeletal muscles develop rapidly because children are more active at this age than at any other age in the life span.

Motor Development

The motor development of preschoolers improves. This is due to physical activity and increasing body growth and development. Preschoolers have an increase in muscle development and develop better balancing skills. Their eye-hand coordination becomes more refined, 15-4. Their reaction time (time required to react to a sight or sound) becomes shorter. Preschool children are able to perform many

15-4 Eye-hand coordination becomes more refined in the preschool years.
© John Shaw

internal organs. Parts inside of the body, such as the heart, lungs, and liver.

reaction time. The time required to respond to a sight or sound.

physical activities. Through play, preschool children's motor skills develop quickly, 15-5.

Gross-Motor Development

At the same time preschool children's large muscles develop, balance develops, too. This complex skill requires both signals from the eyes and the movement of fluids in the semicircular canals of the inner ears. These signals are sent to the brain and then transmitted to the muscles of the body. Based on these signals, the muscles make constant adjustments to maintain balance. Balance keeps a person upright and affects many gross-motor activities. It is also a measure of the eye, ear, and brain health. Several studies have reported a relationship between balancing skills and the ability to start reading, too.

During the preschool years, children differ widely in their balancing skills. Through regular physical activities, preschool children will develop two kinds of balance. **Dynamic balance**, which is balance while moving, is developed when preschoolers walk a line or balance beam. **Static balance**, or balance maintained while being still, is learned when preschoolers stand on one foot with arms outstretched or folded across their chests. Dynamic balance is easier to develop than static balance, 15-6. You

15-5 Strength, coordination, and motor skills are developed through play.

15-6 Balancing is a gross-motor skill made possible by increasing development of the large muscles.
© John Shaw

may realize this if you have ridden a bicycle or watched or participated in dance or gymnastics.

Through muscle development and balancing skills, preschool children become stronger and more coordinated. Their gross-motor skills, such as walking, running, jumping, climbing, throwing, catching, balancing, hopping, and skipping improve. Chart 15-7 shows how these motor skills develop and improve.

You will notice that preschoolers walk more smoothly than toddlers. The chart shows they like to try more challenging ways to walk. They run faster, and their arms and legs alternate in rhythm. Four-year-olds use a forward arm action to jump higher. With increased courage and better balance, climbing becomes easier. They can catch balls that are bounced better than those thrown by others. Three-year-olds begin hopping. Older preschoolers can hop and skip faster and for longer distances than younger preschoolers. Their actions become more advanced in all areas, 15-8.

Two new actions help the preschooler's throwing ability. One is body rotation and the other is weight shift. **Body rotation** is the action of turning the trunk of the body to one side when the hand on the other side is used to throw. **Weight shift** is the change of weight from the back foot to the front foot. Body rotation and weight shift may begin during the third year. They become much more

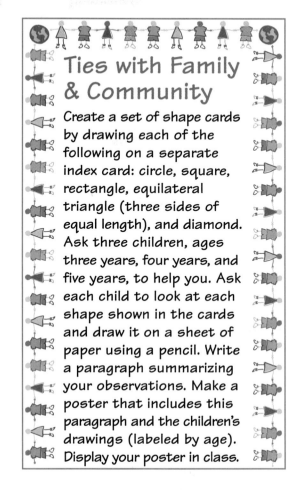

Ties with Family & Community

Create a set of shape cards by drawing each of the following on a separate index card: circle, square, rectangle, equilateral triangle (three sides of equal length), and diamond. Ask three children, ages three years, four years, and five years, to help you. Ask each child to look at each shape shown in the cards and draw it on a sheet of paper using a pencil. Write a paragraph summarizing your observations. Make a poster that includes this paragraph and the children's drawings (labeled by age). Display your poster in class.

dynamic balance. Balance maintained while moving.

static balance. Balance maintained while being still.

body rotation. The action of turning the trunk of the body to one side when the hand of the other side is used to throw.

weight shift. The change of weight from the back foot to the front foot.

Preschoolers' Gross-Motor Skill Development

Walking
❖ Gain skills in balancing.
❖ Hold hands close to the body.
❖ Begin to swing arms in alternate rhythm of foot placement.
❖ Like to walk sideways, backward, and on tiptoes.
❖ Likes to spin around and try to become dizzy, which helps balance (three-year-olds).

Running
❖ Have short stops and starts.
❖ Can turn corners quickly.
❖ Begin to swing arms in alternate rhythm of foot placement.
❖ Increase speed a lot (five-years-old).

Jumping
❖ Have stronger muscles.
❖ Increase distance of broad jump (with girls often lagging behind boys).
❖ Increase height of hurdle jump (with boys and girls are almost equal).

Climbing
❖ Climb with more skill due to longer legs.
❖ Can alternate steps going up stairs (three-year-olds).
❖ Can alternate climbing down steps (four-year-olds).

Throwing and Catching
❖ Begin to turn body to one side (body rotation) when the hand on the other side is used to throw (three-year-olds).
❖ Begin to shift weight from back foot to front foot (three-year-olds).
❖ Can catch balls they bounce better than those thrown by others.
❖ Show increased strength, balance, and coordination and thus improve throwing distance, speed, and accuracy.
❖ Can catch ball with the arms to one side (between ages four and five).

Balancing
❖ Can walk heel-toe on a straight line without falling (three-year-olds).
❖ Can balance on one foot (static balance) for a few seconds (three-year-olds). Can do more static balance feats (four- and five-year-olds).

Hopping and Skipping
❖ Can hop on preferred foot (three-year-olds).
❖ Can hop faster and for longer distances (four- and five-year-olds).
❖ Can skip (between ages four and six).
❖ Can do rhythmic hopping (hopping on one foot and then the other without breaking the rhythmic pattern) and precision hopping (following a certain pathway) (some five-year-olds).

15-7 Compared to the toddler, the gross-motor skills of the preschool child are smoother and less awkward.

15-8 Floor blocks are prefect for the development of gross-motor skills, such as lifting and squatting.
© Nancy P. Alexander

refined by the end of the preschool period. These two changes improve a preschooler's throwing distance, speed, and accuracy.

Fine-Motor Development

Preschoolers' ability to **manipulate**, or work with by using the hands, is still awkward. However, as preschoolers play with small objects, their small muscles develop and fine-motor skills improve. Improved eye-hand coordination also helps fine-motor skills. Chart 15-9 shows what to

manipulate. To work with an object by using the hands.

Sequence of the Development of Fine-Motor Skills

Age	Skills	
Three Years	❖ Builds uneven tower of blocks. ❖ Pours water from a pitcher. ❖ Copies a circle (with some skill). ❖ Draws a straight line.	○ ——
Four Years	❖ Cuts on line with scissors. ❖ Washes hands. ❖ Copies a letter t. ❖ Makes a few letters.	†
Five Years	❖ Folds paper along the diagonal. ❖ Copies a square and a triangle. ❖ Traces a diamond shape. ❖ Laces shoes and may tie them. ❖ Copies most letters.	□ ◇ △

15-9 Fine-motor skills develop in a certain order.

expect in the fine-motor skills of preschool children. (Remember the ages at which children develop may vary. The order of development is almost the same for all children.)

Age Three Years

At age three years, most children can feed themselves using a spoon and fork, but they are still rather messy. They can build towers from small blocks, but the towers are crooked. Three-year-olds can draw straight lines and copy circles. They can unbutton buttons and pull large zippers.

Age Four Years

By four years, movements are steadier. Four-year-olds may try to use knives when they feed themselves. They are able to build straight towers and place blocks with steady hands, 15-10. Four-year-olds begin to cut along lines with scissors. (Scissors used at this age should have rounded tips.) These children can comb their hair and wash their hands. They can also begin to lace, but probably not tie, their shoes.

Age Five Years

At age five years, eye-hand coordination is greatly improved. Right- or left-hand preference is definite by this age for many children. Five-year-olds use a spoon, fork, and knife to feed themselves. They can build towers and place other small toys with skill. They can make simple drawings freehand. Five-year-olds can fasten large buttons and work large zippers. They may even be able to tie shoelaces.

15-10 Small blocks, designed just large enough for preschool hands, aid the development of fine-motor skills.
© LEGO Dacta, the educational division of the LEGO Group

Summing It Up

Preschoolers gain in height and weight much more slowly than toddlers. They begin to look less like babies and their faces begin to look more like those of adults. The waist becomes smaller than the shoulders and hips. Bones grow harder, larger, and longer. Deciduous teeth begin to fall out. Other organs and systems continue to mature. Fat deposits decrease and muscle tissue increases in size.

Dynamic and static balance develop. Large muscles become stronger and more coordinated. Preschoolers are better able to walk, run, jump, climb, throw and catch, balance, hop, and skip.

As preschoolers manipulate small objects, their fine-motor skills improve. Better eye-hand coordination helps skills develop. Their fine-motor skills develop in a certain order that is similar for all children. Three-year-olds can build uneven towers of blocks. Five-year-olds may be able to lace and tie shoes. Hand preference is definite by age five years.

Physical activity is important for preschoolers' growing bodies.

Reviewing Key Concepts

Write your answers on a separate sheet of paper.

1. True or false. Compared to the toddler years, the rate of growth speeds up during the preschool years.
2. Preschool children's weight increases because of _____.
   A. an increase in fat
   B. head (brain) growth
   C. muscle development
3. True or false. At the end of the preschool years, the child's legs equal about half the total body length.
4. Which of the following matures most slowly: brain, digestive tract, or heart?
5. True or false. A four-year-old can cut following a line with round-tipped scissors.
6. True or false. Fine-motor skills refer to how well a child can balance and jump.
7. True or false. Most five-year-olds can do rhythmic and precision hopping.
8. Match the preschool child's motor action to the skills by putting the letter (or letters) before the skill.
   Skills
   _____ walking
   _____ running
   _____ jumping
   _____ throwing
   _____ balancing

Motor actions
   A. uses forward action of arms
   B. shows some body rotation and shifting of weight
   C. uses increased speed
   D. swings arms in alternate rhythm of feet placement
   E. can walk heel-toe on a straight line

9. List four fine-motor skills developed in the preschool period.
10. True or false. Most four-year-olds can tie their shoelaces without help.

Using Your Knowledge

1. **Child Development/Creative Skills.** Write a one- or two-page brochure about the motor skills of preschool children. Illustrations may help. Give copies to local programs serving preschool children for parents and other adults to use. (Ask your teacher to check the brochure before making copies.)
2. **Mathematics/Interview Skills.** Choose one of the age groups listed in Figure 15-1. Survey 10 parents of children in this age group. Record the parent's answers to each of the following questions:
   - What are the age and gender of the child?
   - What are the child's current weight and height?

   Use the data gathered to calculate the average height and weight for children of each gender. How do your figures compare to those of the text?

3. **Interview Skills.** Interview a teacher of preschool children. Ask this person to describe eye-hand coordination of preschoolers at various ages? What changes has the teacher noticed in the children he or she serves from the beginning of the school year until now? Share your findings with the class.

4. **Child Development.** Use a parenting or child development magazine to obtain pictures of children using motor skills. For each picture, identify whether the child pictured is using fine-or gross-motor skills.

5. **Creative Writing/Technology.** Use the computer to compose a short story from the point of view of a preschooler. The story should describe the child's recent experiences with physical growth and development.

Making Observations

1. Observe a group of preschoolers playing. What motor skills have they developed? What motor skills need improvement?

2. Observe the skills of three-year-olds and five-year-olds in handling scissors, pencils or crayons, and a paintbrush. What changes happen in this two-year period? Describe your findings in class.

3. Observe gross- and fine-motor skills of children ages three, four, and five years. Make a chart to record the advancing skills. The chart might look like this—
Age and gender of child_____
Motor Skill—
Hopping
can hop _____
distance hopped _____
can hop rhythmically _____
can hop with precision _____
Jumping
length of broad jump _____
height of hurdle jump _____
forward movement of arms
seen _____
Compare the skills of each age by using the average for each skill.

Thinking Further

1. Why are the preschool years important ones for providing children with many opportunities for gross-motor development? (Think of this question in terms of all areas of growth and development—physical, mental, and social-emotional.)

2. If you were writing a magazine article about gift suggestions to aid in preschoolers' fine-motor development, what gifts would you suggest?

3. Why do preschoolers feel so grown-up? More specifically, what physical changes (appearance and skills) give them this idea?

Chapter 16
Intellectual Development of the Preschooler

Four-year-old Sung commonly uses phrases such as, "Her wants a cookie," "Me goed," and "Me do that." His parents cringe when they hear his grammar mistakes. Each time, they correct him and ask him to repeat the correct words several times. Sung has noticed how angry it makes his parents when he refuses to repeat the words after them. The entire situation is very frustrating for Sung, and sometimes it makes him cry. Sung's parents have noticed he is using correct grammar more often, but he seems to have had less to say lately.

After studying this chapter, you will be able to
✎ relate how new thinking skills emerge in preschool children.
✎ identify the major concepts learned at this stage of mental development.
✎ chart the increasing language skills of preschoolers.

Define...

- preoperational stage
- preconceptual substage
- intuitive substage
- egocentrism
- mental images
- internalized
- abstract
- logical thinking concepts
- classifying
- monologue
- collective monologue

Preschool children build mentally on what they have learned as infants and toddlers. Because preschoolers have better motor skills, their world broadens. Preschoolers can interact with more objects and people. They can participate in more events. This enables them to observe more and develop more advanced ideas about the physical attributes of things in their world. Preschoolers' mental development also broadens their world. They no longer rely only on their senses and motor actions to learn about their environment. Preschoolers can now solve problems mentally. Their more mature brains give them longer attention spans and help them recall more. Growing language abilities are also a major bonus, not only in communicating but also in thinking with words.

Piaget has described the second major stage of mental development as the **preoperational stage**. This is the stage children reach before they acquire logical mental actions, which Piaget calls *operations*. These logical mental actions (operations) require the mind to think through problems and act accordingly. Operations are what most people consider logical thinking. *Logical thinking* includes combining ideas or objects, placing them in order, and doing "if-then" thinking. Preschool children have not entered the logical thinking stage yet. Just as toddlers who are walking are prone to missteps, preschool children who are thinking are prone to thinking errors in logic.

How Preschool Children Learn

The preoperational stage occurs during the preschool years. For some children, it includes the first year or two of school as well. Chart 16-1 shows the two parts of the preoperational stage—the preconceptual and the

preoperational stage. The second of Piaget's developmental stages in which children have begun to do some mental thinking rather than solving all problems with their physical actions.

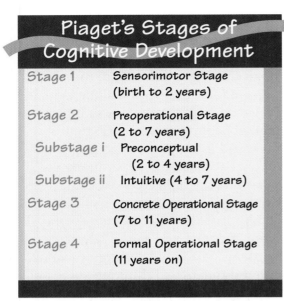

Piaget's Stages of Cognitive Development

Stage 1	Sensorimotor Stage (birth to 2 years)
Stage 2	Preoperational Stage (2 to 7 years)
Substage i	Preconceptual (2 to 4 years)
Substage ii	Intuitive (4 to 7 years)
Stage 3	Concrete Operational Stage (7 to 11 years)
Stage 4	Formal Operational Stage (11 years on)

16-1 The preschool child functions in the preoperational stage.

intuitive substages. The **preconceptual substage** is a substage in which children ages two to four years are beginning to develop some concepts. These children are able to form a mental image of what they see around them. However, many of these concepts are incomplete or illogical. Children may see different members of the same group as identical, such as all collies as Lassie.

In the **intuitive substage**, children sometimes are able to grasp a problem's solution by how they feel about it. Through their intuition, they base their solutions on "feeling" their way through problems rather than on logic. For example, a child standing on the ladder of a slide may say to his or her parent, "I am taller than you," because he or she can see over the parent's head. The intuitive preschooler doesn't use logic, such as, "I may look taller, but my feet are higher than my parent's feet; thus I am still shorter than my parent."

Obstacles to Logical Thinking

Although preschool children mentally are more advanced than toddlers, they do not think logically. There are still quite a few obstacles they must overcome before they can think logically.

First, preschool children, especially those under four, are *egocentric*. Piaget describes **egocentrism** as the preschooler's belief that everyone thinks in the same way and has the same ideas as he or she does. Egocentrism, in this sense, does not mean children are selfish or too concerned with themselves. It means they simply view the world in relation to themselves, 16-2. They may offer others candy from their mouths because they are enjoying it and think others would, too. If children think the slide is tall, they think adults think it is tall, too. They do not recognize that an adult who is taller may see the slide as small.

Secondly, preschoolers center their attention on only one part of an object or event. They do not see all parts at the same time. Look at the example in Figure 16-3. The preoperational child can see that two same-size glasses

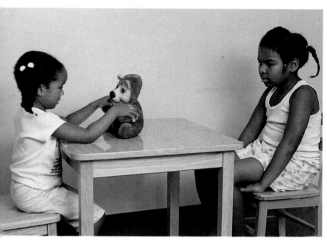

16-2 The three-year-old (left) is asked to describe what she believes is the older girl's view of the bear. She describes the bear's face. This is her view from her side of the table.
© John Shaw

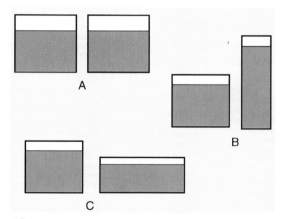

16-3 Preschool children know the amount of liquid in the two equal-sized glasses is the same (A). When the liquid of one container is poured into a tall tube (B) or a wide bowl (C), preschool children incorrectly think the amount of liquid has changed.

hold the same amount of liquid (A). However, when one glass is poured into a beaker of smaller diameter, the child sees the liquid higher up in the beaker (B) and thinks the tall container holds more. The child does not understand it is the thinness of the beaker that affects the level of the liquid. (The child can, however, tell you how the two containers differ in appearance.) The same thinking occurs when the child sees the liquid in the wider diameter bowl and again thinks the quantity of liquid has changed. (C) The child usually thinks *wide* means *more*, so the bowl must contain more liquid than the glass. However, in looking at the lower height of the liquid in the wider bowl, the child may also think it has less liquid than the glass. Suppose the adult pours the liquid back and forth from the original glass to the beaker or bowl. The child

preconceptual substage. A substage of the preoperational stage in which children ages two to four years are developing some concepts.

intuitive substage. A substage of the preoperational stage in which children can solve many problems correctly by imagining how they would act out the solution instead of using logic.

egocentrism. The belief a person has that everyone thinks in the same way and has the same ideas as he or she does.

may continue to say the quantity changes with each pour. The child cannot reason that the quantity remains the same because no liquid was added or taken away. The needed logic for this thought does not usually develop until the school-age years.

Also, preschool children tend to focus on single steps, stages, or events, rather than see the order of changes. Piaget says the focus is like seeing each frame of a film as a separate, unrelated picture rather than a running story. As shown in 16-4, if an object is held upright and falls, it passes from an original state (vertical) to a final state (horizontal). This happens through a series of angled states. Preoperational children, after watching the object fall, will draw only the first or the last state. How something happened or what something was like before a final change took place does not enter their minds, 16-5.

16-5 When asked to recall catching a fish, this preschooler would focus on the fish in the water and the fish in the boat. He would not focus on the in-between stages of getting the fish into the boat.

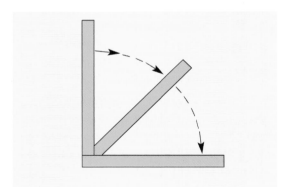

16-4 When preschool children are asked to watch as a rod is dropped and then draw what they have seen, they draw only the first state or last state. They do not draw any of the in-between states.

Preschoolers cannot follow a line of reasoning back to where it starts. They cannot retrace the steps to undo the task. For example, adding two to three equals five. To reverse the problem, a logical thinker would subtract two from five to equal three. Because the preschooler cannot see why subtracting can "undo" addition, Piaget says the preschooler cannot *reverse* (undo an action).

Finally, preschoolers link actions without using logic. Reasoning this way causes flaws in logic. An example is when a mother makes coffee just before a father comes home from work each day. The child may conclude that it is the coffee that brings Dad home.

The preschooler links events to each other when they occur close together in time. A preschooler also links objects without using logic. For example, tell a child that a bug with eight legs is called a *spider*. Then show the child a daddy longlegs and say, "The daddy longlegs has eight legs. What is the daddy longlegs?" The child will probably say, "It is big," "It is brown," or "It bites." The child was given the information but cannot conclude the daddy longlegs is a spider.

New Abilities Emerge

Preschoolers can think in their heads better than before. They do not always have to go through physical actions in order to solve problems. Their problem-solving skills depend on their memories of past sensory and motor experiences, however. The preschoolers' thinking is marked by a number of new abilities—symbolic play, mental images, drawing, and language.

Symbolic Play

Preschool children play many pretend games. While playing, they change things in some way or ways from the real world or dreams. In the pretend games, objects may stand for anything the child wants. Roles may change, too, as the child can take on adult or even animal roles. These mentally changed objects and roles are symbols used to represent the pretend world and the child's role in it, 16-6. Because children make up

16-6 The young boy's hat and climbing frame may be anything he imagines.
© Nancy P. Alexander

their own symbols, such as a leaf for a plate or the child as Baby Bear, pretend play is a mental step beyond imitation.

Mental Images

Mental images are symbols of objects and past experiences that are stored in the mind. They are the pictures in the mind when words or

mental images. Symbols of objects and past experiences that are stored in the mind.

experiences trigger the image. Unlike imitation and other play, mental images are private and **internalized** (thought about only). Mental images are not exact copies of real objects and experiences, but they do relate to the real world. For example, what mental images do you have when you hear the following words: *cat, thunderstorms,* and *flower*?

Drawing

Preschool children no longer scribble. They now attempt to draw objects and depict their world through these drawings, 16-7. Preschoolers intend their drawings to be realistic. They draw what they think or know about a person, not what is visually accurate (like a camera view). For example, a side view of a goldfish in a drawing may show both eyes and even a smiling mouth. Drawing is a step between symbolic play and

Ties with Family & Community

Ask a preschool center director for permission to visit with children about their drawings. (If possible, ask permission to videotape or photograph a few pieces of their art.) Ask the children to tell you about the drawings. (Say, "Tell me about your picture," rather than, "What is it?") Take notes on their responses. Using your notes and the photos or videotape of the art, share with the class what symbols were used in the drawings. Point out ways in which the artists attempted to show reality but were not visually accurate (such as drawing all four wheels on a car as complete circles).

16-7 This older preschool girl's drawing shows she is in an advanced stage of thinking. She uses rather realistic symbols to show her ideas in her drawing.
Wood Designs of Monroe, Inc.

mental images. This is because preschool children draw first and then decide what their pictures represent. This is in contrast to older children who decide what to draw, form a mental image of the object, and then draw it.

Language

Spoken words are symbols used to represent something. The symbols used in language are the most difficult of all symbols to understand. Unlike symbols used in pretend play, children do not decide on language symbols. Words are also more **abstract** (do not relate to what they represent) compared with many other symbols. For example, the word *car* does not look, sound, or move like a car.

Although words are abstract, they do help in talking. Once language abilities develop, the child can exchange ideas with others and thus learn. The child can also think with words. Thinking is faster using words compared with actions, too.

What Preschool Children Learn

Preschoolers have learned a lot by now. However, many errors and gaps still exist in the preschooler's concepts. During these years, learning is exciting and stimulating.

Concepts Children Learn

Children must learn many concepts. Preschoolers must learn more

16-8 By playing with a toy garage, this child can learn about the physical qualities of objects and use logical thinking concepts.
Fisher-Price, Inc.

about physical attributes of objects, begin to develop logical thinking concepts, and deal with causes and effects. Language, too, must expand for children to learn by communicating and thinking with words, 16-8.

Physical Attributes

Preschool children develop concepts about size, shape, color, texture, and other physical attributes (qualities) of objects. They also learn

internalized. Something that only is thought about and not shared with others.

abstract. Words that do not relate to what they represent.

what happens when objects are acted about by people, such as tossed in the air (they fall) or pushed (they roll or scoot). Piaget called this *physical knowledge*. These attributes are in the objects themselves and can be observed.

Preschool children are limited in their thinking about physical attributes for two reasons, however. First, the child may not note the object's most important features. For example, the child must note a zebra's stripes to distinguish it from a horse. If the child notes the zebra's ears, this will not help, as horses have similar ears. Second, because preschoolers tend to look at parts of an object, they cannot always mentally "see" the whole object. Preschool children were shown drawings such as those in 16-9. They recognized the parts but not the whole. (Nine-year-olds could see both.) The ability to see parts as well as the total figure is important for accurate perception.

Logical Thinking Concepts

Logical thinking concepts are those not experienced through the senses but understood mentally. They require the thinker to see a relationship. Logical thinking concepts include classifying; arranging by size; and understanding numbers, spatial, and time concepts. When compared to physical knowledge concepts, logical thinking concepts are much more difficult for preschool children to understand. In fact, most logical thinking concepts are not mastered until the school-age years.

Classifying Objects

Classifying is the ability to choose an attribute and group all the objects from a set (either mentally or physically) that possess that attribute. Because

16-9 Most preschool children will see only parts of these drawings. They do not see the faces in the whole drawings.

most preschool children become good at matching like objects, they can learn to sort. Sorting is a skill that must be mastered before classifying. Classifying is a much more difficult skill to master than sorting.

To classify, the child must see how objects are alike in one attribute while disregarding other attributes. For example, while using geometric shapes in many colors and sizes, the child decides on one attribute, such as *blue*. The child would classify by grouping all blue things regardless of shape or size. Preschoolers are more apt to consider more than one attribute and end up sorting. They might group all the blue circles together and all the blue squares together until they have many groups. This is matching and sorting rather than true classifying. Piaget would say preschoolers cannot really classify although they can point to each blue item.

Arranging by Size

Often preschool children cannot arrange objects by increasing or decreasing size, weight, or volume. Again, arranging by size requires mentally seeing two relationships. For example, suppose the task was to line up three people by height. The person in the middle must be taller than one person (first relationship) but taller than the other (second relationship). You can imagine how difficult this must be for preschoolers!

Toward the end of the preschool years, many children can arrange dowel rods or sticks in order of their lengths. To do this, however, the preschooler must physically lay the rods beside one another and hold all the bottom ends even.

Understanding Number Concepts

Many preschool children can count. However, counting does not show they understand numbers. For example, a preschool child may be able to count to five by saying the numbers. The same child may have trouble when asked to find five apples in a basket or drawn on a page. Young preschoolers do not understand the one-to-one relationship that takes place when counting objects. Even if preschoolers have seen older children or adults count while touching objects, the child may not understand that one (and only one) number is said for each object touched and that all objects must be touched once (and only once).

Once they can count objects successfully, preschoolers still do not completely understand number concepts that also require seeing relationships. Unlike each object that has its own

logical thinking concepts. Concepts that are not directly experienced through the senses but are developed through thought.

classifying. The ability to choose an attribute and group all the objects from a set (either mentally or physically) that possess that attribute.

name, numbers refer to groups. The number does not really refer to just the last object named; but also to the entire group. Thus, the child must mentally see that *one* is in *two* and *two* is in *three*. In fact, true counting is really adding.

Furthermore, number concepts may be made more difficult for young children by the use of many indefinite terms, such as *less, few, many,* and *some*. Adults need to realize how difficult it really is for preschoolers to understand number concepts.

Understanding Spatial Concepts

Preschool children understand the words *up, down, left, right, under, over, here,* and *there*. However, they have problems with spatial concepts. For example, until about five years of age, preschoolers may not know what is on the other side of a wall in their own homes. Preschool children also draw what they think about space rather than what they see. Chimneys on drawings of their houses are also at right angles to the roof, 16-10.

Preschool children think of the location of an object or person in relation to themselves. Learning left and right from another's perspective is hard—especially if the person is facing them. Simple tasks, such as setting a table, help children grasp these concepts.

A relationship between understanding spatial concepts and music has been noted in brain development research. Children who studied a musical instrument (not singing) have

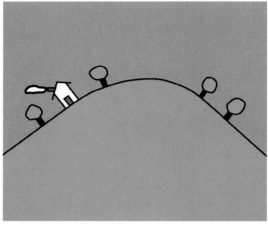

16-10 A preschool child often draws trees and other objects at right angles to the slope of the hill.

better understandings of spatial concepts throughout life. Music learnings, begun at ages three or four years, seem to produce long-term changes in the brain.

Understanding Time Concepts

Preschoolers can recall the recent past. Yesterday is recalled but a week or a year ago may be forgotten. Children link time to events, such as time to eat lunch. They cannot see time passing. There is no physical change in the days of the week. Morning, afternoon, and seasonal changes are gradual. For these reasons, time concepts are hard to understand. They are among the last concepts to develop.

Cause and Effect

Preschool children try to understand cause and effect, 16-11. Asking questions helps them to do this. Many

16-11 By pulling a wagon and checking on it often, this young girl is learning cause and effect in steering.
STEP 2 Corporation

cause and effect questions deal with natural events that may be too complex for young children to understand. Children ask questions such as, "What causes the rain?" and "What will happen to my dead fish?" Although adults may give them scientific answers, these children seem to settle on their own ideas. Some of these ideas are not even part of the real world. For example, they may believe giants cause the rain.

Preschool children may assign human qualities to nonhumans, such as plants, animals, and objects. Sometimes this is used to avoid being punished or having to do something they do not want to do. For example, a preschooler may say, "My teddy bear left my toys outside."

Preschool children often reverse cause and effect. They may say, "Because I am staying in bed, I am ill." Reversing cause and effect may

occur because many causes and their effects happen at almost the same time. In some cases, the preschooler's reversal of cause and effect may come from the difficulty in using the sentence structure to express the concept.

Language Abilities Increase

Some preschool children speak rather well. They use language to express their needs and feelings to others, 16-12. Age three years is an important time for language use.

Preschoolers' speech is as egocentric as their thinking because language often reflects thinking. In other words, they talk as though the listener would understand as they do. Thus, they often

6-12 Children who are deaf express their needs and feelings to others using sign language.
Barrier Free Environments, Inc., Raleigh, N.C.

do not communicate all the needed information. *Egocentric speech* includes telling a story from the middle instead of the beginning because preschoolers assume the listener knows the beginning of the story. These young children may also use pronouns without naming the person, such as, "She is eating." Again, they assume the adult knows who *she* is. The preschooler may even become impatient with the adult's lack of knowledge.

Other types of egocentric speech include repeating words without speaking to anyone. Sometimes children use monologue (talk to themselves as though thinking aloud). Other times they engage in a collective monologue (talking to another person but not listening to what the other person has said). All children go through this stage of language development.

Toward the end of the preschool stage, egocentric speech gradually disappears. This makes communication easier. Better articulation, a larger vocabulary, and advanced grammar also make communication easier.

Articulation of Preschool Children

Most toddlers have some problems making all the sounds in their spoken language. Most children substitute one sound for another for a time. In the English language, children master sounds between ages three and eight years. How fast preschool children master the sounds varies. However,

the order in which they master them is about the same for most children. *Total mastery* means the child can articulate the sound in different positions within words. (Most sounds, but not all, are found in the beginning, middle, and end of words.) Chart 16-13 shows the sounds that most preschool children have mastered.

Vocabulary of Preschool Children

Experts study vocabulary growth. They have found that children know about 900 words at age three years, 1,500 words at four years, and 2,000 words at five years. Words for concrete items (such as names for

Articulation Mastery of Preschool Children

Age	Sound	Word Examples
3 Years	m	monkey, hammer, broom
	n	nails, penny, lion
	p	pig, happy, cup
	h	hand, doghouse
	w	window, bowl
4 Years	b	boat, baby, tub
	k	cat, chicken, book
	g	girl, wagon, pig
	f	fork, telephone, knife
5 Years	y	yellow, onion
	ng	fingers, ring
	d	dog, ladder, bed

16-13 Ninety percent of all preschool children master these sounds by the given age.

objects and people) are learned before those that symbolize abstract ideas (such as names for emotions). Also, preschool children often assign their own meanings to words. A three-year-old may use the terms *less* and *more* to mean *more* or *yesterday* to mean anytime in the past. Brain development research shows the window of opportunity for vocabulary growth never closes.

Grammar of Preschool Children

Sentence structure becomes much more complex during the preschool period. At the beginning of this stage, preschool children do not seem to notice word order. Young children will respond to "Give doll the Mommy," as quickly as they do to "Give Mommy the doll." By five years, children will not respond to, "Give doll the Mommy." Preschool children's use of grammar matures a great deal between ages three and five years.

Brain development research shows the window of opportunity to learn grammar through listening to others closes at five or six years of age. Perhaps this is why grammar problems are difficult to overcome even in the school-age years.

Grammar at Three Years

As shown in chart 16-14, three-year-olds begin to have some ideas about grammar rules. Once they learn the rules, they tend to apply them even to

the exceptions. Three-year-olds may know *-ed* means past tense. Once they know the rule, they apply it to all verb forms. They may even say, "I eated." Adding *-ed* to all verbs simply

Grammar of Three-Year-Olds

The *-ing* verb ending used.
❖ **Rolling, falling**

Past tense for regular verbs (*-ed*) used.
❖ **Rolled, walked**

Past tense for some irregular verbs used.
❖ **Sank, ate**

Verb *to be* used to link noun to adjective.
❖ **Truck is red; I am good**

The *-s* for making plural used.
❖ **Cars, dolls**

The *-'s* for possessive used.
❖ **Bob's, Daddy's**

Articles used.
❖ **A, the**

Prepositions referring to space used.
❖ **On, in**

16-14 Three-year-olds are learning many of the rules of grammar.

monologue. Talking to oneself as though thinking aloud.

collective monologue. Talking to another person but not listening to what the other person has said.

shows the child has learned this grammar rule. In time, the child will learn the exceptions to the rules.

Children may have a hard time with questions because the word order is switched. Three-year-olds use question words like *when* and *why*, but they do not switch the word order. A three-year-old may ask, "When Mary will come?"

Negatives are very difficult for children, too. Once children know about negatives other than *no*, they add extra negatives. Sentences such as *I don't never want no more spinach* are common at this age. Three-year-olds do not understand the concept of multiple negatives.

Grammar at Four and Five Years

Four- and five-year-olds speak in longer, more complex sentences. They lengthen their sentences by using clauses, conjunctions, and prepositions. Instead of saying, "We play games. I had fun," the older preschool child says, "I had fun because we played games."

Four-year-old children may still find the word order of questions confusing. They often form questions by simply moving the question word to the beginning of the statement, such as "What the dog is eating?" By age five years, many children begin using tag questions. *Tag questions* are

asked by making a statement and then adding *yes* or *no* to ask the question. An example of a tag question is, "The baby is small, yes?" Late in the preschool years or early in the school-age years, children begin to form questions using the proper word order. They move the question word to the beginning of the sentence with the verb following next. For example, they would say, "What is the dog eating?"

Grammar Problems

Older preschool children continue to have two problems with grammar. They have trouble with pronouns. They use objective case pronouns where subjective case is correct. For example, the child may say, "Him and me went to town," instead of "He and I went to town." Pronouns may cause problems for children into the school years.

Children also continue to apply grammar rules to every case. They may say *eated* instead of *ate*. Once the child learns the irregular form, he or she may even say *ated*. A five-year-old may learn to use the plural form *feet* and ask, "May I go barefeeted?" The many irregular forms in the English language will trouble some children for years, even if they hear the correct grammar.

Summing It Up

According to Piaget, preschool children are in the preoperational stage and do not yet think logically. They learn by developing some mental concepts, but the concepts are incomplete or illogical. They solve problems by "feeling their way through" instead of using logic.

Preschoolers are beginning to think in their heads rather than depending on actions. Through their new abilities, such as symbolic play, mental images, drawings, and language, they are better able to solve problems and communicate.

Preschoolers develop many concepts about the physical attributes of objects, such as size, shape, color, texture, and other qualities. Older preschoolers are also beginning to learn logical thinking concepts, such as classifying; arranging in order; and understanding numbers, space, time, and cause and effect. Because this tasks involve complex mental relationships, preschoolers will make many errors even into the school-age years.

Preschool is an important time in language development, which is now linked to thinking. Most children at this age are ready to express their needs and feelings to others. Communication is easier because preschoolers can now articulate better and their vocabulary has increased. Sentence structure and grammar rules tend to be difficult for many preschool children as well as older children.

Preschoolers use their increasing intellectual skills as they look at books.

Reviewing Key Concepts

Write your answers on a separate sheet of paper.

1. Two children are playing by each other but are really talking to themselves as they play. This is an example of _____.
   A. egocentrism
   B. symbolic play
2. True or false. Preschool children tend to see the entire picture rather than concentrate on its parts.
3. True or false. It's difficult for preschoolers to subtract numbers because their concept of reversing is not fully developed.
4. A four-year-old begins a seven-hour car trip to his grandparents' home. Many times during the first hour, the child asks, "When will we get there?" The parents respond, "We will be there soon after lunchtime," thinking the statement will help their child understand. A few minutes later the child says, "Let's eat lunch." This is an example of _____.
   A. lack of ability in reversing the operation
   B. associating time with action without using logic
5. Complete each of the following sentences by placing the correct terms in the blanks.
   Terms
   A. symbolic play
   B. drawing
   C. mental images
   D. language
   Sentences
   _____ is a step between symbolic play and mental images.
   _____ is made up of the most abstract symbols.
   _____ are symbols stored in the mind.
   Through _____, children use ideas from

their real world, dreams, and imagination.

6. Briefly describe the preschooler's ability to understand each of the following logical thinking concepts:
   A. classifying
   B. ability to place objects in size order
   C. understanding spatial concepts
   D. understanding time concepts
7. True or false. Preschool children tend to settle on their own ideas for answers to scientific questions.
8. True or false. Preschool children often talk to themselves.
9. True or false. Preschoolers learn words for emotions, such as *love* and *hate*, before they learn words for objects and people.
10. Of the following sentence pairs, choose the sentence a three-year-old is most likely to say.
    A. "Mommy fixed my toy." OR "My toy was fixed by Mommy."
    B. "I'm never going no more to your house!" OR "I'm not ever going to your house again!"
    C. "I like food. I like apples best." OR "I like food, and I like apples best."

Using Your Knowledge

1. **Consumer Skills/Teamwork.** Work with three group members to draw or collect pictures of items that can be used in pretend play. Sort items into two groups. In one group, place purchased items that often stand for one thing in play, such as a doll. In another group, place household items that can be many things in play, such as a box. Mount each group of pictures on a separate poster. Discuss with your group the following questions—
   A. Are purchased items or household items more apt to be used in one way? Which are more likely to be used in many ways?

B. From which type of items do you think children mentally profit more—items that are often used in one way or items that are used in many ways?

2. **Child Development Experiment.** Try the liquid task (as described in 16-3) with a three-year-old and a five-year-old. Report your findings to the class.

3. **Child Development Experiment.** Try one of the following logical concept tasks with preschoolers. Report your findings to the class:

A. Borrow a set of blocks in various colors and geometric shapes from a preschool center. Ask a three-year-old to group together blocks that are alike in some way. Repeat the task with a five-year-old. Were there differences in the ability of the children to classify blocks?

B. Borrow or make a set of rods or dowels in different sizes. (Their lengths should vary at least ¼ inch.) Demonstrate (only once) for children ages three, four, and five years how to put the sticks in order from longest to shortest. Then ask the children to place the sticks in order. What differences do you note in the children's ability to do this task? Are these differences age-related? Explain.

4. **Technology.** Visit at least three Web sites to research language development in the preschool years. Use a computer to compose a report summarizing your research.

5. **Child Development Experiment.** Make an audio recording of the speech of preschool children in play. After listening to the tape, try to answer the following questions:

A. What sound substitutions did you hear?

B. Did you hear complex sentences— both statements and questions? Give examples.

C. What incorrect grammar did you hear?

D. What concepts seemed to be correctly understood by the children? What, if any, incorrect ideas were expressed?

Making Observations

1. Observe a group of three- and four-year-old children. As they play and talk, note what they do or say that shows they still do not think logically. Which concepts seem difficult for these children (time, classifying, and cause and effect)?

2. Observe a group of preschool children playing a pretend game. What symbols did they use? (Examples are material symbols, such as a block for a boat; sound symbols, such as sirens; and action symbols, such as pretending to eat.) In what ways were the symbols realistic? Discuss your findings with the class.

3. Observe a three- or four-year-old. Note errors in articulation and grammar. Compare your findings with charts 16-13 and 16-14.

Thinking Further

1. Why do adults sometimes confuse preschoolers' egocentrism with selfishness? What, if anything, might an adult say or do to help these children develop a less egocentric point of view?

2. How can a preschool teacher who has many dramatic play, art, and literature/language activities justify these as intellectual and not "just play" activities?

3. How is collective monologue an egocentric behavior? Would selfish adults tend to engage in collective monologues? If so, how might an adult monologue differ from the definition of children's monologue?

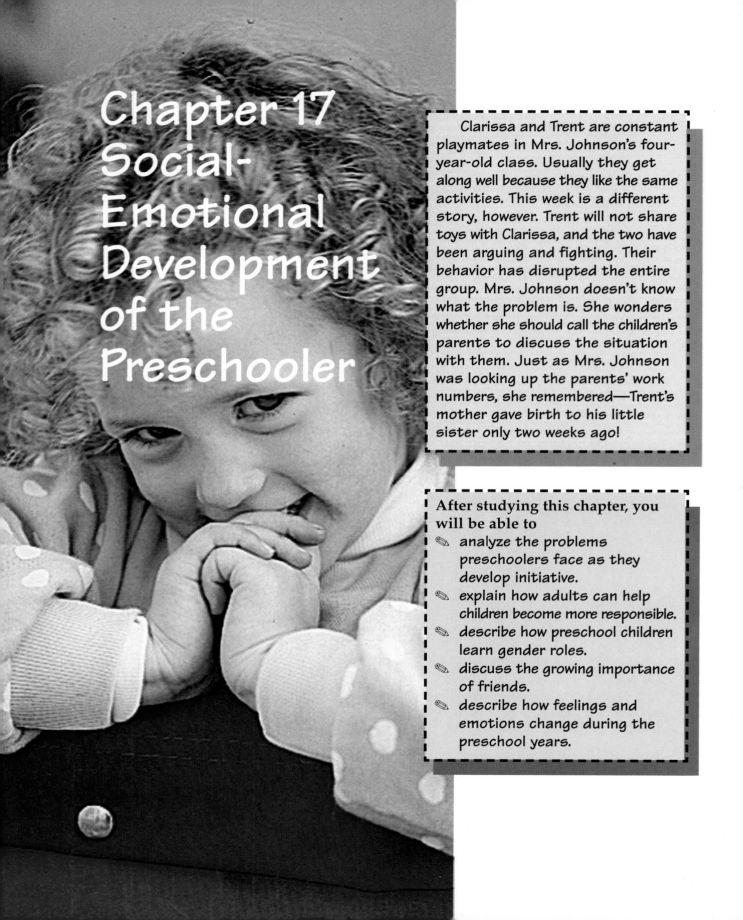

Chapter 17
Social-Emotional Development of the Preschooler

Clarissa and Trent are constant playmates in Mrs. Johnson's four-year-old class. Usually they get along well because they like the same activities. This week is a different story, however. Trent will not share toys with Clarissa, and the two have been arguing and fighting. Their behavior has disrupted the entire group. Mrs. Johnson doesn't know what the problem is. She wonders whether she should call the children's parents to discuss the situation with them. Just as Mrs. Johnson was looking up the parents' work numbers, she remembered—Trent's mother gave birth to his little sister only two weeks ago!

After studying this chapter, you will be able to

✎ analyze the problems preschoolers face as they develop initiative.

✎ explain how adults can help children become more responsible.

✎ describe how preschool children learn gender roles.

✎ discuss the growing importance of friends.

✎ describe how feelings and emotions change during the preschool years.

Define...

initiative
guilt
gender-role learning
sex typing
sexual stereotyping
peers
stressors
emotional dependency
repressed jealousy

Preschool children continue to relate socially with people outside the family circle. As they reach out, they learn more about themselves as individuals within adult and child social groups. Preschoolers start to think and act on their own. They also start to show some responsibility and begin learning to control their emotions. Preschoolers start to understand that temper tantrums are among the ways of showing feelings that are not acceptable to adults. Preschoolers' emotions also become more complex as they understand more about their world.

Developing Social Awareness

Children's social awareness grows during the preschool years. Their feelings about themselves and how they fit into social groups are beginning to emerge. They are becoming more

dependable and can complete simple tasks in the home. Through better use of language and social skills, they start to make friends with other children.

Taking the Initiative

Between ages three and six years, children become even more independent. Because of their improved abilities and limitless energy, they have a strong desire to learn, explore, and do. These children want to experience many things. They may show never ending curiosity, talk a lot and loudly, move all the time, and even attack others to get what they want.

When children are in this stage, which Erikson calls *initiative versus guilt*, they are eager to try new activities. Initiative motivates them to do so. **Initiative** is the ability to think or act without being urged. Developing initiative is important because it sets the stage for ambitions later in life. Yet, initiative can lead to failures. Too many failures may lead to **guilt** (blaming yourself for something done wrong) and fear of trying new things, 17-1.

When the preschool child makes mistakes, he or she may feel badly about himself or herself. If the child feels too guilty, obedience becomes so important the child is afraid to try

initiative. The ability to think or act without being urged.

guilt. Blaming yourself for something done wrong.

Erikson's Stages of Personality Development

Basic trust versus basic mistrust (year 1)

Autonomy versus shame and doubt (year 2)

Initiative versus guilt (preschool years)

❖ Preschool children have growing abilities, much energy, and desire to engage in activities.
❖ They begin trying things on their own initiative.
❖ The sense of initiative learned at this stage leads to ambition and purpose.
❖ Too many failures and too many negative responses from adults lead to guilt and fear of trying new activities.

Industry versus inferiority (middle childhood)

17-1 Showing initiative while avoiding guilt is a major social-emotional task of the preschool years.

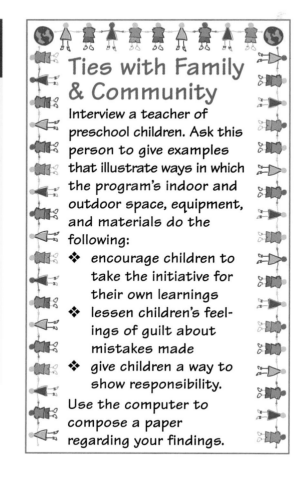

Ties with Family & Community

Interview a teacher of preschool children. Ask this person to give examples that illustrate ways in which the program's indoor and outdoor space, equipment, and materials do the following:

❖ encourage children to take the initiative for their own learnings
❖ lessen children's feelings of guilt about mistakes made
❖ give children a way to show responsibility.

Use the computer to compose a paper regarding your findings.

new things. This fear and guilt stifles initiative. To prevent guilty feelings, children must know it's okay to make mistakes.

Children develop initiative when they are allowed to ask questions, experiment, and explore. However, their initiative can sometimes lead to actions that are dangerous or beyond their abilities. In these cases, adults need to step in and set limits.

Showing Responsibility

During the preschool years, children often take the first steps toward becoming dependable people, 17-2. They begin to show responsibility, a sign of being dependable. Learning to show responsibility takes time and calls for experience. Children will have many successes and failures before they learn responsibility.

Adults help children become responsible by setting examples and giving children chances to learn. For

17-2 As preschool children put their belongings in "cubbies," they are learning responsibility.
Wood Designs of Monroe, Inc.

17-3 Children learn to be dependable when they can help with real tasks in their world.
© John Shaw

this to occur, adults must select tasks the child can do. The child should have both the ability and the time to do each task. He or she also must be shown how to do tasks. Any requirements must be made clear. Adults must follow through with praise or other rewards for successes. They must also offer support after failures.

Preschool children are often given responsibility for household tasks, such as helping in the kitchen, putting toys away, and folding laundry. In preschool programs, children are often required to put away toys, books, and other materials. They help hand out snacks and care for plants and animals. Erikson believes children should take part in the routines of their world in real and important ways, 17-3.

Learning Gender Roles

Learning about yourself is an important part of social awareness. This is because you learn how to fit into certain social groups (family, school, clubs, and others). In order to fit into any social group, people learn what is expected. For example, some behaviors are expected from people based on their gender. **Gender-role learning**

gender-role learning. Learning what behavior is expected of males and females.

means knowing what behavior is expected of a male or a female.

Gender role is a major concept children learn in the preschool years. Until age two years, most children cannot identify whether they are male or female. By age three years, gender-role learning begins. At this age, children know there are physical differences between boys and girls. They are also beginning to sense that boys and girls act differently in many situations.

How Does Gender Role Develop?

Children learn their gender roles by how others treat them and how they see others in their male or female roles. Some families treat boys and girls differently (**sex typing**). In these families, big differences exist in the clothing worn, toys received, and ways parents react to boys and girls. Other families do not distinguish between what a boy and girl can do, play with, or wear, 17-4.

Children most often identify with and imitate models of the same gender. They begin to think and behave as though the traits of another belong to them. They identify with and model themselves after family members and friends. They also may model teachers and characters from television, movie, and storybooks.

Cultural Factors

Society's view of male and female roles is not as clearly defined as it once was. Traditional gender roles see the male as more aggressive and the

17-4 Little girls often learn much about being female from their mothers.

economic head of the family. The traditional gender role sees the female as the wife and mother who stays home. **Sexual stereotyping** is a statement or even a hint that men and women always do or should do certain tasks. You can find examples of sexual stereotyping in books, television shows, and in some people's conversations.

These traditional roles are changing with the increase in the number of women employed outside the home. Also, more men have been sharing household and child care duties. Many people believe that, in order to thrive within today's lifestyle, roles must adapt to the situation. Both men and women may want to show assertive traits (such as sharing opinions) on the job. They both may want to show loving, gentle traits with their children.

Different cultures or groups hold different beliefs about gender roles. Some groups stress differences between male roles and female roles. Others stress similarities between male and female roles.

Extending Social Relations

Preschool children not only improve motor skills and knowledge through social activities, but they also increase their social learnings. These social learnings include sharing, controlling anger, thinking of other's feelings, and joint efforts, 17-5.

17-5 Small acts of kindness grow into concern for others.
© Nancy P. Alexander

Adults Are Still Important

Preschoolers continue to depend on adults to meet many of their needs. Adults serve as social models, too. They teach children by example. Besides responsibility and gender role, adults can model relationships, morals, self-control, manners, and much more.

Other Children Become More Important

Siblings and peers are more important to preschool children than to toddlers, 17-6. (**Peers** are others near the same age.) Preschool children's reactions to other children at this age are different. Some preschoolers have fun playing with other children, others do not.

Making Friends

The ease of making friends depends on a child's friendliness, ability to follow group rules, and lack of dependence on adults. Preschool children also prefer friends of the same gender, 17-7.

Preschool children have a rather self-centered view about friendships.

sex typing. Treating boys and girls differently.

sexual stereotyping. A statement or hint that men and women always do or should do certain tasks.

peers. Unrelated children who are near the same age.

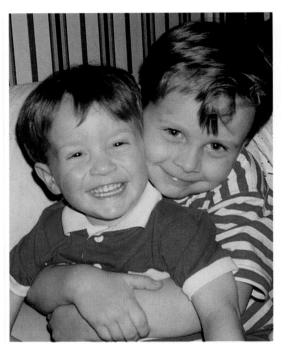

17-6 Warm relationships with siblings are important to the preschool child.

17-7 Most preschool children prefer having friends of the same gender.
Carter's

They see friends as people who play with you, help you, and share their toys. Because of this self-centered view, usually two or three preschool children form a closed circle of friends. After all, if there are too many friends, a child may not get enough from a friend. (For example, a toy may be shared more easily with one child than with several children.) To protect their interests, preschool children will often call out, "You can't play with us." When a friend does not do as the child desires, feelings quickly change. The child takes a new best friend—at least for the moment.

Learnings from Play Groups

The peer group offers many learnings. As preschoolers play together, play experiences become richer. Children get new ideas and can play with more than one child. Group play teaches preschoolers how to behave with peers. Because peers are equals, children can simply refuse to play with a child who doesn't play fairly. Children become less self-centered in peer groups. They hear other children's points of view. Finally, children learn that friends are fun. A child can play with friends, sit and talk with friends, and celebrate with friends, 17-8.

17-8 Preschool children begin to enjoy playing with peers.

Feeling and Controlling Emotions

Preschool children feel many emotions and express them in intense ways. Preschoolers still react to common childlike stressors. **Stressors** are situations that cause stress. These include adults' *nos*, short separations from caring adults, and fear of monsters. Besides these stressors, preschool children will react to many more long-lasting and serious stressors. These may include illness, moving, death, adult quarrels, and divorce.

Preschool children feel many emotions and are expected to control many of their intense feelings. Controlling outward signs of emotions, such as crying, screaming, or hitting, helps children become socially acceptable. However, if children control emotions without admitting their underlying feelings to themselves and others, they may become emotionally troubled. Children need to express feelings. Statements such as, "I am angry," or, "I'm afraid you'll leave me the way you left Daddy," are healthy.

Dependency

Preschool children often feel a conflict between their needs for dependence and independence. Like toddlers, three-year-olds most often show their dependence in emotional ways. **Emotional dependency** is the act of seeking attention, approval, comfort, and contact. In emotional dependency, the child is often dependent only on one or two people. Unlike toddlers, preschoolers are more apt to accept comfort from strangers. However, they still prefer a loved adult or peer.

By age five years, children express more need for help in achieving a goal than emotional dependency. Older preschool children may ask an adult to button their coat or reach a toy on a high shelf. In most cases, the child really does need help. The child also may ask for help that is not

stressors. Situations that cause stress.

emotional dependency. The act of seeking attention, approval, comfort, and contact.

needed. He or she may do this to check the adult's love or concern. In other words, emotional dependency is sometimes disguised as a way to earn attention and comfort.

Fear and Anxiety

Many of the toddler's fears disappear by the preschool years. New fears and anxieties replace the previous ones. Boys often report a greater variety of fears as they grow older. Girls report more intense reactions to the fewer fears they have. Although fears are individual, fears in the preschooler years do share some common features.

❖ Fear of the known, such as vacuum cleaners, disappears. However, fear of the imagined, such as monsters and robbers, increases. Children often associate these fears with the dark.

❖ Fears of physical injuries become more common. Examples include the fear of death by fire, an auto accident, or drowning, and the fear of bites and stings of animals and insects. These fears emerge as children know they can be hurt, 17-9.

❖ Fear of pain caused by medical and dental work occurs.

❖ Anxiety of a general nature is experienced. Children's specific fears may become general anxieties. For example, fear of a tornado may spread to general anxiety during a thunderstorm or even a strong wind.

17-9 Safety precautions may help lessen a preschool child's fear. Floating in an inner tube may help a child who fears water to feel more at ease in a pool.

As you can see, these fears and anxieties are due to the growing mind. Preschoolers understand many new concepts, but their understanding may still be limited. On the negative side, lack of understanding often creates fears and anxieties. For example, a preschool child would not understand that only certain weather conditions cause tornadoes. On the positive side, some fears may help protect children from trying unsafe activities.

Anger and Aggression

Anger and aggression begin around 10 months of age. They peak with displays of temper in the toddler years and continue in the preschool years. Expression of anger and aggression change in the preschool years to some extent.

Preschool children tend to hit or bite less than toddlers, but they threaten and yell more. Increased language skills cause this change. However, boys tend to be more physical than girls, whereas girls tend to be more verbal than boys.

Anger and aggression seem to be directed toward siblings and peers more often than toward adults. Preschool children appear to have learned that aggression toward adults, especially the physical type, is not acceptable. Also, anger and aggression are directed more at siblings and close friends than at casual peers.

Causes of Anger and Aggression

Children often use aggression to get their way or intentionally hurt another. Intentionally hurting someone else is the most serious form of aggression. Adults should seek to determine the underlying causes of such aggression and take action to help the child.

Children may be aggressive to gain attention or affection, 17-10. Determining what a given aggressive act means can be difficult without knowing the context of the act or the traits of a given child. For example, some preschoolers may use a playful shove or hit as an affectionate greeting rather than as an aggressive act. In some cases, the child receiving

17-10 Preschool children may become angry and aggressive as a way to gain attention.

such a greeting may not recognize it as a friendly sign. Fights can start from these innocent behaviors.

Sometimes objects cause a preschooler's anger. Preschoolers are in the initiative stage and often go beyond their abilities only to find that objects, as well as people, may frustrate them. For example, a child may blame a bike for a fall rather than his or her lack of skill. This can result in anger and even aggression toward the object or person. Sometimes this aggression is taken out on other nearby people or objects.

Several conditions cause, or at least strengthen, anger and aggression. Having goals blocked can cause anger. One study shows that preschool children have 90 of their goals blocked each day. Preschool children who like to take charge are affected most by not getting what they want when they want it. The more carefree child often is not too unhappy when goals are blocked, 17-11. This type of child simply changes the goal. If a peer takes a toy they are using, these children simply find another toy.

Jealousy

Jealousy begins when people realize they must share with others the love, attention, possessions, and time once given only to them. Jealousy often develops when there are changes in the family.

The most common time for jealousy is when a new brother or sister is born. Now children must share their parents' love with this new sibling. Babies take a lot of time and energy. Children translate this as love. Children may feel there is more love for a baby and less for them.

17-11 Tears often follow feelings of anger when a goal is blocked. Adults need to be there for the upset child.
© Nancy P. Alexander

Preschool children show fewer attachment behaviors than do toddlers, but attachment has not disappeared. In times of stress, preschool children may try to recapture the early attachment feelings. They may cry, cling, show signs of emotional dependence, and have toileting accidents.

Some preschool children may feel jealousy but ignore the feeling. **Repressed jealousy** is jealousy that is not directly expressed and may even be denied. Children may show this type of jealousy through nightmares or physical problems, such as upset stomachs, headaches, fevers, and change in appetite.

Unlike toddlers, preschool children are better able to understand their parents' explanations. For example, a preschooler is more likely to understand when parents explain why the baby gets so much attention. Preschoolers are able to talk about some of their feelings. They can feel important by helping with a new baby. Preschoolers who are in group programs have more contacts outside the family than do other preschoolers. This often makes it easier for them to adjust to a new family member or situation.

repressed jealousy. Feelings of jealousy not directly expressed and may even be denied.

Summing It Up

Preschoolers who are allowed to try new activities develop a sense of initiative. If they have too many failures or no's from adults, they may feel guilty and fear trying new things on their own.

Adults need to help preschoolers become dependable. Gender roles are not as clearly defined as they once were. However, they are an important part of learning. Children learn gender roles by how others treat them and through their associations with others. They begin to identify with and model the thinking and behavior pattern of others. In this way, they learn family and workplace gender roles.

Preschool children increase their social learnings. They are still dependent on adults, but other children have become more important. Play experiences help preschoolers learn how to get along with others and develop friendships.

The preschoolers' emotions are becoming more complex. They want to be independent, but are still dependent on adults, especially for emotional support. Some of their old fears and anxieties have disappeared, but others have appeared. Anger and aggression surface during the preschool years. Also, family changes bring about feelings of jealousy. However, preschoolers are better able to talk out their feelings, which helps them adjust to the changes.

Reviewing Key Concepts

Write your answers on a separate sheet of paper.

1. True or false. When limits are given to preschool children, they will quit showing initiative and feel guilty.
2. True or false. When adults show preschoolers how to do something, they are teaching them about dependability and responsibility.
3. True or false. Preschoolers need some praise when they meet goals.
4. True or false. Responsibility is learned quickly if parents assign preschool children household tasks to complete.
5. True or false. In gender-role learning, children learn what is expected in the boy or girl role.
6. True or false. A preschool child identifies with and imitates only the father role model.
7. Preschool children tend to have a closed circle of friends because
   A. too many friends overwhelm the child
   B. children's games are usually played with only two or three children
   C. children have a self-centered view of friendships
8. What can children learn from group play? List four learnings.
9. Which of the following fears are most common in preschool children:
   A. loud sounds
   B. monsters
   C. physical injury and pain
   D. flushing toilets and vacuum cleaners
   E. teasing by other children
   F. darkness
10. True or false. Anger in the preschool years is always a sign of frustration.
11. Preschool children direct their anger more at (known, unknown) children and adults.
12. True or false. Jealousy over a new baby is common.

Using Your Knowledge

1. **Teamwork/Critical Thinking.** Work with a small group to find examples of sexual stereotyping in magazine advertisements. Discuss with your group how sexual stereotyping affects gender-role learning. Present your findings to the class.
2. **Art/Creative Skills.** Draw a cartoon that illustrates preschool children's ideas of friendship.
3. **Interviewing Skills.** Interview a preschool child about something scary that happened to him or her. Have the child draw a picture. Write a brief summary of the interview, including quotes from the child about the scary incident. Display the child's drawing and your report on a bulletin board.
4. **Child Development/Creative Skills.** Design a poster for parents on helping preschooler's become responsible.
5. **Technology/Language Arts.** Research on the Internet the development of phobias. Write a short report on your findings.

Making Observations

1. Observe a preschooler interacting with an adult at home or in a group program. What tasks was the child asked to do? How did the adult explain the task? Was the child able to do it, and why or why not? Did the child seem to feel successful?
2. Observe preschoolers in a group program. What emotions were expressed? How did adults handle the intense emotions? Did they help the children find more acceptable ways of expressing feelings?
3. Watch children at play in a group program. List some of the gender-related differences you noted in the children's play activities, discussions, and interactions.

Thinking Further

1. How have gender roles changed over the last two or three generations? Do you think learning gender roles is easier or more difficult for today's children than for children 50 or more years ago? Why?
2. How do you think preschoolers benefit from their interactions with the elderly? How do you think the elderly benefit from the interactions?
3. How might adults lessen the possibilities of jealousy in preschoolers? How can adults help preschoolers deal with their jealousies if they occur? How is uncontrolled jealousy harmful in the teen and adult years?

Chapter 18
Providing for the Preschooler's Developmental Needs

After studying this chapter, you will be able to
- plan ways to meet the developmental needs of preschool children.
- help preschool children care for their own physical needs.
- stimulate preschool children's mental thinking.
- assist preschoolers in meeting their social and emotional needs.

Mrs. Garcia was delighted when her son, Jose, was admitted to the university nursery school on his fourth birthday. In the past month, however, she has become more and more dissatisfied with the program. She tells her neighbor, "Jose is happy, and the teachers says he's bright. The problem is that Jose spends too much time in dramatic play. Every few days he's pretending to be someone else. Four-year-olds should be learning letters and numbers. Perhaps I should enroll Jose in another preschool that uses worksheets and computer programs to teach these skills. Reading and math skills are so important."

Define...

enuresis
compare
contrast
passive observing
problem solving
transformation
class
class complement
reversals
divergent thinking
convergent thinking
cooperation
altruistic behavior
anger
aggression
assertive

As you have seen, preschool children's motor, mental, and social skills develop at rapid rates. These skills help preschoolers meet their own needs. Preschoolers want to do things for themselves and others. They like to use their motor skills to feed and dress themselves and help with everyday tasks.

Mental thinking (as opposed to using physical actions to solve problems) is well underway in the preschool years. Preschoolers can mentally see objects and actions. They can even begin to solve problems in mental ways. Concepts become more correct. Language helps preschoolers expand concepts. Language is also a sign of a preschooler's progress in learning concepts.

Social skills also grow in the preschool years. Preschool children's social world includes many new adults, close friends, peers, and perhaps younger siblings. Adults expect preschool children to become more independent, more responsible, and more in control of their feelings. Peers and siblings treat children more as equals. Peers do not give each other the special favors adults often do. For example, a child will not always be given the first turn when playing with peers as he or she would when playing games with adults.

Preschool children are learning a whole way of life in which needs in one area of development affect needs in other areas. Thus, preschool children's changing physical, mental, and social needs demand a great deal of support and much time from caring adults.

Physical Needs

Preschool children no longer completely depend on adults to meet all their physical needs. As the body matures, motor skills are refined, and the mind grows, preschoolers are better able to help care for themselves. At this age, children want to help meet their own needs. They want to help prepare meals and dress themselves, 18-1.

Children will take the initiative in learning how to meet their physical needs. However, adults must help.

18-1 Preschool children like to help make their own food and do other self-care tasks.
© John Shaw

This is the first chance the child and adult have to work as a team and meet the child's physical needs.

Meeting Nutritional Needs

To meet the preschool child's nutritional needs, adults must plan carefully. Children at this age grow at different rates. In addition, their growth and energy output varies from month to month. On the positive side, preschool children become more interested in foods prepared in different ways. On the negative side, eating junk foods (foods low in nutritional value) may become more of a problem in the preschool years.

You Are What You Eat

The slogan *you are what you eat* is correct. What you eat affects how you grow. Growth slows during the preschool years as compared to the first three years of life. However, a preschooler is not finished growing. In the preschool years, height increases about seven inches, and weight increases about 13 pounds. Other body systems must keep pace with skeletal growth. If the diet does not meet the body's needs, the body may conserve fuel needed for its own upkeep. This may slow the rate of growth. Children are also more prone to diseases when nutritional needs are not met. In addition, their recovery time is slower when ill.

The preschool child is an active child, 18-2. Watch preschool children

18-2 Preschool children have high energy levels.
Courtesy of PlayDesigns (800-327-7571)

at play. Their bodies twist, turn, and bounce as they walk. Because preschool children don't sit still, their energy needs are high. This energy must come from the foods they eat.

Nutritious foods are needed for brain growth, too. General alertness is affected by a person's daily diet. Diet seems to affect emotions, too. When daily food needs are met, the child seems less irritable and restless.

Basic Food Choices

The diets of preschool children should still follow the Food Guide Pyramid for Young Children, 18-3. Three-year-olds should be offered serving sizes similar to (perhaps slightly larger than) those for two-year-olds. (Remember that serving sizes for the milk group are the same at all ages.) According to the USDA, serving sizes in all groups remain constant for Americans ages four years and older. The number of servings needed from a group may change at various points in the life span, however.

Parents may vary their child's diet to suit the child's growth rate, which varies from month to month. They should also consider the child's energy levels, health, and food preferences. When a child needs a special diet for health reasons, adults should consult a doctor or registered dietitian.

Children should eat snacks that provide nutrients as well as calories. Experts say preschool children as well as adults should lessen their intake of sugar, salt, and fats. Why limit these

items? Eating excessive amounts of sugar can lead to tooth decay, obesity, and other health problems. Consuming too much fat and salt early in life may increase chances of high blood pressure in later years. This chance increases if high blood pressure exists in the family's health history. Snack foods are often high in sugar, salt, and fats.

Food Attitudes Are Learned

The food attitudes preschoolers learn may last a lifetime. Offering a variety of foods in a pleasant atmosphere helps preschoolers form good food attitudes.

For the most part, people like variety in their lives. This includes what they eat. Some children may go through phases where they want the same food(s) day after day for a time. Others eat or drink a few of the same foods daily but vary other foods.

Many options are available within each food group. Children should be able to eat foods they like and still meet their nutritional needs. Forcing children to eat foods they don't like can cause them to have negative feelings toward healthy foods. Using food to reward or punish can also have a bad effect. Children who are rewarded and punished with food may learn to eat as a way of bribery. For example, imagine the following conversation:

Adult: "You can't have dessert until you eat your peas!"

Child: "How many cookies do I get if I eat my peas?"

Food Recommendations for Preschoolers

	Three-Year-Olds	Four- and Five-Year-Olds
Grain Group	Servings daily: 6 Serving sizes: ½ to ⅔ slice of bread; ¼ to ⅓ cup cooked cereal, rice, or pasta; ½ to ⅔ ounce ready-to-eat cereal or crackers	Servings daily: 6 Serving sizes: 1 slice of bread; ½ to ⅔ cup cooked cereal, rice, or pasta; 1 ounce ready-to-eat cereal or crackers
Vegetable Group	Servings daily: 3 Serving sizes: ¼ to ⅓ cup chopped raw or cooked vegetables or ½ to ⅔ cup raw, leafy vegetables	Servings daily: 3 Serving sizes: ½ cup chopped raw or cooked vegetables; or 1 cup raw, leafy vegetables
Fruit Group	Servings daily: 2 Serving sizes: ½ to ⅔ piece of fresh fruit; ½ to ⅔ melon wedge, ⅓ to ½ cup juice; or ⅛ cup dried fruit	Servings daily: 2 Serving sizes: 1 piece of fresh fruit; 1 melon wedge, ¾ cup juice; or ¼ cup dried fruit
Milk Group	Servings daily: 2 Serving sizes: 1 cup 2 percent, reduced-fat milk; 1 cup yogurt; or 2 ounces cheese	Servings daily: 2 Serving sizes: 1 cup 2 percent, reduced-fat milk; 1 cup yogurt; or 2 ounces cheese
Meat Group	Servings daily: 2 Serving sizes: 1 to 2 ounces meat, fish, or poultry (cooked and lean); ¼ to ⅓ cup cooked, dry beans; or 1 to 2 eggs	Servings daily: 2 Serving sizes: 2 to 3 ounces meat, fish, or poultry (cooked and lean); 1 cup cooked, dry beans; or 2 to 3 eggs
Fats and Sweets	Limit these.	Limit these.

18-3 Parents should offer foods to their preschoolers as outlined by the Food Guide Pyramid for Young Children. Three-year-old children will eat less (except in the milk group) than older preschoolers.

Preventing Eating Problems

Adults can prevent some eating problems in preschool children. Adults need to know that children and adults have different senses of taste and smell. For example, many adults wonder why some children do not like spinach. There is an acid in spinach (oxalic acid) that leaves a bitter aftertaste in the mouths of children, but not adults. Children often prefer mild flavors and aromas over stronger ones. They tend not to like foods that are too spicy. Children are influenced by other food tastes and qualities, as well.

Food That Looks Good

How food looks may influence whether children think they will like it. Children like attractive-looking foods. Foods of different sizes, shapes, colors, textures, and temperatures look better than foods that look the same. Plates should have some empty space. Full plates can give children the feeling of too much before they take one bite. (Children can have second helpings.) Children also enjoy foods prepared especially for them, 18-4. Special dishes, napkins, or centerpieces may make eating a meal or snack even more special.

Separate Rather Than Combination Foods

Children often prefer foods that are eaten separately rather than foods that are combined. If children see or

A

B

C

18-4 Foods that look fun to eat also seem to taste better.
© John Shaw

taste one food they do not like in a casserole, soup, or salad, they may reject the whole dish. They accept mixtures of fruits more easily than mixtures of vegetables. Children may eat what they choose to mix more readily than adult-prepared mixtures. For example, children may prefer to mix their own salads from several bowls of precut vegetables.

Foods Served at Acceptable Temperatures

Preschool children do not like foods that are served at extreme temperatures. In fact, they can easily burn their mouths on foods that are too hot. Some of these foods (such as hot drinks) can simply be avoided for most children do not like them anyway. Soups are good for children, but young children cannot manage a steamy bowl or cup of soup. One easy solution is to drop a few ice cubes into hot soup just as the child begins to eat. As the ice melts, the temperature of the soup will drop to an acceptable level. Very cold foods present a problem, too. Children eat these foods very slowly, because eating large bites can cause a sharp headache. Thus, there may be more ice cream on the outside of a preschool child than on the inside! Parents can start offering suggestions for managing hot and cold foods during the late preschool years.

Foods Prepared in Different Ways

Children show likes and dislikes for ways to prepare food. A child who turns down cooked carrots may eat a crisp, raw carrot. A salad dressing or dip that is not too tangy may make almost any vegetable or fruit easy to eat. Dressings made from yogurt and cheese help meet the calcium needs of young children, too.

New Foods in Small Amounts

Children will often take one bite or a small amount of a food just to see whether they like it. Give children new foods in small amounts (one slice or a tablespoon). Serve new foods with ample portions of foods children like to eat.

Easy-to-Eat Foods

Foods should be easy for preschoolers to eat. Bite-sized and finger foods are preferred over foods that are harder to eat. Most children at this age cannot cut food. They may not hold spoons and forks the right way. These problems make eating messier for preschoolers than it is for older children and adults, 18-5.

Making Meals Fun

Children enjoy helping to prepare food. By helping, children learn about colors, shapes, tastes, aromas, textures, and appliance names (*blender, oven*). They learn food preparation terms (*cut, boil, poach, bake*) and food names. Cooking teaches math concepts (*measurement, numbers, temperature, time, shapes*). It also introduces children to science as they see changes in foods (*rising, baking, freezing, boiling*). As an added bonus, children often eat what they help prepare.

Children should enjoy eating with others. Meals should be a time to relax, share, and have fun. There should be a quiet time before and after meals. Enough time should be given for the meal itself, because eating with children takes time.

Setting an example of taking turns talking and other table manners allows children to learn at mealtimes. However, punishment and scoldings should not take place at the table. All talk should be pleasant.

An attractive room for eating helps, too. Dishes and flatware suited to the child's hands make mealtime easier and also lessens the chance of accidents. Preschool children may want to help make the table attractive by choosing the napkins, picking a flower from the garden for the table, or helping set the table.

Food becomes a part of many celebrations. Preschool children may look forward to helping prepare a special holiday dish or choosing their birthday menu. Trying different eating styles is fun, too. A restaurant, cafeteria, picnic, clambake, or cookout provides children with more food experiences, 18-6.

18-5 Preschool children still cannot hold a spoon or fork in an adult way.
© Nancy P. Alexander

18-6 Participating in a cookout can enhance a child's appetite and interest in food.

Selecting the Right Clothes

Selecting the right clothes for preschool children is important. Clothes protect the child's body from harsh weather conditions and scrapes and cuts. Clothes are also important to a child's growing self-concept, 18-7.

18-7 Cute clothes enhance the preschooler's self-concept.
© John Shaw

Fit

Fit is an important feature of preschool children's clothes. Clothes must give the active child freedom to move. Fit children by size, not age. Sizes for preschool children's clothes are often given as 4 through 6X or 7. Because preschool boys and girls often have similar measurements, measurements for a given size are often the same for both.

Hangtags and charts on children's sizes often give several measurements (chest, waist, hip, inseam, and others) rather than just height and weight. You may note some overlap of sizes such as toddler size 4 (4T) and children size 4 (4). Often the chest and waist measurements are the same in toddler and children sizes. However, children sizes are often longer, and both the shoulders and back are wider than in toddler sizes. In addition to regular sizes, some clothes for children are sold in more specialized sizes to fit the slender child and the heavier child.

Chart 18-8 shows one example of typical preschool clothing sizes. Clothing varies slightly by retailer, so parents should carefully read the measurements for the best fit.

Fabric and Construction Features

Preschool children's clothes must have most of the same quality fabric and construction features as toddler clothes. (Review the clothing section in chapter 14.) Preschool children

Typical Preschooler's Clothing Sizes

Size	Height in Inches	Weight in Pounds	Chest in Inches	Waist in Inches	Seat in Inches
4	39 to 41½	32½ to 37	22½ to 23	21 to 21½	22½ to 23
5	42 to 44½	37½ to 42	23½ to 24	21½ to 22	23½ to 24
6	45 to 46½	42½ to 47	24½ to 25	22 to 22½	24½ to 25
6X or 7	47 to 48½	47½ to 54	25½ to 26	22½ to 23	25½ to 26

18-8 These sample measurements are used by one retailer to determine sizing. Parents should check for fit by using the measurements on the label or hangtag rather than buying by the child's age.

grow mainly in the length of the arms and legs and the width of the shoulders. For these reasons, their clothes should have the following growth features:

❖ wide hems that can be let out as arms and legs grow
❖ kimono or raglan sleeves that allow for increase in the width of the shoulders
❖ adjustable shoulder straps and waistbands that allow for both length and width increases

Also, because preschool children explore indoors and outdoors, their clothes need more safety features. Outdoor clothing worn after dark should be light-colored or have a trim of reflective tape that will reflect the light from cars or other vehicles. Hoods attached to coats and rainwear should easily detach if caught on large objects. (Children have suffered neck and back injuries from nondetachable hoods.) Floppy headwear can prevent children from seeing traffic or other hazards. Floppy or wide legs and long shoelaces can cause tripping. Long, wide sleeves that are not gathered into a cuff; drawstring ties; long sashes and scarves; and extra large clothes are also dangerous.

Self-Dressing Features

By the end of the preschool years, many children can dress themselves with only a little help from adults. Of course, adults should always be near to help the child and check the child's attempts. Chart 18-9 shows the features that aid self-dressing. In addition to self-dressing features in garments, special toys can help children learn to button, snap, zipper, and do other closings, 18-10. These give children extra dressing practice.

Self-Dressing Features

❖ Large openings, especially for slipover garments

Reason:
Children are not skilled in pulling clothes just right to squeeze through small openings. Children do not like (and may fear) having tight neck openings pulled over their face and ears.

❖ Easy-to-recognize fronts and backs of garments like labels. threads, or tape sewn inside.

Reason:
Children cannot easily hold a garment by the shoulder seams or waist to find the back and front. Children can learn to place slipover garments with the label face down before putting arms in sleeve openings. they can also learn to place the label of step-in clothes (pants and skirts) next to the body before stepping into the garment. Children may need help with wrap dresses, skirts, and jumpsuits.

❖ Front rather than back openings, such as front buttons and attached belts that hook in front.

Reason:
Back closures are hard for children to reach and cannot be seen.

❖ Elastic in waistbands and in sleeves (at wrist).

Reason:
Elastic is easier to manage than are buttons, hooks, snaps, and zippers.

❖ Easy-to-work fasteners. Fasteners children can work easily include zippers with large pull tabs; smooth, flat buttons at least the size of a nickel; and shank or sew-through buttons sewn with elastic thread for a little give. Easy-to-work fasteners also include gripper snaps the size of a dime that do not fit too tightly together and hook-and-loop tape fasteners.

Reason:
Children do not have the fine-motor skills needed to work small, tight-fitting fasteners.

18-9 Self-dressing features help preschool children learn to dress themselves.

Shoes and Socks

Most preschool children grow one shoe size every four months. By the preschool years, children may have more than one style of shoe. Along with size, check for certain features in each style, 18-11. When you buy bigger shoes, you may also need to buy bigger socks. Sock size corresponds to shoe size. Parents should have children try socks on for fit. Socks fit properly if they allow ½ inch of space beyond the child's longest toe.

Clothes and Self-Concept

Preschool children are well on their way to developing a unique personality. Clothes are one way to express their personality. Preschool children show off their clothes and talk about the clothes worn by others. Children may make comments about pockets or trim.

Preschool children should make some choices about their clothes. Perhaps they can choose the color they want from similar outfits. If the outfit is to be sewn, a child could choose between two pattern views or among a few trims. Not only will children enjoy clothes they have chosen, but they also learn to make decisions.

Handling Sleep and Toileting Problems

The routines of meeting sleep and toileting needs are often in place by the end of the toddler years. Most preschool children still have a few problems in these areas from time to time.

Sleep needs are individual. They will even vary from time to time. Most children give up daytime naps

18-10 Many toys make learning to dress fun for preschoolers.
Lakeshore Learning Materials; Carson, Calif.

Style and Fit for Children's Shoes

Style	Fitting Features
Activity shoes	❖ Flexible soles that are ¼-inch to ³/₈-inch thick to absorb the pounding of walking, running, and jumping.
Sneakers and athletic shoes	❖ Arch support in correct position. Check fit with the socks to be worn with the shoes. Socks are often bulky, requiring larger shoes.
Sandals	❖ Adjustable straps and buckles that do not press into the foot.
Dress shoes	❖ As flexible a sole as possible. (Thin soles of dress shoes do not absorb pounding. For this reason, dress shoes should only be worn for short periods.)

18-11 Shoe fit includes more than the right length and width.

during the preschool years. However, they will still need 10 or more hours of sleep at night. If bedtime rules have been enforced in the toddler years, most preschool children accept them. The bedtime ritual is still wanted (and needed). Fears of the dark and monsters still exist, but many preschool children develop their own routines to help ease such stress. (Locking windows or having a doll watch over their sleep may comfort the child.)

Toileting accidents occur once in a while with most preschool children. Daytime accidents are most often caused by waiting too long to visit the bathroom. Adults may need to remind children to go to the bathroom after awakening in the morning or from naps. In addition, they should remind children before going outside, and before and after meals.

Time seems to be the major cure for bedtime accidents. Most children are not night-trained until at least age three years. Any instance of involuntary (by accident) urination of a child over three years of age is called **enuresis**. Sometimes, people use the term to apply to bed-wetting when the child no longer has daytime accidents. There may be many causes of bedtime accidents in the late preschool years (and even in the school-age years). Some problems include deep sleeping, fear of getting up in the dark, and too much liquid before bedtime. In a few cases, physical causes may exist. Most children outgrow these problems within a few

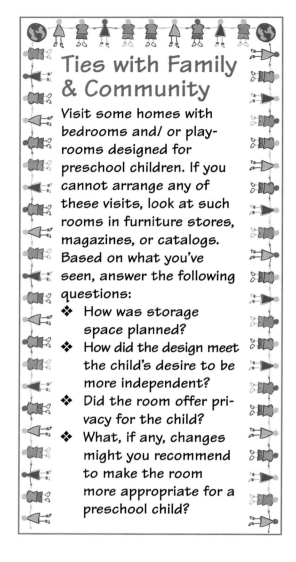

Ties with Family & Community

Visit some homes with bedrooms and/ or play-rooms designed for preschool children. If you cannot arrange any of these visits, look at such rooms in furniture stores, magazines, or catalogs. Based on what you've seen, answer the following questions:

❖ How was storage space planned?
❖ How did the design meet the child's desire to be more independent?
❖ Did the room offer privacy for the child?
❖ What, if any, changes might you recommend to make the room more appropriate for a preschool child?

years. For those who do not, medical help may be needed.

Providing Needed Space and Furnishings

Unlike babies and toddlers who want to be in the almost steady company of adults, preschool children want to be on their own more. Often preschool children have more toys and belongings than younger children. They need to be able to safely reach and return many of their own things. Adults must plan carefully for storage and furnishings.

Preschool children want a little space to call their own. This may be anything from a drawer or chest of drawers to one or more rooms. Even when a bedroom is shared with another child, a screen, storage cabinet, or curtain can divide the room. This allows some private space for times when the child wants or needs to be alone.

Learning Responsibility

Preschool children can learn self-help skills and become responsible for the care of their belongings. However, they need some storage space that is easy for them to use, 18-12. A pegboard wall with holders for equipment helps children store toys neatly and keep them in sight. A window can be flanked with storage shelves. A window seat or desk can be used in front of the window. Strips of hook and loop tape tacked to a wall of the closet or other places can hold lightweight toys. Storage ideas are limited only by the imagination.

Plan storage so preschool children can help themselves. Lower clothes hooks and rods for a child's use. Place often-used toys and items near where they will be used and within the child's reach. There can be some order to their clothes and toys—one the child can understand and follow.

18-12 Storage space helps when adults try to teach children to care for their own things.
© John Shaw

Intellectual Needs

Adults must help preschool children meet their intellectual needs. As they did during the toddler years, adults direct children's attention to things to do and problems to solve. Preschool children may be enrolled in special programs. However, the home and neighborhood play groups are still the most important places for learning. Preschool children's mental abilities can and do develop any time and any place. Think about how

 enuresis. Any instance of involuntary (accidental) urination by a child over three years of age.

much a child can learn from a simple shopping trip. While shopping, the child can do the following:

* observe attributes of items, such as color, size, shape, and texture
* classify items
* learn number skills
* learn language skills in naming and describing items

Learning Through Observing

Children must learn to observe by seeing, hearing, touching, smelling, and tasting. During the preschool years, children should be able to see details. They then can **compare** (see how objects or people are alike) and **contrast** (see how objects or people are different). Games and activities can improve these skills. As an example, give a child a magnifying glass. Help the child look at a leaf, penny, fingernail, piece of food, or other small object. Use a pencil to point to details you want the child to see. Later, ask the child to describe the objects he or she saw. See 18-13 for other suggestions for observation activities.

Observation Activities

Magnifying objects

Show the child a simple magnifying glass. Help the child look at a leaf, penny, fingernail, design, piece of food, or other small object. Use a pencil to point to details you want the child to see. Later, ask the child to describe the objects shown.

Alike and different

Gather pairs of objects or pictures that are exactly alike. Mix up the objects and have the child sort into like pairs. Books can be made where detachable pieces can be matched to those that are attached to the page.

Variation: Have the child explain how some items are the same in some ways and different in others. Examples of objects to compare include a fork and spoon, a poodle and collie, an apple and orange, two different hats, or two different coins.

© John Shaw

Shape sorting

Shape sorters have holes that fit various shapes, such as square, circle, and pentagon. Have the child match an object with the hole through which it will drop. As children master simple shape sorters, more advanced ones can be used.

Variation: (1) Use precut shapes of paper, plastic, or wood to make other shapes, designs, or pictures. Ask older children to name shapes and explain how they recognized each shape. (2) cut shapes out of ½ inch sponges. Using a clothespin, dip in tempera paint, and stamp on paper. (3) Using a pegboard and rubber bands, make shapes.

18-13 Observation activities help children learn to compare and contrast.

Television Viewing

Children also observe by watching television. Attractive characters, animation, movement, repetition, and many sounds used on children's television programs and many commercials cause children to observe. However, passive observing (attending without responding) is not the same as learning. Most television shows do not require responses from children. Even if a show encourages a child to respond, the child may not.

Children need more time to digest an idea than the few seconds a television image may provide. Caring and teaching adults are more important to children's learning than any television program. Thus, television should not be used as a babysitter. However, when a quality program is viewed with a sharing adult who builds on the concepts, a learning boost will likely occur.

Learning Through Problem Solving

Problem solving is a broad term. It most often includes noting a problem, observing and questioning what you see, and solving the problem. Almost from birth, babies are action-oriented problem solvers as they physically try to make items work. By the preschool years, children use both mental and action-oriented problem-solving skills.

Mental problem solving depends on basic skills described in chapter 16.

These basic skills are classifying; reversing; and arranging objects according to increasing or decreasing size, weight, or volume. Knowing about transformations is another basic skill. Transformation is the sequence of changes by which one state is changed to another. For example, a caterpillar is transformed into a butterfly. Heat transforms ice to water. Understanding transformation is logically difficult for preschool children because the child focuses on single steps, stages, or events rather than the process as a whole.

How Adults Can Help Preschoolers Solve Problems

Preschool children, especially three- and four-year-olds, can often sort items. However, most preschool children find classifying objects difficult. Adults can help them solve these problems. For example, adults can help children sort any number of household items. These

compare. To see how objects and people are alike.

contrast. To see how objects and people are different.

passive observing. Watching another's actions without responding.

problem solving. Noting a problem, observing and questioning what you see, and solving the problem.

transformation. The sequence of changes by which one state is changed to another.

items could be laundry, toys, flatware, and groceries. To turn a shopping trip into a lesson, adults might say, "Let's put together all the food that came in boxes and then put all the canned food together. Now let's put the fresh fruits and vegetables together."

Helping Children Classify Items

Adults can help children classify items. After showing the child small blocks that may be classified by color or shape, the adult can ask, "Are any of these alike in some way?" The child may respond by saying that some of the objects are red, smooth, or round. When the child singles out a common attribute, the adult might say, "Would you like to find all the round pieces and put them in this box? Then we'll put all the other blocks that are not round in the other box." When classifying items, there are only two groups. The **class** is a group of items that are alike in some way (the attribute). The **class complement** is the group of all objects that do not belong to the class. See 18-14 for other sorting and classifying activities.

Helping Children Put Items in Order

Preschool children have trouble putting items in order. Many activities

---

Sorting and Classifying Activities

Button sort

Use an egg carton or other sectioned container for sorting buttons into three or more groups. You may have the child sort according to color, size, way sewn on, or shape. (Buttons can be sorted using pieces of paper or boxes if sectioned containers are not handy.)

Variation: Sort many other objects for fun and even as a household task. Flatware, laundry, toys, and groceries can all be sorted.

Make a book

Children can cut or tear pictures from newspapers, catalogs, and magazines. The pictures can be mounted by groups, such as fruit, cars, dogs, and toys. (The child should decide on the groups.)

Does it belong?

After the child can easily classify, bring out another object and put it with the class. Ask the child, "Does this belong?" The child should explain why it does or does not belong.

© John Shaw

18-14 Sorting and classifying activities enhance children's problem-solving skills.

can help children with this concept. Children may line objects up from shortest to tallest or from tallest to shortest. The keys on the piano are ordered by pitch from high to low or low to high. Children can see and hear this. In retelling a story, events must be put in order, 18-15. The number system is a series.

Adults can help preschoolers learn to put items in order through games and activities. However, they should keep two points in mind. First, restrict the number of items to be put in order to five or fewer. Second, make the differences in the items easy to notice.

18-15 After looking at a book, preschoolers often enjoy telling the events in order.

As an activity, adults could read to children about the fabled Three Bears. After reading the story, talk about the sizes of each bear, chair, and bed. See 18-16 for other activities.

Helping Children with Reversals

Before the child can mentally handle reversals (mentally doing and undoing an action), they need to perform some physical reversals. Reversals must be experienced—not taught. An example might be letting the child pour water from one container into a different container and back again, 18-17. See 18-18 for other reversal activities.

Helping Children with Transformation

Transformations happen in the natural world on a daily basis. Adults can point these out to children. For example, while watching birds perch on a feeder or in a tree, an adult could ask the child, "What happened to the bird's wings when it perched?" (They were outstretched and now are folded.) As a transformation activity, the adult and child could look in the family

class. A group of items that have an attribute in common.

class complement. In classifying, any object that does not belong within the class being considered.

reversals. Mentally doing and undoing an action.

Activities for Putting Objects in Order

Make yourself little

Help a child act out different sizes with his or her body. Show how to make yourself little (by crouching down), bigger (by standing), and biggest (by stretching).

Little, bigger, biggest

Gather three boxes—one small, one large, and one even larger. Place the boxes in front of the child so the smallest box is to the child's left, the medium box is in front of the child, and the largest box is to the child's right. Ask the child to find the little box, then the bigger box, then the biggest. If the child makes a mistake and does not correct it, try nesting the boxes to compare sizes for him or her. To vary the game, you may reverse the box order or use four or five boxes that vary in size.

The Three Billy Goats Gruff

Read this story to a child. A copy with illustrations will help the child better see the sizes of the goats. After reading the story, talk about the sizes of the goats that crossed the bridge.

Ordering blocks

Cover three blocks of wood with different grades of sandpaper. Have the child put the blocks in order from least rough to roughest by rubbing them. Then ask the child to put the blocks in order using only sight. For a variation, the child may stack items in order of weight and size.

18-16 These activities enhance children's concepts of order.

18-17 Children learn reversal skills through their play activities.
© John Shaw

photo album or other pictures of the child. The adult could point out changes in size, hair length, and motor skills. He or she could ask the child to point out other changes from one picture to the next. Non-hardening clay and sand are wonderful materials for noting transformations, too. See 18-19 for other transformation activities.

Learning Through Symbolizing

Intellectual needs also are met as the child begins to think in terms of symbols or signs. There are a number of ways children think in these terms.

Reversal Activities

Tower of blocks

Help a child build a tower with blocks. Have the child take the stack of blocks down, one by one, to reverse the order of building.

Lacing cards

Make or buy lacing cards. To make one, draw a picture on cardboard, then punch holes in the cardboard over the outline. Use a shoestring to lace through the holes and create the picture's outline. Children can lace, undo, and relace the card.

Water and sand play

Gather two containers of different sizes and put some water in one. Let the child pour the water from one container into the other and then back. To vary the game, use sand.

18-18 These activities help teach children about reversals.

Transformation Activities

Growing plants

Help a child plant a fast-growing seed, such as a bean. You also may put a sweet potato in water. Look at it each day. Talk about the changes you see. Taking pictures also can help the child see the progress.

I am growing

Look at the family photo album or other pictures of the child. Point out changes in size, hair length, and motor abilities, such as sitting and standing.

Cooking

Ask the child to help you cook. Point out changes that happen. Baked goods increase in size in the oven. Liquids freeze to make ice. Gelatin becomes firm as it sets. Sugar dissolves. Eggs boil and become firm.

Making new colors

Gather paints, crayons, or colored water. Show a child how to make a new color by combining two different ones. Let the child combine different colors.

18-19 These activities help children grasp the concept of transformation.

The way in which children pretend is a form of symbolism. Through play, children take on the representation of another person or object, 18-20. They need many chances to pretend to be other people and objects. Many children begin pretending around their first birthday, but pretending does not reach a peak until the preschool years.

For the most part, children need only a little help in pretending. For example, adults can have the child pretend to be any person or thing. If they suggest an underwater diver, they may see the preschooler putting on a pretend deep-sea fishing outfit. Soon the child will be diving after lost treasures, being careful not to be attacked by sharks.

Helping Children through Symbolizing

I'm a monster!

Begin by asking the child, "How do you think monsters look? How do you think they move? What sounds to you think they make? Show me." (Pretending to be a monster may help children overcome the fear of monsters.)

Variation: Have the child pretend to be any person or thing.

Pantomime

Have the child act out an action. The adult may suggest one, or the child may choose one. Have others try to guess what the action is.

Ballet

Ballet is acting out a story or idea through dance. Plan some music and let the children act out something in the form of dance. The child can choose what to be and how to dance it. You may need to give a few ideas to get the child started.

18-20 These activities help meet children's intellectual needs.

Using Symbols in Art

Children use symbols when they paint, color, or do other art work. Younger children make their art products first and then sometimes decide what they represent. As children mature, the idea comes before the product is made. As is true of all representations, the child decides on the symbol, not the adult.

When children use objects, such as building blocks, clay, or dolls, to represent who or what they want to, a form of symbolism is used. Children's play materials may or may not be like the real world, but they symbolize the real world for them, 18-21.

18-21 Children use play materials to symbolize their real world.
Fisher-Price, Inc.

Using Symbols in Language

Words are highly abstract symbols. One of the issues of early childhood education is whether children should be taught to read and do simple math problems at an early age. Many experts feel most preschool children need more time to deal with their world using less abstract forms of symbols. They question early reading and math for the following reasons:

❖ Young children must arrive at their own meanings and develop their own skills. Repeating without meaning is not real learning. Adults need to provide materials, ask questions, and present problems for children to solve.

❖ Problem solving in the real world gives a practical reason for learning. By setting the table, the child may see the need for counting forks. However, the child may not see the need to count objects in a picture shown by an adult.

❖ Divergent thinking (coming up with different possible ideas) is more often developed through rich, everyday experiences. On the other hand, convergent thinking (coming up with only one right answer or way to do a task) is more often seen in formal lessons. Answers to many of life's problems require divergent minds.

❖ Children need time to deal with their real world.

❖ Some children feel stress as a result of formal lessons. If young children see learning as fun, this attitude may carry over to the years ahead.

Unless the child sees the mental link between a real object and its symbol (such as a real cat and the word *cat*), the symbol means nothing. When learning is meaningless or too difficult, it is stressful rather than fun. For these reasons, children need many experiences with real objects and less abstract symbols (such as pretending to be a cat or drawing pictures of cats) before beginning to read words.

Learning Through Motor Skills

As children move and do things, they become more skillful in both mental and physical ways. Children learn as they move their bodies in space. They learn as they manipulate objects.

Because preschool children are in almost constant motion, they learn many gross-motor skills through play and play activities. However, a few planned activities may be fun and help mental development as well. For example, adults can help children plan an obstacle course of tables, chairs, and sturdy boxes. Have the child go under, around, through,

divergent thinking. Coming up with different possible ideas.

convergent thinking. Coming up with only one right answer or way to do a task.

and/or on top of the obstacles. Other suggestions for games and activities that promote gross-motor skills are found in 18-22.

Fine-motor skills should be enjoyed, too. Some of the best items are art materials, puzzles, small wooden beads to string, pegboards, and lacing cards. Small construction toys, such as plastic snap-together blocks and other building materials, also promote fine-motor skills, 18-23.

Learning Through Language

Preschool children learn language from what they hear—the articulation of sounds, vocabulary, and grammar. For this reason, adults must be the best language models they can be.

18-23 Puzzles and other small objects help children develop fine-motor skills.
© Nancy P. Alexander

Gross-Motor Games

Getting objects
While the baby is watching, roll or move any toy or safe object out of the baby's reach. Encourage the baby to get the object. As the baby's motor skills improve, increase the distance between the baby and the object.

Knock off the toy
When a baby can stand by holding on to a playpen or crib railing, place a stuffed toy on the railing. Encourage the baby to hold on to the railing with one hand and knock the toy off with the other.

Splashing in water
Splashing in a tub or pool helps the baby improve motor skills. Adults must watch babies at all times when children are in or near the water. The adult can hold the baby and encourage the baby to splash and kick.

Cartons
Place a large carton on its side so the baby can crawl into it. Let the baby crawl in and out of the carton.

18-22 Gross-motor games promote children's physical skills.

Preschool children need many daily chances to talk with adults and older children, 18-24. When preschool children play only with age mates or younger children, they do not learn as quickly as they do by talking with adults. For this reason, only and first-born children are often more advanced in language than younger siblings.

Language needs to be a part of all activities. When it is only used to give orders, language learnings are not expanded. When activities and speech are combined, children's concepts and skills grow.

Television and Reading

Adults should monitor the types and amount of television children watch. Although children can hear speech on television programs, it is one-way speech. This is because the child hears but does not respond. Children's shows that urge children to respond ask for one- or two-word responses. Studies show that children who watch less than five hours of television per week do much better in school. (Some children watch five or more hours per day.)

Reading to children every day increases language learnings. Books take us beyond the day-to-day world. Reading helps to expand concepts. It also helps children see books and reading as important. Libraries and bookstores are filled with wonderful

18-24 Looking through a window screen on a quiet, rainy day gives preschool children time to talk with their mother.
Courtesy of Kimberly-Clark

picture books for young children on almost every topic imaginable.

Computers and Learning

Many preschool children have access to computers in their homes and in their early childhood programs. During the preschool years, children are just learning about technology. Most children, even preschoolers, develop a special liking for computers for the following reasons:

❖ Computers are part of their everyday world. Even before the preschool years, many children look at the computer monitor as adults use the computer.

❖ Children are in control as they work on the computer. When they push a button or click the mouse, something happens. They receive instant feedback.

❖ The computer is patient and permits repetition. The child can look at the pictures, hear and see a story, draw and color, play a game, or work on learning shapes, numbers, or colors countless times. The computer is perfectly matched to the child's attention span, too, for the child can leave the computer at any point.

Hardware designed with the young child in mind makes the computer easier to use. Because of children's small hands and not fully developed fine-motor skills, standard mice and keyboards can be difficult to use and somewhat frustrating. Specially designed mice and keyboards are available for young children and children with physical disabilities. This equipment is much more expensive than standard equipment and is quickly outgrown by preschoolers. Yet it is worth considering for the child's comfort and ease of use if the child will be using the computer often.

In order to operate the computer, the hardware must also be at the right height for children. Unless children have their own computers and computer furniture, stable and comfortable stools that have seats at the right height may be the best option. A footstool or footrest is also needed if children's feet do not rest flat on the floor without one.

Many software programs are now available for children that have excellent formats and good content for the ability and interest level of the child. Because software is relatively expensive, it should be selected with care. Some general suggestions are given in 18-25.

Before purchasing, parents should decide what type of program they want. Some examples are drawing and coloring, interactive stories, learning basic skills (shapes, colors, numbers), and learning concepts (such as pictures and names of animals). They should read the evaluations from independent sources rather than from the publishers or distributors of the software.

Parents and caregivers introducing preschoolers to computers need to teach the basics such as names for the hardware—computer, disk drive, and monitor—and how to handle the floppy disks and CDs. They need to install programs, run them, and show children how they work. Until children are skilled at using a program alone, adults need to stay nearby to answer questions. However, adults should give the minimal assistance needed and avoid taking over. Adults also need to keep children safe while using

computers. (This topic is described in chapter 21.)

Social-Emotional Needs

During the preschool years, children's personalities seem to blossom and become more stable, 18-26. Preschoolers begin to learn more about themselves. Questions, such as "Who am I?" and "What can I do on my own?" are more fully answered in the preschool years. Through successes and mistakes, preschoolers test their skills. They begin to see themselves as boys or girls with role differences.

Selecting Software

❖ Does it fit your computer's hardware requirements (Macintosh or PC; DOS or Windows; processor type and speed; memory capacity; disk drive required—CD-ROM or 3.5-inch floppy; hard drive space needed; display type; and sound card type)? The sound and color used in children's software require much memory.

❖ Can the child use it without much adult help (controls work quickly; icons are large and easy to select; graphics make sense; instructions are easy to follow)?

❖ Is it designed for children (under child control; files not intended for child are childproof; children know whether their answers are right or wrong)?

❖ Is it of value to the child (content is good and challenges; child can explore and experiment; content is free of bias; feedback is given; required skills are at child's ability level)?

❖ Is the program enjoyable for the child?

❖ Does it have good design features (high quality music and speech; keeps a record of child's work)?

18-25 Parents should carefully investigate any software purchases.

18-26 Laughter and looks of confidence are signs of a healthy self-concept in preschoolers.
© Nancy P. Alexander

Adults need to meet the social-emotional needs of preschool children. They must often explain reasons for limits or requirements and repeat these. Firmness and fairness must be the adult's rule if the child's self-concept is to remain healthy.

Discipline: Helping with Initiative and Mistakes

Preschool children define themselves in terms of what they can do. In order to find out what they can do, almost all children try many activities. (In other words, they show initiative.) Active preschool children are curious. They do many things on impulse without thinking about the results of their actions. In trying new things, preschool children go beyond their abilities and make mistakes. These mistakes are self-defeating because preschool children see almost everything as within their control. Too many mistakes may bring on guilt.

When children are successful, they need to hear positive statements from adults. Children need adults to tell them what they are like. This refines their self-image and promotes feelings of self-esteem.

Children learn more by their own attempts than by having adults do for them or tell them what to do. Preschoolers learn from both successes and mistakes. Thus, children must be given some freedom to try. Adults must accept that children will try some things even when told no. Some

preschool children decide the pleasure of doing something is worth the punishment. Children can even dream up new activities not presently covered by the rules.

Limits

Preschool children should be given reasonable limits. They need limits for safety purposes and to prepare them for the real world. These rules should be spelled out. When children fail to obey, they need to be disciplined in a loving, yet firm, way.

Honest Communication

Parents and other adults need to communicate honestly when guiding and disciplining children. Being honest helps children build trusting relationships. It also helps children realize they should be truthful.

Children need to be aware that adults, too, make mistakes. Children learn this when they hear adults say, "I goofed!" or "I'm sorry." They begin to understand that all people make mistakes. They also start to see that making mistakes doesn't make them bad.

Sharing Responsibility

Preschool children see tasks as new skills to learn, fun, and a way to please others, 18-27. Adults can help them become more dependable and able to handle more responsibilities.

Some adults offer few, if any, opportunities for children to help. These adults may see preschool children as not having the desire to help.

18-27 Helping others is a fun way to learn and to please.
Courtesy of Park Seed Company

18-28 A child should be given a pet to care for only if the parent thinks the child can handle the responsibility.
© John Shaw

The child may stop in the middle of a task to play. Perhaps the adult thinks children lack the ability. The child may break a dish. A few adults think of children as servants who should perform tasks upon demand and to adult standards. Most, however, agree that family life and school life are made better when both adults and children help each other.

The following suggestions will help children share responsibility:

❖ children may suggest tasks but adults must decide which tasks are safe and within children's grasp, 18-28

❖ physical conditions should help children perform tasks. Low hooks or clothes rods, a place for each item, and a sturdy stool for reaching a cabinet are examples.

❖ adults can talk about tasks planned for the day, and they can tell children what they should do. Young preschoolers often help the adult do a task, but five-year-olds can work alone on some tasks.

❖ adults should not expect perfection. The finished task should remain as it is, or the task can be explained again for the child to do over. (When adults redo tasks, children feel a sense of failure.)

❖ adults can make some tasks seem more fun by creating a game. For example, blocks can be hauled to the "lumberyard" (the shelf).

❖ at times, adults should respect children's priorities. There may be no harm in letting a child do a job 10 minutes later.

Children need to be rewarded for tasks completed. Adults must decide whether work is done for love only (and thus should not involve pay) or work should have pay (with money or other wants fulfilled). Some adults compromise on this issue. They expect certain jobs to be done without pay. Then they may consider other jobs—those elected by the child—to be beyond the call of duty. The extra jobs may involve pay. Whether adults pay or do not pay, children need to be thanked and skills need to be praised.

Aiding Gender Role Learning

Due to changes in society today, many parents and other adults are questioning the more rigid gender roles of the past. As is true with all personal priorities, parents need to be informed about the issues and make decisions. Adults make their feelings about gender roles known to children in many ways. The roles they allow or encourage their children to try and the day-to-day attitudes they convey affect children.

Preschool children learn their gender roles mainly through observing adults of the same gender. They learn as they help their same-gender parent with household tasks and errands. Seeing parents and other adults at work also shows children adult gender roles. Toys and books related to jobs allow children to learn about many gender roles.

Providing Time for Friendships

Living in a social world involves balancing between self-assertion (insisting on one's rights) and cooperation (joint effort). Because preschool children must learn to see from another person's point of view, the balance between a child's will and the wills of others takes a long time, often years.

Seeing differences in people helps children learn to see from another's point of view. The process begins in the infant and toddler years. At this time, children expand their social world beyond parents to include other family members. Friendships with peers help children see even more differences in people, 18-29. Friction, which almost always occurs in play groups, shows children in a direct way that others see issues differently. In peer groups, children also witness altruistic behavior (concern for others). This helps children learn that others are important, too.

Friendship is a way to learn from others. Preschool children's ideas are expanded through play. In play groups children also have fun times, which are an important part of their lives, 18-30.

18-29 Friendships help children really understand others.
© Nancy P. Alexander

18-30 Through their friendship, this boy learns many concepts when he helps his friend's family harvest sweet corn.

Helping Children's Social Relations

Adults can help children's social relations by giving them time to play with friends. These friends may be neighborhood playmates. They also may be friends from the preschool, special interest group (such as swimming or dance class), or house of worship. Adults should allow children to interact with each other and not interfere with little conflicts (except for safety reasons).

Reducing Conflicts

Adults can reduce the conflicts of preschoolers in these ways:

❖ Teach children they do not always have to share, any more than adults do. Sometimes adults expect children to share all their toys, even with casual friends. Adults are not expected to share all their belongings even with close friends.

cooperation. Joint effort; getting along with others and considering their goals.

altruistic behavior. Concern for others.

❖ Model concern for the hurt child rather than shaming the one who has done wrong. Children learn more when adults show real concern for the hurt or wronged child while ignoring the child who was in the wrong. They see that care is given to children who are harmed.

❖ Explain feelings of both children wanting the same toy or wanting to do the same thing. Often toys are given up rather quickly when the adult says, "Maria needs to play with the car for a little while, but when she's ready to give it up she'll let you know."

Helping Children with Emotional Control

Emotions are intense in the preschool years. The growing minds of preschool children broaden their emotions. They also help children control how they express their emotions. People cannot control feelings. They must, however, learn to control how they express these feelings. Better control of expression is a major task of the preschool years.

Adults can help children control how they express feelings by setting an example. Children imitate control, or the lack of control, seen in adults. They also imitate other children and television and movie roles.

Adults need to explain to children it is all right to feel sad, angry, hurt, and happy. They should also tell children it is all right to express some emotions.

("It is all right to cry when we feel sad." "We laugh when we're happy." "You should tell Tabitha, 'It makes me mad when you take my toys. Give them back.'") However, children need to hear that people must not hurt others even when they are wronged. ("Hitting hurts," or "It makes others feel sad when you call them names.") Adults should talk about how all people have to work to control their feelings. There are many books on this topic, 18-31.

Dependency

Knowing when and how to help preschoolers can be difficult. Some children are unable to handle some tasks on their own but do not want the help adults offer. Other children, however, will not let go of help from adults even when they do not need it. These preschool children need to become more independent. It is a

18-31 Preschool children can get ideas from books about how to express their feelings in more positive ways.
© John Shaw

challenge for adults to find a balance between helping and not helping.

Adults can help by loving and respecting children, 18-32. This gives children a secure base from which to try things on their own. When children ask for help, adults should be willing to help. Adults need to judge how much help children need. (Adults must avoid being too helpful or protective.) Physically arrange the house with low hooks, stools, and other aids that make tasks more manageable for children. Adults should plan tasks for preschoolers that are within their abilities. Children need praise and encouragement when they try tasks on their own.

18-32 A close relationship between parent and child provides children with a sense of security and allows them to explore, knowing they will be loved even when they make mistakes.

Fear and Anxiety

Some fear and anxiety helps protect people. However, too much may be harmful. The following ideas may help keep children's fears and anxieties in check:

❖ Accept the expressed fears and anxieties of children. (Never make fun of them.)

❖ Assure children you will help keep them safe. (Never threaten to leave a child, even in a playful way.)

❖ Model courage. Children learn fears from adults.

❖ Handle one fear at a time. Repeat reasons children need not be afraid. Small steps taken slowly in dealing with fears and anxieties may help.

❖ Consult a doctor if fears seem too prolonged or too intense.

Anger and Aggression

Handling children's anger and aggression is not only draining but often stirs up angry feelings in adults. Adults should note the difference in **anger** (a feeling caused by frustration) and **aggression** (an attempt to hurt or an act of hurting someone). They should not try to stop anger in children. Instead, they need to help children try

anger. A feeling caused by frustration.

aggression. An attempt to hurt or an act of hurting someone.

to manage anger in ways other than aggression. Look for reasons the child feels angry. Does the child want attention? Is he or she frustrated in reaching a goal? Is he or she looking for revenge? Understanding motives makes finding ways to manage anger easier.

Competitive situations between peers should be reduced. Enough toys should be supplied so children do not have to wait too long for a turn. Play should be de-escalated. Some games that begin on a rather low key become aggressive. Other games can calm children or encourage cooperation. Watch peer play groups closely. Adults can stop aggression before it occurs (and the child gets some satisfaction from the act). If children need to be corrected, adults should use nonphysical ways. However, a child should know when adults disapprove of aggressive acts. Likewise, adults need to praise cooperation.

Spanking

Studies show that punishment by aggression (spanking), especially for a child's aggressive act, increases aggression in preschool children. Spanking increases the child's anger. This produces a negative, aggressive response from the child. Furthermore, adults are serving as models of aggression—the exact behavior they wish to stop.

Modeling Aggression

Children see aggression modeled in many ways including adults' acts, peers' acts, and acts on television programs, including those by cartoon characters. All studies show that children learn to be more aggressive by example. Even letting a child hit a pillow or kick a tree trunk sends the message aggression is all right. Instead, teach children it is all right to feel angry, but acts of anger must be controlled.

Society tries to teach an attitude of being **assertive** (speaking out, standing up for your rights, and defending yourself), but not being hurtful to others. Trying to find the line between assertiveness and aggression can be most difficult for preschool children. (It can even be difficult for adults at times.) Because of this, preschoolers may act in an aggressive way when they are trying to be assertive.

Jealousy over a New Baby

A preschool child needs help in accepting a new baby into his or her family. Parents should tell the child about the new baby before the event. They should sound pleased, but not overly excited, because children may think new babies are more important than they are.

The new baby should be described in realistic ways in terms of the work involved and other facts. Some preschool children are led to believe the new baby will be an instant, able playmate. If possible, seeing a friend's new baby can help. The child should be involved in plans for the new baby.

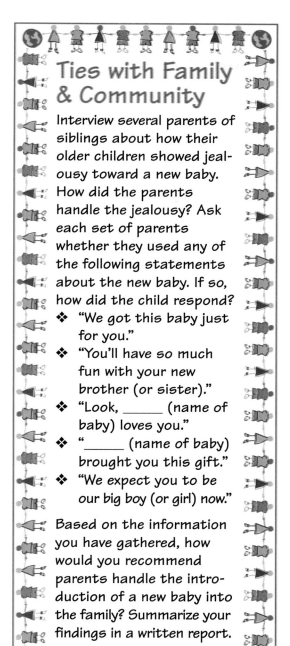

Ties with Family & Community

Interview several parents of siblings about how their older children showed jealousy toward a new baby. How did the parents handle the jealousy? Ask each set of parents whether they used any of the following statements about the new baby. If so, how did the child respond?

❖ "We got this baby just for you."

❖ "You'll have so much fun with your new brother (or sister)."

❖ "Look, _____ (name of baby) loves you."

❖ "_____ (name of baby) brought you this gift."

❖ "We expect you to be our big boy (or girl) now."

Based on the information you have gathered, how would you recommend parents handle the introduction of a new baby into the family? Summarize your findings in a written report.

Preschool children seem to be happier when they can stay in their own home or near their own home and visit their mother in the hospital (even by telephone). They prefer not to be sent to stay with friends or relatives for several days. (A preschool child can imagine only so much, and separations from loved ones are always difficult.)

When the Baby Arrives

Older children need time alone with parents after the new baby arrives. A little time spent with a preschool child says, "I love you, too." Showering an older child with gifts does not make up for time and may be seen as a bribe.

Older children should be allowed to help with the new baby. Adults should sincerely thank those extra feet and hands that help so much, 18-33. However, adults should avoid talking about how grown up older children are. Older children may want to be babies at times. Some children enjoy pretending to care for a baby with a doll. Preschoolers enjoy being told or shown with photos how they were once cared for in the same ways.

assertive. The act of speaking out, standing up for your rights, and defending yourself.

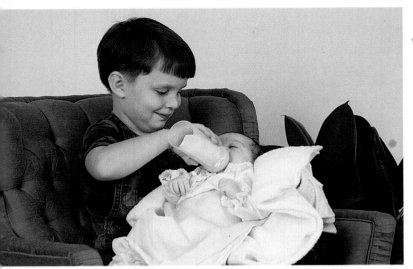

18-33 There are many ways in which an older child can help with a new baby.
© John Shaw

Recognizing Developmental Delays

Preschool children with delays may show some of the behaviors of average toddlers as listed in chapter 14. Because preschoolers are becoming more social, these behaviors as well as gross- and fine-motor skills and language are observed. If preschool children are attending child care or preschool programs, their caregivers are often good judges of developmental delays. Parents should consult with caregivers on a regular basis and observe their own children working and playing with other children of the same age. Knowing some typical preschool behaviors may help parents identify delays and bring their concerns to experts, 18-34.

Typical Preschooler Behaviors

Three years
Walks up stairs
Stands a second on one foot
Rides tricycle
Opens a door
Verbalizes the need to use a toilet
Feeds self

Four years
Hops in place (no real forward movement)
Throws ball
Catches bounced ball
Copies circle
Knows colors (red, yellow, blue, orange, green, purple)
Uses simple sentences with "heard" grammar
Washes hands without help
Plays with other children

Five years
Walks backward heel-toe
Runs on tiptoe
Recognizes his or her own printed name
Tries to write a few letters
Begins to cut foods with a table knife
Recognizes some coins
Answers greetings ("Hi" or "How are you?")
Draws rectangles and triangles
Laces shoe

18-34 Knowing what typical preschooler behaviors are can help to recognize developmental delays.

Summing It Up

Preschool children are active and need to eat nutritious meals and snacks. They learn attitudes about food likes and dislikes from others. Preschool children like food that is easy to eat and looks attractive.

Clothing must fit properly and allow room for the child to move and grow. When selecting clothing for children, adults should look for safety features and those that promote self-dressing. Adults should allow preschool children to make some choices about their clothes.

Bedtime rules and rituals continue to be important. Toileting accidents sometimes occur. Children need to be reminded at times to use the bathroom.

Preschoolers need some space to call their own. Their area should feature storage space that is easy for them to use.

Adults need to offer opportunities for children to learn. They need to provide materials, encourage observation, and present problems for children to solve. Learning by developing symbols is critical for preschoolers because it prepares them for handling more abstract symbols, such as words. Language skills improve through modeling and using language as a part of daily activities.

When guiding and disciplining preschoolers, adults must set limits. When children fail to obey the rules, reasonable actions by a loving, but firm, adult should be taken.

Adults should give children responsibilities that suit their age and ability. They need to be rewarded for completing their responsibilities.

Children learn gender roles at this age. Books and toys help children have a wider view of gender roles in various work situations. Books and toys help children have a wider view of gender roles in various family and work situations.

Adults should see that children have friends to play with and not interfere with their small conflicts. By playing with others, children learn different points of view and ways that others think and behave.

When children have fears and anxieties, adults should never make fun of them. Modeling courage and handling one fear at a time is helpful.

Adults can teach children about anger and control. Adults also need to help children learn how to express their feelings without hurting others. When acts of aggression occur, adults should always use nonaggressive means to end these acts.

Jealousy over a new baby can be lessened if the preschool child is prepared in advance. Spending time alone with the preschool child and having the child help with the baby will ease feelings of jealousy.

Reviewing Key Concepts

Write your answers on a separate sheet of paper.

1. Which statements are true about a preschool child's diet? (You may choose more than one.)
   A. Because of the preschooler's steady growth pattern, he or she needs exactly the same food from month to month.
   B. The preschool child needs food to meet his or her high energy output.
   C. Eating junk food can be more of a problem for preschool children than for toddlers.
   D. Preschool children should be told to eat their vegetables if they want to have dessert.
   E. Preschool children and adults like foods prepared and served the same way.
2. True or false. Forcing children to eat a food they don't like does little or nothing to help them learn to like that food.
3. Which of the following features should garments for preschoolers have?
   A. short zippers
   B. narrow hems
   C. raglan sleeves
   D. wide shoulders
   E. adjustable shoulder straps
4. List three clothing features that could cause accidents.
5. List two ways adults can help children have fewer toileting accidents.
6. True or false. Most television programs do *not* involve children's minds in an active way.
7. True or false. Mental problem solving is mastered in the preschool years.
8. Which of the following activities always involves symbolizing?
   A. manipulating objects
   B. representing objects and people in pretend play
   C. making art products
   D. building with blocks
   E. playing gross-motor games
   F. using words
9. Hardware and software that have been designed especially for preschoolers _____ (are, are not) available.
10. The best resources to help preschoolers learn language skills are _____ (other children, adults).
11. Adults _____ (should, should not) redo tasks that preschool children have done below the adults' standards.
12. List two things adults can do to make children's mistakes less self-defeating.
13. True or false. Gender roles are learned mainly by example.
14. Describe two ways to reduce conflict among preschoolers.
15. True or false. The way adults control their emotions does not affect children's emotional control.

Using Your Knowledge

1. **Consumer Skills.** Borrow some clothes designed for preschool children from parents. Examine each garment for self-help features listed in 18-9.

2. **Parenting and Career Skills.** Make or gather the materials for one or more of the examples of planned activities for preschool children given in the chapter. Use the planned activity with preschool children in a group program. Discuss with the class what did or did not work and why.

3. **Child Devlopment.** Think of some ordinary events or objects, such as Halloween costumes; a tall slide; and a large, playful dog. Describe how each situation may appear to a preschool child.

4. **Technology.** Use the Internet to research books and videos designed for preschool children who are expecting a new baby in the family. What materials are available for parents to use with their preschoolers as they talk about the changes to come? Use the computer to compile a bibliography of the materials you find.

5. **Role-play.** Role-play a situation in which a child is angry and hits a friend. Have one person be an adult who is supervising the children. Have the adult demonstrate both good and poor discipline methods.

Making Observations

1. Observe preschoolers in a child care program eating lunch or a snack. What foods are they provided? Did they seem to like the foods or reject some? Why do you think a certain food was rejected? How did the adult encourage eating?

2. Observe preschoolers in a group program. How do their space and furnishings meet preschoolers' needs? Which features could or should be used in the home?

3. Observe preschoolers playing in a group program. Which materials help them solve problems (classify, put things in order, and symbolize)? Which materials help their motor skills?

4. Observe two or more preschoolers playing. What examples did you see of self-assertion? What conflicts occurred? Why did these conflicts occur? How were they resolved? What examples did you see of cooperation? Why do you think the children were cooperative (ages of children or enough play materials)?

Thinking Further

1. Your text states that food attitudes learned in the preschool years may last a lifetime. What is meant by a food attitude? What food attitudes do you have that perhaps began as early as the preschool years?

2. What types of clothing did you like or did not like as a preschooler? How did your clothing tastes reflect your personality? In your opinion, to what extent should parents permit or encourage their preschoolers to make clothing choices?

3. How can adults support preschoolers' learnings through friendship? When should adults "back off" and allow children to learn how to make friends and resolve conflicts with friends?

Chapter 19
School-Age Children

Gordon, a second grader, rides the bus to school. He has started using some "off-color" language at home and resists having his parents correct him. He knows this language is not acceptable but continues to use it. Gordon loves to read, seeing each new word as a challenge. He also likes building objects with craft kits. He fusses about participating in school programs, making excuses about having to stand next to kids who are "fat and dumb." He has told his cousin Megan she can no longer play basketball with him because girls have to be the cheerleaders.

After studying this chapter, you will be able to
- describe the physical development of school-age children.
- describe the intellectual development of school-age children.
- describe the social-emotional development of school-age children.
- explain how adults and parents can help school-age children meet their developmental needs.

The school-age years are filled with fun, adventure, school, friends, family, and other events. Disappointments, challenges, and hard work are also part of this scene.

Many physical changes happen in children during the school-age years. Their fine- and gross-motor skills improve. In addition excelling in gross-motor activities, older children become skillful at fine-motor tasks like model building and handicrafts.

School-age children begin to think more logically and rely less on perception. This helps them learn new skills. Language skills are refined during middle childhood. Soon, children can articulate all English sounds. Their vocabulary continues to grow.

Children mature a great deal socially, too. Self-evaluation becomes more common during the school-age years. Children judge themselves in relation to others. They deepen their social relations with adults and peers. Adults are still an important part of school-age children's lives. Guiding and directing them during these crucial years are important tasks.

Between ages 6 and 12 years, children are called **school-age children** as they progress from dependent first-graders to independent preteens. Their motor, mental, and social skills develop quickly during this time, which is called the school-age years or **middle childhood.**

school-age children. Children between ages 6 and 12 years.

middle childhood. Another name for the school-age years, the period of development from 6 to 12 years of age.

Physical Development of School-Age Children

Middle childhood is a period of many changes in the body. Although these changes sometimes seem awkward as they happen, they help school-age children become more coordinated.

Body Growth and Development

The slow, steady growth rate continues in school-age children. Toward the end of middle childhood, some children—mainly girls—begin a growth spurt and other body changes of the preteen and teen years. (A **growth spurt** is a period of rapid growth, usually linked with adolescence.) During these years, body proportions change and organ systems mature.

Height and Weight

School-age children's height increases more steadily than their weight. This is because, for the most part, genes determine height. (Height is not easily affected by the environment, except by long-term conditions like malnutrition or certain illnesses.)

Weight seems to parallel height somewhat. Taller children tend to be heavier and shorter children tend to be lighter. The environment also influences weight because of factors like nutrition, illness, activity, and stress.

Boys are taller and heavier than girls until the ages of 10 or 11 years. At this time, most females enter a growth spurt. Many girls are taller than boys at this age. Children are often sensitive to the size difference, especially if they are becoming interested in those of the opposite gender. In reality, the average difference is only about one inch at age 12 years. The difference shows up mainly in a boy who matures slowly and a girl who matures quickly. Most boys catch up in growth during the early teen years.

Body Proportions

During middle childhood, body proportions become even more like those of an adult. A child's waist and head begin to look more in proportion to his or her body. The arms and legs grow longer, which gives the child a lower center of gravity and better balance, 19-1. During these years, the trunk grows until it is two times as long and two times as wide as it was at birth. The abdomen protrudes even less than it did in the preschool years because of the longer trunk.

Bones and Teeth

The skeletal system continues to mature. The bones continue to ossify and grow larger and longer. The most significant growth is in the teeth and jaw. School-age children constantly lose baby teeth and grow permanent ones. Girls often lose and replace teeth before boys do. Changes in the teeth and jaw result in a more mature-looking face.

19-1 School-age children develop more adult proportions. These new proportions make many tasks easier than they were in the preschool years.

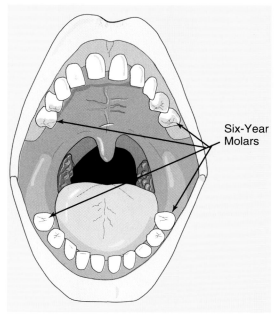

19-2 Six-year molars are the first permanent teeth.

The first two teeth, often the bottom front teeth, fall out during the late preschool years. The last of the 20 baby teeth, the *cuspids* (shown in chapter 7) fall out around age 12. (The tooth fairy is busy during these years!)

Unlike baby teeth, **permanent teeth** are intended to last a lifetime. They are harder and less sharp than baby teeth. The first permanent teeth to come in are called **six-year molars**.

They do not replace any lost teeth. Their name tells the age at which they usually appear. They grow behind the second set of deciduous (baby) molars, 19-2. The next permanent teeth replace lost baby teeth. The permanent teeth change the look of the lower part of the face, 19-3.

growth spurt. A period of rapid growth.

permanent teeth. The set of teeth that begin to come in during the school-age years and are meant to last a lifetime.

six-year molars. The first permanent teeth, which grow in behind the second set of deciduous molars.

19-3 Permanent teeth, which look almost too large for the child's face for a time, change the look of the lower jaw. Young school-age children's teeth are in many stages of growth.
Marcia Hillman Hart

Muscle Growth

Muscles grow and become more firmly attached to bones during middle childhood. However, the muscles are not mature and are easily injured. **Orthopedic problems** (those relating to the bones and muscles) are the most common physical problems of this age.

The skeleton grows more quickly than the muscles. The lag in muscle growth gives a loose-jointed, somewhat awkward look. Children of this age cannot completely keep their muscles from moving. This makes sitting still almost impossible!

School-age children may complain of aches and pains. These muscle aches are called growth pains. **Growth pains** are caused by muscles trying to catch up with skeleton size.

Organ Growth

Brain growth slows during middle childhood. The brain reaches 95 percent of its adult weight by age 10. The wiring is almost complete, and the brain has become more specialized. One area of the brain serves as the visual center, another as the speech center, and so forth. From this time, rewiring the brain is difficult if not impossible.

Other organs continue to mature, too. The heart grows slowly and is small in relationship to the rest of the body. Too much strain on the heart is dangerous.

The eyes mature, enabling the child to have good visual acuity and binocular vision. The ears mature by age seven. The maturity of the eyes and ears aids perception.

Other changes include a decrease in fat deposits. Skin becomes less delicate or fine in texture. Often light hair becomes darker, too.

Motor Development

School-age children enjoy almost all motor activities. They seem to have a surplus of energy. Motor skills continue to improve.

Gross- and Fine-Motor Skills Improve

Motor skills improve during middle childhood. Children who are ages six to eight years enjoy active games that use their large muscles. They are more developed in large-muscle coordination than in small-muscle coordination. For this reason, they enjoy running, jumping, climbing, and playing simple games like tag and catch.

Children ages 9 through 12 years begin to develop interests in more specific motor skills. This is due to increased mental ability as well as improved large-muscle coordination.

They tend to prefer organized sports, skating, or bicycling rather than running or jumping, 19-4.

Motor skills become better in middle childhood for the following reasons:

* faster reaction time. *Reaction time* is the time required to respond to a stimulus like a thrown ball.

orthopedic problems. Problems relating to the bones and muscles.

growth pains. Muscle aches that occur when the muscles grow rapidly to catch up with increasing skeleton size.

19-4 Older school-age children enjoy sports, such as baseball.

❖ improved precision. **Precision** is the ability to perform motor skills accurately. It is shown in skills such as balancing, steadiness, and aiming at a target.

❖ greater speed and improved strength.

❖ improved flexibility. **Flexibility** is the ability to move, bend, and stretch easily.

Older school-age children have highly developed fine-motor skills. Improved skill helps them do arts and crafts, write, play musical instruments, dress themselves, and handle other tasks that need fine-motor precision. These skills seem to increase steadily during the school years. Improvement in writing ability is shown in 19-5.

Skill Performance

In the early part of middle childhood, boys perform better than girls in tasks requiring power, force, and speed. After girls begin their growth spurt, they often equal or excel boys of the same age in these tasks. Girls of all school ages tend to perform better than boys in tasks requiring flexibility or rhythm. Experts do not know whether these motor differences in the genders are due to genes or environment. Studies do show a girl or boy who is highly skilled in one motor activity will likely excel in others.

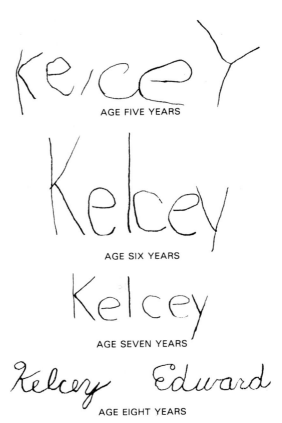

AGE FIVE YEARS

AGE SIX YEARS

AGE SEVEN YEARS

AGE EIGHT YEARS

19-5 Fine-motor skills increase each year, as seen in writing attempts.

Providing for School-Age Children's Physical Needs

Although most school-age children have outgrown the need for direct physical care, they still have many needs that adults must meet. As children begin to think for themselves and as peers become more important, meeting needs becomes more complex. For example, school-age children see having a coat that fits in with what everyone else is wearing as more important than whether the coat will keep them warm.

Encouraging Health and Safety Practices

Good health habits, such as diet and physical activity, strongly influence how school-age children develop physically. Health habits affect their weight, posture, complexion, hair, and energy levels. Adults must promote safe living habits. They can do this by explaining good habits, setting examples, and offering chances for practice.

A Healthful Diet

Eating nutritious foods helps the school-age child's body meet its growth needs and increased energy demands, 19-6. Healthful diets help school-age children resist infections. School-age children also need to store some nutrients for the rapid growth that will occur in their teen years.

Parents can base the diets of their school-age children on the Food Guide (see chapter 5 to review the Guide). Chart 19-7 gives nutrition recommendations for school-age children. As each child's needs may differ slightly, adults may need to adjust the child's diet somewhat. They should consult with the child's doctor or a registered dietitian for advice.

When children start school, adults are no longer in control of what they eat at lunchtime. Some schools publish

19-6 Nutritious foods are more important for proper growth.
Cherry Marketing Institute

their weekly menus to help parents plan other meals and snacks of the day. However, children may not always eat what is on their lunch plate. Even children who carry their lunches to school may give or throw away some of their food. Parents and school staff should urge children to make nutritious food choices while away from home.

Snacking is often unsupervised. By this age many children buy snacks with their spending money. These

precision. Ability to perform motor skills accurately.

flexibility. The ability to move, bend, and stretch easily.

Food Recommendations for School-Age Children

	Number of Servings*	Serving Sizes
Bread, Cereal, Rice, and Pasta Group	6 to 11 daily	1 slice of bread; ½ to ¾ cup cooked cereal, rice, or pasta; 1 ounce ready-to-eat cereal or crackers
Vegetable Group	3 to 5 daily	½ cup chopped raw or cooked vegetables; or 1 cup raw, leafy vegetables
Fruit Group	2 to 4 daily	1 piece of fresh fruit; 1 melon wedge, ¾ cup juice; or ¼ cup dried fruit
Milk, Yogurt, and Cheese Group	2 to 3 daily	1 cup milk; 1 cup yogurt; or 2 ounces cheese
Meat, Poultry, Fish, Dry Beans, Eggs, and Nuts Group	2 to 3 daily	2 to 3 ounces meat, fish, or poultry (cooked and lean); 1 cup cooked, dry beans; or 2 to 3 eggs
Fats and Sweets	Use sparingly.	Use sparingly.

*Food needs in the school-age years vary. The number of servings needed depends on the child's age, size, health, and activity level. Ask a doctor or registered dietitian for specific recommendations for a certain child.

19-7 School-age children need a nutritious diet to meet their growth and energy needs.

often include junk foods. Children who eat too much junk food can lose their appetite for nourishing food. Junk food can also increase tooth decay and cause obesity. (Obese children can have serious social adjustment problems by nine years of age.)

Adults can promote healthy snacking by keeping nutritious, ready-to-eat snacks on hand. Examples are cheese cubes, fresh fruit, and raw carrots or celery sticks. Adults can urge children to prepare their own nutritious snacks, too. Because school-age children like to eat, they often enjoy cooking. Many good cookbooks are written for this age group. They contain simple recipes that children can prepare on their own.

Physical Activity and Other Good Health Practices

In addition to providing nutritious foods and promoting a good diet, adults can promote other health practices. School-age children need moderate physical activity daily or at least three to four times a week. Physical activity is a major contributor to physical fitness. Adults must see that children spend time being active each day rather than always sitting in front of the television or computer.

The average school-age child also needs eight to nine hours of sleep each night. School-age children need sleep on a regular basis. If they don't sleep enough, they are unable to concentrate and do quality work. They also become irritable.

Safety Practices

Safety rules need to be modeled and practiced. For example, adults must insist on seat belts and bicycle helmets, 19-8. Adults need to keep the home safe from potential hazards. Most home accidents are due to falls and fire. Other dangers include those from poisoning, drowning, firearms, and electricity.

Selecting the Right Clothing

Like children of all ages, school-age children need clothing that fits and is well constructed. School-age children are active, so clothing should have growth features and be able to

19-8 Bicycle helmets keep children safe as they ride.

withstand stress and strain. Most school-age children have developed self-dressing skills except for a hard-to-reach button or a specially tied bow. Younger school-age children may still need to have clothes with some self-dressing features. Shoe and sock sizes change on the average of every six months for children ages 6 to 12 years.

Children of this age develop their own preferences for color and style. They are concerned about how peers view them. The right clothing and shoes help make children feel part of the group, 19-9. If clothing and shoes are too different from what others wear, children may feel rejected. Compliments from others on their clothing help boost children's self-confidence.

Providing Needed Space and Furnishings

School-age children want and need space of their own. Adults should think about the following features when planning a space for school-age children:

- ❖ space that may be used for many purposes—playing, working on hobbies, studying, daydreaming, sleeping, and dressing. Children often want space for their friends to visit for the afternoon or even overnight.
- ❖ storage space for clothes and shoes, play and hobby equipment, and books. Display areas for photos, pennants, collections, hobbies, and keepsakes are often prized.
- ❖ space that is attractive to school-age children. They like to choose their own color schemes and accessories, 19-10.
- ❖ easy-to-clean rooms help children who are just learning home-care skills.
- ❖ furniture and accessories the child can use as a teen and young adult may be a wise investment.

19-9 School-age children want to dress in much the same way as their peers.

19-10 School age children prefer bedrooms planned with their interests in mind.
Seabrook Wallcoverings, Inc.

Intellectual Development of School-Age Children

Thinking mentally involves thinking with symbols rather than having contact with a concrete object or event. School-age children can think using even more abstract symbols than preschoolers.

Between ages 7 to 11 years, children's thinking depends more on logic and less on perception. Piaget called this third stage of mental abilities the

Piaget's Stages of Cognitive Development	
Stage 1:	Sensorimotor Stage (Birth to 2 years)
Stage 2:	Preoperational Stage (2 to 7 years)
Stage 3:	Concrete Operational Stage (7 to 11 years)
Stage 4:	Formal Operational Stage (11 years on)

19-11 The school-age child functions in the concrete operational stage.

concrete operational stage, 19-11. The term *concrete* means that logic is based on what the child has experienced at some previous time.

Piaget called the last stages of mental abilities **formal operations** (ages 11 and older). In formal operations, a person can reason more abstractly.

The difference between concrete and formal operations can be seen in how a child plays a game of checkers or chess. At the concrete operational stage, the child can play checkers or chess by the rules. He or she makes each move based on what is on the

concrete operational stage. Piaget's third stage of mental development, in which children begin to think logically, but base their logic on past experiences.

formal operations. Piaget's final stage of mental development, in which a person can reason abstractly.

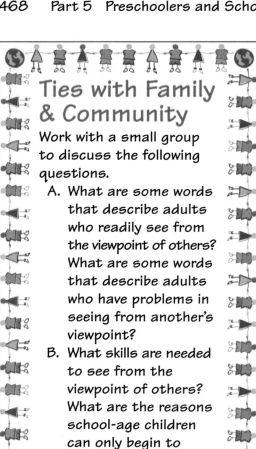

Ties with Family & Community

Work with a small group to discuss the following questions.

A. What are some words that describe adults who readily see from the viewpoint of others? What are some words that describe adults who have problems in seeing from another's viewpoint?

B. What skills are needed to see from the viewpoint of others? What are the reasons school-age children can only begin to develop the skill of seeing from the viewpoint of others?

C. Give some incidents in which not seeing from the viewpoint of others has led to funny or serious situations.

Develop a group presentation to share with the class points brought up in your group's discussion.

board at that time. He or she does not think in terms of the next three to five moves. Older players in the formal operational stage can think ahead and plan strategies. A person in formal operations plans game strategy by thinking, "If my opponent does such and such, then what will my options be?"

How School-Age Children Think

School-age children are in the stage between *preoperational thinking* (before logic) and reasoning on the most abstract level. They are slowly using more advanced thinking skills.

Seeing from the Viewpoint of Others

School-age children begin to see others have ideas that differ from their own. Realizing that others have different ideas leads children to question their previous thoughts and search to find the right answers. School-age children work to prove or deny answers by using logic.

Piaget believed contact with peers is the greatest help in freeing children from egocentric thinking. For real communication with others, a person must recognize the point of view of others and notice how it compares or contrasts with his or her own ideas.

Focusing on More Than One Part

During the school years, the child comes to focus on more than one aspect of something at a time. This means the child can see more than one change in an object at one time. Refer again to Piaget's liquid task with a tall, thin glass and a short, wide glass, shown in chapter 16. In the school-age years, the child knows the greater width in the first glass makes up for the greater height in the other glass. Because the child can note both diameter and height changes at the same time, it is easier to understand how the same amount of liquid looks taller in a thinner glass.

Using Reversibility Logic

School-age children are better able to understand reversibility logic. As you read earlier, reversibility is the ability to follow a line of reasoning back to where it started. They can carry out a task in reverse order. There is the understanding that if something is put back the way it was to begin with, it will be the same. The child who flattens a clay ball knows the clay can be made into a ball again. (In math, this concept is carried out in subtraction.)

Reversibility also means knowing that one change, such as in height, can lead to another change, such as in width. The child knows the clay can be bigger in diameter because it is flatter. (In math, this concept is carried out in division.)

Noting Transformations

School-age children can mentally put together a series of events to see changes in an object. When they watch a liquid being poured from one glass to another, they see the liquid in the first glass, then the liquid as it is being poured into the second glass, and then finally the liquid in the second glass. Once the transformation is noted, children know the liquid in the second glass is the same as the liquid in the first glass. They know this even though the two glasses are different shapes.

Being able to note transformations helps children understand other concepts. For example, school-age children can accept their parents were once babies. They can believe a tree grew from a seed. They understand many natural transformations, such as water turning to ice, 19-12.

Using Deductive and Inductive Reasoning

The school-age child uses deductive reasoning. **Deductive reasoning** is reasoning from the general to the specific. For example, the child is presented with a general statement that all fish live in water. If the child knows that guppies are fish, then he or she can deduce that guppies live in water, 19-13.

deductive reasoning. Reasoning from the general to the specific.

19-12 Playing in the snow helps children understand the transformation snow makes into water as it melts.

19-13 School-age children begin to use deductive reasoning to form their own concepts about the world around them.

Older school-age children may begin to use inductive reasoning. **Inductive reasoning** is reasoning from specific facts to general conclusions. Inductive reasoning is called **scientific reasoning** because it is the form of logic commonly used by scientists. Inductive reasoning is most often found in children over 11 years of age. These children can weigh several ideas they have tested and draw a conclusion. For example, a child may know that people make ice cubes by putting water in a freezer. The child may put fruit juice in the freezer and find that it becomes solid, too. After trying other liquids, such as soft drinks or milk, the child may use inductive reasoning to conclude that cold temperatures change liquids into solids.

What School-Age Children Learn

Because school-age children are beginning to use logic in their thought processes, they are able to learn many new things. Logic helps them learn school subjects like language arts, reading, math, geography, science, and the arts. School-age children's concepts are clearly more advanced than preschool children's concepts. However, they still have trouble grasping some concepts, such as events in history, scientific logic, and value systems.

Physical Knowledge Concepts

As you recall, physical knowledge concepts include concepts about size, shape, color, texture, and other qualities of objects and people. It also includes knowing what happens to objects when they are acted upon, such as hit, squeezed, or dropped. Physical knowledge concepts become more advanced in school-age children because their perception has matured, 19-14. Their senses mature, making sight, sound, smell, and touch more accurate. The brain, too, processes what is seen and heard in more defined ways.

Perception

Perception in school-age children changes in many ways, especially in accuracy. Accurate perception aids physical knowledge concepts.

❖ They do more in-depth exploring of their world. By age nine years, a child uses the eyes or fingertips to trace the outline of an object rather than glancing at it quickly. This more thorough examination helps them note details in objects.

❖ Children learn what information to act upon and what to ignore as they examine an object. If the child is identifying geometric shapes, the color of the shapes is ignored.

inductive reasoning. Reasoning from specific facts to general conclusions.

scientific reasoning. Another name for inductive reasoning, the form of logic commonly used by scientists.

A   B

19-14 Both parquetry blocks (A) and design cubes (B) can be arranged in various designs and patterns to promote the learning of physical knowledge concepts.
© John Shaw

❖ They learn to correctly pair **visual** (seen) and **auditory** (heard) stimuli, such as written letters and their sounds or written music notes and their pitches.

Memory

School-age children have an improved memory, which helps them develop physical knowledge concepts. These children are beginning to see the need for a good memory. Remembering the attributes of objects, people, and places is important. Without remembering these attributes, children cannot identify, describe, classify, or order them. Children also develop methods to help them remember. Such methods include singing the alphabet or learning a rhyme about the number of days in the months of the year.

Logic

Logic allows school-age children to form better, more accurate physical knowledge concepts. For example, the ability to use logic helps children master the concept of conservation. **Conservation** means that changing the shape, direction, or position of an object or objects does not alter the quantity. Children must be able to understand conservations before they can form accurate physical knowledge concepts related to length, mass, weight, or volume. Understanding some of these concepts begins during the early school-age years. Other conservation tasks cannot be solved until age 11 years or even later.

Perception, memory, and logic work together to help a child develop physical knowledge concepts. With increased physical knowledge, the child is better able to give more meaning to words, drawings, and other symbols.

Logical Thinking Concepts

The ability to mentally understand relationships among objects becomes well developed in the middle childhood years. School-age children better understand classification, order, numbers, space, distance, time, and speed. These logical thinking concepts become more accurate as children replace perceptual thinking with logic.

Classification

As you read in chapter 16, classification is the grouping of objects into a class and its complement. As school-age children classify, the attribute (shape, color, way used) that defines the class remains stable. For example, school-age children do not group by shape and switch to color in the process. School-age children also include all objects that meet the attribute for that class. By middle childhood, children fully understand the class and the complement, 19-15.

School-age children learn hierarchical classification. **Hierarchical classification** is having classes within other classes; that is a class may have many subclasses. The large class of *animals* can be broken down into subclasses such as *birds* and *fish*. Both the groups *birds* and *fish* can be further subdivided, too.

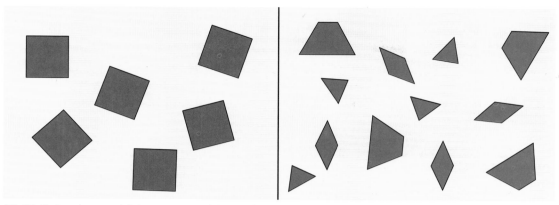

19-15 School-age children group things that are alike—the class of squares. They also place the class complement (other shapes) in a random way.

Order

School-age children can show relationships among objects by putting them in order. This involves using differences among the objects to order them. Differences might include those seen (color, shape, size), heard (pitch, loudness), and felt (texture and temperature). Other differences involve time or order of events. These older children can now arrange even objects with small differences. School-age children use ordering in their daily lives, because now the concept of *series* is used in daily life, such as in calendars, lists, and alphabetizing.

Number

During the last part of the preschool stage and the early part of middle childhood, children learn many basic concepts about numbers. They need to learn number concepts like *greater than, less than, equal to,* and *others.* Some of these basic ideas must

be grasped before children can understand math, 19-16.

Children also learn that groups are changed in number if more objects are brought into the group (adding). They also learn the number changes if objects are taken away from the group (subtracting).

Space

School-age children have many correct ideas about space. They can tell whether objects are open or closed

visual. Referring to the sense of sight.

auditory. Referring to the sense of hearing.

conservation. The concept that changing an object's shape, direction, or position does not alter the quantities of the object.

hierarchical classification. Having classes within other classes.

19-16 Many materials are available for teaching number concepts. Because math is a logical concept, children need to wait until the late preschool and early school-age years to work with math symbols.
© John Shaw

and whether they are far or near. They can also see the relationship of two or more objects. They understand such concepts as *close to, connected, behind, in front of, above, below, left,* or *right.* They know, too, that distant objects like a flying jet do not get smaller as they move farther away.

Distance, Time, and Speed

Children who are younger than age eight years have problems grasping distance, time, and speed concepts. They mainly have trouble understanding the ways these concepts relate. Time and distance are often confused. For example, the young school-age child may say that walking some place is far, but that running makes it near.

Children often learn clock time and calendar time in the first or second grade. However, they do not understand calendar time well until age 10 or 11 years. The time of historical

events seems difficult to grasp until the teen years. Stories written for children often reflect their understandings of time. Stories for the young child often begin with "Once upon a time." Stories for school-age children give hints about seasons or years. Books for late childhood years mention exact time periods.

Cause and Effect Relationships

School-age children begin to resolve many cause and effect relationships. As children become less egocentric, they begin to understand that humans do not cause natural happenings. They begin to have more of a scientific approach to their thinking.

The earlier belief that nonliving objects have lifelike qualities is given up for scientific answers. However, some aspects of nature (sun and stars, oceans, mountains) that are thought of as powerful may be seen as lifelike by older children.

Language Is Mastered

Around six or seven years of age, children's speech becomes more social. They want to talk with their friends and adults. The speech of school-age children is not as involved or intellectual, however, as many adult conversations.

Vocabulary

Active vocabulary continues to grow in middle childhood. Children of this age give more exact definitions than do younger children. If you asked children to define the word *orange*, preschool children would often say, "You eat it." School-age children would give a more exact definition, such as, "It is a color or a fruit." Definitions of words are often used as part of tests given to children during the school years, 19-17. Reading helps the vocabulary grow, as does learning to spell words and write sentences.

Articulation

Articulation of all English sounds is often mastered by age eight years. Children with the most articulation problems at the end of the preschool years often continue to have speech problems in the school years. Speech problems are also related to reading problems. This is because children need to articulate, say sounds in order to decode the sounds of letters, a skill that is needed for reading and spelling.

19-17 *School-age children build both their active and passive vocabularies by reading and writing.*

Grammar

Around age nine years, children have mastered the grammar they hear. They use their own set of grammar rules to make plurals, use pronouns, and show tense. These rules may or may not be those that are accepted by grammar experts.

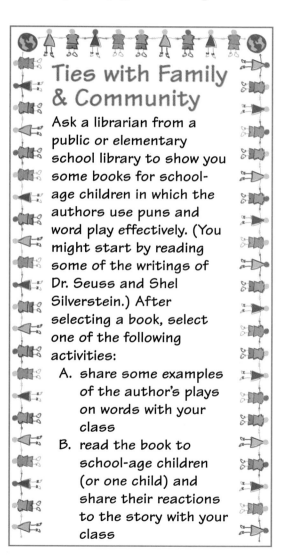

Ties with Family & Community

Ask a librarian from a public or elementary school library to show you some books for school-age children in which the authors use puns and word play effectively. (You might start by reading some of the writings of Dr. Seuss and Shel Silverstein.) After selecting a book, select one of the following activities:

A. share some examples of the author's plays on words with your class

B. read the book to school-age children (or one child) and share their reactions to the story with your class

19-18 One way that school-age children play with words is by saying jump-rope rhymes.

Changing grammar habits after this age requires relearning.

Middle childhood is also the age of having fun with words. Children learn different word rhymes, raps, and chants, 19-18. Name-calling can even become a word contest that may turn a fight into laughter. Humor is expressed more in words during the middle childhood years. Children come to enjoy many kinds of jokes, riddles, and simple puns.

Helping School-Age Children Meet Their Intellectual Needs

School-age children need time to play, enjoy hobbies, be with peers, and daydream. They also have intellectual needs to meet. School meets many of the mental needs of children. However, home is an important learning environment, too. Children need a rich out-of-school world of things to do and see. Even day-to-day activities can be rich in learning experiences.

Guiding Intellectual Development

Adults can help school-age children meet their intellectual needs in many ways. For example, adults can do the following:

❖ provide opportunities for children to participate in activities that require effort over longer periods. Such activities might include learning to play an instrument or being involved in sports. It might include beginning a hobby, such as stamp collecting, model building, or other projects.

❖ allow children to choose the activities they find most rewarding.

❖ encourage children to learn. However, adults should not overuse rewards and praise. The feeling of doing a good job is often the best reward.

❖ show an interest in and support the school's program.

❖ show interest in their own activities. Adults whose skills and satisfactions grew over long periods of time are children's best models.

Adults can enrich children's language in many ways. Sharing ideas and experiences with children can be mutually rewarding. Reading to children and listening to them read is helpful. Adults can encourage children to express themselves correctly. Children learn the language they hear, speak, and read.

There are many language games that are fun as well as helpful. Individual word puzzles of all types are available, too. These include crossword puzzles, word finds, and scrambled words.

Preparing the Child to Enter School

Between late August and September each year, several million five- and six-year-olds enter school. Many older children also enter new schools because their families have moved. Starting school is exciting and perhaps scary for many children.

Entering school is a new developmental task for children. They must deal with new people—both children and adults. They also must deal with new concepts and skills and with a different daily structure, 19-19. School-age children spend 44 percent of their waking hours at school.

Adults need to help children make the transition from home to school as enjoyable as possible. Stress may accompany the new hours and routines. Adults need to realize children may manage anxiety at school, but they may show anxiety and stress at home. Extra patience is needed during the adjustment time. This is a poor time to add new learnings or tasks, such as

19-19 The people, concepts, and schedules of elementary school differ from those of the preschooler's world.
© John Shaw

music lessons or a new pet, to a child's life.

Adults can help children have a good basis for their school experiences in many ways. For example, they can do the following:

❖ develop a secure and trusting relationship with their children
❖ allow children to have more independence
❖ teach children to accept the authority of adults other than parents
❖ help children overcome separation anxiety

School also means getting along with peers for many hours. Children sit, line up, work, eat, and share with other children. Unlike the preschool play groups, where children choose their own friends and play when they want, school relationships are more teacher directed. Children who are adaptable and have had contacts with others find it easier to adjust than those who haven't had this opportunity.

Getting the Child to School

Adults need to make transportation plans clear to children. Younger children who walk or catch a bus need instructions. Some adults or older children who are known to the child should be nearby. Children should be reminded not to talk to or go with strangers. They should know their full name, parent's names, address, and phone number.

School should be viewed as a natural course of events—everyone goes to school. Adults should create a normal routine for the first few days of school. Overdoing photos, sounding anxious, getting the child ready too early (or too late), or serving a special breakfast are not ways to make school a matter-of-fact event.

Adults should say goodbyes at the bus stop, on the schoolyard, or at the classroom door. These goodbyes should be warm but not clingy. The teary-eyed child often regains control soon after the adult is out of sight, 19-20.

If the first days go well, children look forward to school. Experiences that are not good may lead to situations where the child wants to avoid school and will use every excuse to stay at home.

19-20 Saying goodbye in the schoolyard helps children enter the classroom in a composed, positive state.

Reinforcing School Tasks

School children need daily encouragement and help. Adults must continue working with and helping their children. Help is not effective if given only a few days after the teacher shares negative reports with parents. The schools and parents and other adults close to children have the same goal. They all want to give children the best possible education. Children are best helped when all those concerned work as a team.

Adults have a number of responsibilities concerning their children's schooling. Among these are the following:
* see that children attend school regularly and follow the rules
* take an interest in what children are learning

❖ talk with children about schoolwork, look at their papers, and stay in close contact with the school

Adults and children need to plan a quiet place for study. Space with a desk or table for doing work like writing is important. Many children also enjoy a place to stretch out while reading.

A certain amount of time needs to be set aside for doing homework. This amount varies with the age of the child. Elementary school children need time to play and perhaps have a snack or evening meal before doing homework. Homework should be done before watching television or other activities. School-age children who do not have homework can use the set time for reading or being read to, drawing, or doing other activities that complement school tasks. Household tasks can fit with school tasks, too. For example, adults may plan a cooking project to reinforce fractions.

Adults can ensure that children follow through on any activities the school sends home with the child. They need to supervise children's homework, but not do it for them. In the elementary school, homework most often is assigned to reinforce skills learned in class. Doing children's homework makes them rely on adults to solve their tasks. It also prevents the child from getting needed practice. (If homework is often too difficult, adults should talk to the teacher.)

Guiding Television Viewing

Parents should limit television viewing and leisure activities on school nights. Several studies show that as hours of television viewing increase, grades drop at the same rate. Children who do not watch as much television tend to concentrate better and use their imaginations more. Also, school-age children who learn to budget their work and leisure times develop healthy lifelong work and play habits.

Television can be a useful tool for learning and entertainment, however, in limited amounts. It is not healthful to let television watching replace many other worthwhile activities, especially involvement with others and hands-on activities.

Assisting Computer Use

Most school-age children are becoming comfortable with computers and use them for learning and fun. Quality software and Web sites can be used to support school learnings and enhance problem-solving, decision-making, creativity, concepts, language learnings, and even social skills. With good software and access to the Internet, children can do the following:
❖ access information
❖ communicate (send and receive e-mails, "talk" with experts, and compose stories and poems)
❖ publish their work
❖ visit interactive sites

Teachers need to help parents learn to assist their children in the use of computers. Parents need to see software and Web site evaluations (as discussed in chapter 18) and have lists of software and Web sites used in their children's classrooms. Teachers need to explain to parents how children can use computers in doing homework and projects and in having fun. Many librarians have helpful computer information for parents, too. Much literature on children's computer use is available through parenting magazines, children's magazines, and newspapers and on the Internet. This information provides reviews of software and Web sites and makes suggestions for online activities.

Although computer use is a useful tool, parents and other adults must keep children safe while using the computer. Safety is discussed in chapter 21.

Social-Emotional Development of School-Age Children

A whole new social experience begins in middle childhood. Children need to make many new adjustments. School-age children have to be much more independent. They are concerned about what others think of them. Getting along with age-mates is fun, but sometimes difficult. They find that mastering skills needed in order to fit into society can be stressful.

In many ways, social development becomes the most important aspect of development in middle childhood. The peer group becomes more and more important as children progress through the school years. Relationships with peers affect all aspects of development. School-age children's physical skills are often judged by how well they can play sports and games with peers. Through their school activities, they make daily judgments of their own learnings compared with those of peers. Some school and youth organizations use peer-group projects. Peer groups also act as a source of socialization. Each group teaches its own rules of conduct needed for acceptance.

Developing the Self-Concept

School-age children take a close look at themselves, 19-21. They become keenly aware of their **shortcomings** (areas in which a person wants or needs to improve) and failures. Self-evaluation becomes more complex for the following reasons:

❖ School-age children become almost totally concerned with what others think of them. Peers can judge harshly. Adults cannot often change how peers judge each other.

❖ Abilities in reading, mathematics, music, computer literacy, and other skills are more difficult for them to measure. Earlier, they could tell how they compared with other children in their motor skills like playing baseball. Now it is much

19-21 School-age children often spend much time alone thinking about themselves.
© John Shaw

harder to compare because their school studies are more abstract.

❖ School-age children are generally evaluated in comparison to other children's skills. School grades are earned more in comparison to other children's work than in comparison to the child's own previous work.

Showing Social Awareness

During middle childhood, children begin to show a greater awareness of what is going on around them.

School-age children develop a sense of work and industry as they learn some of the skills needed to become ready for adult life. Social relationships grow and become more complicated.

Sense of Work and Being Industrious

As you read in chapter 17, Erikson described the preschooler's sense of initiative as thinking and acting without being urged. The preschool child's ability to initiate experiences prepares the child for later development. In the school-age years, children enter Erikson's fourth stage of development, industry versus inferiority, 19-22. **Industry** means joining others in striving to become a competent member of society. **Inferiority** is feeling incompetent and less valuable as a member of society.

Like initiative, industry involves doing and making things. However, industry builds on the strides made in the initiative stage. Thus, it differs from initiative in three major ways.

shortcomings. Areas where a person wants or needs to improve.

industry. A sense of joining others in striving to become a competent member of society.

inferiority. A feeling that one is incompetent and less valuable as a member of society.

Erikson's Stages of Personality Development

Basic trust versus basic mistrust (first year of life)

Autonomy versus shame and doubt (second year of life)

Initiative versus guilt (preschool years)

Industry versus inferiority (middle childhood)

Middle childhood is the time for developing the tools of society in preparation for adult work. If children are encouraged to use these tools, they develop a sense of industry. If too little is expected or if children are criticized for their efforts, a sense of inferiority develops. Inferiority results in poor work habits, avoidance of competition, and the inability to cope with later tasks.

19-22 Being industrious while learning to avoid feelings of inferiority is the major social-emotional task of the school-age years.

These include the following:

❖ Industry involves the drive to accomplish school tasks and other projects, whereas initiative involves learning tasks that will reduce the need for adult help.

❖ Industry involves joining others and working as a team member, whereas initiative is more personal.

❖ Industry focuses on recognition from peers and important adults, whereas initiative focuses on pleasing self and parents.

If school-age children are successful in this stage, they feel confident and productive. Being industrious increases children's feelings of self-esteem and responsibility. They see that what they do makes a difference. If children's efforts and work are demeaned or ignored, the outcome may be a lasting sense of inferiority.

School-age children want to satisfy themselves while being acceptable to society. The play of earlier years is replaced with more meaningful work (at least by adult standards). However, play is still important in middle childhood.

Children learn their lifelong attitude toward work at this time. Those with a sense of industry see work as the way to learn new ideas and skills and to perform in worthwhile ways. These children also see work as a way to win approval from others. Parents, teachers, and peers encourage the learning of skills. Even social organizations like 4-H, Boy Scouts, or Girl Scouts make learning skills the route to success and higher status, 19-23.

School-age children like to learn to do things with and for others. They are learning and practicing cooperation as they enjoy the interaction with others.

Peers Become Important

As children spend more time with peers, they depend less on adults for company. Children in the elementary school years like to form groups. The nature of friendships changes as children mature.

19-23 Youth organizations, such as cheerleading groups, encourage and recognize children for their hard work and skills.

19-24 In the school-age years, children begin developing close relationships with a few special peers.

Close friendships are beginning to develop in the early school years, 19-24. By age eight years, there is more separation of genders. Peer groups are informal and often include children who live near each other. Groups are often within walking or cycling distance. The groups change as families move in and out of the neighborhood.

In this stage, children often see a friend as someone who helps them. They seldom think in terms of how they can help the friend. Give and take does occur, but it serves the individual rather than the mutual interest of friends.

Between the ages of 9 and 11 years, more close friendships form. Boys choose boys for friends, and girls choose girls. Children also show dislike for the opposite gender. However,

girls may become interested in boys around age 11 years. Similar interests and tastes determine friendships more often than physical nearness. Some formal groups, such as team sport groups, form at this time, also. The nature of these friendships becomes one of cooperation and helping each other in order to achieve group goals.

Peer Groups Serve a Purpose

Peer groups are important to children and may serve the following purposes:

❖ Belonging to a peer group gives children a feeling of sharing and loyalty. Special friends may huddle, talk, giggle, argue, and fight as they share times together. Children feel a sense of security and self-esteem when working or playing with others in their group.

❖ Peer groups reinforce self-concept. School-age children are highly concerned about how they appear to others. In peer groups, children tag others with labels, such as captain of the team or the last one chosen. These labels make children aware of how others feel about them. Once they absorb these peer attitudes, children react to themselves as others have reacted to them.

❖ Peer groups provide emotional support. Adults cannot provide the comfort that children feel when they realize others their age share similar feelings. Their group members understand how they feel.

❖ Peer groups share information with each other. Children learn from their peers as they work on group projects. They not only want to be part of the group, but they want to be the best in the group. This makes children want to learn all they can from their peers.

❖ Through their peer groups, they learn how to deal with rules and get along with others. Even the earlier play groups become more organized as children participate in games with rules. These groups teach children that social relation-ships involve rules and rules help groups work as teams. Peer group codes contain more rules about what not to do than what to do. Children learn consequences of what can happen, such as being removed from the group, if rules are broken.

❖ Peer groups help school-age children gain self-control and depend less on adults. The peer group serves as a sifter for thinking through adult-taught priorities. Peers help children decide which priorities to keep and which to adjust. As children consider priorities, they learn to conform to others at times and stand firm in their own beliefs at other times.

Controlling Emotions

By the time they enter school, children show patterns of emotional behavior. These patterns are fairly well established. Their emotional development and personality continue to merge. Thus, the emotions felt by school-age children affect all their behavior, which influences their personality.

Love

All school-age children need love. They show love to adults and peers who care for them and accept them as they are, 19-25. School-age children do not seek relationships in which they must give too much in return. They do care for others who share common interests.

The need for love is shown in school-age children's great desire to be accepted by others—adults and peers. These children, however, do not express their love as openly (with hugs and kisses) as younger children. School-age children show love for adults by kindness and doing activities with them. They show affection for peers by wanting to be with them and sharing secrets. They also show affection by staying in touch through the telephone and notes and giving small presents.

School-age children who do not feel loved have a narrowed emotional range. They experience little or no joy,

19-25 School-age children show their love to family members and other close people by spending time with them.

grief, or guilt. Thinking abilities are hurt because these unloved children cannot concentrate. These children often turn to antisocial behavior, such as hostile acts.

Fear and Anxiety

Some of a child's earlier fears and worries become less threatening. There is a greater separation of fantasy and reality. Thus, fear of the dark disappears after age 7 years. Fear of the supernatural declines by age 9 or 10 years. Fears of physical harm (disease, injury, or death) continue from the preschool years into the school-age years. School-age children's fears and anxieties also center on the future, embarrassment, and people and their actions, 19-26.

The fears and anxieties of middle childhood often do not disappear with age. Some studies report over half of the school-age children's fears and anxieties persist into adult years.

Anger and Aggression

Expressions of anger and aggression change with age. School-age children do not display their anger as physically as younger children do. They are better able to control their bodies and express themselves verbally. By this time, they know what is and is not acceptable. Therefore, children in middle childhood show their anger in less direct ways. For example, anger may be expressed in the forms of

Fears and Anxieties in Middle Childhood

The future

❖   any new situation, such as a new school or new neighborhood
❖   the world in general, such as war, pollution, and economic changes

Embarrassment

❖   school failure
❖   remaining unchosen for a team sport, part in a play, or other event
❖   mistake made in a game, recital, or other performance
❖   poor personal appearance
❖   physical examinations and fear of changing clothes in a locker room or public place
❖   personal shortcomings

People and their actions

❖   family quarrels
❖   divorce/disagreement of parents
❖   fear that custodial parent may leave
❖   kidnappers and child enticers
❖   abuse
❖   gangs and bullies

19-26 The major fears and anxieties of middle childhood are the future, embarrassment, and people and their actions.

disrespect, sulkiness, and scapegoating (blaming others for their own mistakes). School-age children also show anger by gossiping, plotting, and even imagining the downfall of their enemies. Withdrawal from a situation, such as quitting or using less ability, may be another sign of anger. Some older children are physically aggressive, and their acts can have devastating outcomes.

As children grow older, they become angry about different things. Like preschool children, school-age children are angered when their wants are denied or their possessions are threatened. However, unlike preschool children, school-age children are also angered by what they see as wrongs to others. In later years, anger at social wrongs may be turned into positive social action.

Helping School-Age Children with Their Social-Emotional Needs

Although the peer group becomes a more major part of school-age children's social lives, adults are still important. Adults need to help children in their activities and schoolwork. Parents often foot the costs of children's training or participation in activities. They arrange for safe transportation to and from these activities. Adults give children support and encouragement in their emotional development.

School-age children enjoy just being with familiar adults. Elementary school children are still interested in doing things with and for their families, 19-27. These children also enjoy being with other adults, such as teachers and youth leaders.

Guiding and Modeling Behavior

Adults model their personal priorities and attitudes about almost all aspects of life. School-age children watch and listen to important adults in their lives. They pattern many of their thoughts and actions after these adults. School-age children still need a certain amount of guidance.

Balance Dependence with Independence

School-age children often question adults' guidance. Yet, school-age children need adults to listen to them and, at times, to advise and set limits. Adults must learn the balance between letting go and being there for children. This is not easy. Adults do not know whether they should protect children from problems with friends or let them cope on their own. Adults may be torn between trying to enforce their teachings and allowing children to make some of their own decisions.

Extend Gender Role

Adults help extend the gender role development in the school years. Mothers and other female adults close to school-age girls affect the girls' feminine gender role learnings, 19-28. These learnings include goals in the world of work. Fathers and other male adults close to school-age boys affect boys' masculine gender role learnings. Fathers and other adult males who model warmth and sureness in their

19-27 Taking part in family activities is still important to school-age children.
© John Shaw

scapegoating. Blaming others for one's own mistakes.

19-28 These boys learn about gender roles for males as they imitate their father by "shaving" with toy razors.

Ties with Family & Community

Discuss with two professionals who work with school-age children how the world of work and home-care tasks have changed during the last two or three decades. (School counselors, principals, and family and consumer sciences teachers are good resource people.) Ask each adult how these changes have altered the value of skills needed by adults in society. How have these changing skills affected the knowledge and skills needed by school-age children? What courses have been added to the school curriculum in the last thirty years to address these concerns? Share your findings with the class in an oral report?

masculine roles directly affect femininity in girls. Warm, masculine-type models also help girls in their teens relate well to males in their age group. The same is true for female adults and their affect on school-age boys' learning.

Encourage Work and Industry

In middle childhood, children develop attitudes that prepare them for adult work. To help children develop positive feelings about work, adults must help the child focus on abilities rather than on their faults. They should set reasonable standards.

When standards are too high, children feel they can't reach them and won't try. If standards are set too low, children may not work at their potential. Even small successes help children feel good about their work, which increases their self-esteem.

Adults can help by encouraging children to succeed in school. Children do better in school when they have loving, caring parents who want them to do well than when parents show little or no concern.

Expand Children's Horizons

Adults should plan activities that can develop children's physical, mental, and social skills. By the school years, children begin to develop more unevenly. A child who has developed advanced reading skills may lag in motor skills. Children still have a wide range of talents, so they could achieve in many fields. On the other hand, children should not be expected to excel in all areas. Adults need to encourage children to test and expand their abilities.

Adults can suggest hobbies where children can succeed, 19-29. Children enjoy the steps involved in hobbies, such as making and finding objects. They like to display their new learnings.

Keep Family Communication Open

It is important for parents and children to talk and express their feelings openly. If good communication patterns are established during middle

19-29 Hobbies, like insect collecting, can be a fun learning experience.
© Nancy P. Alexander

childhood years, later teen-parent relationships will be much better.

During the early school years, children view their parents as the greatest in every way. By age 9 or 10 years, they begin to see their parents' mistakes. Relationships between parents and children become somewhat strained. However, good communication can help ease the strain.

To communicate clearly, adults must talk to children honestly and openly. They need to explain why they feel a certain way and show willingness to listen to their children's feelings. Parents may be upset because their child went to a friend's home after school without telling them. They should explain they become worried when they do not know where their child is. Parents should also let the child have input on how to avoid the problem in the future.

Listening

Listening is an important part of communication. Parents may pick up on children's emotions by listening to their comments. A child may say, "You always pick on me!" Parents can use such comments as a chance to ask children what is on their mind. They may learn that certain actions bother their children. Parents may also clear up misunderstandings at these times.

When children realize their parents will listen, they are more likely to come to their parents with problems. Children will have some problems with friendships or school. They often look to parents in these situations. Giving advice and assuring children can help them bounce back from problems. Children see their parents as people who have weathered some of the same problems.

Throughout the school years parents are still admired. This is true even though children feel that parents create many of their problems. Open communication allows children to build strong bonds with their parents that will last a lifetime.

Enjoying Family Ties

School-age children think of their families as home base. They think of home as a place for food, clothing, and shelter and psychological security.

Psychological security is a feeling that someone cares and will help when needed.

The family provides a balance between letting go and holding on in the school years. In this role, the family provides security for trying new skills. They also need to be available when children need support.

Family activities can extend the skills children learn in school-age peer groups. In addition to direct help, parents can help by organizing the child's schedule, seeing that needed equipment is ready (washing uniforms, buying ballet slippers), and driving children to and from activities.

School-age children enjoy just being with family. They want to learn home-care skills. Children are pleased when they are old enough and skilled enough to do many things they were not allowed to do in the preschool years. Children also enjoy family times, 19-30. They enjoy family meals, weekend outings, yearly vacations, and family celebrations. The special plans and surprises are all part of taking a major role in family rituals. School-age children may even think about how they will continue these customs when they are adults.

Providing Time for Friendships

Children need time to be with friends. Some adults have so many other plans for children they don't have a chance to form friendships.

19-30 Family outings strengthen family ties.

19-31 Parents who encourage children to spend time in their yard or home with peers help friendships form.

Making friends welcome in the home and encouraging peer activities is important, 19-31. Parents must understand children will like their best friends almost as much as the family and will want to include them in family outings.

Because the peer group is so important, fears of rejection are real in middle childhood. Every child, at one time or another, feels rejected by peers. You often hear school-age children say, "Nobody likes me," or "I can never do anything right!" Such statements from a child who is usually accepted are best ignored. However, adults do need to help when children experience general rejection, especially if the rejection lasts over a week. How to help depends on the child, but the following ideas often work:

❖ Try to discover the problem behind the rejection. The problem may be the child's physical appearance. The problem may also be the lack of certain skills— physical or athletic skills, academic skills, or social skills.

❖ Give children direct help in overcoming the problem. The child may need better grooming tools and lessons. The child may also need coaching in a new skill or step-by-step suggestions on how to make friends.

❖ Plan games and activities where there is not so much pressure on a child's skills. Play dodge ball rather than softball.

psychological security. The feeling that someone cares and will help when needed.

Loss of Friendship

Children also need help when they lose their best friends through conflict, new interest, or moving away. School-age children can suffer great pain, even depression, from such a breakup. Depression can cause a decrease in eating, sleeping, working, or playing.

Adults can help in many cases. Children may talk to adults about the loss of a friend. Adults should choose words carefully when they discuss the breakup. For example, they should not say, "It's not as bad as you think. You'll feel better soon." Many children will tune out well-meaning adults at this point. Instead, adults should try to talk about the emotions felt without mention of getting over them.

Adults need to stay neutral if the breakup was caused by conflict. Joining a child's anger or hurt places all the blame for the breakup on the former friend. It may also say to the child, "You made a poor friendship choice."

Adults can prepare children in advance for breaks in friendships. Preparation should begin in the preschool or early school years. Parents can begin by talking about why people become friends and sometimes end friendships. Adults can also tell children about some of their friendships and breakups (or read stories about loss of friends and the hurt it causes). Preparation can also include encouraging children to play with more than one child so the loss of one friend will not be too crushing.

Helping Children Control Their Emotions

Adults should continue to guide and help children control their emotions in middle childhood. They should explain to children that all people have strong feelings. Adults can talk about some of their own emotions, too. School-age children may also be helped when they read about the struggles of other children and adults to control feelings. Adults can also point out that a person needs to control his or her emotions out of respect for others.

Children need to observe parents modeling control of their own behavior. They learn by watching adults handle frustration and anger. Parents should talk about the child's problem. If they use nonphysical means to let the child know he or she has done wrong, they model acceptable ways of behavior. These are better methods than physical punishment, which shows loss of control.

Control of emotions can be helped in indirect ways, too. Physical activity and creative tasks help children release their anger. Children show less fear of the physical world as they gain skills and knowledge. Fear of water is overcome when a person learns to swim well. As children improve skills, they develop healthy self-concepts. Having healthy self-concepts helps children overcome many social fears because children are not as worried about being embarrassed or rejected.

Helping Children Improve Their Self-Esteem

Children's feelings about themselves are influenced by how others, who are important in their lives, treat them, 19-32. Parents and other adults who provide love, appreciation, and encouragement form the base for a positive self-esteem.

Every child has special talents and abilities. Parents and adults need to praise and encourage those traits. They can offer positive feedback for what the child is doing well. Saying, "You did a good job," is an important message for children to hear.

Parents need to communicate their love and acceptance to their children. School-age children still seek parental affection and approval. Children need to know they are important to their family.

Adults should discipline children privately, not in front of their peers or others. If criticism must be given, the act should be criticized and not the child. In this way, they learn that what they have done was wrong but they can still be trusted and loved as a person.

Parents and adults need to help school-age children continue to build their confidence. They need to help children learn to believe in their own abilities. With their love, praise, and support, adults can help school-age children in their struggle for self-esteem.

19-32 When children are treated well by friends and loved ones, it helps them feel good about themselves.

Recognizing Developmental Delays

Although it is hoped that children's developmental delays have been recognized and successfully treated prior to the school years, many school-age children have delays. Some of these children's delays were identified at younger ages, but these children have not yet caught up with their peers. Unfortunately, some children's developmental delays may not be recognized until the school-age years.

Many teachers are seasoned judges of developmental delays in physical, intellectual, and social-emotional areas. Most teachers have had some training in child development. Also, because they teach so many children, teachers are often more experienced than parents in recognizing whether children are average or delayed.

Parents are usually informed of delays during the formal parent-teacher conferences or sometimes through more informal contacts with teachers, coaches, or scout leaders. Although developmental delays are not the only reason children fail to achieve in school, parents should note the achievement of their children. Parents who note their children do not seem to be achieving should contact their children's teachers as soon as possible. Through the sharing of information about children's home and school life, problems can be more accurately identified and actions planned.

Although the pace of growth and development slow in the school-age years, many changes still occur in this six-year period.

Summing It Up

School-age children's physical development continues slowly and steadily. They go through many body changes that seem to make the body appear awkward. The skeletal system is maturing. Bones are growing and hardening. Permanent teeth are coming in and changing the look of the face. Motor skills become better because of faster reaction time, precision, and improved flexibility. Their fine-motor skills begin to be highly developed.

Adults should encourage good health habits, such as a healthful diet, physical activity, and adequate rest. Parents and adults need to emphasize good safety habits and basic rules of safety in the home.

School-age children are beginning to think more logically. They are beginning to realize others have ideas different from their own. Deductive and inductive reasoning become more accurate. Children's understanding of physical knowledge and logical thinking concepts improves. School-age children can use reversibility skills to see more than one change in an object. They can join a series of events to see a transformation. By middle childhood, children have mastered most of the rules of language, including grammar and articulation.

Parents and adults need to provide activities that will help the school-age child grow mentally. Common experiences can help children learn. Helping children prepare for school and creating an environment that encourages learning is important.

Children face the challenge of industry versus inferiority. They show greater social awareness during middle childhood. Adult and peer relationships deepen. Peer groups are important. Children's feelings about themselves are reinforced by how peers treat them. Their sense of work and industry increases as they develop attitudes that prepare them for adult work. The major emotions of love, fear and anxiety, anger, and aggression are fairly well set and affect their behavior.

Parents and adults can encourage their school-age children to take part in peer activities and help them get along with friends. Activities that challenge their physical, mental, and social skills can be planned. Adults can model emotional control when dealing with discipline problems. Creating an atmosphere of open communication builds strong bonds between adults and children. With their love, respect, and guidance, adults can help children maintain a strong self-concept.

Reviewing Key Concepts

Write your answers on a separate sheet of paper.

1. True or false. Boys are taller and heavier than girls throughout middle childhood.
2. True or false. The first permanent teeth to erupt replace lost baby teeth.
3. List four reasons school-age children need an adequate diet.
4. Upon hearing another person's point of view, a child in the concrete operational stage thinks his or her own ideas are _____ (always right, possibly wrong).
5. True or false. When noting change in an object, school-age children begin to take in more than one aspect of the change at the same time.
6. Give two examples of deductive reasoning.
7. List three reasons entering school for the first time is stressful.
8. _____ (Physical, Mental, Social) development is the most critical aspect of development in middle childhood.
9. Children can learn healthful work attitudes when adults encourage them _____ (to just get by, to do their best) in everything.
10. List six purposes of the peer group.
11. Which of the following statements are true? (You may choose more than one.)
    A. School-age children need adults to make most decisions for them.
    B. Adults need to encourage children to be independent.
    C. Adults affect the gender role learnings of children, even in the school years.
    D. Because peer influence is so great during the school years, it matters little what attitudes or priorities adults convey by their actions or words.
    E. Family activities, such as vacations, should stop during middle childhood because children need and want to be with peers.

Using Your Knowledge

1. **Art/Child Development.** Make a collage of pictures of children from ages 6 through 12 years. What physical changes do you notice?
2. **Art/Child Development.** Create a poster called "Qualities Needed In Motor Skills." Divide the poster into five areas labeled *reaction time*, *precision, speed, strength*, and *flexibility*. Find pictures or draw sketches of activities that fit each quality.
3. **Polling/Mathematics.** List common gross- and fine-motor activities. Ask a class of fourth- or fifth-grade students to choose their three favorite activities from the list. Tabulate the results. Which activities were chosen most often? Were these gross- or fine-motor skills?
4. **Consumer Skills/Technology.** Visit the Web sites of various manufacturers of computer products for children. Compare the features of three software products designed for school-age children. Based on your findings which item would you recommend most, and why?

5. **Interviewing Skills.** Compile a list of 12 interview questions to ask a professional who works with school-age children who have developmental delays. If possible, record the interview on audio- or videotape. Share the tape or describe your findings to the class.

Making Observations

1. Observe school-age children eating their school lunches and choosing snack foods. How nutritious are the foods they eat (not just buy)? What problems do you see with their diets in terms of sugars, fats, or lack of nutrients? What physical problems, if any, can you observe?

2. Observe school-age children playing a table game like checkers, chess, or cards. What evidence of the use of logic (strategy) do you see? How would this be different for a five-year-old attempting to play the game?

3. Observe the play of 6- and 7-year-olds and that of 11- and 12-year-olds. How does play differ between these age groups in terms of motor skills?

4. Observe a group of school-age children. What rules are being set for acceptance in the group? Which aspects of development are being the most critically judged by peers (body appearance, physical skills, intellectual abilities, or social skills)? Explain your answer. What is happening to children on the fringe of the group?

5. Observe school-age children in the classroom. Which emotion or emotions seem the hardest to control? Give examples of displays of anger, aggression, fear, or anxiety you observe that may be the child's way of asking for love and attention.

Thinking Further

1. How do you think girls who mature early feel when they are taller and more mature looking than their classmates or when they excel in skill performance over these same peers?

2. Some parents give their kindergartners a crash course (often a few weeks or even a few days before school starts) in learning the alphabet, naming colors, counting, and writing their names. Do you think this is helpful or harmful to children? Why?

3. Why do you think school-age peers judge each other so harshly? What societal factors do you think contribute to this behavior?

Part 6
Guiding and Caring for Children

All children need help as they grow and develop. Parents are not the only people who guide and care for them. Many other adults in child-related careers care for children, too. Guiding and caring for children of any age is an exciting experience. Many important skills are needed to provide warm, appropriate care and guidance for children. The skills needed may vary according to the specific career or age group of the children.

In **chapter 20**, you will learn how children expand and refine their learnings through play. You will find many suggested activities and materials for providing learning experiences that children will enjoy.

Chapter 21 will help you become more aware of the risks to children's health and safety. You will also learn many ways to protect children.

Selecting quality group programs is a difficult task. In **chapter 22**, you will study various child care programs and the qualities that make some programs better for children than others.

In **chapter 23**, you will learn more about children who have special needs. These children have needs that differ from those of average children. To help meet these needs, adults must use special parenting and teaching techniques. Adults must also foster all facets of a child's growth and development.

Every family faces problems and challenges. A few children and families have problems so severe they challenge the health of children and the strength of families. In **chapter 24**, you will study both ordinary challenges and more severe problems. You will also learn some ways to confront these **family concerns and problems.**

Finally, **chapter 25** will review child-related careers. You will also learn how to determine whether any of these careers is right for you.

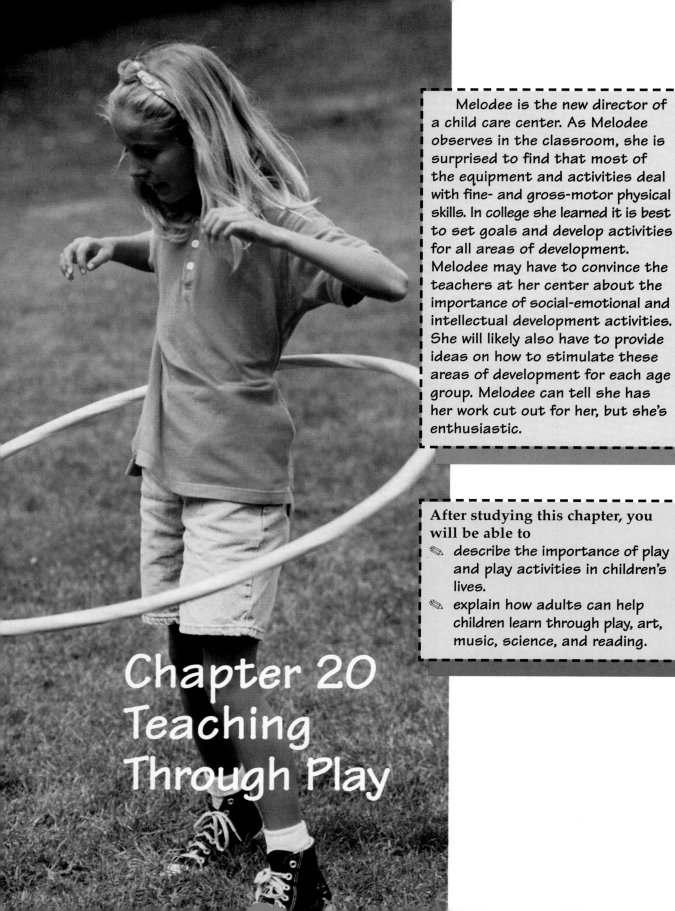

Melodee is the new director of a child care center. As Melodee observes in the classroom, she is surprised to find that most of the equipment and activities deal with fine- and gross-motor physical skills. In college she learned it is best to set goals and develop activities for all areas of development. Melodee may have to convince the teachers at her center about the importance of social-emotional and intellectual development activities. She will likely also have to provide ideas on how to stimulate these areas of development for each age group. Melodee can tell she has her work cut out for her, but she's enthusiastic.

After studying this chapter, you will be able to

✎ describe the importance of play and play activities in children's lives.

✎ explain how adults can help children learn through play, art, music, science, and reading.

Chapter 20
Teaching
Through Play

Define...
active-physical play
manipulative-constructive play
imitative-imaginative play
play therapy
language-logic play
prop box
visual arts
manipulative stage
scribbling
representation stage
transparencies
percussion instruments
rhythm instruments
melody percussion instruments

20-1 While playing with bubbles, a child can express what he or she knows as well as learn more about the nature of air and bubbles.
© John Shaw

Children are curious. They want to explore new objects, places, and people. Children are also eager learners. They ask countless questions as they strive for self-direction. Children express their learnings in many ways, such as through play, art, music, science, and literature.

Learning and expressing are closely related. Learnings are reflected in the way children express themselves. Their expressions expand and refine their learnings, 20-1.

Children need adults to encourage self-expression and help them learn. Adults can see what each child is ready to do. They can provide the time, space, and materials for activities. They can give children ideas, if needed. For the most part, children learn more from their senses and actions than from being told. Adults need to provide play experiences that teach children as well as those that simply amuse them.

Children and Their World of Play

Through play, children interact with the world of people and objects. Play can even take the form of ideas, such as word play and problem-solving games. Play is a self-chosen activity that children do for its own sake. Most of all, play is fun.

Importance of Play

Years ago, experts had not studied the value of play. They had not given it an important place in a person's life. Play—even for children—was not accepted in early history because children were expected to work. In the more recent past, play was seen as something children and adults did in their spare time. Today, experts know that play is important.

Play and Physical Development

One reason play is important is it helps a child's physical development. Play improves muscles and nerves. Activities help the heart and lung systems. Active children who play often are more likely to maintain a healthy weight. Play also improves balance and coordination, 20-2. Active children and adults tend to feel better physically than those who are not active.

Play and Mental Development

Children learn through play. In turn, children's play reflects what they have learned. Play helps children learn concepts about their physical world. Play also brings children in contact with objects. Children can cause objects to do many things. They observe the results of actions. Children soon see how objects differ. They also learn how objects are made and about their physical limits.

20-2 Pretend play can promote motor skills and help children learn about the roles of others.
Joe Blanco/Blanco Photography

Logical Concepts

Through play, children learn logical concepts. For example, children classify objects as they set up a grocery store or repair shop for pretend play. Children arrange objects in size order as they nest measuring cups in their play kitchens. Number concepts form as the child sees that adding more blocks makes a higher tower or longer train. In filling a sand pail, children see that small objects fit inside, but large ones will not. They may conserve as they pour objects from one container to another. Other logical concepts also develop.

Symbol Systems

Symbol systems are used in play, too. In symbol-type play, the child selects the most important aspects of an experience. For example, when playing with dolls, a child mostly feeds, bathes, clothes, and rocks the doll. When pretending to be a wild animal, a child may make loud sounds and engage in pretend attacks. Children make props to go along with their pretend play that are symbols for objects in the real world. Symbol-type play helps a child prepare for the more abstract written and spoken language symbols.

Language

Play helps children learn language. For the infant, the sound of peek-a-boo comes to signal the return of a person. Infants begin with babbling sounds, which are often heard during their play with adults. Toddlers may repeat one or two words as they march around the room or pretend to read a book. Preschool children try out new rhythm and sound patterns in language. They often repeat favorite lines of stories and nursery rhymes. School-age children try rhymes, jingles, and other forms of language sound patterns.

Humor and Creative Thinking

Humor is mental play. This type of play cannot begin until the child is well underway with his or her thinking skills. Usually it begins between the second and third year. When a child makes a change from reality or the usual, such as drawing a dog with wings, the child is showing humor. This type of humor is often called absurdities. Young children very much enjoy the type of absurdities found in Dr. Seuss' books (such as green eggs or an elephant hatching a bird's nest). As children develop, they see humor in language itself. School-age children, for example, like simple puns and idioms taken literally.

Play also improves creative thinking. Through play, children try new ideas. For this reason, children who play are apt to become artists and scientists as adults. During play, children can make mistakes without being corrected. Making mistakes is part of the creative process. Because they do not feel pressure, children enjoy learning new concepts through play. They also learn more through play than through any drilling process.

Play and Social-Emotional Development

Children become aware of others through play. Through this greater awareness, they develop trusting relationships. Babies play games only with people they trust, such as parents and other caregivers. Parents who play with their children during the childhood years seem to be close to them in later years.

In the preschool and school-age years, children play more frequently with peers than with adults. Playing with peers teaches children the concepts of rules, rights and property, sharing, and settling disputes. Children also learn acceptable and unacceptable behavior, as well as skills in teamwork and being a leader. In play, children

20-3 Playing as a group helps social development.
Del Monte Corp.

learn to detect others' feelings, too. Children who play well with others seem to have the most friends, 20-3.

Children work out many of their feelings and problems in play. They also use playtime to make things happen their own way. For example, preschool children often feel limited in what they can do or make happen. By playing dinosaurs, they can identify with the dinosaur's size and strength and make up for their own shortcomings.

Stages of Play

Children's play reflects changes that take place in their physical, mental, and social-emotional development. In a real way, play pulls together all aspects of development. For this reason, one expert referred to play as the highest level of child development.

Children go through stages of play as they grow. These stages build on each other. Babies do not begin to play in advanced stages. Older children learn to play in higher stages, but they can still play in earlier stages, too. When older children play with younger children, the stage of play most often fits the younger children. When children play with new objects, the stage of play may also become less advanced.

Stages of play are described in terms of the child's play with objects and people. Chart 20-4 shows stages of play with objects and people and how these two areas compare to each other. Because experts do not agree totally on these stages, the chart shows only one way to view the stages of play.

Types of Play

There are many types of play. One way to think about play is by its stages. Another way to think about play is by the basic skills involved. Types of skills involved in play include active-physical play, manipulative-constructive play, imitative-imaginative play, and language-logic play.

Stages of Play

Age	Play with Objects	Play with People
From a few months to school-age years	❖ Practice play—Babies explore objects by picking them up or tracking them with their eyes. Play activities are repeated.	❖ Solitary play—Babies ignore other children who are nearby. Sometimes babies treat others as objects to be pushed or walked on, to be poked in the eyes or nose, or to have hair pulled. ❖ Onlooker play—Toddlers watch others play but do not join in their play. ❖ Parallel play—Children play near other children and often play with the same or almost the same toys. They note that others have interests and skills much like their own. However, there is no real interaction among children.
From age 3 years through elementary grades	❖ Symbolic play—Children engage in fantasy play. They pretend they are someone else. Also, they project mental images on objects. For example, a stick can become a horse.	❖ Associative play—Two or more children play at a common activity. The children share ideas. However, the play is not well organized. For example, one child may decide to run a food store and another may be a mother, but the mother never shops at the food store.
Peaks at age 9 or 10 years	❖ Rule play—Children make rules to govern their games or carefully follow the rules already established.	❖ Cooperative play—Two or more children share common goals and play complementary roles, such as the chaser and the chased.

20-4 The stages of play can be described in terms of how children play with objects and how they interact with peers in play situations at each age.

Active-Physical Play

In **active-physical play**, children use gross-motor skills. These skills use the large muscles for movements like walking, running, hopping, jumping, twisting, bending, skipping, galloping, catching, throwing, balancing, pushing, pulling, and rocking.

Through active-physical play, children learn about the space around them. They also learn about objects in this space and the movement of the body. Names for movements and positions in space take on meaning. These names include *forward, backward, big, little, fast, slow, under, over, up, down, behind, in front of, through, beside,* and *between.*

Through play, children improve and test many physical skills. They learn how strong they are by pushing, pulling, lifting, and carrying. Children learn to spring to lift their body and catch themselves on impact. Upward movement is a skill they often need. Catching themselves the right way when they land protects the body from injury. Active-physical play also improves reaction time and balance. Reaction time improves as the body matures and the child practices. Children need balance for almost every gross-motor movement, 20-5.

Active-physical play helps children become more graceful. Grace improves when the gross-motor skills are developed. Grace is pleasing to see. It also helps a person engage in many more fun activities.

20-5 Balance, which children need for most activities, develops slowly.
Wood Designs of Monroe, Inc.

Manipulative-Constructive Play

Manipulative-constructive play involves fine-motor skills. These skills develop after the basic gross-motor movements. For example, the fine-motor skill of writing develops after the gross-motor skill of walking. However, some fine-motor skills do start to develop early in life. Crawling babies can pick up small objects (such as gravel and paper) on a carpet. They then can carefully put them in the mouth, ear, and nose. Eye-hand coordination is also involved in manipulative-constructive play.

Many toys and materials promote fine-motor skills. These include jigsaw puzzles, small blocks and construction materials, beads for stringing, pegs and pegboards, art tools, woodworking tools, and cooking tools. Toys that promote fine-motor skills are made for little, unskilled hands as well as for more skilled hands, 20-6.

Besides promoting fine-motor skills, manipulative-constructive play helps a child's ability to mentally picture objects. It also helps children make abstract models of what they see.

20-6 Some building toys are made for advanced fine-motor skills.
LEGO Dacta, the educational division of the LEGO Group

Imitative-Imaginative Play

In **imitative-imaginative play**, children pretend to be objects or persons other than themselves. They carry out this play verbally and/or in actions. There are three stages of imitative-imaginative play—imitative play, dramatic play, and socio-dramatic play.

Imitative Play

Imitative play begins at about two years of age, or just as children begin to use symbolic thought, 20-7. Symbolic thought allows the child to let one thing stand for another. For example, a stack of books may become a spaceship. In a similar way, symbolic thought also allows the child to do one imitative action to an object, such as feed a baby doll. Toddlers and young preschool children engage in imitative play for very short periods. However, they tend to repeat the same imitative play symbols and actions over days, weeks, and even months.

Dramatic Play

The second stage, dramatic play, begins when the child is three or four years of age. Dramatic play involves

active-physical play. Play that uses gross-motor skills.

manipulative-constructive play. Play that uses fine-motor skills.

imitative-imaginative play. Play in which children pretend to be persons or objects other than themselves.

20-7 For toddlers and young preschoolers, symbolic play is simple. Often, they use only one object and one action to symbolize the real object or event.
Angeles Group

role-playing with more than one child. Each child's role, however, is independent of the others' roles. For example, three children may be space creatures, but each child plays the game in his or her own way. These children may engage in collective monologue. Dramatic play often involves several behaviors associated with a role, such as a father who makes repairs, goes to work, and mows the grass.

Socio-Dramatic Play

In the last stage, socio-dramatic play, a group of five- to seven-year-olds plays with a theme. They assign roles to each child. Instead of just being space creatures, the children may pretend to look for new planets together. In this form of play, each child has a special role, 20-8.

Imitative-imaginative play has great value. Children learn to imagine or picture themselves as if they are other people and objects (symbolizing). This kind of play helps memory because children must recall events in play. It also helps language because children must listen and speak during play. There is much freedom in expression, too, as children try to bridge the gap between what they know and do not know. Children can use their bodies to extend their language.

20-8 As older children play house, they take on specific roles of adults. Symbolic play is much more advanced than in the earlier years.
Angeles Group

For example, a child may say, "I'm a barber," while using the fingers as if to snip hair. Much planning and decision making takes place as children choose roles, props, and actions in their play. Adults often see children's leadership roles emerging.

Children can use play to try out many roles. In this way, children get some feel for others' real-life roles. Children join in holiday and other rituals as they act out roles, 20-9. Many adult work and family roles began in childhood as play roles.

20-9 The mood and meaning of holidays are captured through role-playing.
Libby, McNeill and Libby, Inc.

Through play, children can also express fears, resentments, and even hostile feelings in ways that are socially approved. In fact, role-play can even have some healing qualities. For example, play therapy is the use of play between a child and a trained counselor to help the child resolve certain problems.

Language-Logic Play

Language-logic play is the form of mental play most often seen in school-age children. There are many different types of language and word games. In some language games, children compete using vocabulary skills. Other language games include humor that is based on language, such as puns. Logic games, such as chess and checkers, require much thought about one's actions. Children must think ahead and plan strategies for sports and table games, 20-10. Logic games also include object puzzles and word problems.

play therapy. Use of play between a child and a trained counselor to help the child resolve certain problems.

language-logic play. A form of mental play common in school-age children that involves words and logical concepts.

20-10 *Because school-age children have logic skills, they can plan strategy for board games and even play with adults.*
© Nancy P. Alexander

The Adult's Role in Children's Play

Adults have a major role in children's play. They must provide time, space, and materials. They need to allow for a great deal of free expression. Adults' attitudes toward play influence how a child views an activity. What adults do and say can promote or hamper children's creativity. Adults should provide play experiences that are important to children. To help children learn through play, adults also need to allow freedom to play, allow time to explore, display the right attitude toward play, and select toys with care.

In addition, sometimes parents can join in their children's play when

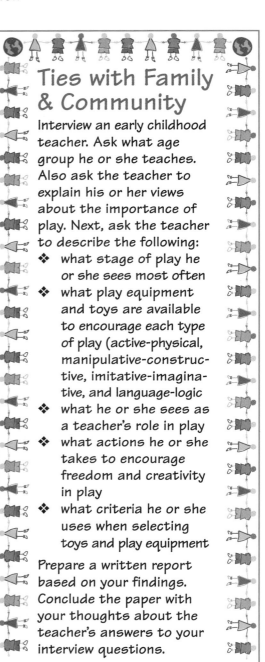

Ties with Family & Community

Interview an early childhood teacher. Ask what age group he or she teaches. Also ask the teacher to explain his or her views about the importance of play. Next, ask the teacher to describe the following:

❖ what stage of play he or she sees most often
❖ what play equipment and toys are available to encourage each type of play (active-physical, manipulative-constructive, imitative-imaginative, and language-logic
❖ what he or she sees as a teacher's role in play
❖ what actions he or she takes to encourage freedom and creativity in play
❖ what criteria he or she uses when selecting toys and play equipment

Prepare a written report based on your findings. Conclude the paper with your thoughts about the teacher's answers to your interview questions.

invited by the children. At these times, parents should let children choose the activity and lead the play.

Usually when an adult takes too much of a lead or becomes too involved, children stop playing and simply watch the adult.

Allow Freedom to Play

During play, children should be allowed as much freedom as possible, 20-11. Toys that have only one use, such as coloring books, can restrict children's play. Adults restrict play by setting many rules for safety or other reasons. Peers, too, restrict play by telling each other what and how to play. Although play can never be totally free, adults should help keep restrictions to a limit.

Allow Time to Explore

For the most part, adults should give children time to explore materials on their own. Adults can observe play and, at times, add ideas or materials.

20-11 Children should have as much freedom as possible in their play.

Children should decide whether to use them. One example of how to add ideas and materials is modeling an action, such as pretending to eat make-believe food. Adults can increase a child's language skills by adding to a child's growl. They may say, "Growl! I am a tiger looking at you with my big, green eyes." Adults can also explain new concepts. They can describe airplanes as objects that go quickly down a special road called a runway so they can fly in the air. They can use blocks and a toy plane to explain. Adults need to rotate toys or add new toys from time to time.

Display the Right Attitude Toward Play

Adults need to see the importance of play and express that feeling to children. Think of the attitude an adult expresses to a child when the adult says, "Can't you see I'm busy? Go away and play." Toys and play need to be seen as important, too.

Select Toys with Care

In daily play, children will use their toys extensively. For this reason, adults should select toys with care. Toys should be safe and fun. (See chapter 21 for more details about toy safety.)

Toys should be developmentally appropriate. Many infants and toddlers like texture toys, squeeze toys, stuffed toys, large balls, dolls, and toys that make sounds. Preschool children like toys for gross-motor play (balls, pedal toys, climbing toys) and fine-motor play (puzzles, beads, pegs). They also like floor blocks, dress-up clothes, puppets, toy cars, trucks, planes, animals, and people. Children can use prop boxes for role-playing, too. A **prop box** contains a set of real objects related to a certain role for children to use in play. For example, a prop box might contain the props needed to role-play a store clerk or nurse. Board games, computer games, and sports equipment are popular with school-age children. Older school-age children often like collectible toys, too.

Because each child is unique, children like different types of toys. Children's toy collections should be balanced, however. Children need to have various toys that aid all aspects of development.

Adults need to avoid giving too many toys that "perform." Examples of performing toys are battery-operated toys which perform one or more actions when switched on and toys that talk for the child. These toys do not allow much child involvement or stimulate creativity. Children need toys that let them be the "performers." Children can use open-ended toys, such as building blocks, art supplies, and balls in many ways, 20-12.

Toys should be planned for different play settings, such as indoors, outdoors, and travel. Travel toys must be chosen with much thought. These toys must be held in children's hands or laps. They must

20-12 In their play, these children are using balls in one of many creative ways.
Courtesy of GameTime, Fort Payne, Ala., USA

be safe in a moving car. They cannot make too much noise for a small space or distract the driver. Toys must be able to withstand the temperature of a closed car. Some toys and games are designed for travel. These toys include cassette tapes of songs and stories, magnetic game boards, and toys that attach to car seats or the back of the vehicle's front seat.

All toys should reflect positive social attitudes. Toys and equipment should be antibiased. The toys should represent people of both genders, all ages, and all cultural groups in a positive way. Toys should avoid stereotyping of any kind. For example, both male and female clothes (and even some gender-neutral clothes) should be provided for children's dramatic play. Props for role-playing should extend beyond the kitchen and reflect many other home tasks and work roles. Dolls and manipulatives with illustrations should reflect the diversity of society. Art materials should be available to represent various skin tones. Holiday materials should be included for various cultures.

Toys should also be nonviolent in nature. Guns and knives, for example, encourage playful aggressive acts in children. Sometimes, too, young children cannot tell the difference between a real weapon and a realistic toy or can mistake a real weapon for such a toy with devastating consequences. Toys should encourage cooperation with and respect for others.

Adults must be wise when purchasing toys. They should keep in mind children usually have too many toys. These toys are expensive, and thus overbuying goes against good consumer sense. Play space and storage space must also be considered.

Older children can learn many useful skills and have fun while making toys. Sometimes children spend as much time making toys as they do playing with them. Making toys also teaches children to save and recycle useful items often thrown away.

Providing Enrichment Activities for Children

Adults can provide many learning experiences that enrich children's lives. They can encourage creativity with the types of play they provide and the ways they value these activities. Experiences in art, music, science, and literature help children learn aesthetic, creative, and scientific concepts. These experiences can also help children appreciate both natural and created beauty. Having rich and fulfilling experiences in these areas also reinforces other basic learnings and helps children develop.

Art

Art is important in children's lives. **Visual arts**, such as painting, molding, and photography, create products that appeal to the sense of sight. Visual arts help children in many areas of development. For example, fine-motor skills improve as children handle paintbrushes, scissors, and crayons.

The arts increase intellectual learnings, too. Sensory experiences help children expand their concepts of color, line, shape, form, texture, and size. Because children create what they know, visual arts cause children to think about their world. Children then record their ideas in their finished products.

Finally, art helps children develop in social-emotional areas. Children

prop box. A container that holds a set of real objects related to a certain role for children's use in play.

visual arts. Forms of art that create products that appeal to the sense of sight.

make choices about what they want to do and how they want to do an art activity. Art helps them to express feelings, too. Taking pride in their art and knowing that others accept their products builds their self-esteem, 20-13.

Stages of Development in Visual Arts

Experts study the stages of children's development in the visual arts by watching children use art materials and looking at their finished products. A child's total development determines how he or she uses crayons, paints, clay, and other art materials. At first,

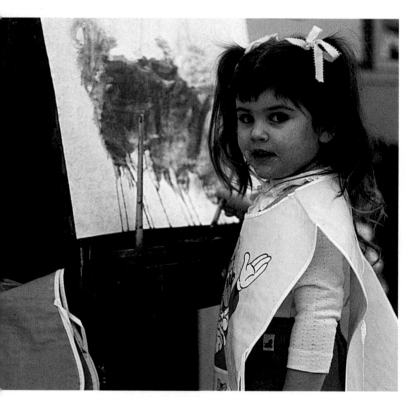

20-13 Children express their feelings through art.

children play with the art materials. They then use the materials to represent objects, experiences, and feelings. For these reasons, development is divided into the manipulative stage and the representation stage.

Manipulative Stage

In the **manipulative stage**, children play with art materials rather than use them to create artwork. Early in this stage, children under two years of age enjoy art for motor reasons. They cover paper with marks and pinch, pat, and even eat clay.

Soon the child begins to see what happens as a result of certain actions. At about 24 to 30 months, children begin the second step in this stage, called scribbling. **Scribbling** consists of dots, straight and curved lines, loops, spirals, and imperfect circles. Scribbling is important because the child must make the eyes and hands work together.

About 30 to 42 months, the third step in the manipulative stage occurs. The child begins to use basic shapes, such as crosses, rectangles (including squares), and ovals (including circles).

manipulative stage. First stage in children's visual-arts development in which they play with art materials rather than use them to create artwork.

scribbling. The second step in the manipulative stage of visual-arts development in which writing consists of dots, straight and curved lines, loops, spirals, and imperfect circles.

They combine shapes in drawings, too. Many of these shapes are lost in the layers and layers of crayon marks and paint.

In the transition step between the manipulative and representation stages, children ages 42 to 60 months create their first symbols. Because the child often decides what the symbol is after it is made, the symbol may or may not be named. The face is often the first and favorite symbol seen in children's drawings. Even when children draw a body, it appears to be an afterthought. Children add lines to the face to draw arms, hands, body, and legs. They use circles for feet or shoes, 20-14. The head remains the

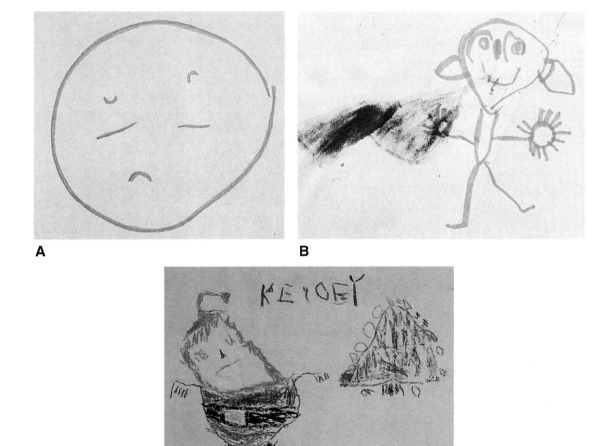

A

B

C

20-14 Human figure drawing begins with the head (A). Later, the child adds single lines to show trunk, arms, legs, fingers, and feet (B). Finally, the child adds details to the drawing (C).

largest part of children's drawings for years. Although drawings contain symbols, there are no spatial relations among objects. Symbols seem to float.

Representation Stage

Most five- or six-year-old children have reached the **representation stage**. In this stage, children create symbols that represent objects, experiences, and feelings. Adults can see a child has entered this stage when the child decides what the symbol is before creating it. ("I'm going to draw a tree.") Another signal is the child shows spatial relations among objects. In a simple spatial relationship, the child shows what is on the ground by using a baseline. (A *baseline* is a line of grass, dirt, or water drawn near the bottom of the paper. The baseline can also be the lower edge of the paper itself.) The sky often appears as a strip of color across the top of the paper. The child envisions air between the objects on the baseline and the sky, 20-15. A child may draw two or more baselines, which show objects at varying distances. The objects closest to the child always are drawn on the baseline closest to the lower edge of the paper.

Other spatial relations in the representative stage include folding over. *Folding over* is showing a spatial idea by drawing objects perpendicular to the baseline, even when it means drawing objects upside down, 20-16. Some children draw a mixture of side and top views in one drawing. A child may draw a table and chairs with the

20-15 A baseline of ground or water is the first way children show spatial relationships among objects.

20-16 Children often show objects that are across from each other by drawing objects at right angles to a baseline. This results in upside-down objects.

chairs showing from the side view and the whole top of the table showing, too.

In an effort to depict what they know about objects, rather than what is visually true, children's symbols often have certain features. Many times they *exaggerate* (or increase) size to show importance. A child may exaggerate the size of his or her parent in a drawing. Certain body parts may be exaggerated, too, such as arms that reach to the clouds to catch a ball or fly a kite.

Children often draw symbols pictured as transparencies. **Transparencies** are pictures that show the inside and outside of an object at the same time, much like an X ray. A drawing of a house may have windows on it, but it may show people and furniture inside the house as well. In other types of transparencies, children mix the profile and front views of an object. For example, a profile view of a person may show both eyes.

After age seven or eight years, representation becomes more advanced. Children draw a more detailed human face that shows expression, 20-17. Visual depth also becomes a part of these more advanced drawings, 20-18. Children draw the perspective of objects as they see it, not as they think it should look. By nine or ten years of age, children can draw objects from their perspective and from the perspective of others.

20-17 School-age children add many details to the human face.

 representation stage. Second stage in children's visual-arts development in which they create symbols to represent objects, experiences, and feelings.

transparencies. Pictures that show the inside and outside of an object at the same time, much like an X ray.

20-18 School-age children begin to include visual depth in their drawings.

The Adult's Role in Stimulating Art Experiences

Adults can stimulate art experiences by introducing children to artistic skills and art activities suited to their stages of development. They should provide art materials that allow children to explore and enrich their art skills. Adults can encourage children in their artwork in many ways.

In introducing children to art activities, adults should provide children with the right environment and supplies, 20-19. They must show children how to use artistic tools, such as scissors and paintbrushes. Once children understand how to use tools, adults should let children do their own work. They should not make models for children to copy or add to the child's work. Children's work reflects their

skill in handling tools and their way of seeing the world. See chart 20-20 for suggested art activities.

Adults should encourage children by showing interest in their artwork. They can help children try new techniques by saying they have confidence in the children. Adults can show interest by joining children in art activities. (However, adults should never compete.) They can also display children's artwork, which increases self-esteem.

Reacting to Children's Art

When children show adults their artwork, what should adults say? A good response is to ask the child to tell them about the work. Adults can say, "Can you tell me about your drawing (painting, clay project, or other)?" This is a better response than asking, "What is it?"

When children don't know what they should draw or color and ask for ideas, adults can suggest three ideas. The child then can choose the one or ones that appeal the most. This may even inspire more creative thinking, and the child may come up with his or her own ideas.

Music

Sounds in many pitches, rhythmic patterns, and degrees of loudness are the parts of music. These parts surround people from birth. Children hear sounds and respond to them by paying attention, moving, and making

Environment and Supplies for the Visual Arts

The Environment

Space
- ❖ Find a place to draw, paint, model clay, cut and paste. The space must be easy to clean, such as a kitchen, playroom, or outside.

Storage
- ❖ Use a large cardboard box to store supplies. You may decorate the box with the child's favorite artwork.

Display
- ❖ Hang pictures on the refrigerator with magnets, mount pictures on a bulletin board, or display them in a picture frame. Change artwork frequently.

Keeping artwork
- ❖ Select a few products and store them in scrapbooks or photo albums.

The Supplies

Paper
- ❖ Buy newsprint and construction paper, shelf paper, and paper bags.

Crayons
- ❖ Buy large crayons (suited for small hands) in the eight basic colors. (For young children, nontoxic, washable crayons are best.)

Paint
- ❖ Buy dry tempera that is mixed with water for brush painting and with liquid starch for finger painting.

Pudding Finger Paint
Prepare instant vanilla pudding to which a few drops of food coloring has been added.

Scissors
- ❖ Buy quality child-sized scissors. Scissors are available for left- and right-handed children. Depending on a child's age, select either blunt or pointed styles.

Paintbrushes
- ❖ Buy three or four brushes with short handles and bristles that are about one inch wide.

Paste
- ❖ Buy white paste or glue that works on paper and cloth. You may also make your own paste.

Flour Paste
1 cup flour
½ cup water
Combine flour and water. Mix well until creamy. Store in covered container.

Clay
- ❖ Buy Plasticine® (clay that remains soft due to oil) or play dough. You may also make play dough using these recipes.

Peanut Butter Play Dough
2 cups peanut butter
1 cup flour
1 cup confectioner's sugar
Combine and mix.

Play Dough
2 cups flour	2 tablespoons salad oil
1 cup salt	4 teaspoons cream of tartar
2 cups water	food coloring

Combine and cook until mixture thickens into a soft ball. When cool enough to handle, knead. Store in an airtight container.

Collage materials
- ❖ Collect alphabet cereal, pasta, dried beans or peas, seeds, boxes, cloth, yarn, ribbon, paper, flowers, leaves, twigs, straws, and other objects that children can glue to a flat surface.

Art smock and cleanup supplies
- ❖ Use an old, long-sleeved shirt. Cut sleeves to child's wrist length and put on backwards. Button only the top button. Use a piece of vinyl to cover the worktable.

20-19 The right environment and supplies enhance art learnings.

Art Activities

Squeeze-bag art

Use a self-locking, clear food storage bag. Put a few tablespoons of finger paint inside. Smooth the bag until paint covers the inside of the bag with a solid film. Press air out, lock the bag, and seal the bag with tape. Place the bag on a flat surface. The child can draw on it with fingers. To renew drawing surface, rub the bag lightly with your hand.

Deodorant-bottle pens

Gather deodorant bottles that have rings and balls. Remove the rings and balls. Fill bottles with tempera paint mixed with water, then replace the rings and balls. (Do not use starch in tempera.) Children can roll paint on paper to make designs.

20-20 Children enjoy art activities such as these.

sounds. Thus, musical development is like all other development. Those children who have had a rich world of sound and movement will have a good background for later learnings and pleasure.

For young children, there is a oneness between movement and music. Even toddlers move to music without being prompted by adults. Because young children need chances to move, music can be a fun way to support this need.

Benefits of Music Experiences

Music provides chances for sensory and expressive experiences.

Listening to music is the basis of all musical learning. As children become more attuned to the sounds around them, they learn to translate the sounds in musical ways. They may say that sounds have a high or low pitch or an even or uneven rhythm. Also, listening to the sounds of music can improve children's listening skills in general.

Making music is fun. Even babies invent ways to make sounds. They shake or hit objects and make sounds with their voices and hands. When children are able to care for musical instruments, adults should encourage them in learning to play them.

Many instruments require more finger strength and skill than young children have. For these reasons, the first instruments children use are often percussion instruments. The tones of **percussion instruments** are produced when struck. Percussion instruments without a definite pitch, such as most drums, are called **rhythm instruments**. In contrast, **melody percussion instruments**, such as xylophones, produce various pitches when certain bars are struck, 20-21. By using these instruments, young children see how sounds are made, play rhythmic patterns, and perhaps play simple melodies. With special training, some young children become quite skilled in playing an instrument. In fact, many professional musicians began playing instruments between three and five years of age.

Singing seems to make children feel good. They often sing or chant to

20-21 Rhythm instruments are the best instruments for young children.
Lakeshore Learning Materials; Carson, Calif.

tell what they are doing. ("Feed...ing ba...by.") They use the same words for singing as they do for speaking. Thus, singing helps language learnings.

Although young children do enjoy singing, they often cannot carry a tune. They are not able to match their voice pitch to the notes of the music. Until young children find a singing voice, they simply talk in a sustained hum they call singing. When the singing voice is found, the range is often limited to about six tones (from middle C to A). By practicing and

listening, children can develop singing skills over time.

Preschool children may also have problems singing with other voices or with musical instruments. In order to sing with others, a child must hear his or her own voice, the voices of other singers or instruments, and the unison sound.

The Adult's Role in Guiding Music Experiences

To guide music experiences, the adult must introduce children to music activities suited to their interests. These areas include listening, singing, playing instruments, and moving to music, 20-22. In addition to providing activities, adults can provide an environment that is rich in sound. They can model enthusiasm and appreciate a variety of music.

Perhaps the adult's most difficult role is listening to and praising children's musical attempts. Children need adult encouragement if they are to practice enough to gain musical

percussion instruments. Musical instruments that produce a tone when struck.

rhythm instruments. Percussion instruments without a definite pitch, such as most drums.

melody percussion instruments. Instruments that produce various pitches when certain bars are struck, such as xylophones.

Music Activities

Hearing sounds

Play tapes that feature sounds in nature and sounds that manufactured products make. Talk about the tones heard in terms of sound qualities like *high-low, loud-soft, near-far,* and *continuous-discontinuous.* Also talk about the direction of the sound.

Story sounds

Read stories that mention sounds. Ask children to make the sounds mentioned in the story using their voices, their bodies, or objects.

Matching sounds

Play different tones using an instrument. Ask the child to match his or her voice to the pitch. (Notes should be between middle C and one octave above middle C.) For a variation, match rhythms by tapping a simple rhythmic pattern and having the child echo the pattern. After the children echo several patterns, ask a child to play a pattern and let you echo.

Finding the sound

Have children pretend to be kittens or other animals that make sounds. Have the kittens hide while mother cat (one of the children) pretends to be asleep. After the kittens have hidden, the mother cat awakens and meows to her kittens. Kittens meow in response, and the mother cat must find the kittens by following the sounds. For a variation, have the children point in the direction of a sound they hear. You may also have children locate a loudly ticking clock or metronome you have hidden.

20-22 *Music activities provide rich sensory and expressive experiences.*

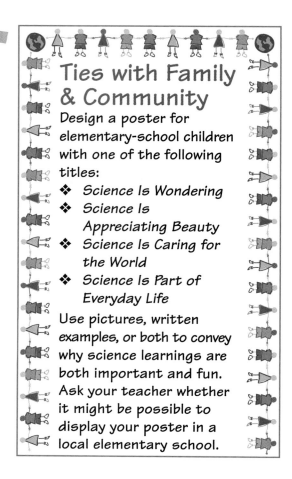

Ties with Family & Community

Design a poster for elementary-school children with one of the following titles:

❖ *Science Is Wondering*
❖ *Science Is Appreciating Beauty*
❖ *Science Is Caring for the World*
❖ *Science Is Part of Everyday Life*

Use pictures, written examples, or both to convey why science learnings are both important and fun. Ask your teacher whether it might be possible to display your poster in a local elementary school.

skills. Especially during the school years parents and other adults may listen to many less-than-perfect performances. However, with loving acceptance children can become skilled musicians or, at least, learn to appreciate music.

Science

Children are born scientists. They wonder and seek answers. They test their answers repeatedly. The raw materials of science surround children in their homes, yards, group programs, and schools.

What Is Science?

To children, science is wondering about the world and everything in it. Before they can wonder, children must progress through a few steps. They must be aware, then focus on an object or happening by ignoring other things, and then observe, 20-23.

Science is part of everyday life. Children experience science when they catch a cricket, put it in a jar, and watch it. They experience science when they watch water freeze and see snow melt. Children can learn about science when they ask, "Why do I need to eat my green beans?" or, "How do clouds move?"

Science is appreciating beauty. Most children are awed by the world of living and nonliving matter. They are eager to share what they find with others, 20-24.

Science is caring for the world. For the most part, children translate beauty into caring. However, because of their young minds, children may not know living things can be hurt or even killed. They may not understand

20-23 All scientists—both children and adults—observe in order to learn.
Lakeshore Learning Materials; Carson, Calif.

20-24 Children like to share special objects they find in nature.
© Nancy P. Alexander

that resources such as water, land, and air can be damaged. They may not realize people can spoil beauty when they are not careful.

The Adult's Role in Encouraging Science Activities

Adults should encourage children to wonder, appreciate the beauty of their world, and focus on science in everyday life. Adults can call attention to the beauty of many science concepts. These include light coming through a prism, colors on butterflies' wings, the smell of roses, and the songs of birds. Adults can also read books on nature to children. They can visit zoos, gardens, and forests together. (Some places have special children's tours.) Adults can help children form collections of beautiful things, such as seeds, rocks, and shells.

Children usually explore and ask questions without being led by adults. However, adults can use some methods to help children explore. They can ask children to name the sense(s) used in learning about many objects— a bell, a rainbow, the rain, foods, a frog, or any other object. Adults can encourage children to classify objects. Adults may ask, "How are these two objects alike? How are they different?" Adults should also ask many questions to encourage children to test ideas. Adults may ask, "What goes through a sifter?" "What do magnets pick up?" "Which objects float?" "What would happen if. . . ?"

Lessons on caring for nature should begin early. Adults can begin by giving children tasks in caring for living things starting in the toddler years, 20-25. (The task must match the child's age.) Adults should also model care for the environment. This includes saving energy in the home and reminding children to turn off lights and running water. Families should also help with cleanup work around the home and in their community.

Focus of Science Activities

Science activities should focus on what children see and question around them. Science should never be a magic show. Instead, adults should explain science so children can learn about the world. For this reason, the topics and their order may differ from child to child. Generally speaking, topics should focus on children's questions and play activities.

20-25 Children must learn to care for the treasures of nature, such as animals, early in life.

Children like living creatures of all sizes. They need to watch, listen to, and touch animals, when appropriate. Most of all, children need to develop a respect for living things.

Children should focus on substances (physical matter of things). As children play, they handle liquid, granular, and solid substances. Activities can focus on the attributes of substances. An adult may ask, "What is water like?" See 20-26. Other activities can focus on what objects can be made from (or with) a substance or how the substance is used. When children are doing these activities, they are learning physical knowledge concepts.

Children can overcome some fears with science facts. For example, many children fear thunderstorms. By the early school years, children can understand the causes of thunder and lightning with adults' help. Adults can explain thunder as a loud noise caused by lightning, which rapidly heats the air causing it to expand. (To demonstrate the sound, blow up a paper bag, hold the neck of the bag tightly, and hit the bag with the other hand. As the air expands and breaks the bag, there is a pop.) Lightning is a flash in the sky caused by energy (electricity) being released. In a dark room, you can create "lightning" (static electricity) by rubbing two inflated balloons on your clothes, then holding the balloons close to each other. A spark should jump between the two balloons much as lightning does within a cloud or between a cloud and the ground.

Children should focus on fun activities that can involve many learnings, 20-27. For example, cooking is one of the best ways to learn many science concepts, and both preparing and eating food is fun.

Children's books and magazines are filled with science learnings and activities. Television programs and the Internet are great learning resources, too. Children's interests can be easily matched with these resources.

20-26 Children need to have many firsthand experiences with substances like water.
© John Shaw

20-27 Cooking activities can help children learn about science.
© John Shaw

Literature

Literature opens up a world of magic and new ideas for children. What child is not enchanted with stories and poems? Literature entertains and is an important learning tool for children. Through books, children learn pleasant lessons in concepts and language.

Benefits to Children

Books enrich life and help children appreciate beauty. Books answer children's endless questions and cause them to want to learn. Through quality stories and poems, children hear the rhythm of language, the rise and fall of the voice, and tongue-tickling phrases.

Reading to children builds their active and passive vocabularies. Children then may make up their own stories and poems at an early age, 20-28. A young child made up

Disappearing Candy on Halloween

Once there was a jack-o'-lantern who sat in a windowsill and thought, "I'll never get to go somewhere. All I do is sit on a dumb windowsill on Halloween night while kids get to go trick-or-treating. Then they get candy. All I get is lighted with a match!" But the jack-o'-lantern was wrong. That night, a little girl picked up the jack-o'-lantern and put candy in him. Every once in a while there would be a "Crunch! Crunch!" Then the neighbors would say, "You are getting sleepy." When the girl got tired of trick-or-treating, she went home. She decided to eat her candy. Then she reached inside the jack-o'-lantern and pulled out nothing. She picked up jack-o'-lantern and stared with her eyes as big as saucers. She asked, "What has happened to my candy?" She began trick-or-treating again. Meanwhile back at the house, jack-o'-lantern thought, "Well, I guess Halloween is not so bad as long as you are patient and have bushels of candy."
—Kelcey, age seven

The Sad Pumpkin

Once there was a pumpkin. He hated any pie. One day someone gave him some pie and he began to cry. The cook asked, "Why are you crying?" He said, "Because I hate this pie." And when the cook heard this, she too began to cry. The maid came in, and when she saw the mess she said, "What's the meaning of this? I really cannot guess." And when the maid heard, she too began to cry. When the wise man came in, he gave a big, long sigh. He said, "This pumpkin hates it 'cause it's pumpkin pie."

—Keith, age seven

20-28 Children who are read to often use their rich source of background material for original works.

this poem while watching water flow from a water hose. "Water drip, water fall, running down my outside wall." (Keith, age three years.)

Children who have learned to love books can express themselves through dramatic play, art, music, and other experiences, 20-29. They are able to express themselves and their feelings in many forms.

Young children like to hear stories about others their age and about people and things with which they are familiar. They better understand themselves by hearing stories that draw on their backgrounds. Older children may want to expand their learning by reading about topics that are less familiar to them.

Selecting Books for Children

In order for books and other literature to stretch the mind and stir creativity, adults must choose them with care. A children's librarian can help adults make good choices.

Books need to be on the child's level. Babies and toddlers enjoy

20-29 *Children enjoy drawing their favorite stories.*
Maggie Scudella

hearing nursery rhymes. Toddlers and preschool children enjoy picture books with quality pictures. First picture books need only simple captions (or perhaps no captions at all). Later picture books have simple plots. In picture books the pictures tell the story. Books for older children have more involved plots and more written description. Now the mind creates the pictures.

Children should experience books with delight. Story time should help children relax. Adults should hold children as they read or seat children close to them. They should also read in interesting ways, using inflections and different voices. Children should be able to see pictures clearly. Adults can encourage remarks or laughter as they read.

Adults can plan some follow-up activities after reading a story or poem. These activities do not have to immediately follow the story. However, they should occur while the book is still fresh in the child's mind. Follow-up activities include talking about the story, finding details in the pictures, and relating the book to the child's own experiences. Other activities are drawing, making a model, or enjoy a cooking activity related to the story. Children can also do activities discussed in the book, such as going to the zoo. This makes the story or poem more meaningful to them.

Children learn much from their play.

Summing It Up

Play helps children develop in many ways. Children's play tends to reflect the changes in their developmental levels. Basic skill types of play include active-physical, manipulative-constructive, imitative-imaginative, and language-logic play.

Adults need to allow children freedom to play and time to explore. Their attitude should reflect the importance of play. Adults should choose safe and fun toys. Selections should also be based on the age of the child and type of play settings. Children can also make many toys from objects found at home.

Adults should promote learning experiences in art, music, science, and through literature. Children can learn many skills that enrich their lives through these activities.

As their art skills develop, children will progress through stages. Adults need to provide the right environment and supplies to help children with their art activities. They should be supportive and show interest in their children's artwork.

At an early age children move to the sound of music. Most children enjoy singing and making music. Adults can introduce music activities and provide an environment that is rich in sound and movement.

Children's exploring and observing leads to many questions about science concepts. Adults can encourage children's curiosity about the world and help them seek answers to their questions.

Children who have stories and poems read to them increase their language development and self-expression. Adults should choose books and literature with the child's age and interests in mind. Follow-up activities help to reinforce learnings.

Reviewing Key Concepts

Write your answers on a separate sheet of paper.

1. Play helps children with which of the following?
   A. physical development
   B. mental development
   C. social-emotional development
   D. All of the above.
2. Match the type of play with the basic skills.
   Types of play
   _____ active-physical play
   _____ manipulative-constructive play
   _____ imitative-imaginative play
   _____ language-logic play
   Skills
   A. symbolizing skills
   B. fine-motor skills
   C. gross-motor skills
   D. high-level mental skills
3. True or false. Different types of skills develop through different types of play.
4. True or false. Visual arts are mainly important for social-emotional reasons.
5. True or false. Scribbling has no value in the child's art development.
6. True or false. When children use a baseline in their artwork, they are showing spatial relationships.
7. True or false. Children begin to use transparency symbols in their artwork when they are between two and three years of age.
8. Listening to the sounds of music _____ (can, cannot) improve children's general listening skills.
9. True or false. Rhythm instruments are often the first musical instruments children use.
10. True or false. Children's science learnings are mainly made up of special activities planned for children.
11. True or false. Children's spoken language reflects what has been read to them.
12. Explain how books can help children appreciate beauty.

Using Your Knowledge

1. **Role-Play.** Work with a small group to role-play the various stages and types of play as described in the chapter.
2. **Mathematics/Consumer Skills/Technology.** Review the recipes for finger paint, paste, and play dough (not peanut butter play dough) given in Chart 20-19. For each recipe, calculate the cost of the ingredients if you were to buy them in a grocery store. Next, shop online to price commercially prepared finger paint, paste, and play dough. Compare the prices of the homemade and store-bought supplies. How would the costs compare if you already had on hand the items needed to prepare the recipes yourself?
3. **Creative Skills/Career Skills.** Help an older preschool or school-age child make a simple musical instrument. The books *Music and Instruments for Children to Make* (Book 1 and Book 2) by John and Martha Faulhaber Hawkinson are good resources. Your music teacher

may also have more resources you could use.

4. **Technology/Consumer Skills.** Shop online or visit a local library to search for books adults can use to guide children in science activities. Use a computer to create a bibliography listing at least three such books. For each book, include the title, author, copyright date, publisher, and a brief paragraph describing the book.

5. **Language Arts/Career Skills.** Select and read a book to a child. Use a follow-up activity with the story. Report to the class how the child responded to the story and follow-up activity.

Making Observations

1. Observe children of different ages at play. Using Chart 20-4 as a reference, identify each stage of play you observe. Also identify the type or types of play involved. Support your findings with information from the text.

2. Observe a teacher encouraging children's creative development in visual arts or music. How does the teacher guide the children's development? How are the children reacting? What skills are children developing? Do the children seem to enjoy the experiences? Why or why not?

3. Observe children as they select books in a preschool center. Listen to the children talk with each other about the books. Describe the types of books that interest young children. (Note subject matter; illustrations; novelty items, such as pop-up pictures; or fun language, such as rhymes.)

Thinking Further

1. If you watch a group of children during free-play time, you will note they show preferences for active-physical, manipulative-constructive, imitative-imaginative, and language-logic play. What connections do you see between the children's personalities and their play choices? Which type of play did you prefer as a child? Do you see any connection between preferred play as a young child and your preferences for study, leisure, or work activities now? Explain.

2. The text states, "a child's total development determines how he or she uses crayons, paints, clay, and other materials." Make a collection of children's creative artwork. How is the child's physical, intellectual, and social-emotional development reflected in each piece of art?

3. Why is play one of the best ways to learn? Can you still learn through play? Give some examples.

Helena's family child care home serves children ages six months to six years. Helena doesn't know how to handle a toy safety issue. The preschoolers want to play with smaller, more advanced toys that are inappropriate and unsafe for the younger children. Helena considers these options: offering only toys that are appropriate for all children, limiting use of smaller toys to younger children's naptimes, or provide a separate area for the older children to play with these toys. Helena decides to call her state's agency in charge of family child care homes to ask for advice.

Chapter 21
Protecting Children's Health and Safety

After studying this chapter, you will be able to

- explain ways to protect children from diseases and illnesses.
- create a safe environment for young children.
- teach young children simple safety practices.
- discuss the steps in preparing a child for medical care in the doctor's office, in the hospital, and at home.

Define...

- dental caries
- orthodontist
- immunity
- antibodies
- naturally acquired immunity
- artificially acquired immunity
- antigens
- immunization
- active immunity
- passive immunity
- symptoms
- contagious disease
- allergy
- allergen
- childproofing
- restraint systems
- certified child safety seats
- safety recall
- LATCH system
- child passenger seat technician (CPS)
- filtering program
- first aid
- diagnosis
- terminally ill

Today's advances in health and safety are greater than ever before. However, growing up is still risky business. Each day, infants and children face the risks of illness, injury, and even death. Sometimes people can control these risks while other times they cannot. In particular, careful supervision and childproofing can help children avoid many risks altogether. Adults who care for children have a huge responsibility when it comes to keeping them healthy and safe.

Protecting Children from Disease and Illness

How can a disease, an injury, or an abnormal condition affect a child? Any one of these may cause pain, life-long physical health problems, and damage to self-esteem. When health problems are prevented, detected early, or treated properly, children have a better chance of leading a healthy and happy life.

Nutrition, Rest, Cleanliness, and Physical Activity

What are a person's basic needs? For good health, a person must meet his or her needs for good nutrition, rest, cleanliness, and physical activity. People must meet these basic needs throughout life. However, paying careful attention to them may be more important in childhood than at any other time, 21-1.

Basic health care is important because it helps children grow and develop properly. In turn, good health provides children energy for their daily activities. When a disease or

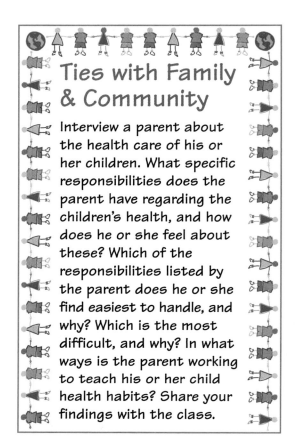

Ties with Family & Community

Interview a parent about the health care of his or her children. What specific responsibilities does the parent have regarding the children's health, and how does he or she feel about these? Which of the responsibilities listed by the parent does he or she find easiest to handle, and why? Which is the most difficult, and why? In what ways is the parent working to teach his or her child health habits? Share your findings with the class.

21-1 Children who are in good health are happy and ready to learn.
© John Shaw

injury occurs, children who are otherwise healthy tend to recover quickly and completely. Also, neglecting health needs for long periods causes health problems that medical science cannot repair.

Adults need to help children meet their basic physical needs starting early in life. In addition, adults must model good health practices. These actions positively affect children's health. Parents' actions may also help children develop good, lifelong health care habits.

Medical and Dental Care

The goal of health care is to keep children well. To do so, doctors examine children regularly, not just when they are sick. You have read about well-child checkups in earlier chapters of this text. These checkups may find possible health problems before they become serious. They may even prevent problems altogether.

Doctors check children's growth and development. They protect children from certain diseases. They also note eating, sleeping, and playing habits. Doctors answer parents' questions about their child's development.

Because well-child checkups are so important, doctors suggest a schedule for regular visits. The schedule varies slightly among doctors, but the American Academy of Pediatrics suggests some general guidelines. The AAP recommends at least nine well-child checkups during the first three years, not including checkups made between birth and discharge from the hospital. This schedule usually included 1-, 2-, 3-, 6-, 9-, 12-, 18-, 24-, and 36-month checkups. A yearly examination is recommended after three years of age. Babies of nursing mothers may have extra checkups during their early weeks to make sure they are gaining weight properly (a sign they are getting enough milk). Also, premature babies are often seen by their doctors more frequently because their health and development are more vulnerable than full-term babies.

Dental care by pediatric or family dentists should begin by the first birthday and be repeated every six months afterward. Dentists clean teeth. They inspect and X ray teeth, if necessary, for **dental caries** (decayed places in teeth). Dentists repair damaged teeth and teach children how to care for their teeth. After the permanent molars come in, many dentists recommend sealants. These are plastic coatings that protect the chewing surfaces of the teeth and thus, prevent dental caries.

If a child's teeth are irregular, the child's dentist may refer him or her to an orthodontist. An **orthodontist** is a dentist who specializes in correcting irregular teeth. For example, an orthodontist may make crooked teeth straight. When teeth are straight, a pretty smile is not the only benefit. Straight teeth allow people to chew food properly and clean teeth more easily. Having straight teeth also decreases the chance of tooth and gum disease, 21-2.

Dental hygiene should begin at birth. The American Academy of Pediatric Dentistry recommends wiping a baby's gums and teeth with water-dampened gauze or a soft, clean baby washcloth after each feeding for the first year. For children ages one to seven or eight years, they recommend the following:

❖ Brush teeth twice daily with a baby toothbrush. If only one brushing can be done daily, it should be before the baby goes to sleep each night.

❖ Brush without toothpaste until the child is two years of age or learns to spit. (Low fluoride toothpaste should be used until three years of age to keep children from swallowing

dental caries. Decayed places in teeth.

orthodontist. A dentist who specializes in correcting irregular teeth.

21-2 Even teeth that look right at first glance may need straightening for good dental health.
American Association of Orthodontists

too much fluoride, which can discolor the teeth.) Begin with a tiny smear of toothpaste and gradually increase the amount to the size of a pea by six years of age.

❖ Brush in a circular motion on both the inside and outside surfaces of teeth and gums. Brush top to bottom and back to front. Brush the top of the tongue. Brushing

should last a couple of minutes. Swish with water.
❖ Rinse mouth after eating if not brushing.
❖ Floss adjacent teeth as soon as they erupt.
❖ Avoid offering bottles in bed. If a bottle is needed, use boiled unsweetened water at night.
❖ Give milk and juice only at mealtimes. Sweet drinks, such as fruit juices, should be served only in a cup. Offer milk from a cup beginning soon after 12 months of age.
❖ Because brushing is a complex fine-motor skill, children cannot begin brushing their own teeth until they are about five years old. (Of course, before this age they can begin practicing toothbrush use after each brushing.) Parents should continue to supervise and help with brushing until children are seven or eight years old.
❖ Adults should practice good dental hygiene. This sets an example for the child. It also reduces the spread of bacteria from the parents' mouth to the child's mouth in kissing.
❖ Wash toothbrushes once a week in a dishwasher, or with soap and water. Store brushes bristle-end up. Replace brushes every three to four months.

Immunization

Immunity is the body's defense against disease. Scientists speak about several types of immunity. The body has some *general immunities*, which defend against many diseases. These defenses include skin, some types of cells, fever, and inflammation. For the most part, however, the body needs *specific immunity* to defend against a particular disease. To form these immunities, the body must develop or receive specific **antibodies**, which are proteins in the blood that fight disease.

Specific immunity can be one of two types. **Naturally acquired immunities** (sometimes called *natural immunities*) are developed after direct contact with infection or by receiving antibodies from the mother during pregnancy or breast-feeding. Naturally acquired immunities can be quite long-lasting, sometimes lasting a lifetime.

Natural exposure to some diseases is dangerous or deadly, however. A person wouldn't risk exposure to these diseases as a way to build immunity. Instead, the person might receive **artificially acquired immunities** (sometimes called *acquired immunities*). These immunities form as a person's reaction to antibodies or an antigen received through medical care. **Antigens** are substances made in a laboratory and transferred to people in the form of an injection (shot). An antigen is made from the bacteria, viruses, or toxins that cause diseases, but it is not as strong as the disease itself. When the antigen is injected into the body, the body builds antibodies to fight it. These antibodies will remain in the body to protect the person

against the illness in the future. Doctors call this type of protection **immunization**. Other terms with the same meaning are *vaccination* and *inoculation*. For some illnesses, the body needs a series of immunizations to build a strong defense.

Specific immunities can also be described as active or passive. **Active immunity** is when the person's own

immunity. Having agents that prevent a person from developing a disease.

antibodies. Proteins in the blood that fight disease.

naturally acquired immunities. Immunities that are developed after direct contact with infection or by receiving antibodies from the mother during pregnancy or breast-feeding; also called *natural immunities*.

artificially acquired immunities. Immunities formed as a reaction to antibodies or an antigen received through medical care; also called *acquired immunities*.

antigens. Substances made in a laboratory and transferred to people in the form of an injection (shot) to help their bodies form antibodies against a disease.

immunization. An injection of antigens given to a person to provide immunity from a certain disease.

active immunity. Immunity in which a person's own body must produce antibodies to a disease.

body must produce antibodies. This occurs during direct exposure to the illness or the antigen in an immunization. Active immunity takes several days or even weeks to become effective. This is the time when the body needs to react by making antibodies. Once developed, this immunity lasts several years or a lifetime. **Passive immunity** results when antibodies are produced by one person's exposure to a disease and then passed to another person. This is what happens when mothers pass antibodies to their unborn babies across the placenta. It can also happen for a few days after birth when mothers breast-feed their newborns. A person can also receive a transfusion of antibodies that were made by someone else's body. These antibodies can be made into an antiserum and given when people need immediate immunity and cannot wait for their bodies to build antibodies. An example would be when a person is bitten by an animal with rabies. Passive immunity lasts only a few weeks.

To fully describe immunity, scientists refer to both types of specific immunities in one name. For example, when they speak of immunization, scientists would call it artificially acquired active immunity.

Immunizations prevent some serious diseases. These diseases once caused serious illness and death, mainly among children. They include tetanus, diphtheria, pertussis (whooping cough), polio, measles, rubella (German measles), mumps, and chicken pox.

Infants should begin receiving immunizations at birth. Most doctors agree immunizations that begin at birth give children the most protection from disease. Immunizations should protect the baby without competing with antibodies received from the mother. The immunization schedule in chart 21-3 is based on current knowledge.

Children's doctors keep records of immunizations. Doctors check these records before giving more doses. Schools and camps also require them as official records. Parents should keep a record, too, for their own information.

Medical Attention During Illness

Sometimes children need special medical attention. Many childhood illnesses end quickly without cause for worry. However, many **symptoms** (signs of an illness or injury) may reveal a need for prompt medical help. Chart 21-4 lists some major symptoms for which adults should consult a doctor. Even if they notice vague symptoms, adults should call a doctor if the child's behavior seems abnormal.

passive immunity. Immunity in which a person obtains antibodies formed by another person's body.

symptoms. Signs of an illness or injury.

Recommended Childhood Immunizations

Age	Immunization	Comment
Birth to 2 months	HepB-1	Timing of first dose depends on mother's hepatitis B status.
1 to 4 months	HepB-2	Timing of second dose depends on age at first dose.
2 months	Hib-1; IPV-1; DTaP-1; P-1	IPV can be given as early as age one month in high-risk areas or during outbreaks.
4 months	Hib-2; IPV-2; DTaP-2; P-2	Two-month interval is recommended between first and second doses of IPV.
6 months	Hib-3; DTaP-3; P-3	
6 to 18 months	HepB-3; IPV-3	
12 to 15 months	Hib-4; MMR-1	MMR should be given at 12 months in high-risk areas.
12 to 18 months	P-4; Var	Var may be given to susceptible children at or after 12 months. Unvaccinated children who do not have a reliable history of chicken pox should be immunized at the 11- to 12-year visit. Susceptible people age 13 years and older should receive two doses at least one month apart.
15 to 18 months	DTaP-4	
24 months and 30 months	HepA-1 and HepA-2	Recommended in selected areas of U.S.
4 to 6 years	IPV-4; DTaP-5; MMR-2	DTaP and IPV should be given at or before school entry. DTaP should not be given at or after the seventh birthday.
11 to 12 years	MMR	MMR should be given at entry to middle or junior high school, unless two doses were given after the first birthday.
14 to 16 years	td	Repeat every 10 years throughout life.

Vaccine Abbreviations:

- ❖ HepB—hepatitis B virus vaccine
- ❖ Hib—Haemophilus influenzae type b conjugate vaccine
- ❖ IPV—inactivated polio virus vaccine
- ❖ DTaP—diphtheria and tetanus toxoids and acellular pertussis vaccine
- ❖ P—pneumococcal vaccine
- ❖ MMR—live measles, mumps, and rubella viruses vaccine
- ❖ Var—Varicella (chicken pox) vaccine
- ❖ HepA—hepatitis A virus vaccine
- ❖ td—adult tetanus (full dose) and diphtheria toxoid (reduced dose) for people ages 7 years and older

21-3 This schedule recommends infants start their immunization program at birth.

Symptoms Indicating Possible Illness

Area of Concern	Symptom
Blood	❖ large amount lost in bleeding ❖ bleeding will not stop
Body movement	❖ convulsions ❖ immobility in any part of the body ❖ shaking ❖ stiffness of the body
Bones and muscles	❖ swelling ❖ pain ❖ difficulty in movement
Brain	❖ dizziness ❖ visual problems ❖ strange actions or appearance ❖ unconsciousness ❖ headache
Breathing	❖ difficulty in breathing ❖ slow or rapid ❖ continued coughing, sneezing, or wheezing
Digestive system	❖ sudden decrease in appetite ❖ nausea and/or vomiting (forceful vomiting as opposed to spitting up foods) ❖ vomits for several hours with inability to retain fluids ❖ abdominal pain or tenderness ❖ sudden increase or decrease in number of bowel movements ❖ stools or urine unusual in amount, color, odor, or consistency
Eyes	❖ irritated or red ❖ sensitivity to light ❖ blurred vision
Fever	❖ rectal temperature of 101°F or above ❖ mild fever that lasts several days
General behavior	❖ unusually quiet, irritable, or drowsy ❖ strange behavior after a fall or other accident ❖ if already ill, has a rise in fever or new symptoms appear ❖ sharp screaming ❖ ear rubbing, head rolling, or drawing of legs toward abdomen
Nose	❖ nasal discharge (note color, amount, and consistency); congestion, or bleeding
Skin	❖ dry or hot ❖ excessive perspiration ❖ rash or hives ❖ severe cuts or abrasions ❖ deep bruising ❖ flushed or pale in color
Throat	❖ sore ❖ red ❖ choking

21-4 When certain symptoms appear, children may need medical help.

In order to understand a child's condition, doctors need specific information. The adult should think of questions the doctor may ask, such as the following:

❖ What are all the child's symptoms? (Give exact information, such as, "Louisa has vomited five times in the last two hours. Each time she has lost about one cup of fluid.")

❖ When did you first notice these symptoms?

❖ Has the child recently been exposed to a **contagious disease** (disease that can be caught from another person)?

❖ Have you treated the child's illness in any way? How? Have you given the child food, liquid, or medication? When? Does the child take any medication regularly?

❖ Do you know whether the child is allergic to any medication? (A new doctor will not know about a child's allergies.)

❖ What is the name and phone number of your pharmacy? (The doctor may phone in a prescription.)

Adults need to write down all this information before calling a doctor, except in extreme emergencies. They should also take pen and paper to the phone to write the doctor's instructions. After receiving instructions from the doctor, adults should ask him or her the following:

❖ Is there anything I should know about giving this medication or treatment? What other measures should I take (such as keep the child lightly covered; use a humidifier; keep the child in bed)?

❖ When should I expect an improvement?

❖ What changes would merit another call or office visit?

Adults should repeat the instructions for the doctor to be sure they have understood the directions correctly. They should follow the doctor's advice exactly. If questions arise after the call, adults should not hesitate to call the doctor again and ask him or her to clarify.

Childhood Diseases

Adults who care for children should be aware of diseases that are often contracted during childhood. These are called *childhood diseases*, 21-5. Most childhood diseases are contagious. Until immunizations were developed for prevention and modern drugs were found effective for treatment, many children died or were left impaired by some of these diseases. Even today, many children suffer negative effects and even die from these diseases. This can occur when adults are unaware of the diseases and their symptoms and do not follow medical advice for prevention or treatment.

contagious disease. A disease that can be caught from another person.

Childhood Diseases

Condition	Cause	Symptoms	Comments
Bronchitis	reaction of air tubes in the chest	cough after a cold that lasts for more than 2 weeks	Seek medical treatment.
Chicken pox	virus	fever; runny nose; cough; and rash (pimples, blisters, and scabs)	Seek medical treatment. Keep child away from others for 6 days after rash begins. Vaccine can prevent.
Colds	virus	runny nose; scratchy throat; coughing; sneezing; watery eyes	Seek medical treatment if child looks and/or acts very ill.
Conjunctivitis	virus and bacteria	watery eyes; mucus in eyes; red/pink color in whites of eyes; eyelid redness	Seek medical treatment. Keep child away from others for 24 hours after treatment has begun.
Diaper rash	secondary infection may be caused by bacteria or yeast	redness, scaling, and pimples or sores in diaper area	Seek medical advice if rash persists or worsens. If rash is caused by infection, keep child away from others for 24 hours after treatment has begun.
Diphtheria	bacteria	headache; fever; severe sore throat with white fluid over tonsils and throat; cough; bloody nasal discharge	Seek medical treatment. Keep child away from others for 2 weeks after fever starts or when throat cultures are clear. Vaccine can prevent.
Earaches	bacteria and virus	fever; pain; difficulty in hearing; drainage from ear	Seek medical treatment.
Haemophilus influenza type b (Hib)	bacteria	fever; lethargy (tired); vomiting; poor appetite; earache; breathing and swallowing difficulties; cough; purple area on skin near eyes	Seek medical treatment. Keep child away from others until fever is gone or physician okays contact. Vaccine can prevent.
Hepatitis B	virus	fever; jaundice (yellowing of skin and whites of eyes); loss of appetite; nausea; joint pain; rash	Seek medical treatment. Keep child away from others until fever is gone and skin rash is dry.
Impetigo	bacteria	red, cracking, oozing blister-like pimples often seen on the face	Seek medical treatment. Keep child away from others until 24 hours after treatment has begun.

(Continued)

21-5 Childhood diseases can be serious illnesses in the early years.

Childhood Diseases (Continued)

Condition	Cause	Symptoms	Comments
Measles	virus	fever; cough; runny nose; watery eyes; brownish red and blotchy rash that begins on face and neck and spreads downward; white spots in mouth	Seek medical treatment. Keep child away from others for 6 days after rash begins. Vaccine can prevent.
Meningitis	virus and bacteria	fever; lethargy (tired); poor appetite; vomiting; irritable (fussy); headache; stiff neck	Seek emergency medical help. Physician will determine if child can have contact with others. Vaccines may prevent.
Mumps	virus	Fever; swelling of one or more salivary glands; earache; headache	Seek medical treatment. Keep child away from others for 9 days after onset of swelling. Vaccine can prevent.
Pertussis (whooping cough)	bacteria	runny nose; coughing spells; vomiting	Seek medical treatment. Keep child away from others for 3 weeks after onset of cough. Vaccine can prevent.
Polio myelitis	virus	fever; vomiting; irritable (fussy); headache; stiffness of neck and back; paralysis in some cases	Seek medical treatment. Physician will determine when child may have contact with others. Vaccine can prevent.
Reye's Syndrome	virus (often within 3 to 5 days after other viral infections)	vomiting; sudden fever; mental confusion; lethargy; drowsiness; irritability (fussy); body rigidity; coma	Seek emergency medical help. Aspirin has been linked to onset in over 90% of cases. For this reason, never give medicines containing aspirin to children.
Roseola infantum	virus (seen in children under 2 years as suggested in the name "infantum")	fever followed by rash	Seek medical treatment. Keep child away from others until fever is gone.
Rubella	virus	red rash; enlarged lymph nodes; joint pain	Seek medical treatment. Keep child away from others for 6 days after rash begins. Vaccine can prevent.
Scarlet fever (scarlatina)	bacteria	fever; rash that causes skin to peel	Seek medical treatment. Keep child away from others until 24 hours after treatment has begun.
Strep throat	bacteria	sore throat; skin infections	Seek medical treatment. Keep child away from others until 24 hours after treatment has begun.

21-5 Childhood diseases can be serious illnesses in the early years.

Allergies

Allergies affect over one-fourth of all children and are the greatest cause of chronic long-term health problems in young children. An **allergy** is a condition that results when a child's immune system is very sensitive to an allergen and reacts negatively when it comes into contact with it. An **allergen** is a substance that causes an allergic reaction, 21-6.

Common symptoms of allergies include: frequent "colds" and ear infections, chronic congestion (stuffy nose), headaches, frequent nosebleeds, dark circles under the eyes, wheezing, skin rashes, frequent upsets to the stomach, and irritability (fussiness).

Allergies may be life-threatening, but more often make the child feel badly.

Allergies are treated by removing or limiting contact with the substance (not having a pet or staying inside as much as possible when the pollen count is high), using drugs for allergies (antihistamines, decongestants, and bronchodilators), and receiving injections for some allergens, which is called *desensitization therapy*.

Accident Prevention

Accidents claim the lives of more children than any of the major killer diseases of childhood. Several factors lead to the high accident rate among

Types of Allergens

Allergies	Agent	Symptoms
Ingestants	❖ foods (often milk, citrus fruits, chocolate, wheat, and eggs) and medicines taken by mouth	❖ digestive upsets ❖ respiratory problems
Inhalants	❖ pollens, molds, dust, and animal dander	❖ respiratory problems
Contractants	❖ soaps; cosmetics; fibers in clothing, carpets, drapes, and upholstery; plants; and medicines applied to skin	❖ hives and rashes
Injectables	❖ insect bites and stings, thorns, and medicines that are injected	❖ respiratory problems ❖ digestive problems ❖ hives and rashes

21-6 Children may suffer from one or more of these types of allergies.

children. Some equipment and toys are not safe. Most homes have some hazards even after adults attempt to correct them. Children are energetic and curious. By the toddler years they have the gross- and fine-motor skills to reach almost anything and get into it. Thus, children depend on adults to protect them. Adults can do this by creating a safe environment and supervising their children. They can also model and teach safety practices.

How Do Accidents Happen?

Parents worry about how to protect their children from violence and strangers who kidnap. Many parents do not think about the two major threats to their children's safety—home hazards and lack of constant and adequate supervision. Children are much more likely to be injured in an accident at home than by a stranger's crime.

Children are the most prone to accidents before they are old enough to learn about safety practices. For this reason, adults need to take extra care to prevent these accidents. They can do this by removing hazards, supervising children, taking safety measures, and making children aware of the need for safety.

Creating a Safe Environment

Infants are totally dependent on safe equipment and clothing and on their parents' constant attention to

21-7 When using baby equipment, such as a jogging stroller, parents must be well informed about safety features and guidelines for safe use.

safety matters, 21-7. Creating a safe environment is also crucial for toddlers and preschool children. These children cannot make sound safety judgments. Children may not understand why they must be careful. They may be too busy reaching their goals to remember warnings. Adults must do all they can to keep the environment safe for children. In such an

 allergy. Condition that results when a person's immune system is very sensitive to a particular allergen and reacts negatively when exposed to it.

allergen. A substance that causes an allergic reaction.

environment, accidents are reduced and children can play without being too concerned about safety. Older children can help protect themselves.

Supervising Children

Safety gadgets do not take the place of adults' eyes and ears. Children depend on adults for their safety. Accidents happen more often when adults do not supervise children carefully. When adults are talking on the phone, watching television, working on the computer, visiting a friend, feeling ill, or in any way preoccupied, accidents are more likely. They happen more often in the late afternoon and early evening hours when parents make dinner or do other household tasks.

Accidents happen more often when supervision is unsuitable or lacking. For example, accidents happen more often when older children supervise younger ones. Accidents also happen when children (especially school-age children) are home alone while their parents work or run errands.

Anticipating Possible Hazards

Creating a risk-free environment is impossible. Even if it were possible to remove all hazards, this would not teach children to face and cope with risks. However, risks must not be too great, or serious accidents may happen. To prevent serious accidents, adults must look for possible hazards.

Children's developmental changes lead to certain types of accidents. Babies face hazards at birth. These hazards multiply as babies' motor skills, curiosity, and independence increase. Chart 21-8 shows accidents that are likely to occur during each stage of development. Adults must watch each child's development carefully. As they see growth stages occur, the adult must take certain safety measures. A child who can crawl up one step or onto any low object can soon climb an entire flight of steep stairs. Falls are common when babies first climb. However, an adult can keep the child safe by blocking off stairs before a child can climb a whole flight.

Helping Children Meet Goals in a Safe Way

Adults should help children meet their goals in safe ways. Young children learn about the world by climbing and putting objects in their mouth. Adults need to provide children with safe environments rather than change the children's goals. When babies want to climb, adults should let them climb up and down a single carpeted step or off and on a chair. This environment is safe for them to explore, even if they take small tumbles. In addition, it helps children meet their goals. Also, small risks teach them to cope with possible dangers. Adults should block off a steep staircase, however, because this poses a great risk for the child.

Accidents Children Are Likely to Experience

Age of Child	Child's Traits Leading to Possible Accidents	Major Accidents
Birth to 3 months	❖ skin is much more sensitive to heat than adults' skin ❖ wiggles and rolls off flat surfaces but cannot move away from danger ❖ puts objects into mouth and swallows them	❖ bath scalding ❖ falls ❖ injuries from swallowing small objects ❖ drowning ❖ strangling on cords or smothering from items like dry cleaning bags or balloons ❖ suffocation under blankets, pillows, or soft objects
4 to 6 months	❖ skin is more sensitive to heat than adults' skin ❖ moves by rolling over and may crawl or creep ❖ grasps any object and places it in the eyes, ears, nose, or mouth ❖ hits objects, including breakable ones	❖ bath scalding and burns from hot water faucet ❖ falls ❖ injuries caused by swallowing small objects or putting them into eyes, ears, or nose ❖ injuries from broken objects like glass or plastics
6 to 12 months	❖ sits alone ❖ grabs anything in sight ❖ looks for objects hidden or fallen out of sight (around 10 months) ❖ puts objects in eyes, ears, nose, or mouth ❖ hits, pokes, and pushes objects ❖ may walk with or without help	❖ falls from stairs or high places ❖ injuries caused by pulling on cords of kitchen appliances, pulling or grasping containers filled with hot foods or beverages ❖ burns from open heaters and floor furnaces ❖ injuries caused by swallowing small objects or putting them into ears, eyes, or nose ❖ injuries from dangerous objects like knives, sharp-edged furniture, breakable objects, and electrical outlets ❖ mishaps while using walkers, strollers, and riding toys
1 to 2 years	❖ walks ❖ climbs ❖ throws objects ❖ pulls open drawers and doors ❖ takes items apart ❖ puts objects in mouth	❖ falls on stairs, in tubs or pools, and off high objects like crib railings or tables ❖ burns from grabbing handles of pots on stove ❖ poisoning from medication and cleaning agents ❖ injuries from dangerous objects like knives, electrical outlets, breakable objects, toys with small parts, and sharp-edged objects inside and outside ❖ injuries caused by being on driveways and roads and in outside storage areas

(Continued)

21-8 Children of various ages differ in the type of accidents they are most likely to experience.

Accidents Children Are Likely to Experience (Continued)

Age of Child	Child's Traits Leading to Possible Accidents	Major Accidents
2 to 3 years	❖ can rotate forearm to turn doorknob ❖ likes to climb on objects ❖ likes to play with and in water ❖ fascinated by fire ❖ moves at fast speed ❖ does not like to be restrained ❖ likes ride-on toys	❖ injuries caused by getting into almost anything that is not locked or equipped with special devices ❖ injuries caused by falls from high places, jumps onto dangerous surfaces like concrete, falls off ride-on toys and swings ❖ burns from cigarette lighters, matches, and open flames ❖ injuries caused by playing in driveways and roads and darting across streets ❖ injuries caused by swallowing small objects or putting them into eyes, ears, and nose ❖ eye injuries due to dust and sand ❖ swings; falls result in broken bones
3 to 6 years	❖ explores neighborhood ❖ plays rougher games ❖ plays with other children ❖ tries to use tools and equipment of the home	❖ poisoning from medicines and household products ❖ injuries from using home, shop, and garden tools ❖ injuries related to action games, bicycles, and rough play ❖ various injuries from interesting hazards like old refrigerators, deep holes, trash heaps, and construction sites ❖ drowning ❖ burns from electrical outlets, appliances, and open flames ❖ traffic injuries
6 to 12 years	❖ participates in sports ❖ likely to try stunts on a dare in traffic as a pedestrian or on bicycle ❖ interested in firearms and fireworks ❖ uses tools in home and yard care	❖ sports-related injuries ❖ drowning ❖ firearm and fireworks accidents ❖ traffic injuries

21-8 Children of various ages differ in the type of accidents they are most likely to experience.

Childproofing the Environment

Adults must note dangerous objects in children's worlds. Moving unsafe objects out of a child's reach or preventing dangerous situations is called **childproofing** the environment.

Childproofing should start before the baby is born. Professional childproofing is a service available in many large cities. A professional childproofer inspects the home so he or she can assess the need for safety devices and do the childproofing. The service is expensive but includes the costs of the advice, safety devices, and installation.

Many parents childproof their own environment, however. To childproof the adult must do the following:

* Childproof every part of the environment—inside and outside the home and vehicle.
* Stay at least one step ahead of a child's development. A child who is just learning to stand may grasp a tablecloth for balance and pull off dangerous objects, such as hot soup.
* Move the way children do and where children move. Thus, if children are going to crawl in the kitchen, parents need to get down on their hands and knees and look for dangers from the child's perspective.
* Check the child's belongings, including baby furniture, baby care equipment, supplies, and toys, 21-9.
* Choose pets carefully.

21-9 Children rely on their parents and caregivers to provide safe playthings.

* Stay up-to-date on the latest safety and product information.

Indoor Safety

The indoor environment is often the greatest hazard to a child. Each home is alike in some ways (doors, windows, electrical outlets) and different in others (stairs or no stairs, furnishings). Thus, parents must look for dangers in their own homes. Babies not only

childproofing. The process of moving unsafe objects out of a child's reach or preventing dangerous situations.

differ in their development at certain ages but in their traits. Sometimes a baby's personality calls for additional childproofing measures. For example, some babies are extra curious and explore everything. Others are climbers who will try to scale everything in your home. Still other babies put more things into their mouth than others.

No home is safe. Problems can be found in the home structure, general furnishings, each room, and items kept in or near the home. Refer to the appendix at the end of this text for a list of indoor dangers and how to prevent them.

Preventing Poisonings

Poisonings of children under five years of age account for more than half of all accidental poisonings in the home each year. At this age, children like to examine objects. When attractively packaged household items catch their attention, children will often eat or swallow these products. Products that look (or even taste) like candy are especially enticing.

If adults take safety measures, children are less likely to be poisoned. Adults need to learn which products are dangerous, 21-10. They must read all product labels and heed warnings.

Poisons Cause Accidents

Cleaning Products	Garage and Garden Products	Medications	Personal Products
air fresheners	antifreeze	acetaminophen	aftershave
ammonia	caustic lime	amphetamines	cosmetics
bleach	fertilizer	analgesic creams	deodorant
cleaners	gasoline, kerosene,	antibiotics	hair coloring products
dishwasher and dish-	lighter fluid, oil, and	anticonvulsants	hair remover
washing products	other petroleum	antidepressants	lotion
disinfectant	products	antidiarrheals	mouthwash
drain opener	oils	aspirin	nail polish and polish
floor wax	paint	blood pressure drugs	remover
furniture polish	pesticide	camphor	perfume
laundry products	putty	cold preparations	permanent wave
lye	strychnine	diabetes drugs	solution
metal polish	varnish	heart drugs	powder, talcum (baby
oven cleaner	weed killer	iron, vitamins with iron	and body powder)
rust remover	windshield solution	oil of wintergreen	rubbing alcohol
spot remover		pain relievers	shampoo
toilet bowl cleaner		sleeping pills	soap
water softener		tranquilizers	
		vitamins	

21-10 Many common substances are poisonous.

Store household products high above floor level (rather than under sinks) to keep them away from crawling babies. Lock up household products when children can walk and climb. (Once children can climb, their reach is almost without limits. If adults must leave an unsafe product unattended, they must store it in a safe, out-of-reach place. Do not leave the unattended product within reach, even for a minute.

Poisonous products must be kept in their original containers with the labels intact. Never transfer poisons to food or drink containers (such as a box, jar, or bottle). Do not put a safe substance in a container that originally held a poisonous product. For example, do not put water in a bleach bottle because a child might then assume the contents of all bleach bottles are safe. Keep medication in childproof containers. Store household products in safety containers. Adults must carefully check containers after each use to ensure the container is in good condition and closes properly.

Do not keep products that are *lethal* (deadly) in the house. The risks are too great. For example, one teaspoon of oil of wintergreen contains six grams of salicylates. This equals the amount in 20 adult aspirin. This amount of oil of wintergreen would kill a child.

Medication is safer when adults take the following safety measures:

* Flush old medications down the toilet rather than throwing them in the garbage.
* Replace childproof caps carefully after use.
* Lock medication in a cabinet, a small chest, or suitcase.
* Never give a child medication in the dark.
* Never refer to medication as *candy*.
* Do not give medication in baby bottles or juice glasses.
* Do not take medication (even vitamins) in front of young children.
* When carrying medication, store a limited amount in a childproof container and keep it in a purse or pocket. Keep your purse and the purses of visitors out of children's reach.

Standing Water Safety

Young children are not clumsy, but their body proportions make them top-heavy. If young children lose their balance near water, they may fall in and be unable to get out. Children can drown in even an inch of water. Never leave unattended buckets of water (for mopping or other chores), filled bathtubs, sinks, or washing machines. Use a latch on toilet lids or install locks high on the outside of all bathroom doors. Eliminate or plan barriers to other standing water containers, such as indoor fountains or aquariums.

Firearm Safety

Guns kill more than 10 children every day. Most firearm accidents happen when children discover a loaded gun at home. Firearm safety, in part, involves adults teaching children that guns are not toys and must not be handled by children. Children, however, are curious and often want to experiment even with "forbidden" objects. Thus, childproofing ensures the safest environment for the child and his or her visitors. The safest childproofing measures include the following:

❖ Taking ammunition out of firearms
❖ Locking the firearms out of the reach of children and using quality trigger locks
❖ Storing the ammunition in a locked container apart from firearms
❖ Keeping keys to firearms and ammunition cabinets in an area separate from other household keys
❖ Locking gun-cleaning supplies for they are poisonous

Outdoor Safety

Adults must check that outdoor areas are safe for children, too. Common unsafe objects in the outdoor area include rocks, broken glass, ruts, holes, and bumps. Nails and other sharp objects can puncture children. Areas may become slippery and unsafe when wet.

If the outdoor area has pools, ponds, wells, or deep holes, adults should be sure they are enclosed by a fence the child cannot climb. The areas also should be closed and safely locked or covered to provide complete safety. To prevent falls from decks, use safety netting from the top of the railings to the deck floor. A safety gate or deck gate should be installed at the top of the steps. Open steps (common for decks) are also more risky for young children than closed stairs. Remove doors and trunk lids from old refrigerators, freezers, stoves, and cars if they are near children's playing areas. This prevents children from getting trapped inside and suffocating.

Plant Safety

Outside plants present a special safety problem. Many plants, flowers, vegetables, shrubs, and trees are poisonous or have poisonous parts, 21-11. It is not always obvious to adults

21-11 Before allowing their children to play outdoors, parents should check to make sure the plant life in the area is not poisonous for children.

when children have eaten a plant leaf, however, many plants are dangerous when eaten. Some plants, because of their chemical makeup, harm the digestive tract in ways similar to eating ground glass. Other beautiful plants are deadly. Eating even one leaf of these plants may kill a child. Children need close supervision when playing outside, especially in wooded areas, gardens, and greenhouses. Remember, too, that many plants are treated with poisonous pesticides and fertilizers.

Indoors, adults should remove poisonous houseplants where children live or visit. Parents can check with their pediatrician or the Poison Control Center to learn which types of plants are poisonous. Adults should choose only nonpoisonous houseplants and keep these out of children's reach.

Safe Play Areas

Making sure children will not wander out of a safe area provided for their play is a great task. Yards with enclosed fences are best. Gates should be locked or equipped with child-proof safety devices to keep children from opening them. For example, attach a screen door latch on the outside of the gate. Adults may also fit a gate with a bolt from the inside to the outside where the nut is attached. Because these devices require an adult to reach over a gate to unlock it, they are out of a child's reach.

When young children play in driveways or carports with pull/push toys or riding toys, adults should watch them closely. An extension ladder laid across the driveway a few feet from the street can help remind a child to turn around. Adults can replace the extension ladder with a play stop sign for older preschoolers. Remember, ladders and signs are only reminders, not safety devices. Children still need close supervision.

Traffic Safety

For young children, traffic safety is another outdoor concern. Young children are not able to see ahead or react with caution to moving traffic. This is especially true when they are riding tricycles and bicycles. Traffic safety skills are not completely mastered until about age 11 years. Children first must know that traffic can be unsafe. Traffic safety skills depend on perceptual judgments of space, speed, direction, and distance. In addition, these perceptions must interact. A child's brain and body must react quickly and correctly.

Scoldings and warnings will not solve these safety problems. Rather, adults must set limits for play areas, supervise children closely, model safe behavior, and teach safety. (Teaching safety is discussed later in this chapter.) With experience and guidance, children will gradually learn traffic safety rules and practices.

Vehicle Safety

Car accidents are the leading cause of death for infants and children. Experts say protecting children with proper restraint systems could reduce that rate by 90 percent. **Restraint systems** include car seats, seat belts,

and other devices that hold children safely in place while traveling in a motor vehicle. Approved restraints have passed crash tests and are designed especially for children of a certain weight.

Infants and young children should be secured in certified car safety seats *every* time they travel in a motor vehicle, 21-12. This is the law in all 50 states and the District of Columbia. This law extends to taxis as well as personal cars. Additionally, the Federal Aviation Agency (FAA) recommends child safety seats be used in planes for children under four years of age.

Certified child safety seats are restraint systems for infants and young children that have been tested and approved by federal agencies. Certified child safety seats are commonly known as *car seats*. (As the next section describes, child safety

21-12 When properly used every time, child safety seats can save lives.

seats vary by the height and weight of the child.) Infant feeding seats and carriers offer no crash protection and should not be used in vehicles. Car beds should be used only with premature infants whose condition does not enable them to ride upright. In these cases, only federally approved car beds should be used.

While in a motor vehicle, adults should *never* hold a child in their arms or on their laps. This provides no protection for the child in the event of a crash. Some adults may mistakenly think child safety seats are unnecessary for babies and young children. They may feel they can hold children on their laps and protect them during a crash. This is untrue. In a crash or hard stop, any loose objects will fly about inside the car. These moving objects exert tremendous force. For example, in a 30-mile-per-hour crash, a 10-pound baby moves forward with a force of 300 pounds. Such force is impossible for an adult to contain, meaning the baby will fly out of the adult's arms. At the same speed, an adult who weighs 125 pounds is thrown forward with a force of between one and two tons. This means a baby who rides on an adult's lap is apt to be crushed in a crash. A baby sharing a seat belt with an adult is in equal danger, even when the car is moving slowly.

Types of Child Safety Seats

All child safety seats have a chairlike frame (seat back is higher than the child's head) made of a high-impact material. They are covered with a polyester-filled cushion. The frames have multiple slots for adjusting the harness and vehicle seat belts. The harness and vehicle seat belts keep the car seat securely in place inside the vehicle.

Many types of child safety seats are available. To provide protection, a seat must be selected to fit the child's age, height, and weight, 21-13. *Infant-only seats* are rear-facing and recline at a 45-degree angle. Some of these seats come with detachable bases, making it easy to remove the seat while leaving the base still secured in the vehicle. *Convertible seats* are bigger and heavier than infant-only seats. These seats can be used from infancy through the preschool years. *Convertible seats* face the rear in a semireclining position for children under 30 or 35 pounds and then face forward in an upright position for heavier children. As the name suggests, *forward-facing seats* can only

restraint systems. Car seats, seat belts, and other devices that hold children safely in place while traveling in a motor vehicle.

certified child safety seats. Restraint systems for infants and young children that have been tested and approved by federal agencies; also known as *car seats*.

Selecting Child Restraint Systems

	Birth to 1 Year	1 to 4 Years	4 to 8 Years[1]
Weight[2]	5 to 20 or 22 pounds	20 to 40 pounds	40 to 80 pounds
Height[3]	Up to 27 inches	28 to 34 inches	35 to 57 inches
Type of Seat	Infant-only or rear-facing convertible seat	Convertible rear-facing seat until at least one year[4] or forward-facing after one year[5, 6]	Belt-positioning booster seats
Seat Position	Rear-facing in middle of the back seat	Rear- or forward- facing in the back seat	Forward-facing in the back seat
Notes on Correct Use	❖ Baby's head must be 2 inches below top of the seat. ❖ Correct incline of seats made before 2002 may require a tightly rolled towel under the seat where the back seat and car cushion meet. ❖ Harness straps should come through the slot at or below shoulder level. ❖ Chest harness clip should be at infant's armpit level. Angle indicators, built-in angle adjusters, harness adjusters, and head support systems are required for seats built beginning in 2002.	❖ Harness straps should come through the slots at or above child's shoulders. ❖ Use top harness slots of safety seat for front-facing children. ❖ Chest harness clip should be at the child's armpit level.	❖ Use with vehicle's lap and shoulder belt. ❖ Shoulder belt should cross the chest and rest snugly on the shoulder. ❖ Lap belt should cross the upper thigh area. ❖ The American Academy of Pediatrics recommends shield booster seats be used without the shield.

[1] Although children may outgrow booster seats before 9 years of age, all children age 12 years and under must ride in the back seat of vehicles and be buckled.
[2] Weight is more important than age in selecting the correct safety seat.
[3] Height is most important for seat to fit properly with the head in a safe position and straps crossing the child's body in safe places.
[4] Many new convertible seats are designed to hold infants and toddlers up to 30 or 35 pounds in a rear-facing position. A rear-facing position are a must for infants but are also recommended for toddlers under 30 to 35 pounds. In a head-on collision, a rear-facing seat allows the force of the crash to spread evenly over the spine. Because the spine is so prone to injury in young children, a rear-facing seat can mean the difference between minor and severe spinal cord injury. Parents need to know that 20 pounds and 1 year is the bare minimum for using any forward-facing seat.
[5] Some newer models of forward-facing only seats can be used by children from 20 to 60 pounds.
[6] Some high-back booster seats with built-in harnesses can also be used for children 30 to 40 pounds.

21-13 Parents should choose the proper type of restraint based on their child's age, weight, and height.

be used in a forward-facing position. These seats are not suitable for infants, but can be used for older children.

Although the law may permit older children to ride in the back seat with a standard seat belt, adults need to understand that seat belts were designed for adult bodies. Buckling an older child into the center back seat in no way matches the safety of proper equipment. Regular seat belts do not protect children who weigh less than 80 pounds for the following reasons:

❖ Young children can slip through a regular seat belt because they do not have long, heavy legs to anchor them.

❖ Regular seat belts can ride up to a young child's abdomen, where there are no bones to protect the child from the strain of the seat belt if a crash occurs. In a crash, the child's internal organs could be damaged.

❖ The standard shoulder harness of a regular seat belt can move across a child's face or neck, which is unsafe. Young children need a harness designed for their size and body proportions to protect the neck and head.

To protect older children, *booster seats* are used to position children who are between 35 and 37 inches tall and who weigh between 40 and 80 pounds. Booster seats are used to elevate the child so the vehicle seat belt will be fastened in the right position. Thus, they are often called belt-positioning

booster seats. Some parents prefer the newer combination seats, which can be used by preschool children with the harness until they are large enough to safely use the same seat without the harness as a booster seat.

Choosing a Child Safety Seat

Adults may buy new child safety seats in many stores. Because babies can arrive unexpectedly, parents should choose, obtain, and install the child safety seat several weeks before the baby's due date. They will need to use the child safety seat from the baby's very first trip—home from the hospital.

Parents will not want to buy a car seat more than a few months in advance, however. This is because car seats are often subject to safety recalls. In a **safety recall**, the manufacturer of a product issues a notice stating the product has been found to be unsafe. For safety reasons, consumers are asked to stop using a recalled product unless the manufacturer can provide additional parts that will make the product safe.

Before purchasing a car seat, parents can call the Auto Safety Hot Line or check online at the National Highway Traffic Safety Administration Web site, 21-14. For new purchases, they

safety recall. Issuing of a notice by the product manufacturer stating the product has been found to be unsafe.

21-14 Parents can use the Internet to research baby and toddler products, such as child safety seats, before they make a purchase.
Apple Computer

should always send the registration card that comes with the seat back to the manufacturer. In turn, the manufacturer will notify the buyer of any problems or recalls.

In some towns and cities, adults may rent or borrow restraint systems from various programs or agencies. Parents may also borrow or buy used child safety seats. This practice is not advised, however, because the safety of the seat is unknown. Any child safety seat that is more than six years old or has ever been in even a minor accident is unsafe. If parents know a seat's owner and history, they might

decide to borrow a newer, accident-free seat from family or friends. They will need the owner's manual for the seat, however. If the manual is not available, parents can order another manual from the manufacturer.

Installing and Using a Child Safety Seat

Unless child safety seats are installed and used properly, they offer little or no protection for a child in a crash. For this reason, the American Academy of Pediatrics advises adults to read the directions to install child safety seats carefully. Photos on the packaging should not be followed because these may be misleading. Adults should also read their vehicle owner's manual to ensure they are using the seat belts correctly. This is true whether the seat belts are used to restrain an older child or secure the child safety seat of a younger one.

A new child safety seat attachment has been developed to make child safety seats easier and safer to use. This system, called the **LATCH system** (LATCH stands for Lower Anchors and Tethers for Children), must be installed in all new cars beginning with model year 2002. For older cars, parents can check with the dealer about prices for installing the LATCH system. In the LATCH system, hardware is mounted into the vehicle to hold straps that are attached to a LATCH-designed child safety seat. These straps hold the car seat in place without the use of the vehicle seat belt.

For LATCH systems and other child safety seats, parents may want to seek help from a certified **child passenger seat technician (CPS)**. This professional can provide information on child safety seats and inspect them after installation. Parents can consult the National Highway Traffic Administration to find CPS technicians in their area. The American Academy of Pediatrics Web site also provides useful information on child safety seats for all children, including those who are premature or have special needs. This Web site also provides an online shopping guide for child safety seats.

All restraint systems are designed for the back seat of the vehicle. Placing children in the back seat is important because passenger-side air bags are now in many models of cars. If these air bags inflate, children under age 12 years who ride in the front seat are in danger of death or serious injury. This is true even if they are in certified child safety seats.

Air bags are designed to work with lap/shoulder belts to protect teens and adults. In almost all cases involving injury and deaths to infants, rear-facing safety seats are placed very close to the dashboard. This causes the air bag to hit the safety seat with an intense force when it inflates. The force breaks the child safety seat, causing head and brain injuries to the child. Injured toddlers and older children facing forward were often unbuckled or not wearing the shoulder portion of the safety belt. In other cases, these children were simply too close to the dashboard because they were playing with something on the dashboard or because they slid or flexed forward during precrash braking. Neck and head injuries often occur when the body is closer than 12 inches to the dashboard at the time the air bag is triggered. Death can also occur, especially to young children.

If adults have a vehicle with no back seat, such as a sports car or truck, they should realize these are not safe vehicles for children. If using another vehicle is not an option, these adults should have the passenger-side air bag turned off and properly use the rear-facing seat in the vehicle seat. For older children in forward-facing seats, adults should use the air bag but move the vehicle seat back as far as possible. They should advise children not to lean toward the dashboard.

Each time before starting any vehicle, an adult must make sure the child is buckled into the restraint system properly. Each buckle and strap

LATCH system. Attachment that will be installed in new motor vehicles to make child safety seats safer and easier to use.

child passenger seat technician (CPS). Professional who provides information on child safety seats and inspects them after installation.

exists for a purpose. Proper use of these is important to the child's safety. For this reason, adults should take time when needed to adjust restraint systems to fit the child properly.

Additionally, adults should set an example by always wearing a seat belt and driving safely. Children are less likely to resist using restraint systems if they and others in their lives have always used them. These children do not see using restraint systems as a choice. Children who have not always used restraint systems must be taught to do so.

An added benefit to restraint systems is that studies find children behave better in cars when they are restrained. Perhaps restraint systems cause children to feel less car motion (which is tiring) and enable them to see out the windows better. Restraint systems also allow children less mobility and freedom to misbehave.

Other Safety Measures

The proper installation and use of restraint systems is essential to children's safety. In addition, adults should set some other guidelines for safe travel in motor vehicles. First, they should make sure doors are locked at all times. They should never allow passengers—especially children—to ride in the following ways:

- ❖ with any part of the body hanging out an open window
- ❖ in cargo areas of cars, vans, or trucks
- ❖ kneeling on the floorboard of the vehicle

If adults need to attend to a child's needs, they should pull the vehicle to the side of the road. They should not try to reach into the back seat while driving to offer assistance. Using common sense and following the rules of the road will also keep children safe.

Baby Items and Toy Safety

Children's products cause many injuries each year. Many injuries can be avoided if adults choose baby items and toys carefully. Also, adults must realize that even safe items and toys become dangerous when misused. This means supervision and safety lessons are crucial.

Selection

Selecting safe baby/toddler items and toys is important, 21-15. Some safety features are now required by law. For example, the slats in cribs and playyards must be spaced no more than 2 ⅜ inches apart. The law requires paint on baby items and toys to be nontoxic. Items and toys made prior to the enactment of a law may not meet the law's standards. Also, certain homemade toys may be unsafe if they do not follow the guidelines of the law.

Most new toys that are unsafe for infants and toddlers must carry warnings, such as "Not Intended for Children Under Three Years of Age." Other items, such as lawn darts, cannot be sold in toy departments or toy stores because they are dangerous for children to use.

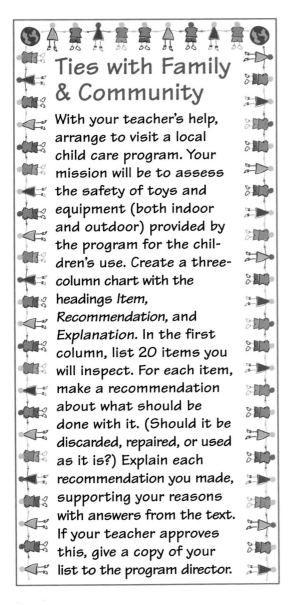

Ties with Family & Community

With your teacher's help, arrange to visit a local child care program. Your mission will be to assess the safety of toys and equipment (both indoor and outdoor) provided by the program for the children's use. Create a three-column chart with the headings *Item*, *Recommendation*, and *Explanation*. In the first column, list 20 items you will inspect. For each item, make a recommendation about what should be done with it. (Should it be discarded, repaired, or used as it is?) Explain each recommendation you made, supporting your reasons with answers from the text. If your teacher approves this, give a copy of your list to the program director.

When selecting baby/toddler items and toys, adults should do the following:

❖ Examine items for safety features carefully. Safety features are especially important on items for babies and toddlers.

❖ Read labels carefully and heed recommendations.

❖ Check toys for durability. Make sure small parts are secure on all toys—even for older children.

❖ Find age-stage appropriate toys. Age is only a clue to stage. Toys should be appropriate for the child's physical skills (ability to use the toy), mental abilities (understand how to use the toy), and interests. They should also have the needed age-stage safety features, 21-16.

❖ Throw toy packaging away. Plastic; styrofoam; small, plastic ties; and other packaging materials are safety hazards for young children. These materials are not meant to be played with and should be discarded. The only exception is the identifying or safety information on baby or toddler items. Parents may want to keep this information in a file folder. This allows them to check recall information or file a complaint.

Supervision

Adults should consider each toy in terms of how much supervision the child will need to use it, 21-17. If a great deal of long-term supervision is needed, the toy may not be appropriate for the child's stage. Parents should consider putting the toy away for a later date.

Supervision involves answering these questions:

❖ Can an adult teach the child to use the toy properly?

Safety Standards for Baby/Toddler Items

Item	Safety Standards
Baby vehicle (carriage or stroller)	❖ Should be pretested for balance and weight distribution. ❖ Safety brake can be quickly set. ❖ Protective bumpers should pad.
Bassinet	❖ Sturdy bottom and wide, stable base. ❖ Smooth surfaces. ❖ Secure leg locks. ❖ Firm mattress with snug fit.
Bed (toddler)	❖ Use detachable rail with openings no more than 3½ inches apart. ❖ Put padding on floor next to bed in case child rolls out.
Changing table	❖ Sturdy. ❖ Guardrails that are at least 2 inches high. ❖ Safety strap. ❖ Toiletries are out of reach of babies.
Crib	❖ Slats must not be more than 2⅜ inches apart. ❖ Height of crib side from bottom of mattress to top of railing no less than 26 inches. ❖ Child has outgrown crib when side rail is less than three-fourths of child's height. ❖ Children 35 inches and taller must be removed from portable cribs. ❖ Latch on drop sides should be releasable only on outside and require a double kick. (This prevents young children and large dogs from tripping the latch.) ❖ Crib sides should lock at maximum height. ❖ Paint should be lead free. ❖ Teething rails are preferred. ❖ Crib should not have horizontal bars inside, because a baby can climb on them. ❖ Bumper pads with 6 or more ties are the safest. They are not recommended until the baby can raise the head and should be removed once the baby can stand. ❖ Corner posts are 1/16 inch or shorter or 16 inches or higher for canopy beds. ❖ Place cribs away from windows, heaters, lamps, wall decorations, cords, and climbable furniture. ❖ Remove crib mobiles and hanging toys at 5 months. ❖ No cutout designs on head- or footboards. ❖ Buy cribs designed after 1987.
Crib mattress	❖ When rail is in lowest position, the top of the mattress support and the top of the rail should be no less than 9 inches for standard crib and 5 inches for portable crib. ❖ Mattress should be covered with durable plastic with air vents. ❖ Torn mattress covers should be discarded. ❖ Mattress should fit snugly in crib. Space between crib and mattress should be smaller than two adult fingers held together. ❖ Should be firm rather than soft. ❖ Move mattress to the lowest point once child can pull himself to standing.

(Continued)

21-15 Baby items must meet these standards to keep children safe.

Safety Standards for Baby/Toddler Items (Continued)

Item	Safety Standards
Diaper pails and wastebaskets	❖ Keep out of reach of children. ❖ Choose models with child-resistant lids.
High chair	❖ Wide-spread legs improve stability. ❖ Tray should lock in place. ❖ Crotch snap and wrap-around seat straps are needed. ❖ Nonskid rubber mats (available for bathtubs) placed on seat help prevent baby from sliding.
Playyard	❖ Slats should be no more than 2³/₈ inches apart. ❖ If playyard has mesh netting, the weave should be smaller than tiny baby buttons and pierced earrings. ❖ Floor should not collapse. ❖ Hinges on folding models should lock tightly. ❖ Check playyards for rivets (screwlike fasteners). If a rivet sticks out ¼ inch or more, stop using the playyard. Pacifier strings and clothing can catch on rivet and cause strangulation.) ❖ Stop using playyard when child can crawl out of it.
Vaporizer	❖ Has Underwriters' Laboratories (UL) seal. ❖ Cold water models are safer than steam models.
Miscellaneous	❖ Replace metal hangers with strong plastic hangers. ❖ Remove dry-cleaning bags or any dangerous product wrapping.

❖ Can an adult watch the child as he or she uses an electrical toy?

❖ Can toys meant for older children be kept out of the reach of younger siblings?

Use and Storage

Adults need to think about the space needed to use and store equipment. In some cases, the size of a piece of equipment during use and non-use is about the same, such as stringing beads, a xylophone, and a stuffed animal or doll. In other cases, toys in use require much more space than they do when stored, such as a puzzle with many pieces, large floor block sets, and toy tea sets and dishes. Adults must ask themselves other questions, too, such as:

❖ Is there a safe place to ride a wheeled toy?

❖ Is there a place to store outdoor toys when not in use?

❖ Are there places to store toys to prevent accident-causing clutter?

❖ Are special storage cabinets or shelves needed? (Storage items can be expensive, too.)

Safety Features for Toys

For Infants and Toddlers

Size should be larger than the child's two fists. Even large toys can break, exposing small parts. The law bans small parts in new toys intended for children under age three. Older and handmade toys may still have small parts.

Nonbreakable. Toys that break may expose small parts or break into small pieces. Toys made of glass or brittle plastic are the most unsafe.

No sharp edges or points. The law bans new toys with sharp edges or points intended for children under age eight. Broken toys often have sharp edges. Wires with sharp points are often inside stuffed toys.

Nontoxic. Painted toys should be labeled nontoxic. Avoid all painted toys for children who put playthings in their mouth.

No long cords or strings. Toys with long cords or strings should not be used with infants and young children who can wrap them around the neck.

Nonflammable, flame retardant, or flame resistant. Dolls and stuffed toys should be made of materials not likely to ignite.

Washable and hygienic materials. Dolls and stuffed toys must be clean when bought and must be easy to keep clean.

No broken or uninflated balloons. These balloons are the most dangerous objects for suffocation.

No toys or games with marbles or balls that are smaller than 1¾ inches in diameter. These items are a choking hazard.

No parts that are small enough to fit inside a cardboard bathroom tissue tube. (Special measuring tubes are also available.) The law bans small parts intended for children under age three years. Older and handmade toys may still have small parts.

No detachable clothing on dolls or stuffed animals. Fasteners are very small clothing items and thus present a choking hazard.

No toys with springs or hinges. Springs and hinges can pinch fingers.

Sounds at acceptable levels. The law requires a label on toys that produce sounds above a certain level. The label warns, "Do not use within one foot of the ear. Do not use indoors." Toys making sounds that can result in hearing damage are banned.

For Older Children

Safe electric toys. Electric toys must meet requirements for maximum surface temperatures, electrical wiring, and display of warning labels. Electrical toys that heat are intended for children over age eight.

Items used for age intended. Chemistry sets, hobby sets, balloons, and games and toys with small parts are extremely dangerous if misused or left within the reach of younger children.

Sturdy, safe, large outdoor equipment. Space between moving parts is wide enough not to pinch or crush fingers. Bolt ends would be covered with plastic end caps. Swing seats should be lightweight and have smooth, rolled edges. All swing sets, gyms, and other large equipment should be anchored firmly to the ground.

Paints and crayons marked with designation ASTM D4236. The designation means the material has been examined and is either nontoxic or carries a warning.

No toys that are projectiles. Projectiles cause many eye injuries.

Safe tricycles and bicycles. Tricycles and bicycles should have proper assembly. Seats should be adjusted to the rider's height. (Adults should never purchase a tricycle or bicycle for the child to "grow into.") Pedals should have skid-resistant surfaces. Reflectors (at least two inches in diameter) should be used on bicycles. Helmet should be worn at all times.

21-16 When selecting toys for infants, toddlers, and older children, adults should note special safety features.

21-17 Crayons are appropriate for this preschooler, but are inappropriate for toddlers because parents must supervise them more closely.

Photo provided by and reproduced with permission of Binney and Smith

Maintenance

Baby-toddler items and toys should be checked to ensure they do not have the following:

* recalls issued by the manufacturer or the U.S. Product Safety Commission
* sharp points; jagged edges; and loose parts
* any removable parts that are small enough to fit inside a child's mouth
* rust on outdoor equipment, which weakens the structure
* stuffed toys and dolls that must be repaired and cleaned
* batteries not secured by a cover with a screw to prevent removal by the child

Adults should remove any broken toys from use. Children can seriously injure themselves with broken toys. Adults must properly dispose of those that cannot be fixed. They should repair any other broken items before they are put back into use.

Adults can add a few safety devices to baby items and toys, too. If a toy chest is not properly ventilated, drill a few air holes. Place a piece of adhesive tape around the wheel edge of skates to slow them. To remind children not to hold the chains of a swing too low (and thus be thrown off balance), mark chains with tape on the proper holding place.

Pet Safety

Because pets can bite, transmit diseases, and cause allergic reactions, adults must choose them carefully. Adults should choose breeds of animals that are less apt to bite. Dogs that are one year and older and cats that are nine months and older have developed immunity to many diseases. These animals make better children's pets than puppies and kittens. If children show an allergy to a pet, adults must keep the animal away from them.

Veterinarians (animal doctors) should see pets on a regular basis. The veterinarian will advise on regular care of the animals. A sick pet should be examined at once.

Children should learn how to treat a pet, 21-18. Adults should not expect young children to care for a pet. This responsibility exceeds their development.

21-18 Pet safety includes teaching children how to handle and care for pets.
© Nancy P. Alexander

21-19 By providing a taller chair and footrest, parents could easily adapt this computer workstation to reduce their child's far reach to the mouse.
Apple Computer

In the lower elementary grades, children can begin to learn some pet-care duties from adults. Adults must also remind children to wash their hands after each time they handle a pet, pet housing (such as a fishbowl or cage), or pet items (toys and feeding containers).

Computer Safety

Millions of children use computers on a daily basis at home and at school. With the increase in children's computer use, both physical safety and protection from adult content have become a concern. Parents can take steps to make computer use safer for their children.

Protecting Physical Safety

Children's posture and eyes can suffer when using computers.

Computer work areas in homes are often designed with the adult in mind. Instead, the work area should be arranged with all users in mind, 21-19.

To prevent posture strain, the work area should be at the right height for the child to reach the keyboard and mouse with ease and still keep his or her feet flat on the floor (or on a step stool or footrest if the chair or stool is too high). The monitor (screen) should be adjusted so the child does not have to tilt his or her head backward or forward. (Adults can readjust the monitor position for each user). If the child uses books or other written materials at the computer, a document holder should be located close to the monitor so the child does not twist his or her neck.

Special care should be taken to prevent eye problems, too. To protect the eyes, adults should do the following:

❖ Adjust the room lighting to match the lighting of the monitor. Bright overhead lights are often too bright. Use a dimmer switch on the overhead light, use a lamp using less wattage, or use a lamp with a three-way bulb that is on the lowest setting during computer use.

❖ The screen should be glare-free. Reposition work area or use a glare-reduction filter on the computer. The filter should have the American Optometric Associations (AOA) Seal of Acceptance.

❖ Children need to take breaks. Experts suggest a 10-minute break each hour. This is because lengthy viewing times can result in eye problems. Problems seeing clearly at various distances can occur if focusing at particular viewing distance for too long. Computer users often don't blink enough while staring at a monitor. Eye irritation is more likely to occur with reduced blinking, as blinking allows eye fluid to wash over the eyes.

Protecting Children from Unacceptable Content

The content of software and the Internet is constantly growing and varied. Most people have mainly positive experiences in using the computer, but there are risks.

One thing to keep in mind is that anyone in the world can publish on the Internet. Thus, some content can be erotic, violent, or even illegal. Children can access this content whether they are seeking it on purpose or happen onto it by accident.

Another danger happens when children connect online to strangers who have bad intentions. Adults have posed online as children to befriend children and lure them to meet face-to-face. At these meetings, some of these adults have taken advantage of or kidnapped the children. Thus, parents have two roles in children's computer use—protecting children from the dangers and guiding children toward the benefits.

Some of the ways parents can control and guide include the following:

❖ locate computers in an open area of the house where use can be observed

❖ monitor what software children are using

❖ make sure there is a balance between computer use and other activities

❖ set rules and guidelines for the child's computer use, 21-20.

❖ set a good example as an adult. Children watch parents' behaviors on the computer as well as in other activities of life.

❖ plan special projects for children on the Internet. Special projects reduce time spent exploring the

Computer Safety Rules for Children

To promote the safety of children when using computers, parents should set rules such as the following:

❖ Use the computer only at times approved by adults. (Late-night or unsupervised use should be off limits.)

❖ Do not give out any personal information or send any photos. (Children should use a penname when on the Internet.)

❖ Do not use chat rooms or bulletin boards unless approved by adults.

❖ Tell parents about any uncomfortable images, information, or message and never respond to such messages.

❖ Do not meet in person with anyone you have communicated with online without a parent with you.

21-20 By setting rules to govern their children's computer use, parents can help protect their children from the dangers of the Internet and guide them toward the benefits.

Internet aimlessly. Some experts estimate that as much as 90 percent of exposure to inappropriate content occurs accidentally while children are exploring without a specific goal.

In addition, parents may need to create technological barriers by using a **filtering program**. This is a program that prevents a child from accessing inappropriate material on the Internet. These programs can do the following:

❖ block access to Web sites with adult content

❖ block access to the Internet totally during set hours

❖ create a log of visited sites

❖ track Internet discussions in chat rooms

❖ monitor software downloaded to a personal computer

Adults have several options when it comes to filtering systems. They can use any of the following:

❖ a closed system filtering program in which parents first approve the sites their children can visit

❖ a server-level filtering system

❖ a closed system and server-level filtering system together

❖ Internet filtering by restricting children's access to search engines that are not designed for children

Adults need to know that no filtering program is foolproof. Children are best protected by both filters and adult supervision. Parents should talk to their children about the dangers of the Internet and be available to talk to children when questions or problems arise regarding Internet use.

Safety Devices and Safety Measures

To help prevent possible accidents, adults must always be a step ahead of children. They must childproof the environment before the child is able to get into trouble. For example, adults cannot wait until a child can open doors to restrict the child's access to a door that leads to a steep flight of stairs. Adults should never rely on norms or past experiences to tell them when to childproof. Children develop at different rates, even within the same family. Also, some children explore more than others.

Safety devices can help prevent accidents. These include electrical outlet covers and safety latches on cabinets and drawers. Using safety knobs that fit over standard knobs that require an adult's grip to open them are also important. Although these devices are helpful, they do not take the place of careful supervision. Fire and smoke detectors need to be installed. Fire extinguishers must be ready for use.

Medical emergencies arise from both illnesses and accidents. Adults need to recognize symptoms requiring emergency treatment, 21-21. Adults must also take proper action. These steps include:

❖ Apply first aid. **First aid** is emergency treatment for an illness or accident that is given before professional medical help arrives. Training in first aid can be very helpful to parents and is required as part of teacher training. First-aid supplies, including a first aid chart or book, should be kept current and nearby as well, 21-22.

❖ Call the Emergency Medical System. Adults need to keep emergency phone numbers updated and quickly available, 21-23. When

Symptoms Requiring Emergency Treatment

Seek emergency treatment when a child:

❖ looks or acts very ill or seems to be getting worse quickly
❖ acts very confused
❖ breathes so fast or hard that it interferes with making sounds or drinking
❖ has uneven pupils
❖ has a high fever (for infants under 4 months a rectal fever of 101°F or higher; for children over 4 months a fever of 105°F or higher)
❖ has forceful vomiting (for infants under 4 months – once; for children over 4 months – continuous vomiting)
❖ has severe headache or neck pain or stiffness
❖ has a seizure for the first time or has a seizure that lasts more than 15 minutes
❖ has a blood-red or purple rash NOT associated with an injury
❖ has hives or welts that appear rapidly
❖ has a stomachache that causes screaming or doubling up or has a stomachache after a blow to the stomach region
❖ has bleeding that does not respond to first aid
❖ has black or blood-mixed stools
❖ has not urinated for 8 hours
❖ has continuous clear drainage from the nose after a head injury
❖ has a fracture (broken bone)

21-21 Adults who note these symptoms should seek emergency medical treatment for the child.

filtering program. A program that prevents a child from accessing inappropriate material on the Internet.

first aid. Emergency treatment for an illness or accident that is given before professional medical help arrives.

First-Aid Items

❖ adhesive bandages (various sizes)
❖ adhesive tape
❖ antiseptic for cuts and scratches
❖ calamine lotion (for insect bites)
❖ gauze bandages and squares
❖ scissors
❖ syrup of ipecac (used to induce vomiting for some, but not all, poisonings)
❖ first-aid chart or book (for quick reference)

21-22 A few first-aid supplies are needed to treat minor mishaps.

Emergency Phone Numbers

Local emergency number (if you have one): 555-1243

Ambulance: 555-7820

Dentist: 555-6473

Doctor: 555-7654

Drugstore: 555-8901

Fire department: 555-8041

Hospital: 555-7302

Neighbors: Mrs. Rodriguez 555-4060
Mr. Petersen 555-3867

Police department: 555-8938

Poison control center: 555-8392

Relatives: Grace Taylor (Grandma 555-2323
Mr. and Mrs. Mason (Uncle Dan and Aunt Dianne) 555-3374

Taxi: 555-4222

21-23 Posting the correct emergency phone numbers near the telephone saves time in a crisis.

an emergency occurs at school or in child care, staff must read and follow the child's Emergency Medical Form; seek emergency medical help if needed; stay with the child until a parent arrives; and complete an incident report.

❖ Continue first aid until professional help arrives and then do not interfere with the assistance.

Sometimes emergency situations occur due to fire, explosion, or weather situations. In these cases, parents or teachers should conduct evacuation or safety plans that have been practiced with children. They should comfort and reassure children who are frightened. A parent or teacher should have a flashlight and first-aid kit next to the evacuation door(s) or in the safety area for easy access. (A tote bag filled with these supplies makes it easy to carry while helping children.)

Safety Lessons

Teaching safety is an ongoing process that begins almost at birth and continues for life. The first lessons occur in the home and yard. They expand to include the total environment, such as school, water, traffic, and job safety.

Adults are models for children. A child will absorb the adult's approach to everyday actions and safety measures, such as buckling seat belts and looking before crossing streets. Adults may even exaggerate behavior to make safety measures clearer for the child. They may stop, look, and say, "I don't see a car coming, so we can cross now," before walking across a street.

Adults should carefully explain the boundaries of play. They must show as well as tell children what they can and cannot do. Such warnings are helpful only if they are stated in positive ways. An adult may say, "Grass is for playing, and streets are for cars and trucks." Warnings stated in negative ways may tempt children to act in unsafe ways. Also, warnings that are repeated too often lose their meanings.

All warnings should be coupled with reasons, or the child may think a given action is okay if the adult is not watching. For example, adults should explain the importance of safety devices like seat belts, crash helmets, and life jackets. They should also explain how to use these devices properly, 21-24.

Adults need to insist on obedience. Children want and need to be protected. Parents require obedience when they take action against wrong doings instead of simply threatening

21-24 Safety devices protect a person's life.
Louisiana Department of Wildlife and Fisheries

children. Taking action does not call for physical punishment. It can mean making the child stay in the bedroom or come inside for a short time. Insisting on obedience is a way of saying, "I care about you."

Practice Safety Measures

Adults should practice safety measures with children. These measures might include a fire drill or a safe walk to school. Adults can also read books on safety to children. They can watch special segments on safety in children's television programs. To support the safety lessons, adults can have children talk about, act out, or draw the safety actions.

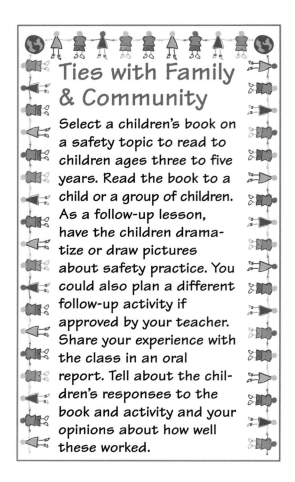

Ties with Family & Community

Select a children's book on a safety topic to read to children ages three to five years. Read the book to a child or a group of children. As a follow-up lesson, have the children dramatize or draw pictures about safety practice. You could also plan a different follow-up activity if approved by your teacher. Share your experience with the class in an oral report. Tell about the children's responses to the book and activity and your opinions about how well these worked.

Preparing a Child for Routine or Hospital Care

Medical care should be part of children's lives on a routine basis as well as when problems arise. Going to the doctor or dentist can be stressful for both child and adult. However, there are ways to ease the stress.

Routine Care

Depending on their ages, children react in different ways to routine care. Children under two years of age often cry while being examined. (They may begin crying when undressed and placed on cold scales.) Two- and three-year-olds often cry, too. They may also hide from, kick, or push the doctor. (Hiding, kicking, and pushing are attempts to get rid of those who are checking or treating them.) Older children are better able to understand what going to the doctor means. These children are apt to become anxious ahead of time. They may become more anxious in the car or walking in the office. They often cry or kick during routines that are not comfortable. Many children are relaxed about procedures that are painless. Following the visit, older children may act bossy. This may help relieve the feelings of powerlessness they felt during the visit.

Adults can lessen some of the stress of routine care in several ways. First, they can select capable and caring health care professionals. Adults should feel free to ask questions. They should also feel the doctor answers these questions completely and clearly. The doctor and dentist should appeal to the child, too. Children often like doctors and dentists who greet them by name and in a friendly way. They also like caregivers who notice something personal, such as a child's new haircut or pretty dress. Talking to the child during the checkup and

21-25 Waiting rooms that appeal to children make medical care less stressful.
© John Shaw

remaining calm, even if the child doesn't, are other positive qualities. Colorful waiting rooms and examination rooms also appeal to children, 21-25.

Adults should bring books and toys to appointments to make waiting more pleasant for the child. They should also bring a change of clothes, if needed. They should ask before giving a child candy or gum, which changes the color of the mouth and throat. This may make **diagnosis** (identifying the cause) of an illness more difficult. Adults should arrive at the appointment with information and prepared questions.

Adults can reassure the child it is okay to feel sick. Pain or other sick feelings may frighten a child. Adults can explain a little about procedures and relate them as much as possible to everyday life. They may say, "X-rays are pictures," and, "The dentist will look at your teeth." Too many explanations, such as, "The doctor will use a large machine to make the X-ray," can add to a child's fear.

Helping the Child During the Examination

During the actual examination, the following will help the child feel more comfortable:

❖ Adults should stay with the child and stand where the child can see them. (Dentists, however, usually prefer adults stay in the waiting room.)

❖ Use a soft, soothing voice. A child may stop crying to hear whispered words.

❖ Hold the child if the doctor asks.

❖ Do not tell the child a procedure will not hurt if, in fact, it will. Instead, tell the child, "It will be all right," or "Soon it will be over." If the child cries, reassure him or her that crying is all right. Say, "I know this hurts, but it will stop hurting soon."

❖ Do not distract a baby or child by making noises, such as jingling keys. Such sounds interfere with a doctor's ability to hear internal sounds. Some babies and children cry louder when an adult tries to distract them. (Perhaps they feel the distraction means the proce-dure will be painful.)

diagnosis. Identifying the cause of a person's illness.

Hospital Care

Hospital care is often a special problem for both parents and children. Parents see hospitals as places where people experience separation from loved ones, pain, and even death. Hospitals may also seem large and *impersonal* (not concerned about the child as a person). Parents tend to feel they are no longer in charge of their child's care once the child enters the hospital. Also, doctors or nurses often ask parents to assist during painful treatments, which can be almost unbearable for parents.

Parents or other adults may also feel guilty about the cause for needed hospital care. For example, they may feel they could have prevented a fall if they had watched more carefully. Adults might think they should have sought care earlier to keep symptoms from becoming more serious.

Children may also fear being cared for in a hospital. A child under four years of age might be most concerned with the fear of separation from parents. Older children worry about what doctors will do to their bodies. Children react to medical tests and treatments in the hospital in even more intense ways than they react to office visits. This can be because of the new people caring for the child. Also, the child may endure more frequent and painful tests and procedures. Hospital stays are longer than office visits, and the surroundings are unfamiliar, too. Children may think of hospital care as punishment.

Easing the Stress of Hospital Care

Parents can ease the stress of hospital care in many ways. First, they should find out as much as possible about the stay. This will prepare them to better help the child. If possible, they should tell the child about the stay ahead of time. The talk should focus on good points (time in the hospital will help the child feel better). However, adults should never be dishonest about what they tell the child. This can damage the child's ability to trust.

Allowing children to explore the idea of hospital care through play can be helpful. too. Using a toy doctor's kit and reading books about hospital care may relieve some of children's fears. Some hospitals have playrooms where children can act out hospital care. (The rooms also provide art activities, games, and books.)

An arranged hospital tour of the children's area may make the child feel more comfortable. The nurse who will care for the child should give the tour, if possible. Children need to develop friendships with those they'll be seeing most often, 21-26. This helps hospitals seem less threatening.

Parents should plan to room-in with babies and young children when possible. Many hospitals provide a bed or reclining chair, food service, phone, television, and magazines for the parents of hospitalized children. Members of service groups may help

21-26 A warm feeling between a child and a nurse makes hospital care easier.
© John Shaw

parents by serving snacks or shopping for small purchases. They may also volunteer to sit with the child for a while so the parent can take a break.

During the Hospital Stay

While the child is in the hospital, parents can often meet the child's nonmedical needs, which may include feeding, bathing, and toileting. They should go with the child for tests and treatments when allowed. In some hospitals, parents can go with the child to the surgery room and stay with the child until he or she is unconscious. Parents may also be present in the recovery room as the child awakens.

During a hospital stay, children need items that comfort them and remind them of home, 21-27. Adults should bring some of the child's toys, pajamas, or other items to the hospital. If the child can have visitors or phone calls, adults can arrange for friends, adults, and siblings to stay in contact.

Older children may want to keep a scrapbook or box to help them remember their stay. The book or box might include pictures, hospital bracelets, covers to disposable thermometers, and syringes without needles. Children can show hospital items when telling others about their stay. Like talking about any other experience, talking about a hospital stay is healthy for children.

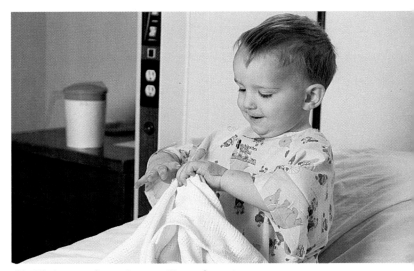

21-27 Items from home, like a favorite blanket, make a child's hospital stay more comfortable.
© John Shaw

Caring for an Ill or Injured Child

Parents and adults who work with children will need to care for ill or injured children at some time, 21-28. Children will experience many scrapes, bumps, and bruises as they learn what their bodies can and cannot do. Young children, especially those under age seven or eight years, have many common illnesses, such as colds and digestive upsets. Adults often handle such small problems. Doctors also expect adults to follow through with care for more complex problems.

There are several common conditions adults must frequently treat in children. See 21-29 for practices doctors recommend. Adults should use a current first-aid chart or book to give first aid for major injuries. Taking a first-aid class is also very helpful.

21-28 If adults know some simple first-aid steps, they can treat many minor accidents at home.
© John Shaw

Giving Medication and Proper Care

For many illnesses, adults are expected to give medication. They should use accurate measuring devices. A medically defined teaspoon contains exactly 1 teaspoon of liquid, but a household teaspoon varies from ½ teaspoon to 1½ teaspoons of liquid. For this reason, adults should use medically defined measuring devices to give liquid medicines. This ensures they will give the correct dosage each time. Incorrect dosages may prevent infections from clearing up (from too little medication). They may also cause a child to be poisoned (from too much medication).

Adults should give medication to children in ways that make it easy for them to take. Babies may suck medication through a nursing nipple with ring attached. Some may take medication from a dropper or syringe (without a needle) inserted far back at the side of the mouth. Older children often receive medication from a medical measuring spoon. Before children can swallow tablets, adults can crush the tablets and mix them with sugar or a bite of food. An older child can learn to swallow a tablet by tipping the head back. This action causes the tablet to sink in the back of the throat. Children can also learn to swallow a capsule by bending forward. This causes the lightweight capsule to float toward the back of the throat.

Keeping an active child in bed is a challenge for most parents. As children

Caring for Children's Health Problems

Fever

Fever is a temperature above normal body temperature. This is 97.6°F when taken under the arm (auxiliary), 98.6°F when taken orally, and 99.6°F when taken rectally.

Fevers under 101°F usually do not need treatment. Very young infants may be an exception. Ask the child's doctor for guidelines.

For higher fevers, use ibuprofen (unless child is dehydrated* or vomiting) or acetaminophen but *not* aspirin. (Dosages are best based on weight, but child's age may be used for dosage unless the child is very light or heavy for age.) Sponge bathing can be done with medication or in place of medication if child is vomiting. To sponge bathe, use only tepid water (85°F to 90°F) in a room that is about 75°F. Keep child's room cool; dress child lightly; encourage the non-vomiting child to drink fluids, avoid fatty diets that are difficult to digest, and keep child from exerting himself or herself.

Diarrhea

Mild cases: Continue normal diet.

Moderate cases: Use commercial rehydration fluids in generous amounts unless the child is vomiting and cannot keep these down.

Severe cases: May require IV fluids administered at the hospital.

Do not make special fluids to treat diarrhea, offer boiled milk or salty broth, treat with antidiarrheals, or prevent child from eating if hungry.

Call doctor if child is dehydrated,* has blood in stool, has a high fever (over 102°F), or diarrhea continues more than 24 hours.

Vomiting

Offer fluids frequently. (Toddlers and preschoolers can drink commercial rehydrating fluids and school-age children may have a 50/50 blend of sports drink and water. Avoid caffeine and high-sugar drinks.) If child vomits after taking fluids, offer nothing for one or two hours and then try ice chips or spoonfuls of liquid. After several hours without vomiting, begin solids, such as toast, oatmeal, bananas, applesauce, cooked fruits, or soft-boiled egg. Do not offer raw fruits or vegetables, bran cereals, or dairy products until the child is able to keep down other solids. Call the doctor if baby vomits after every feeding in a 12-hour period or if vomiting is associated with swelling or a sharp abdominal pain, blood or bile in vomit, confusion or listlessness, signs of dehydration,* or combined with diarrhea for more than 12 hours.

Runny Nose

Use a nasal aspirator (rubber bulb syringe) to suck mucus from nose. Make saltwater drops by combining ¼ teaspoon salt with 4 ounces water. Place a few drops in each nostril five times per day. The drops will cause sneezing, which will clear the nasal passages. Use a cool-air humidifier in the child's bedroom. Call the doctor if other symptoms appear.

Scrapes and Scratches

Wash with soap and water; rinse well. If desired, apply an antiseptic spray, cream, or ointment to the affected area. Cover with an adhesive strip or small piece of sterile gauze held with adhesive tape. Call the doctor if the wound is deep, puncturelike, or does not heal as it should.

*Dehydration is the loss of fluid due to diarrhea, fever, and vomiting. Signs of dehydration include high fever, little urine output, dry mouth, crying with no tears, and "sunken eyes."

21-29 Doctors often expect adults to care for these health problems.

begin to feel well, they do not want to stay in bed. Quiet games, books, television, music, and paper and crayons can help children pass time. Visits from adults and other children (if the illness is not contagious) also help.

When children are ill or injured, they need a little extra attention. Babies and young children often need lots of holding and rocking. Older children may need their illness or injury and the treatment explained to them. Most children enjoy little surprises, too. These might include a small gift; a special dish (if they can eat); or a get-well card. Above all, adults should appear cheerful and confident so they will not cause children to worry. If the child's attitude is positive, this can also speed recovery.

Caring for a Terminally Ill Child

Despite great advances, medical science cannot cure every illness. Among those who are **terminally ill** (have diseases that will result in their deaths) are children. Terminal illnesses in children include some congenital problems, such as heart and liver diseases and cystic fibrosis. Other diseases, such as AIDS and forms of cancer, are also terminal illnesses.

Facing the death of a child is one of the most profound emotional experiences a family can ever encounter. Often the family feels this period more keenly than the ill child. They feel a sense of loss before the death

occurs. They show this by going through the stages of coping with death. Families show denial. ("The doctors are wrong.") They may try bargaining with their faith. ("Just let my child live and I will...") Families feel depressed thinking about the loss and its impact. Finally, they accept the idea of their child's death. Although family members feel sad, they usually want to appear cheerful for the child's sake or the sake of others. They also want to remain hopeful.

Helping the Ill Child Cope

Besides trying to cope with their own feelings, family members must help and seek help for the ill child. How a child perceives his or her condition depends greatly upon his or her age. Children begin to understand death in the preschool years, but their understanding is rather limited until the school-age years. What and how much should a family tell a child? That is a personal decision best made after the family discusses the child's case with professionals and each other.

Parents need to find out how much the sick child wants or needs to understand about his or her illness. Older children often realize what may happen. They may fear possible tests and treatments, the separation that death brings, and being left alone. Ill children may be concerned about their parents' feelings of loss. Families must allow sick children to do all they can physically tolerate and as much as possible for themselves. They should try to help their terminally ill child experience his or her remaining life to the fullest.

Helping the Family Cope

Family members need the help of professionals during this time of crisis. Many hospitals that treat terminally ill children hire professionals such as medical staff, religious leaders, and social workers to help the family. Parent support groups are also available. Members of these groups often provide much comfort. These people have gone through or are going through the same problems.

The family needs the help of friends at this time, too. Friends should learn as much as they can about the disease and its treatments. This will help them better understand what family members share with them. The role of friends can be described best as listening rather than advising. Certainly friends should express their concern and sorrow, but they should carefully choose their words. For example, saying, "I understand how you feel," may prompt a hurt response, such as, "How could you? Your child is healthy!"

If possible, friends should offer help. They should consider the family's needs and suggest a concrete way to assist. This might be an offer to cook the family dinner or drive a healthy child to an after-school activity. Such offers are easier for the family than the vague offer of, "Let me know if there is anything I can do." Most of all, friends must remember that family members will need emotional support during the weeks and months before and after the child's death.

terminally ill. Having a disease that will result in death.

Summing It Up

Protecting and maintaining children's health and safety is one of the major responsibilities of adults. In addition to teaching and modeling good health practices, adults need to provide a safe and healthy environment.

In order to monitor growth and development, adults should have children checked by health care professionals on a regular basis. Getting children vaccinated will protect them from many diseases. Children need prompt medical attention when they show certain or prolonged symptoms of illness.

Adults need to anticipate and remove possible hazards in their home. Childproofing the environment will help prevent many accidents.

Preparing children for routine or hospital care will help lessen their fear and anxiety. Ill or injured children should be treated as doctors recommend. Families experience severe emotional stress when a child is terminally ill. Caring friends and others can help family members at this time.

Reviewing Key Concepts

Write your answers on a separate sheet of paper.

1. True or false. Good nutrition serves as a physical support when an accident or injury occurs.
2. List the two best ways for adults to prevent accidents.
   A. Warn or threaten a child.
   B. Create a safe environment.
   C. Prevent the child from doing dangerous acts.
   D. Let the child learn lessons from dangerous experiences.
   E. Teach safety.
   F. Remove all unsafe items from the home and yard.
3. True or false. The type of accidents a child commonly has changes with the child's age.
4. Why does the time of day affect the number of accidents children have?
5. Poisonings of children under the age of five years account for what percent of all accidental poisonings in homes each year?
6. True or false. Poisonings from plants are harder to detect than poisonings from household products.
7. Which of the following is the number one cause of death for infants and children?
   A. plant poisonings
   B. household poisonings
   C. household falls such as on stairs
   D. car accidents
   E. diseases
8. Explain why holding a child on your lap or sharing a seat belt in a car is unsafe for the child.
9. List five ways parents can protect and guide children in computer use.
10. List four ways an adult can lessen the stress of routine medical care for a child.
11. Give three reasons that hospitals are stressful for the parents of sick children.
12. True or false. Teaspoons from household flatware are suitable for measuring liquid medication.
13. List two guidelines for helping the family of a terminally ill child.

Using Your Knowledge

1. **Teamwork/Creative Skills.** On your own, list 10 guidelines you think parents should follow in promoting their children's health. Share your list with a small group of classmates, and listen to the lists of other members. Then, work with your group to create a "Top 10 List" that includes the best ideas of each member. Plan a creative way to present your group's list to the class.
2. **Technology/Consumer Skills.** Go shopping online, in person, or in catalogs to research the latest child-proofing devices. Describe your top three picks to the class and explain how each of these devices works.
3. **Technology/Consumer Skills.** Compare the specifications and prices on two closed filtering programs. Which one would you recommend, and why?

4. **Creative Skills/Safety Practices.** Design a poster that illustrates a safety practice young children can learn. If approved by your teacher, display your poster in a local elementary school.

5. **Technology/Safety Practices.** Use the computer to create a list of emergency telephone numbers for your home. Place a copy of this list near each telephone. (Use chart 21-23 as a guide for the numbers needed.)

Making Observations

1. Observe a group of toddlers or preschoolers at play. What traits of this age group make them prone to accidents? Give specific examples. How did adult actions or the environment prevent or lessen potential accidents?

2. Visit the home of a 6- to 12-month-old infant. What signs of child-proofing are evident? What additional measures of child-proofing would you recommend?

3. Observe toddlers or preschoolers in a doctor's waiting room. What environmental factors lessened children's stress? Did any environmental factors increase the stress? How did parents increase or decrease stress in children?

Thinking Further

1. Explain the difference between a *risk* and a *hazard*? For a given child, can a hazard ever become a risk? Are some risks necessary for growth and development?

2. If a young married couple plans to have children soon, what advice could you give them regarding choosing a vehicle? Be specific.

3. Why are people often fearful of medical procedures or hospital care? How are the causes of these fears perhaps similar to those of young children? How might the causes be different?

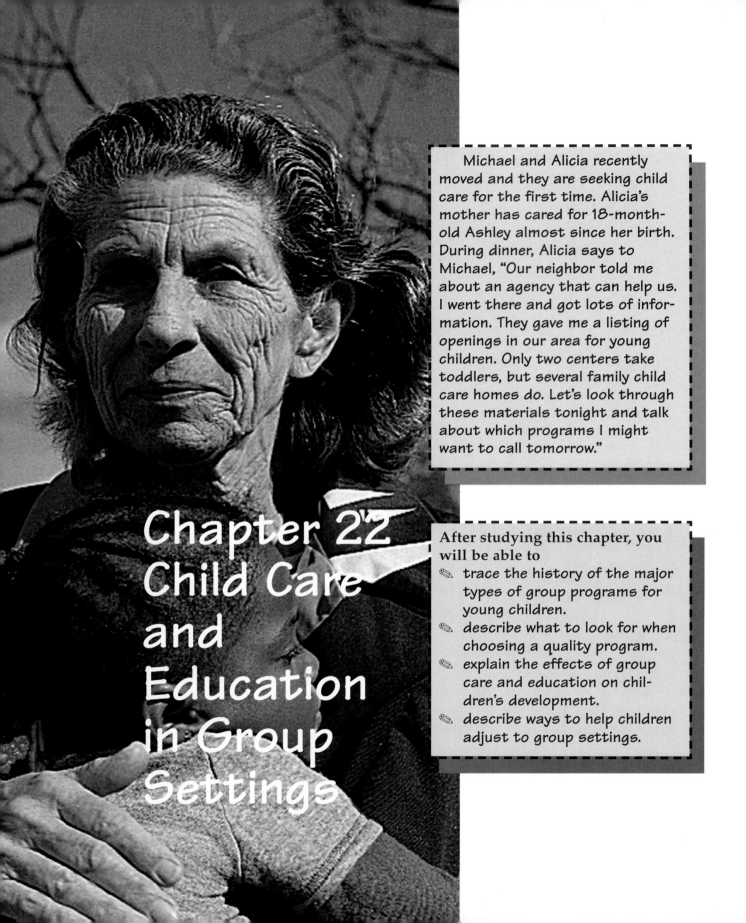

Michael and Alicia recently moved and they are seeking child care for the first time. Alicia's mother has cared for 18-month-old Ashley almost since her birth. During dinner, Alicia says to Michael, "Our neighbor told me about an agency that can help us. I went there and got lots of information. They gave me a listing of openings in our area for young children. Only two centers take toddlers, but several family child care homes do. Let's look through these materials tonight and talk about which programs I might want to call tomorrow."

Chapter 22
Child Care and Education in Group Settings

After studying this chapter, you will be able to
- trace the history of the major types of group programs for young children.
- describe what to look for when choosing a quality program.
- explain the effects of group care and education on children's development.
- describe ways to help children adjust to group settings.

Define...

child care programs
in-home child care
au pairs
nannies
family child care
center-based child care
for-profit programs
not-for-profit programs
work-related child care programs
school-age child care programs
  (SACC)
child care resource and referral
  agencies (CCR&R)
kindergarten
private programs
fingerplays
nursery schools
Montessori schools
Head Start
regulations
public programs
adult-child ratio
developmentally appropriate
  practices (DAP)
developmentally inappropriate
  practices (DIP)
field trips
culture shock
bias
hidden added costs
hidden cost credits

Why do some parents enroll their children in group programs? Some may work outside the home and need child care while they are gone. Others may need relief from caring for children full-time because of health (or other) reasons. Still others may use group care to challenge their children in all areas of development.

Programs for young children have not always been common. Today, the picture has changed. In the last three decades, the number of group programs has increased. Why? One reason is the public's growing concern about the need for quality education for children. Another reason is the growing number of parents in the workforce. Yet another reason is that quality group programs can affect children in many positive ways.

Along with the increased number of children enrolled in group settings, the types of programs have changed. Programs are now available to meet the needs of infants and toddlers as well as school-age children. These programs also serve more children from diverse cultures and children with special needs.

Types of Group Programs

There are all kinds of group programs for children, including child care programs, kindergartens, nursery schools, and Head Start programs, 22-1. Descriptions of how these programs differ follow.

Child Care Programs

The term **child care programs** refers to programs that operate to care for children for extended hours,

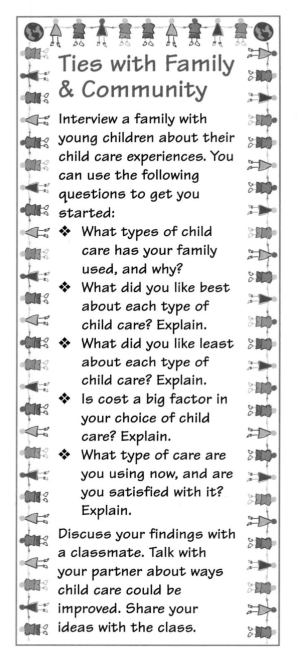

Ties with Family & Community

Interview a family with young children about their child care experiences. You can use the following questions to get you started:

❖ What types of child care has your family used, and why?

❖ What did you like best about each type of child care? Explain.

❖ What did you like least about each type of child care? Explain.

❖ Is cost a big factor in your choice of child care? Explain.

❖ What type of care are you using now, and are you satisfied with it? Explain.

Discuss your findings with a classmate. Talk with your partner about ways child care could be improved. Share your ideas with the class.

22-1 Group programs vary from those that only care for basic needs to those that provide many special activities to enhance development.

usually between 9 and 12 hours a day. The main purpose of child care programs is to provide basic care for children when parents are not available. More and more child care programs are providing education as well as care services, however. Child care programs offer services for children from infancy to preschool age. They even may serve school-age children at times when school is not in session.

Historical Overview

In Europe in the late 1700s and early 1800s, child care programs were called *Infant Schools.* These programs served poor children from toddlerhood to ages five or six years, at which age children entered the workforce.

By the middle of the nineteenth century, child care for children of poor parents existed in urban areas of the United States. Many of these programs included programs to teach adults how to care for their home and children. Federal funds aided child care programs during the Great Depression of 1929 and World War II.

After World War II, child care programs declined until the 1960s. At that time, women entered the workforce in great numbers. Some experts now note quality child care programs do not exist for all the children needing care. Currently, the increase in the number of children needing care is larger than the increase in quality child care placements.

Types of Child Care Programs

Parents use four main types of child care—in-home child care, family child care, center-based child care, and school-age child care. The type of care parents choose depends on many factors. These include the number and ages of children, cost of care, family goals for children, location of employment, work hours, and types of child care available in the local area. No one type of child care is best for every family; each type has its advantages and disadvantages, 22-2. In each type of child care, the quality of care may range from high to inadequate. Thus, parents must carefully check any child care arrangements before contracting for care. They should also check regularly on their children's care throughout their enrollment.

In-Home Child Care

In-home child care takes place in the child's own home. This type of child care can be provided by parents, relatives, or nonrelatives.

In some families, one parent stays at home to care for the children. Even among families in which both parents work, however, 24 percent of all children under school-age are cared for in their homes by a parent. In-home care by a parent is more common for infants and toddlers than it is for preschoolers. Parents can provide this type of care by working alternate schedules so one parent is always home, taking children to work with them, or working from home.

Almost one-fourth of the children in child care are cared for by a relative. A little less than half of this relative care is done in the child's home.

Only about 6 percent of all children in child care have care provided by non-relatives in the home. Three types of caregivers who provide in-home child care are housekeepers, au pairs, and nannies. Housekeepers are often employed on an hourly basis and take care of the children and clean the house. Au pairs and nannies are mainly hired to care for children.

Au pairs provide child care for a host family as part of a cultural exchange program. This exchange program might last anywhere from six months to a year. In addition to

child care programs. Programs that operate to care for children for extended hours, usually between 9 and 12 hours a day.

in-home child care. Child care that takes place in the child's own home.

au pairs. Persons who provide child care for a host family as part of a cultural exchange program.

Comparing Types of Child Care Services

Type of Care	Advantages	Disadvantages
In-home child care—A person is hired to care for children in the children's home.	❖ The children receive all the caregiver's attention. ❖ Chances of health and safety problems are small. ❖ Children can be cared for when they are ill. ❖ Children are not taken outdoors in inclement weather or early hours. ❖ Children stay in the home atmosphere.	❖ Quality care can be a problem. ❖ Adults must make alternative plans if the caregiver cannot work. ❖ Adults must pay Social Security employer taxes. ❖ Education activities are rarely offered unless the person is well trained and does not have major housekeeping duties.
Family child care—A small number of children are cared for in another person's home.	❖ A good selection of family child care services may exist. ❖ Usually all children receive the attention they need. ❖ This type of program suits after-school care. ❖ Hours of operation often are flexible and meet parents' needs. ❖ Children from the same family who are different ages may be cared for together. ❖ Children stay in a homelike atmosphere.	❖ Quality care may not be given in all family child care programs. ❖ Most family child care programs are not licensed. ❖ Parents must make alternative plans if the caregiver cannot work. ❖ Children must leave the house each day. ❖ Children may not be allowed to attend the program if they are sick. ❖ Education activities may not be offered.
Center-based child care—A fairly large number of children are enrolled in a center.	❖ Caregivers emphasize cooperative play and social living. ❖ Centers often are licensed so quality may be ensured. ❖ The center director makes any alternative plans needed. ❖ The center may provide special services, such as an educational program. ❖ Facilities and equipment are designed for children. ❖ Education activities are often offered.	❖ Parents often are concerned about their children's health and safety. ❖ The day may involve too many structured activities, especially for younger children. ❖ A home atmosphere is usually missing. ❖ Every child may not receive the attention he or she needs. ❖ Hours and days of operation are not flexible. ❖ Often payment is expected in advance and even for days when the child is absent. ❖ Often ill or injured children cannot attend the center. ❖ Children must leave their home each day. ❖ Some centers are costly.

(Continued)

22-2 Each type of child care service has its advantages and disadvantages.

Comparing Types of Child Care Services (Continued)

Type of Care	Advantages	Disadvantages
School-age child care—Part-time care for school-age children while parents are employed or not at home.	❖ Children do not experience the risks of self-care. ❖ In quality programs, children receive care, recreation, diversion, and education.	❖ Part-time quality group care is difficult to find, especially in rural areas, and may be rather expensive on a per-hour basis. ❖ Most SACC programs are designed for children grade 3 and below. (Programs are needed for children to age 12 or 13 years.) ❖ Some children do not like a structured program after attending school all day.

child care, au pairs also do light housekeeping. For their services, au pairs receive room, board, and transportation from the host family. Most au pairs are young, single women without children. They often have limited child care knowledge and experience. Although the au pair works for the family, he or she is a live-in guest of the host family. An au pair should be treated as a member of the family and should not be expected to work "around the clock." Host families are expected to provide cultural experiences and free time for au pairs.

Nannies are professionals who contract with a family to provide in-home child care. They typically care for children from birth to age 10 or 12 years. Like au pairs, most nannies are young, single women. However, nannies are not cultural exchange persons. They may live in the home or

come to the home daily. Nannies do not do housework beyond preparing meals for the children. Nannies are employed by the family. They have set responsibilities and hours even if they live with the family. Nannies often have training beyond high school in child care, health and safety, and nutrition. Some have a college degree and are certified. (These nannies are called: Certified Household Managers, Certified Professional Nannies, or Certified Professional Governesses.) Because of their training, nannies often earn more than housekeepers, au pairs, or babysitters. While some nannies stay with the same family for

nannies. Professionals who contract with a family to provide in-home child care.

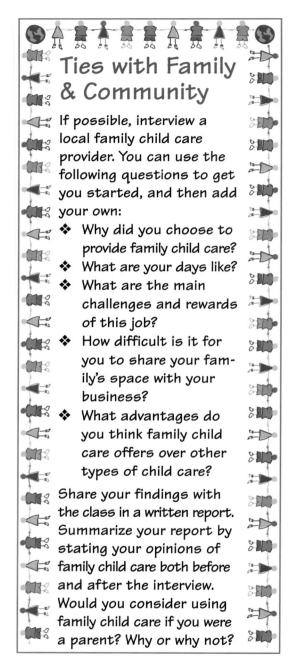

Ties with Family & Community

If possible, interview a local family child care provider. You can use the following questions to get you started, and then add your own:

❖ Why did you choose to provide family child care?
❖ What are your days like?
❖ What are the main challenges and rewards of this job?
❖ How difficult is it for you to share your family's space with your business?
❖ What advantages do you think family child care offers over other types of child care?

Share your findings with the class in a written report. Summarize your report by stating your opinions of family child care both before and after the interview. Would you consider using family child care if you were a parent? Why or why not?

years, many see their jobs as short-term. These nannies often complete their schooling and then direct child care centers or teach in group programs.

Family Child Care

Family child care is care provided by a person for a small number of children in his or her own home. Some family child care homes are run much like child care centers. For example, these homes might offer a structured schedule, menu, and activities. Other family child care homes are run by a parent of young children. This parent stays home with his or her own children and provides care for other children, too.

Many parents need family child care for various reasons, 22-3. These families might need more flexible hours than often provided by large group programs. Other families need family child care because larger programs may not be available in their locale. Furthermore, many parents want family child care because they see it as more homelike—similar to the type of care they would provide if not employed. Many family child care homes may follow less of a schedule than child care centers. Children in family child care may do many homelike activities. They may "help" the provider do housekeeping tasks, visit with friends who come to the home, and even go on shopping trips. Due to the many advantages of family child care, the military and some large corporations are seeking ways to increase the number of regulated family child care homes for their employees' children, 22-4.

Advantages of Family Child Care Placements for Some Children

Children	Advantages of Family Child Care
Infants and toddlers	Using family child care for infants and toddlers is much less expensive than using child care centers. Also, infants and toddlers need much individual attention, which may be available in a family child care home.
Children who are prone to mild illnesses, such as colds, sore throats, and ear infections	Pediatricians often advise parents of these children to limit the children's contact with large groups of children. Because family child care homes have fewer children, these may be a better choice than child care centers.
Children who need part-time care	Part-time care is more often available in family child care homes than in child care centers. Centers try to maximize their profits by filling as many placements as they can with children who need full-time care. Some centers charge the same rate for part-time care as full-time care, while many family child care providers charge a reduced rate for part-time care.
School-age children	Most center-based child care programs are designed for young children. These programs do not meet the needs of children who are school-age. Furthermore, most older children need only part-time care.
Children who live in rural areas	Many rural areas do not have much selection in center-based care. In these areas, many more children attend family child care homes.

22-3 Quality family child care may be the best child care option for many families.

State laws limit the total number of children family child care homes can serve. Often this is six or seven children, including the caregiver's own children. If the children are all under two years of age, the total number is four or five children.

An estimated 70 percent of all family child care homes do not report their business to the state; thus, they do not have a state license or certificate of registration to operate. If the state is unaware of a family child care home, it cannot regulate the care provided there. Some of these non-regulated homes have too many children or do not provide safe care. Parents cannot be certain of the care provided in

 family child care. Care provided by a person for a small number of children in his or her own home.

22-4 In family child care centers, siblings can be cared for together in a homelike setting.
Bonnie Mori

unlicensed homes. They should instead seek a family child care home that is licensed or registered. In this type of home, they can be assured of at least a minimum standard of quality.

Center-Based Child Care

Center-based child care is a large group program in which child care is provided in a center (not a home). Center-based child care is planned for children whose parents are full-time employees. About 31 percent of all children under school-age with working parents attend center-based child care programs.

Centers differ in the number of children they serve. Many centers serve 20 or fewer children who are cared for in a building with one or two large rooms. Others enroll several hundred children who are placed in age-related groups and cared for in a multiroom building that resembles a school setting. State laws set the standards for all aspects of center-based child care programs (building requirements, staff, and program).

Most center-based child care programs are for-profit programs. This means they are set up to make money. Individuals or family corporations own them as a business. A few for-profit center programs have grown into national chains. Other center-based child care programs are not-for-profit programs. These programs are set up to make only enough money to cover costs. These may be funded by parents as cooperatives or by religious or service groups. Other not-for-profit centers are sponsored by businesses, hospitals, branches of the armed services, and colleges. Parents usually pay lower fees at a not-for-profit program than at a for-profit program. Programs sponsored by businesses for their employees' children are often called work-related child care programs.

School-Age Child Care

School-age child care programs (SACC) provide child care for 5- to 16-year-olds when school is not in session—before and after school, on school holidays or vacations, and during the summer. SACC programs are needed today because almost 80 percent of households with school-age children have working parents. Although schools provide care for children much of the day, the school day is shorter than the standard workday. Self-care is not a good choice for most families, so quality SACC programs are definitely needed. Part-time care is difficult to find in other child care programs because these are designed mainly for the full-time care of younger children.

The majority of SACC programs are affiliated with schools or agencies that serve youth. In the schools, space is often provided to other sponsors, such as the YMCA, to operate these programs. Other groups that operate SACC programs are religious groups, park and recreation facilities, housing authorities, military bases, family child care homes, child care centers, and companies. In some SACC programs called *clubs*, parents choose from a menu of activities for their children.

The basic goals of SACC programs are the following:

❖ care (protection, shelter, food, and guidance)
❖ recreation (supervised play or specific skill development, such as dance, ball games, or swimming)
❖ diversion (crafts, drama, field trips), 22-5
❖ education (help with homework or lessons in music or dance)

As is true of all types of child care, parents have trouble finding quality SACC programs and affording the costs for quality. For providers, the main challenges are finding suitable

22-5 Some school-age child care programs provide materials for children to do craft projects.

center-based child care. A large group program in which child care is provided in a center rather than in a home.

for-profit programs. Programs that are set up to make money.

not-for-profit programs. Child care programs in which income only covers costs.

work-related child care programs. Child care programs funded by businesses for their employees' children.

school-age child care programs (SACC). Programs that provide child care for 5- to 16-year-olds when school is not in session.

housing for a part-time program and planning details if space must be shared.

Trends in Child Care Programs

Several trends are seen in today's child care programs. These include the following:

❖ More infant and toddler care. (The need is great, because the majority of women return to their jobs within the child's first year. Programs for the youngest children are still most difficult to find. Quality infant and toddler programs are really scarce for they are very expensive and thus not affordable for many families, 22-6.)

❖ Growth in SACC programs. (Most SACC programs are in urban and suburban areas and serve children Grade 3 and below. More programs are needed, especially those whose activities interest older children.)

❖ Many businesses are becoming involved in child care. (Some businesses, especially those employing many women and the military, are providing work-related child care programs for their employees. Many other businesses are promoting the growth of child care programs within their communities and paying some of the costs of child care.)

❖ Growth in **child care resource and referral (CCR&R) agencies.** These agencies promote local child care programs and help parents find child care. They are funded by the state or by community business and civic groups. In CCR&R agencies, experts research the need for and availability of local child care. Information is given to providers and would-be providers to help them know what type of care is most needed and how to provide quality care. Although CCR&R staff members do not recommend a given program to parents, they share listings of local providers and information on the programs and current openings. They also help parents learn to select quality programs.

Kindergartens

Kindergarten programs are publicly and privately operated educational programs for four- and five-year-old children. In the United States, kindergartens are part of each

22-6 Quality infant/toddler programs are in demand.
Environments, Inc.

state's public education system. Private schools also sometimes offer kindergarten. Kindergarten serves as an entrance to school education and gives children the chance to play and develop through various activities.

Background of Kindergartens

Friedrich Froebel founded kindergartens as private programs in Germany. (**Private programs** are programs owned by individuals, churches, or other nongovernment groups.) The programs enrolled children from ages three to seven years and provided teaching suggestions for mothers with younger children.

Froebel felt a school for young children should be different from a school for older children, 22-7. He planned many of the activities that occur in kindergartens and other programs for young children today. Examples include activities with building blocks, beads, art materials, sand, math concepts, animals, plants, stories, and music. Another example is **fingerplays**, or poems and rhymes that are acted out with the hands. These activities were unlike the drill methods used in other schools of Froebel's time. In fact, Froebel's statement that "play is the highest level of child development" was scorned by many of his time.

Kindergartens came to the United States with German immigrants in the mid-1800s. Soon, English-speaking groups began to adopt the concept of kindergarten. People began to see the

22-7 Kindergartens allow more time for play and creativity than schools for older children.
© John Shaw

child care resource and referral agencies (CCR&R). Agencies promote local child care programs and help parents find child care.

kindergarten. Programs publicly and privately operated for four- and five-year-old children; serve as an entrance to school education.

private programs. Programs owned by individuals, churches, or other nongovernment groups.

fingerplays. Poems and rhymes that are acted out with the hands.

good effects of kindergarten on the lives of young children. Because of this, public schools began to include kindergarten as part of public education. Many states now mandate kindergarten attendance. Over 95 percent of five-year-olds attend kindergarten.

Over the years, kindergartens have changed some to meet children's needs. Some people have expressed concern about efforts in some programs to teach reading and other abstract learnings. Many feel this causes too much stress on children. The challenge of kindergartens is to fit the needs of children today and lead slowly toward children's next years in school.

Nursery Schools

Nursery schools provide education and physical care for children under age five years. Besides these services, many nursery schools serve as research sites for child development experts. They also offer training opportunities for students, teachers, and caregivers. Parents sign releases that allow for the study of their children and adult training in the classroom. All observing and reporting in nursery schools should follow ethical guidelines.

Most nursery schools are privately owned, but a few operate in public schools. Usually, nursery schools are high-quality programs that are directed by child development experts. These experts also oversee the activities, which ideally build on life within the

22-8 Nursery schools offer many rich play activities.

family, 22-8. Thus, most activities are firsthand experiences. Children play in a setting that is rich with materials, equipment, other children, and adults who are caring and well trained.

Unlike child care programs, nursery schools often operate for half-days. For this reason, nursery schools are a good fit for stay-at-home parents who want to offer their child a quality group experience. Parents often get detailed reports on their child's development. Sometimes nursery schools are a good match for parents who work part-time, too. Parents who work full-time are less likely to use half-day nursery schools because they must make other arrangements for their children for the rest of the workday.

The Origin of Nursery Schools

Nursery schools began in England in the early 1900s to help needy children. When nursery schools started in the United States, child development was becoming a science. The schools opened as laboratory schools directed by staffs of research and teaching hospitals and colleges. The schools studied children. They also trained mothers and teachers to care for and teach children.

Today's Programs

Some nursery schools still study children and provide career training. These laboratory schools operate in colleges, universities, and some high schools across the nation. However, today the term *nursery school* is used rather loosely, and child care programs may call themselves *nursery schools.* These so-called nursery schools only provide physical care for children. Thus, parents who are considering nursery schools should find out exactly what services each provides.

Montessori Schools

Another type of group program is a Montessori school. **Montessori schools** encourage young children to learn independently through the use of highly specialized materials rather than direct input from teachers.

Children usually enter Montessori schools between ages two and one-half to three years. Montessori classrooms are formed from a group of children within a three-year age span. Children in this group are not separated by age, grade, or level. They are free to move about the classroom, work with other children, and use any materials they understand, 22-9. Teachers trained in Montessori methods guide the children's use of materials. However, they do not use direct teaching. In this way, Montessori schools strive to put each child more in charge of his or her own learnings.

22-9 Low, open shelves allow children to be more in charge of their own learnings.
American Montessori Society/Montessori Greenhouse School

nursery schools. A public or private program for children under age five that provides education and physical care.

Montessori schools. Schools that encourage children to learn independently through the use of highly specialized materials.

Sensory learnings that involve specialized materials are a major focus of the program. Activities center on what children learn to see, hear, touch, taste, and smell in the world around them. Self-help activities, such as preparing food and washing hands, also are a big part of the program. Materials are designed to teach mathematics and language concepts, too.

Named for their founder, Maria Montessori, the first Montessori schools opened in Rome, Italy, in the early 1900s. Montessori was a medical doctor who had worked quite successfully with children with mental disabilities. This success led her to plan an all-day program for poor children between ages 30 months and 7 years. She named her school the *Casa dei Bambini,* which means *children's house.*

Montessori believed children differ from adults and from each other. She also felt children can absorb and learn from their world as they work at tasks. (Montessori did not like Froebel's ideas about the child's need for play. She believed the child works for work's sake, while adults work to complete a task.)

Montessori schools were begun in the United States to teach children following Montessori's methods. However, today some Montessori schools in the U.S. include some components of other American early childhood programs. These include creative art, dramatic play, science activities, and gross-motor play using playground equipment. Other Montessori schools still follow a more traditional Montessori approach.

Head Start

In the 1960s, Americans became concerned with the effects of poverty in America. Studies showed how important the early years were to a child's development. **Head Start** was launched in 1965 as a federal program for children from low-income families. These children needed food and medical care, as well as help in learning important concepts and language skills, 22-10.

Parents and families are a key part of planning and operating local Head Start programs. Community

22-10 Children in Head Start programs are encouraged to engage in a lot of dramatic play. This helps them develop concepts needed for later school learnings like reading.
© Nancy P. Alexander

involvement is also important. In addition to educational activities, Head Start offers activities and services to help meet the unique needs of children from low-income families. Some of these activities help children build self-esteem. Others focus on helping children and families work together to solve problems. Activities and learnings that relate to culture are a key part of Head Start programs.

Choosing a Group Program

Group programs cannot replace the teachings of home life. However, when quality group life is used to support and enrich home life, children can grow in many ways.

Children learn personal priorities away from home as well as in the home. Adults need to look for programs that promote their beliefs and priorities.

Parents should choose programs that meet the needs of their family. The needs of families differ, and not all programs will meet each family's needs equally well. A good fit is needed between family and program. All families should consider a few basic guidelines when choosing a group program for children.

Regulations

Regulations are standards that govern a group program. Regulations cover housing, equipment, staff, services, and business operations. Some regulations, such as fire safety, apply to all programs. Other regulations apply only to private programs. Still other regulations apply only to public programs. **Public programs** are those funded by local, state, or federal monies. Examples of public programs are public schools and Head Start programs.

Parents must be sure the program they choose meets all applicable regulations. However, regulations are minimum standards. Compare this idea to passing a test. Some students pass with high grades, others barely pass, and many others fall between these groups. In the same way, even though a program meets regulations, it may still be of poor quality. The one exception to minimum standards is accredited programs. Accredited programs are not only licensed but have met even higher standards of quality set for by a professional organization. Thus, accredited programs are like high achievers on tests.

Head Start. A federally sponsored program that was launched to meet the needs of children from low-income families.

regulations. Standards that govern a group program.

public programs. Child care programs funded by local, state, or federal monies.

Also, some regulations are easier to check than others. If a fence is required around the outside play area, this is easy to check. On the other hand, evaluating the warmth and nurturance provided by a staff member is much more difficult.

Finally, some regulations are simply on record with little or no enforcement. For example, many regulations cover family child care, but homes are seldom checked to see if they meet these regulations.

Housing and Equipment

The type of housing and equipment varies with a program's goals. For example, a family child care home, kindergarten, and Montessori program have different housing and equipment because they have different goals and activities. Furniture, equipment, and materials should meet the needs of the children in the program, 22-11. No matter what type of housing and equipment are provided, these should be safe and meet health standards. The conditions must be sanitary. Adequate space for comfort and activities is a must. The housing and equipment should convey the message "It's nice here!"

Staff

Children have many needs and must have plenty of adult help and supervision. Group size should be kept small with adequate adult coverage. *Group size* refers to the number of children in one room who will interact

22-11 Housing and equipment in a good program provide plenty of space; neat, cheery surroundings; and activities suited to a child's development.
LEGO-Dacta, the educational division of the LEGO Group

with each other throughout the day, 22-12. Younger children and children with special needs must have the most physical care and supervision. Therefore, their groups must be very small. Older children require less physical care; thus they can be cared for in groups that are somewhat larger.

Regulations also state how many adults must be on duty in each child care program. The **adult-child ratio** (read as adult to child ratio) is the number of adults per number of children. An adult-child ratio of 1:10 (read as adult to child ratio of 1 to 10) means 1 adult per 10 children. This ratio can be reversed by saying child-adult ratio is 10:1 (read as child to adult ratio is 10 to 1). This means exactly the same thing—there are 10 children for each adult.

Recommended Group Sizes and Adult to Child Ratios

Age of Children	Group Size*	Adult to Child Ratio*
0 to 1 year	6	1:3
1 to 2 years	8	1:4
2 to 3 years	12	1:6
3 to 6 years (excluding first grade)	18	1:9

* Numbers for group size and children per adult should be reduced if children with special needs are included.

22-12 For safety and quality programming, group programs for young children should adhere to recommended group size and adult-child ratios.

Parents must read descriptions of centers carefully when it comes to adult-child ratio. The terms *low* or *high ratio* can be easily confused. Parents should look for a high adult-child ratio, which is also a low child-adult ratio. They may also wish to ask exactly what the ratio is rather than relying on these descriptors. Refer to 22-12 again for recommended adult-child ratios. For all age groups, a higher adult-child ratio is needed when children with special needs are enrolled in the program.

In addition to teachers or caregivers, group programs need staff to direct the center, prepare meals, clean, and perform other special duties. These people, as well as regular volunteers, are called *support staff*. Support staff are vital to quality programs but are not counted when the adult-child ratio is calculated.

Children need adults who are in good physical and mental health. Children must feel secure, loved, and wanted. To feel loved, children must know they matter to others. They need to have adults who hug, comfort, listen to, and talk with them, 22-13. Children even need adults to say no and correct them when needed.

22-13 Staff members must care deeply for the children they teach.
© John Shaw

adult-child ratio. The number of adults per number of children in a group setting.

Adults also must guide children in their care. Children need adults to help them develop during their early years. In order to meet children's needs, adults must apply their knowledge of child development at each stage. For example, adults who care for infants must cuddle them and accept their dependency. Toddler caregivers must encourage them to explore and learn. Adults who serve preschool children must welcome their curiosity, questions, and energy.

Staff members must also work well with adults. They must be able to work together as a team. Staff members must also be able to communicate well with parents. They must be sensitive to parents' concerns and convey needed information about each child to his or her parents.

Parent Communication and Participation

In high-quality programs, staff members promote parent involvement. When parents and teachers work together, it is best for children's development. For better communication and participation, teachers or caregivers need to do the following:

❖ convey the importance of parents. Parents need to know they play the most important role in their children's life. They need to feel respected by the staff as the child's first teacher. Studies show the parent-child relationship influences the child's development more than any other aspect of a child's life.

❖ know more about each family they serve. Part of knowing includes understanding how a family's culture might influence parenting practices and child development. Culture also influences how parents view behavior because cultures differ in their priorities and beliefs. Thus, those who work with young children need to understand culture and how it affects families. Even within the same culture, however, not everyone sees the "ideal child" in the same way. Thus, the teacher must get to know each child's family.

❖ find ways to work with parents as a team. To do this, the teacher must know a great deal about child development and understand and be open to a parent's specific goals for a child. The teacher must also examine his or her own beliefs, attitudes, and goals. If the goals of the teacher and parent differ, the teacher should find ways to meet both sets of goals, 22-14.

❖ know the ways in which parents prefer to communicate with and participate in their children's group program. Parents have the right to say no to all communication and involvement. Teachers must accept this choice but leave the door open for them to later change their minds. For the parents who will participate, teachers need to offer some options, 22-15.

Goal area: Discipline

Teacher's Goal and Reason: Children should begin to learn self-control. Through learning self-control, children use problem-solving skills to resolve conflicts and gain self-esteem.

Parents' Goal and Reason: Child should respect authority. A child has to respect parents, just as adults have to respect the authority of their employers.

Using Both Goals: After discussing both goals, the teacher may suggest how both can be met. For example, children will be asked to resolve some of their conflicts with the teacher's help. They will also be expected to follow rules and show respect for other people and property. In some situations (such as safety issues), children will be expected to do exactly what the teacher says.

22-14 Teachers and parents should work as a team in setting goals for children in a group program.

Program Activities

Program activities vary with the goals of early childhood programs. Goals should be determined in keeping with **developmentally appropriate practices (DAP).** A DAP program is one that uses knowledge about the following:

* child development
* the strengths, needs, and interests of each child within the group
* the social and cultural contexts in which children in a given program live

The opposite of DAP are **developmentally inappropriate practices (DIP).** A program with many DIP is not a desirable environment for young children. Parents should avoid placing their child in this type of program, if possible.

It can be somewhat difficult to determine whether a program's practices are DAP or DIP. To judge whether a certain practice is developmentally appropriate or inappropriate, you would have to consider the

developmentally appropriate practices (DAP). Child care and education that uses knowledge about child development and considers each child's strengths, needs, interests, and culture.

developmentally inappropriate practices (DIP). Child care and education that do not use knowledge about child development and focus mainly on the group instead of each child.

Communicating and Involving Families

Family Communication

Parent Room or Reception Area
❖   Photos and stories of program activities are displayed on a bulletin board.
❖   Materials including videos on child development and the group program are available for parents to read and view.
❖   Handouts for parents are available.

Group Meetings and Workshops
❖   Orientation meeting for parents and children.
❖   Discussion groups on child development, program activities or policies, or community concerns.
❖   Make-and-take workshops. (Parents, who are provided materials and directions, make a take-home learning game for their child.)

Open House
❖   Parents see facilities and view displayed materials, such as children's drawings and stories.
❖   Parents may participate in some of the children's activities.
❖   Parents and extended family members meet staff members and other families.

Individual Conferences
❖   Teachers and parents set goals for child in the group program.
❖   Teachers and parents review child's work, accomplishments, strengths, and needs.

Home Visits
❖   Teachers see child and family in home setting.
❖   Parents share some of the child's home life.

Parent Visits to the Program
❖   Parents see their child in the program.
❖   Parents learn more about the program's goals and activities.

Newsletters
❖   May contain descriptions of current program activities, suggestions for home learning and fun activities, information on new books, Web sites, TV shows, or community events.
❖   Often sent to parents weekly or monthly. Some programs also post this on the program's Web site.

Informal Notes to Family Members
❖   Used as a way to share a child's activity or achievement.
❖   Can be sent to a family member for a special event or to show concern.

Family Participation

Serve on an Advisory Board
❖   Plan activities for program.
❖   Advise director or administration on desired program goals, such as services needed for children or families.
❖   Discuss general concerns of parents.

Volunteer in the Program
❖   Regular volunteers for assisting in programs or making learning materials for children's use.
❖   Occasional volunteers for helping teachers during children's outings or special activities in which extra adult help is needed; helping with fundraising activities; sharing talents, hobbies, or work role with children; or helping with special cleaning, painting, or repair jobs at the program site.

22-15 Teachers can find a variety of ways to communicate with parents and invite their participation in the group program.

development of the children and the circumstances surrounding the practice. For example, asking two-year-olds to sit still for a 15-minute story would likely be considered as a DIP. However, this same activity would be a DAP for five-year-olds. (Sitting still this long might still be a DIP for a given five-year-old with a short attention span.) In choosing the right group program, parents should know the major DAP that make for high-quality early childhood programs, 22-16.

Generally, a program that uses DAP promotes all areas of development. This type of program builds confidence and gives children the feeling they can handle tasks themselves.

Programs with DAP use day-to-day routines to help children learn. In these programs, eating serves more purposes than curbing hunger. Snacks and meals offer a time to learn about foods and styles of eating. Eating also offers the chance to practice table manners and talk with others. Self-care is also part of daily routines. Children want to become independent by learning to take care of themselves. Many programs encourage self-help skills.

In programs with DAP, activities are often planned as ways to help children develop. These program activities often include the following:

❖ language learnings. Language skills are improved by talking, listening, and reading (or looking at) good books.

❖ math learnings. Math skills are developed by counting, matching shapes in puzzles, and seeing who is taller.

❖ social learnings. Social learnings increase as children try new roles and help each other, 22-17. Holidays and birthdays are fun social events, too.

❖ science learnings. Learning about living and nonliving worlds is most exciting for young children. Children learn through activities with pets, plants, food, and others.

❖ creative fun. Children enjoy expressing themselves through art, dramatic play, and music.

❖ motor skills. Gross-motor skills are developed through active play, especially outdoor play. Fine-motor skills are improved as children manipulate materials such as art materials, puzzles, and building materials, 22-18.

Many good programs invite adults who are not on staff to share their special skills with children. These volunteers (including parents) can teach the children and be role models for them. When a parent shares skills, this builds the self-esteems of both the parent and child.

To provide firsthand learnings, staff can plan **field trips**, or outings

field trips. Outings that take children to places off a child care program's property.

Contrasting Developmentally Appropriate and Inappropriate Practices

	DAP	DIP
Program Goals	Goals are planned for physical, mental, and social development. Children are seen as individuals who differ developmentally and will grow and change at their own rates. Children are also seen as having their own unique styles of learning and their own interests.	Goals are planned mainly for mental development. Although children may differ developmentally at time of program entrance, they should achieve age-norms by the end of the program. Children's unique styles of learning and interests are not seen as important; children must conform to group instruction.
Housing/ Materials	Room is arranged with learning or activity centers (art, book, science, manipulative, blockbuilding) throughout. Materials are mainly for play. Most materials have no right or wrong answers (dramatic play props, art materials, sand, and water). Many materials invite children to play together in small groups.	Room is often arranged with tables with an assigned place for each child facing the teacher's desk. Materials are often workbooks or duplicated sheets for teaching beginning reading and arithmetic. Drill software is often used on computers.
Curriculum Content	Children's activities help them develop gross- and fine-motor skills, literacy skills, social and scientific concepts, and creative abilities.	Children's learnings are mainly focused on developing reading and arithmetic skills. All other activities are not seen as important.
Assessment	Teachers assess children mainly through observations and note what they observe about each child in anecdotal records, check sheets, etc. Teachers also collect samples of children's work (art work, photos of children's block structures, and videos of children in many types of activities). Often a portfolio (much like a scrapbook) is kept which includes the teacher's observation for each child records and the samples of work and is shared with the parent(s).	Teachers give "paper and pencil" tests and even end-of-the-year standardized tests. Scores that compare each child with the norms (how the typical child does) are shared with the child's parent(s).
Teaching Methods	Teachers permit children to work on their own or in small groups as much as possible. Through the teacher's constant observations, he or she decides when the children need a little help or when the housing or materials need changing.	Teachers do a great deal of group "telling." Drill methods are often used for learning (such as colors, letters, and numbers).
Guidance of Children	For a given child, teachers encourage self-control based on his or her stage of development. Teachers help children achieve self-control through simple explanations ("Hitting hurts."), modeling the desired behavior, and redirecting ("Chairs are for sitting. You may climb on the _____.") Teachers use positive comments when children use self-control.	Teachers expect all children to sit still and listen most of the day. When they do not conform, they are often punished (time-out chair, etc.). Treats are sometimes given as a bribe to keep children doing what teachers expect.

22-16 Programs with DAP are based on child development and on what is known about each child. In contrast, programs with DIP are based on teacher expectations for the group of children, and these expectations are often directed mainly toward early academic achievement.

22-17 Dramatic play is a way to "try on" real life roles, such as husband and wife.

22-18 Many materials are good for fine-motor development.

that take children to places off the program's property, 22-19. Field trips are a fun way to teach children about their community. For example, a field trip to the fire station helps children learn about the firefighters who protect their community. This field trip can help children experience firefighting in a way they cannot through regular classroom activities and materials.

Cultural Diversity in Group Programs

Children in group programs reflect the great cultural diversity of society. They are members of families that differ in language, social customs, beliefs, and goals for their children. Some children entering group programs may experience **culture shock**, an uncomfortable response to an unfamiliar culture. Children may also sometimes encounter **bias**, a belief or feeling that results in unfair

culture shock. An uncomfortable response to an unfamiliar culture.

bias. A belief or feeling that results in unfair treatment of another person or makes such treatment seem right.

22-19 Children enjoy field trips to interesting places.

treatment of another person or makes such treatment seem right.

As young children work to develop self-awareness, they notice differences between themselves and others, too. In a carefully planned program, children have the chance to build self-identity, respect diversity, and develop anti-bias attitudes. In such a program, adults do the following:

❖ **Affirm each child's identity.** Learn how to pronounce each child's name and say useful words in the child's language. Help children learn to describe themselves and their activities. Respond to children's questions and comments about culture in positive ways.

❖ **Respect diversity by making the program culturally rich.** Children need to live in a classroom that represents people from many cultures, 22-20.

❖ **Help children learn that biased behaviors hurt.** Adults might read books on feelings, and describe feelings when hurtful things are said and done. Adults can also help children find ways to include others during play and avoid competitive situations, such as "boys versus girls" or games with winners and losers.

Providing Child Care and Education for Children with Special Needs

More and more children with special needs are enrolling in child care and education programs. To meet the needs of all children, many group programs for young children practice *inclusion*. This means placing of children with special needs and other children in the same group, while providing special help for the children who need it.

Inclusion seems very natural in programs for young children. In these programs, diversity of all kinds is seen as positive. Furthermore, teachers and caregivers in programs often work in teams. Thus, it seems natural for a teacher or caregiver to work with other adults who provide

Characteristics of a Culturally Rich Program

Materials

- ❖ books about all types of children and families, books that show positive roles, and books that celebrate various cultural activities and customs
- ❖ housekeeping centers filled with dolls of both genders and various cultural/ethnic groups; tools, play foods, and cooking utensils from various cultures
- ❖ puzzles, pictures, and posters depicting families from various cultures
- ❖ crayons, paints, and paper to represent all skin tones
- ❖ musical instruments and recordings from various cultures
- ❖ toys and games from around the world
- ❖ photos of multicultural activities shared in the program

Activities

- ❖ reading stories, singing songs, learning poems, cooking foods, or playing games that have their origins in various cultures
- ❖ learning words, phrases, songs, or rhymes in various languages
- ❖ using art materials to depict oneself and others, various celebrations, and multicultural program activities
- ❖ sharing an object from home or telling about a family activity
- ❖ attending parades and festivals in the community
- ❖ making a book of multicultural activities using photos, children's artwork, and child-dictated stories of these activities

People

- ❖ welcoming volunteers of all cultural/ethnic groups and generational groups
- ❖ having parents from various cultures share favorite foods, songs, or stories
- ❖ seeing people of various cultures and both genders engaged in their work roles

22-20 The ideal multicultural community begins in group programs for young children.

help for children with special needs.

In inclusionary programs, the room must be arranged with children's special needs in mind, 22-21. For example, space must be provided for the ease of movement of children with wheelchairs and walkers. Teachers and caregivers also learn how to help the children with this equipment.

Planning activities requires teamwork. All children work on many of the same concepts and skills. However, some activities must be adapted for children with special needs. Activities are easiest to modify when they involve a single child. For example, a child with disabilities could enjoy puzzle time with other children by using a puzzle with fewer pieces or larger knobs. This accommodation is easy to make.

The learning needs of all children can be met in class activities, too. For example, a teacher may include squatting and singing in a beanbag toss

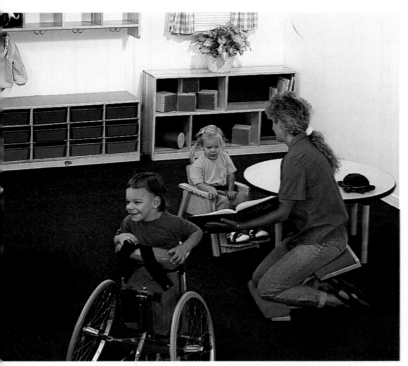

22-21 Group programs need to meet the special needs of children, as well as including them in class activities.
RIFTON for People with Disabilities

game. Many children could do all parts of the activity, while children with special needs could enjoy at least parts of the activity. The nature of each child's needs determines what he or she can do. A child with physical disabilities might not be able to squat or toss the beanbag, but could learn the song. A child with hearing loss would enjoy squatting and tossing the beanbag, even if he or she couldn't hear the song. Thus, teachers can plan activities that meet the goals of all children and truly include children with special needs.

Other Considerations

Some families need child care programs that offer some special services. These services might include transportation to and from the program, child care for the mildly ill, or extended-hour care. Programs with these services are not always conveniently located. If several families need the same services, they may be able to persuade programs to add these services. Work-related child care programs are good examples of how businesses have met the special child care needs of their employees.

Good programs for young children cost money. Costs of programs are rising due to increased costs of staff salaries, buildings, equipment, and supplies. Costs of programs vary with the type of program, days and hours of care, age-group served, and location.

Families may or may not have to pay all program costs. For-profit programs earn most, if not all, of their income by charging fees. These programs cost families the most money. Not-for-profit programs often are funded mainly by nonfamily sources, such as the state and federal government or service groups. Often families either pay little or none of the costs for this care. Not-for-profit programs that are operated as cooperatives (co-ops) are funded by families. In co-ops, parents offer their time and services to help keep costs low. Work-related child care programs are usually funded by both the business and through parent fees.

Families must decide what they can afford and seek the best program for their money. Often families spend 10 percent or more of their total gross income to meet child care costs. Besides the direct costs, families need to look at the costs in terms of **hidden added costs**. These are costs that add to the direct costs. Examples are costs of transportation, supplies, and disposable diapers (if cloth diapers would have otherwise been used). Services or items donated to a child care program are hidden added costs, too. Families must also consider **hidden cost credits**. These are credits that lower direct costs of child care. They include money that may be added from a second income. They also include money saved in the cost of utilities, food for at-home care, and child-care tax credits.

Quality of Group Programs

Only high-quality programs can have good effects on children. However, adults cannot judge a program by simply meeting the staff or checking the indoor and outdoor areas. Also, they cannot judge a program by noting the papers that say the program meets state standards, 22-22. The only way to be sure of a program's quality is to observe the day-to-day activities.

Families need to quickly recognize programs that are unsafe for children.

The following are signs of poor programs:

❖ parents cannot visit without asking in advance (Programs should welcome parents' visits at any time.)

❖ staff members are not trained to work with young children

❖ the program does not take special interest in children's needs (Programs with large groups of children and few adults are more likely to have this problem.)

❖ adults push children to perform above their abilities, causing them stress

Adults need to remember that children are defenseless clients of programs they attend. That is, young children cannot measure the quality of a program for themselves or take action if the quality is poor. Children depend on their parents to find quality programs for them.

See 22-23 for a checklist to use when evaluating a child care facility. As many children often spend a great deal of their early life in child care, adults must make sure the staff and care facilities meet the needs and priorities of their family.

hidden added costs. Costs of child care that add to the direct costs.

hidden cost credits. Credits that lower the direct costs of child care.

22-22 Having safe outdoor areas for play is only one standard of a quality program.
Landscape Structures, Inc.

Effects of Group Care on Children

Families are concerned with the effects group care has on children. They want to do what is best for their children. Experts have studied the effects of group care on children's health, mental development, and social development.

Effects on Health

There has been some concern over the health of young children enrolled in group programs. Studies do not agree on the number of common illnesses in enrolled children versus children not enrolled. Centers that enroll 50 or more children seem to have a higher rate of illness as compared to programs with lower enrollments. However, there seems to be no increase in serious illness in children who attend programs that follow good health practices. Families should consult their doctors about what is best for their children. For some children with chronic illnesses, pediatricians may advise less exposure to others through in-home child care or family child care programs.

Effects on Mental Development

Group programs do not seem to have either a positive or negative effect on the mental development of children from middle-class homes. As a whole, group programs offer more activities in certain areas than do most homes. Programs like Head Start can help the mental development of children from low-income families. If gains from such programs are to remain stable, however, there must be home and school follow-up for many years.

Effects on Social Development

Since the early 1900s, experts have been concerned that group programs might weaken bonds between children and families. Many recent studies do not find the child-family bond damaged because of care in

Child Care Program Checklist

Overall Evaluation

_____ Does the program meet regulations?

_____ The child care center is licensed.

_____ The family child care home is licensed or registered.

_____ The licensed center or family child care home is accredited.

Safety

_____ Does the inside and outside appear safe?

_____ The outside area is fenced.

_____ Both the inside and outside areas are childproofed.

_____ Equipment and materials are in good condition.

_____ Is the center or home clean and orderly?

_____ Is at least one staff member trained in first aid?

_____ Are parents required to complete health records and emergency forms?

_____ Has the facility been inspected by the fire department and health department?

Equipment and Materials

_____ Is the equipment the right size for children?

_____ Is the furniture the right size for children?

_____ Are the equipment and materials right for the children's ages and special needs?

_____ Is a variety of equipment and materials available?

_____ Is there enough equipment and materials for all children in the program?

_____ Do the materials invite a child to play?

_____ Are there shelves for the equipment and materials when they are not in use?

_____ Is there enough space for children to play?

Group Size and Number of Staff

_____ Are different age groups of children cared for separately or are mixed-age groups developmentally compatible?

_____ Does the adult-child ratio for each age group meet state laws and guidelines?

_____ Is there an adequate number of staff members with children at all times?

_____ Does the group size meet state laws and guidelines?

_____ Does the program employ additional staff to cook and clean?

Staff

_____ Are all staff members warm and loving with the children?

_____ Staff members kneel to a child's level to speak with them.

_____ Staff members look at children when they speak with them.

_____ Staff members smile often.

_____ Staff members use pleasant voices and words.

_____ Staff members seem calm and unhurried.

_____ Do staff members provide appropriate activities for physical, mental, and social-emotional development?

_____ Do staff members welcome parents at any time?

_____ Do staff members talk with each parent every day at pick-up and drop-off times?

_____ Are routines (eating, toileting, napping, and putting on outside clothes) handled pleasantly?

_____ Is self-care encouraged when appropriate?

_____ Are some special activities planned each day?

_____ Have staff members passed criminal records checks?

(Continued)

22-23 Adults need to carefully check out prospective programs for children.

Child Care Program Checklist (Continued)

Special Services

_____ Is transportation provided?

_____ Can parents arrange for extended care?

_____ Does the program enroll special needs children?

_____ Does the program have ways to serve mildly ill children?

Costs

_____ Is the cost reasonable compared with programs offering similar services?

_____ Are there hidden costs, such as an extra charge for supplies?

_____ Can the program costs be reduced for low-income families, families with several children enrolled, or parents who can provide services like volunteer time?

_____ Is the payment plan workable?

group programs. One example is a recent two-year study of children between three and one-half months and two and one-half years. The study found that constant, daylong separation of children from families did not change the importance of family in the child's life.

Some studies do show children are more aggressive as a result of group programs. Contact with peers tends to increase aggression in children because they must stand up for themselves. How teachers handle this aggression seems to affect how much children continue to express it. When children are enrolled in group programs, parents can help by reducing other possible aggression-promoting influences. One way to do this is to limit children's exposure to media portrayals of aggression. On the positive side, children in group programs have the opportunity to learn needed social skills that will help them in the future, 22-24.

Helping Children Adjust to Group Care

The change from home care to group care is a time of adjustment for children who are six months of age and older. These children often have separation anxiety. Even school-age children may feel a bit uneasy for the first few days away from home, 22-25. (Younger children—those between six weeks and six months are usually not distressed by receiving care from someone else.)

Adults need to make the adjustment seem casual. They can make a child anxious by talking too much about the change. Adults may be anxious, too, but must do their best to stay calm and confident. An adult's demeanor should show he or she is sure of the child's ability to adjust. The adult may say, "I know there are many new boys and girls, but you will make new friends. Everyone is new for a while."

22-24 In group programs, children must learn to share with others.

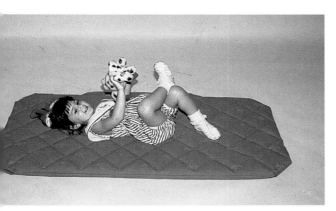

22-25 A favorite toy often eases the stress of nap time away from home.
Angeles Group

About a month before enrolling a child in a group program, the adult should explain what the program is like. He or she may explain there will be other children, toys, and activities. They should also visit the program, if possible.

Some children do not adjust well to group care, even after a few weeks. In these cases, parents should investigate the cause. Unannounced visits to the program might reveal problems. Parents should also ask the adults in charge what problems they have noted and what efforts they are making to help the child adjust. Children should be encouraged to share with parents what about the program makes them uncomfortable. Parents should take their answers seriously.

Suppose parents find no problems with the care, but the child still has adjustment problems. In this case, parents should find other ways to help the child adjust. They might offer the child more chances to play with other children. They could ask their child's doctor for advice.

If parents find problems with the care their child is receiving, they should start to look for a new placement right away. Their children's safety and well-being should be the primary concerns. If possible, parents can remove the child from group care temporarily and start this care again gradually. This may not be possible for working parents. These parents should offer extra love and support as they search for a more acceptable group program. Parents should monitor the situation closely until a new program can be found.

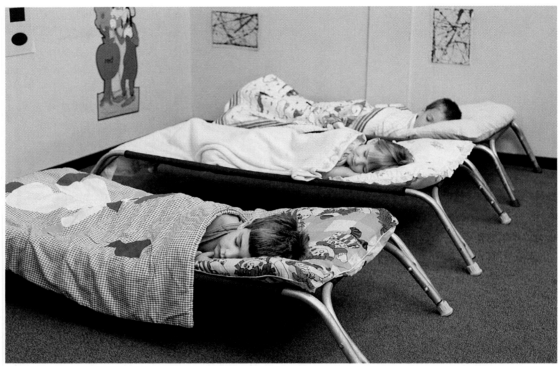

Young children in group programs need a clean, quiet, and sanitary area for napping.

Summing It Up

Parents have several options when it comes to child care and education for their young children. They can choose in-home child care, family child care homes, group programs, or school-age child care programs.

Large numbers of group programs for children exist throughout the country. Some are called child care centers. Others are called kindergartens, nursery schools, Montessori schools, and Head Start programs. All of these have a history of meeting particular needs of children and families.

Because many children spend a great portion of their life in group programs, adults must choose these programs carefully. By learning about the key factors on which they should focus, parents can increase the chance they will find a quality program that is a good match for the child and the family. Getting involved in programs also help adults find out whether they are of high quality.

Studies show that children in group programs do not seem to have any more serious illnesses than those not attending programs. Children's mental development does not seem to be positively or negatively affected through group programs. However, group programs often offer more activities that provide needed help in these areas. According to one study, being in a group program does not change the importance of the family in the child's life. The interaction with others may make children more aggressive and yet better able to stand up for themselves. This is a worthwhile coping skill for their future.

Adults need to help children adjust to group care. Visits to the program by the adult and child are recommended. If children are not adjusting easily to group care, adults might try other programs. Adults may shorten the time children spend in group care. Having others play with children in their own homes or in the home of a friend is helpful, too.

Reviewing Key Concepts

Write your answers on a separate sheet of paper.

1. Group programs for children are growing both in _____ and _____.
2. The types of nonrelative caregivers who provide in-home child care are _____, _____, and _____.
3. Match the names of the types of group programs with their descriptions. (You may use each name more than once.)
   A. child care programs
   B. kindergartens
   C. nursery schools
   D. Montessori schools
   E. Head Start programs
   _____ may be operated by businesses for their employees' children
   _____ are based on the methods used to help children with mental disabilities
   _____ are the oldest types of group programs
   _____ are funded by government monies to help children from low-income families overcome some of their problems
   _____ based on the idea "play is the highest level of child development"
   _____ stresses that children absorb from their world as they work at tasks
   _____ have served as a laboratory setting for the study of children
   _____ today, most operate as for-profit programs
   _____ have a focus on sensory learnings and self-care tasks

_____ are part of the public education system in the United States
4. True or false. The adult-child ratio pertains to the number of children housed together.
5. List four criteria for making program activities DAP.
6. Cultural diversity in child care and education programs for young children can be reflected through the chosen _____, _____, and _____.
7. True or false. Inclusion is the placement of children with special needs in regular classrooms.
8. Name one hidden added cost and one hidden cost credit in enrolling a child in a group program.
9. List five guidelines for choosing a quality child care program.
10. True or false. Children in group care seem to have been proven to be at a higher health risk for serious illnesses than children who stay at home.
11. Suggest three ways families can help their young children adjust to group care.

Using Your Knowledge

1. **Interviewing Skills.** Interview a nanny, au pair, or other in-home child care provider. What does he or she see as the challenges and rewards of this job? How is the person compensated, and what duties are expected of him or her?
2. **Teamwork/Career Skills/Group Discussion.** Work with a partner to brainstorm activities and services that might be needed in a school-

age child care program. Share your ideas in a class discussion.

3. **Technology/Writing Skills.** Conduct Internet research to learn regulations in your state for licensing of group programs and family child care homes. Then, use the computer to compose a brief paper summarizing your findings and your reactions. Based on what you have learned, how easy do you think it is for child care programs to be licensed? What changes do you think should be made in the current requirements?

4. **Consumer Skills/Career Skills.** Shop in stores, online, or in catalogs for materials, equipment, and toys for child care programs. What items do you note that are culturally rich? What items do you note that have been adapted for children with various special needs? Share your findings with the class.

5. **Teamwork/Community Connections.** Work with your classmates to compile a directory of local child care programs. The directory can include the program's name, owner, address, phone number, admission requirements, hours operated, and comments on special services or licensing. Be sure to include programs of all types mentioned in the chapter, if possible. If your teacher approves, create copies of this directory and place them in pediatricians' offices, the Chamber of Commerce, the public library, and other places where parents may read it.

Making Observations

1. Observe activities in two types of group programs for children. How were the programs similar? What differences did you note?

2. After carefully studying chart 22-23, observe a child care program. Use the checklist to rate the program. Explain why you would or would not enroll a child in this program based on your observation.

Thinking Further

1. Today there are many types of early childhood programs. What factors should parents consider in choosing a program? Which factor or factors do you consider most important? Why?

2. Visit two different types of child care programs for young children in your area. Discuss in class your findings about how these programs, their goals, and their services differ.

3. Suppose you were the parent of a preschooler and were deciding whether to return to your career or stay at home with your child. What factors should enter into your decision making? Be specific. What is the most important factor to consider? Why?

3. Suppose you are a kindergarten teacher. Some of your students have been in preschool programs, while others have not. What differences might you notice in these two groups of children, especially during the first few weeks of school?

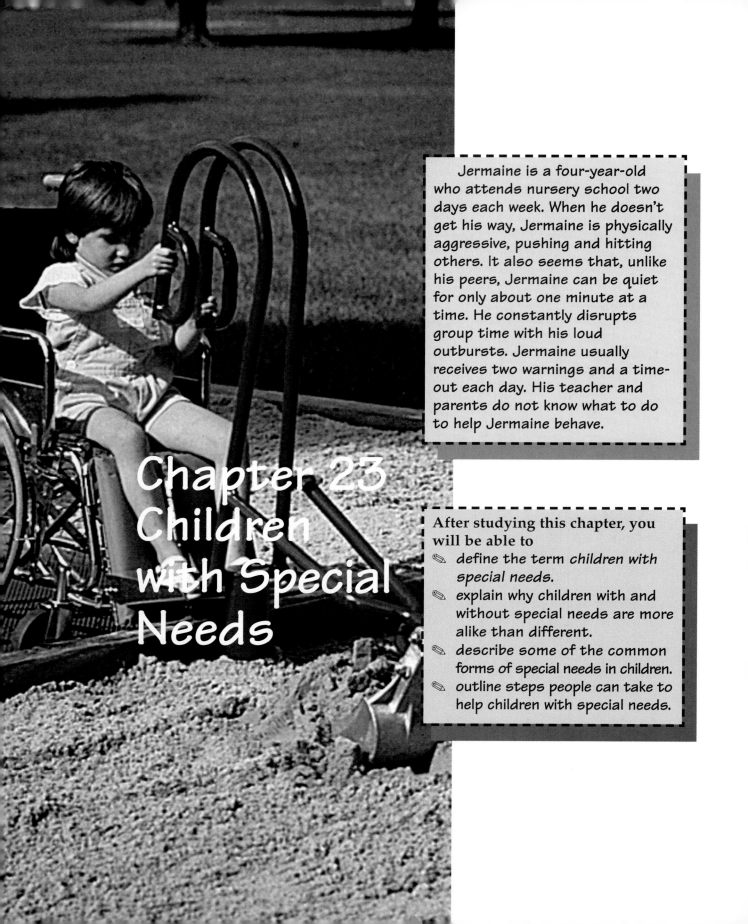

Jermaine is a four-year-old who attends nursery school two days each week. When he doesn't get his way, Jermaine is physically aggressive, pushing and hitting others. It also seems that, unlike his peers, Jermaine can be quiet for only about one minute at a time. He constantly disrupts group time with his loud outbursts. Jermaine usually receives two warnings and a time-out each day. His teacher and parents do not know what to do to help Jermaine behave.

Chapter 23
Children with Special Needs

After studying this chapter, you will be able to

✎ define the term *children with special needs.*

✎ explain why children with and without special needs are more alike than different.

✎ describe some of the common forms of special needs in children.

✎ outline steps people can take to help children with special needs.

Define...

- child with special needs
- borderline
- profound
- chronic
- correctable
- hearing impaired
- IQ tests
- gifted and talented children
- physical disability
- visually impaired
- legally blind
- speech impaired
- mental disability
- learning disabilities
- spatial orientation
- dyslexia
- developmental dyscalculia
- behavioral disorders
- aggressive behavior
- withdrawn behavior
- attention-deficit hyperactivity disorder (ADHD)
- attention-deficit disorder (ADD)
- hyperactivity
- Individualized Education Plan (IEP)
- Individualized Family Service Plan (IFSP)

Each person is unique. Therefore, children differ in the rate, pattern, and degree of their growth and development. Through research, child development experts have learned which developmental milestones most children generally attain within each

stage. A child whose development follows these patterns exhibits *typical development*. What makes these developments *typical* is that most children attain them within the same stage.

The development of a **child with special needs** differs from that of the development typical for most children who are his or her age. Some children develop behind most other children in one or more ways. These delays are often caused by a disability or disorder. Other children with special needs develop far ahead of most other children in one or more areas.

Children with special needs may have abilities that differ from most children in seeing, hearing, motor skills, speech, thinking, and social behaviors. As with all children, each child with special needs is unique. Special needs can vary widely. As a general rule, however, developmental differences are seen between children with special needs and other children in one or more of the following ways:

❖ First, a child can have special needs in one area or more than one area. (One child may differ from typical development in art only. Another may differ from typical development in both art *and* music.)

child with special needs. A child whose development differs from that of the development that is typical for most children of the same age.

❖ Second, skills may be accelerated or delayed in rate of appearance or may not follow the typical pattern of development. Observations and tests are used to identify a talent or problem. (For example, a doctor might test a child's hearing and score his or her abilities.)

❖ Third, the test results report the degree of a talent or problem. Words such as *borderline* and *profound* describe a child's talents or problems. **Borderline** means a talent is just above average or a problem is mild. **Profound** describes a talent as extreme or a problem as severe.

❖ Fourth, a problem (not a talent) may be described as *chronic* or *correctable*. **Chronic** means the problem may exist for a long time, perhaps a lifetime. (A missing limb presents a chronic, lifelong problem.) Some problems may be **correctable**, which means they can be overcome with the appropriate support. (Speech problems are thought of as correctable if a child can overcome them with therapy.)

Children Are More Alike Than Different

Children with special needs and other children are more alike than they are different. All children have the same basic needs. They need physical care, adults to rely on, and love, 23-1. In addition, however, children with

23-1 All children need safe playthings, a stimulating environment, and nurturing adults.
© John Shaw

special needs require care that differs or exceeds the care required by most other children.

Children with special needs and other children are also more alike than different because they most often follow the same patterns of development. Of the 3 percent of children who do not reach developmental milestones on time, only one-fifth follow a different pattern and sequence of development than other children. Some of these children may even lose skills they once had attained, such as language skills. However, the vast majority of children with special needs are like typically developing children in their pattern of development. Children with special needs, however, may develop at a different rate than other children. For example, children with a slight hearing loss often learn to talk the same way most other children do, except they learn more slowly.

In addition to the rate (or speed) of development, children with special needs and other children develop abilities in the same areas—motor skills, thinking abilities, and social-emotional skills. Differences in the degree of development are often noted, however. For example, a highly gifted child will develop logical thinking skills sooner than other children and will likely reach higher levels of abstract thinking than most adults do.

Children with special needs and other children are also alike in many other ways, 23-2. Almost all children like to spend time playing with friends and enjoying themselves. Children with special needs differ from other children only in the area or areas affected by the special need. For example, a child who is unable to walk may perform on the same academic level as most other children his or her age. In addition, a child may be disabled in one area, but gifted in another. For example, a child who is **hearing impaired** (has hearing loss) may excel in sports.

Children with Special Needs

As you have read, children with special needs and other children are more alike than different. Children with special needs will vary in the rate, pattern, or degree of development in one or more areas. Some children

23-2 Children with and without special needs are more alike than they are different.
Courtesy of GameTime, Fort Payne, Alabama, U.S.A.

borderline. A term used to identify a talent as just above average or a problem as mild.

profound. A term used to identify a talent as extreme or a problem as severe.

chronic. A term used to indicate that a problem will be long-lasting and perhaps lifelong.

correctable. A term used to indicate that a problem can likely be overcome with the appropriate support.

hearing impaired. A term used to indicate that a person has hearing loss.

develop faster or achieve higher degrees of development than most other children. These children are often described as *gifted* or *talented.* Developmental delays, differences in patterns of development, and lower degrees of development are called *impairments, disabilities,* and *disorders.*

Observations and/or tests are used to identify children with special needs. Some special needs are noted at birth, such as visible physical disabilities. Most special needs are not apparent right away, however. In many cases, parents or teachers may question some of the child's behaviors. Parents should bring these behaviors to the attention of the child's doctor. The doctor can examine the child and decide whether further testing is needed. In many cases, certain tests can be done to determine the type and degree of the special need.

One test that is frequently used for measuring mental ability is the IQ test. *IQ* stands for *intelligence quotient.* **IQ tests** measure how quickly a person can learn, how able a person is to reason using words and numbers, and how easily a person can find solutions to problems. Thus, IQ tests measure what is called *intelligence.* As you have learned in math, a quotient is the answer to a division problem. Years ago, when children answered IQ test questions, they would be given a score called the *mental age.* (The mental age meant a given child performed like the typical child of that age. This means a child with a mental age of six years performed like a six-year-old, but could be actually a four- or five-year-old.) The mental age was divided by the chronological age (child's actual age). This division yielded a quotient that was multiplied by 100 (to avoid the decimal) and called an IQ. If the child's mental age and actual age were similar, the child had an average IQ of 100 or nearly 100. If the mental age was a year or more older than the actual age, the child had an above-average IQ. If the child had a mental age a year or more younger than the actual age, the IQ was below average. Today, a special chart compares the mental and chronological ages rather than using the math problem to determine the IQ.

Intelligence tests are more accurate when given to only one person at a time. Although intelligence tests can be given to preschool children, the results are more accurate when given in middle childhood and later (at about nine years and older). Intelligence tests for infants and toddlers are not accurate. These very young children cannot sit still to take the test, nor do they have the skills needed to understand what to do or how to respond to the tester. An IQ score is more accurate when children have the ability to remember, reason, comprehend, respond verbally, make patterns, and work puzzles.

Children with Gifts and Talents

Almost every child has a talent he or she can do better than most other children. A child might read, swim, or jump rope better than other children. Because all children have gifts, the words *gifted* and *talented* are difficult to define. **Gifted and talented children** are defined as children who show high performance in one or more of the following areas:

❖ general mental ability (the child shows above average intelligence)
❖ specific academic aptitude (the child excels in one or more subject areas)
❖ creative or productive thinking (the child writes or invents)
❖ leadership ability (the child plans or organizes)
❖ high skill in visual or performing arts (the child excels in art, music, or dance)
❖ high psychomotor ability (the child excels in sports)

Some children seem to be gifted or talented in almost all areas. Others are talented in one or two areas only, 23-3.

Statistics on gifted and talented children show about 16 out of every 100 children are above average. About 3 children of these 16 are gifted. About 2 to 5 percent of all school-age children—some 2 to 5 million children—qualify for special school programs for gifted and talented children (called GT programs).

23-3 This young girl is gifted in the area of music. Giving children extra attention in their gifted areas helps them advance their talents.

 IQ tests. Tests that measure how quickly a person can learn, how able a person is to reason using words and numbers, and how easily a person can find solutions to problems.

gifted and talented children. Children who can or who do show high performance in one or more of six key areas.

Why are some children gifted? Giftedness seems to be due partly to genes. Certain talents seem to run in families. For example, musical ability ran in the Mozart family. Giftedness also is due to an environment that encourages a child to pursue his or her gifts. Wolfgang Amadeus Mozart had a father who encouraged him to play music at a young age.

Just as all children are unique, so are gifted and talented children. However, gifted and talented children often have some shared traits that set them apart from their peers, 23-4. Experts use test scores; art products; or judged performances in music, dance, or sports to see if a child is gifted and talented.

Children with Physical Disabilities

There are many types of physical disabilities. A **physical disability** is a limitation of a person's body or its function. Examples of physical disabilities include having limited mobility (ability to move about); missing limbs; bone, joint, and muscle diseases; and damage to the brain or nervous system. Any of these problems cause delays in gross-motor development. Children with these types of physical disabilities may need special aids, such as artificial limbs, walkers, crutches, braces, or wheelchairs, to participate fully in daily life, 23-5.

Two other areas of physical disability are vision and hearing problems. As with other disabilities, these can range from mild to profound. Children with vision or hearing loss may need special supports, such as eyeglasses or hearing aids.

Children who are **visually impaired** have problems seeing. Some vision problems can be corrected with eyeglasses. Some people may only see light, colors, shadow forms, or large pictures. Other problems are so severe they make a person unable to see. A person who is **legally blind** has a level of vision loss that makes him or her eligible to receive certain services. (A person is often designated as *legally blind* if his or her best eye has a corrected visual acuity of 20/200. The same designation is used if the person's visual field is 20 degrees or less in the better eye.) Children who are legally blind might learn to use the Braille system of raised dots to help them read.

Signs of possible vision loss include squinting, holding objects close to the face, and rubbing the eyes often. Having poor *distance judgment*

physical disability. A limitation of a person's body or its function.

visually impaired. A term used to indicate that a person has vision problems or vision loss.

legally blind. A term that indicates a person meets criteria for vision loss that entitle him or her to receive special services.

Traits of a Gifted and Talented Child

Traits	Examples
The child uses advanced vocabulary at an early age.	At age two years, a child says, "I see a kitten in the backyard and he's climbing our fence," instead of just saying, "I see a kitten."
At age two or three years, a child may learn to read on his or her own.	Most gifted children do not read at an early age. This may be because they see no need to read. However, those who do read learn on their own.
The child is quite observant and curious.	As a toddler, the child remembers where all the toys are stored on the shelf. At age two and three years, the child begins to ask many questions that begin with *what*, *where*, *how*, and *why*. They may ask, "How does the water get out of the bathtub?" "Where does the water go?" "Why does water go down?"
The child remembers many details.	The child can recall many past experiences with details that adults may have forgotten.
The child has a long attention span.	At age one year, the child may look at a book for five minutes. Other children may just glance at the book. By the school-age years, the child may spend hours on a project and even be totally unaware of other events.
The child understands complex ideas.	Children who are gifted want to learn so much that the topics that interest them change often.
The child develops critical thinking skills and makes careful judgments.	Children who are gifted note when something seems illogical. For example, seeing water drops form on the outside of a glass, the child may ask, "How does the water get there? It did not rain on the glass." Children who are gifted also are more critical of themselves. They may say, "I should have done better. That was a silly mistake."
The child shows talents early.	A child gifted in visual arts may draw facial expressions like sadness or surprise at a young age. At this same time, friends are drawing circles for the eyes and nose and a curved line for the mouth.
The child does not like repetition.	A child who is gifted likes the new and unsolved. The child may become bored when asked to do 50 basic math problems.

23-4 Each gifted child is unique but may share some common traits with other gifted children.

23-5 This young girl enjoys taking part in free play with the help of her walker.
© John Shaw

(missing steps and bumping into objects) or using *self-stimulation play* (making rocking movements or noises) are also signs.

People who are hearing impaired may have hearing loss that ranges from mild to profound (deafness). Hearing aids may help a child with hearing loss learn to hear and communicate. In severe cases, hearing aids cannot help. Sign language can be a very useful way for these children to communicate with others.

Signs of possible hearing loss are being unresponsive to sounds, making speech sounds incorrectly, or major delays in talking. Many children who are hearing impaired use their sense of touch more than other children. They also watch other peoples' faces and mouths closely.

Children with Speech Disorders

Some children differ from most other children in the sound of their speech. Children who are **speech impaired** speak in ways that draw attention, are not easily understood, or cause the speaker to have a poor self-concept. Children who are speech impaired can have problems in one or more of the following three areas:

❖ articulation. Children may use one sound for another, distort sounds, or leave out or add sounds in words.
❖ voice problems. Children's voices may be too high or too low in pitch, too loud or too quiet, nasal, or husky.
❖ rhythm problems. Children may repeat sounds or words, be unable to get speech out, or speak rapidly.

Profound problems in speech are very noticeable, but smaller differences are more difficult to detect. Parents may not hear these differences because they are used to their child's speech. In other cases, parents have the same speech problem as the child, which the child learned through imitating their speech. Doctors and teachers are often better able to hear consistent irregularities in a child's speech. Children with suspected speech problems need to be evaluated by a *speech pathologist*. This professional is trained to evaluate and treat speech problems.

Children with Mental Disabilities

A **mental disability** is often defined as having intellectual abilities that, when compared with others of the same age, are a year or more delayed. Mental disabilities vary from mild to profound. Causes include gene disorders, prenatal and birth problems, and injuries to or infections of the brain after birth. A lack of basic experiences in the environment may also cause mental delays. There is a wide variance among children with mental disabilities, but many share the following signs:

❖ delays in motor skills
❖ smaller vocabulary and shorter sentence length
❖ a grasp of simple, but not highly complex ideas
❖ avoidance of difficult tasks
❖ short attention spans
❖ more-than-average fondness for repetition
❖ difficulty making choices

Because the brain is involved in all aspects of development, children with mental disabilities need to be diagnosed and treated early in life. The windows of opportunity for brain wiring close

rather early in life. Children with mental disabilities need the help of highly specialized teachers. Working with mentally disabled children is not simply a matter of teaching skills more slowly. These teachers often must use innovative methods to break skills down into steps the children can practice.

Learning Disabilities

Learning disabilities are defined as problems in one or more areas of spoken or written language, mathematics, and spatial orientation. (**Spatial orientation** is the ability to see relationships between objects in space.)

Some learning disabilities include dyslexia and developmental dyscalculia. **Dyslexia** is a disability that affects a

speech impaired. A term used to indicate that a person has speech problems.

mental disability. The condition of a person whose intellectual abilities are a year or more delayed when compared with the abilities of other people of the same age.

learning disabilities. Problems in one or more areas of spoken or written language, mathematics, and spatial orientation.

spatial orientation. The ability to see the relationship between objects in space.

dyslexia. A learning disability that affects a person's ability to read, write, and spell.

child's ability to read. Children with dyslexia also have problems writing and spelling. They may find it difficult to connect words with their written forms. These children may reverse words and letters when they read or write them. They may confuse the order of letters in words or read words backward. More boys than girls have dyslexia. **Developmental dyscalculia** is a learning disability that affects a child's mathematical abilities. This problem is similar to dyslexia except that it involves mathematical skills rather than reading skills.

Children with learning disabilities may have average and/or above-average intelligence. However, they may perform at lower levels due to their disabilities.

Causes of Learning Disabilities

What causes a child to have a learning disability? Studies show learning disabilities are not caused because parents do not help children learn. They also show they are not caused because children are spoiled, lazy, stubborn, or mentally disabled. Learning disabilities seem to result from physical problems. For example, dyslexia is associated with a disorder of the body's central nervous system. Other causes include prenatal problems, such as lack of oxygen for the

fetus. Problems during birth itself also may cause learning disabilities. Other causes are accidents, high fevers, and breathing or nutritional problems after birth.

In the past, learning disabilities were rarely noted before the school years. This is because a disability often shows up when formal learning begins. Some children can hide their disability, even in the lower grades. They may memorize words in a reading text rather than really reading them. The signs shown in 23-6 seem to be common for many children. However, the difference is that a child with a learning disability thinks in a disordered way. This happens at the same time his or her peers are ready to learn and think more clearly. Learning problems are part of the everyday life of a child with a learning disability.

Greater awareness of learning disabilities has made better help available. Also, the increased number of children in early childhood education programs makes it possible to detect learning disabilities at earlier ages. More widespread use of testing

developmental dyscalculia. A learning disability that affects a child's mathematical abilities.

Basic Traits of Children with Learning Disabilities or Disorders

Traits	Examples
Brain messages are jumbled even though the sense organs are normal	❖ Reverses letters when reading, writing, or speaking. For example, may read *on* as *no*, write 24 for 42, or say *aminal* for *animal*. ❖ Confuses related words, such as saying *breakfast* instead of *lunch*. ❖ Stops often in mid-sentence and starts a new idea. ❖ May have trouble identifying the question asked, such as confusing the questions, "How are you?" and "How old are you?".
Poor spatial orientation	❖ Has problems doing tasks that involve spatial concepts like *up, down, left, right, top, bottom, above,* and *below*. ❖ Doesn't see items that are within the line of vision. ❖ Has trouble judging distances. ❖ Gets lost often. ❖ Has problems writing on a line. ❖ Has problems with jigsaw puzzles.
Seems awkward or clumsy	❖ Has trouble tying shoes or buttoning small buttons. ❖ Is poor at sports. ❖ Trips or loses balance because of misjudging distance. ❖ Has poor timing. ❖ Cannot coordinate several tasks at one time.
Has a short attention span	❖ Cannot listen to a story or finish a project.
Is overactive	❖ Is always moving, to the point of bothering others. ❖ Fidgets constantly through quiet activities.
Acts disorderly	❖ Needs more attention than most children of the same age and seeks this attention by misbehaving. ❖ May misbehave to convince others that the behavior is bad instead of unintelligent.
Is inflexible	❖ Becomes upset when any routine changes. ❖ Becomes anxious in new places or around new people. ❖ Rejects objects that are different (for example, refuses a cracker that is broken). ❖ Demands that others cater to his or her needs, even when it is not possible.

23-6 In general, children with learning disabilities face more problems in learning than do other children because they do not think in the same way as other children do.

programs has also contributed to diagnosis of these disabilities.

Children with Behavioral Disorders

A **behavioral disorder** is a pattern of problems that surfaces in a person's behavior. Disorders are often marked by extremes of behaviors. As with other special needs, behavior disorders vary in terms of severity. The causes of a disorder are often a puzzle. In some cases, severe and constant stress seems to be the cause. Brain injuries and other physical causes also sometimes exist. Experts are in the early stages of solving the puzzle of behavioral disorders. There are several common behavioral disorders.

Aggressive behavior is an outward behavioral disorder. Children with this disorder name-call, fight, and bully without being provoked into such actions. They cannot seem to control these behaviors.

Withdrawn behavior occurs when children do not relate well with others. They may resist change and panic when changes occur. They often have poor self-concepts and do not always think realistically.

Two related disorders have to do with the ability to pay attention. People must use attention and memory to learn, retain information, and solve problems. To pay attention, a person has to focus one or more of the senses on a certain aspect of the environment (listen to a recording) and ignore irrelevant information (a humming fan).

Although all people sometimes become distracted, some people are highly distractible. Two disorders that involve attention are **attention-deficit hyperactivity disorder (ADHD)** and **attention-deficit disorder (ADD)**. ADHD involves the lack of attention and **hyperactivity** (behavior that is extremely active beyond normal energy level). ADD involves the lack of attention, but does not include hyperactive behaviors, 23-7. For this reason, ADD is sometimes called *hypoactivity disorder*.

ADHD and ADD are difficult to diagnose. In children, diagnosis is based on observation rather than medical tests. Similar symptoms appear in childhood anxiety and depression. Although the problems with lack of attention and learning disabilities are different, they often occur in the same children.

Some researchers state that 10 percent of all children have either ADHD or ADD. Others claim the numbers are much lower. Hyperactivity is often misdiagnosed; some experts say only one to three percent of children who are labeled hyperactive are truly hyperactive in a medical sense. Hyperactivity is present, however, in 75 percent of the cases involving attention disorders. Attention disorders affect boys four to five times more often than girls.

Several techniques are being tried to help children with attention disorders. These include the following:

❖ restricting stimuli (having fewer items to see and hear, at the same time)
❖ establishing and adhering to a routine
❖ giving short, clear instructions
❖ using praise and rewards
❖ providing experiences that are challenging but manageable, 23-8

❖ offering physical activities
❖ watching diet, especially food coloring
❖ giving medications to calm hyperactivity

When carefully monitored by doctors, medications have proved valuable in some cases. Giving medication without careful observations has been criticized for several reasons,

Traits of Children with Attention Disorders

Attention-Deficit Hyperactivity Disorder

are inattentive; easily distracted; forgetful
act as if "driven"
are fidgety (may run, climb, or move in other ways constantly; get out of their chairs or their places in group settings)
constantly change activities often without completing anything
do sloppy and incomplete work
speak out in class
will not wait for their turns
have frequent and intense emotional outbursts (fight, have self-imposed isolation, defiant, can't take criticism)
are clumsy and accident-prone
have excessive activity in sleep

Attention-Deficit Disorder

are inattentive; easily distracted; forgetful
act disinterested ("tune-out") or daydream
fail to finish a task or play activity
appear not to listen
cannot organize work

23-7 Children who cannot pay attention are often diagnosed with attention disorders. Some are also hyperactive.

behavioral disorders. A pattern of problems that surfaces in a person's behavior.

aggressive behavior. An outward behavioral disorder in which people name-call, fight, or bully without being provoked into such actions.

withdrawn behavior. Behaviors that show a separation from the rest of society, such as not relating well to other people, not wanting changes to occur, and lacking self-esteem.

attention-deficit hyperactivity disorder (ADHD). A disorder that involves the lack of attention and extremely active behavior that exceeds a typical high energy level.

attention-deficit disorder (ADD). A disorder that involves the lack of attention but does not include hyperactive behaviors.

hyperactivity. A pattern of extremely active behavior in which a person is overactive, restless, and has a short attention span.

23-8 Teachers can promote all children's development by offering them appropriate activities, materials, and encouragement.
© John Shaw

however. First, it is often the first treatment tried. Second, these medications have side effects, such as slowing children's appetite and growth and causing sleeplessness, listlessness, and a stuporlike state. Third, frustrated adults may view these drugs as a way to control children who have high energy levels but do not actually need the medication.

Help for Children with Special Needs

All children with special needs should have special help. The first step in providing this help is to identify children with special needs. Family members often are shocked when

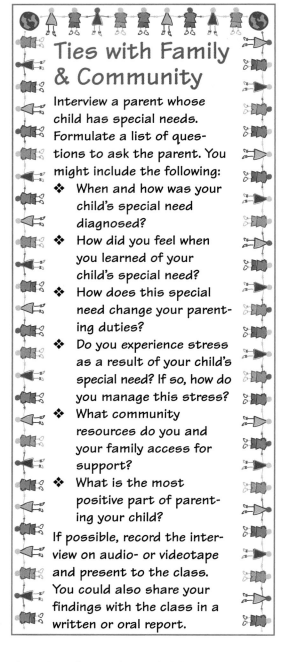

Ties with Family & Community

Interview a parent whose child has special needs. Formulate a list of questions to ask the parent. You might include the following:

❖ When and how was your child's special need diagnosed?

❖ How did you feel when you learned of your child's special need?

❖ How does this special need change your parenting duties?

❖ Do you experience stress as a result of your child's special need? If so, how do you manage this stress?

❖ What community resources do you and your family access for support?

❖ What is the most positive part of parenting your child?

If possible, record the interview on audio- or videotape and present to the class. You could also share your findings with the class in a written or oral report.

they first learn their child has special needs. This news is even more shocking when the special need is a disability. Sometimes families face this adjustment when a child is born. Other times, the problem may not be noticed until sometime during the school-age years when the child seems to fall behind or differ from peers. For still other parents, an accident or illness disables a child. Even giftedness or talent shocks parents because the active minds or special talents of these children often baffle adults. It may take parents some time to adjust to this news and learn how to meet their child's special needs.

How Many Children Have Special Needs?

An estimated one child in 10 children has special needs. Some special needs are more common than others, however. For example, about 3.5 percent of all children have speech disorders, but deafness affects far fewer children (about .075 percent of all children).

Anywhere from 3 to 45 percent of all children have learning disabilities, depending on the way the term *learning disabilities* is defined. This definition may differ from one professional to another. State laws may also play a role. These laws vary in the definitions used to determine which students have special needs and are therefore eligible for a free public education. (Laws require that all children with special needs receive a free and appropriate public education.)

What Kinds of Help Are Needed?

All children with special needs will require extra help or help that differs from that of most other children. According to new brain development research, intensive help is needed and should be begun early for the assistance to be most effective.

Parents generally start to seek help through a pediatrician. The doctor can refer the child for needed tests, 23-9. Once testing is complete, doctors can explain the child's condition to parents and discuss ways to help the child.

23-9 Experts use tests to pinpoint each child's disability or gift.

Laws require public schools to educate children with special needs who are between the ages of 3 and 17 years, 23-10. Laws also require that an educational plan be designed for each student with special needs. This plan, called an **Individualized Education Plan (IEP)**, is tailored to the child's specific educational needs. It includes goals for the child and a placement agreement. The most common placement is *inclusion* (full-time placement in a regular classroom) rather than *mainstreaming* (an older term for placing the child in the classroom only part of the day).

Parents, teachers, and school administrators design the IEP together and agree to carry it out. Parents also meet with their child's teachers on a regular basis, 23-11. The child is also retested on a regular basis, and the plan is adjusted as needed to fit the child's changing educational needs.

States may, but are not required to, provide services for children with special needs who are younger than three years of age. If these services are provided, laws require that an **Individualized Family Service Plan (IFSP)** be written. Unlike the IEP, which focuses on the child's needs, the IFSP focuses on the entire family's needs. The IFSP is written to coordinate all needed services for each family that are related to the child's development.

Members of the family often join support groups. Many of these groups are national with local chapters. At the national level, these groups provide family members with the latest information on children with special needs. National groups also seek money for research and assistance for families who need costly training or equipment. At the local level, groups support the goals of the national groups. They also provide helpful contacts and services among those with similar needs.

23-10 Special programs that meet the needs of children are available through public funds.
© John Shaw

23-11 Parents who have children with special needs help plan their children's education.
© John Shaw

Individualized Education Plan (IEP). An educational plan that is tailored to the specific educational needs of a child with special needs.

Individualized Family Service Plan (IFSP). A plan that focuses on the needs of a family with a child younger than three years of age who has been identified as having special needs.

Summing It Up

Children whose development differs in rate, pattern, or degree have special needs. These needs can occur in the areas of seeing, hearing, motor skills, speech, thinking, or social behaviors.

Children with special needs and other children are more alike than different. All children have the same basic needs, although children with special needs do need extra help in certain areas.

Children who are gifted and talented show high performance in one or more areas. These areas include mental ability, specific academic aptitude, and creative or productive thinking. Other areas of high performance may be in leadership, visual or performing arts, or psychomotor abilities. Gifted children tend to show their talents early and share some common traits, such as an early use of vocabulary and a memory for details. Gifts and talents may be due to both heredity and environment.

Developmental problems are sometimes called disabilities, impairments, or disorders. The most common types of developmental delays include physical disabilities, speech disorders, mental disabilities, learning disabilities, and behavioral disorders.

Tests can help identify how to best help a child with special needs. Federal funds are available for the education of children with special needs. When problems are indicated, an Individualized Education Plan or Individualized Family Service Plan is written. Both plans set up a program of education that will best meet the child's special needs.

It can be challenging to parent a child with special needs. Learning how to meet the child's special needs is important. Support groups help, too, because they provide contact with others in similar circumstances.

Reviewing Key Concepts

Write your answers on a separate sheet of paper.

1. Special needs (are, are not) seen in degrees and may or may not last a lifetime.
2. True or false. Some forms of special needs are difficult to define.
3. Delays have to do with the _____ (rate, pattern, degree) involved in reaching developmental milestones.
4. Name three areas in which children may have gifts and talents.
5. Match each of the following traits with the type of special need it best fits.

   Traits
   _____ asks many complex questions at a young age
   _____ watches others' faces very closely
   _____ uses one sound for another sound
   _____ shows poor distance judgment
   _____ writes *saw* for *was*
   _____ likes repetition
   _____ can't identify right and left
   _____ uses a large vocabulary
   _____ hits without being provoked
   _____ has many advanced interests
   _____ lacks self-esteem
   _____ plays a musical instrument at an early age with much skill
   _____ has delayed motor skills and finds complex ideas hard to grasp

   Special need
   A. gifted and talented
   B. visually impaired
   C. hearing impaired
   D. speech impaired
   E. mentally disabled
   F. learning disabled
   G. behaviorally disordered

6. Name three signs of a possible learning disability in children.
7. Order from 1 to 5 the steps for helping a child with special needs.
   _____ testing
   _____ writing an IEP
   _____ referral for testing
   _____ finding a suitable program to help the child
   _____ retesting and writing a new IEP from time to time

Using Your Knowledge

1. **Language Arts.** Read the biography or autobiography of a famous person who is gifted or talented. Report to your class on the person's accomplishments and struggles.
2. **Language Arts.** Read the biography or autobiography of a famous person with disabilities. Report to your class on the person's accomplishments and struggles.
3. **Technology/Consumer Skills.** Shop online to find toys and play equipment designed for children with physical disabilities. What features of these items make them easier to use by a person who is physically disabled?

4. **Technology/Writing Skills.** Research on the Internet to learn more about ADD or ADHD. Write a short report describing recent advances that have been made in diagnosing or treating these disorders.

5. **Teamwork/Community Resources.** Work in a small group to investigate the resources available in your community for the families of children with special needs. Create a directory of all the resources you locate, including name, address, contact person, phone number, and a brief description of services offered.

Making Observations

1. Observe a special education classroom or an inclusionary classroom. Note ways in which children with special needs and other children are alike.

2. Observe children with special needs in a group setting. List all the instances you observed of the children receiving special help.

3. Observe a program that serves children with special needs. How does the program differ from a regular classroom in terms of housing and equipment, class size, staff to child ratio, subjects taught, teaching methods, and other factors? How is it the same as a regular classroom?

Thinking Further

1. Do you know children with any special needs? What special needs do they have?

2. What types of problems do families face when they have children with special needs?

3. What is the overall goal of the special help given to children with special needs? Does this differ from the overall goal for meeting the needs of most other children?

Chapter 24
Concerns of Children and Families

Four-year-old Felicia attends the child care center where Brandon works. Although she was once happy, lovable, and energetic, Felicia's behavior has changed. Now she has unpredictable outbursts of aggression and anger. She throws things at others and destroys their work. At other times, Felicia is withdrawn and refuses to talk to anyone. For the past two weeks, she has clung to her mother's leg upon arriving at the center each day. Brandon wonders what the problem is and how to help Felicia.

After studying this chapter, you will be able to

✎ describe four sibling relationships and explain how a child's birth order affects development.

✎ describe how parental employment affects children.

✎ explain how stress from family moves can hurt children and how to lessen these effects.

✎ describe ways adults can help children handle divorce, remarriage, and death.

✎ point out problems single parents and teen parents face.

✎ describe ways to protect children from neglect and abuse.

✎ list resources available for helping children in crisis.

Family life is complex these days. Sometimes stressful events occur that cause tensions and problems that affect family life. These problems affect children.

Children need to grow up in a strong family. When divorce, remarriage, or death upsets the family, adults need to help children cope. When the family must relocate, adults must reassure children they will soon feel secure in their new environment.

Some parents must balance family and work issues. Single and teen parents face additional challenges when raising and supporting their children.

Child abuse and neglect cause serious emotional and psychological problems for children. Many carry the problems with them all their life. Adults must protect children from abuse.

The relationships children have with family members play an important role in their development. Sibling relationships are especially important. Children learn a lot by playing and living with brothers and sisters.

Sibling Relationships

In most families, children grow up with siblings. The average American family has two children. This means most children interact with at least one brother or sister. In some families, children have several siblings.

Sibling Interactions

Siblings influence each other's lives in many ways. They play the roles of playmates, teachers, learners, protectors, and rivals. Sibling relationships teach children about social give-and-take.

Playmates

Brothers and sisters are built-in playmates for each other. In play, siblings learn to set goals and cooperate. Siblings also share hours of fun, 24-1. Brothers and sisters remember these fun times throughout their adult years.

24-1 Siblings often look back fondly on the relationship they shared as children.

Teachers and Learners

Older children often act like teachers while younger siblings play the part of eager learners. As teachers, siblings explain, define, describe, show, and offer examples. Most brothers and sisters show interest in their younger sibling's efforts. They help them reach their goals as well.

Older siblings also model social skills. These social skills include learning gender roles. Younger siblings learn gender roles faster than firstborns and only children. Having a sibling also helps children learn the difference between good and bad social behavior. From a child's point of view, a sibling shows good social behavior if he or she plays nicely, helps with chores, and doesn't tattle.

Protectors

If you have ever seen an older child run to a younger sibling's defense, you know that siblings protect each other. Siblings protect each other most often in the following situations:

❖ when siblings have an age gap of three or more years
❖ when siblings come from large families
❖ when children are unsupervised outside, on the way to and from school, or with a babysitter
❖ when peers attack a younger sibling in a physical or verbal way

Older children can help adults watch younger brothers and sisters (although adults never should leave children alone). As a bonus, older children who help parents care for siblings are better prepared for parenthood and child-related careers, 24-2.

Rivals

Two or more children in a family compete in both physical and verbal ways. Younger children and boys fight physical battles more often than older children and girls. Younger children plead, whine, and sulk. Older children often command, boss, and call each other names.

Why does rivalry occur? Children may compete for the love and attention of parents and friends for several

Space

Parents need to control the space children use. Each child needs space for his or her belongings. High shelves keep toddlers away from older children's toys and books. Adults should teach children to share, but they should not expect them to share all the time. Children should share in the same ways adults share—sometimes, but not in all cases. Also, children should have some time to play without siblings. Playing alone and with friends is healthy. Siblings, especially younger ones, can pester children when they are always around.

Fights

Adults should ignore fights unless children are in physical danger or property may be damaged. If adults settle each dispute, children may feel rewarded with the adults' attention. If the fight must be stopped, adults should tell children to stop without adding a threat. If children do not obey this command, adults should physically separate the children.

Family Togetherness

Parents should stress the importance of family togetherness and support. Families should take part in some activities everyone enjoys. Adults must teach children to take pleasure in another's good fortune. Adults should explain that family members love one another although they sometimes get angry at each other. Above all, adults should praise loving behavior, 24-3.

24-2 Caring for a brother or sister prepares children for future parenthood.
© John Shaw

reasons. They may be jealous of siblings who seem more capable than they are. They also may not be able to see a situation from another's point of view. To young children, *fair* means *equal*.

Adults cannot prevent rivalry, but they can lessen it by giving each child lots of love. Each child needs positive feedback. Parents must not compare one child to another. Children are different, and comparing them usually makes one child resent the other and feel angry toward parents.

24-3 Adults should praise children's loving behavior toward one another.
© Nancy P. Alexander

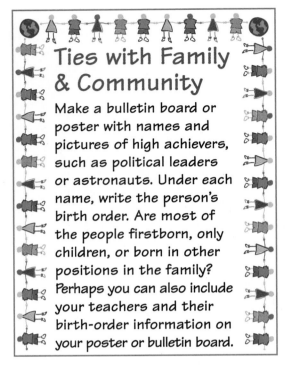

Ties with Family & Community

Make a bulletin board or poster with names and pictures of high achievers, such as political leaders or astronauts. Under each name, write the person's birth order. Are most of the people firstborn, only children, or born in other positions in the family? Perhaps you can also include your teachers and their birth-order information on your poster or bulletin board.

Birth Order and Development

To some degree, the order of children's birth affects their social roles and personalities. Facts about birth order cannot be applied to all children, however. Personality traits also depend on the gender of the children, the number of older and younger siblings, the attitudes of parents, and a family's culture. Larger age gaps between a child and the next older sibling reduce the effects of birth order on development.

Only Children

About 10 percent of children are only children. This figure has doubled since the 1950s. Two reasons for this increase are more women in the workforce and delayed childbearing.

Many myths surround only children. Some believe only children are lonely, spoiled, selfish, less bright, and more dependent on parents. Only children seldom live up to these ideas. Like all children, only children are distinct persons with their own personalities. However, they usually are not lonely if playmates are a part of their lives. In fact, they learn to spend time alone as well as with others. Only children often are less selfish or jealous than other children. This is because they are less threatened by the loss of attention or possessions. Only children usually have high intelligence quotients (IQs). See 24-4 for a list of some common traits of only children.

Firstborn Children

You will see in 24-4 that firstborns have many of the same traits as only children. This is partly because most firstborns are only children for a little while (except siblings from a multiple birth). Like only children, firstborns are often bright. They often teach younger siblings, and teaching benefits their intellect. Firstborns are also mentally creative because siblings look to them for ideas.

Some parents call their firstborns *experimental children* because the

Traits Affected by Birth Order

Only Children
have high IQs
achievers
perfectionists
high self-esteem
relaxed
not jealous
unselfish
socially outgoing
are leaders as adults

Firstborns
have the highest IQs
are achievers (stay in school most years)
creative
have lots of zeal and drive
ambitious
anxious
conservative
mature
conformists
want company in times of stress
angry and irritable at times
less popular
leaders as adults

Middle Children
have slightly lower IQs than only children and
    firstborns
less highly driven
attracted to nonacademic areas like sports
    or the arts
cheerful
easygoing
relaxed
patient
adaptable
gentle
tactful
outgoing
popular
charming
see themselves as less skillful than older
    siblings
feel lost in the middle at times

Youngest Children
have the lowest IQs as compared with only
    children and older siblings
are underachievers
seek pleasure
relaxed
secure
calm
kindhearted
popular
negotiators
good companions
need to feel loved and cherished as adults

24-4 Birth order can affect a child's mental and social-emotional development.

parents must try untested ideas on them. This means they are not treated the same as later children in the family. Firstborns are punished more severely and rewarded more liberally than later children. New parents often are more anxious and less sure of their parenting skills than parents of more than one child.

Firstborn children are not less popular with other children as are only and later-born children. These first children tend to use high-power social tactics like bossing, threats, and physical force to protect younger siblings. These tactics do not make them popular with peers.

Middle Children

Birth order findings seem to best fit families with four or fewer children. For this reason, the term *middle children* refers to the second child in a family of three siblings. It also refers to both the second and third children in families of four siblings. Findings on middle children, shown in 24-4, do not fit large families (five or more siblings) or families with multiple-birth siblings, such as twins.

Middle children seem to have lower IQs than those of only and first-born children. When children are spaced closer than three years, adults tend to spend less time with middle children. Adults spend more time with these children when the age gap is three or more years.

Socially, middle children seem to adjust easily to new situations. When

other children are born, middle children do not feel as displaced as firstborns. This may be because they always have shared their parents. They've even shared hand-me-down clothes and toys. On the negative side, they may feel caught in the middle. Some middle children feel they must constantly compete with older siblings. A middle child may also feel a younger child steals attention as the family baby.

Youngest Children

As shown in chart 24-4, youngest children do better socially than mentally. Their IQs are usually lower than those of their siblings. This may be because they rarely play the role of teacher with siblings.

Youngest children are often relaxed and cheerful. Parents usually are comfortable with their parenting skills by the time this child is born. Youngest children deal with more personalities from the time they are infants than do older siblings. Plus, they are used to receiving attention and care from older siblings, 24-5.

On the negative side, parents may treat the youngest child more like a baby because they know he or she is their last child. Siblings tend to take care of the youngest child, too. These factors may cause the youngest to be more dependent and less mature. Youngest children are more likely to resort to sulking, tattling, teasing, and fighting.

A Child's Identity

Birth order does not need to affect a child's later success. Adults can

24-5 Youngest children receive plenty of attention from older siblings.

avoid the pitfalls of birth order by focusing on the child, not the child's place in the family. Comments referring to birth order can create bad side effects, such as dependency. ("She's just a baby.") Other comments may cause stress. ("You're the oldest so you should know better.")

Adults also need to treat each child fairly. Unfair treatment includes showing favoritism and forgetting to praise all children. Spoiling the youngest and expecting too much from firstborns and only children are also unfair treatments. Adults need to promote their children's best traits. They also need to help children overcome the negative effects of birth order. If adults treat children as individuals, children will develop their own identities.

Children of Multiple Births

As you read in chapter 4, the number of multiple births has grown since the early 1990s. Many people ask whether parenting multiple-birth children is different from **singletons** (children born one at a time.) In many ways it is. Parents must meet more sets of needs at once. In meeting these needs, tasks, time, and costs often double or triple. Most parents soon realize they need extra help, especially right after birth.

Multiple birth children react to the world differently than singletons. This is because they spend a lot of time with each other, go through school together, and may look alike. For these reasons, children of multiple births share perhaps the closest of all

 singletons. Children born one at a time, as opposed to children of multiple births.

24-6 Twins and other multiple-birth children often have very close relationships.

human relationships. Their relationship even may be closer than that of parent and child, 24-6. These siblings have few problems remaining close. Instead, they may have problems developing **separate identities** (feelings of being distinct people rather than a unit). Those who have the most problems with this are identical children and same-gender, look-alike fraternal children. Treating multiple-birth siblings as distinct children rather than as a unit will help each child form a separate identity.

When fostering these separate identities, adults need to preserve the siblings' special bond. Identical children share more than the same birthday—they share a common genetic makeup.

Stories and research abound concerning identical children with similar health problems, interests, and traits, even when raised thousands of miles apart. Being more alike than different is often normal for them. Adults should allow children to choose how much alike or different they wish to be. In this way, multiple-birth children will work out separateness and closeness just as other siblings do.

Parental Employment

Today, 92 percent of all families with children have one or both parents employed. Some families need or want two incomes. Many single parents, whether mothers or fathers, are forced to work in order to support their children. Changes in welfare laws have caused many parents to look for work. Many parents see careers outside the home as rewarding.

Not all parents work outside the home. Some have family businesses, such as farms and stores. More and more people are working from home. Many home-based workers have computers, cellular phones, modems, video teleconferencing, and faxes in their home offices, 24-7. This equipment allows them to conduct business without leaving home. When families are involved, working at home takes special planning. Parents must set aside time and space to complete work tasks in an efficient way.

24-7 This mother can use her computer to work from home while her young child naps.
Apple Computer

Effects on Children

How does a parent's job affect a child's development? Research shows that babies have fewer adjustment problems if mothers return to work before they are three months old or after age two years. Babies develop strong attachments to their caregivers between 3 and 24 months. Another awkward time to enter the workforce is when children are ages 11 through 13 years. At this time, children are coping with many changes in their life. Having a parent return to work may be too much.

Some studies show today's children receive as much attention from their working parents as yesterday's children did from their full-time mothers. This may be true. Working parents use more timesaving home appliances today, so keeping a home doesn't require as much of their time. Working parents use conveniences, such as eating out, more often than other parents. They may also try to make up for the hours away from home by spending meaningful time with their children each day.

Children of working parents enjoy some advantages over children with at least one parent who stays home. Children with working parents tend to miss fewer days of school. They usually enjoy meaningful and well-planned free time with parents. They also help with household chores and learn home-care skills. These children may live in homes with more structured times and more clearly stated rules. In this environment, children often show more confidence. Another advantage of working parents is that children interact more with others and spend more time with other adults and children, 24-8.

When both parents work, children think in broader terms about gender roles. Children who grow up in these homes do not think of women only as homemakers and men only as wage

separate identities. Feelings of being distinct people rather than a unit.

24-8 In many families in which both parents work, fathers are more involved with their children.

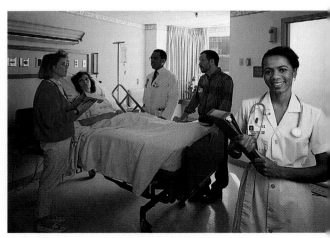

24-9 When parents are happy with their work, they tend to enjoy parenting more.
Photo courtesy of Washington Hospital Center, Washington, D.C.; Photographer Jim Douglass

earners. They see their mother arrive home from a day at work and help their father prepare dinner.

Effects on Parents

Finding a balance between work and family is sometimes difficult. Working does affect the emotional state of parents. Sometimes, working brings happiness. Often it brings **role strain**, a feeling of having too many tasks to do at one time. Working may also cause a parent to feel role guilt. **Role guilt** is a feeling of not doing the best job at work or at home because of role strain. When parents are happy with either working full-time or staying home, then children seem to adjust well, 24-9. However, if either parent is unhappy, it creates family stress.

Most parents do have some problems as a result of their work. They cannot always find time to relax. They may have trouble with child care arrangements. Some parents end up spoiling children as they try to make up for time away from home. Parents often feel guilty for not being able to attend some school functions that occur during work hours.

Balancing Family and Work

By planning carefully, parents can lessen the stress of parenting while holding a job. Working parents need to budget their time carefully. Letting some minor tasks slide may be necessary. They should plan family time, which is essential, in their daily schedules. Parents need to give their children some **quality time** (time when parents are totally attentive to their children) each day. Also, parents should check on the next day's clothes, lunch, and homework before children go to bed. This helps avoid morning panic.

What do working parents do if a child is sick, the caregiver is ill, or the child care center is closed? Parents must think about this in advance. If an older child must stay home alone after school, parents must talk about safety measures before problems occur.

Working parents should meet and talk with teachers. They should attend as many of their children's school-related events as possible. Likewise, parents should include their children in their work life. They can set up a visit to their worksites, explain their jobs, and share stories about their day at work.

Working parents still need to set limits for their children. Parents cannot make up for time away from the family by letting children do what they want to do. As with other children, children of working parents want and need guidance.

Parents who return to work after a time spent with children need to recognize and accept the feelings of their children. Children show feelings in many ways. Two- through four-year-olds may regress (act less mature than before) for a few weeks after the parent returns to work. Children usually express their feelings during the early evening hours when everyone is tired and hungry. The children often want to reconnect at this time and share the entire day's events. However, parents may need to relax for a few minutes after long hours at work. After spending a few quiet minutes, parents can devote their complete attention to the family.

Children in Self-Care

In the 1800s, the problems of the children of working parents began to surface. These children wore their house keys around their necks. They stayed home alone for a portion of a day and cared for themselves until a parent returned from work. During World War II, they were called *latchkey children*. Today, they are called **children in self-care**.

About seven million children under age 13 are in self-care. When teens are included in this number, it increases greatly. The number of children in

role strain. A feeling of having too many tasks to do at one time.

role guilt. A feeling of not doing the best job at home or work due to role strain.

quality time. A time when parents are totally attentive to their children.

children in self-care. Children who are at home alone after school or for a portion of the day and must care for themselves during that time.

self-care continues to increase for the following reasons:

❖ more dual-career and working single-parent households
❖ decrease in the number of extended families in which other adults are in the home
❖ high costs of child care
❖ lack of quality before- and after-school programs designed for the school-age child

Children, their parents, and the community all are affected by self-care. Some of these effects are positive and others are negative, as shown in 24-10. There are ways parents can decrease risks and increase the positive effects.

First, and foremost, parents should plan for self-care by deciding carefully whether their child can handle being in self-care. Parents must check state laws about the age at which children can be legally left at home. (State laws vary, but the legal age is often around 12 years.) They should learn whether the laws set different legal ages for self-care and caring for younger siblings. The care of younger siblings takes even more maturity, and may be legal only at an older age as set by the state.

If the child is of legal age to provide self-care, parents should consider the following when deciding about self-care:

❖ **How mature is the child?** Although many children are developmentally able to stay home alone at about 12 or 13 years, maturity is the key factor. Is the child afraid of staying home alone? Can the child handle unexpected situations without panicking? Has the child shown responsible behavior in other situations?

❖ **How safe is the home?** Any object in your home that requires adult supervision during use is dangerous for older children. Most injury-related deaths occur when children are out of school and unsupervised.

❖ **How safe is the neighborhood?** An unsafe neighborhood can result in fears, injury or death, and involvement in illegal actions. (Rate of juvenile violence is highest in the afternoon between 3 and 7 p.m.)

❖ **How do children feel about self-care?** Do they feel prepared and confident to provide this care? Are they concerned or afraid? What do children feel would make them feel safer or less safe about self-care? What can parents do to help?

Once parents have chosen self-care for their children, they need to teach their children the skills needed to provide self-care. As a part of this process, parents and children should do the following:

❖ Make sure the child learns safety rules, 24-11.
❖ Work out a way for the parent to know the answers to the three *w*s: *where* are the children? *what* are they doing? *who* are they with?
❖ Set rules about the use of appliances, TV, computer, stereo, videos, and other equipment; having friends over; and leaving the house.

Effects of Self-Care

Positive Effects on Children

- ❖ Children can show initiative and industry. (This is especially true for 8- through 13-year-old children. These children are old enough to understand rules and are less prone to peer pressure than teens.)
- ❖ Children may develop more self-esteem.

Negative Effects on Children

- ❖ Minor emergencies can become life threatening. For example, a young child may open a window "to let the fire out."
- ❖ Children are at greater risk for sexual abuse from older siblings and adults.
- ❖ Children may have increased feelings of being separated from or rejected by parents (who are at work) and friends (with whom they cannot play). This may lead to emotional or social problems.
- ❖ Feelings of anxiety may be especially strong for 8- through 13-year-old children who fear burglaries.
- ❖ Children may be overexposed to television and have no guidance while watching.
- ❖ Lack of adult guidance may lead to a child's poor food choices and improper nutrition.
- ❖ Academic achievement may drop due to excessive television viewing. Also, parents may not be able to help children with homework until they return from work; then both children and parents are tired.
- ❖ Children have increased risks of exposure to alcohol and other drugs.

Positive Effects for Parents

- ❖ Child care costs are reduced.
- ❖ With careful planning for the self-care situation, the adult-child relationship may be close, and children may more quickly learn self-care and how to be more responsible.

Negative Effects for Parents

- ❖ Parents have many feelings of guilt and concern.
- ❖ Loss of work productivity occurs while checking or refereeing children over the telephone. This is especially true during after-school hours.

Positive Effects for the Community

- ❖ Community leaders may challenge people to consider the needs of children and their families, such as low-cost child care and after-school programs.
- ❖ Challenges people to provide training for parents and children who must rely on self-care.

Negative Effects for the Community

- ❖ A greater risk of accidents, including home fires, exists.
- ❖ Rates of vandalism, arson, shoplifting, and vagrancy may rise during hours when children are in self-care.

24-10 Self-care has both positive and negative effects.

Rules for Safe Self-Care

❖ Keep house keys with you at all times.
❖ If walking home from school, walk with friends; come straight home unless other plans are first approved by parent.
❖ Call parent upon your arrival.
❖ Do not enter the house if things do not look right.
❖ Tell parents if anything or anyone frightens you.
❖ Call 911 in case of emergency (know how to define an *emergency*) and know how to give address and directions to your house.
❖ Upon entering the house, use locks and set alarm system if you have one.
❖ Never open the door at home but instead talk through the door.
❖ Answer phone calls (it may be the parents calling).
❖ Never tell people at the door or over the phone you are home alone.
❖ Arrange an emergency evacuation plan.

24-11 If children will be in self-care, parents must make sure the children understand these important safety rules.

❖ establish a routine for children to follow.
❖ begin self-care gradually, if possible. Start with a short period when the parent must do a quick, nearby errand or visits with a neighbor briefly. As the child shows confidence, parents can gradually increase the time to cover the amount of time between school and their arrival home. (The average weekly home-alone time is 6 hours.) In the beginning, parents should call to check on children more often, too.

Parents need to understand that self-care is *always* more risky than adult supervision. For this reason, parents should advocate for quality school-age child care (SACC) programs in their area. A parent may find other community-based youth programs suitable for older school-age children. If a SACC program or youth program is not available, parents can join a McGruff House or other block-parent program that helps children in self-care during emergencies or if they become frightened. Parents can also help establish a homework help line.

Coping with Family Moves

Today, the United States is a *mobile society*, which means people move from place to place often. Earlier in history, more people lived in extended families. Today, more than one-fifth of the population moves each year. On the average, each person moves 14 times in a lifetime.

Although some people enjoy moving, most feel some stress. Usually the stress lasts only a few weeks or months. However, for others, it may last a couple of years. Stress lessens when the following are true:

❖ moves do not occur too often
❖ no added stress is present, such as death of a family member or divorce
❖ parents are pleased about the move
❖ children have siblings who can act as playmates until they make new friends
❖ school-age children move at the beginning or end of a school term
❖ school-age children have good grades and do well in school
❖ children have special skills or interests (such as sports or hobbies) that help provide some stability

Stress occurs because moving is a change. People need time to adjust to a new community, city, school, job, and people. Moving can cause loneliness. Children may feel less certain about the past if they move often. They may ask, "Did I know this person when we lived in our old town?" "Where was my bedroom when we lived in our old house?"

Adults can reduce the stress of moving for children. Pointing out the positive reasons for moving is a good start. For example, parents may let children know whether the family will have more income or the children will go to better schools. Moving can enable children to widen their interests, make more friends, and learn more about other people. However, adults need to be honest about the move. They need to mention the bad as well as the good. For example, the family will miss old friends and their house. Adults should also explain each step that will happen as they move. Children will ask many questions. They may even want to act out certain events, 24-12.

If possible, parents should take children with them to see the new home and school before the move. Otherwise, a few pictures of the new area may help make the change easier.

Children should help with packing. It is often best to pack young children's items last. A few favorite

24-12 Young children may need to act out moving as a way to prepare for the real move.
© John Shaw

toys should be placed in the car or in luggage carried with the family.

Adults need to plan more time to be with children both before and after the move. With all they have to do to prepare for a move and get settled in a new place, it can be challenging for parents to find extra time to set aside for their children. This is important, though, because children need special family times to help them feel secure at this stressful time.

Coping with Death

Death is a basic part of life, and even young children need to learn to come to terms with it. Quite a few children lose a parent before they finish elementary school. Many more face death of a close friend, relative, or even a pet during childhood.

Children gradually begin to understand death. At about six or seven months, the baby has separations from caring adults. These separations, most of which are brief, are the earliest times of loss in a child's life. Early separation may set the stage for later responses to separation, loss, and even death. Until age three or four years, children have little, if any, understanding of death. Preschool children's concepts of death are still limited. They try to learn the physical facts of death. They find many facts difficult to believe, and thus, they question the facts. Some concepts that give children trouble include the following:

❖ Life can stop.
❖ Death is forever.
❖ People and pets cannot come back to life, even if children really want them to.

Preschool children usually do not explore religious beliefs about death. However, they may repeat statements they have heard others say. Adults should teach children to express grief, 24-13. Toddlers and preschool children may act in what may seem to be improper ways to a death or its rituals. This is because they do not know how to express their grief. Experts say that, when it comes to death, the feelings of preschool children and adults are very much alike. Both children and adults feel anger, protest, sadness, and loneliness. Both want to be in close contact with others. Adults need to be honest about the loss and their feelings, although they don't need to overburden the child. They need to allow children to talk about death and grieve in their own ways, even through pretend play. In time, most children come to terms with their loss and the stress lessens. Through their experiences, they learn more about death and grief.

24-13 When children lose a loved one—even a pet—they must find ways to express their grief.
© John Shaw

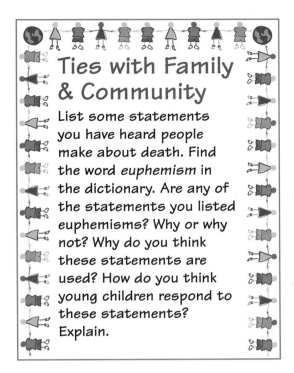

Ties with Family & Community

List some statements you have heard people make about death. Find the word *euphemism* in the dictionary. Are any of the statements you listed euphemisms? Why or why not? Why do you think these statements are used? How do you think young children respond to these statements? Explain.

Helping Children Cope with Grief

Usually, adults do not talk about death with children unless a person or pet dies. If a child asks about death, adults should answer all questions honestly. Many books suggest ways to explain death to a child. Adults need to help children understand and deal with death and grief, 24-14.

If a family member or close friend is terminally ill, adults should prepare the child for the upcoming death. Simple, truthful statements are best. An adult may say, "You know Grandma is very sick. The nurses and doctors are trying to help, but Grandma is getting sicker. She may die soon." Adults should not tell children a terminally ill person is on vacation.

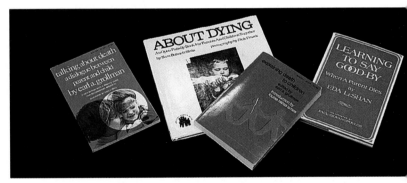

24-14 Carefully chosen books may help answer some questions about death.
© John Shaw

When Death Occurs

When death occurs, adults should explain at the child's level what has happened. They should say what they believe to be true about death.

Children become worried if they feel adults are keeping facts from them or avoiding their questions. Adults should explain death well enough so children do not expect the person (or pet) to return. An adult may say, "Father is dead. This means he doesn't move or breathe any more." Adults should not tell children a deceased person is sleeping. They also should explain religious beliefs simply. Children need to know they have not caused the death. (For example, they may think they have caused the death by having a fight with the person.)

Adults should be prepared to answer questions and repeat facts for a long time after a death. At first, for example, a child may seem to understand that Grandma has died. However, a week later the child may ask, "When is Grammy coming over?"

As children begin to understand death, they may become afraid a parent will die. Parents can reassure their children they will probably live a long time. However, they should never promise children they won't die. If a parent did die after such a promise, the child might feel betrayed and develop a lack of trust in others.

Adults should also help children express their grief. They should let children know it is okay to be sad and cry. Adults should set an example by not trying to hide their own sadness. Adults should give children time to experience sadness and loss. For this

reason, a pet that has died should not be replaced too soon.

Parents need to decide whether the child should be included in such rituals as funerals. The decision depends largely on the child's age and maturity, the child's wishes, and the family's beliefs. Some feel that seeing the open coffin makes death more real. Others feel this is too traumatic for a child. If the child will be participating in any rituals, an adult should explain these in advance so the child will know what to expect.

Coping with Divorce

In the United States, many couples divorce. Statistics show about 10 percent of all children currently live with a divorced parent, and about 1 in 60 children will see their parents divorce in a given year. The divorce rate for married teens is nearly twice that of older married couples.

The divorce rate has been declining for several years. However, divorce statistics are not a reliable indicator of the break-up of families. First, many couples separate although they are still legally married. It is not known how many couples are in this category. Next, the number of unmarried couples living together has greatly increased. Of couple households with children (87 percent), nearly half (41 percent) are unmarried. Because unmarried partners do not file legal paperwork when they separate, the

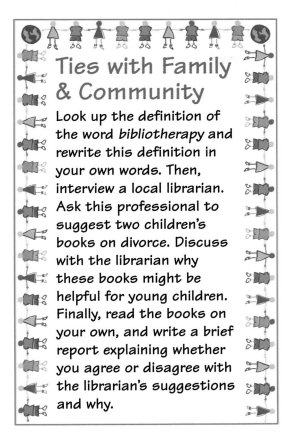

Ties with Family & Community

Look up the definition of the word *bibliotherapy* and rewrite this definition in your own words. Then, interview a local librarian. Ask this professional to suggest two children's books on divorce. Discuss with the librarian why these books might be helpful for young children. Finally, read the books on your own, and write a brief report explaining whether you agree or disagree with the librarian's suggestions and why.

exact number of separations among these families is not known. However, research indicates that unmarried-partner households do have a much higher rate of break-up than married-partner households.

Causes of Divorce

Why do so many people divorce? Many factors contribute to the high rate of divorce. Today's more mobile society brings people of differing backgrounds to meet and marry. Some of these couples find their differences are too great for them to get along well as marriage partners. Being pregnant before marriage as well as marrying as a teen also increases the risk of divorce. Studies show living together prior to marriage does not reduce a couple's chance of divorce.

Marital problems often result from financial strain. Other stresses are related to family or work demands. These stresses can build and affect the marriage. When one spouse is unfaithful, violent, or addicted to drugs or alcohol, the other spouse may seek divorce as a way to regain a healthy home life.

Society also contributes to divorce by emphasizing personal happiness. Some spouses may seek divorce as a way to escape an unhappy situation rather than staying married and trying to work out problems. Society also places less stigma on divorce today than in the past.

Effects of Divorce

Divorce affects both adults and children. Adults have to overcome their negative feelings and adjust to a new lifestyle. When children are involved, adults often have a continual relationship with the former spouse and in-laws.

Children are affected during the separation process and often for years following the divorce. Even children who were infants when their parents divorced deal with these issues in their school-age years.

It is difficult to predict how divorce will affect a particular child.

Reactions to Loss of a Parent Through Death or Divorce

Two- and Three-Year-Olds

whine, cry, and cling

act fretful

have sleep and appetite problems

may regress (This occurs most often at a time of day when the absent parent was often with the child.)

Four-Year-Olds

whine and cry

hit or bite others

feel they caused the divorce or death

Five-Year-Olds

feel anxious

seem moody and restless

act aggressively

want physical contact with others

deny the loss and even pretend parents will be together again

have problems in creative play

School-Age Children

daydream more and worry more about the future

deny the loss

feel angry and bitter (blame parent whom they think is responsible)

feel lonely, abandoned, and rejected by the absent parent

show antisocial behavior, such as lying or stealing

have more headaches and stomachaches

have school problems, such as not being able to pay attention

show premature detachment, rejecting the parent who is gone and the qualities shared with this absent parent (For example, if the parent had athletic ability, the child may reject sports.)

become the confidant of the remaining parent and thus have too much adultlike pressure

Common Behaviors and Feelings: Boys

act oblivious and inattentive

have a drop in school achievement

act more aggressively

have more problems during the divorce process and for the first two years after the divorce

do better if they have a positive relationship with the absent parent

Common Behaviors and Feelings: Girls

feel grief and frustration

cry

withdraw

blame themselves

are more troubled a year after the divorce than at the time of the divorce

24-15 How a child is affected by the loss of a parent through death or divorce depends on the child's age and gender.

Age and gender tend to affect how children cope, 24-15. Divorce usually confuses young children. They do not understand the divorce process, but they know one parent is not living with the family. A child's personality affects how he or she will cope, too. Some children are more positive than others and have fewer coping problems.

The family's standard of living often changes after a divorce. The income of single mothers drops about 73 percent, but the income of single fathers rises by about 42 percent. Almost 90 percent of all children live with their divorced mother, which often means their standard of living drops. This affects all family members.

Coping with the Effects

Parents seeking to divorce may find professional counseling helpful. Counselors or members of support groups can discuss the effects of divorce on parents and children. Parents may need help coping with their personal feelings and meet their children's new needs. Both parents may have new stresses, such as changes in residence, jobs, income, or roles.

Adults should not discuss problems of the marriage or divorce with children. Children cannot understand these complex issues. Because they cannot help solve the problems of marriage, they should not be burdened with them. However, adults should give children honest answers. They may say something like, "Your dad (or mom) and I once were happy together. We no longer are happy living together, so we have decided never to live together again. We both love you, and we will always love you. We will always take care of you." Parents may need to repeat this message many times. They should not explain why they are unhappy. It is more important to reassure children that both parents will continue to love and care for them.

When children are in their late teen years, parents may explain more about the marriage failure. Even then, it is best for parents to state their feelings rather than discuss the flaws of the other parent. A parent might say, "I was very hurt," or, "I felt misunderstood."

Once custody plans are firm, parents should tell children about them (if they are old enough to understand). Custody battles can hurt children. For this reason, parents should shelter children from the details of custody decisions. Parents can explain the custody plan and that both parents feel it is best for the family. They should not discuss other details with children.

Family Members Need Support

Children also need neutral people to support them. These people can help children express their sadness or anger in acceptable ways. Support people also can help children cope with loneliness and a new lifestyle. They can serve as role models, too.

Both parents and children may need a support system for many years. Long-term effects occur more often if there are prolonged tensions in the relationships or other major problems. Children have more problems if they are girls, if their parents divorce during their school-age years, or if their parents suffer role strain. Mothers often experience more role strain because they usually have primary custody in addition to less income. Studies show 44 percent of divorced mothers report more conflicts with their children. An equal percentage of divorced fathers report a better relationship. Role strain can be reduced with understanding of causes, with support when needed, and with some loving apologies for unnecessary conflicts.

Each parent should be careful not to express hostile feelings about the other parent to children or in their presence. A parent should never ask children to choose sides or relay messages to the other parent.

Children need to know their parents still love them. Both parents should explain the divorce is not the child's fault. They should not expect children to handle the divorce in an adult way. Children may feel stress if they are expected to act too maturely for their age. On the other hand, these children still need consistent, firm discipline.

When the family structure changes, parents should alert teachers and other adults who work with children. These adults can help children cope if they are aware of the home situation.

Single Parenting

Almost a third of all families are headed by single parents. Women head five times more of these single-parent households than men. The number of men who are single parents is continuing to increase, however, 24-16.

How do single-parent families form? In some cases, single parenting is caused by death of a spouse or divorce. These circumstances change a two-parent family to a single-parent family. While some single-parent families are formed in this way, many are also formed by parents who have never been married. Among single parents, over 40 percent of mothers and 30 percent of fathers have never

married. Because these families start with just one parent, they may have somewhat different concerns than other single-parent families.

Problems Single Parents Face

Single-parent families face many of the same problems as other families. Families with one parent may experience some of these same problems in different ways from other families. In addition, they experience some problems that are unique to their family structure.

24-16 The number of men who are single parents is increasing.
© John Shaw

Financial problems are often the greatest problems single parents face. This is because the parent who heads the household is often the only parent who pays the children's expenses. Although both parents have a legal responsibility to contribute financially, few parents who live separately from their children actually do. In some cases, the matter is never taken before the court, so a child support order is never issued. A **child support order** is a judgment of the court that states how much the parent who does not live with the children should pay toward the children's expenses. Even when a child support order is issued, however, it can be difficult to enforce if the parent does not willingly pay. For these reasons, half of single-parent families have incomes below the poverty level. This is especially true of single parents who are younger, have never been married, are less educated, or have more than one child to support. Families with more than one of these risk factors are even more likely to live in poverty.

Men and women who are single parents report different types of problems. Single fathers often report problems with housework and the physical aspects of child care, such as cooking and buying clothes. Single mothers often say their biggest problems are disciplining the children and not earning enough money.

Many single parents have strong emotional reactions to the circumstances that made them single parents. They may feel anger, resentment, depression, fear, or sadness at having to carry so much responsibility alone. Single parents report more **social isolation**, or feelings of being alone. They may have no one to talk to about problems and feelings. Because they must fulfill all the responsibilities of parenting and running a household without a partner, single parents often have less time of their own. They are less able to spend time with friends or in activities they enjoy. In cases in which two-parent families lose a parent through death or divorce, family life is disrupted. Feelings of grief and confusion may also be present.

Helping Children Cope

Besides coping with their own feelings, single parents must help their children cope. Parents are the base from which children grow. When death or divorce ends a two-parent family, children feel the loss of a relationship and role model. In these families, children's daily routines change as one parent takes over the duties two parents once shared. The way a child reacts to these changes depends on

child support order. A judgment of the court that states how much a parent who does not live with his or her children should pay toward their expenses.

social isolation. Feelings of being alone.

his or her age and personality. Most of these homes become stable within two years of a divorce or death.

In never-married families, children may have other issues with which they must cope. If both parents are actively involved, these problems are lessened. When one parent is absent, however, children may wonder whether they caused the parent to abandon them. They may wonder why other children have two parents and they have only one. These children may feel a lasting sense of loss, especially if they have never known or no longer have contact with the second parent. They may feel angry toward this parent for not being involved. Some children blame the remaining parent for not staying with the other parent.

In all single parent families, a few long-term effects may continue. In homes where fathers are absent, boys may rebel or do poorly in school. Teen girls may become overly aggressive or shy around boys.

Single parents need support. They may need outside help with problems such as finances, child care, and housework. Adults may need to talk about their feelings with other adults. Some single parents find support or social groups, such as Parents Without Partners, are helpful. In any event, parents should not rely on their children as a sole source of friendship. This is unfair to the children and unhealthy for the parent-child relationship.

Children in single-parent families also need extra support. They need time to work out their feelings. Adults should allow children to express their feelings through actions and words. Books on the topic may be helpful. Children in single-parent families need adult role models of both genders. These can be relatives, friends, neighbors, or adults from an organization such as Big Brothers/Big Sisters. Forming relationships with other children in single-parent families can help, too.

Remarriage and Stepparenting

Many divorced people remarry within a few years of being divorced. Many widowed parents remarry, and parents who have not been married may marry, too.

The younger people are at the time of becoming single parents, the more likely they are to remarry. Over 80 percent of those divorced before age 25 will remarry within 10 years. Within this same time frame, less than 70 percent of those divorced at age 25 and older will remarry. Other factors that influence the potential for remarriage include how long the first marriage lasted and whether the divorced person has children. Women under age 30 who have young children are the most likely to marry a new partner.

In most cases, one stepparent enters a single-parent family. (In more than half of cases, stepfathers join a single-parent family headed by the mother.) A new living arrangement changes daily living patterns. Single parents often are proud they can run a household by themselves. After remarriage, they may have problems sharing the parenting roles with a spouse.

Preparing for Family Changes

Before single parents begin a new stepfamily, they should speak to family counselors. Social workers or religious leaders may conduct such sessions. Older children may want to take part in some of the sessions.

All children beyond infancy need to be prepared for the new marriage and family life. Each remarrying parent should share with his or her children that he or she loves the new spouse and wants the marriage to work out well for everyone. Telling children the new marriage will last, be better, or be fun is not an honest approach.

Children also need to know they are not the only ones who live in stepfamilies. Many stepchildren face the same issues. They may not know what to call the stepparent. They may worry about whom to invite to school or other special functions. Books on stepfamilies may help children adjust, 24-17.

Perhaps one of the most difficult tasks for a stepparent is knowing how much to discipline stepchildren. It is more difficult to discipline stepchildren than biological children. Stepparents

24-17 Books on stepfamilies help children realize that other families have similar concerns.
© John Shaw

are often afraid to correct their stepchildren for fear the children will not like them.

It is usually difficult for children to adjust to a new family structure. The adjustment is even more difficult if the new stepparent has children of his or her own that will join the household, too. However, both parents can help the children adjust over time. When these new family relationships work out, the added family ties are worth the effort.

Teens as Parents

Programs to reduce teen births are ongoing in almost every state. Young Americans seem to be getting the message. The overall birth rate for teens has fallen almost 20 percent since the 1991 high. Today, the teen birth rate is about 49 births per 1,000 females between ages 15 and 19 years. This is the lowest rate in the 60 years. Births for the youngest teens (ages 10 to 14 years) have dropped to the lowest level in 30 years. The decline in the teen birth rate is seen in all cultural and ethnic groups.

Despite these declines, however, the teen birth rate is still high. The Children's Defense Fund reports that 1 in 8 babies is born to a teen mother.

Teen parenting is a risk. Becoming a parent in the teen years has no advantages over having children between the ages 20 and 34 years. The risks of teen pregnancy and parenting affect many aspects of the teens' lives, and it is impossible to reverse the consequences. See chart 24-18 for the consequences of teen parenting. Many of these problems relate to health, financial concerns, and lifestyle changes. Most teens who choose to parent their babies become single mothers. Being a single, never-married parent results in the highest risk for the child's overall well-being.

Health Risks for the Teen Mother and Her Baby

Teens' bodies are still growing and developing—only babies in the womb and infants develop more quickly. Because of all these physical changes, proper nutrition is crucial for a teen. When a teen is pregnant, the baby depends on the mother for nutrition. This depletes her body of nutrients. Poor nutrition before or during pregnancy puts the mother and her baby at risk.

In earlier chapters, you read about the health risks associated with smoking, STDs, and pregnancy. Smoking rates are declining for some of the population, but they are increasing for teens. More teens have STDs, too, and these are rarely treated before an unplanned pregnancy. Teen mothers' risk of STDs is high. One reason is that most teens become pregnant by men between ages 22 and 25 years. These men usually have had multiple partners, which makes them more likely to be carriers of STDs.

The lack of medical care is another health risk for teen mothers. All mothers-to-be need early and continuous prenatal care. They also need medical care for about two months after delivery. Although the rate of prenatal care has increased, some teens still do not receive care they need early in pregnancy. Reasons for this risk are that teen mothers-to-be:

❖ may think they are not pregnant
❖ feel their parents will be upset
❖ are afraid the relationship with the baby's father will end
❖ lack money for medical care or do not know where to go for help
❖ cannot find transportation to a medical facility
❖ do not know that medical care is not necessary
❖ are afraid of medical procedures

Both mother and baby are affected by these risks. Even with good health care, teen mothers experience other health risks. These include longer labors and more C-section deliveries than mothers aged 20 to 29 years. Compared to all mothers, teen mothers are at the highest risk of postpartum depression (PPD).

Consequences of Teen Parenting

For teen mothers

- ❖ Health risks are greater for younger teen mothers and for all teen mothers who don't receive quality prenatal and postnatal care.
- ❖ Over half of women who become mothers in the teen years never complete high school.
- ❖ Teen mothers lack entry-level skills for the job market. Their income is usually 50 percent below that of mothers who have their first child at 20 to 29 years.
- ❖ Teen parents who marry are at high risk for divorce. Statistics show that
  —one in five marriages end in divorce after the first year
  —one in three marriages end in divorce after two years
  —three in five marriages end in divorce after six years
- ❖ Married teen mothers report major marital problems. These problems include the following:
  —more sexual activity than they desire
  —loneliness (Many times a teen husband maintains his social life while the wife assumes more child care responsibility. Also, most teen wives tend to lose touch with girlfriends.)
  —lack of support (Many times, older men who father many babies are not interested in marriage or parenting. The teen mother may not receive companionship, parenting support, or child support.)

For teen fathers

- ❖ Teen fathers have poor school performance and many times drop out of high school.
- ❖ Teen fathers often lack education and training. For these reasons, they usually cannot earn adequate incomes to support their family.
- ❖ Unmarried teen fathers report not being able to see their babies when they wish. Married teen fathers report problems with the child's maternal grandparents.
- ❖ Teen fathers show less self-esteem than other teens because of less education and more financial problems.

For children of teen parents

- ❖ The mortality rate is high for babies of mothers who are age 15 years or younger. This death rate is trice as high as that for babies of mothers between ages 20 and 34 years.
- ❖ Babies of teen parents are a greater risk for congenital problems.
- ❖ Children of teens have lower achievement in school because of
  —having birth defects
  —being born too soon or too small
  —having less family income
- ❖ Children of teens are at a higher risk of being abused because of
  —having birth defects
  —being born too soon or too small
  —having parents who do not know when a child is ready to do or learn a task (A study shows that a group of teen parents thought babies could use the toilet at six months of age.)
  —crying when parents want to sleep, study, or socialize or when parents are depressed

For society

- ❖ Often extra child care tasks and the need for more income burdens the grandparents of the teens' child.
- ❖ Teen parents lose productive income because of their lower-income jobs or unemployment.
- ❖ Society pays the costs of assistance programs to teen parents.
- ❖ Society pays for assistance to children and loss of productive income in the next generation if children do not overcome their problems.
- ❖ Societies may be more violent if children are abused.
- ❖ The numbers and problems faced by single-parent, divorced, and remarried families may increase.

24-18 The risks of teen parenting affect parents, children, and society in general.

Thus, postpartum care is needed to protect both physical and mental health.

The **mortality rate** (rate of death) for the babies of teen mothers is high. Many of the babies who survive have low birthweights. These small babies have higher rates of SIDS and grow slowly throughout childhood. Studies show they have more learning problems in school and more social problems with peers.

Health risks increase even more for both mother and baby if the teen mother is younger than 15 years or has had more than one pregnancy in the teen years. Many teens have a repeat pregnancy before age 20 years.

Financial Concerns

Prenatal care and delivery are expensive. Most teens are not covered by insurance. Even if they are covered by their parents' policies, the costs of pregnancy and childbirth may not be covered. Health problems add to the costs for mother and baby. The added expense of a baby is a real burden for teens, most of whom are financially strapped. Parents must pay for a baby's food, clothing, equipment, and perhaps child care. These costs increase as babies grow.

Some teens turn to their parents for help. This is usually stressful both for them and for their parents. Some teen parents require public assistance in the form of medicaid, Temporary Assistance to Needy Families (TANF), food stamps, and housing subsidy.

Recent changes in welfare laws will make assistance more difficult to receive on a long-term basis.

Sadly, these financial problems can continue into adulthood. Studies show teens who become parents usually have financial problems all their lives. Over half of all teen mothers never finish high school. Teen fathers may drop out of school to get a job. Because they have not completed their education, teens do not have entry-level job skills. This means they usually qualify for only low-paying jobs. Even teens who finish high school rarely complete college, which also keeps them from earning adequate pay. College graduates earn almost twice as much in income over the course of their lifetimes as high school graduates.

Teen parents find completing their education difficult or impossible for the following reasons:
❖ Adequate child care is unaffordable.
❖ Teen parents feel out of place in a traditional program because they are older than other students.
❖ The need for a job, even a low-paying one, may keep teen parents out of school.
❖ Teen parents' time to study is limited because of their parenting responsibilities, 24-19.

Many teen-parent families live in poverty. Living in poverty causes problems that adversely affect the lives of teen parents and their children.

24-20 Teen parenthood has changed this teen father's lifestyle in major ways.
© Nancy P. Alexander

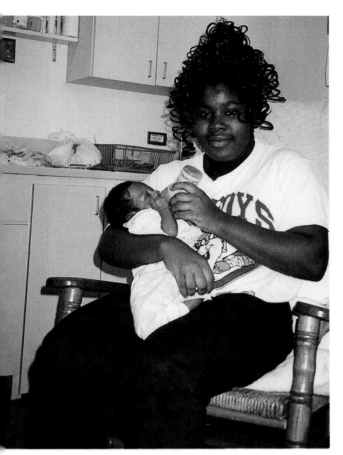

24-19 Even healthy, happy babies take so much care that teen mothers find little time to study.

Lifestyle Changes

When teens become parents, their lives change in dramatic ways. Those who marry because of a pregnancy may find themselves in unhappy marriages. They may encounter problems living with their baby in their parents' homes. Most have financial pressures. Many also socialize less often with friends because they have

more responsibility, 24-20. Teen parents usually lead stressful lives.

Life with Mom and Dad

Teen parents who continue to live with their own parents report additional friction at home. A teen's parents may have a difficult time adjusting to his or her early parenthood. They may be disappointed and concerned. They may insist the baby's other parent stay out of the baby's life. Grandparents of the baby often feel the most stress because they are juggling child care, work, and other family obligations.

 mortality rate. Rate of death.

24-21 Participating in after-school clubs or activities is valuable, but it's something many teen parents do not have the time to do.

They may need more money to help their child and grandchild. They also may feel stress because they must deal with a crying baby or curious toddler later in life.

Social Life Changes

Before pregnancy, a teen's life focuses on school, social activities, and family, 24-21. Once a teen becomes a parent, life changes. Now the teen focuses on the medical aspects of pregnancy, the costs of a baby, and ways to meet the baby's needs. Teen parents have little time to study or spend with friends because baby care takes too much time. Baby expenses leave little or no money to spend on nonessential items.

Many teen mothers say they feel isolated. Although friends usually stand by teen mothers, they may not maintain the same social contact. This often happens during the pregnancy and after the baby is born. This leads to depression and frustration.

Family Violence

Teen frustrations may initiate family violence. Spouse abuse may occur in unhappy marriages. Children of teens are at high risk for abuse. Teens' needs do not mesh with their children's needs. Teen parents rarely have enough support in parenting tasks. They often do not know about child development and may expect children to reach unreasonable goals. The parents' frustration with a child's "lack of progress" often leads to child abuse.

Although teen parents face challenges, many overcome them and have positive experiences as young parents. However, this happens only through hard work. Each parent must be determined to do all he or she can to help the baby and family. Teen parents also need people they can turn to for help. They need emotional, practical, and financial support to overcome the obstacles they face. Today, more community programs are available to help teens finish school and learn to become successful parents and wage earners.

Why Wait?

From the time of birth, human beings want acceptance, loving relationships, and deep intimacy. Although human beings have a strong sexual aspect to their nature, sex cannot by itself satisfy their desires to become truly social beings. A relationship built on sex is very unstable. Sex does not create intimacy—rather sex is one expression of an intimacy that already exists.

Furthermore, some people desire sex for reasons that are not even related to intimacy. For example, some people use sex to avoid a close relationship with their partners; that is, they spend less time in other aspects of the relationship or use sex to end conflicts rather than engage in

problem solving. Others may use sex to get back at their parents, prove themselves, or get the "sexual high" as depicted in the media.

Many teens (and even adults) ask the question: Why should I wait for marriage to have sex if I'm in love? First, what many mistake as love is a passing feeling that does not last. Entering a sexual relationship can make a person feel emotionally tied to the other person. Imagine how painful this would make a break-up.

The results of a sexual relationship can be life-altering and permanent. Two of the most troubling risks are unplanned pregnancy and STDs. (For example, about 63 percent of all STDs occur in people younger than 25 years of age. Among teens, the number of AIDS cases alone doubles every 14 months.) Many birth control methods are available, but the idea of "completely safe sex" is a myth. The only guaranteed way to avoid unwanted pregnancies and STDs is **abstinence**. This choice involves postponing a sexual relationship until marriage. More people realize they have the right to say no to the following:

❖ unwanted pregnancies that will forever change their lives

❖ STDs that may result in sterility, health problems, or death

abstinence. The choice to postpone a sexual relationship until marriage.

❖ emotional scars that may follow a broken relationship
❖ conflicts with parents and other adults who care for them
❖ conflicts with their own consciences, goals, and personal priorities

Child Neglect and Abuse

Even the thought of neglect or abuse of children evokes emotion in almost everyone. Some people feel outraged. Others are confused by the problems involved in preventing neglect and abuse. Those who work in child protection agencies are frustrated in trying to fight these crimes.

Neglect and abuse threaten children's health and welfare. Adults who abuse children cause them physical, mental, or emotional harm. Many children die from these adult actions.

Untold numbers of children suffer neglect and abuse by parents, friends, relatives, or child care workers. Statistics never tell the whole story. Many cases are never reported. Some reported cases are not investigated due to heavy caseloads of social workers. Still other cases are never confirmed (cannot be proven). Thus, the number of cases is higher than data indicate. Furthermore, cases are confirmed based on legal definitions of neglect and abuse as given in a state's child protection laws. Some experts believe these legal definitions should be expanded to include more cases.

Child neglect and abuse are very serious problems. The rate of reported abuse has declined to under 12 victims per 1,000 children, but even one case is too many. One-fourth of all children suffer more than one type of abuse. Of the children who die from abuse and neglect, over 80 percent are younger than age five years. Half of these young children are under one year of age.

Most neglect and abuse occurs in the home and is done by a person the child knows and trusts. Of reported cases, 87 percent involve at least one parent. Another 10 percent of cases involve a relative as the abuser. Child-care or foster-care settings account for 2 percent of cases. Thus, less than 1 percent of reported child abuse occurs at the hands of a stranger.

What Are Child Neglect and Abuse?

Child neglect refers to harm or endangerment of a child caused by an adult's failure to do something legally expected of him or her. States' legal definitions of neglect vary, but most focus on the failure of adults to provide for the child's needs or give a proper level of care with respect to food, clothing, shelter, hygiene, medical attention, or supervision. There are several types of neglect, which include the following:

❖ Physical neglect refers to endangering a child's health or safety by failing to provide supervision and basic survival needs, such as clothing, food, and shelter. (As you read in chapter 10, a particular kind of physical neglect involving failure to feed a baby or small child sufficiently is called "failure to thrive" syndrome.)

❖ **Educational neglect** is failure to conform to state legal requirements regarding school attendance.

❖ **Medical neglect** is harm or endangerment of a child caused by failure to seek treatment for health problems or accidents.

❖ **Moral neglect** is failure to teach the child right from wrong in terms of general social expectations, such as stealing is wrong.

❖ **Emotional neglect** is inadequate care and attention, violence or drug use in the home, or failing to meet the child's emotional needs at each stage of development.

In contrast to neglect, **child abuse** refers to an act committed by an adult that harms or threatens to harm a child's well-being. Specific definitions of the types of child abuse follow.

❖ **Physical abuse** (even when done in the name of discipline) is violence that results in pain, injuries, or both to a child.

❖ **Sexual abuse** is any act of a sexual nature that involves an adult and a child. Some states define sexual

child neglect. Harm or endangerment of a child caused by an adult's failure to do something legally expected of him or her.

physical neglect. Endangering a child's health or safety by failing to provide supervision and basic survival needs, such as clothing, food, and shelter.

educational neglect. Failure to conform to state legal requirements regarding school attendance.

medical neglect. Harm or endangerment of a child caused by failure to seek treatment for health problems or accidents.

moral neglect. Failure to teach the child right from wrong in terms of general social values.

emotional neglect. Inadequate care and attention, violence or drug use in the home, or failing to meet the child's emotional needs at each stage of development.

child abuse. An act committed by an adult that harms or threatens to harm a child's well-being.

physical abuse. Violence that results in pain, injuries, or both to a child.

sexual abuse. Any act of a sexual nature that involves an adult and a child.

abuse as any act of a sexual nature between a child and someone who is at least five years older than the child. Chart 24-22 explains some of the myths and realities related to sexual abuse.

❖ **Emotional/verbal abuse** is any act in which an adult makes excessive demands, harasses, belittles, or verbally threatens the child. Emotional/verbal abuse lowers a child's self-esteem.

What Happens to the Victims?

Although some children who suffer abuse and neglect are resilient, most are left with deep and long-lasting scars. These scars affect every aspect of development. In many cases, the idea that "time heals all wounds" does not seem to apply to those who have been neglected or abused as children.

Physical Scars

Many neglected children lack adequate food, clothing, or housing. Poor hygiene and other unsafe living conditions exist. Many babies fail to thrive.

Abused children are often beaten, bruised, burned, and/or cut. Their bones and teeth may be broken. Even without physical marks, they suffer pain from slapping and other physical attacks. People who are sexually abused suffer internal and external

Myths and Realities of Sexual Abuse

Myth	Reality
❖ Sexual abuse is rare.	❖ Sexual abuse occurs frequently and takes many forms, such as pornography and incest.
❖ The offender is an unknown, dangerous person.	❖ In 85 percent of cases, the offender is a known person, such as a relative or friend.
❖ The incident occurs suddenly, such as when an adult is momentarily out of the room.	❖ The abuse usually is repeated over and over again and may occur for several years.
❖ Child sexual abuse usually is a violent attack.	❖ More often, child sexual abuse is subtle "force." The offender may call it a "new game."
❖ Children often make up stories of sexual abuse.	❖ Children rarely make up stories of sexual abuse. In fact, they are often reluctant to tell about sexual abuse because they fear the offender or feel guilty for being involved.
❖ Children who recant stories of sexual abuse were lying about the first report.	❖ The abuser may have pressured children to change their stories.

24-22 Adults need to know the realities of sexual abuse in order to help children and prevent and treat this serious problem.

injuries, may contract STDs, and may become pregnant.

The statistics show the youngest children are most prone to die from physical neglect and abuse. For example, death can occur due to **Shaken Baby Syndrome (SBS)**, a condition in which a baby or young child has been violently shaken. Shaking a baby causes a "whiplash" motion in which the brain hits the skull repeatedly. These hits cause veins in the brain to break, filling the area around the brain with blood. This blood collects around the brain in the skull and causes swelling. This swelling damages brain cells and puts pressure on the brain stem, which controls breathing and heartbeat. Many shaken babies develop cerebral palsy, paralysis, brain seizures, blindness, deafness, and learning and behavior problems. Between 15 and 30 percent of children with SBS will die from their injuries.

Mental Scars

Mental scars are common when children are neglected and abused. Some mental problems come from brain injuries. Many others result from educational neglect and the inability to concentrate during learning tasks due to abuse. Lack of brain stimulation during the windows of opportunity can also have a negative effect. Studies indicate that about 30 percent of abused children have some type of language or learning problem. In

addition, over half of all abused children have difficulty in school.

Emotional Scars: New Brain Development Research Findings

The brains of infants and toddlers are forever altered by abuse. Physically abused babies have brains that are tuned to track nonverbal cues that may signal the next abusive attack. Abused children closely track the "ups and downs" of adults' emotional states. Brain-stress hormones, such as cortisol, prune the brain wiring. By age three years, the regions of the brain responsible for emotions are 20 to 30 percent smaller for abused children than for other children. Abused children have less brain development in the brain center for joy and other light-hearted emotions. In these children, the slightest stress results in hyperactivity, anxiety, impulsive behavior, and difficulties in paying attention and using self-control.

Emotional scars occur after three years of age, too. Older children often lack self-esteem, and have feelings of anger, anxiety, shame, guilt, or

emotional/verbal abuse. Any act in which an adult makes excessive demands, harasses, belittles, or verbally threatens the child.

Shaken Baby Syndrome. A condition in which a baby or young child has injuries as a result of being violently shaken.

depression due to the abuse or neglect. Over half of abused children have social and emotional problems.

Treatment for Victims

When a case of abuse or neglect is confirmed, children can begin to receive help and treatment. This is the first step toward being an abuse or neglect survivor rather than remaining a victim.

Physical treatment for the abused or neglected child is the first priority. As a doctor examines and treats the child, he or she will take a history (from the child, an older sibling, and/or parents) and document the examination. Records will include the doctor's observations, lab reports, and photographs or drawings.

Caseworkers or advocates from a child abuse prevention agency may also be involved in helping the child. These professionals make decisions about the child's welfare and advocate on his or her behalf. As caseworkers make decisions about the children, they keep the following questions in mind:

❖ What is the relationship of the child to the abuser?
❖ What risks are present for further abuse?
❖ What role, if any, should the courts have in this case?
❖ Should the child remain with the family?
❖ What support services could help both the child and family?

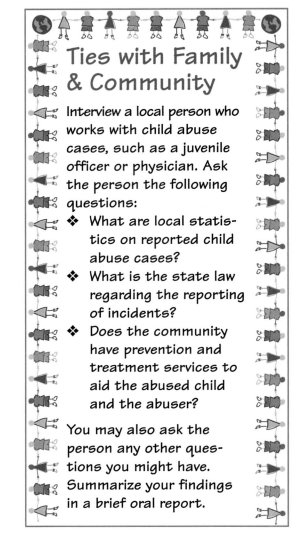

Ties with Family & Community

Interview a local person who works with child abuse cases, such as a juvenile officer or physician. Ask the person the following questions:

❖ What are local statistics on reported child abuse cases?
❖ What is the state law regarding the reporting of incidents?
❖ Does the community have prevention and treatment services to aid the abused child and the abuser?

You may also ask the person any other questions you might have. Summarize your findings in a brief oral report.

The services recommended will depend upon the particulars of the case and the age of the child. Foster care, residential treatment facilities, child advocacy centers, counseling, Head Start programs, group therapy, family intervention therapy, and individual therapy are examples of support services that are often used.

In working with abusers, courts and caseworkers consider the severity of the abuse or neglect, the abuser's relationship to the child, and any past history of abusive or neglectful behaviors. Abusers may be restricted from seeing the child or have their parental rights ended. They may also be convicted of a crime or ordered to receive therapy. This therapy could include treatment for mental illness and/or substance abuse, individual or group counseling, or attendance in classes for abusers. The reason behind these treatments is to deter the adult from choosing further abusive or neglectful actions.

What Are the Causes of Neglect and Abuse?

Why would an adult neglect or hurt a child? There is no simple cause-effect explanation. Sometimes very different reasons cause the same results. For example, neglect may occur when parents cannot afford to meet a child's needs or when parents think only about their own needs. Sometimes neglect occurs when parents do not know how to provide proper care for children. Neglectful and abusive parents come from all levels of income, intelligence, and education. Generally, abusive parents do not have obvious signs of problems that others can see. Abusive parents may seem nice, quiet, and kind when they are at work or around friends.

Yet, experts who have looked closely at neglect and abuse have noted some risk factors. These experts believe it is important to look at the entire family system for answers, 24-23. Although experts cannot weigh the degree of risk for each factor, studies show that drug and alcohol abuse is present in 40 percent of reported neglect and abuse cases. Furthermore, experts cannot always predict from the factors what form the abuse will take. Two exceptions are the following: a parent who physically abuses a spouse is likely to physically abuse a child, and a person who has a history of sexual abuse is more likely to sexually abuse others.

Experts consider abuse a complex, interactive process. For this reason, some parents may abuse only one child in the family or may abuse a child only during times of high parental stress. An example of an interactive process is: An unplanned pregnancy leads to more financial stress for a family who already lives near the poverty level. To save costs, the mother doesn't get prenatal care. Her baby is born at a low birthweight. The tiny baby has feeding problems that cause him or her to cry for hours at a time. The parent, who already has problems in coping, abuses the infant "to stop him from crying." This does *not*, however, mean the child is to blame for the abuse. Abusers are *always* responsible for their actions.

Risk Factors for Neglect and Abuse

Society
- Poverty
- Overcrowding
- Illegal drug culture
- High crime area
- High unemployment rate
- Few social services
- Unaffordable health care

Parent/Family
- Unwanted pregnancy
- Single parent
- Teen parent
- Physical, sexual, or emotional abuse as a child
- Emotional neglect as a child
- Use of violence to express anger
- Lack of self-esteem
- Emotional immaturity
- Poor coping skills
- Alcohol or illegal drug abuse
- Marriage problems
- Financial stress
- Recent stressful events (divorce, recent move, death in family)
- Illness (physical or mental health, especially depression)

- Lacks parenting skills including no preparation for the extreme stress of a new baby
- Lacks knowledge of child development; thus has unrealistic expectations for the child
- Heavy parenting responsibility (multiple births or single children less than 18 months apart in age)
- Weak bonding or attachment to a child (often due to child's care in ICU after birth)
- Use of physical punishment (called corporal punishment)
- Isolation (lack of family or friend support)

Child
- Under the age of five years, especially under age of one year
- Low birthweight or premature
- Looks like or has traits like a disliked relative
- Irritable or cries a great deal (colic; ADHD)
- Disobeys parents or argues a great deal (older child)

24-23 Certain risk factors are commonly found in cases of child abuse and neglect.

How Can Neglect and Abuse Be Prevented?

Neglect and abuse have many causes. These complex problems do not have a single, quick solution. Work must be done on many fronts to put an end to them. Preventing neglect and abuse will take the efforts of individuals, families, communities, and society at large. Each person's involvement counts in the fight against these crimes.

Public Awareness

First, people need to be more aware of abuse and neglect. They need to understand which behaviors are abusive or neglectful. They need to learn more about how these problems threaten children and affect families' lives. People also need to be aware of the legal consequences of abuse and neglect. They need to be informed about how they can help in the fight against these crimes.

Many organizations are leading the way to increased public awareness about child abuse and neglect. These organizations provide a variety of information on prevention and support services. Some of these agencies host Web sites at which people can learn more about abuse and neglect, 24-24.

Social Changes

Abuse and neglect are more likely in a society in which people feel undervalued, financial problems abound, and violence is condoned. To effectively prevent abuse, some of these societal problems must be addressed. Needed changes include the following:

❖ societal rejections of violence and aggression
❖ better economic security for families
❖ reduction in the numbers of mothers who do not receive adequate prenatal care

❖ provision for high-quality child care facilities, including crisis child care programs that provide respite for parents through child care
❖ increased emphasis on respecting children, their needs, and their rights

Being active in groups that work for any of these changes can help prevent abuse. Making elected officials aware of needed changes is important, too.

Professional Support

Doctors and other professionals who come into contact with families need to be aware of risk factors that lead to abuse. They should note any risk factors they observe in specific families and connect high-risk families to the appropriate social programs.

For example, during a prenatal visit, a doctor might ask about how the pregnancy affects others in the family to determine whether there are other problems the family is facing. The doctor could make referrals for the family to seek other needed support services and social programs.

Web Sites for Information on Child Abuse and Neglect

AVANCE Family Support and Education Program	<www.avance.org>
Child Abuse Prevention Network	<www.childabuse.com>
ChildHelp USA	<www.childhelpusa.org>
Family Life Development Center	<www.human.cornell. edu/centers/fldc/>
MELD: Programs to Strengthen Families	<www.meld.org>
National Exchange Club Foundation	<www.preventchildabuse.com>
Prevent Child Abuse America	<www.preventchildabuse.org>

24-24 These Web sites provide valuable information regarding child abuse and neglect.

During well-child checkups, doctors can talk with parents about child development. They can answer questions and offer advice about expected behaviors and issues such as toilet learning, teething, crying, and sleep or eating problems. Understanding child development can help parents form more realistic expectations of their children. When parent expectations exceed children's abilities, it can lead to frustration. This is a problem because frustrated parents are more likely to lash out at their children with abusive behaviors. Appropriate expectations of the child can reduce this frustration and prevent some abusive outbursts.

Doctors can also assess a child's home life by asking simple questions, such as the following:

❖ What is it like for you taking care of your child?
❖ Do you get time for yourself?
❖ Do you get any help with your children from family or friends?
❖ Do you think your baby cries too much?
❖ How do you deal with your child's behavior problems?

It is not enough to just assess, however. Support services must be available in the community. One type of support program is home visitation. In *home visitation*, a professional comes to the home to monitor the health of mother and infant, provide one-on-one parent education, and suggest other helpful community programs parents can access.

Education

Adults need to continue to learn more about children and their care. This education should include life skills training for children, teens, and young adults and education in child development and parenting. Learning more about healthy relationships, communication, stress and anger management, and coping skills will also help people prepare themselves to work with or care for children.

In addition, parents can also benefit from learning parenting techniques from such parent-education programs as Parent Effectiveness Training (PET), Parent Nurturing Program (PNP), and Systematic Training for Effective Parenting (STEP).

Recognizing and Reporting Neglect and Abuse

To end neglect and abuse, people must recognize and report it. Knowing what behaviors are abusive or neglectful is the first step. As a citizen, however, the responsibility does not stop there.

Adults should be alert to signs that abuse or neglect may be occurring. Some common signs children exhibit are listed in 24-25. When adults notice these signs and suspect abuse or neglect, they should report this to an agency that can help. The local or state departments of human services are a good place to start. Adults can also call child abuse hot lines to report suspected abuse. The numbers for

Signs of Child Neglect and Abuse

Anyone who suspects child abuse or neglect should report it to proper authorities so the child can receive help. In fact, the law in most states requires certain people to report suspected abuse or neglect. The following signs will help you identify children who need help.

Neglect

A child may be physically neglected when he or she

- ❖ is malnourished
- ❖ fails to receive needed health care without a parental objection
- ❖ fails to receive proper hygiene (is not washed or bathed; has poor oral hygiene; has ungroomed skin, nails, and hair)
- ❖ has insufficient clothing or clothing that is dirty, tattered, or inappropriate for the weather
- ❖ lives in filthy conditions and/or inadequate shelter

A child may suffer mental or educational neglect when he or she

- ❖ lacks moral training
- ❖ lacks constructive discipline
- ❖ fails to receive positive examples from adults
- ❖ fails to have adequate supervision
- ❖ is left alone for hours
- ❖ fails to attend school regularly because of parents
- ❖ fails to receive parent stimulation toward learning or education suited to his or her ability
- ❖ is not allowed to take part in wholesome recreational activities

A child may be emotionally neglected if he or she

- ❖ experiences constant friction in the home
- ❖ is denied normal experiences that produce feelings of being wanted, loved, and protected
- ❖ is rejected through indifference
- ❖ is overly rejected, such as through abandonment

(Continued)

24-25 People must know the signs of neglect and abuse so they can help children with these problems.

these hot lines are listed in local phone books as well as in national directories of toll-free numbers.

Some professionals who work with children are known as **mandated reporters** of child abuse. These professionals are legally bound to report any known or suspected cases of

mandated reporters. Professionals who are legally bound to report any known or suspected cases of abuse or neglect to the proper authorities.

Signs of Child Neglect and Abuse (Continued)

Abuse

A child may be physically abused if he or she

❖ seems fearful or quiet around parents but has no close feeling for them
❖ is wary of physical contact initiated by an adult
❖ has little or no reaction to pain and seems much less afraid than most children the same age
❖ has unexplained injuries or shows evidence of repeated injuries, such as having bruises in various stages of healing or repeated fractures
❖ is dressed inappropriately, such as an injured child dressed in pajamas who was reportedly injured on a bicycle or a child dressed in a turtleneck in the summer to cover bruises
❖ has long bones that, when x-rayed, show a history of past injuries
❖ has injuries not reported on previous health records
❖ has parents who have taken the child to many hospitals and doctors without appropriate explanation
❖ has parents who refuse further diagnostic studies of their child's injuries
❖ has parents who show detachment or see the child as bad or "different" during medical treatment
❖ has parents who give too many minute details about the cause of injury
❖ tries to protect parents when they are questioned about the child's injuries

A child may suffer verbal abuse if he or she

❖ lacks self-esteem
❖ is either too quiet and polite or uses harsh and improper language when dealing with others, especially those who are smaller or younger
❖ expresses long-term feelings of damage and isolation

A child may be sexually abused if he or she

❖ has extreme and sudden changes in behavior, such as loss of appetite or sudden drop in grades
❖ has nightmares and other sleep problems
❖ regresses to previous behaviors, such as renewed thumb sucking
❖ has torn or stained underwear
❖ has infections (with symptoms like bleeding or other discharges and itching) or swollen genitals
❖ fears a person or shows an intense dislike of being left alone with that person
❖ has an STD or pregnancy
❖ has unusual interest in or knowledge of sexual matters

abuse or neglect. Mandated reporters include health care workers, teachers, counselors, social service workers, and child care providers. In many states, mandated reporters can be charged with a criminal offense if they fail to report known or suspected cases of abuse or neglect.

Depending on state laws, other adults may not be mandated to report abuse or neglect. However, these adults should still feel compelled to make a report. Reporting abuse is the only way these adults can help protect the child from further mistreatment. They must remember that children are defenseless victims in these cases. In most cases, the name and information of someone who makes a report remains confidential.

When a report is made, the appropriate state agency will document the facts. If there is enough evidence, a caseworker will investigate the case. He or she will make a visit to the home and talk to all the family members. If the case is confirmed, steps will be taken to help the child and work with the adult to end the cycle of abuse.

Even in cases where enough evidence is not presented, the report will still be kept on file. It is still important to make the report because this helps to build a case. Over time, if more reports are made about the same abuser, the case will be more likely to be investigated and confirmed.

Adults must stop abuse by reporting suspected cases or stopping abusive cycles. Children must not be allowed to go through life being neglected, abused, or both. They need to receive help as soon as possible in order to end the harm and heal the wounds they have already received.

Another important piece of the puzzle lies with the abusers themselves. These adults play perhaps the biggest role in stopping abuse. They need to recognize that what they are doing is wrong and find help to stop. When abusers sincerely want to change their behavior, the chances for success are much higher. If parents feel out of control and think they may abuse a child, they can call a national organization called Parents Anonymous. Members of this group form local chapters, and they can provide support services any time. Parents can also call a crisis hot line to ask for help.

Resources for Children in Crises

Many resources are available to help children in crises. Some of the resources directly assist children and their families. Others provide information, registries, referrals to local support groups, or counseling.

Some of these resources are departments and agencies of federal, state, or local government. Other resources are national private agencies funded by membership dues and contributions. Still other resources are the work of religious groups, hospitals and medical associations, mental health centers, crises intervention centers, law enforcement agencies, legal associations, counseling services, schools, and civic/volunteer organizations.

Many agencies have online bookstores for purchasing books and other materials designed for aiding children and families facing different problems.

When searching for items on a specific topic of interest, a bookstore might also offer resources for parents, children, or families. Other book titles and materials can be located through online publishers and libraries. You can also use your telephone book, library, or the Internet to find other resources.

Siblings and families are the main force in shaping a child's physical, intellectual, and social-emotional development.

Summing It Up

Children's lives are influenced by their siblings. They learn by interacting with them. Children's birth order tends to affect their social roles and personalities. Multiple-birth children strive to develop their separate identities.

When both parents work outside the home, all family members must cooperate to care for the home and plan time to spend together. How children adjust depends on how much time the parents spend with their children each day, when they enter the work force again, and how they feel about working.

The numbers of children in self-care are increasing. Self-care has many negative effects and may be illegal for children younger than 12 years. If self-care is a must for older children, parents must teach them how to safely care for themselves when the parents will be away for short periods.

Families in the United States tend to move a great deal. Moves can be less stressful for children if parents feel positive about the moves and help their children get used to the new place.

It is difficult for children to understand the concept of death and to deal with grief. Adults should answer children's questions truthfully and at the child's level of understanding. They need to understand that children grieve losses, too.

Divorce can have many causes, and its effects can be lasting. Parents need to help their children who are faced with these new stresses. When the family structure changes, such as through divorce or remarriage, families must adapt to these changes. Children need to be prepared for a new marriage and the changes this will create. Single-parent families have challenges that are unique in addition to the ordinary problems all families face.

Pregnant and parenting teens face many additional risks and problems, too. Because of the high-risk nature of teen relationships, many marriages end in divorce. Some teen family structures survive through dedicated work and much effort.

Abuse and neglect are major problems that threaten children's health and well-being. Some social changes have been suggested to help protect children from neglect and abuse. Many signs of abuse and neglect are observable, but others are not as easily observed. When people report suspected cases of abuse or neglect, the children and adults involved can get the help they need. Treatments are available both for the abused children and the abuser.

Reviewing Key Concepts

Write your answers on a separate sheet of paper.

1. List the four main types of sibling interactions.
2. True or false. Only children are always spoiled.
3. True or false. A parent should not allow multiple-birth children to wear identical outfits, even if the children want to wear these outfits.
4. Name four possible advantages that children whose parents work outside the home have over those whose parents do not.
5. Name two positive effects and two negative effects self-care may have on children.
6. True or false. Most children readily adapt and look forward to family moves.
7. List the three physical concepts about death that children must learn.
8. True or false. Most teen parents stay together for the sake of the baby and work out their financial problems.
9. True or false. Parents should give children a detailed explanation about why their marriage has failed so they can better accept it.
10. Explain the difference between child abuse and child neglect.
11. True or false. In an abusive family, certain children are more likely to be abused than others.
12. True or false. An abusive parent often acts mentally ill outside the home.

Using Your Knowledge

1. **Creative Writing Skills.** Write a fiction story on the joys and trials of being an only child, the oldest child, a middle child, a youngest child, or a multiple-birth child.
2. **Art/Career Skills.** Design a pamphlet for parents featuring tips for preparing a child for self-care. As part of the pamphlet, encourage parents to find or initiate school-age child care programs.
3. **Library Skills.** Ask an elementary school librarian for children's books on one of the following topics: family moves, death, divorce, single parenting, and stepfamilies. For each book, give the bibliographical information, the age for which the book was written, and a few statements giving the main content.
4. **Technology.** Research online about children in self-care and use the computer to compose a report on what you've read.
5. **Interviewing Skills.** Interview a resource person from a local social service agency. Ask this person about specific services of the agency as they pertain to children and families.

Making Observations

1. Observe older siblings with their younger siblings. In what ways, either directly or indirectly, do older siblings influence their younger brothers and sisters?
2. Observe a family in which the parent or parents work outside the home. What advantages do you see for the child or children? What disadvantages do you see? Do you feel the parent or parents show any role strain? Explain.
3. Observe a child who has recently experienced the stress of a move, death, or a family divorce. What seems to be the child's greatest stressor? How is the child coping? How are parents, teachers, family friends, peers, and others helping the child cope?

Thinking Further

1. A young couple is trying to decide whether to have another child as a companion to their only child. They do not really want another child, but they have heard that only children are often spoiled and friendless. What would you advise this couple? What do you think might happen to a child who was wanted only as a companion for an older child?
2. Do you think role strain is solely caused by demands in a person's life or also by personality? Explain. What are some specific ways parents can lessen role strain?
3. In general, why are family moves, deaths, and divorces all difficult for children? What factors can affect children's adjustment to these situations?

Your friend Charmayne is concerned because she does not know what career she wants to pursue in the future. She is 17 years old and earns average grades in math, English, and family and consumer sciences courses. She volunteers for a local child care center after school twice a week. Both adults and children like Charmayne very much. The director of the child care center thinks she is good with children, too.

Chapter 25
Making
Career
Decisions

After studying this chapter, you will be able to
- identify steps in self-assessment.
- explain how to research careers and develop a career plan.
- describe how to find a job.
- describe careers in child-related fields.
- explain how personal and professional qualifications affect your career choice.
- identify skills needed for job success.

Define...

lifestyle
self-assessment
personal priorities
aptitudes
abilities
career plan
resources
short-term goals
long-term goals
resume
personal references
direct intervention
consultants
licensing personnel
entrepreneur
personal qualifications
career burnout
leader
professional qualifications
work ethic
codes of professional ethics
formal leadership
informal leaders
Family, Career and Community
  Leaders of America (FCCLA)

A career is more than just a job title. Choosing a career will affect many factors in your **lifestyle** (typical way of life). Your career choices will likely influence where you live, what skills you must develop, with whom you will associate, what free time you will have, and what your financial picture will be.

You live in a world of change. No one can be sure of all the changes people will face in coming years. However, today's trends can guide you to explore promising career options. For example, most careers today involve knowledge-based work as opposed to work with one's hands. In general, the information-age economy needs a new type of employee. This employee is one who

❖ can change and cope with the stress of change
❖ learns quickly and is willing to learn new skills continuously
❖ possesses skills from more than one field that can be useful in one career

Additionally, career success today is thought of more in terms of the career skills gained than in keeping the same job until retirement. Today, success also means finding work that is rewarding and fulfilling to you. This type of work promotes your physical, mental, and emotional well-being. Making career decisions is a lifelong process of living and learning.

Many people who are interested in children and their development will seek a child-related career, 25-1. These people will choose from one of the many careers that involve children in some way. Other people will seek

lifestyle. The typical way of life for a person, group, or culture.

25-1 An interest in helping children learn and develop musical skills led this man to start a business instructing children on the piano.

careers in other areas. No matter which career field you choose, you will need to develop many skills that are important for all careers. These skills include human relations, communication, teamwork, and leadership skills. People should start developing these skills in childhood and continue building them throughout life.

In addition, the boundaries between work and personal life sometimes blur. This blurring goes beyond being "plugged in" to work during nonworking hours through communication devices, such as cell phones, e-mail, and pagers. Workers often find it challenging to balance their many work and personal roles. As you prepare for the world of work,

it is good to learn more about how to balance multiple roles. Succeeding at this task will make you happier and more successful in each role you fill.

Heading Toward a Career

Your life is an expression of what you are now and can become in the future. The decisions you make about how and with whom to spend time are personal statements about what you feel life is and can be. Some of the most important choices you will make in your life will be related to your chosen work.

People constantly face choices. For the most part, these choices don't seem like choices or at least important ones. Most people simply do what they think is expected. Sometimes choices are made from very limited alternatives. Thus, people often act in rather unthinking ways.

In life, however, some choices are crucial and require much careful thought. Career decisions fall into this category. When career decisions are made without much thought, people are likely to be unproductive and unhappy. Career decisions are also important because they influence many other choices. These include educational and training choices, considering the timing of marriage and parenthood, and making decisions about major purchases.

Identifying Your Interests, Aptitudes, and Abilities

The most difficult and important step in career planning is identifying your interests, aptitudes, and abilities. Another name for this step is **self-assessment**. By doing self-assessment, you learn more about who you are as a person and what type of job would suit you well. It's worth the effort because self-assessment often leads to finding a career that is personally fulfilling. Without this step, some people pursue a career that turns out to be unsatisfying. These people are often disappointed and feel they have wasted the time and money they used for training and education toward this career. Self-assessment could have helped these people identify a better career match.

Interests

What do you care about? What are you proud of? What challenges you? In answering these questions, you are talking about your interests. Some of your deeper interests are called **personal priorities**. These are ideas, beliefs, and objects that are important and meaningful to you. Your family, culture, and experiences have helped to shape your personal priorities. Your personality traits also play a large role.

You might wonder how interests relate to the world of work. Try to view yourself in a particular career. How do you see yourself? What feelings do

you think you'd have about doing this type of work? Talk with people in a given career who are passionate about what they do, 25-2. What brings them satisfaction in their work? Do you think you'd feel a similar satisfaction from such work? The answers to these questions will teach you much about yourself.

Many people seek a career that aligns with their personal priorities and interests. This type of job brings a sense of fulfillment as well as an income. Many workers find it easier to stay in a career field of interest than in a less enjoyable career field. Being interested in your work is only one factor, however. Not all interests will lead to a promising career. Some interests are best pursued as hobbies or volunteer opportunities.

Aptitudes

Aptitudes are natural talents. People are born with aptitudes—these are a part of their heredity. Think of the talents you have that seem to come naturally to you. Some of your aptitudes will be quite obvious to

self-assessment. A step in career planning that involves identifying your interests, aptitudes, and abilities.

personal priorities. Ideas, beliefs, and objects that are important and meaningful to you.

aptitudes. Natural talents.

25-2 If you are interested in becoming a school teacher, perhaps you can ask some of your teachers about the work they do.

you. However, you may even have some aptitudes of which you are not aware. Suppose you have a natural talent for nurturing children. This aptitude might go unnoticed unless you have an opportunity to interact

with children. If you're around children, you might notice within yourself this natural capacity for nurturing. Others might also observe this aptitude and point it out to you.

Most people enjoy doing things that come naturally, so a person's aptitudes often become interests. For example, if you have an aptitude for sports, playing soccer might be one of your main interests. Aptitudes and interests can differ, however. You might not have an interest in a certain area even if you are talented in that area. Likewise, you might be interested in many areas in which you have no natural talents.

When it comes to careers, aptitudes do have an influence. To do well in a career, you will need to develop certain skills. These skills will enable you to perform the tasks of your chosen career. You will likely develop career skills most quickly and easily in areas in which you have natural talents.

For this reason, consider your aptitudes when choosing a career field. In a career field in which you have no aptitude, you may have to work harder to develop the needed skills. Sometimes, in fact, a person may find it impossible to develop skills in areas in which he or she has no aptitude. Choosing a career that aligns with your aptitudes may be very helpful. Even if you select a career that draws upon your aptitudes, you will still need training and practice to develop all the career skills you will need.

A school counselor can give you an *aptitude test*. Your answers to this test will identify the areas in which you seem to have aptitudes. An aptitude test may reveal some career areas that might suit you well.

Abilities

Abilities are skills that have been learned or developed. People are not born with abilities. Instead, abilities are acquired through effort and practice. Abilities can be developed to help a person use an aptitude. For example, if you have an aptitude for leading others, you can develop leadership abilities to help you succeed at it. Abilities can also be developed in place of aptitude. Even a person who is not naturally inclined to teach children can learn ways to interact well with them.

In careers, two types of abilities are needed. The first set includes rather general skills desired of all employees in all fields. For example, communication skills are needed in all jobs. The second kind of abilities is career specific. For example, if you are going to illustrate children's books, you need to develop abilities in drawing and graphic design.

For the most part, you will develop career-specific skills only after choosing a career path. For example, until you chose to pursue a career in illustration, you would not necessarily know to develop drawing abilities. People gain career-specific abilities in colleges, universities, training schools, and on-the-job programs. For entry into some careers, certain tests are also required after training is complete. These tests measure a person's career-specific abilities.

Skill development seldom ends with employment, however. Most workers are expected to continue to develop skills as they work. Many workplaces continue teaching new skills to their employees. Employers also sometimes pay all or part of the costs of needed training or education. Continued learning enhances a person's abilities on the job.

Learning About Careers

Once you have chosen the career field of interest, it is time to find out more about this field. As you learn more, you will form a more realistic picture of what it is like to work in the field and what future opportunities might exist in this career field. From this information, you can decide whether this field is truly a fit for you. You can learn more by getting a market overview, researching the education and training you would need, and taking an inside view at the career field.

 abilities. Skills that have been learned or developed.

A Market Overview

After doing a self-assessment, you will have a better idea about what career field you might like to enter. The next step is analyzing the labor market for career opportunities. Learning about the entire field is a good idea in case a specific career is becoming *obsolete* (no longer useful). You don't want to waste time and money preparing for a career in which jobs will soon cease to be available. Instead, you should try to enter a field that is growing or at least holding steady. Gather facts as you search, 25-3.

Career Information

When you are seeking information about a particular career field, you will want to learn about the following as it pertains to that particular field:

❖ career titles and positions within the field
❖ education or training needed
❖ experience needed
❖ other requirements (tests, credentials, etc.)
❖ current and expected employment opportunities
❖ working conditions and environment
❖ typical work hours
❖ special expectations (travel, technology skills)
❖ starting pay
❖ potential pay
❖ related careers

25-3 Making a wise career choice means getting the facts about a career.

Many resources related to careers are readily available online. Those published by the state or federal government are often reliable. Many other organizations publish career information on their Web sites. You can also keep up with the labor market by reading national and local newspapers and business magazines. Trade or professional journals published within a certain career field can also give you an idea about employment trends in the field.

Seeking Education and Training

Before you can enter your chosen career field, you will first need the required education and training. If you know what career you would like to pursue, you can find out exactly what the requirements are. Some training programs have entry-level requirements. If you are aware of these requirements while you are still in high school, you can begin to work toward them. Taking this step-by-step approach will help you enter the career field as soon as possible.

When you know what education or training you need, you can search for the best place to acquire it. Your school counselor can help you with this search. Most colleges and other training programs have toll-free phone lines and online information. You might also wish to meet with faculty at colleges or other training programs. After reviewing the requirements for your chosen career, you can make your career plan more final.

An Inside View

Getting an inside view is the best way to learn about a particular career. An inside view is the best test for comparing career expectations with your interests, aptitudes, and abilities. There are a few ways you can get an inside view of various careers.

Talk to People in the Career Field

Talk to employers and business owners about the outlook for the career you are considering. Get as many perspectives as possible. Ask each employer what qualities he or she desires in new employees for this career. Perhaps you can talk with a person who is working in your career of interest. Find out what the person likes most and what is most challenging for him or her. You may also want to learn more about the job duties and typical job demands. Ask what advice this professional might share with you about preparing to enter this career in the future.

Gain Related Experiences

Another way to get an inside look at careers you are considering is to get involved. Your experiences will help you learn more about children and decide if a child-related career is right for you. For example, if you are interested in a child-related career, you might consider taking a babysitting class. Your babysitting experiences will teach you about providing care for young children, 25-4. Another way to gain experience is to work as a

25-4 Babysitting is one of the best ways to earn experience caring for children.
© John Shaw

volunteer in a child care center, children's program, or summer camp. Getting involved with professionals is helpful, too. You may be able to serve as an assistant in a child-related business. Some people find volunteer positions. Others find paid positions that help them learn and earn money.

Join Professional Organizations

Joining professional organizations will help prepare you for a career. For example, if you are interested in a child-related career, you may want to join the National Association for the Education of Young Children (NAEYC) or the Association for Childhood Education International.

Most professional organizations publish journals and newsletters to keep members informed on current issues in the field. They also publish other materials for the further training and education of members. Almost all organizations have meetings and conferences to keep members connected and help them continue to develop professionally.

Joining professional organizations also helps you share with others your interest in children. For example, student membership in a professional organization may convince school officials of the need for high school child development classes. As a member of an organization, you may be able to work with others toward improving the quality of child care programs. Joining a group says to parents and the community, "I am joining with others in an effort to provide the best for our community's children."

Develop a Career Plan

After you have done a self-assessment, learned about careers, and chosen a possible career area, you are ready to "tie it all together." You can do this by creating a career plan. This is a detailed list of steps a person

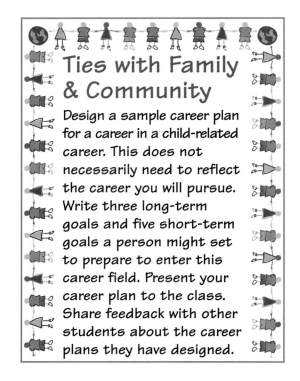

Ties with Family & Community

Design a sample career plan for a career in a child-related career. This does not necessarily need to reflect the career you will pursue. Write three long-term goals and five short-term goals a person might set to prepare to enter this career field. Present your career plan to the class. Share feedback with other students about the career plans they have designed.

must complete in order to enter a chosen career field. A career plan will serve as your guide. It will help you identify what goals to set as you pursue your chosen career.

You will also need to identify your resources, which are tools you can use in achieving your goals. Your goals and resources should be realistic. You will want to be challenged but not feel overwhelmed. Perhaps your goal seems realistic but the resources seem unrealistic. If this is the case, talk with your school counselor and the admissions office at colleges or training schools. Financial aid and other resources are often available to those who are motivated to achieve.

Keeping a log of achievements can be most helpful. This log will help you track your progress and motivate you to accomplish other goals. Reviewing your log can also help you prepare materials for job searches.

Short-Term Goals

Fulfilling a career plan begins with first steps. **Short-term goals** are achievements you desire in the near future. Short-term goals often take one year or less to accomplish. When planning for a career, short-term goals are the many steps you will need to take as you work toward entry in your career field of choice. Short-term goals help you focus on what you need to attain now and help you note progress. See Figure 25-5, in which short-term career goals are those to be attained during the high school years.

Long-Term Goals

Long-term goals are the major achievements toward which you strive. These goals are somewhat like the destination of a trip. They describe where you want to be in your career. Long-term goals take much more time to achieve than short-term goals. These goals often take a year or more to complete.

Long-term goals will keep you focused on the needed abilities, experience, and credentials for a career. Refer to 25-5 again to see examples of long-term goals in a career plan. *Credentials* are proof of having certain

skills, such as a college degree, license, certificate, or designation. In addition, long-term goals also serve as a guide to planning short-term goals. For example, a long-term goal might be to earn a college degree. Suppose the college of choice had a minimum high school grade point average for admission. A logical short-term goal would be to attain a grade point average that meets or exceeds this minimum.

Job Search Skills

Being qualified is one part of finding a child-related career. Another part is looking for and securing a job. Finding the job you want takes effort. There are many steps involved. Knowing what to expect and how to handle yourself at each stage will increase your chances of job-search success.

Defining Your Search

First, determine what kind of job you want. If you are unsure, a teacher or parent may help you decide what

career plan. A detailed list of steps a person must complete in order to enter a chosen career field.

resources. Tools you can use in achieving your goals.

short-term goals. Achievements you desire in the near future.

long-term goals. Major achievements toward which you strive; usually take more than a year to achieve.

Sample Career Plan

Goals	Resources	Log of Accomplishments
Short-Term Goals		
Graduate in the top 10 to 15% of class with a GPA of 3.0 or better.	❖ Get tutoring help as needed through the online high school-college tutoring project. ❖ Develop a regular study schedule.	I set aside 10 hours per week to work on homework this month.
Take courses to learn about children and parents.	❖ High school child development and parenting courses.	Completed Child Development in the spring semester (A-). Enrolled in Parenting for fall semester.
Participate in FCCLA and Writing Club.	❖ School has both of these organizations.	Joined both clubs in fall semester. Helped with children's activity for FCCLA in November. Wrote an article for the paper during "Week of the Young Child" about the importance of parents.
Gain experience in working with young children.	❖ Local SACC program, Head Start, and private child care programs. ❖ Local children's summer camps seek teens as aides.	Accepted as a volunteer in the SACC program. Served 8 hours per week. Applied to be a summer camp aide.
Long-Term Goals		
Earn a bachelor's degree in early childhood education.	❖ Degree offered at local college.	Maintained 3.0 in high school classes this semester to meet local college entrance requirements.
Earn a teaching certificate.	❖ Workshops on college campus help prepare students for tests.	
Work with children beyond requirements of degree.	❖ Student work in campus nursery school is an option.	
Communications skills, including computer skills.	❖ Take additional courses in this area as electives.	Worked a summer job to save money for a computer.
Develop teamwork and leadership skills.	❖ College organizations.	Interviewed a college advisor in early childhood about ways to build these skills.

25-5 A career plan shows a person's goals for educational training, work experiences, and other activities required and desired for entry into a chosen career.

25-6 A teacher or career counselor can help students decide what child-related career they wish to pursue.

kind of job might suit you best, 25-6. Once you decide, you can look in the right places for jobs in that field. If you want to be a camp counselor, you might look for job ads in local newspapers. You may also call local park districts, schools, or houses of worship to ask whether they offer camp programs. Once you find out where the camps are located, you can call each camp to ask who handles hiring counselors and how to apply.

Writing a Resume

To apply for jobs, you may need to write a resume. A **resume** is a short, written history of your education, work experience, and other qualifications for employment. Prospective employers will look at your resume to understand more about your experience. Your resume will help them decide whether you are qualified for a job.

Securing an Interview

Next, you will need to set up a job interview. Some places will allow you to set an interview appointment over the phone. Others prefer a written letter requesting an interview, 25-7.

Completing a Job Application

At some point, often just before the interview, you will fill out a job application. The application asks for such information as your name, address, Social Security number, educational background, and past jobs. It often asks for personal references, too. **Personal references** are people who know you well enough to discuss your qualifications for a job. Employers may call personal references to find out more about you before making a hiring decision. You should not list relatives as personal references. However, you can ask past employers, teachers, and other adults you know well if they will serve as references for you.

Interviewing for the Job

At the interview, you need to put your best foot forward. Your personal appearance should be neat. As a rule, jeans do not make a good impression at an interview. Clean, neat dress pants,

resume. A short, written history of a person's education, work experience, and other qualifications for employment.

personal references. People who know you well enough to discuss your qualifications for a job.

1603 Green Street
Southland Township, Wisconsin 66732
April 15, XXXX

Ms. Anna Martinez
Program Director
Big Lake Day Camp
Rural Route 3
Southland Township, Wisconsin 66732

Dear Ms. Martinez:

I am interested in working as a counselor-in-training at Big Lake this summer. My counselor at Southland High School, Mr. O'Brien, suggested I write you.

I know this job would be a good learning experience for me. I also have much to offer you as an employee. I have taken three child development classes in high school. In two of the classes, I worked four hours per week in the school child care center. I planned many activities for children, including plays, crafts, games, and snacks. I enjoy being with children and helping them learn. In fact, I hope to open my own child care center when I graduate from college.

May we meet for an interview? I will call your office next week to see whether we can schedule an appointment. If you would like to speak with me sooner or have any questions, please call me at 555-7472. Thank you for your time and consideration.

Sincerely,

Willa Holtz

Willa Holtz

25-7 People often use written letters to request a job interview.

dresses, or suits are appropriate (depending on the type of job you want). Good posture, a pleasant smile, and eye contact are also important in an interview.

You may want to rehearse the interview with someone before you go. This will help you prepare answers to some of the questions interviewers often ask. Examples of questions include the following:

❖ Why are you interested in this job?
❖ Why did you choose a child-related career?
❖ Where do you see yourself professionally in five years?
❖ List your strengths and weaknesses.

Be sure to speak clearly and be yourself. It's also a good idea for you to prepare some questions for the interviewer. These questions should focus on learning more about job duties or the place you are seeking work. Asking these questions shows you are interested in the job and the employer. Avoid asking any questions about pay, vacation time, or other benefits until you have been offered the job.

After the interview, you might be offered the job. However, employers often have other applicants to interview before making hiring decisions. If there are many applicants, you might be asked to interview a second or third time before the employer makes a decision.

Awaiting a Response

Unless you are told differently, the employer will probably contact you within two weeks. If the employer offers you a job, respond promptly and politely as to whether you will accept or decline. If you decline the job or you are not offered the position, it is still important to be polite and friendly. The employer may consider you for a future position.

Careers in Child-Related Fields

If you are interested in children and their development, then a career in a child-related field might be for you! Many opportunities exist for

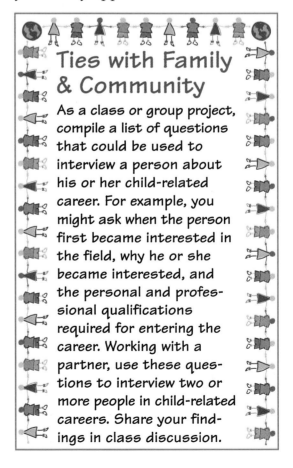

Ties with Family & Community

As a class or group project, compile a list of questions that could be used to interview a person about his or her child-related career. For example, you might ask when the person first became interested in the field, why he or she became interested, and the personal and professional qualifications required for entering the career. Working with a partner, use these questions to interview two or more people in child-related careers. Share your findings in class discussion.

working in a career that involves children in some way, 25-8. Child-related careers are constantly growing. The widespread effort to improve children's quality of life is one trend that makes child-related work a good career choice. Many of today's parents work outside the home, which puts child care workers and early childhood teachers in high demand. In addition, consumers expect more goods and services tailored to children's needs, which increases the demand for workers who create and provide these goods and services.

Learning more about the many types of careers that relate to children can help you decide whether this field is right for you. To be successful in child-related careers, workers also need certain personal and professional qualifications.

Types of Careers

One way to describe child-related careers is in terms of the amount of contact with children. In some careers, adults work with children directly, which is **direct intervention**, 25-9. People in such careers include teachers and pediatricians. In other careers, adults serve as consultants. **Consultants** share their knowledge about children with other adults. For example, college child development professors may serve as consultants to

25-8 Many people find child-related careers to be interesting and rewarding.

25-9 Teaching is one career that involves direct intervention with children.
© John Shaw

teachers of young children. In other careers, professionals develop and sell products for children, 25-10. These adults use their knowledge of children to design and sell toys, clothing, furniture, and educational products. These workers do not have direct contact with children, but still need to understand children and their needs in order to do their jobs well.

Careers in child-related fields also include general career fields. Six areas to consider are health and protective services; care and education; entertainment; design; advertising,

marketing, and management; and research and consulting.

Health and Protective Services

It takes many health care professionals to keep children healthy.

direct intervention. Careers in which people work directly with children.

consultants. Professionals who share their knowledge, such as knowledge about children, with other adults.

25-10 Product development and sales are booming child-related careers.
Angeles Group

Demand for workers in children's physical and mental health services has increased. Adults in these services have the knowledge and skills needed to provide quality health care. They also understand children's health needs. Careers in children's health care include the following:

❖ pediatricians—doctors who specialize in the care of children, 25-11
❖ pediatric dentists—dentists who specialize in the care of children
❖ pediatric and school nurses—nurses who specialize in the care of children
❖ child psychologists—professionals who specialize in the emotional and mental health of children

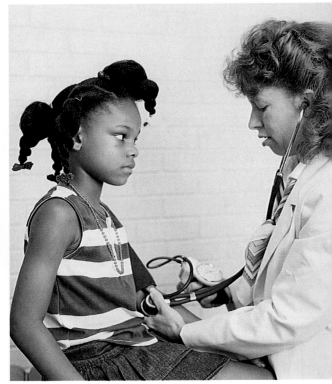

25-11 Being a pediatrician is one of the many careers in health and protective services.
© John Shaw

❖ dietitians—specialists in nutrition who may plan the diets of healthy children and children with special food needs
❖ school food service personnel—people who plan school menus and prepare and serve food to meet children's needs

Other health professionals, such as eye doctors, speech pathologists, hearing specialists, sports medicine doctors, physical therapists, emergency room and hospital personnel, and pharmacists also serve children regularly. These workers need to know how their work with children should differ from their work with older patients. Special training may be needed.

In addition, adults with careers in protective services work to find injustices to children and to correct problem situations. Positions include juvenile officers and judges, child welfare workers, and licensing personnel. **Licensing personnel** are professionals who check the quality of services for children, such as the quality of child care centers. Jobs in protective services are increasing as society becomes more concerned about the rights and needs of children.

Care and Education

More young children are enrolled in group settings than ever before. Private programs are growing in number. Government agencies on both federal and state levels are committed to children's education, 25-12. Public support for child care and early childhood education can be seen in the growth of public school kindergartens and programs for even younger children.

The following care and education careers can be found in both public and private settings:
❖ child care providers—people who care for infants, toddlers, preschool children, and school-age children (when school is not in session)

25-12 *Teachers with special knowledge are needed in education careers.*
© John Shaw

❖ teachers and teachers' assistants— people trained to teach or assist teachers in public and private school programs
❖ special education teachers— teachers who work with children who have special needs
❖ administrators—directors of child care and education programs as well as principals and supervisors of school programs
❖ parent educators—people who teach parents about child development and parenting

 licensing personnel. Professionals who check the quality of services provided for children.

- family life educators—people who provide direct services to children and families or train professionals how to provide services for children and families
- children's librarians—librarians are trained to work in school libraries or in children's sections of other libraries
- high school teachers and college professors—teachers who instruct high school or college students in child-related courses, such as health, education, and development
- child and youth leaders—people who work with children in religious programs or youth organizations, such as scouting groups, recreational programs, and camps
- recreational instructors—people who guide or teach children in such areas as music, art, sports, and hobbies

Career opportunities in child care and education are increasing rapidly. In some areas of the country, demand for workers in this field even surpasses the number of workers available. More quality child care and education programs are needed. As these programs are created, more people will be needed to staff them. Child care workers and teachers will likely remain in high demand in the future. Demand for professionals with special skills will be even higher, 25-13. Examples are teachers of children with special needs and computer teachers.

25-13 Teachers who can provide instruction in two or more languages are in demand as society seeks to meet the needs of diverse cultural groups.
© Nancy P. Alexander

Entertainment

In recent years, the business of children's entertainment has expanded greatly. Many new children's television programs, movies, and live programs have been produced. A wider variety of children's books and games (including video and computer games) are available. People in entertainment careers include producers, directors, technicians, writers, and performers, 25-14.

Design

Because children differ from adults, they need items designed especially for them. These items should be designed to meet children's physical, mental, and social-emotional needs. Items designed for children

25-14 Clowns have entertained children for years.
© Nancy P. Alexander

include clothing, personal care items, dishes and flatware, furniture, books, and toys, 25-15. Designers plan indoor and outdoor spaces for children, such as playgrounds and child care centers. These spaces feature equipment or fixtures (including sinks, water fountains, and commodes) sized for the children who will use them. People who design child-related products and spaces must understand child development. They also need creative skills and an understanding of design principles.

Advertising, Marketing, and Management

As more children's products are produced, businesses need many employees who understand children's needs. These businesses need people

25-15 Children need products like toys designed for them.
Hasbro, Inc.

who are trained to advertise and market the children's products they produce. Another growing career choice is managing the businesses that produce and sell children's products. Positions for advertising, marketing, and managing can be found in corporations, agencies, firms, and small businesses.

Research and Consulting

Many fields, such as health, education, entertainment, design, and business, conduct research on children and their needs. Research studies provide knowledge that allows people to serve children well. The field of research is growing so quickly that a massive amount of information is now available. For example, over 100,000 research studies on children's education are published each year. The challenge is passing on this information to those who will be working directly with children.

Consultants work on behalf of children. They serve as a link between researchers and others in child-related careers, 25-16. Consultants relay information to those in direct intervention, product development, and sales. Some adults consult on a daily basis. Child development experts who provide state and federal lawmakers with information are an example. Other adults work as consultants when called on for written or oral input. With research continuing to increase, consultants will continue to be in demand.

25-16 Consultants interpret research findings to others involved in child-related careers.
© Nancy P. Alexander

Entrepreneurship

Many child-related careers offer chances for self-employment. A person who creates and owns a business is called an **entrepreneur**. Family child care homes are the most common child-related businesses started by entrepreneurs. However, some people own and operate child care centers as well. Entrepreneurs can also start many other types of businesses. Examples are child photography, recreational instruction, private medical practice, and writing for and about children.

Entrepreneurs need many skills other than those directly related to their specialties. For example, a person who owns and operates a child care center must know much more than how to teach and care for children. This entrepreneur must be able to manage money, including handling budgets and fees, paying expenses, and making purchasing decisions. This professional would also advertise; hire staff; oversee enrollment; know and follow laws and regulations; maintain the facilities; communicate with parents; and supervise the staff.

Many people find owning a business rewarding, 25-17. They like having the freedom to run their businesses in their own ways. They also like the variety of being able to fill different roles, such as teacher, manager, and budget director. There are drawbacks, however. Entrepreneurs may have to use their personal money for starting costs or if the business goes into debt. They must make key decisions about the business and live with their choices. Another drawback is that many owners work longer hours and have fewer vacations than they would if they were employed by others.

If you have the skills, knowledge, and energy, you might enjoy starting a business of your own. Entrepreneurship in a child-related field can be satisfying and rewarding. Creativity, knowledge, and hard work can make your business profitable, too.

Personal Qualifications for a Child-Related Career

Personal qualifications are all the traits you possess that cannot be learned in career training. Personal traits are harder to define and measure than learnings that result from career training. For this reason, little research has been done on personal qualifications. Thus, only general traits are discussed.

Concern for Children

For a person in a child-related career, the most important personal qualification is a deep concern for children, 25-18. Sometimes, in the effort to perform well, people lose sight of the most important concern of all—the children. If you work directly or indirectly with children, you must always make decisions based on what is best for them.

25-17 Owning a business is hard work, but many people find it rewarding.
© John Shaw

entrepreneur. A person who creates and owns a business.

personal qualifications. All the traits you possess that cannot be learned in career training.

25-18 People who work with children should be concerned about their safety and welfare.
© John Shaw

Many other qualities are almost as important as concern for children. First, you need to genuinely like children and respect them as individuals. You need to be kind and patient with children and their families. You must be able to tolerate children's noise and activity. You should enjoy children's physical, mental, and social worlds. This includes children's games, songs, stories, and even humor. You need to feel comfortable helping young children with physical needs. This might include helping with toileting or dressing. It might mean letting a child show you a scraped knee or loose tooth.

Finally, you must be able to accept physical closeness from young children. Children want to touch adults' clothing, jewelry, and hair. Sometimes they may do so with paint, dirt, or food on their hands. Children need adults who will hold them, hug them, and comfort them.

Flexibility

In working with children, it is important to remain open to new ideas. Flexibility is important, too, because children can be unpredictable. Research shows the constant changes required in working with children often cause people to have career burnout. **Career burnout** is a state in which a person becomes emotionally tired of a career. It may even lead to health problems from stress. A person who is flexible will be less likely to have career burnout. He or she will adapt more easily to change.

Leadership

Being able to lead others is very important when working in a child-related career. A **leader** is a person who influences or motivates the thoughts, feelings, or actions of others. Children see adults and teens as leaders. A leader should be self-confident, which helps the children feel secure. A leader provides clear instructions for the group or individual child. You need to be able to set limits and be firm with children. Children are not yet self-disciplined and need your help to meet goals. Being able to listen patiently is important, too. Children may need to try several times before they say something in ways adults understand. Leadership skills are also needed in working with adults, such as other staff members or the children's parents.

Professional Qualifications for a Child-Related Career

Professional qualifications are the physical, mental, and social-emotional skills you need to perform in a career. People most often learn these skills from training or entry-level work experience, 25-19. Training might

25-19 Babysitting could be considered as an entry-level job for future child care positions.
Jacob Cullen Darlinger

include classes in high school or college as well as on-the-job training. For example, before you may study to become a pediatrician, you need a college degree in certain areas (often premedicine). You need to score at a certain level on tests that measure your knowledge. You might also need to submit references, interview with faculty at medical school, and pass physical examinations.

Child development is the science of understanding children. If you want to have a career in a child-related field, you must know about child development. Because physical, mental, and social-emotional development are related, you study all aspects of child development. However, professional training for a career often stresses one aspect of development more than others. Pediatricians deal more with physical aspects of development. They must be aware of how other aspects of development affect a child's health, however.

In addition to learning about child development, you will become

career burnout. A state in which a person becomes emotionally tired of a career.

leader. A person who influences or motivates the thoughts, feelings, or actions of others.

professional qualifications. The physical, mental, and social-emotional skills you need to perform well in a career.

specialized in your career area. For example, teachers must have specialized knowledge in the following and other areas:

❖ how children learn
❖ what to teach and in what order to teach certain facts and skills
❖ the best methods and materials for teaching the facts and skills
❖ how to evaluate children's knowledge

For some careers, people must learn specialties within a specialty. Specialties require in-depth learnings. Pediatric ophthalmologists are children's eye doctors. These adults learn general medicine and then learn to treat diseases of the eye. Finally, they learn to care for children's eye problems. Because so few adults have specialties within specialties, these adults often serve as researchers or consultants. They may directly handle only the most difficult cases.

The level of a job determines the amount of training needed. There are many levels of positions within the field of child care. The career ladder in 25-20 shows some of these levels. Teachers' assistants and some associate teachers do not need college degrees. They may have had some training in high school, vocational classes, community college, or college. Supervisors generally have at least bachelor's degrees in child development, early childhood education, or related areas. Many supervisors and most directors have a master's degree in a

25-20 People are needed at various levels in the field of child care.

specialized area of child development. Consultants may have more than one master's degree or a doctoral degree.

Job Training

The amount of training a job requires depends on the level of responsibility it demands. Teachers have greater professional responsibilities than teachers' assistants. Some careers require study in schools and colleges and supervised work in the career field, 25-21. People may earn professional qualifications for other careers, such as entertainment, through on-the-job training.

working in the many child-related careers. This type of exchange often occurs at professional meetings.

Skills for Job Success

At this point in your life, you may not know exactly what type of career you want. You still have time to make this decision. However, you need to start today to develop some skills all employees seek in job candidates. It takes time and experience to develop these skills. If you begin now, you will be much more prepared when it is time to enter the job market.

Human Relations Skills

Human relations skills include basic attitudes toward others, work ethic, and manners. These skills are perhaps the most important you will develop both personally and professionally. Human relations skills affect how you get along with other people. Whether people have or lack these skills often determines whether they will get desired jobs, keep their jobs, or be promoted. People also damage relationships with family and friends due to the lack of human relations skills. For these reasons, it is important to build your skills in relating to others.

Basic Attitudes Toward Others

Although a person's basic temperament is largely determined by genes, basic attitudes begin to develop early in life. Their development is

25-21 *Professional qualifications help this teacher meet both the regular and special needs of the children she serves.*
© John Shaw

In addition to basic career training, adults in child-related careers are expected to keep up with the latest knowledge and practices in their field. Keeping up in a child-related career may require more classroom study, seminar attendance, or independent study. It may also involve on-the-job training in a different setting. In addition, it may involve exchanging knowledge and practices among those

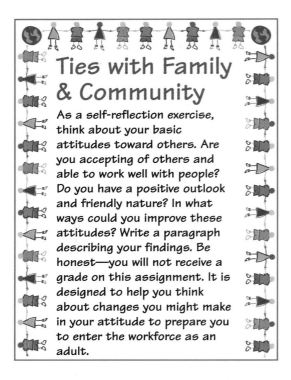

Ties with Family & Community

As a self-reflection exercise, think about your basic attitudes toward others. Are you accepting of others and able to work well with people? Do you have a positive outlook and friendly nature? In what ways could you improve these attitudes? Write a paragraph describing your findings. Be honest—you will not receive a grade on this assignment. It is designed to help you think about changes you might make in your attitude to prepare you to enter the workforce as an adult.

influenced by role models, such as family members, friends, and others. The media plays a role in the formation of these attitudes, too. Basic attitudes are closely tied to self-esteem.

Parents, teachers, and youth leaders often encourage children to develop positive attitudes. For example, they teach children to show respect and solve conflicts peacefully. As people enter the adult years, they become responsible for their own basic attitudes and how these affect others.

To a great extent, work performance is linked to attitude. Employers need employees with good attitudes. These people are friendly, cheerful, and considerate of others in the workplace. In turn, they are liked and respected.

Respecting differences is a key part of a positive attitude. Getting along with coworkers, supervisors, and clients or customers is essential, 25-22.

Employees with bad attitudes complain about everything and everyone. They often argue with coworkers, superiors, and clients or customers. Others with bad attitudes are sullen and withdrawn. These negative attitudes result in reduced job performance for everyone involved. Even if not explicitly said, employees can be fired for having bad attitudes.

Work Ethic

Work ethic refers to a standard of conduct and priorities for job performance. A good employee is said to have a *strong work ethic*. This person understands what behaviors are appropriate for the workplace. He or she is honest,

25-22 When workers feel good about themselves, they find it easy to work with others in a positive way.

hardworking, and dependable. A dependable employee shows up for work, comes to work on time, and works steadily through the workday except for normal breaks. An employee with a strong work ethic strives to get along with others. He or she does the best work possible and cares about the quality of work done. This employee works independently. Employers want employees who have a strong work ethic.

Other employees do not have a strong work ethic. These employees are less likely to succeed. They do only what is asked of them, and nothing more. These employees have little concern with their performance or the quality of their work. They are not dependable and often miss work, arrive late, or waste time throughout the workday. Employers seek to avoid hiring workers who lack a strong work ethic. These employees are also subject to being fired because they cost the company through their poor work behavior.

In addition to personal work ethic, many professions have written standards of conduct for workers in a certain career field. These standards are called codes of professional ethics. An employee is expected to follow any code of professional ethics that apply to his or her profession. In some careers, violating the code of professional ethics can result in suspension or termination from the job or career.

Manners

Manners are about comfort. You want to be comfortable around others, and you want others to be comfortable around you. Employers must trust you will not embarrass them in any situation. Furthermore, good manners help others take you seriously. The following basics should always be practiced:

- ❖ consider people's feelings
- ❖ use manners in meetings, telephone conversations, e-mail messages, and memos
- ❖ apologize if you must interrupt a meeting, conversation, or someone's concentration on a task
- ❖ keep any conflicts situation-related rather than attacking a person
- ❖ keep your voice moderated in loudness and pitch
- ❖ talk and visit with everyone
- ❖ be thoughtful to coworkers and clients

Communication Skills

Over 96 percent of the executives of the nation's largest corporations say their employees must have good communication skills. Over 83 percent

> **work ethic.** A standard of conduct and priorities for job performance.
>
> **codes of professional ethics.** Sets of standards created by various professions to govern the conduct of employees in these careers.

of Fortune 400 companies identified writing skills as their organization's greatest weakness. In general, communication skills are listed as the scarcest skills in the workforce.

Employers expect employees to do the following:

❖ have good listening skills
❖ be good readers
❖ communicate in both speaking and writing situations using standard English grammar and correct spelling
❖ have needed computer and other technological skills

Although the specific skills will vary some with the career, some commonly needed skills are given in 25-23. Which communication skills

Commonly Needed Communication Skills

Listening Skills
❖ following directions
❖ grasping information
❖ clarifying information
❖ asking questions

Speaking Skills
❖ giving instructions
❖ responding to phone calls, voice mail, and personal conversations
❖ participating in meetings and conferences
❖ making presentations

Reading Skills
❖ understanding office signs and maps (such as evacuation plans)
❖ grasping office memos, letters, and manuals
❖ comprehending business reports; mastering specialized vocabulary, codes, and labels; interpreting statistical data; and understanding graphs and diagrams

Writing Skills
❖ writing messages and memos
❖ making records
❖ composing business letters
❖ drafting business reports

Computer-Based Skills
❖ organizing work tasks
❖ writing e-mail messages for business purposes
❖ using the Internet for gathering work-related information
❖ word processing
❖ making spreadsheets
❖ creating databases
❖ preparing materials through desktop publishing
❖ creating drawings and images (computer graphics)
❖ preparing multimedia presentations

25-23 Many communication and computer skills are needed for today's workplace.

have you mastered, and which do you have yet to develop? If you can boost your communications skills, you can greatly increase your chances of job success in your chosen career. On the other hand, if your communication skills are weak, no matter how much career-specific ability you have, you will lose credibility.

Nonverbal communication can have positive or negative effects on others, too. Appearing to be alert and interested, focusing on the speaker, smiling, and greeting others with a friendly voice and firm handshake tells others you think they are important. Falling asleep, yawning, slouching, looking away, or getting into someone's physical space convey negative impressions.

Being a Team Player

For many years, the American economy encouraged and rewarded individual effort. The information-age economy has resulted in a more group-oriented workplace. Workplace teams are now pooling their knowledge, making group decisions, and reaching team goals. Most careers involve some team efforts.

Developing teamwork skills takes time and should be begun in the early years of schooling. Working on group projects is the best way to learn to be a team player. These projects may be assigned as part of a class. Teamwork skills can also be built in clubs, organizations, youth groups, and volunteer activities.

Good team players are people who get along well with others. They gradually develop the following skills:
- being respectful of others' ideas
- taking responsibility for certain tasks and being accountable to team as well as self
- being adaptable and open to new ideas
- sharing roles with team members
- dealing with personality clashes and managing conflicts over ideas

Team members must participate by listening and speaking. They also take different roles, such as: presenting agenda; keeping the team focused on goals; encouraging every member to participate; analyzing ideas presented; and keeping records of ideas and decisions. Team members work to develop problem-solving and decision-making skills. They learn to brainstorm, compromise, build consensus for ideas, and evaluate results of decisions.

Leadership Skills

No matter what career you choose, at some time you will need to be a leader. Sometimes people take formal leadership roles. Your community's mayor and a store manager practice formal leadership. These people have been chosen by others to lead a group. At other times, people take informal leadership roles. Informal leaders lead or guide others even though they are not officially chosen to lead. People may be informal leaders within an organized group as well as outside of one.

Leadership skills have their roots in the early years of life. As children, future leaders often received *unconditional love* (love without strings attached) from their parents and other adults. They were given many chances to develop autonomy and responsibility. This type of upbringing fosters feelings of self-confidence even in the face of risks. Young leaders-to-be often have leadership role models in their lives, too. Thus, they learn by imitating others' actions.

Most effective leaders are also good team players. They have what it takes to get along with others and work together. In addition, effective leaders have many other qualities in common, 25-24.

Like other personal qualities, leadership qualities are a part of your whole life, not just your working hours. For some people, leadership is an aptitude. These people seem to have more natural leadership talent than others. If leadership is not one of your aptitudes, you can improve your ability to lead through practice. Babysitting or providing child care could give you practice at making decisions and being responsible.

You can also gain leadership skills by joining a school organization. You might even run for office and serve as a leader in the organization. One

Qualities of Effective Leadership

Effective leaders often fit the following descriptions:

❖ have a positive outlook and motivate others; they excite people about possibilities
❖ handle responsibility by following through to complete tasks, accepting blame for mistakes, and keeping promises
❖ are honest; followers trust them because they don't take advantage of others
❖ show acceptance of others; they are flexible and open to others' ideas
❖ are aware of differing points of view and work to resolve conflicts
❖ share reasons and explain their positions
❖ seek good group interaction through open and ongoing communication
❖ listen to get other people's perspectives and seek common ground
❖ know how to set and articulate goals to help the team achieve its purpose
❖ assign responsibilities to others
❖ develop team support by getting all members to participate
❖ make sound decisions and are confident in their choices

25-24 Which of these effective leadership skills do you possess? Are there others you could develop?

organization you might consider is **Family, Career, and Community Leaders of America (FCCLA)**. FCCLA is a national organization for students in family and consumer sciences courses. The group's mission is "to promote personal growth and leadership development through family and consumer sciences education." FCCLA strives to help members develop skills for life as family members, wage earners, and community leaders, 25-25.

Managing Multiple Roles

Most adults have more than one role. Many are workers, spouses, family members, parents, consumers, and community members. Some adults have even more roles that include their membership in organizations and other groups. Each role comes with expectations. A person who is a parent, for example, is expected to provide care for his or her children. Workers are expected to perform their job tasks.

Conflict can occur between these many roles and their demands. For emotional and physical health, a person must achieve a sense of balance between his or her roles. When roles do not balance well, role strain can occur. (Refer to chapter 24 to review this concept.) People who face role strain are often stressed, guilty, and unhappy. Stress comes from an overload of tasks and responsibilities. Stress can also occur because of conflict among these due to time limits. Guilt results when one tries to do it all but is unable to achieve everything. Stress and guilt often create more problems. The most common problem is a *spillover* from one role to another, 25-26.

25-25 As a part of her local FCCLA chapter, this high-school student assists elementary-school students with a special project.
Shelli Templeman, Hart County High School FCCLA Chapter, Munfordville, KY

formal leadership. Leadership used by elected or appointed officials and managers in organized groups.

informal leaders. People who lead or guide others even though they are not officially chosen to lead.

Family, Career, and Community Leaders of America (FCCLA). A national organization for students in family and consumer sciences courses.

Signs of a Spillover

Signs of spillover from job
- ❖ worrying about work while away from work
- ❖ being too tired to enjoy family life or to do household tasks
- ❖ not having time for leisure activities or not enjoying them
- ❖ bringing work home
- ❖ receiving complaints from family and friends about long work hours
- ❖ being irritable over little things

Signs of spillover from personal life
- ❖ being sleepy at work
- ❖ thinking about other things while at work
- ❖ feeling your employer expects too much of you
- ❖ being late for or absent from work; spending time on the job dealing with family or other personal matters; and asking to leave early to deal with nonwork matters
- ❖ making lots of careless mistakes
- ❖ reacting in overly sensitive ways to others and hurting other people's feelings

25-26 Spillovers between work and other aspects of life will always occur to some extent because everyone is human. Frequent negative spillovers are damaging both to work and to other aspects of life.

How does one achieve a well-balanced life? Suggestions include the following:

- ❖ Get in touch with your personal priorities. Determine what you really want from life. Make sure your personal priorities are reflected in how you live, not just in what you say. Many people report family is their highest priority. For these people, quality time with family may take priority over other tasks and events. Knowing your personal priorities allows you to be intentional about choices rather than just letting things happen.

- ❖ Rank your personal priorities. Devote more time to priorities of greater importance and less time to those of lesser importance. When two roles conflict, use ranking to select which one to meet first. Use remaining resources to meet other demands.
- ❖ Relax your standards where possible. You probably cannot compromise regarding your job duties. However, you might choose to let some household tasks go longer than you would like. Each person has limited time and resources. Expecting yourself to be perfect in every area will inevitably lead to role guilt and role strain.

❖ Get organized. Get a daily or weekly planner and schedule important events. A written schedule helps you think about tasks in advance and make time available for special events. Planning ahead also helps you prepare for what lies ahead.

❖ Establish daily routines. Routines make the day go more smoothly. For example, morning panic can often be avoided by taking time each night to get everything ready for the next day.

❖ Take time to mentally shift gears. Arrive at work early in order to have a few minutes of down time before the workday begins. After work, use commute time or take a short break upon reaching home, if possible, before starting other tasks or interacting extensively with others.

❖ Ask for help. Family members will often take on some tasks to relieve a loved one's role strain. They are glad to help because they share a sense of devotion to the family. Having help when needed makes it possible to manage multiple roles without undue strain.

❖ Combine activities. When possible, meet more than one goal through a single activity. For example, quality family time may be combined with "fitness time" if children walk with their parents. Quality family time may also be combined with meal preparation

and eating time. Community activities, family time, and fitness may be combined in a "walk-a-thon."

❖ Communicate with others. Talking with someone can alleviate tension and prevent spillover. Sometimes others can offer helpful ideas to better manage role demands. If spillover begins to occur, communicating honestly with a loved one can help a person manage negative feelings and regain perspective.

❖ Take care of yourself at work. Organize your tasks and focus for effectiveness and efficiency. Relax on breaks by eating, exercising, or socializing. Do your work but do not allow others to give you their work.

❖ Reconsider role requirements. If the role expectations are still too great, seek help. If your work is the problem, talk to your employer. Discuss possible options that may be helpful, such as *flextime* (job in which workers have options on work schedules), job benefits including child or elder care, or even a less demanding job within the business. Another option is to look for another job.

Leaving a Job in the Right Way

Few people stay in the same work-place for a career lifetime. People change jobs for many reasons. Sometimes people discover after working in a certain career that it is not a good match for them. Others "outgrow" their jobs due to more education and learning. Some people find their present work is more than they expected or can do. Many job changes occur when a family moves due to one spouse being transferred. Some people are laid off due to business problems. A few people are fired or asked to resign.

If you plan to voluntarily leave a job, it is best if you already have found another job. You should not use your work time at the current job to search for another job. However, you can look for another job in your nonworking hours. In most cases, quitting your current job without another job is less responsible than securing another job first.

Even when leaving your current job, you have an obligation to treat your employer fairly. See Figure 25-27 for guidelines to follow when you wish to leave a job.

Regardless of why you are leaving, you should strive to end the job on a positive note. Leaving in this way will help others remember you in a good light. In the future, you might need a reference or recommendation from your employer or coworkers, too. Tips for leaving on a positive note include the following:

❖ leave when the business is less busy, if possible. For example, an accounting firm would not want to lose employees during "income tax season."

❖ avoid bragging about your new job. Your employer and coworkers do not want to hear all the wonderful things about your new position. You might instead point out what you will miss about your

Obligations When Leaving a Job

Before leaving your current job, you should do the following:

❖ consult your employee handbook or personnel policies to learn the correct procedure for terminating (ending) employment. Adhere to this procedure as you notify the employer you wish to leave the job.

❖ provide ample notice so the employer can find a suitable replacement. The personnel policy may address the required time of notice. If it does not, you will need to decide how much notice to give. An acceptable amount of notice depends on the level of skills required in the job. Employers often need more time to fill a high-skill job than an entry-level job. Two weeks' notice is generally the minimum for an entry-level job.

❖ complete a letter of resignation and any other termination forms, if required by the employer. You should address your notice to your direct supervisor.

❖ try to complete all current tasks. Employers expect and are paying for your work through the final day. You may be expected to help train the employee who will take your place.

25-27 To leave a job in the most professional way, an employee should follow these tips.

current job, supervisor, and coworkers.

❖ show appreciation to your supervisor for his or her help and thank others who have helped you learn needed skills or were good role models.

Employees and their employers do have certain rights that are protected by law. If you are fired or laid off, you will need to learn about these rights. In these cases, it might be wise for you to seek legal advice. Some Web sites and other publications provide information about the legal rights that apply to the termination of a job.

Summing It Up

Choosing a career is a crucial decision that affects a person's lifestyle. Teens and young adults need to begin making career decisions early. To make a wise choice, you should begin with self-assessment. After learning about careers, you should be able to find one or more matches between your interests, aptitudes, and abilities and the requirements for a career. From this information, you can design a career plan.

Careers in child-related fields continue to grow. Adults can work in a number of child-related career areas. These include health and protective services; care and education; entertainment; design; advertising, marketing, and management; research and consulting; and entrepreneurial services.

To work well with children, people need a basic knowledge of their development. Personal and professional qualifications are required to enter a child-related field. After becoming qualified for a child-related job, you must use organized, efficient job search skills to find a job.

No matter what career you choose, it's important to develop some general skills that are needed in every field. These include human relations, communication, teamwork, leadership, and role-management skills. Developing these skills is a lifelong process. Leaving a job the right way is also important for career success.

Reviewing Key Concepts

Write your answers on a separate sheet of paper.

1. Self-assessment involves identifying your _____, _____, and _____.
2. Career plans have _____ goals and _____ goals.
3. In general, careers in child-related fields are _____ (increasing, decreasing) in number.
4. List 12 child-related careers that are available in your area.
5. _____ are professionals who usually share their knowledge about children with other adults rather than working directly with children.
6. Name three items people can design and sell for children.
7. For each of the following career areas, list two specific careers within that area:
   ❖ health and protective services
   ❖ care and education
   ❖ entertainment
   ❖ design
   ❖ advertising, marketing, and management
   ❖ research and consulting
8. List three personal qualities needed by adults working directly with children.
9. Professional qualifications are mainly (taught, not taught).
10. All adults involved in careers in child-related fields must have a basic knowledge of _____ in order to be effective.
11. True or false. Some job skills are used for success in many careers.
12. Describe three responsibilities workers have when leaving a job.

Using Your Knowledge

1. **Personal Development/Career Skills.** As an individual project, list some of your interests, aptitudes, and abilities. For each item listed, ask yourself how your traits match the desired personal and professional qualifications of those entering careers in child-related fields.
2. **Role-Play/Career Skills.** Work with a partner to role-play several interview situations. Conduct yourselves as you would during an interview. Take turns being the interviewer and the person being interviewed. After your role-plays, form a small group and discuss insights you gained while doing the role-play.
3. **Career Skills/Interviewing Skills.** Choose a career within one of the six child-related career areas described in the chapter. Consult your school guidance counselor about finding information regarding this career. Based on your findings, prepare a chart listing the occupation, as well as the personal and professional qualifications needed by people wishing to enter this career.
4. **Art/Career Skills.** Make a poster showing how membership in a local FCCLA chapter could aid the development of leadership skills needed for job success.

5. **Communication Skills/Technology.** Use a computer to compose a pretend letter of resignation following the guidelines described in the chapter.

Making Observations

1. Observe people working in child-related careers. What skills do they use? What aspects of the child's development (physical, mental, and/or social and emotional) do they especially need to know for this career?
2. Observe your friends as they become involved with children in different settings. What skills are they developing? Would these skills be helpful in parenting?
3. Observe a national, state, or local leader. List the leadership skills you have observed. Give example(s) of each skill.

Thinking Further

1. Why would it be good to take one or more courses in child development regardless of career choice?
2. If you wanted to inquire about particular careers in child-related fields, how would you proceed? What questions would you need to have answered?
3. Why is it wise to get involved in child-related fields even before completing high school? How can early involvement even help you after you complete your training or education for the career?

Glossary

A

abilities. Skills that have been learned or developed. (25)

abstinence. The choice to postpone a sexual relationship until marriage. (24)

abstract. Words that do not relate to what they represent. (16)

acquired immunodeficiency syndrome (AIDS). A disease caused by the HIV virus, which attacks the body's immune system. (5)

active immunity. Immunity in which a person's own body must produce antibodies to a disease. (21)

active vocabulary. The words a person uses in talking or writing. (8)

adoption. The process by which a child of one pair of parents legally becomes the child of other parents (or parent). (2)

adoption agency. A state-funded or private agency licensed by the state to handle adoptions. (2)

adult-child ratio. The number of adults per number of children in a group setting. (22)

age norm. A range of ages at which average children reach developmental milestones. (7)

age of viability. The age at which most babies could survive if they were born (28th week of pregnancy). (4)

age-appropriate behaviors. Proper or expected ways to express emotions at certain ages. (9)

aggression. An attempt to hurt or an act of hurting someone. (18)

aggressive behavior. An outward behavioral disorder in which people name-call, fight, or bully without being provoked into such actions. (23)

allergen. A substance that causes an allergic reaction. (21)

allergy. Condition that results when a person's immune system is very sensitive to a particular allergen and reacts negatively when exposed to it. (21)

altruistic behavior. Concern for others. (18)

amniocentesis. A prenatal test in which a needle is inserted through the woman's abdomen into the amniotic sac and a sample of the fluid is removed for cell study. (5)

amnion. A fluid-filled sac that surrounds the baby in the uterus. (4)

anemia. A low level of oxygen-carrying substances in the blood. (6)

anger. A feeling caused by frustration. (18)

antibodies. Proteins in the blood that fight disease. (21)

antigens. Substances made in a laboratory and transferred to people in the form of an injection (shot) to help their bodies form antibodies against a disease. (21)

anxiety. Fear of a possible future event. (9)

Apgar test. A test that checks the baby's chance of survival. (6)

aptitudes. Natural talents. (25)

articulation. Making the sounds of a language. (12)

artificial insemination. ART procedure that involves introducing sperm into the vagina or uterus by a medical procedure rather than by sexual relations. (3)

artificially acquired immunities. Immunities formed as a reaction to antibodies or an antigen received through medical care; also called acquired immunities. (21)

assertive. The act of speaking out, standing up for your rights, and defending yourself. (18)

assisted reproductive technologies (ART). Methods infertile couples can use to help them conceive. (3)

attachment. Closeness between people that remains over time. (9)

attachment behaviors. Actions one person demonstrates to another person to show closeness to that person. (9)

attention-deficit disorder (ADD). A disorder that involves the lack of attention but does not include hyperactive behaviors. (23)

attention-deficit hyperactivity disorder (ADHD). A disorder that involves the lack of attention and extremely active behavior that exceeds a typical high energy level. (23)

attributes. Distinctive characteristics of an object, such as size, shape, color, and texture. (12)

au pairs. Persons who provide child care for a host family as part of a cultural exchange program. (22)

auditory. Referring to the sense of hearing. (19)

authoritarian. Parenting style in which the main objective is to make children completely obedient. (2)

autonomy. A form of self-control in which a person seeks to do his or her will. (13)

axons. Long, thick cables that transmit all the signals from a neuron to other neurons. (1)

B

babble. To make a series of vowel sounds with consonant sounds slowly added to form syllables. (8)

baby blues. A mild postpartum mood disorder that goes away on its own. (5)

behavioral disorders. A pattern of problems that surfaces in a person's behavior. (23)

bias. A belief or feeling that results in unfair treatment of another person or makes such treatment seem right. (22)

binocular vision. Type of vision that involves fusing an image so it appears as one image using both eyes. (8)

birth control methods. Methods couples use to prevent conception. (3)

body proportions. The relative size of body parts. (7)

body rotation. The action of turning the trunk of the body to one side when the hand of the other side is used to throw. (15)

bonding. Developing a feeling of affection. (5)

borderline. A term used to identify a talent as just above average or a problem as mild. (23)

Brazelton scale. A test used to determine whether a baby has problems interacting with the environment, handling motor processes, controlling his or her physical state, or responding to stress. (6)

breech birth position. The buttocks-first position in which some babies enter the birth canal. (5)

C

career burnout. A state in which a person becomes emotionally tired of a career. (25)

career plan. A detailed list of steps a person must complete in order to enter a chosen career field. (25)

cartilage. Soft, elastic, flexible tissue that provides structure for the body. (4)

cell. The smallest unit of life that is able to reproduce itself. (4)

center-based child care. A large group program in which child care is provided in a center rather than in a home. (22)

certified child safety seats. Restraint systems for infants and young children that have been tested and approved by federal agencies; also known as *car seats*. (21)

certified nurse midwives (CNM). Nurses who have special training in delivering babies during normal pregnancies. (5)

cesarean section. A delivery method in which the mother's abdomen and uterus are surgically opened and the baby is removed. (5)

character. An inward force that guides a person's conduct. (1)

child abuse. An act committed by an adult that harms or threatens to harm a child's well-being. (24)

child care programs. Programs that operate to care for children for extended hours, usually between 9 and 12 hours a day. (22)

child care resource and referral agencies (CCR&R). Agencies promote local child care programs and help parents find child care. (22)

child development. The scientific study of children from conception to adolescence. (1)

child neglect. Harm or endangerment of a child caused by an adult's failure to do something legally expected of him or her. (24)

child passenger seat technician (CPS). Professional who provides information on child safety seats and inspects them after installation. (21)

child support order. A judgment of the court that states how much a parent who does not live with his or her children should pay toward their expenses. (24)

child with special needs. A child whose development differs from that of the development that is typical for most children of the same age. (23)

child-centered society. A society that sees children as important and works for their good. (1)

childproofing. The process of moving unsafe objects out of a child's reach or preventing dangerous situations. (21)

children in self-care. Children who are at home alone after school or for a portion of the day and must care for themselves during that time. (24)

chorion. Membrane that surrounds the baby in the uterus. (4)

chorionic villus sampling (CVS). A prenatal procedure for finding abnormalities in the unborn by testing a small sample of the chorion. (5)

chromosomes. Threadlike structures that carry genes in living cells. (4)

chronic. A term used to indicate that a problem will be long-lasting and perhaps lifelong. (23)

class. A group of items that have an attribute in common. (18)

class complement. In classifying, any object that does not belong within the class being considered. (18)

classifying. The ability to choose an attribute and group all the objects from a set (either mentally or physically) that possess that attribute. (16)

closed adoption. An adoption in which the identity of the birthparents and adopting family are not revealed to each other. (2)

codes of professional ethics. Sets of standards created by various professions to govern the conduct of employees in these careers. (25)

cognition. The act or process of knowing or understanding. (8)

colic. A condition in which a baby has intense abdominal pain and cries inconsolably. (6)

collective monologue. Talking to another person but not listening to what the other person has said. (16)

communication. The skill needed to understand others and to be understood by them. (12)

compare. To see how objects and people are alike. (18)

concept. An idea formed by combining what is known about a person, object, place, quality, or event. (8)

conception. The union of the ovum and sperm cells. (4)

concrete operational stage. Piaget's third stage of mental development, in which children begin to think logically, but base their logic on past experiences. (19)

congenital problem. A physical or biochemical problem that is present at birth and may be caused by genetic or environmental factors. (5)

conservation. The concept that changing an object's shape, direction, or position does not alter the quantities of the object. (19)

consultants. Professionals who share their knowledge, such as knowledge about children, with other adults. (25)

contagious disease. A disease that can be caught from another person. (21)

contrariness. The tendency to oppose almost everything others do or say. (14)

contrast. To see how objects and people are different. (18)

convergent thinking. Coming up with only one right answer or way to do a task. (18)

coo. A light, happy sound babies begin to use to communicate between six and eight weeks after birth. (8)

cooperation. Joint effort; getting along with others and considering their goals. (18)

coordination. The working together of muscles to form movements. (10)

correctable. A term used to indicate that a problem can likely be overcome with the appropriate support. (23)

crawl. To move by pulling with the arms but not lifting the abdomen from the floor. (7)

creeping. Moving by using the hands and knees or the hands and feet with the abdomen off the floor. (7)

cruising. Walking by holding something for support. (7)

cultural diversity. Having more than one culture represented. (2)

culture. The way of life within a group that includes language, beliefs, attitudes, personal priorities, rituals, and skills. (1)

culture shock. An uncomfortable response to an unfamiliar culture. (22)

D

deciduous teeth. The first set of teeth, which will later be replaced by permanent teeth. Also called nonpermanent or baby teeth. (7)

deductive reasoning. Reasoning from the general to the specific. (19)

deferred imitation. The ability to recall someone's behavior and later imitate it. (12)

democratic. Parenting style in which parents set some rules but allow children some freedom. (2)

dendrites. Short, bushy cables that allow each neuron to receive signals sent by other neurons. (1)

dental caries. Decayed places in teeth. (21)

dependence. Reliance of one person on another to meet his or her needs. (9)

depressants. Substances that slow the functions of organs and the nervous system. (10)

depth perception. The ability to tell how far away something is. (8)

development. The gradual process of growth through many stages, such as infancy, childhood, adolescence, and adulthood. (1)

developmental acceleration. When a child performs like an older child. (1)

developmental delay. When a child performs like a younger child. (1)

developmental dyscalculia. A learning disability that affects a child's mathematical abilities. (23)

developmental tasks. Skills that should be mastered at a certain stage in life. (1)

developmentally appropriate practices (DAP). Child care and education that uses knowledge about child development and considers each child's strengths, needs, interests, and culture. (22)

developmentally inappropriate practices (DIP). Child care and education that do not use knowledge about child development and focus mainly on the group instead of each child. (22)

diabetes. A disorder caused by the body's inability to use sugar properly. (5)

diagnosis. Identifying the cause of a person's illness. (21)

dilation. The first stage of labor, during which the cervix opens. (5)

direct intervention. Careers in which people work directly with children. (25)

direct observation. Watching children in their natural environments. (1)

discipline. The use of methods and techniques to help teach children self-control. (2)

disposition. A person's general mood. (9)

divergent thinking. Coming up with different possible ideas. (18)

dominant traits. Traits that always show in a person even if only one gene of the pair is inherited for that trait. (4)

dynamic balance. Balance maintained while moving. (15)

dyslexia. A learning disability that affects a person's ability to read, write, and spell. (23)

E

educational neglect. Failure to conform to state legal requirements regarding school attendance. (24)

egocentrism. The belief a person has that everyone thinks in the same way and has the same ideas as he or she does. (16)

embryo. Term used to describe a baby in the embryonic stage of development. (4)

embryonic stage. The second stage of prenatal development, which lasts about six weeks. (4)

emotional dependency. The act of seeking attention, approval, comfort, and contact. (17)

emotional neglect. Inadequate care and attention, violence or drug use in the home, or failing to meet the child's emotional needs at each stage of development. (24)

emotional/verbal abuse. Any act in which an adult makes excessive demands, harasses, belittles, or verbally threatens the child. (24)

emotions. Thoughts that lead to feelings and cause changes in the body. (9)

enriched environment. An environment that offers a person many chances to learn. (10)

entrepreneur. A person who creates and owns a business. (25)

enuresis. Any instance of involuntary (accidental) urination by a child over three years of age. (18)

environment. The sum of all the conditions and situations that affect a child's growth and development. (1)

environmental factors. Those factors caused by a person's surroundings. (5)

episiotomy. An incision made to widen the birth canal and prevent tearing. (5)

extended family. Family in which several generations live together. (2)

eye-hand coordination. The ability to coordinate what a person sees with the way the person moves his or her hands. (11)

F

failure to thrive. A condition in which a child fails to grow at a healthy rate. (7)

fallopian tubes. Two hollow tubes that connect to the uterus and have fingerlike projections that reach toward each ovary. (4)

Family and Medical Leave Act. Law that protects the rights of the workers of large companies to take up to 12 weeks of unpaid leave per year for various family-related reasons. (3)

family child care. Care provided by a person for a small number of children in his or her own home. (22)

family life cycle. A series of six stages through which many families go over the years. (2)

family planning. Decisions couples make about the desired number and spacing of future children. (3)

Family, Career, and Community Leaders of America (FCCLA). A national organization for students in family and consumer sciences courses. (25)

fertility counseling. Medical evaluation that seeks to determine the reasons for fertility problems and explore available treatment options. (3)

fetal alcohol syndrome (FAS). A condition in infants that occurs when mothers drink heavily during pregnancy. (5)

fetal stage. The third stage of pregnancy, lasting from about nine weeks after conception until birth. (4)

fetus. Term used to describe a baby in the fetal stage of development. (4)

field trips. Outings that take children to places away from a child care program's property. (22)

filtering program. A program that prevents a child from accessing inappropriate material on the Internet. (21)

fine-motor skills. Being able to use and control the small muscles, especially those in the fingers and hands. (7)

finger foods. Foods a baby can self-feed using the fingers. (10)

fingerplays. Poems and rhymes that are acted out with the hands. (22)

first aid. Emergency treatment for an illness or accident that is given before professional medical help arrives. (21)

flexibility. The ability to move, bend, and stretch easily. (19)

Food Guide Pyramid for Young Children. A child-friendly version of the Food Guide Pyramid developed by the USDA to address the needs of children ages two to six years for nutritious foods and physical activity. (14)

forceps. A curved instrument that fits around the sides of a baby's head and is used to help the doctor ease the baby down the birth canal during a contraction. (5)

foregone income. Potential income given up by a parent who leaves the workforce and stays home to raise a child. (3)

formal leadership. Leadership used by elected or appointed officials and managers in organized groups. (25)

formal operations. Piaget's final stage of mental development, in which a person can reason abstractly. (19)

for-profit programs. Programs that are set up to make money. (22)

foster families. Families in which adults provide temporary homes for children who cannot live with their birthparents. (2)

fraternal. Term describing children from multiple pregnancies who develop from two ova and differ in genetic makeup. (4)

G

gamete intrafallopian transfer (GIFT). ART procedure in which a mixture of sperm and eggs is placed in the woman's fallopian tubes, where fertilization can occur. (3)

gender-role learning. Learning what behavior is expected of males and females. (17)

genes. Sections of the DNA molecule found in a person's cells that determine the individual traits the person will have. (1)

genetic factors. Traits that are passed through the genes. (4)

genetics. The study of the factors involved in the passing of traits from one generation of living beings to the next. (1)

germinal stage. The first stage of prenatal development, which lasts about two weeks after conception. (4)

gifted and talented children. Children who can or who do show high performance in one or more of six key areas. (23)

grammar. The study of the preferred word usage and order in a given language. (12)

gross-motor skills. Being able to use the large muscles to roll over, sit, crawl, stand, and walk. (7)

growth pains. Muscle aches that occur when the muscles grow rapidly to catch up with increasing skeleton size. (19)

growth spurt. A period of rapid growth. (19)

guidance. The words and actions parents use to influence their children's behavior. (2)

guilt. Blaming yourself for something done wrong. (17)

H

Head Start. A federally sponsored program that was launched to meet the needs of children from low-income families. (22)

hearing impaired. A term used to indicate that a person has hearing loss. (23)

heredity. The sum of all the traits that are passed to a child from blood relatives. (1)

hidden added costs. Costs of child care that add to the direct costs. (22)

hidden cost credits. Credits that lower the direct costs of child care. (22)

hierarchical classification. Having classes within other classes. (19)

hyperactivity. A pattern of extremely active behavior in which a person is overactive, restless, and has a short attention span. (23)

I

identical. Term describing children from multiple pregnancies who develop from one fertilized ovum and have the same genetic makeup. (4)

illegal market adoption. An adoption in which adoptive parents pay money to an agency, independent source, or birthparents other than medical and legal costs that are approved by state law. (2)

imitating. Copying the actions of someone else. (8)

immunity. Having agents that prevent a person from developing a disease. (21)

immunization. An injection of antigens given to a person to provide immunity from a certain disease. (21)

in vitro fertilization (IVF). ART procedure occurs when some of the mother's eggs are surgically removed, fertilized with sperm in a laboratory dish, and then implanted in the mother's uterus. (3)

independent adoption. An adoption in which a person, such as a lawyer or physician, works out the details between the birthparents and adoptive parents. (2)

independent. Wanting to do things for oneself. (9)

indirect costs. Resources used to meet child-related costs that could have been used to meet other goals. (3)

indirect observation. Observation done by methods other than watching children, including asking other people questions about the children and observing the products children make. (1)

individual life cycle. A description of the stages of change people experience throughout life. (1)

Individualized Education Plan (IEP). An educational plan that is tailored to the specific educational needs of a child with special needs. (23)

Individualized Family Service Plan (IFSP). A plan that focuses on the needs of a family with a child younger than three years of age who has been identified as having special needs. (23)

induction. A technique in which parents discipline by reasoning and explaining. (2)

inductive reasoning. Reasoning from specific facts to general conclusions. (19)

industry. A sense of joining others in striving to become a competent member of society. (19)

inferiority. A feeling that one is incompetent and less valuable as a member of society. (19)

infertile. Unable to conceive after a year of trying. (3)

inflections. Changes of pitch. (8)

informal leaders. People who lead or guide others even though they are not officially chosen to lead. (25)

in-home child care. Child care that takes place in the child's own home. (22)

initiate. To begin. (9)

initiative. The ability to think or act without being urged. (17)

intellectual development. How people learn, what they learn, and how they express what they know through language. (8)

intensive care nursery (ICN). Special nursery that can provide immediate intensive care just after birth for babies who need it. (6)

internal organs. Parts inside of the body, such as the heart, lungs, and liver. (15)

internalized. Something that only is thought about and not shared with others. (16)

intolerance. A negative physical reaction caused by eating a food. (10)

intuitive substage. A substage of the preoperational stage in which children can solve many problems correctly by imagining how they would act out the solution instead of using logic. (16)

IQ tests. Tests that measure how quickly a person can learn, how able a person is to reason using words and numbers, and how easily a person can find solutions to problems. (23)

J

jaundice. A liver condition that can make the skin, tissues, and body fluids look yellow. (6)

joint custody. The shared legal right of parents who are not married to provide care and make decisions about their children's lives. (2)

K

kindergarten. Programs publicly and privately operated for four- and five-year-old children; serve as an entrance to school education. (22)

L

labor. The process that moves the baby out of the mother's body. (5)

Lamaze method. A delivery method in which the pregnant woman is trained to use breathing patterns to keep her mind off pain. (5)

language. A symbol system in which words are used as labels for people, objects, and ideas. (12)

large-muscle development. The development of the trunk and arm and leg muscles. (11)

LATCH system. Attachment that will be installed in new motor vehicles to make child safety seats safer and easier to use. (21)

leader. A person who influences or motivates the thoughts, feelings, or actions of others. (25)

learning disabilities. Problems in one or more areas of spoken or written language, mathematics, and spatial orientation. (23)

Leboyer method. A delivery method that focuses on making the baby as comfortable as possible during and immediately after delivery. (5)

legally blind. A term that indicates a person meets criteria for vision loss that entitle him or her to receive special services. (23)

licensing personnel. Professionals who check the quality of services provided for children. (25)

lifestyle. The typical way of life for a person, group, or culture. (25)

lightening. A change in the baby's position in which the uterus settles downward and forward and the baby descends lower into the pelvis. (5)

logical thinking concepts. Concepts that are not directly experienced through the senses but are developed through thought. (16)

long-term goals. Major achievements toward which you strive; usually take more than a year to achieve. (25)

love withdrawal. Discipline techniques in which parents threaten children with being unloved or suggest some form of parent/child separation. (2)

low birthweight. Term that describes babies who weigh less than 5½ pounds at birth. (5)

M

mandated reporters. Professionals who are legally bound to report any known or suspected cases of abuse or neglect to the proper authorities. (24)

manipulate. To work with an object by using the hands. (15)

maternity leave. Time a woman takes off from work for the birth or adoption of a child. (3)

medical neglect. Harm or endangerment of a child caused by failure to seek treatment for health problems or accidents. (24)

mental disability. The condition of a person whose intellectual abilities are a year or more delayed when compared with the abilities of other people of the same age. (23)

mental images. Symbols of objects and past experiences that are stored in the mind. (16)

middle childhood. Another name for the school-age years, the period of development from 6 to 12 years of age. (19)

miscarriage. The expulsion of a baby from the mother's body before week 20 of pregnancy. (5)

mistrust. The most serious form of not trusting, which includes a lack of trust and feelings of suspicion. (9)

monologue. Talking to oneself as though thinking aloud. (16)

monotone. Sounds all in a single pitch. (8)

Montessori schools. Schools that encourage children to learn independently through the use of highly specialized materials. (22)

moral neglect. Failure to teach the child right from wrong in terms of general social priorities. (24)

mortality rate. Rate of death. (24)

motor development. The use and control of muscles that direct body movements. (7)

multicultural families. Families with members from two or more cultural groups. (2)

multiple pregnancy. Pregnancy in which two or more babies develop. (4)

muscle development. The lengthening and thickening of muscles. (11)

N

nannies. Professionals who contract with a family to provide in-home child care. (22)

natural childbirth. A delivery method in which the pregnant woman learns about the birth process and uses breathing and relaxation techniques to reduce fear and pain. (5)

naturally acquired immunities. Immunities that are developed after direct contact with infection or by receiving antibodies from the mother during pregnancy or breast-feeding; also called *natural immunities*. (21)

neonatal intensive care units (NICU). Heated, completely enclosed beds for newborns who need intensive care. (6)

neonate. Medical term for the baby from birth to one month of age. (6)

neonatology. A branch of medicine concerned with the care, development, and diseases of newborns. (6)

neurons. Brain cells that send and receive electrical impulses amongst each other that direct the various tasks of the brain. (1)

not-for-profit programs. Child care programs in which income only covers costs. (22)

nursery schools. A public or private program for children under age five that provides education and physical care. (22)

nurturance. Providing all aspects of care for a child, which includes meeting physical, emotional, and social needs. (2)

nutrient density. The level of nutrients in a food in relation to the level of calories in the food. (14)

nutrients. Substances in food that give people energy and help them grow. (10)

O

obedience. Acting within the limits set by others. (14)

object concept. The ability to understand that an object, person, or event is separate from one's interaction with it. (8)

object constancy. The ability to learn that objects remain the same even if they appear different. (8)

object identity. The ability to learn that an object stays the same from one time to the next. (8)

object permanence. The ability to learn that people, objects, and places still exist even when they are no longer seen, felt, or heard. (8)

obstetricians. Doctors who specialize in pregnancy and birth. (5)

open adoption. An adoption that involves some degree of communication between birthparent(s) and adoptive family. (2)

orthodontist. A dentist who specializes in correcting irregular teeth. (21)

orthopedic problems. Problems relating to the bones and muscles. (19)

ossification. Hardening of bones caused by the depositing of the minerals calcium and phosphorus. (7)

ovum. The female sex cell; also called the *egg*. (4)

P

parentese. High-pitched style in which parents speak to their children. (12)

passive immunity. Immunity in which a person obtains antibodies formed by another person's body. (21)

passive observing. Watching another's actions without responding. (18)

passive vocabulary. The words a person understands but does not say. (8)

paternity leave. Time a man takes off from work (usually without pay) for a set period after a child's birth or adoption. (3)

pediatrician. A doctor who cares for infants and children. (6)

peers. Unrelated children who are near the same age. (17)

perception. Organizing information that comes through the senses. (8)

perceptual learning. The process of developing perception. (8)

permanent teeth. The set of teeth that begin to come in during the school-age years and are meant to last a lifetime. (19)

permissive. Parenting style in which parents give children almost no guidelines or rules. (2)

personal priorities. Ideas, beliefs, and objects that are important and meaningful to you. (25)

personal qualifications. All the traits you possess that cannot be learned in career training. (25)

personal references. People who know you well enough to discuss your qualifications for a job. (25)

phenylketonuria (PKU). A disease that can cause mental retardation if left untreated by diet. (6)

physical abuse. Violence that results in pain, injuries, or both to a child. (24)

physical disability. A limitation of a person's body or its function. (23)

physical neglect. Endangering a child's health or safety by failing to provide supervision and basic survival needs, such as clothing, food, and shelter. (24)

placenta. An organ filled with blood vessels that nourishes the baby in the uterus. (4)

plasticity. The ability of the brain to be shaped and reshaped, which is greatest early in life. (1)

postpartum care. The care the mother receives during the six to eight weeks following the birth of her baby. (5)

postpartum depression (PPD). A less frequent, but serious form of depression that may occur after giving birth. (5)

postpartum psychosis (PPP). A rare and extremely severe mental illness that may result after giving birth. (5)

power assertion. A discipline technique in which parents use or threaten to use some form of physical punishment. (2)

precision. Ability to perform motor skills accurately. (19)

preconceptual substage. A substage of the preoperational stage in which children ages two to four years are developing some concepts. (16)

pregnancy-induced hypertension (PIH). The name for high blood pressure caused by pregnancy. (5)

premature. Term that describes babies who are born too soon. (5)

prenatal development. The development that takes place between conception and birth. (4)

preoperational stage. The second of Piaget's developmental stages in which children have begun to do some mental thinking rather than solving all problems with their physical actions. (16)

preschool children. Children between the ages of three and five years. (15)

principles of growth and development. Statements of the general patterns in which growth and development take place in people. (1)

private programs. Programs owned by individuals, churches, or other nongovernment groups. (22)

problem solving. Noting a problem, observing and questioning what you see, and solving the problem. (18)

professional qualifications. The physical, mental, and social-emotional skills you need to perform well in a career. (25)

profound. A term used to identify a talent as extreme or a problem as severe. (23)

pruning. The process of weeding out underused or weak connections between neurons. (1)

psychological security. The feeling that someone cares and will help when needed. (19)

public programs. Child care programs funded by local, state, or federal monies. (22)

Q

quality time. A time when parents are totally attentive to their children. (24)

quickening. Movements of the fetus that can be felt by the mother. (4)

R

reaction time. The time required to respond to a sight or sound. (15)

recessive traits. Traits that typically do not show in a person unless both genes for the trait are inherited. (4)

reduplication babbling. Repeating the same syllable over and over again. (8)

reflexes. Automatic, unlearned behaviors. (6)

registered dietitians. People who have special training in nutrition and diet and meet the qualifications of the American Dietetic Association. (14)

regression. Going back to an earlier stage of development. (14)

regulations. Standards that govern a group program. (22)

repressed jealousy. Feelings of jealousy not directly expressed and may even be denied. (17)

resources. Tools you can use in achieving your goals. (25)

restraint systems. Car seats, seat belts, and other devices that hold children safely in place while traveling in a motor vehicle. (21)

resume. A short, written history of a person's education, work experience, and other qualifications for employment. (25)

reversals. Mentally doing and undoing an action. (18)

Rh factor. A protein substance found in the red blood cells of about 85 percent of the population. (5)

ritual. A pattern of activities repeated at a regular time each day, such as bedtime. (14)

role guilt. A feeling of not doing the best job at home or work due to role strain. (24)

role strain. A feeling of having too many tasks to do at one time. (24)

rooting reflex. Reflex that helps babies search for food by turning the head and moving the mouth in response to a touch on the cheeks or mouth. (6)

S

safety recall. Issuing of a notice by the product manufacturer stating the product has been found to be unsafe. (21)

scapegoating. Blaming others for one's own mistakes. (19)

school-age child care programs (SACC). Programs that provide child care for 5- to 16-year-olds when school is not in session. (22)

school-age children. Children between ages 6 and 12 years. (19)

scientific reasoning. Another name for inductive reasoning, the form of logic commonly used by scientists. (19)

self-assertion. Doing as one chooses rather than what others want. (14)

self-assessment. A step in career planning that involves identifying your interests, aptitudes, and abilities. (25)

self-awareness. The understanding a person has about himself or herself as a person. (10)

self-esteem. Feeling good about yourself and what you can do. (13)

self-restraint. The ability to control yourself. (14)

sensorimotor stage. The first of Piaget's stages of cognitive (intellectual) development in which children use their senses and motor skills to learn and communicate with others. (8)

sensory stimulation. Using the five senses to learn about the environment. (10)

separate identities. Feelings of being distinct people rather than a unit. (24)

separation anxiety. Anxiety common in babies caused by the fear that loved ones who leave them will not return. (9)

sequenced steps. Steps in growth and development that follow one another in a set order. (1)

sex typing. Treating boys and girls differently. (17)

sexual abuse. Any act of a sexual nature that involves an adult and a child. (24)

sexual stereotyping. A statement or hint that men and women always do or should do certain tasks. (17)

sexually transmitted diseases (STDs). Infectious illnesses that are passed primarily through sexual intercourse. (5)

Shaken Baby Syndrome (SBS). A condition in which a baby or young child has injuries as a result of being violently shaken. (24)

shortcomings. Areas where a person wants or needs to improve. (19)

short-term goals. Achievements you desire in the near future. (25)

siblings. Brothers and sisters. (9)

single-parent families. Families headed by one adult. (2)

singletons. Children born one at a time, as opposed to children of multiple births. (24)

six-year molars. The first permanent teeth, which grow in behind the second set of deciduous molars. (19)

skeletal system. The body system that includes the bones and teeth. (7)

small-muscle development. The development of small muscles, especially those in the hands and fingers. (11)

social isolation. Feelings of being alone. (24)

social-emotional development. Type of development involving a person's disposition, interaction with people and social groups, and emotions. (9)

socialize. To train a child to live as part of a group, such as the family, culture, or society. (1)

solids. Foods that are semi-liquid and mushy for feeding an infant by spoon. (10)

spatial. Pertaining to space. (14)

spatial orientation. The ability to see the relationship between objects in space. (23)

speech impaired. A term used to indicate that a person has speech problems. (23)

sperm. The male sex cell. (4)

static balance. Balance maintained while being still. (15)

stepfamilies. Families formed when a single parent marries another person. (2)

sterile. The condition of being permanently unable to conceive or carry fully biological children. (3)

stillbirth. Loss of a fetus after 20 weeks of pregnancy. (5)

stimulants. Substances that speed up the functions of organs such as the heart and nervous system. (10)

stimuli. An agent, such as light or sound, that directly influences the activity of the sense organs. (8)

stressors. Situations that cause stress. (17)

sudden infant death syndrome (SIDS). A syndrome in which a baby dies without warning in his or her sleep. (6)

surrogate mother. A woman who bears (sometimes both conceives and bears) a child for a couple. (3)

symptoms. Signs of an illness or injury. (21)

synapse. A tiny gap between a dendrite of one neuron and the axon of another across which electrical impulses can be transmitted. (1)

T

teachable moment. A time when a person can learn a new task because the body is physically ready, caregivers encourage and support, and the child feels a strong desire to learn. (1)

temper tantrums. Sudden emotional outbursts of anger commonly displayed by toddlers. (13)

temperament. The tendency to react in a certain way to events. (9)

terminally ill. Having a disease that will result in death. (21)

toilet learning. The process by which adults help children learn to use the toilet to manage their elimination needs. (14)

training pants. Special underpants or pants made of disposable diaper material that help lessen the mess of accidents during toilet learning. (14)

transformation. The sequence of changes by which one state is changed to another. (18)

transitional stage. A stage of development in which a person is passing from one stage to another. (14)

two-parent family. Family consisting of a father, a mother, and their biological child or children who live together. (2)

U

ultrasound. A prenatal test in which sound waves bounce off the fetus to produce an image of the fetus inside the womb. (5)

umbilical cord. The cord that connects the baby to the placenta. (4)

uterus. The organ in which the baby develops and is protected until birth. (4)

V

vacuum extraction. Technique that uses suction to help the doctor move the baby down the birth canal as the mother pushes. (5)

visual. Referring to the sense of sight. (19)

visually impaired. A term used to indicate that a person has vision problems or vision loss. (23)

vocabulary. The words a person understands and uses. (8)

voluntary grasping. The intentional grasping of objects. (7)

W

weaning. The gradual process of taking a baby off the bottle or breast. (10)

weight shift. The change of weight from the back foot to the front foot. (15)

well-baby checkup. A routine medical visit in which the doctor examines a baby for signs of good health and proper growth. (6)

windows of opportunity. A prime period in a child's life for developing a particular skill if given the chance to do so. (1)

wiring. Network of fibers that carry brain signals between neurons. (1)

withdrawn behavior. Behaviors that show a separation from the rest of society, such as not relating well to other people, not wanting changes to occur, and lacking self-esteem. (23)

work ethic. A standard of conduct and priorities for job performance. (25)

work-related child care programs. Child care programs funded by businesses for their employees' children. (22)

Z

zygote. The single cell formed at conception; also called a *fertilized egg.* (4)

Photo Credits

GameTime, Fort Payne, AL, U.S.A., opening photo chapter 23

©*Nancy P. Alexander,* opening photo chapter 22

PlayDesigns, opening photos chapters 13 and 17

Presbyterian Church (USA) Foundation/Presbytarian Survey, opening photo chapter 1

Appendix

Indoor Dangers		
Danger	**Possible Causes**	**Childproofing Measures**
Environmental **Carbon monoxide**	• Wood-burning, coal, gas, kerosene, and propane heating devices emit more carbon monoxide than electric heating. • Homes with attached garages are at higher risk because vehicles emit carbon monoxide as waste. • Cooking on a barbeque grill nearby the house increases risk because carbon monoxide is released in the smoke.	• Maintain fireplaces and heating system. • Keep home well ventilated. • Keep grill farther from the home and close doors and windows when using the grill. • Install a carbon monoxide detector on each floor in the home. Replace or repair as needed. • Learn the warning signs of carbon monoxide poisoning. Seek help at once if these are noted.
Fire	• Problems with household wiring, electrical appliances, chimney fires, and space heaters are main causes of fires. • Accidents with matches, lighters, cigarettes, and candles often lead to fires. • Cooking accidents can cause fires.	• Install smoke detectors in every bedroom and near the kitchen. Check monthly and install new batteries twice yearly. • Have working fire extinguishers near kitchen and fireplaces. • Keep matches, lighters, cigarettes, and candles out of the reach of children. • Never leave lit candles or food cooking on the stovetop unattended. • Plan escape routes from various rooms of the house. Teach fire safety and escape routes to even very young children.

(Continued)

Indoor Dangers *(Continued)*		
Danger	**Possible Causes**	**Childproofing Measures**
Environmental *(Continued)* **Lead paint (Used in buildings built before 1978.)**	• Lead poisoning comes from breathing lead dust or fumes or eating paint chips. (Lead causes brain damage.)	• Lead paint must be removed by a professional or covered with an approved sealant.
Structure **Doors, sliding glass**	• Child may walk into or through glass. • Fingers can be pinched.	• Block off door, if seldom used, but be sure door can be used in case of an emergency. Put colorful decals on glass at the child's eye level. • Use doorstop high on doorjamb.
Doors, swinging	• Fingers can be pinched. • Children may lock themselves in the room. • Inside doors can lead to unsafe places. • Inside doors can lead to outside.	• Use doorstops and door holders to protect fingers. • Keep unlocking tools handy and learn how to unlock. Consider removing doorknob locks and install hook-and-eye locks if needed. • Use high hook-and-eye locks on outside of door when not in room or storage area. • Utilize safety gates. • Use door monitor that sounds an alarm. Keep doors to the outside locked but keep keys nearby but out of child's reach.
Electrical Outlets	• Child can be electrocuted by putting fingers or objects in outlets.	• Use outlet safety devices. The best are outlet covers that replace existing plates. When unplugged, a sliding cover snaps into place over outlets. • Use power strip covers. • Outlets can be sealed with electrical tape. • Use devices that replace outlet covers that keep cords plugged in for freezer, television, washer, dryer, and refrigerator. • If safe, place heavy furniture in front of outlets never or seldom used.

(Continued)

Indoor Dangers *(Continued)*		
Danger	**Possible Causes**	**Childproofing Measures**
Structure *(Continued)* **Fireplaces**	• Child can be burned or cause fire in the fireplace to spread throughout the house. • Child can be injured in a fall against hearth.	• Install fireplace grill and keep it in place. • Keep keys for gas fireplace out of reach. • Keep fireplace logs, tools, and matches out of reach. • Cover sharp corners of hearth.
Heaters and radiators	• Child can be burned.	• Keep guards around open heaters, radiators, and floor furnaces.
Stairs	• Child can be injured in a fall. • Child can be trapped or fall through openings in stair railings.	• Move furniture away from staircases. • Install a hardware-mounted safety gate at the top of stairs and three steps from the bottom of stairs. Gate should carry the seal of the Juvenile Products Manufacturers Association. • Attach a safety netting against railings.
Windows	• Child can fall through or out of windows.	• Never put furniture or other climbable objects in front of windows. • Don't depend on locked screens to prevent falls. • Open casement windows from the top. Open low windows no more than 4 inches. Use window stops to prevent wider openings. • Install window guards with approved release mechanisms for all upper-floor windows and first-floor windows that open onto unsafe surfaces. (For secure mounting, window frame must be in good condition.) • Plant shrubs or use soft edging, such as wood chips, under windows.

(Continued)

Indoor Dangers *(Continued)*		
Danger	**Possible Causes**	**Childproofing Measures**
Furnishings **Appliances, small**	• Appliances can fall on child if dangling cord is pulled. • Dangling cord can strangle child. • Child can be electrocuted by playing with cord near socket or water.	• Drape cords behind appliances while in use. • Put cords out of reach when appliances are not in use. • Store appliances out of children's reach.
Blinds	• Double cords on Venetian blinds and continuous-looping drapery cords can loop around neck, causing strangulation. • Venetian blinds bought before Sept. 2000 have inner cords that can form loops when not locked into position.	• Cut cords and install safety "break-away tassels." • Place cords on hooks called *cleats* to keep them out of reach. • Continuous-looping drapery cords should be anchored near the floor to keep the cord taut. • Keep cribs, playyards, and other furniture away from windows. (Deaths can occur when children play with cords or crawl on furniture and jump or fall off with the cords around them.) • Use cordless blinds with a spring-loaded system.
Curtains	• Suffocation can occur if curtain is wrapped around head.	• Keep babies and young children away from curtains. • Move cribs and playyards out of reach of curtains. • If purchasing new curtains, consider buying short ones.
Fans	• Fingers can be cut by twirling fan blades. • Injury can result if fan falls on child.	• Place window screening between fan blades and grills. • Keep fans out of child's reach.
Floor lamps	• Injury can result if child pulls lamp over.	• Place floor lamps behind sturdy furniture. • If buying new, consider smaller table lamps or overhead lighting.

(Continued)

Indoor Dangers *(Continued)*		
Danger	**Possible Causes**	**Childproofing Measures**
Furnishings *(Continued)* **Rugs, area, and throw**	• Children can slip or trip over loose rugs.	• Use nonskid pads under rugs or buy rugs with nonslip backing. • Tape loose edges of rug to the floor.
Wastebaskets	• Children can find many harmful objects inside.	• Never place anything in a wastebasket that could harm a child. Flush unused medications down the toilet. Take unsafe items directly to an outside garbage can. Tie knots in plastic can liners. • Use child-resistant covers on all outdoor garbage cans.
Room Dangers **Bathroom**	• Child can drown in toilet. • Children can bump into hardware. • Children can be burned by hot water or hot hardware in the bathtub. • Children can fall or drown in the bathtub. • Child can be electrocuted by nearby electric devices when using tub or sink. • Child can be poisoned or harmed by personal care items, medicines, and cleaning products.	• Install a toilet lid lock. • Install a safety cover on the doorknob or a hook-and-eye lock near top of door outside the bathroom door to prevent children from entering without an adult's knowledge. • Put a rubber-covered guard over tub faucet and knobs. • Use nonslip mat in the tub. • Supervise children at all times when they are bathing. • Set water heater below 120°F. • Run cold water after bath water briefly to cool faucet. • Paint hot water faucet with red fingernail polish to help your children remember which faucet is hot. • Use only 2 to 3 inches of water when bathing a child. • Keep personal care products (including baby wash and baby shampoo), medicines, and cleaning products out of child's reach. Lock these away when not in use. Keep them from child's reach when in use, and put them away promptly after use. • Unplug bathroom appliances when not in use. Never store these plugged in near a bathtub or sink.

(Continued)

Indoor Dangers *(Continued)*		
Danger	**Possible Causes**	**Childproofing Measures**
Room Dangers *(Continued)* **Kitchen**	• Sharp utensils or glass items (if broken) can cut child. • Doors on large appliances can pinch fingers. Child can crawl inside large appliances and be trapped. • Child can be burned with hot beverages, foods, or appliances. • Children can be poisoned.	• Use safety locks to keep cabinet doors locked. Use plastic safety latches on drawers. • Store these items in highest and hardest-to-reach places. • Set aside one cabinet as a safe place for toddlers to play. Store safe and interesting objects in this cabinet. • Use appliance latches and keep these latched when appliances are not in use. • Use a safety gate to keep children out of kitchen unless supervised by an adult. Other options are to place child in a playyard nearby or strap the child into his or her high chair and offer safe toys for play. • Use heat-resistant stove guard to block access to burners. Cover stove knobs with guards. Use back burners instead of front burners when possible and turn handles of pots and pans toward the center of the stove. • Never carry a child while cooking or carrying hot items. • Keep cleaning products and chemicals locked in high cabinets.
Living room, den, family room, and bedrooms	• Unstable furniture can fall on child. • Furniture with sharp edges or glass components can cause scrapes and cuts.	• Remove unsteady items, such as end tables and plant stands, when possible. • Anchor heavy bookcases, shelves, and entertainment centers to the wall with nylon straps screwed into wall studs. • Pad sharp edges of furniture. • Remove furniture with glass components. Large glass-front cabinets can be turned toward the wall.
Nursery	See Figure 21-25 "Safety Standard for Baby/Toddler Items."	

(Continued)

Indoor Dangers *(Continued)*		
Danger	**Possible Causes**	**Childproofing Measures**
Other Items **Beverages**	• Hot beverages can burn babies. • Consuming alcoholic beverages can harm children.	• Keep hot beverages out of reach of children. • Do not carry hot beverages around children or leave these sitting unattended. • Keep bottles of alcoholic beverages locked out of children's reach.
Tools	• Many tools are heavy or sharp and can cause injuries if used improperly.	• Lock dangerous tools out of children's reach. • If children show interest in tools, buy play tool sets or tool sets made for children.
Insects, **spiders, and** **rodents**	• These can bite and spread disease. • Repellents can be poisonous. • Rodent traps can injure a child.	• Exterminate for pests. • Be careful not to allow children into exterminated areas until sprays have been cleaned off surfaces. • Keep traps out of children's reach.
Houseplants	• Many houseplants are poisonous.	• Ask your local extension agency or plant nursery to learn which plants are safe for homes with young children. • Keep all houseplants out of reach of children and teach children not to touch or eat the plants.

Index

why